American Poets

FROM THE PURITANS
TO THE PRESENT

Also by Hyatt H. Waggoner

The Heel of Elohim:
Science and Values in Modern American Poetry

Hawthorne: A Critical Study

William Faulkner:
From Jefferson to the World

Emerson As Poet

The Presence of Hawthorne

American Visionary Poetry

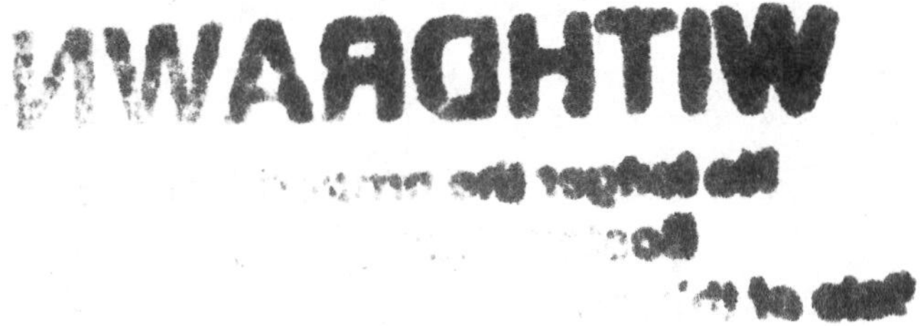

American Poets

FROM THE PURITANS TO THE PRESENT

Revised Edition

Hyatt H. Waggoner

LOUISIANA STATE UNIVERSITY PRESS
BATON ROUGE AND LONDON

Manufactured in the United States of America

Reissued by the Louisiana State University Press in 1984
Louisiana Paperback Edition, 1984
10 9 8 7 6 5 4 3

Library of Congress Cataloging in Publication Data

Waggoner, Hyatt Howe.
American poets, from the Puritans to the present.

Bibliography: p.
Includes index.
1. American poetry—History and criticism. I. Title.
PS303.W3 1984 811′.009 83-19624
ISBN 0-8071-1146-5
ISBN 0-8071-1163-5 (pbk.)

No jingling serenader's art,
Nor tinkle of piano strings,
Can make the wild blood start
In its mystic springs.
The kingly bard
Must smite the chords rudely and hard,
As with hammer or with mace;
That they may render back
Artful thunder, *which conveys*
Secrets of the solar track,
Sparks of supersolar blaze.

— Emerson (roman added)

Give me initiative, spermatic, prophesying, man-making words.

— Emerson

No one will get at my verses who insists on viewing them as a literary performance.

— Whitman

Every thing and every being in the world is something greater and something other than all we happen to know about it and than we consider it to be; yes, even more than that — it is something greater and other than all that we shall ever come to know about it. The poets are those who better than other people can inform us thereof.

— Simon Frank, Russian philosopher, 1877–1950, as translated by Nicholas S. Arseniev

The idea of an art detached from its creator is not only outmoded; it is false.

— Albert Camus

Poetry has always easily kept abreast of the utmost man can do in extending the horizon of his consciousness, whether outward or inward. It has always been the most flexible, the most comprehensive, the most farseeing, and hence the most successful, of the modes by which he has accepted the new in experience, realized it, and adjusted himself to it. . . . It has always at last been in poetry that man . . . succeeds in making real for himself the profound myth of personal existence and experience.

— Conrad Aiken

Contents

Preface to the Revised Edition

WHAT I said on pages xiv and xv in the Preface to the first edition of this book remains true of the final chapters in "After Modernism," especially of the last one, in which I try to bring the story of our poetry up to the present. That is, concentrating on lengthy treatments of poets who seem to me to be "representative" has once again forced me to omit, or merely mention in passing, poets whose work I have high respect for and find great enjoyment in, some of whom could be described as "favorites" of mine. (An example would be Mary Oliver, whose poems I enjoy reading more than those of several of the poets I have included.) To the extent that I have not let personal taste determine inclusion and exclusion, I have tried to be "objective."

Still, of course, deciding which poets among contemporaries will come to seem most important from a "representative" point of view involved "subjective" judgments that may well prove, in time, to have been quite wrong. When dealing with poets of the past, respect for critical consensus can be a guide, but when dealing with poets of the recent past and present, on whose work no critical consensus has yet evolved, one can only make the best guess he can—and hope for time and opportunity for yet another revised edition.

My new debts for this Revised Edition are chiefly to Howard Munford, who read the new chapters as they were written, to Florence Hubbard, who typed them, and to Margaret Fisher Dalrymple, for her inspired editing.

Rochester, Vermont
1984

H. H. W.

Preface to the First Edition

WHEN I first began to work on this book some five years ago, I had no idea it would turn out the way it has. Persuaded that our native poetic resources are far richer than we know, and particularly that the New England poets of the nineteenth century, so long despised and unread, ought to be partially reclaimed for mature readers, I planned to write a sort of old-fashioned "appreciative" history of our poets and their poetry.

The one thing I was really clear about when I began was what I *didn't* want to do. I *didn't* want to produce a "thesis" book which would rate and classify the poets according to a contemporary ideology foreign to their own outlooks and poetic purposes. (A work which seemed to me to do just this, R. H. Pearce's *The Continuity of American Poetry,* had been published in 1961.) And I didn't want to write a series of "close readings" of a "New Critical" sort and call the result a "history."

When I applied for a Guggenheim Fellowship in 1963 to continue work on the book, I wrote of my intentions in this way:

> I do not want this to be a "thesis" book. I want rather to try to see the poets as nearly as possible in their own terms, to see life with their eyes and feel it in terms of their values. Thus my emphasis will be on individual poets, their visions and their craft. I look upon them principally as men speaking to other men — to us — across the centuries. As yet I have discovered no intellectual formula that will embrace them all and I doubt that one will emerge in my further studies. Intellectual history will thus be subordinated to individuals, and the details of literary history I plan to relegate largely to notes.

Already, it would seem, I was beginning to think of the work to be done in Emersonian terms, approaching the history of our poetry through individual poets rather than the other way around, that is, treating poets in terms of "movements," "forces," and "social trends." For a while after this I toyed with the idea of using as my title Emerson's phrase, "artful thunder," or else alluding to his *Representative Men* by calling my book "Representative Poets." But as yet I had no real idea of what I would gradually discover during the course of my combined sabbatical-Guggenheim year, 1964–1965: that Emerson is the central figure in American poetry, essential both as spokesman and as catalyst, not only the founder of the chief "line" in our poetry but essential for an understanding of those poets not numbered among his poetic sons.

The realization of Emerson's centrality came to me slowly, held back no doubt by certain existing preferences, prejudices, and intentions — my desire, for instance, to rehabilitate, so far as a fresh look at their work would permit, the "schoolroom poets." Seeing Emerson as central could only make the accomplishment of that intention more difficult. Or my sympathy with and admiration for the great "Modernist" poets of the period from 1910 to, say, 1950 — the poets I had grown up reading and admiring — how could *they,* who had begun their work and shaped their viewpoints in the high tide of the rebellion against the "idealism" of the nineteenth-century British and American tradition in poetry, how could *they* be saved from being down-graded if Emerson's essay "The Poet" were admitted to be, what it had come to seem to me to be, the single most important critical document for anyone whose aim was to understand the development of our poetry?

But the realization did arrive, however slowly. Resistance to it was overcome not by any contrary thesis but by the weight of evidence. As I continued to immerse myself in the poetry, letting the modern "secondary material" — the scholarly and critical *treatments* of the poetry, with which I was already largely familiar — recede ever further into the background of my attention, the evidence that Emerson was in fact central, at least until early in our own century, whether we liked to admit it or not, grew and grew. Reading all the poetry and much of what might illuminate it — letters, journals, biographies — of each of the fifty-two poets I treat at length made the conclusion that Emerson is central seem to me inescapable.

But if this were so, then several of the chapters I had written before all the implications of what I had discovered had become clear to me would have to be redone. I went back and reread all of Emerson's poetry once again, for the second time in three years, and rewrote the chapter on his work. In the light of new evidence and fresh conviction, the chapter on Whitman seemed also to need redoing; and many other chapters had to be extensively revised. Since I was now teaching and administering once again, these revisions delayed the book for more than a year.

I hope that as a result of the delay the book is better, even though it is also, as a result of the revisions, further from my original intention for it than it was when I finished the first draft. There is now a sense, I suppose, in which it *could* fairly be called a "thesis" book, *i.e.,* a book dominated by one idea, which determines the selection and interpretation of the "evidence." But if so, it seems to me that the "thesis"—Emerson's centrality in our poetry — was discovered in, not imposed on, the material. Long before Leslie Fiedler's *Waiting for the End* (1964) came to my attention in 1966, I was aware of facts about our poets that make Fiedler's unprecedented statements about the centrality of Emerson seem to be understatements:

> Easiest of the lines of American verse to forget, or remembering, to despise, is the line of Ralph Waldo Emerson. . . .
>
> Without understanding Emerson, however, it is impossible to deal with two notable early modern American poets, Frost and E. A. Robinson, who seem otherwise unaccountable eccentrics; nor can one understand the place of Emily Dickinson between Emerson's time and our own; nor, finally, can one appreciate the true meaning of Edward Taylor, that recently rediscovered American metaphysical poet who is Emerson's ancestor, as Emerson is Emily Dickinson's. . . .
>
> It is clear, as a matter of fact, that the sole line of American poetry which has an unbroken line of development as old as our country itself is the one that runs from Taylor to Emerson to Dickinson to Frost and beyond; and it is Emerson who brought it to full consciousness, at the very moment when the schools of Longfellow and Poe and Whitman were defining themselves for the first time.

Fiedler's insights here are valid and important, and if he had followed them up — but his book is primarily about culture and fiction, so he had no reason to do so — he might have anticipated, in print, much more of what I had to discover the hard way. And there are many other signs, besides Fiedler's insightful book, that Emerson is being read, *really* read, these days, after a period half-a-century long in which most of those who shape our literary views have known him only at second or third hand, in caricature. Thus Kenneth Burke has recently discovered that Emerson proposed a "method" of transcendence — "I-Eye-Aye" — and R. P. Warren has included in his latest collection of poems a series called "Homage to Emerson: On Night Flight to New York." That Burke's implied respect for Emerson is strongly tempered by a tone of amused superiority toward Emerson's "innocence," and that Warren takes Emerson more seriously in his poems than he does when he is discussing him before audiences, are to be expected. To take Emerson *wholly* seriously in his own terms today is still to lay oneself open to the charge of being as "innocent" as Emerson himself is thought to be. But what really matters is that people like Burke and Warren are at last rereading Emerson.

One result of Emerson's taking over this book the way he has, to the extent of supplying not only its point of view but its organization, I still regret. Making "representative poets" the center of attention, as I have, and treating their work at some length, as seemed necessary if the method were to justify itself at all, has required that a good many poets whose work I enjoy and respect, whose work indeed may even be superior in some ways to the work of some poets I have treated, have had to be omitted from the discussion, or could have been included only if this book had been extended to several volumes.

This problem became more acute as I went along. I discussed every Puritan poet I wanted to discuss, and I felt little distress about relegating all but one of the Hartford Wits to an end note. I was not much distressed by having to omit such nineteenth-century poets as Ellery Channing, Henry Timrod, and Paul Hamilton Hayne. But I had hoped to present a number of the discoveries I have made while browsing among ignored or forgotten poets in the Harris Collection of American Poetry and Plays at Brown; to talk about the once-popular work of William Reed Huntington, for instance, who published in the 1890's. I would very much have liked to discuss the unique virtues of the late-nineteenth-, early-twentieth-century chaste late-romantic, Lizette Woodworth Reese. And having to leave out of account such more recent poets, several of them favorites of mine, as John Wheelwright, S. Foster Damon, John Peale Bishop, Richard Eberhart, Jeremy Ingalls, and Delmore Schwartz was really distressing.

Worse yet, to be forced by the method I had chosen to discuss contemporary poetry without treating the work of such poets, several of them personal friends, as Daniel Hoffman, Daniel Berrigan, Brother Antoninus, Vassar Miller, Chad Walsh, Charles Philbrick, Edwin Honig, Howard Nemerov, James Dickey, and many others — this was personally as well as critically embarrassing. At this point in the writing I was almost ready to abandon the method and bring all of these, and some others, in for treatment, if only in a sentence or two. But I decided I had to follow the light I had been given. Every method has its limitation, achieves its special emphases at a cost. The price I have paid for trying to illuminate the main lines of the development of American poetry by concentrating on lengthy treatments of "representative" poets is not being able to talk about some of the poetry that means most to me personally. But perhaps another time, another book.

Nevertheless, if the way Emerson "took over" the book proved an embarrassment in this way, there was a compensation for the distress. Focusing on Emerson seemed to me originally, and still seems, to throw more light on the question of what's *American* about American poetry than any other approach could have. If we take Emerson as pivotal, then it appears that Anne Bradstreet in her "Contemplations" and, much more clearly, Edward Taylor in such lines as his "Oh! What a thing is Man? Lord, Who am I?" begin to sound the notes that have characterized American poetry for more than three centuries now. Our poetry has been, and continues to be, more concerned with nature than with society or culture, and more concerned with the eternal than with the temporal. Characteristically, it has tested the validity of society and culture by the standard of what is natural, or, to say what amounts to the same thing in a different way, has tested the temporal and secular by the standard of the eternal. Even when most strongly in rebellion against their religious heritage, as Stephen Crane was, our poets have tended to take a "supramundane" point of view. Most of our chief poets have been religiously unorthodox, to be sure, with a strong tendency among them toward antinomianism; but very few if any of them have been religiously indifferent or unconcerned, or properly to be described as "secular."

One of the reasons why our poets, with not very many or very important exceptions, have seemed so little concerned with the nature and fate of actual society as such — or, if concerned, have been only negatively related, as opposed, in flight or in rebellion — becomes apparent as early as the Puritan poets of the seventeenth century, if we let Emerson determine our perspective. A recent book on the peculiar theological emphases of the American Calvinists makes this point succinctly. As Norman Pettit has written, in *The Heart Prepared: Grace and Conversion in Puritan Spiritual Life:*

> For Calvin, the test of the elect had been by profession of faith, an upright life, and participation in the sacraments; but for the Congregational founders of New England an inward test of personal experience was now also required.

The "test of personal experience"—with the strongest possible stress on "personal" — has been, it seems to me, as characteristic of our poetry as of our religion. Deprived of the security offered by place, position, class, creed, and the illusion of a stable, an unchanging society, our poets, like our religious seekers, have had to discover meaning where none is given and test its validity personally. American poets have characteristically seen man as Robinson saw him in "The Man Against the Sky." Almost all, and certainly all the greatest of them, have turned from society toward theology and metaphysics for their answers to the question Taylor was the first to ask, "Lord, Who am I?"

Most of our poets have displayed the attitude toward poetic convention and poetic language appropriate to a poet who is using poetry to "discover" and to "say" something, to write as a "prophet," in short, rather than as an artisan or "maker." Thinking of the poet as a "namer" and a "sayer" — to use Emerson's terms — American poets have generally taken a rather top-lofty attitude toward the traditions, conventions, and "rules" that supposedly govern the practice of their craft. They have turned inherited poetic forms and traditional genres to their own purposes or abandoned them entirely. They have used, and not been used by, words, ready always to invent new ones if the old ones did not serve.

Whitman, more extreme and outspoken in this respect than most, still was taking a characteristically American stance when he said, "No one will get at my verses who insists on viewing them as a literary performance." American poets have typically been very little concerned with what may be called the merely "literary" standards. They have been more concerned, that is, with "discovery" than with "performance." A man facing the unknown must necessarily "discover" before he is able to "perform." American poets have faced the world armed chiefly with their innocence, their "not knowing." From the beginning, the most representative American poets have anticipated the characteristic that more than anything else distinguishes the American poetry of our own day from that of the past and of other societies: in it *nothing* is known, nothing given, everything is discovered or created, or else remains in doubt.

Emerson gave this situation its classic formulation in "The Poet" and "Circles," certainly the two most characteristic and, in my view, the greatest prose statements ever made about the relation between American poetry and American life.

I am indebted for the free time necessary to complete this book to the John Simon Guggenheim Memorial Foundation for the grant of a Fellowship in the academic year 1964–1965, and to Brown University both for the sabbatical leave which, with the help of the Guggenheim Fellowship, stretched into fifteen months, and for a grant from its Faculty Research Fund to pay for the final typing of the manuscript and for assistance in checking for accuracy in the quotations.

My deepest debts to persons are to Professor George Monteiro and Professor Joseph Yokelson, who read the first typed version and made many helpful suggestions. I also feel very grateful to Clare Beghtol, Louise Habicht, Susan Hines, Jacqueline Pourciau, and John Patterson, my students, who helped keep me literate and accurate; to Irma Perry of Rochester, Vermont, who typed the first, handwritten, version; and to Jacqueline Taylor of Brown who typed the second, much revised, version. Virginia Wharton, copy editor for the publisher, did the sort of job on the typescript that makes a writer grateful for his good fortune.

To say that I am deeply indebted to my wife, Louise, is, in this case, no mere following of an academic convention. Without her

Acknowledgments

Atheneum Publishers: "Vision" from *The Compass Flower* by W. S. Merwin, copyright © 1977 by W. S. Merwin, reprinted with the permission of Atheneum Publishers. "Vision" was first published in *The New Yorker.*

Beacon Press: *I Wanted To Write a Poem* by William Carlos Williams, reprinted by permission of the Beacon Press, copyright © 1958 by William Carlos Williams.

Brandt & Brandt: *Sheepfold Hill* by Conrad Aiken, published by Thomas Yoseloff, The Sagamore Press, copyright © 1945, 1946, 1949, 1952, 1958 by Conrad Aiken, reprinted by permission of Brandt & Brandt.

Doubleday & Company, Inc.: (1) "On the Quay," copyright © 1962 by Beatrice Roethke as Administratrix of the Estate of Theodore Roethke; lines from "They Sing, They Sing," copyright © 1956 by The Atlantic Monthly Company; from "In Evening Air" and "Meditation at Oyster River," copyright © 1960 by Beatrice Roethke as Administratrix of the Estate of Theodore Roethke; and from "Journey to the Interior," copyright © 1961 by Beatrice Roethke as Administratrix of the Estate of Theodore Roethke; all from *The Collected Poems of Theodore Roethke*, reprinted by permission of Doubleday & Company, Inc. (2) Excerpts from *The Zodiac* by James Dickey, copyright © 1976 by James Dickey, reprinted by permission of Doubleday & Company, Inc. (3) "The Cancer Match" from *The Eye-Beater, Blood Victory, Madness, Buckhead and Mercy* by James Dickey, copyright © 1969 by Modern Poetry Association, reprinted by permission of Doubleday & Company, Inc.

Ecco Press: "It Was Raining in the Capital" from *The Double Dream of Spring* by John Ashbery, copyright © 1976 by John Ashbery, reprinted by permission of The Ecco Press.

Farrar, Straus & Giroux, Inc.: (1) *Life Studies* by Robert Lowell, copyright © 1956, 1959 by Robert Lowell. *For the Union Dead* by Robert Lowell, copyright © 1956, 1960, 1961, 1962, 1963, 1964 by Robert Lowell. (2) "Henry Sats" from *77 Dream Songs* by John Berryman, copyright © 1959, 1962, 1963, 1964 by John Berryman, reprinted by permission of Farrar, Straus and Giroux, Inc.

Grove Press, Inc.: *Selected Poems of H.D.*, published by Grove Press, Inc., copyright © 1957 by Norman Holmes Pearson.

HARCOURT, BRACE & WORLD, INC.: (1) *95 Poems* by E. E. Cummings, copyright © 1958 by E. E. Cummings. (2) *Honey and Salt* by Carl Sandburg, copyright © 1963 by Carl Sandburg. (3) *Advice to a Prophet and Other Poems* by Richard Wilbur, copyright © 1961 by Richard Wilbur. All reprinted by permission of Harcourt, Brace and World, Inc.

HARVARD UNIVERSITY PRESS: *On the Mystical Poetry of Henry Vaughan* by R. A. Durr, copyright © 1962 by the President and Fellows of Harvard College.

HOLT, RINEHART AND WINSTON, INC.: (1) *Complete Poems of Robert Frost,* copyright 1916, 1923, 1928, 1930, 1934, 1939, 1945, 1947 by Holt, Rinehart and Winston, Inc., copyright 1936, 1944, 1951, © 1956, 1958, 1962 by Robert Frost, copyright © 1964, 1967 by Lesley Frost Ballantine, reprinted by permission of Holt, Rinehart and Winston, Inc. *In the Clearing* by Robert Frost, copyright © 1956, 1959, 1962 by Robert Frost, reprinted by permission of Holt, Rinehart and Winston, Inc. (2) *Selected Letters of Robert Frost,* edited by Lawrance Thompson, copyright © 1964 by Lawrance Thompson and Holt, Rinehart and Winston, Inc., reprinted by permission of the Estate of Robert Frost and Holt, Rinehart and Winston, Inc. (3) "One Who Rejected Christ" from *Poems About God* by John Crowe Ransom, copyright 1919 by Holt, Rinehart and Winston, Inc., copyright 1947 by John Crowe Ransom, reprinted by permission of Holt, Rinehart and Winston, Inc. (4) "I Am the People, the Mob" from *Chicago Poems* by Carl Sandburg, copyright 1916 by Holt, Rinehart and Winston, Inc., copyright 1944 by Carl Sandburg, reprinted by permission of Holt, Rinehart and Winston, Inc.

HOUGHTON MIFFLIN COMPANY: (1) *Preludes and Symphonies* by John Gould Fletcher, reprinted by permission of Mrs. John Gould Fletcher and Houghton Mifflin Company. (2) *The Complete Poetical Works of Amy Lowell.* (3) *Collected Poems 1917–1952* by Archibald MacLeish.

INDIANA UNIVERSITY PRESS: "An Offering for Dungeness Bay" from *Sleeping in the Woods* by David Wagoner, copyright © 1974 by Indiana University Press, reprinted by permission of Indiana University Press.

ALFRED A. KNOPF, INC.: (1) *Selected Poems* by John Crowe Ransom. (2) *Collected Poems* by Elinor Wylie. (3) *Collected Poems* and *Opus Posthumous* by Wallace Stevens, protected by copyright and reprinted here by special permission of the publisher.

LIVERIGHT PUBLISHING CORPORATION: (1) *The Collected Poems and Selected Letters and Prose of Hart Crane*, reprinted by permission of Liveright Publisher, N.Y., copyright 1933, © 1958, 1966 by Liveright Publishing Corporation, N.Y. (2) *Collected Poems of H. D.,* published by Liveright Publishing Corporation, copyright 1925, © 1953 by Norman Holmes Pearson.

THE MACMILLAN COMPANY: (1) *Collected Poems* by Marianne Moore, copyright 1935 by Marianne Moore, renewed 1964 by Marianne Moore and T. S. Eliot; *Collected Poems* by Marianne Moore, copyright 1944 by Marianne Moore. (2) *Collected Poems* by Edwin Arlington Robinson, copyright 1915 by Edwin Arlington Robinson; *Collected Poems* by Edwin Arlington Robinson, copyright 1921 by Edwin Arlington Robinson, renewed 1949 by Ruth Nivison; *Collected Poems* by Edwin Arlington Robinson, copyright 1934 by Edwin Arlington Robinson. (3) *Collected Poems* by Sara Teasdale, copyright 1922 by The Macmillan Company; *Collected Poems* by Sara Teasdale, copyright 1915 by The Macmillan Company, renewed 1943 by Mamie T. Wheless; *Collected Poems* by Sara Teasdale, copyright 1926 by The Macmillan Company, renewed 1954 by Mamie T. Wheless; *Collected Poems* by Sara Teasdale, copyright 1933 by The Macmillan Company. (4) *Collected Poems* by Vachel Lindsay, copyright 1923 by The Macmillan Company, renewed 1951 by Elizabeth C. Lindsay; *Collected Poems* by Vachel Lindsay, copyright 1917 by The Macmillan Company, renewed 1945 by Elizabeth C. Lindsay; *Collected Poems* by Vachel Lindsay, copyright 1920 by The Macmillan Company, renewed 1948 by Elizabeth C. Lindsay; *Collected Poems* by Vachel Lindsay, copyright 1925 by The Macmillan Company; *Collected Poems* by Vachel Lindsay, copyright 1914 by The Macmillan Company, renewed 1942 by Elizabeth C. Lindsay, all reprinted with permission of The Macmillan Company. (5) *The Spoon River Anthology*, *The Great Valley*, *Toward the Gulf*, and *Songs and Satires* by Edgar Lee Masters, reprinted with permission of Mrs. Edgar Lee Masters.

HOWARD NEMEROV: "The Flame of a Candle" from *The Blue Swallows*, published by University of Chicago Press, copyright © 1967 by Howard Nemerov, reprinted by permission of Howard Nemerov.

NEW DIRECTIONS PUBLISHING CORPORATION: (1) *The Collected Earlier Poems* of William Carlos Williams, copyright 1938 by William Carlos Williams; *The Collected Later Poems* of William Carlos Williams, copyright 1944, 1948, 1950, © 1963 by William Carlos Williams; *Pictures from Brueghel and Other Poems* by William Carlos Williams, copyright 1954 by William Carlos Williams, all reprinted by permission of New Directions Publishing Corporation. (2) *Personae* by Ezra Pound, copyright 1926, 1954 by Ezra Pound, reprinted by permission of New Directions Publishing Corporation. (3) "Human Being" from *Life in the Forest* by Denise Levertov, copyright © 1978 by Denise Levertov; "Candles in Babylon" from *Candles in Babylon* by Denise Levertov, copyright © 1982 by Denise Levertov. Both of the above reprinted by permission of New Directions Publishing Corporation.

OXFORD UNIVERSITY PRESS: *Collected Poems* by Conrad Aiken, copyright 1953 by Conrad Aiken.

RANDOM HOUSE, INC.: (1) *Selected Poetry* by Robinson Jeffers, copyright 1924 by Peter G. Boyle, copyright 1925 by Horace Liveright Incorporated, copyright 1935 by the Modern Library Incorporated, copyright 1927, 1928, 1929, 1932, 1938 by Robinson Jeffers, copyright 1931, 1933, 1937 by Random House, Inc., copyright renewed 1951, 1953, 1955, 1956, 1957, and 1959 by Robinson Jeffers. (2) *Promises* by Robert Penn Warren, copyright © 1955, 1957 by Robert Penn Warren; *You, Emperors and Others* by Robert Penn Warren, copyright © 1958, 1959, 1960 by Robert Penn Warren; *Brother to Dragons* by Robert Penn Warren, copyright 1953 by Robert Penn Warren.

CHARLES SCRIBNER'S SONS: (1) *Poems, 1922–1947* by Allen Tate. (2) "Miniver Cheevy" from *The Town Down the River* by Edwin Arlington Robinson; *The Children of the Night* by Edwin Arlington Robinson.

THE SIXTIES PRESS: *The Suspect in Poetry* by James Dickey.

VIKING PENGUIN INC.: "A Man of Words" from *Self-Portrait in a Convex Mirror* by John Ashbery, copyright © 1972, 1973, 1974, 1975 by John Ashbery, reprinted by permission of Viking Penguin Inc.

WESLEYAN UNIVERSITY PRESS: "Trying to Pray" from *The Branch Will Not Break* by James Wright, copyright © 1963 by James Wright, reprinted by permission of Wesleyan University Press.

RICHARD WILBUR: "The Proof," copyright © 1963 by Richard Wilbur. This poem originally appeared in *The Atlantic*.

W. W. NORTON AND COMPANY: "Turning a Moment to Say So Long" and "Corsons Inlet" from *Collected Poems, 1951–1971* by A. R. Ammons, copyright © 1972 by A. R. Ammons; *Tape for the Turn of the Year* by A. R. Ammons, copyright © 1965 by Cornell University, Norton edition published 1972; "Hibernaculum" from *Selected Longer Poems* by A. R. Ammons, copyright © 1980, 1975, 1972 by A. R. Ammons. All of the above are reprinted with the permission of W. W. Norton and Company.

PART ONE

Beginnings

CHAPTER I

Puritans and Deists

Dear Austin. We just got home from meeting — it is very windy and cold — the hills from our kitchen window are just crusted with snow, which with their blue mantillas makes them seem so beautiful. . . . Father and mother sit in state in the sitting room perusing such papers only, as they are well assured have nothing carnal in them.

— Emily Dickinson, writing her brother Austin, November 16, 1851

My poetry is carnalized metaphysics.

— E. E. Cummings

The truth is that the ultimately moral character of the universe, whether it is personified in the form of a righteous and transcendent God or is conceived as immanent in the world-process itself, has been a part of all advanced religious cultures. It has been, until recent times in the West, a universal belief of civilized humanity. . . . That values are subjective and relative, that the world is not a moral order, is the fashionable belief of the intellectuals of our time.

— W. T. Stace, *Religion and the Modern Mind*

Now it is such a total commitment, appropriate to a "question of great consequence," a commitment which is based upon but goes beyond rational considerations which are "matters of speculation"; a commitment which sees in a situation all that the understanding can give us and more; a commitment which is exemplified by conscientious action building on "probabilities," which Butler thinks to be characteristic of a religious attitude.

So taking Part I of the Analogy [*Bishop Joseph Butler,* The Analogy of Religion Natural and Revealed to the Constitution and Course of Nature] *along with the Introduction, Butler suggests that religion claims (a) a fuller discernment, to which we respond with (b) a total commitment. Such a commitment without any discernment whatever is bigotry and idolatry; to have the discernment without an appropriate commitment is the worst of all religious vices. It is insincerity and hypocrisy.*

— Ian T. Ramsey, *Religious Language*

Puritan Verse

IN approximately three and a half centuries American poetry has come full circle — and now shows signs of starting around once more. The sense of evil, of the darkness of experience, of the alien unknown and uncontrolled in which man is immersed, has been expressed for us, in our times and our terms, by most of the finest modern poets. Stevens in "The Snow Man" and Williams in "These" express our sense of alienation from the Real that forms the center of meaning in Eliot's early poetry. Frost speaks for many besides himself in "Design":

> I found a dimpled spider, fat and white,
> On a white heal-all, holding up a moth
> Like a white piece of rigid satin cloth —
> Assorted characters of death and blight
> Mixed ready to begin the morning right,
> Like the ingredients of a witches' broth —
> A snow-drop spider, a flower like froth,
> And dead wings carried like a paper kite.
>
> What had that flower to do with being white,
> The wayside blue and innocent heal-all?
> What brought the kindred spider to that height,
> Then steered the white moth thither in the night?
> What but design of darkness to appall? —
> If design govern in a thing so small.

The sense of the "domination of black," as Stevens called another of his early poems, has been the predominant strain in the poetry of the first half of our century. It has not been unopposed, of course. It has been countered in all sorts of ways: by Cummings with his transcendentalism; by Eliot himself in his later poetry with his orthodox Christian faith; by Frost, first with his explorations of the various meanings and possibilities of endurance, and then, toward the end of his career, with his heterodox and antinomian Biblical religion; by Hart Crane with his immanentist Emersonian mysticism. But the very multiplicity and variety of the answers have only emphasized the difficulty and persistence of the question: Does man's life have any lasting meaning at all?

"Is there a Meaning, a Purpose, or a Law?" asked Robinson, at the beginning of the century, and he could not find an answer. Other poets again and again have felt that the question needed to be answered, and they have attempted throughout their poetic careers to arrive at an answer. But no answer has seemed quite sufficient, none has wholly satisfied or been widely convincing. Only insofar as our youngest generation of poets have thrown off modernism entirely, both its formal practices, and its assumptions, attempting to start afresh on entirely different premises, do we have a body of poetry that does not at least start by assuming with Eliot that "April is the cruellest month."

Our poets have spoken for our time, and they have not been alone in what they have said. Joyce, Proust, Kafka, Virginia Woolf, Hemingway, and Faulkner in the novel, the Existentialists in philosophy, and the neo-orthodox theologians in religion — these have all shared the poets' vision of the prima facie meaninglessness of man's existence. They have felt and expressed his inability to get any answers to the important questions or, despite the triumphs of technology, to control his destiny. Man, they have all said in effect, finds himself thrown into a world that makes no sense, that reduces him and his meanings to nothing, a world that can only be characterized in its quintessential reality as the Absurd. If there is any meaning beyond the satisfactions of the hour that suffice for the unaware and the self-deluded, the meaning will have to be created or, with difficulty, creatively discovered, for it is not given, not supplied, not in any sense simply there to be appropriated.

This dark strain was a submerged minor note in nineteenth-century American poetry. Here and there we find it just under the surface. Now and then it breaks into the open and becomes dominant, as it does in a very special sort of way in Poe and Melville and in many of the poems of Emily Dickinson. But to find it most powerfully and meaningfully expressed we must go outside the poetry, to the fiction — to Hawthorne, Melville, and the late work of James. Earlier, in the verse of the eighteenth-century Enlightenment, it was hardly present at all.

But it was present when American poetry began, with the Puritans. Between the Puritans and the early work of Eliot or Stevens, a whole world of faith *seemed* to have been lost, to be sure. The Puritans were Pauline Christians; their faith admitted, officially, of no doubts. Eliot and Stevens began by assuming that such a faith was impossible and devoted themselves to the problem that resulted, in the one case rediscovering an authentic version of the faith, in the other finding a substitute for it in the *creative* possibilities of the imagination. But they began where the Puritans began, with an imagination dominated by the presence of evil.

The Puritans responded to the pressure of their awareness of darkness and man's powerlessness with the assertion of a dogmatic faith in man's — or at least their — triumph over meaninglessness. But the very shrillness and rigidity of their expressions of faith betray the pressure of the challenge to it. With so much darkness everywhere, the light they had demanded to be guarded with rigorous devotion. Their light was intense and single, a narrow searchlight beam probing the blackness to light up the little group of the Elect. It did not affect the surrounding darkness at all.

In our time the Existentialists rediscovered what a good deal of nineteenth-century thought seemed to have forgotten, that death is the supreme and final reality in life, the "normative possibility" that must structure all our values. "To accept death . . . is to take my preoccupations for what they are worth, nothing. From this detachment springs the power, the dignity, the tolerance of authentic personal existence." Thus an Existentialist philosopher today. But the Puritans needed no philosophers to tell them this. They already knew it. The elegy was their favorite type of poetry, or at least the form they composed oftenest when they turned their hand to verse, as a great many of them did.[1]

The Puritans valued poetry for its usefulness — but not in any crude utilitarian sense. They would not have understood an art for art's sake doctrine, not because they had contempt for art but because for them life was all of a piece and lower values should properly be subordinated to higher ones. The use of poetry was to help one to live well — and die well. For this purpose even the simplest poetic memorial of the humblest versifier might serve. An elegy on the death of Elizabeth Tompson reduces the central motif of Puritan poetry to its baldest terms in its opening lines:

> Upon the Death of yt desireable young virgin, Elizabeth Tompson, Daughter of Joseph & Mary Tompson of Bilerika, who Deseased in Boston out of the hous of Mr legg, 24 august, 1712, aged 22 years.

A lovely flowr Cropt in its prime
  By Deaths Cold fatall hand;
A warning hear is left for all
  Ready prepard to stand.

For none can tell who shall be next,
  Yet all may it expect;
Then surely it Concerneth all,
  Their time not to neglect.

On a considerably higher level of sophistication Philip Pain devoted his *Daily Meditations* (1666), which is probably the first book of American poetry printed in this country, to the theme he developed in Meditation 9:

Man's life is like a Rose that in the Spring
Begins to blossom, fragrant smells to bring.
Within a day or two, behold Death's sent,
A public Messenger of discontent.
  Lord grant, that when my Rose begins to fade,
  I may behold an Everlasting shade.

For Pain, life took on meaning only as death was confronted:

ETERNITY! O soul-amazing thought,
That never to my senses yet was brought
Rightly to understand it. Oh, the height,
The breadth, the length, the depth of what I slight!
  Help, Son of *David,* mercy on me have.
  This is a coming; I must to the grave.

This is minor verse, to be sure, but not doggerel, as *The Bay Psalm Book* is, and not trivial in the quality of its vision. Hardly anything is known of Pain beyond a reference to his early death by drowning, but he is worth remembering — and reading, once at least — for his expression of that aspect of Puritan experience that produced, as a less direct result, the crabbed dogmatics of Wigglesworth's *Day of Doom.*

*

ANNE BRADSTREET

More literary in motivation than Wigglesworth and longer-lived than Pain is Anne Bradstreet. The best way to become interested in her poetry today is to start by reading John Berryman's *Homage to Mistress Bradstreet.* This vivid and moving tribute by a contemporary poet to a poetic ancestor brings the wife and mother alive as her own verse seldom does even in the best known of her few personal poems like "To My Dear and Loving Husband." In Berryman's poem we get the existential life that is generally so deeply buried under the theology and the borrowed imagery of Mrs. Bradstreet's own verse writing. And our interest in the woman may carry over, as motive and stimulus, to the work.

Very little of the verse in her first volume, published in London in 1650, seems today to justify the title, *The Tenth Muse Lately Sprung up in America: Or Severall Poems, Compiled with Great Variety of Wit and Learning, Full of Delight.* But "Contemplations," which was published only after her death in the revised and augmented collection that appeared in 1678, shows her growing in self-confidence and skill. "Contemplations" could be called our first nature poem, though *she* would not have thought of it that way. When she contemplates the splendor of a New England autumn, with its colors that seem "painted" but are really "true," she finds her senses "rapt" and hardly knows what she ought to feel:

> I wist not what to wish, yet sure, thought I,
> If so much excellence abide below
> How excellent is He that dwells on high,
> Whose power and beauty by his works we know.

If this foreshadows Bryant, other parts of the poem introduce themes and images that have continued to engage our poets through several centuries. Attachment to "the things of this world" and detachment, *contemptus mundi,* are explored here with sensitivity and intelligence. "The sweet-tongued philomel," knowing nothing of time, is spared man's dread: "winter's never felt by that sweet airy legion." Watching fish jumping calls forth two of her finest lines:

> Look how the wantons frisk to taste the air,
> Then to the colder bottom straight they dive.

For man, perhaps April is, as Eliot would later put it, the "cruellest" month:

When I behold the heavens as in their prime,
  And then the earth, though old, still clad in green,
The stones and trees insensible of time,
  Nor age nor wrinkle on their front are seen;
If winter come, and greenness then doth fade,
A spring returns, and they're more youthful made.
But man grows old, lies down, remains where once he's
    laid.

By birth more noble than those creatures all,
  Yet seems by nature and by custom cursed —
No sooner born but grief and care make fall
  That state obliterate he had at first;
Nor youth, nor strength, nor wisdom spring again,
Nor habitations long their names retain,
But in oblivion to the final day remain.

Shall I then praise the heavens, the trees, the earth,
  Because their beauty and their strength last longer?
Shall I wish there or never to had birth,
  Because they're bigger and their bodies stronger?
Nay, they shall darken, perish, fade, and die,
And when unmade so ever shall they lie;
But man was made for endless immortality.

"Contemplations" is probably Anne Bradstreet's best poem, worth reading for more than just its anticipations of later poets, but unfortunately it is not typical of the bulk of her work.

If we come to most of it hoping for a revelation of the quality of American life as it was experienced by an intelligent woman of poetic sensibility, we shall mostly be disappointed. The intelligence and the sensibility are there, but the preoccupations in the verse leave almost no place for them. Here and there we find a memorable line or two; sometimes a readable whole poem. But the overwhelming majority of the lines, unfortunately, are very flat, built of the clichés of classic and Biblical imagery. Even "Contemplations" is weakened by the predominance of too-much-expected adjectives: "stately" oaks and elms, "goodly" rivers, "gliding" streams, and "shady" woods. In the personal poems that later readers have always preferred, like "Upon the Burning of our House," the sentiments seem for the most part to be standard for the time, the things Puritans knew they *ought* to feel — and so *did* feel, of course:

> Then streight I 'gan my heart to chide:
> And did thy wealth on earth abide?
> Didst fix thy hope on mouldring dust,
> The arm of flesh didst make thy trust?

Her house, her worldly treasures, have burned, and the heartache of the loss gets momentary, and in the first line vivid, expression:

> And when I could no longer look,
> I blest his Name that gave and took,
> That layd my goods now in the dust:
> Yea so it was, and so 'twas just.

But chiefly — or so we would gather from the poem — the catastrophe was the occasion for a little sermon she delivered to herself. She saw, or thought she ought to see, and so no doubt in some measure did see, no genuine conflict of values between things temporal and things eternal, for all *real* values were eternal. So she concludes:

> The world no longer let me Love,
> My Hope and Treasure lyes Above.

The otherworldliness of Puritan poetry is less attractively, but more interestingly, exhibited by Michael Wigglesworth in his immensely popular poem *The Day of Doom.* Unlike Mrs. Bradstreet, Wigglesworth was not interested in poetry as poetry or in contemplating nature. He rhymed his dogmas because they were easier to remember that way. Both he and his readers were agreed that verse was a useful aid to the cultivation of a devoutly God-fearing life. Further to intensify the mnemonic effect of his ballad stanzas — which were also, when printed differently but without other change, the "common meter" of the familiar Protestant hymns — he added internal rhyme in the long lines:

Still was the night, serene and bright,
  when all men sleeping lay;
Calm was the season, and carnal reason
  thought so 'twould last for aye.

"Carnal reason" takes no thought of death; by it "vile wretches" are led to a wholly false sense of security. The wellsprings of Puritan piety were never more baldly — and, for us, less attractively — laid bare. Their very nearly Gnostic dualism of spirit and flesh, good and evil, God and the world, the eternal and the temporal, is adequately suggested by "carnal" placed before the kind of reason we might call worldly, or secular, or even, from their point of view, short-sighted. All that partakes of the flesh is *carnal* — low, debased, evil or the source of evil. St. Paul had found the source of evil in his "members," and Puritans read Paul too well. His Hellenism — the Greeks, unlike the Hebrews, were dualists — and his traces of Gnosticism were adopted and magnified by American Puritans, with a result that gives some plausibility to the old notion that Paul, not Jesus, "invented" Christianity.

The theology Wigglesworth rhymes is thoroughly world-denying and to most modern minds, I would suppose, thoroughly repulsive — when it does not strike one as simply ridiculous. Though supposedly based on the Johannine "God so loved the world that he sent his only-begotten son" to atone for our sins, it turns out to be not "the world" that is loved but only a tiny remnant, the Elect. Even the children of the Elect — not to mention the vast majority of mankind who cannot claim to be among the Elect — if they should chance to die before being baptized, must go to eternal torment.

Concerning *their* fate, Wigglesworth seems to have felt a little uneasy. It must be right that they should suffer forever, but perhaps they should not suffer so *much* as mature, unrepentant sinners. The concession he made to them, allowing them to dwell in "the easiest room in Hell," was a sop to conscience, though Wigglesworth would not of course have thought of it that way.

Two centuries later Oliver Wendell Holmes, writing from the standpoint of an urbane Unitarianism, would dismiss Calvinist theology in "The Deacon's Masterpiece" as an amusing relic of an unenlightened past, logically tight but based on assumptions that could not stand scrutiny. A century later still, contemporary scholars would be busy examining Puritanism with considerably more sympathy than Holmes had shown, though with a final effect of detached objectivity, refraining from passing judgment, for the most part.

But to the reader of poetry who wishes to share the values of the poetry he reads, as he must if he is to enter into it and let it enter him, a theology which strikes him as at once incredible and perverse, monstrous in its perversion of a gospel of love into a set of beliefs expressive of sadistic hatred, this theology is not irrelevant to his judgment of the poetry. "Suspension of disbelief" is possible only within certain broad limits; it is an inappropriate reaction in the face of what seems stupid or vicious. When theology is the whole substance of the poem, as it is in *The Day of Doom,* and when it is hammered home with the rude energy and dogged literalness that characterize Wigglesworth's writing, the reader must take a stand, not because he cares more about theology than about poetry but precisely because he cares enough about poetry to take it seriously.

Only Calvinists of a thoroughly Puritan stripe — and one doubts, with Holmes, that there are many left — could fail to be appalled by the theology. Life as it is examined here in the light of death and judgment is revealed to be a pointless test — pointless because the final marks were recorded before the test was taken, since God chose the Elect who would pass the test before time began. God becomes a cruel, arbitrary Oriental despot, choosing "whom He will," and Jesus, when he is not a passive tool of his Father's absurd plan of salvation, is a dreadful judge, articulating the rationalizations of a specious "logic" intended to justify injustice. The more Wigglesworth succeeds in making clear and vivid to us the details of the beliefs he hoped to inculcate, the more he fails as a poet who can speak to us — as a man speaking to other men across the silences. His poem remains a grotesque curiosity, though as a poet he is not without energy and even some skill.

Some of the best Puritan poetry is in the form of elegies, many of them written by amateurs who tried their hands at verse only a few times in their lives, and then in the form most expressive of their convictions. Death now affords the occasion as well as determining the perspective. A double motive is at work in them, to memorialize the dead and to search for the meaning of life by examining completed lives.

Quite often the search took the form of anagrams and acrostics based on the subject's name. If we find the method peculiarly inappropriate, as most of us are likely to — death the occasion for a display of ingenuity and wit? — we have only to reflect for a moment on the theology that produced it to find that it "makes sense," in a way. Since everything that happened was thought to be foreordained and the work of God, either directly, or indirectly through the agency of the Devil, whom God permitted to operate, everything must be in some way a *sign* to be interpreted, a revelation of the Divine Will. Thus what later came to be called the General Revelation — Nature, properly interpreted by Reason — reinforced and extended the Special Revelation of Scripture. Nothing happened by chance and nothing was without meaning.

But if this were so, then it would be not simply in the larger events and general pattern of a person's life that one might try to find meaning. Just as Scripture assures us that the very hairs on our heads are numbered, so the very letters of our names may be divinely ordained and thus revelatory of the Divine Will. In short, while the popularity of the elegy in general testifies to the Puritans' conviction that the meaning of life can best be read in the light of death, the popularity of the anagrammatic or acrostic elegy is expressive of their belief that life contains no neutral territory where God or the demonic powers do not operate. The poetic form is related to their search for what they called "Special Providences," identifiable particular manifestations of God's concern for His world.

The anagrammatic method then "makes sense" of a kind, but the kind it makes is narrowly logical. Holmes's point in "The Deacon's Masterpiece" again: Once we scrutinize the premises, the system falls apart. To remember that while Puritan Milton was writing "Lycidas," his American coreligionists were composing acrostic elegies is to recall how provincial American Puritanism quickly became. To make anagrams a method of discovering the Divine Will is to trivialize the concept of Revelation. Where *everything* becomes a Special Providence, the idea of Providence itself would seem to lose all meaning. The error here is not so much logical as cultural, aesthetic, and rational in the existential sense. The epistemology is all wrong: verbal ingenuity seems to be placed on a par with reason, insight, and intuition as a method of discovering truth. As a mathematician might say of a mathematical formula, it is not that the anagrammatic method can be proved to be *untrue* but that it is aesthetically (or rather, morally and religiously) *unpleasing*. No one who has ever taken the idea of Divine Revelation seriously, however he may have emphasized its transcendence of reason, has ever thought of it as simply trivial and arbitrary.

But "trivial" and "arbitrary" are precisely the adjectives that describe the anagrammatic method of discovering meaning. It is not difficult, if one is allowed a little freedom to add and subtract letters, to see, as Benjamin Tompson did, that the name "Elizabeth Tompson" contains the significant anagram "o i am blest on top." But since it also contains "O I am not blest" and others equally unsuitable for memorial verse, how do we know which one is *truly* revealing? As well toss dice or read tea leaves. The ingenuity that discovered "Tis Braul I Cudgel" in the name Claudius Gilbert and "i am gon to all bliss" in Abigaill Tompson would seem pretty clearly to be the poet's, not God's: clearly, that is, unless we assume that man initiates literally nothing, that all actions are God's, in which case, absurdity enters in by another door, for then not only man's wit but his striving, too, has none of the personal and human meaning the elegists attribute to their subjects; and God Himself becomes such a very bad poet.[2]

The elegies make somewhat more interesting reading than most Puritan verse because they concern specific individuals. Interest in their subjects, or, if the subjects are known to us, that plus interest in how the subjects impressed their contemporaries, can sometimes carry us through much crude poetry. But the general feature of the first century of New England verse is that it tells us almost nothing of the concrete, existential experience of people, places, or things. For this, for the kind of thing that poetry can do best, we generally have to go to the prose — and even that is not usually very rewarding.

One would think, for example, that a poem written in 1638 to celebrate the poet's first sight of the new land would give us at least some idea of what such an experience must have been like. We should like to know, and poetry should be able to tell us. But Thomas Tillam's "Uppon the first sight of New-England" begins like this:

> hayle holy-land wherein our holy lord
> hath planted his most true and holy word,
> hayle happy people who have dispossest
> your selves of friends, and meanes, to find some rest
> for your poore wearied soules, opprest of late
> for Jesus-sake, with Envye, spight, and hate,
> to yow that blessed promise truly's given
> of sure reward, which you'l receve in heaven

and goes on in similar vein for fourteen more lines. What we get from reading it is not any sight of the new land, or any insight into what the experience of sighting it must have been like, except that it produced a sense of thankfulness; what we get is only religious abstractions. No word of the poem would have had to be changed if its subject had been sighting a South Sea island or the shores of Antarctica instead of Massachusetts. Reading it, we wonder if it might have been saved as a poem if William Carlos Williams had guided the pen for just a line or two.

Puritan poetry in effect tends to find this world so radically imperfect as not to be worth saving or grieving for — or memorializing. Anne Bradstreet counted it a sin in herself that she should grieve at the loss of her house. Her "real" house was elsewhere. The Puritan poet placed very little value on "the world's body." Though he searched his experience for signs of God's will and man's destiny, typically he was not interested in the things themselves that became for him signs, but only in what the signs signified. The world was thin, not thick, and he chose to look right through it to things Divine. Though he held to a theology intended to magnify the role of Christ in the Atonement, the Puritan poet very often denied, by implication, the meaning of another, more central, Christological doctrine, the idea of the Incarnation itself. For both the form and the content of his poetry imply a denial that spirit or meaning, in life as in art, must get embodied, enfleshed, must risk entanglement with matter, if it is to become substantial, just as matter must become involved in transcendence if it is to be redeemed. Cummings has spoken of his poetry as "carnalized metaphysics." The way the Puritan poets used the word *carnal* tells us one reason why their poetry is so seldom successfully incarnational.

As a pilgrim struggling toward a Celestial City wholly elsewhere, the Puritan poet might have found true symbols distracting. His attitude toward poetry was deeply ambivalent: he valued it for what it might do to promote sanctity, but he distrusted it for what it might do to reconcile us to the things of this world. The result of his ambivalence is apparent in the poetry he wrote.

EDWARD TAYLOR

Of all the Puritan poets, only Edward Taylor makes much use in his poetry of what the Puritans called "carnal" things, and even he is generally only *using* them as transparent signs, not valuing them for what they are in themselves. Though he is by far the best of the Puritan poets and though many of his traits as a writer, particularly the way he uses homely imagery, justify the label "metaphysical" that has been given him, yet he often exhibits the bigotry and idolatry that characterize so much of Puritan verse. Only when we think of his style in the largest sense — of the purely poetic aspect of his poetry — are we likely to think of him as belonging in the company of the chief American poets.

When we do think of him this way — when we close the book and remember only certain lines and phrases — we are likely to decide that he occupies a minor but respectable place in our main tradition. For in his attitude toward language and poetic forms Taylor shows us what will later become recognizable as the peculiarly American attitude, an attitude compounded of perhaps equal parts of Puritan eschatology and Transcendental seeking. Taylor's verbal coinages, archaisms, and often personal meanings, his readiness to drop the meter when the thought demands it, his way of twisting, ignoring, or distorting any convention that gets in his way — all this and more makes us think of Emerson and later American poets. If his doctrines are Puritan, his attitude toward language and forms of verse might just as well be called Transcendental.

Even at his poorest, when he seems to be doing little more than rhyming doctrine or history, he suggests traits we find more fully exhibited later in Emerson, Whitman, Dickinson, William Carlos Williams, and Cummings, traits of American Transcendental poetry, in short. His cavalier attitude toward the conventions with which he was acquainted foreshadows Emerson's definition of what true poetry should be, "metre-making argument." Even thematically, there is a sense in which he is in the main stream of American verse. His central question, "Oh, what a thing is man! Lord, who am I?" has been asked over and over by the chief American poets, from Emerson to Roethke. Like Robinson's, his only real interest in man comes when he sees him against the sky; like R. P. Warren, he is interested in definition of the nature of man's sin and his glory.

But all this is very abstract. When the modern reader turns back to the poems themselves, apart from the half a dozen or so best, he is likely to be more disappointed than pleased by most of what he finds. He finds, for instance, relatively little of that tension between attachment to things temporal and longing for things eternal that characterizes most religious poetry of a high order. In the bulk of his poetry Taylor does not have to face the problem of trying to wean himself from a loved but dying world. Most of his poems open with that problem already solved by the Puritan theology and ethos. If the tension between love of the things of this world and longing for Heaven existed in the man, as presumably it must have, it does not generally get into the poetry, except sporadically, and when it does it is denigrated.

One of the best of the Preparatory Meditations, written as devotional exercises before Taylor's monthly administrations of the Lord's Supper, will illustrate the point. Meditation 33, First Series, is often considered one of the finest poems Taylor ever wrote, partly at least because in it there seems to be an acknowledgment of the conflict between the temporal and the eternal; but even here, Taylor does not grant the attachment anything like equal value with the detachment. According to Taylor's dating, the poem was written the day his first wife died. There are evidences in the poem of Taylor's grief at the loss—perhaps the anticipated loss[3] — of his "true love," his "deare," but chiefly Taylor takes this occasion to upbraid himself for loving a mere "Toy" instead of giving all his love to Christ.

The poem is keyed to First Corinthians, 3:22, which Taylor quotes as including "Life is youres." (Actually, he took only a little liberty with the text, condensing to get at what was for him the heart of the matter: "Whether Paul, or Apollos, or Cephas, or the world, or life, or death, or things present, or things to come;

all are your's.") The important point, as Taylor saw it, was that the Faithful are inheritors of eternal life, so that, in effect, Christ *is* their life. Grief then, even grief for one's wife, would be inappropriate. Not attachment but detachment would seem to be our proper relation to the things of this world. For Taylor, this *contemptus mundi* theme must have seemed to be enforced by the preceding verse, "Therefore let no man glory in men. For all things are your's." Prompted by the occasion and habituated as he was to the Puritan tendency toward literalism in interpreting Scripture, Taylor would have read this, "Let no man glory in *men,*" that is, in the "things of this world," the "mites" and "Toys" mentioned in the poem. To make this interpretation Taylor had only to ignore the larger context, which makes it clear that Paul was here advising the quarreling churchmen in Corinth to put aside disputes about whose followers they were and concentrate on the essentials of the faith they had received, from whatever source. Judging from the poem that follows, Taylor seems to have felt that the chief meaning of the passage was that he should not be grieved by the thought of his wife's death.

That he actually was grieved the poem makes very evident, especially in the lines:

> Nature's amaz'de, Oh monstrous thing Quoth shee,
> Not Love my life? What Violence doth split
> True Love, and Life, that they should sunder'd bee?

In these lines loss and promise remain in tension. But if his "true love" for his wife conflicts with his love of Christ, Taylor sees this as a sign of a weakness he should try to conquer. What his *real* "life" is, he has already declared, in his opening stanza:

> My Lord my Life, can Envy ever bee
>   A Golden Vertue? Then would God I were
> Top full thereof untill it colours mee
>   With yellow streaks for thy Deare sake most Deare,
>   Till I be Envious made by't at myselfe,
>   As scarcely loving thee my Life, my Health.

The play on "deare" suggests that the unruly affections are not yet fully under control, but if the heart is torn, the mind knows what the heart *ought* to feel: Christ is the Lord, the Life, the Health — the true "deare." The second stanza implicitly acknowledges the reality of the conflict by the very vehemence of its denial that there should be a conflict:

> Oh! what strange Charm encrampt my Heart with spite
> Making my Love gleame out upon a Toy?
> Lay out Cart-Loads of Love upon a mite?
> Scarce lay a mite of Love on thee, my Joy?

Toward the end of the poem, as Taylor hopes for reunion with his wife in Heaven, "life," which had seemed until now perfectly clear — the promise of eternal life to the faithful — becomes ambiguous: "I and my Life again may joyned bee." In Heaven, he will be able to love Christ as he should, without ceasing to love his wife. Only the assurance of immortality can prevent his being distracted by attachment to mere mites and toys from complete devotion to Christ — "Oh! Graft me in this Tree of Life . . . that I may live." In the end, Taylor is reconciled to his loss, assured that in the light of faith it is really no loss: He has given his wife to be the bride of Christ:

> Give me my Life this way; and I'le bestow
> My Love on thee my Life, and it shall grow.

He has made a kind of promise — *not* to be grieved, *not* to be further distracted from things eternal. We are a long way here from Anne Bradstreet's poem on the burning of her house, in which the conflict of values was almost completely suppressed, but the same theology may be seen at work, denying the significance of a conflict actually felt. One way to state the superiority of Taylor's poem over Bradstreet's is to say that in the earlier poem, except for one line, we have to *guess* that the poet felt grief at the loss of her worldly goods and so turned to God all the more strongly, while in Taylor's poem a real conflict is implicitly acknowledged even while it is being explicitly denied. At his best, Taylor does a great deal more than merely versify doctrine.

But only a handful of Taylor's poems are as good as this one. Generally they tend to be both clotted and incoherent, sometimes incoherent even as statement. A good deal of the time he seems to be making his poems simply by collecting every possible illustrative image he can think of and simply adding them all up. The famous and justly praised "Huswifery" does not prepare us for the bulk of the work in this respect. For the most part, he picks up and drops his metaphors without showing much real concern for them. Meaning is what matters, and this world gets its meaning wholly from outside.

One of his best known, and best, poems will illustrate the point. His "Preface" to "God's Determinations" celebrates the greatness of God, the Creator, in imagery that is, for the most part, effective:

> Upon what Base was fixt the Lath, wherein
> He turn'd this Globe, and riggalld it so trim?
> Who blew the Bellows of his Furnace Vast?
> Or held the Mould wherein the world was Cast?

Throughout the first dozen lines the images used to convey Taylor's wonder at God's making the world are all drawn from *man's* activities in making things — pottery, ironwork, buildings, clothing. But then Taylor turns from making to other activities ("Who in this Bowling Alley bowld the Sun?," perhaps his greatest line) and to objects that in one way or another image the power of a God who

> Can take this mighty World up in his hande,
> And shake it like a Squitchen or a Wand.

The most tightly knit part of the poem, lines three through fourteen, has sometimes been printed as a separate poem. So presented, no explanation is needed, for the excerpt is in no way dependent on what precedes or what follows. And even within these twelve lines, the organizing principle is chiefly external, being supplied by the story of the creation in Genesis. Within the poem — either the whole poem or the excerpt — there is no reason why housebuilding should precede sewing and follow iron-making. And the most memorable line of the group, drawn from bowling, would seem to have no connection with anything that precedes or follows.

There is a kind of curious and perverse appropriateness about Taylor's usual way of organizing his poetry. Taylor uses images allegorically, and from the point of view of the intrinsic quality of the images themselves, often incoherently because "nothing

Man" and his world have no meaning, no reality even, except as they point to God. Taylor's images for the most part are not symbols but signs, pointers, for by definition symbols have intrinsic interest and implicit meaning. From Taylor's point of view, interest in fallen man and his activities or in nature, which had been blasted along with man by the Original Sin, could very easily become excessive. To value highly things carnal was evidence that one was not one of the Elect. "For here have we no continuing city, but we seek one to come."

Taylor's longest poem of those that have been transcribed from his manuscripts, his "Metrical History of Christianity," is about as unreadable as a doggerel poem can be. For more than four hundred crowded pages it versifies the legendary history of those who persecuted, and those who suffered for, the faith. Only occasionally does it rise from verse to poetry, in the normative sense, and then chiefly either to praise God for the wisdom He displays in arranging history as he has, or to dwell with loving interest on the sufferings of persecutor or martyr. Thus the fate of Herod:

> But God goes on and Justice doth thus smite
>   Him with a Slow and burning Fire that makes
> His bowells rot, a greedy Apetite,
>   Worms eating him alive, sore Belly akes
>   A nasty Priapism doth abound
>   In him, and he doth stinck above the ground.

Such passages as this have their own sort of macabre interest, but they are relatively rare, certainly not typical of the poem as a whole. As a whole, this poem is, I think, the dullest poem I have ever tried to read.

Compared with the "Metrical History," "God's Determinations" is easy going. It is in no sense dramatic, as we should expect it to be from the fact that it consists of speeches assigned to various characters — the saint, the unregenerate soul, Christ, and others. It is not dramatic because the content of the speeches is determined by purely doctrinal considerations, not at all by any individualizing of the speakers. And neither is it marked by any special lyric intensity or vividness. But it is more coherent than many of the Meditations, and its exposition of the whole range of Christian doctrine is sometimes marked by interesting psychological insights. Some of the speeches by the soul who fears he is not Elect, for instance, along with the replies of the assured saint, contain very perceptive notations of the dynamics of religious belief. As a whole, though, the poem is just dull.

Taylor's elegy on the death of Samuel Hooker seems to me one of his best organized and sustained poems of any length. It is a dignified and sometimes moving poem, except in the passages where Taylor's bigotry takes over. (Why does everyone comment on Wigglesworth's bigotry and no one on Taylor's? Their theology is the same, and the rigor with which both held to it seems equal.) When Taylor praises Hooker for his "orthodoxy," the poem becomes unintentionally funny. Almost everyone, it seems, except Taylor and Hooker and a tiny group of the faithful — almost everyone is damned, doomed to unending God-inflicted torment — for New England is already, in 1697, in "Declension" from earlier orthodoxy. Not only (of course) all non-Christians, not only Christians with the bad luck to be born "Papists" or Anglicans, but Presbyterians (apostasy) and even liberal Congregationalists (Stoddardeans) — not to mention Quakers, Baptists, Antinomians, and others — all these and more are damned. One would think that it ought to have depressed Taylor at times to consider how few, how very few, were those whom God in His infinite power and justice had been able to save. Hawthorne wrote the proper comment on all this in his "The Man of Adamant": the righteousness of the Puritans, he said in effect in the story of the man whose heart finally turned to stone, was indistinguishable from self-righteousness. Theologically, though not, to be sure, in their polity, Puritans were immersed in caves of self the better, as they supposed, to pursue their separate salvations.

Taylor's very best poems are not weakened, as the elegy on Hooker is, by bigotry. The well-known and justly praised "Prologue" to the "Preparatory Meditations," a half dozen or more of the Meditations themselves, "The Glory of and Grace in the Church Set Out," from "God's Determinations," and a few of the miscellaneous poems, of which "Upon a Spider Catching a Fly" and "An Address to the Soul Occasioned by a Rain" are perhaps the best, deserve and reward more than one reading. In them Taylor is more than a devotional poet and more than the writer of lines useful for illustrating the nature and consequences of Puritan belief. He is the initiator of a great tradition.

Taylor's anticipations of what was destined to become the main tradition in American poetry — insofar as American poetry is not simply a rather inferior branch of British poetry — are somewhat more apparent in the way he uses language and his attitude toward poetic forms than they are in the substance of his poems. Philosophically, the way from Taylor to Emerson is considerably longer than that "from Edwards to Emerson," to borrow Perry Miller's classic phrase. (Reading Taylor, I have often found myself wishing that he had had Edwards' mind, or that Edwards had had his poetic gift, and had been a poet.)

"Upon a Spider Catching a Fly" will sufficiently illustrate Taylor's foreshadowing of Emerson's most typical and effective manner — as well as his theory — in the matter of poetic style. Taylor's short lines, the absence of all ornament and flourish, the impression he creates of a *mind* at work concerned to *say* something important, the colloquialisms combined with syntactical inversions — all this and more suggests Emerson's practice at his best. Taylor's lines "This goes to pot, that not/ Nature doth call," for instance, are recognizably close in *manner* to Emerson's closing lines in "Merlin I":

> There are open hours
> When the God's will sallies free,
> And the dull idiot might see
> The flowing fortunes of a thousand years; —
> Sudden, at unawares,
> Self-moved, fly-to the doors,
> Nor sword of angels could reveal
> What they conceal.

Taylor's style in "Upon a Spider" is perhaps even closer to these lines from Emerson's "Bacchus." Note the inversion in Emerson's last line:

> Water and bread,
> Food which needs no transmuting,
> Rainbow-flowering, wisdom-fruiting,
> Wine which is already man,
> Food which teach and reason can.

It is at once curious and suggestive that many of the features of Taylor's verse that make him seem inferior to George Herbert, whom he so often parallels and apparently echoes, bring him closer to Emerson. Where Herbert is smooth, Taylor is rough; where Herbert is coherent, Taylor is often seemingly, or perhaps really, incoherent; where Herbert works within recognized forms and standard meanings of words, Taylor often seems impatient with form, even the form he has chosen, and quite ready when necessary to bend language to his purposes, even if he has to make up a word or invent a new meaning for an old one. Clearly, Taylor is a lesser poet than either Herbert or Emerson, for entirely different reasons, but comparison of his work with Herbert's tends to lead to the conclusion that Taylor's is hardly worth reading, being only a very inferior imitation; while comparison with Emerson makes him seem a sort of poetic pioneer.

Comparisons are strategic as well as instructive. Whether Taylor ought to be thought of as a late and provincial metaphysical or an early practitioner in a poetic tradition that later diverged more and more widely from British tradition until it produced Whitman and Dickinson — this is a question everyone will want to answer for himself, in his own way.

Deists

JOEL BARLOW

In the seventy-eight years between the death of Edward Taylor and the publication of Joel Barlow's *The Columbiad,* the Puritan faith that had shaped the poetry of the first hundred years was destroyed. To the conservatives of the time, fearful that the softening influence of rationalism would destroy the faith entirely, it seemed that the death of the old way was the work of freethinking infidels and Jacobins inspired by the Devil and the French Revolution.

But it might with at least equal justice be said that Puritanism had committed suicide. The very rigor of its self-defense exposed its inner contradictions. As it fought off doubts within and doubters without, it came to seem to many what it had always seemed to Anglicans and others, a superstitious set of beliefs designed chiefly to absolutize the interests of those who held them by destroying those of everyone else. By Barlow's time what seemed to the religious conservatives a battle between orthodoxy and infidelity, seemed to the religious liberals a struggle not only between superstition and enlightened knowledge but between the right of the few and the right of all men to have hope.

Barlow wastes no time in *The Columbiad* attacking Puritanism. He simply ignores it as irrelevant. Assuming the natural goodness of man as the Puritans had assumed his natural depravity, he placed his hope in Reason, Science, and free institutions. In sprightly, often deft, heroic couplets he redefined the work of the Christian pilgrim: It was now to build the City of God on earth. Reason and freedom would be his tools, but tools used in the service of an unchanged end — universal love. Men find it difficult to accept the guidance of Reason at first; its radiance comes as a shock, but eventually

> All nations catch it, all their tongues combine
> To hail the human morn and speak the day divine.

With a rare hexameter Barlow emphasizes his point: a "human" morn, not a dawn conceived in terms of what Taylor called "nothing Man." But the human morn expresses the immanence of the Divine by the very quality of its humanity: it initiates "the day divine." If Barlow's liberalism looks forward to Emerson and Whitman, there is also a sense, less obvious but not unimportant, in which it may be seen as inverting Puritanism in order to salvage what could be saved from the wreck, a sense of man's high destiny, particularly in America, where the old corruptions and inequities of Europe no longer prevailed.

> Here social man a second birth shall find,
> And a new range of reason lift his mind,
> Feed his strong intellect with purer light,
> A nobler sense of duty and of right,
> The sense of liberty; whose holy fire
> His life shall temper and his laws inspire,
> Purge from all shades the world-embracing scope
> That prompts his genius and expands his hope.

It would be easy to see Barlow as reversing everything Taylor stood for and asserting its opposite. Reading his rational, often witty, and smoothly polished lines, so lacking in the sense of tension and difficulty that marks, and sometimes mars, Taylor's best work, we may come to this conclusion. But it would be only partially justified. On hope, for instance. Barlow is a very hopeful poet; but so, in a different way, is Taylor. The locus of Barlow's hope is in the future, in a Utopian society to be achieved when man has had time to use his reason freely, as he would have in the past if he had not been prevented by evil institutions. Taylor's hope rests on his faith in God; its locus is beyond time. Both are hopeful poets, hoping for different things.

So with other contrasts. If Barlow and other men of the Enlightenment located the Celestial City on earth, in the future, still they took seriously its "celestial" character: it was for them an ideal of a juster, freer, happier society in which man could realize his full potential as a creature made in the image of God. Their conception of it was "secular" compared with Taylor's, but it would be better to speak of a shift of emphasis than of a reversal of ideals. Whether the Kingdom would come in time or out of it has always been a moot question for Christian orthodoxy. Barlow might have claimed — as Jefferson, whose thought was very similar, did claim — that the end result of his revisions in inherited doctrine was to recover the true essence of the faith.

At any rate he was convinced that what was needed was not faith and prayer but for man to use his God-given powers to their limit. He had no doubt that in this new Eden of the West, where no Fall had occurred, man *would:*

> But when he steps on these regenerate shores,
> His mind unfolding for superior powers,
> FREEDOM, his new Prometheus, here shall rise . . .

And with freedom would come that natural, indeed inevitable, unfolding of man's natural powers that kings and churches had hitherto prevented. "Progressive are the paths we go": The dialectic of history is certain; the very geography of America will inevitably produce a new and finer type. Barlow takes the determinism implicit in the Puritan notion of the Predestination of the Elect and the Damned and gives it first a biological, then a social and racial, emphasis, but his version retains its character as Providential. As he explains in the Argument to Book II, modern knowledge shows

> That the human body is composed of a due proportion of the elements suited to the place of its first formation; that these elements . . . produce all the changes of health, sickness, growth, and decay; and may likewise produce any other changes which occasion the diversity of men; that these elemental proportions are varied, not more by climate than temperature and other local circumstances; that the mind is likewise in a state of change, and will take its physical character from the body and from external objects . . .

The new land, in short, will produce the new Adam, unfallen and in no need of divine redemption through a vicarious atonement. We think of Whitman, who exulted that he was "formed from this soil," and of Stevens' Crispin in "The Comedian as the Letter C": "Nota: his soil is man's intelligence . . . Crispin . . . planned a colony."

Man's religion in the past has been the product, Barlow tells us in the poem, of his fear —

> He bows to every force he can't control . . .
> Hence rose his gods, that mystic monstrous lore
> Of blood-stained altars and of priestly power,
> Hence blind credulity on all dark things,
> False morals hence, and hence the yoke of kings.

This false religion has made man "despise the earth" which produces him. In the new land, though, free of the yoke of kings and priests, he will "reject all mystery" and become at last mature:

> Man is an infant still; and slow and late
> Must form and fix his adolescent state,
> Mature his manhood and at last behold
> His reason ripen and his force unfold.

Only when this has happened will he realize his true potential —

> Soaring with science then he learns to string
> Her highest harp, and brace her broadest wing,

With her own force to fray the paths untrod,
With her own glance to ken the total God,

and so to celebrate adequately at last the "harmony divine" immanent in the world. Again we think of Emerson and Whitman and their continued expression of Barlow's Enlightened vision. But as we do so, we are aware of a depth of meaning in their re-expression of it that is quite lacking in Barlow. Or we think of Warren's *Brother to Dragons* and of what Jefferson had to learn in that poem. Barlow's rationalism, though it rests on and promotes noble sentiments and generous ideals, comes at last to seem too easy, even naive. Evil is surely not so easily disposed of.

But *The Columbiad* is more interesting and significant than noting the limitations of Barlow's rationalism would imply. Many readers are likely to find it the first really *readable* long poem in American literature. Barlow handles the heroic couplet with ease and skill. If he uses it imitatively, so, in a sense, did everyone who used it after Pope, who would seem to have completed the exploration of all its possibilities. It serves Barlow well for humor, of which he has a good deal, and exhibits nicely the strength of his thought, which lies in its clarity and coherence. If it is sometimes facile, it moves in a sprightly way. If it lacks depth of suggestiveness, it is urbane and reasonable. Barlow is our closest equivalent in poetry to Jefferson in prose. Though he had a more limited imagination than Jefferson, and closed himself to new ideas sooner, his growth from Calvinistic Federalism, as we see it in *The Vision of Columbus,* to Deistic, physiocratic progressivism in the later version of the same poem, *The Columbiad,* is impressive. Here was a man who, up to a point at least, could learn from experience. His ideas often strike us as crude, when we paraphrase them, but his way of holding — and expressing — them entitles him to be called a genuine poet.

Barlow's best poem is less ambitious than *The Columbiad.* "Hasty Pudding" is surely too long, but its best parts are, as they are intended to be, really funny. It deserves a place among the better pieces of light verse written in America. Its opening lines show that Barlow is no amateur versifier:

Ye Alps audacious, thro' the Heavens that rise,
To cramp the day and hide me from the skies;

Ye Gallic flags, that o'er their heights unfurl'd,
Bear death to kings, and freedom to the world,
I sing not you. A softer theme I chuse,
A virgin theme, unconscious of the Muse,
But fruitful, rich, well suited to inspire
The purest frenzy of poetic fire.

The medial caesuras, end-stopped lines, and antithetical balance all mark this as a competent handling of the Popean heroic couplet,[4] but more than that can be said for it. Classical echoes are worked for all they are worth, with a mock-heroic effect. From the invocation of the first lines, through the allusion to the *Aeneid* in "I sing not you" ("*Arma virumque cano:* Arms and the man I sing"), through the ambiguity of Barlow's description of his subject, the humor derived from incongruity of matter and manner is skillfully handled. Corn meal mush ("hasty pudding") *is* a softer subject than that which Virgil chose to celebrate. And Barlow exploits the ambiguity contained in much conventional language of love — eating, loving, food for the body, food for the soul — with a fine consistency here and in the succeeding dozen or so lines. *Softer, virgin, fruitful, frenzy, fire,* and, in the next verse paragraph, *raptures, sweets, mingled, married,* and *heat* all maintain the sex-eating ambiguity. And it is most appropriate for, as Barlow says, he is *in love* with hasty pudding: "I sing the sweets I know, the charms I feel."

This is witty and skillful verse. The tight form serves Barlow well. The unitary nature of the couplet itself tends toward the aphoristic expression that the humor demands and that Barlow's thought finds its natural expression in even when he is not being humorous. The line tends to be a unit within the unit of the couplet, and the half line within the unit of the line. The result is a set of possibilities of symmetrical relationship so logical that they may be diagrammed; thus,

1 2
1a 1b 2a 2b
Bear DEATH to KINGS, and FREEDOM to the WORLD,

where "death" and "freedom," and "kings" and "the world" are at once parallel (equal grammatically) and antithetical (very different, semantically). Or in this line,

> Glide o'er my palate, and inspire my soul,

in which the medial caesura adds to the shock created by making the act of eating hasty pudding a source of religious inspiration. Barlow is being effectively funny here, but he was soon to express the same idea — "thought" as "ideology," springing from a material base — seriously in *The Columbiad,* in which Columbus is granted the supposedly hopeful vision of the new land creating a new and superior race by the very physics and chemistry of its soil and climate.

PHILIP FRENEAU

Barlow held his ideas lightly, had wit, and managed at his best to put his personal impress on inherited verse forms. Not so Philip Freneau. "The poet of the Revolution" and the pioneer spokesman for certain preromantic attitudes and interests held his religious and political ideas very solemnly and seldom wrote more than a line or two at a time that is in any way memorable. Deist and Anti-Federalist that he was, Freneau suffered in his own time and has been undiscriminatingly praised in ours for reasons having little to do with the quality of his poetry. If Washington had never referred to "that rascal Freneau," it may be doubted that "liberal" scholar-critics of the recent past would have been moved by ideological sympathy to claim so much for him.

Nevertheless, though he ought certainly to be thought of as a minor poet whose work for the most part is no more than competent versifying, Freneau ought not to be completely forgotten. He was more than an apprentice at poetry, as most of his political and religious opponents, the Hartford or Connecticut Wits, were. He was a competent journeyman, born perhaps in the wrong time, when a style of poetry and of thinking was about to be replaced by another that would make his own seem irrelevant. Freneau had the misfortune to be a "transitional" poet, imitative in the old mode, not yet fully aware of, or able to create, the new romantic mode.

As a worker in the British neoclassic sensibility and style, like Barlow, Freneau frequently seems to be saying what Pope or Charles Churchill had said earlier and better. Even his titles can repel us with their solemn, dry abstractness — "On the Universality and Other Attributes of the God of Nature," for example, or "On the Uniformity and Perfection of Nature." By the time we have read the second poem through to the concluding stanza, we are likely to find ourselves remembering that Pope had said this long before Freneau, more briefly, more coherently, and more wittily:

> No imperfection can be found
> In all that is, above, around, —
> All, nature made, in reason's sight
> Is order all, and *all is right.*

The generally accepted opinion about which of Freneau's poems are most worthy of being remembered, insofar as opinion is reflected in the choices of anthologists, seems to me in no immediate need of major correction. Freneau's most readable verse is to be found neither in his philosophic poems nor among his poems on the Revolution, but in his Gothic long poem "The House of Night," which foreshadows Poe, and in his poems on the American scene, which sometimes suggest Bryant. Among the latter, "The Wild Honey Suckle" is worth reading once if only to get the full impact of its memorable final couplet:

> The space between, is but an hour,
> The frail duration of a flower.

These are probably the best lines Freneau ever wrote, but he wrote other poems worth at least one reading, among them "On a Honey Bee," which, unlike most of Freneau's work, suggests in a number of its lines Emerson's later "The Humble-Bee" in style, though its sensibility and theme are very different. There are also, in the same category, "The Indian Burying Ground," with its pointed and economical opening stanza, and "Stanzas: Occasioned by the Ruins of a Country INN, unroofed and blown down in a storm," which is interesting to read as Freneau's rationalistic rehearsal for Emerson's great Transcendental poem "Bacchus." Freneau begins, "Where now these mingled ruins lie/ A Temple once to Bacchus rose," and ends with the hope that the inn may be rebuilt so that the "jovial crew" may gather once again under its sheltering roof. Emerson later would likewise praise the god of intoxication and take his stand against a socially approved prudent and rational sobriety, though with a higher end in mind than conviviality and momentary forgetfulness of nature's storms and darkness.

If Freneau accomplished little that compels our interest, he anticipated not only Emerson but also Bryant and Poe — in theme and subject, and even, occasionally, in style. Whether he was born at the wrong time, culturally speaking, to write greater poetry, or whether, instead, we should say he lacked the "individual talent" to make his own creative and original — and expressive — contribution to the "tradition" of late eighteenth-century British poetry is a question I suspect must remain unanswered.

CHAPTER II

Five New England Poets: The Shape of Things To Come

Longfellow sometimes wrote "lyrics of strange and compelling beauty."

— Robert Frost to Gorham Munson

Caged in the poet's lonely heart,
Love wastes unheard its tenderest tone;
The soul that sings must dwell apart,
Its inward melodies unknown.

— Oliver Wendell Holmes, "To My Readers"

Above all, he [James Russell Lowell] was through and through an American, true to the principles which underlie American institutions. His address on Democracy, *which he delivered in England, is one of the great statements of human liberty.*

— Biographical Sketch, probably by Horace E. Scudder, in the Household Edition of Lowell's poems

It is so much easier to forget than to have been Mr. Whittier.

— Winfield Townley Scott

In an age when all literate people *read* and a great many tried their hands at *writing* poetry, Michael Wigglesworth was a literate Puritan minister who used verse to vivify doctrine. Edward Taylor, our first poet of genuine merit, was a Puritan minister with a flair for versifying, using verse to enrich his own devotions and to occupy his spare time in work for the greater glory of God. Barlow was a statesman and man of affairs who responded to the felt need for a national literature by writing an epic to celebrate the new land. Not one of them thought of himself, or was thought of by others, as principally a poet.

But however Bryant and the other "schoolroom poets" earned their livings, however they spent most of their time, they all in greater or lesser degree, and sooner or later, came to think of themselves and to be thought of by others as poets. Bryant and Whittier were editors, Longfellow, a professor of languages, Holmes, a medical doctor, and Lowell, a professor and ambassador. But even in their own time they came to be known as our chief practitioners in the highest branch of literature. They were our answer to the charge that America had no culture worth mentioning. Symbols of America's coming of age culturally now that she had grown beyond colonial status politically, they lived to see their bearded portraits hung on the walls of schoolrooms and the schools themselves named after them.

Despite such gestures of public recognition and acclaim, they were for the most part not outrageously overvalued by their own age. They were minor poets, and most of their critics knew it — and when it was appropriate said so. If there was ever a genuine need to debunk them in order to achieve a juster estimate of their lasting worth, it is not now. Insofar as they shared, with minor poets in every century, the attitudes and unexamined ideas of a period not ours, they are very hard for us to respond to sympathetically: Except in their very best work, they generally seem irrelevant or simply dull, when not ridiculous. What is needed is an attempt to salvage something of value from their massive Collected Poems.

WILLIAM CULLEN BRYANT

Bryant wrote a dozen or so memorable poems, most of them very early in his life and most of them dark poems. None of the progressive opinions held by the liberal editor of the New York *Post* appear in any of them. They begin a New England tradition in poetry that gets its best expression in Dickinson, Robinson, Frost, and Robert Lowell.

"The Journey of Life" is typical. In it we may see foreshadowings of Robinson's "Credo" and Frost's "Desert Places":

Beneath the waning moon I walk at night,
   And muse on human life — for all around
Are dim uncertain shapes that cheat the sight,
   And pitfalls lurk in shade along the ground,
And broken gleams of brightness, here and there,
   Glance through, and leave unwarmed the death-like
      air.

The trampled earth returns a sound of fear —
  A hollow sound, as if I walked on tombs;
And lights, that tell of cheerful homes, appear,
  Far off, and die like hope amid the glooms.
A mournful wind across the landscape flies,
  And the wide atmosphere is full of sighs.

And I, with faltering footsteps, journey on,
  Watching the stars that roll the hours away,
Till the faint light that guides me now is gone,
  And, like another life, the glorious day
Shall open o'er me from the empyreal height,
  With warmth, and certainty, and boundless light.

The voice here is that of one of the children of the night whose fate Robinson was later to describe and suffer. The "broken gleams" that cannot warm the cold dark air are like the fragmentary words the later poet hears only as "lost, imperial music," understood as giving promise of a clearer message to come but quite without power to prevent the present virtual hopelessness. The distant lights that flicker away leave the speaker alone in his desert place to cultivate not stoicism, as Frost would later do, but hope. But even the hope can only be waited for: It is present in the closing lines only as a promise. So Robinson would later write, "It is the faith within the fear/ That holds us to the life we curse."

Hope deferred is the substance of another poem equally typical of Bryant at his best. "The Death of the Flowers" begins with present loss:

The melancholy days are come, the saddest of the year,
Of wailing winds, and naked woods, and meadows
    brown and sere.
Heaped in the hollows of the grove, the withered leaves
    lie dead;
They rustle to the eddying gust, and to the rabbit's tread.
The robin and the wren are flown, and from the shrubs
    the jay,
And from the wood-top calls the crow, through all the
    gloomy day.

The seasonal rebirth of nature is known but not sensed in the present. The flowers are simply gone:

> The rain is falling where they lie, but the cold November
> rain,
> Calls not, from out the gloomy earth, the lovely ones
> again.

In the last stanza the speaker turns from nature to the human world with its similar desolation and similar hope. He thinks of "one who in her youthful beauty died" and finds it appropriate that one "So gentle and so beautiful, should perish with the flowers." The most significant relationship between the flowers and the girl — the promise of rebirth for both, the hope that April is not the cruellest month — is never stated in the poem, fortunately, though it motivates and controls the implicit metaphor as the reason why it is "not unmeet" that the beautiful and short-lived girl should have been laid in the earth in the autumn with the flowers. The restraint with which Bryant handles his theme in this poem is unusual for him, but it springs from a quite typical honesty. The mind knows what it knows about the progress of the seasons, and what it knows makes it possible to cherish hope, but evidence and hope are not to be confused. The present days remain "the saddest of the year."

Honesty, not irony in the modern manner, is what distinguishes "Hymn to Death." The opening lines implicitly confess the difficulty of what will be attempted — "My voice unworthy of the theme it tries" — the "theme" being the idea that death should be welcomed as a friend, not thought of as "the last great enemy," as it is called in the Bible. Just how difficult a task this would be for Bryant, there is no need to conjecture. In the lines mistakenly prefixed to the first printed version of "Thanatopsis" he had written:

> And 'tis the eternal doom of heaven
> That man should view the grave with fear.

And in the same stanzas he had called the fear of death not only divinely imposed but natural and "sacred":

> There is a sacred dread of death
> Inwoven with the strings of life.

So that when he undertakes in "Hymn to Death" to show that "the world" has slandered death, there is something artificial about the attempt. "I come to speak Thy praises" introduces a debater who, aware of the one-sidedness of the proposition he has chosen to defend, will nevertheless carry the defense as far as possible. "True it is, that I have wept/ Thy conquests," yet the challenge to defend death has been accepted: "Raise then the Hymn to Death. Deliverer!"

But the ingenious defense of death as the friend of virtue ("the wicked, but for thee,/ Had been too strong for the good") has overlooked one fact all along, that death comes to the virtuous as well as to the wicked. The body of the poem ends abruptly with the recognition of this fact, which is the sole subject of the long (thirty-five line) conclusion:

> Alas, I little thought that the stern power
> Whose fearful praise I sung, would try me thus
> Before the strain was ended. It must cease —
> For he is in his grave who taught my youth
> The art of verse, and in the bud of life
> Offered me to the muses. Oh, cut off
> Untimely! . . . .
> . . . .
> . . . . Rest, therefore, thou
> Whose early guidance trained my infant steps —
> Rest, in the bosom of God, till the brief sleep
> Of death is over, and a happier life
> Shall dawn to waken thine insensible dust.

The death of the revered father while the wicked continue to flourish is the emotional fact which invalidates the plausible arguments elaborated in the body of the poem, the *overlooked* fact that proves them but "desultory numbers." The poem is dramatic: It dramatizes the speaker's discovery that the fact of death is not easily disposed of by argument. The conflict it poses is not resolved, as other major conflicts within Bryant's thought and between his thought and his sensibility were not to be resolved, but this poem is the better for the lack of resolution. It records an argument emotionally unacceptable and an emotional fact only partially understood. Honesty forbids that either one should be denied.

> Shuddering I look
> On what is written, yet I blot not out
> The desultory numbers — let them stand,
> The record of an idle revery.

An unresolved conflict of a different sort may be seen in "Thanatopsis." Two voices present this meditation on death, the voice of the poet, who introduces Nature's voice in the opening lines and interprets it in the closing lines, and the voice of Nature itself in the body of the poem; and the two voices seem not to be saying quite the same things about Nature's meanings. Though the poem deserves its fame for the somber beauty of many lines and whole passages, yet it is questionable whether it can be called a unified poem.

Bryant wrote the central section first, in which Nature speaks without interruption, then added the opening sixteen and a half lines and the closing fifteen and a half as introductory and concluding comment. The original poem was stoical and naturalistic in its outlook, offering as consolation to those who are "sick at heart" with fear of death only the reminder that "All that breathe/ Will share thy destiny." Nature's voice tells man that he will be "resolved to earth again" and "mix[ed] forever with the elements." Not only everything individual but everything human will be destroyed — "lost each human trace" — when man has died and become "brother to the insensible rock/ And to the sluggish clod . . ."

The mood in this part of the poem suggests the Book of Ecclesiastes. "One generation passeth away, and another generation cometh: but the earth abideth for ever," wrote the Preacher. Bryant has Nature define itself as "the great tomb of man," so crowded with the graves of the dead that we cannot walk, even in the wilderness itself, without treading upon them —

> . . . The golden sun,
> The planets, all the infinite host of heaven,
> Are shining on the sad abodes of death,
> Through the still lapse of ages. . . .

In short, there seems to be little or nothing in what Nature says in the poem that would lead us to call the Preacher's conclusion unjustified: "For in much wisdom is much grief: and he that increaseth knowledge increaseth sorrow."

But of course to sharpen grief or increase sorrow was far from Bryant's conscious intention. He added a hopeful introduction and a consoling conclusion. Together, they almost succeed in transforming a naturalistic poem into a religiously consoling one. The opening lines promise the balm of Nature's "healing sympathy" to those who approach Nature in loving communion. Nature's voice, the poet tells us, will console and strengthen us "When thoughts/ Of the last bitter hour come like a blight" over our spirits.

The closing lines interpret Nature's words as meaning that a virtuous life is a sufficient basis for hope:

> So live, that when thy summons comes to join
> The innumerable caravan, which moves
> To that mysterious realm, where each shall take
> His chamber in the silent halls of death,
> Thou go not, like the quarry-slave at night,
> Scourged to his dungeon, but, sustained and soothed
> By an unfaltering trust, approach thy grave,
> Like one who wraps the drapery of his couch
> About him, and lies down to pleasant dreams.

The question one must ask about this ending is whether or not it has been adequately prepared for. What is there about the vision of the earth as a tomb, or about being mingled with insensible rocks and sluggish clods, that must be seen as sustaining and soothing? If we may — having lived a virtuous life — approach death with "unfaltering trust," should there not have been some hint earlier in the poem as to the *object* of our trust? If our trust should be in Nature, how shall we conceive Nature so as to justify placing our trust in it? Finally, do not "dreams" imply both a dreamer and an awakening? ("He is not dead but sleepeth.")

Such questions may seem captious, but it is difficult not to think that Bryant has tacked an implicitly religious conclusion onto a naturalistic poem, that he has therefore not earned his consolations, and that they rest on something outside the poem, not in it — on his religious heritage, in short. Ecclesiastes knew better than to try to find comfort in the bitter knowledge he gained from surveying the seasons of man's life: "Let us hear the conclusion of the whole matter: Fear God, and keep his commandments: for this *is* the whole *duty* of man." It seems relevant that God is not mentioned in the poem, nor is there any suggestion that behind the flux of Nature's becoming there is being.

The plea for virtuous living and trustful dying in the concluding lines is essentially Deistic, but Bryant's mature faith was conservative Unitarian. In many later poems he was explicit about the object of his trust, the implication of comparing dying to sleeping, and the way Nature must be viewed if it is to be a source of consolation. For instance, in the late hymn "Blessed Are They that Mourn" he writes:

> For God has marked each sorrowing day,
> And numbered every secret tear,
> And heaven's long age of bliss shall pay
> For all his children suffer here.

And again, in "The Earth Is Full of Thy Riches," on Nature as symbolic language:

> Lord, teach us, while the admiring sight
> Dwells on Thy works in deep delight,
> To deem the forms of beauty here
> But shadows of a brighter sphere.

Two conclusions would seem warranted: that the original portion of "Thanatopsis" is much better poetry than we find in the explicitly religious poems just quoted; and that the hymns offer better reason for conceiving of dying as being like sleeping and having pleasant dreams than anything said in the original part of "Thanatopsis." This does not, of course, mean that the faith in personal immortality Bryant expressed in the hymns is the only way of conceiving of death that can lessen the "blight" cast by fear of death. *The Tibetan Book of the Dead* and Emerson's "Hamatreya" both offer profounder meditations on death than "Thanatopsis" does, both suggest the idea of "merging" with Nature or spirit (but not Nature conceived as "sluggish clod"), and both conceive of death as involving loss of self. Neither the book nor the poem is sentimental, as the concluding consolatory lines of "Thanatopsis" seem to me to be. "Thanatopsis" is a memorable poem, in some passages a great one, but it is still a flawed poem.

"To a Waterfowl," on the other hand, is perhaps almost as good as its ardent admirers have claimed. What *this* poem means it says explicitly and clearly, and nothing in the imagery or the statements in the rest of the poem contradicts what the voice tells us is the meaning of his image. The God who guides the waterfowl in its migratory flight, keeping it safe from the hunter, will similarly guide us through life to a final refuge. "To a Waterfowl" preaches the same message of "unfaltering trust" that the final version of "Thanatopsis" was meant to inculcate, but it does so coherently. Poetically, at least, its trust is well-grounded in experience. Here Bryant *earns* his conclusion.

There is an almost classic simplicity and fitness about the images. The end of day, approaching darkness, a single bird flying toward an unknown destination, the emptiness of the sky in which he is lost to view — all these images work to create the hope first expressed generally in the fourth stanza and then repeated in more specific and personal terms, as though it had "sunk in," taken on more real because more personal meaning, in the last stanza.

The general movement of the poem at once follows the flight of the bird across the sky and the life of man from unknown to unknown. It moves from "rosy" and "crimson" through "desert" (featureless) and "illimitable" to "far," "cold," and "thin," to "dark night" and "abyss": from brightness to the darkness and nothingness which make hope necessary. It balances safety and danger, home and desert, shelter and the abyss. Even while it asserts its faith, it acknowledges the power of unfaith: "Yet stoop not, weary, to the welcome land." One would *think* the bird would be weary after flying all day. The man knows what it means to be weary, and the reader is reminded, too, even as he reads the denial.

Or "Lone wandering but not lost." "Wandering" suggests "lost," but the statement denies the suggestion. Or "the abyss of heaven." "Heaven" — both the sky and Heaven in common speech and here — is both empty and limitless or indefinable. As *empty* it threatens, like the "far height" and "the cold, thin atmosphere"; as *limitless,* it is the source of hope beyond words, offering escape from the hunter death.

Bryant never wrote so well again. "Forest Hymn," "The Prairies," "Monument Mountain," "A Winter Piece," "To a Fringed Gentian," and a few others are poems worth rereading, but most of his work seems quite flat and thin today. Perhaps one of the reasons why he wrote most of his poetry, and all of his best poetry, before he was forty, was that he found he had nothing to say which was not contradicted by something else he wanted to say. Contradictions could remain unresolved in "Hymn to Death" without spoiling the poem, but it is doubtful that Bryant knew clearly just why or how the poem succeeded.

All his life Bryant continued to believe in nationalism, democracy, science, and Progress, to re-express the message of Barlow, in fact. But in his early years, until he got his feelings under control and ceased to write memorable poems, he also *felt* life in terms not too different from Edward Taylor's. The imagistic incoherence that has often been noted in his poems parallels if it does not reflect the incoherence of vision of a poet who could write "The Ages," celebrating Progress, yet propose a return to Nature as the cure for the "guilt and misery" of which he found the world full. Bryant reflected too completely and uncritically the thought of his age to write more than a few fine poems. But in those few he is the worthy initiator of a tradition still with us.

HENRY WADSWORTH LONGFELLOW

Bryant had just two things to say as a poet: that despite the reality of Progress, the "guilt and misery" of the world demand to be countered by a faith beyond the evidence, and that Nature supports such a faith, offering a balm to the troubled heart. Longfellow had just one thing to say, and he tried as best he could to deny it: that time is inherently and inevitably man's enemy, bringing only loss and nothingness. Longfellow is a very melancholy poet whenever he writes from the center of his sensibility. There are American poets with a sharper and more meaningful sense of tragedy, but none sadder, none with fewer resources of spirit to counter the blackness.

He did what he could to cheer himself and reassure his age by repeating the clichés about Progress and Enlightenment. But though his words of cheer convinced many and helped win him the position Oliver Wendell Holmes accorded him as "our chief singer," he himself remained unconvinced. Though even so generally perceptive a reader as his friend James Russell Lowell summed up his impression of the role Longfellow played in his age by calling his art "consoling," the Faust figure in "The Golden Legend" really speaks for Longfellow when he says:

> This life of ours is a wild aeolian harp of many a joyous
> strain,
> But under them all there runs a loud perpetual wail, as of
> souls in pain.

When he took his own advice and looked into his heart and wrote, he recorded the voices of the night or wrote of the sound of the sea, which reminded him of his lost youth and of the "mystery of grief and pain" found "in the very heart" of life. *Evangeline* ends with lines strangely out of tune with the message of faith proclaimed so loudly throughout the body of the poem:

> While from its rocky caverns the deep-voiced,
> neighboring ocean
> Speaks, and in accents disconsolate answers the wail of
> the forest.

The more he was unconvinced, the louder he needed to shout the stereotypes on which he hoped Hope might firmly rest. The last lines he wrote, a week before his death, rebuked the heart, with its vain attachment to the past, and proclaimed the triumph of Enlightenment and Liberalism in the inevitable march of Progress:

> Out of the shadows of night
> The world rolls into light;
> It is daybreak everywhere.

Everywhere but in the poet's heart perhaps. Though "The Bells of San Blas," which ends with these lines, is one of Longfellow's better poems, strengthened by a dramatic interplay between the voice of the bells and the voice of the poet, who interprets the voice of the bells, yet even here the hopeful conclusion seems relatively unprepared for, tacked on. To the "me," the speaker of the poem, the bells have sung "a strange, wild melody" of decay and loss; they have spoken of an age "that is fading fast" in such a way as to "touch and search" the heart. Nothing they have said has really prepared us for the *jubilate* of the last lines. What the poem *intends* to mean is that the liberal "new faith" has happily triumphed over Catholicism. What it actually means is that it is very saddening to think of the old unenlightened times "when the world with faith was filled," but still one ought to rejoice — just why, the poem does not say.

If there is some disparity between intended and achieved meanings in "The Bells of San Blas," there is absolute incoherence in Longfellow's most famous poem, "The Psalm of Life." It is deeply revealing of the nature of the poet's fame and of the age that honored him that this should have become his best-loved poem; for though it intends to mean that life is worth living after all, what it effectively *does* mean is that life *must* be worth living but the poet can't think why. One stanza in the poem comes through clearly and remains in the end without contradiction:

> Art is long, and Time is fleeting,
> And our hearts, though stout and brave,
> Still, like muffled drums, are beating
> Funeral marches to the grave.

Generations have been consoled by the comfort offered by the other stanzas, but the price of comfort in this case is shutting off thought. The propositions are as mixed as the metaphors. The basic exhortation is that we must "Act, — act in the living Present!" We must "trust no Future" and "let the dead Past bury its dead"; the present is all that concerns us. But three stanzas before this we have been told that our destiny is "to act, that each to-morrow/ Find us farther than to-day" — in other words, to act in the present for the sake of the future. And in the stanza following we are told both that we should take comfort from the lives of those in the past and that we should live so as to guide and inspire men of the future. What then *is* the relationship of past and future to the present, of memory and hope to present action? The poem can tell us only, "Learn to labor and to wait" — labor for what, wait for what, or how this waiting is consistent with not trusting the future, it does not say.

The propositional confusion is mirrored in the metaphors. One example will suffice.

Lives of great men all remind us
We can make our lives sublime,
And, departing, leave behind us
Footprints on the sands of time;

Footprints, that perhaps another,
Sailing o'er life's solemn main,
A forlorn and shipwrecked brother,
Seeing, shall take heart again.

If we try to picture these images as images, what happens? How long will footprints left in sand last? Will the next tide wipe out the whole record of the past? And even if the men of the future arrive before that happens, how will they be able to *see* them while out at sea, "sailing o'er life's solemn main"? And how can the shipwrecked brother be "sailing" and *at the same time* "shipwrecked"? Either the ship has been wrecked or it has not. If not, he is sailing and can't see the footprints on the beach; if so, he is not sailing any longer but walking and being inspired.

It is relatively easy but ordinarily not worthwhile to make fun of poor poetry. But "A Psalm of Life" is too bad a poem and yet too typical of the age to be simply forgotten. To the generations that grew up knowing it by heart it meant a message of courage and hope which needed no definition and discouraged inquiry into their sources and reasons — for the propositions which expressed and motivated them seemed axiomatic. Men with better minds than Longfellow settled for Activism in a time bemused by the idea of Progress. Carlyle made a doctrine of work, and Marx thought progress toward the Utopian future at once inevitable and demanding the utmost sacrifice. Only a few wondered, as did Hawthorne, Thoreau, and Melville, whether we were riding on the train or being run over, or whether the celestial railroad built by the new faith were taking us to heaven or to hell. For the many to whom Longfellow spoke effectively, it seemed best not to question the direction of the action or probe too curiously into the nature of the choices necessarily involved. It was enough to take heart and be up and doing.

That this is just what the poem meant, that such a summary does not do the poem an injustice by omitting some hint of the seriousness and difficulty of our choices, is suggested by the greater clarity with which the poet said much the same thing in "Excelsior." Critically, James Thurber said all that needs to be said of this poem in his satiric illustrations for it. Only a very bad poem could be so completely destroyed by a few drawings. The point enforced by the little allegory of the poem is that one must, like the youth who carried the banner with the strange device — "Excelsior," higher — go onward and upward.

Why, the voice in the poem does not say. Instead, he reports a voice from the sky which is no more informative: It merely repeats, serenely, "Excelsior." Meanwhile the dauntless young man is dead, as the old man had foreseen —

> There in the twilight cold and gray,
> Lifeless, but beautiful, he lay.

This, apparently, if the *plot* means anything, is where idealism will get you. But Longfellow, as usual when faced with the need or desire to speak hopefully, did not take his story seriously, any more than he had taken his metaphors seriously in "A Psalm of Life." Longfellow, we may conclude, was a very sad poet who became not simply banal but incoherent and confused when he tried to cheer himself or others. "Excelsior" and "A Psalm of Life" may well be the worst famous poems ever written.

Several of Longfellow's longer poems are better, but for the most part they are not very good, and for similar reasons. In the first place, the lack of intelligence so glaringly apparent in "A Psalm of Life" is also apparent in the longer poems, though usually not to the point of producing absurdity. Ardently admiring Goethe, Longfellow rewrites the Faust story in "The Golden Legend," but in doing so he completely ignores Goethe's meaning: *his* Faust makes a pact with the Devil for no apparent reason. Or in "The Divine Tragedy" he retells the Gospel story of Christ's Passion and Resurrection in the words of the Evangelists, with a minimum of creative change and with no implied criticism or interpretation, leaving us wondering whether he has abandoned his Unitarian theology for orthodoxy or is simply not interested in the meaning of the events, or supposed events, he records.

Christus, composed of "The Divine Tragedy," "The Golden Legend," and "The New England Tragedies," is his most ambitious poem, intended to interpret the whole development and meaning of Western history. Longfellow left the work unfinished; what remained undone was precisely those parts Longfellow would have found hardest to do, and almost certainly would have done least well: the introductory and transitional material supplying the rationale of his three-part scheme of interpretation. But we can guess what he intended. The three periods — ancient, medieval, and modern — would be characterized by the three theological virtues, hope, faith, and love, with St. Paul's order significantly reversed for the first two. The unconnected parts, as we have them and from statements outside the poems, indicate that he must have intended to say the ancient world was lifted out of its despair by the hope it found in Christ; the medieval world elaborated this hope into a mighty structure of polity and theology, all based on and expressive of its faith; and the modern world, though less hopeful and less faithful — or credulous — has nevertheless discovered for the first time the real meaning of the hope and the faith — love.

But this is largely conjecture, resting as much on evidence outside the poems as on the faint implications of the poems themselves. Perhaps it is fortunate that the grand plan was never completed, considering the muddle Longfellow always got into when he tried to philosophize. Though the general interpretation as we have reconstructed it seems worthy enough for a long poem, a direct expression of it in philosophic verse might well have led to the kind of thinking we have in "Excelsior" and "The Psalm of Life." In a curious way then, the very *lack* of explicit thought in *Christus* as the poet left it contributes to whatever power the separate poems have. "The Divine Tragedy" is the least valuable of the three. As a symbolic gesture, its patchwork of quotation and paraphrase becomes a kind of liturgical re-enactment, a gesture of fidelity to which criticism is irrelevant, a genuflection. "The Golden Legend" has thought in it, but not of a sort that would helpfully advance the plan for *Christus* as a whole. The medieval world, supposedly the Age of Faith, emerges from the poem as perplexed, doubtful, torn between head and heart: a rehearsal for the nineteenth century, in short. So far as the poem works with us at all, it is only as we read the Faustian Prince Henry's meditations as Longfellow's own:

> It is the sea, it is the sea,
> In all its vague immensity,

Fading and darkening in the distance!
Silent, majestical, and slow,
The white ships haunt it to and fro,
With all their ghostly sails unfurled,
As phantoms from another world
Haunt the dim confines of existence!

. . . .

Above the darksome sea of death
Looms the great life that is to be,
A land of cloud and mystery,
A dim mirage . . .
Leaving us in perplexity,
And doubtful whether it has been
A vision of the world unseen,
Or a bright image of our own
Against the sky in vapors thrown.

The two New England tragedies that make up the third part of *Christus* are very much better. They contain in fact some of Longfellow's best writing. Here for once he had something to say and said it well. The burden of these tales of the Puritans is the Pauline — and perfectly orthodox — idea that love is the greatest of the three theological virtues. But the Puritans betray the virtue to which they ought to be dedicated, as their persecutions of the Quakers and of the witches show. "John Endicott" exposes their bigotry and "Giles Corey of the Salem Farms" their superstitious cruelty. Both are competent, thoroughly readable narrative poems, too little known by those who continue to read anything by Longfellow. They suffer only by comparison with Hawthorne's "Endicott and the Red Cross," "The Gentle Boy," "The Man of Adamant," and "Young Goodman Brown."

Evangeline and *Hiawatha* were very famous in Longfellow's time and deserve a better fate than being read only by school children, as is now the case, when they are read at all. The first suffers from Longfellow's customary sentimentality and from the fact that between the opening tragedy of the dispossession and separation and the final tragedy of the reunion at death, nothing happens which is ultimately of any significance — for Evangeline or for the reader. Not enough was given in the tale as Longfellow heard it to make a long poem, but a long poem it must be. Between the high points at beginning and end the poet doggedly fills in the details of a life of almost incredible dedication and frustration, but the reader quickly foresees that the continual near-meetings will come to nothing and is tempted to skip to the end to get the suffering over with.

I have already quoted the closing lines of the poem, which record the "disconsolate" voices of the forest and the sea, but such are not the tone of the official voice of the poem. That voice records without comment the words of the priest, telling Evangeline to "have faith, and thy prayer will be answered!" Her prayer *isn't* answered, but the narrative voice seems not to notice the fact. Instead, he records, also without irony, the voice of Nature, telling Evangeline "that God was in heaven, and governed the world he created." That He was doing a rather poor job of governing in this case, from the *human* point of view, would seem obvious to the modern reader, but not, apparently, to Longfellow. Instead, he records the "inexpressible sweetness" that fills Evangeline's heart every time it seems possible that her indefatigable pursuit of her lost lover may be successful. One would think that at last the girl might have learned from disappointment not to hope.

Instead she becomes a "Sister of Mercy" carrying a taper through the night in her visits to comfort the sick among the poor and acquiring an inner light that made the recipients of her charity think they saw "Gleams of celestial light encircle her forehead with splendor." Hawthorne may have found here hints for his treatment of Hester in *The Scarlet Letter,* begun a couple of years after he read the poem; at any rate, he was, as he wrote Longfellow, much moved by it. Like Hester, Evangeline visited the sick carrying a light and seeming to be surrounded by a halo, but the distance between Hawthorne and Longfellow is measured by the essential difference between the two strikingly similar portraits. Hawthorne did not suppose, or try to get the reader to believe, that Hester's development in charity canceled the tragedy of her life. Hawthorne's portrait is drawn without the luxury of sentimentality.

Evangeline is a "romantic" tale in which "romantic" becomes almost a synonym for "escapist," for a refusal to take a good hard look at the facts and what they imply. Still, it has many passages of moving and authentic poetry, and for the most part the pathos does not turn into bathos. It is not difficult to see why Hawthorne was moved by it in an age less suspicious of its tender feelings than ours. With the excision of a few passages it might seem almost worthy of the fame it once had. *With* these passages, however, it must seem to most of us fatally flawed by a feature perfectly typical of Longfellow: What comes through in the poem is the terrible pathos of a life dominated by loss and longing; the message of cheer and comfort, on the other hand, seems wholly bogus and completely unrelated to the facts as recorded.

Hiawatha is "romantic" in a somewhat different sense: it idealizes the Indians and is nostalgic for a simpler culture, closer to Nature; but it is not, for the most part, sentimental. The Indian legends are recorded faithfully enough to be convincing, and though Hiawatha and his associates are sometimes made to seem more like Victorian Bostonians than like Ojibways and Dacotahs, for the most part there is no necessity for making the myths more comforting than they are because they are *Indian* myths. Longfellow has been blamed for his ending, in which, as Hiawatha dies, a missionary priest brings the message of a higher and truer religion which Hiawatha then commends to his people, but only a complete relativist about religious matters ought to find this necessarily false or sentimental. It is at least true enough to history to be in a quite different category from the appliquéd moralizing of *Evangeline*.

Longfellow's generally fatal lack of intelligence, as well as the core of feeling that was all he really had to work with as a poet, are both exhibited in one of his better poems, "The Chamber Over the Gate." The chamber is the one in which, in the Biblical story, David wept for his son Absalom, who had died while in rebellion against his father. But Longfellow, typically, ignores all the *meaning* of his source, using only the literal scene, which supplies him his title, and the emotion of grief. His story involves no conflict of loyalties, no moral problems, no forgiveness of disloyalty. "The light goes out in our hearts" in the poem simply because of death: it could be anybody's death, for it has nothing to do with the *quality* of life. "That 't is a common grief/ Bringeth but slight relief." The closing lines, from the Bible, have almost none of the meaning their original context gives them — "Would God I had died for thee, O Absalom, my son!" The grief in the poem is genuine and the poem has a valid meaning of its own, but the Biblical trappings are largely irrelevant to it.

Longfellow raided Western literature for themes and subjects, but he found very little in it but what he brought to it, a "disconsolate" — one of his favorite adjectives — sense that life was no more than a funeral march to the grave. It is partly for this reason that generally his simplest, least ambitious, most personal, and shortest lyrics are his best. Comparison with writers of more intelligence is usually fatal to him, but all too frequently he enforces the comparison by borrowing from them or imitating them. His Shakespearean dramas have all the "teachable" qualities of Shakespeare without any of the genius. The examples of Shakespeare and Goethe overwhelmed him, and the adulation so quickly won with his first volume, *Voices of the Night,* encouraged him to believe that he could at once be the Voice of the People and the bardic Voice of Truth.

His best poems seem therefore to have been written almost despite himself, without his knowing what he was doing or what they really meant. In a dozen or more short poems Longfellow is more than a merely competent story-teller and versifier. In them he writes of the "autumn within" as he thinks of his lost youth and listens to the sound of the sea. "The Fire of Driftwood" builds its metaphor of life as a fire without need to underscore "the secret pain" that fills the hearts of those aware of the gloom beyond the hearthside, or to add any message of comfort. "The Tide Rises, The Tide Falls" may seem pointless until we realize that the traveler whose footprints are effaced on the sand and who is seen no more is man, every man. Here, as in all of Longfellow's best poetry, "Sleep and oblivion/ Reign over all."

"The Ropewalk" is almost the only poem Longfellow ever wrote that gives us a *reason* for life's sadness, apart from the inevitability of death. (It is also one of the few in which Longfellow resisted the temptation to moralize. In it he lets his picture speak for itself, perhaps because he could not bring himself to acknowledge the full implication of what he had done.) The spinners of the rope walk backward "While the wheel goes round and round/ With a drowsy, dreamy sound" like that of "sleep and oblivion." They cannot see where they are going, and though they are laboring, nothing in the poem would tempt us to describe them as "up and doing."

"The Jewish Cemetery at Newport" is notable for its restrained expression of sympathy for the sufferings of the people it concerns, but it too presents men walking backward to the grave. Though it might offend the feelings of a Jew for whom Judaism is a living religion with meaning for the future, there is no anti-Semitism here, for the poem implies that the fate of the backward-looking people is really man's fate. Inevitably man looks backward to a lost youth, an age of faith, as he is swept onward by time to an alien land.

The stridency, the general irrelevance to their context, and the self-contradictory nature of Longfellow's efforts to deny this melancholy vision are the proof that the part of him able to produce successful poems remained unconvinced by the arguments he eagerly seized upon. Only when he forgot the arguments and wrote out of the recurrent, almost continuous, mood of sadness did he write really well. "Snow-flakes" succeeds in part just because it does not try to tell us why the snowstorm is more truly revealing of life's meaning than are the hope and promise of spring.

> This is the poem of the air,
> Slowly in silent syllables recorded;
> This is the secret of despair,
> Long in its cloudy bosom hoarded,
> Now whispered and revealed
> To wood and field.

Here Longfellow walks in the company of Emily Dickinson and Robert Frost, overshadowed but not obliterated by their presence. Like Bryant, what he found when he looked into his heart was not what the age, or he himself, wanted to confront. Bryant stopped writing, except for an occasional poem. Longfellow looked into foreign literature and wrote, as pleasanter and more likely to bring him the fame he coveted. Since he had neither Bryant's genuine concern for liberal social causes to distract him, nor Frost's cultivated toughness to help him to endure, the blackness he saw and upon occasion memorably expressed was too much for him. He retreated into the serene opulence of the public image of "our chief singer," whose voice, as his friend Holmes also said, "wins and warms . . . kindles, softens, cheers [and] calms the wildest woe and stays the bitterest tears!" The benign confidence of the white-bearded figure on the schoolroom wall was won at a high price.

OLIVER WENDELL HOLMES

Oliver Wendell Holmes, friend of Longfellow and of most of the other famous literary figures of the age, was at once a more intelligent and attractive man and, finally, a less interesting poet. Combining the practice and teaching of medicine with a lifelong devotion to poetry and philosophy, he became not just Boston's but America's most famous after-dinner speaker and occasional poet.

Whatever the occasion, he could turn out a graceful and fitting poem for it. In full-fledged revolt against what in rural and small town New England was still counted as religious orthodoxy, he devoted himself to an attack on the old and an exploration of the possibilities of the new ways of thinking and feeling. Wit, urbanity, and charm were not more conspicuous in the man than in the verse, and in both, an essential kindness prevented any sharp edges in his satire. When he attacked ideas, he tried to do so without hurting those who held them. He epitomized the best that Boston Brahmin culture could produce. But very little of his verse survives the public occasions that produced it.

Unlike Longfellow, who preferred feeling to thinking and kept the two as separate as he well could, Holmes admired and tried to practice wholeness. He faced the issues of his day and thought about them intelligently. But the positive solutions at which he arrived provided meager inspiration for verse. He versified copiously, but generally not about the things that meant most to him. Refusing for himself (though he professed to admire it in his friend) Longfellow's sentimentalism, and lacking ability to feel the poetry in the *ideas* that came as he explored to the limit the implications of immanence, he could ordinarily write verse effectively only when it was "light," only when it came from the top of the mind. The more serious subjects he thought about constantly, with mixed feelings, but generally left unversified. When he wrote about them it was usually in prose.

An exception to this, the only important exception, is "The Chambered Nautilus." Here he begins by distinguishing between the way "poets" would treat the sea shell he is contemplating and (by implication) the way he, a man of science, will treat it.

"Poets" — that is, romantic poets, who make a practice of not distinguishing between fact and fancy — "feign" that the shell is a ship, that the sea it sails is "unshadowed," that summer is always "sweet" and "enchanted," and that there are "sea-maids" sunning their hair on coral reefs. Like Prufrock much later, the speaker cannot believe in mermaids any more, though unlike Prufrock, he does not express any nostalgia for the lost belief, at least not in this poem. He does elsewhere, however, and perhaps this would be a richer poem if he did here too.

His concern is not with such "romancing" but with the simple practical moral lesson the shell can teach us. The living creature that secreted the shell around itself built a larger "house" each year, growing physically as we must mentally and spiritually until at last, at its death, the walls that shut it from heaven, that kept it from attaining the absolute in life, were at least less restrictive than formerly. Though the house it built for itself becomes a "crypt" or burial vault when the creature dies with heaven still unattained, the promise contained in the expanding form of the shell is not canceled, only qualified. The image illustrates the basic law of life, movement, growth, *toward,* but never in this life *attaining,* the ideal.

The voice the poet hears speaking from "the deep caves of thought" tells him that we should do likewise, welcome the challenge of the new, leaving the old "temple" precisely in order to fulfill its own implicit promise. "Shut thee from heaven with a dome more vast" suggests Holmes's basic paradox. The liberal theology of the "new temple" will share the characteristic of all theologies — it will shut man from heaven, reduce the Absolute to finite formulas; but at the same time it will be closer to adequacy, its dome "more vast." It too will presumably become a "crypt," but a better one because more open to the skies. As Holmes said elsewhere, in an early poem not reprinted in his three-volume *Poetical Works,* "We trust and doubt, we question and believe,/ From life's dark threads a trembling faith to weave."

Holmes was fond of saying that a faith which feared *thought* was doomed. For the Nautilus not to have moved on to more spacious mansions would have been to value security over adventure; but the security would have been supposed, not real, and could only have been attained at the cost of a death farther from heaven than necessary. The lesson the shell has to teach us is not, finally, that we should prefer facts to "fancy" but that openness to life is better than closedness, that life is an adventure with no limits that can be established. As the crypt opens to the sky, the dome of the new temple opens toward heaven. As Holmes said in one of his medical addresses on the fact and limits of biological mechanism, "In conclusion, we recognize our spiritual natures as having only incidental and temporary relations with the material substance and general forces of the universe." The new temple pointed to God not less surely but more surely than the old. Starting by saying, in effect, let's have no more poetic make-believe, let's have *facts,* the poem ends, like the shell it meditates on, by opening up new vistas for imagination and feeling to inhabit.

Much more typical of most of Holmes's best work is the famous "Deacon's Masterpiece." It is typical in a number of ways. Most of the doctor's serious poems are very flat, but in his light verse his wit comes to his rescue. Again, except for "The Chambered Nautilus," Holmes is almost always more effective in attack than in defense: The absurdities of old thought and ways he saw clearly enough, but the virtues of the new were present to him less clearly, at least so far as his imagination was concerned. His heart was loathe to follow where his mind led: He found it difficult to make poetry from either alone. Even of the Puritan system of belief, which repelled both heart and mind, he said once, "A faith which breeds heroes is better than an unbelief which leaves nothing worth being a hero for."

But if his heart ordinarily failed to find completely satisfactory lodging in the shape of things to come, no such problems faced him in "The Deacon's Masterpiece." Its attack on tightly logical systems of thought is in the name of reasonableness. One would have to go outside the poem to show that it foreshadows James's pragmatism — and that of the doctor's son, Chief Justice Holmes — for the poem contents itself with satirizing the mistakes of an overconfidence in "logical" reason, leaving the better way of thought merely implied. But the better way *is* implied. If a philosophy or theology is not too tightly constructed, it is possible, because of its very openness, to repair it, to patch it up as need be. The deacon's masterpiece, by contrast, was invulnerable to attack or decay at any point. Equally strong everywhere, it could neither break down nor be repaired: It had simply to vanish. "Logic is logic. That's all I say."

That's all Holmes *wanted* to say, or thought he needed to say —

to the perceptive. "Logic" is not enough. Deductive reasoning can be so skillful as to make any system, even the most repellent or ridiculous, invulnerable to attack — until its premises are denied, at which point it simply vanishes as a system one must take seriously, without ever having been "disproved." If anyone wanted to apply the poem's point to Calvinism, he was free to do so — but since Calvinism was not mentioned, no latter-day Calvinists' feelings would be hurt.

But the shay *was,* after all, a "deacon's" masterpiece, and it disappeared just as the parson got to "fifthly" in his sermon. Those who wanted to take the hint could do so. Jonathan Edwards had died just a hundred years before the poem was written and published, and he had "proved," in his most famous work, *The Freedom of the Will,* that the will is not free, though man remains responsible before God for his actions. Holmes had no answer to Edwards' logic: he simply refused to believe the conclusion it dictated. As he said once in a lecture, after stressing the powerful case that could be made for mechanism or determinism on the basis of biological evidence, "I reject . . . the mechanical doctrine which makes me the slave of outside influences, whether it work with the logic of Edwards, or the averages of Buckle; whether it come in the shape of the Greek's destiny, or the Mahometan's fatalism; or in that other aspect, dear to the band of believers . . . 'election.' "

But, it has been asked, if Holmes had Edwards in mind as the "deacon" who built the masterpiece that is the subject of the "logical story" told by the poem, why is the date of its completion given as 1755 instead of 1754, the date when Edwards' *Freedom of the Will* was published, as Holmes naturally knew? Chiefly on the basis of this puzzling discrepancy, some commentators have been led to question whether the poem refers to Calvinism at all. But of course it *does.* For Holmes, Calvinism, which Edwards had defended in his famous work, was *par excellence* the system so tightly logical that one was powerless to answer it in logical terms: One was forced simply, as Holmes said, not to answer but to "reject" it. He rejected it, just as he rejected Oriental or any other form of fatalism and as he rejected scientific determinism, for which, as he often pointed out, the evidence kept piling up and piling up.

The point is really that the poem satirizes *any* logical system containing clear thinking that appears to lead inevitably to a conclusion repellent to one's sense of truth. Life is larger than logic, and intelligence — for Holmes, more flexible. It is not only Calvinism that leads to conclusions that must be rejected even though we can't prove them wrong. But Calvinism was certainly, in Holmes's mind, the best and most pertinent illustration of a system at once perfectly logical and perfectly mistaken. The narrowness of Calvinism is of course suggested in the poem by the New England dialect of the deacon. But in its deepest implications, the poem anticipates Frost's pragmatic rejection of rationalism in "The Bear."

The poem treats its subject humorously, but privately Holmes thought Calvinism not just mistaken but vicious. He objected to it not as one who was irreligious might, as an extreme example of religious superstition, but on moral and, precisely, religious grounds. It not only, he thought, denied man his dignity, it denied God his sublimity, reducing him to an unjust Oriental potentate. But most of all it offended the moral sense, especially in its doctrine of Election. "Any decent person," he once wrote — in prose, typically —

> ought to go mad if he really holds . . . such opinions. Anything . . . that makes life hopeless for the most of mankind . . . ; anything that assumes the necessity of the extermination of instincts which were given to be regulated, no matter by what name you call it, no matter whether a fakir, or a monk, or a deacon believes it, . . . ought to produce insanity in every well-regulated mind.

This is a more pointed and viable comment on Calvinism than anything he ever said in his verse. The closest he ever came to speaking his full mind on the subject when he spoke as a poet was in "Urania: A Rhymed Lesson," in which he characterized the Calvinist mind negatively enough but in such general terms that the sting of the criticism is largely removed:

> Dark is the soul whose sullen creed can bind
> In chains like these the all-embracing mind.

We have to guess whom he has in mind as the liar when he cautions,

Trust not the teacher with his lying scroll,
Who tears the charter of thy shuddering soul;

that is, who denies man's freedom and dignity, belittling man to enhance God. "O what a thing is man?" Edward Taylor had asked. Holmes answered, a creature made in the image of God and created to be free, whether he likes his freedom or not:

Made in his image, thou must nobly dare
The thorny crown of sovereignty to share.

But these statements were made in an early poem that Holmes decided not to preserve in his collected works. Holmes was not only genuinely kind, as I have said, so that he tried to keep his satires as general as possible, with the result that they usually strike us as harmless in both senses, as not likely to hurt anyone and not having much point; he was also, despite his wide culture, at bottom a provincial. Boston, he *felt,* though he *knew* better, was the world. His criticism of the "orthodoxy" of his Puritan forefathers seemed to him tantamount to a criticism of Christianity itself; and a criticism of Christianity was tantamount to an attack on religion. But there are other versions of Christianity besides Calvinism, and other religions besides Christianity.

Religion he thought essential. All he wanted to do was to purify his ancestral religion of its errors, in effect, to save it from itself. Chiefly this meant to him cleansing it of the "meanness" of Calvinism. Predestination, total depravity, suspicion of man's natural instincts, all these must go. Man's freedom and dignity and the essential goodness of the created world must become articles of faith. Like Emerson, he wanted not to minimize or deny the role of the Absolute in our lives but to magnify it by increasing wonder. Man, he was sure, has an immortal soul and an eternal destiny, and Nature, properly understood, reveals God. "Thus . . . we arrive," he concluded a lecture on the latest trends in medical science,

> independently of Revelation, at the doctrine of Miracles. . . . All being is . . . one perpetual miracle, in which the Infinite Creator, acting through what we often call secondary causes, is himself the moving principle of the universe he first framed and never ceases to sustain.

Jonathan Edwards ought to have been pleased with this, recognizing that both its method and its conclusion paralleled his own. Other passages in Holmes's writing, particularly those stressing man's power and dignity, he would not have liked so well, of course, but an impartial judge of the dispute could easily make a strong case in purely Biblical terms that it was Edwards and not Holmes who lacked "orthodoxy" on this matter. He might point out that it was not the Old Testament or the four Gospels or even the record of the early church in the Book of Acts that stressed man's depravity, but Paul and Augustine and Calvin. Attacking Calvinism in mid-century Boston was almost like beating a dead horse, or rather, a dying back-country horse. There were social and personal reasons, but no real religious reason, why Holmes had to make his satirical verse so bland.

But the personal and social reasons were real enough. The contrast between the earliest verse and the bulk of the later work makes clear what happened to him as a poet. The earliest poems are less skillfully versified and constructed but there is much more in them of the kind of thought we find later only in the prose. The career that Holmes chose for himself, or allowed himself to be chosen for, that of after-dinner poet, put a premium on charm and a penalty on depth. He found he had a natural talent for the role of cultivated entertainer that had become his. Paradoxically, the genial wit and charm that will keep a few of the later poems alive with the kind of life that anthologies have, became a means of evasion. More and more as he specialized his role, the verse became less than the man. It was in an early poem he chose not to preserve, "The Secret of the Stars," that he wrote what seems to me his most memorable line:

> What thou shalt tell us, grant us strength to bear.

JAMES RUSSELL LOWELL

Thinking sadly, in "The Cathedral," of an earlier time, both personal and cultural, when "sense" and "soul" were more in tune, when thought did not conflict with and sterilize feeling, Lowell wrote, "I might have been a poet." He *was* a poet — but a minor one who never realized his potentialities. "The Cathedral" is one of the rewarding long meditative poems in American literature,[1] marked by a more sophisticated awareness of the nature of the challenge of the new scientific thought to the old faith than any poem of its time; but it is written in very tired language. Reading Lowell today is likely to awaken a stronger sense of unrealized potential than is the case with any other of the "schoolroom poets." No other one of them brings us so close to Whitman or, in thought, to Henry Adams, or to Lowell's English contemporaries Tennyson and Arnold, yet leaves us in the end so far away from them.

Lowell was much more *thoughtful,* as a poet, than Bryant, and had a much richer sensibility. He could respond to much more than the sight of Berkshire nature and the thought of the past and death. He was very much more intelligent and, in any but a most superficial sense, well-read than Longfellow. In contrast to Holmes, he was, to use an old but useful distinction, a *poet* while the genial doctor was, ordinarily, a facile versifier. His learning was both broad and deep and his taste cultivated, so that a comparison with Whittier throws the latter's provincialism and rustic self-culture into sharp relief. Yet as a poet he seemed to his own time, and still seems to many, to have accomplished less than any of these. Why?

Not because he lacked the courage to try all the larger, more impressive forms developed in the past and practiced by his age. While Holmes's sense of his own limitations kept him, generally, within the realm of light and occasional verse, so that reading his work as a whole we have a sense both of its severe limitations and of its frequent success within those limitations, reading Lowell straight through is next to impossible. Most of the poems in the five-hundred-odd pages of double columns of small print in his volume of collected verse are simply failures, and a large number of the longer ones are quite unreadable — long winded, repetitious, and imitative of Wordsworth and the other English Romantics and Victorians.

He wrote odes in the traditional manner, but only the one devoted to Harvard's commemoration of those she sent to the Civil War remains in any degree readable. He tried long meditative and philosophic poems in the manner of Wordsworth, but of these only "The Cathedral" is likely to hold us today, and even that has great flat stretches. He tried retelling the Arthurian legends, as Tennyson was doing, but "The Vision of Sir Launfal," though it pleased his age, has seemed to ours to moralize its subject too easily. Aware that, as he put it, he had pursued the Muse without ever catching up with her, he turned to fresh matter and wrote about it in a fresh manner in his poems in New England dialect. But even in this area, where he was not in competition with older poets he revered, he could not quite *find* himself. The elaborate prose machinery of *The Biglow Papers,* intended to bolster the dialect poems, shows that he did not adequately realize the significance of the one area in which he was really a pioneer.

Yet his poems, especially the later ones, are sprinkled through with excellent things. The parts of *A Fable for Critics* commonly anthologized, dealing with his contemporaries, are memorable for incisive critical judgments expressed in epigrams that often seem as apt today as when they were written. But these parts are only about half of the poem, the rest of which is humor of a type that no longer seems funny, if it ever really did.

The best parts of *The Biglow Papers* mingle humor, sentiment, and social criticism in a language at once accurate and expressive, anticipating Mark Twain's later and more convincing demonstration that the vernacular could be made an effective literary instrument. But the Notices, Introduction, Glossary, Index, and Notes are so elaborately overdone that they would bury the poem if one had to read it entire, as published — either series. The first and second series together would run to well over three-hundred pages if printed in single-column and normal-sized type. Lowell seems never to have known when to stop.

His exploration of New England folk materials resulted in one poem that is thoroughly readable all the way through, not just in excerpts. "Fitz Adam's Story" is a fine poem of its kind, and its kind is not negligible. Its discursiveness is justified by the richness of its portrayal of back-country scenes and character types. When it describes a formal parlor in a country inn, for instance, it reminds us of Mark Twain's description of the parlor of the Grangerfords in *Huckleberry Finn*; indeed it might be argued that it is in a way better, for though the voice here is aware of the humorous aspects of the scene he so vividly conveys to us, the humor never moves into burlesque at the expense of reality.

The heart of the story tells us of the reception Deacon Bitters got when he died and went to Hell. The grimly orthodox deacon is a very succinct and pointed epitome of a chapter in New England history. He is the Puritan become the sharp-dealing Yankee trader, dropping the inwardness but keeping the husks of his faith. Calvinist piety has been metamorphosed into "the Protestant ethic" without losing any of its grimness, losing only its meaning and justification. When the deacon gets to Hell he discovers that even the Prince of Darkness will not tolerate *his* brand of meanness.

For a sense of just how well Lowell has handled his material here, one should compare it with Faulkner's version of the same folk tale in *The Hamlet.* Flem Snopes and Deacon Bitters are both meaner than the Devil, and both are rejected from the realm of the properly damned. Lowell's version contains the same high-spirited folk humor that distinguishes Ratliffe's dream in the novel, expressed in memorable epigrammatic verse:

A pious man, and thrifty too, he made
The psalms and prophets partners in his trade,
And in his orthodoxy straitened more
As it enlarged the business at his store;
He honored Moses, but, when gain he planned,
Had his own notion of the Promised Land.

A little anthology of passages from Lowell's later poems could easily be made up in such a way as to demonstrate that he was thoroughly aware of all the currents of thought and feeling in his age and that his own attitudes toward them were both mixed and discriminatingly intelligent. In his nationalism and his attitude toward the use of American experience in poetry he often echoes Emerson's "American Scholar" and parallels Whitman.

"What marvelous change of things and men!" he wrote in the Ode celebrating the hundredth anniversary of the fight at Concord Bridge, a poem he might well have entitled an "Ode to Freedom." Yet the welcome he extended to the future remained discriminating. As he wrote in "The Elm," another anniversary poem, "Sure the dumb earth hath memory . . . Present and Past commingle . . .

So charmed, with undeluded eye we see
In history's fragmentary tale
Bright clues of continuity,
Learn that high natures over Time prevail,
And feel ourselves a link in that entail
That binds all ages past with all that are to be.

In his often ironic comments on a future he both welcomed and feared he has much in common with Henry Adams, who also had mixed feelings about the triumph of democratic secularism over the age of faith. He was able to respond to the challenge presented to Boston Brahminism by Lincoln and to hail him as "New birth of our new soil, the first American," but he anticipated Eliot's Prufrock in fearing that the "springs of wonder" might dry up in "This age that blots out life with question marks." Pondering a fleeting intuition of oneness with nature, a sense of being at home in the world, he could not repress the doubt that immediately came:

> Or was it not mere sympathy of brain?
> A sweetness intellectually conceived
> In simpler creeds to me impossible?

"Too conscious" of thought's destructive implications, he debated with himself endlessly and walked forth from the cathedral "saddened, for all thought is sad." He wondered whether there might be "no corner safe from peeping Doubt," but he knew that "Nothing that keeps thought out is safe from thought." He was as aware as Adams that theirs was "no age to get cathedrals built," yet he was as sure as Robinson that life would be both "brutish" and "fruitless" if we could not now and then divine

> A mystery of Purpose, gleaming through
> The secular confusions of the world,
> Whose will we darkly accomplish, doing ours.

"Credidimus Jovem Regnare," "Tempora Mutatus," "Agassiz," and "The Cathedral" remain readable poems only because the thought in them is so firm. They may be, as Eliot once said of similar nineteenth-century verse he considered bad, "ruminative," discursive rather than objective and dramatic; but unless one wants to dismiss all such poetry by definition, without a hearing, he had better take these poems seriously. In them, Lowell speaks in a voice more nearly his own than any he had achieved in his earlier verse, but his themes and his treatment of them prompt us to compare him here with such English contemporaries as Arnold and Tennyson. And here at least he is not destroyed by the comparison.

Nor is he, I think, in "Rhoecus," about which opinion has been mixed over the years. The introduction shows us Lowell groping for an understanding of the function of myth, and coming as close as any of his contemporaries, even Emerson, to a formulation that would seem adequate today. The fables created by the myth-making mind, Lowell writes, are not, of course, to be confused with history, but they contain "revelations" of a truth more inward than outward, yet not the less true therefore. They point "surely to the hidden springs" of distinctively human truth, whatever liberties they may take with fact. Indeed, "in whatsoe'er the heart/ Hath fashioned for a solace to itself," creating out of falsehood its "needful food" of truth, there are "pure gleams of light/ And earnest parables of inward lore."

The fable of Rhoecus and the Dryad which follows Lowell's interesting introduction very aptly illustrates its point. Rhoecus was shut out from a deep experience of the beauty all around him, shut up in himself so that he was "alone on earth," because his response to nature was divided and impure:

> We spirits only show to gentle eyes,
> We ever ask an undivided love.
> And he who scorns the least of Nature's works
> Is thenceforth exiled and shut out from all.

The point of this might be explicated in contemporary terms by reference to Martin Buber's *I and Thou.* Buber does not limit the experience of *meeting* to persons; we may, he argues, truly *meet* a tree. When we do, the tree ceases to be the *object* of our experience, or the sum of the things we know about it, or the sum of the ways we may use it. It stands over against us as a being existing in its own right, demanding our intransitive attention. "I encounter no soul or dryad of the tree, but the tree itself." That we do not experience dryads or glimpse tangible souls in trees is Lowell's point, too, made in his introduction. But that nature contains an element that transcends the ultilitarian and the purely rational, transcends what may be either *used* or rationally *known,* both Lowell and Buber are saying. To experience transcendence requires, as Lowell implies and Buber argues, an openness and self-forgetfulness akin both to aesthetic contemplation and to love, requires "gentle eyes" and an "undivided love," love for the "not me" in itself, as an existent being independent of us.

"Rhoecus" makes clear at once the background in romantic theory of Buber's contemporary philosophy, and the contemporary relevance of romantic metaphysics. But Lowell did not often write so well. For one thing, his own love of nature was usually not "undivided." He was too well aware of the direction of the drift of contemporary thought to trust nature's beneficence or to wish always to read its meanings to the end.

> What we call Nature, all outside ourselves,
> Is but our own conceit of what we see,
> Our own reaction upon what we feel.

As he wrote in "Credidimus Jovem Regnare," we once believed that God reigns over, and is rendered "visible" in, his handiwork, nature, but with this belief gone, "Life saddens to a mere conundrum." It was becoming unclear whether nature meant nothing, or the wrong things. All that was clear was that it was no longer self-evidently the handiwork, and thus the intelligible sign, of God. "Now Pan at last is surely dead."

Unable to see nature with the eyes of the great romantic poets whom he revered, not at all sure that, as Bryant had put it, nature contains a balm for troubled hearts, Lowell wavered between a theism for which he was nostalgic and a naturalism which he could not bring his heart to accept. "Beset by doubts of every breed/ In the last bastion of my creed," he experienced hopelessness amounting, in his own words, to despair as he continued to express his purely emotional allegiance to a world of faith now lost, to "those serene dawn-rosy days/ Ere microscopes had made us heirs/ To large estates of doubts and snares." The world seemed more and more like one "huge interrogation mark."

How then could he write well of nature, to which he knew one must give one's heart if one were to experience its meanings, if his mind told him his heart was naive, that there were no meanings, or none acceptable to the heart? Uncertain of the answer, he wavered between restating Bryant and anticipating Robinson. To keep himself and his readers from thinking about the unanswerable questions, he wrote a great deal, especially long poems full of elaborate rhetorical tricks and jokes calculated to distract the mind and leave the heart to brood undisturbed in its sad recess.

The dilemma Lowell found himself in is reflected in his poetry in all sorts of ways, but especially, and most harmfully, in his language. Only in the very late poems did he ever come close to finding his own voice and then it was too late for the kind of poetry he had always wanted to write, too late for nature lyrics, too late for anything but the meditative verse of the self-mocking "Cathedral" or the rumination of "Credidimus." In the earlier work Lowell had spoken in three distinct voices, none of which was suitable for the expression of the serious themes that were dearest to him. The New England dialect of *The Biglow Papers* was fine for the creation of characters like Hosea Biglow, but there were things Lowell wanted to say that his back-country Yankee could not plausibly be made to feel or think. The joking colloquialisms of *A Fable for Critics* were just right for humor and satire expressive of a part of Lowell's own attitudes. But what of his deepest and most serious responses to life? For these he had only the voice he had inherited from his romantic predecessors; and, in part perhaps because his fundamental attitudes were so deeply mixed, he could create no other, find no new idiom for what he felt.

In the great bulk of his poetry written in a serious tone Lowell's language is more literary and derivative than that of any of the other "schoolroom poets." Even Longfellow in his best work was more successful in finding his own voice. Whittier, too, whose power when he succeeds is almost never what we should call *verbal,* never a matter primarily of control of tone and diction, speaks in words that more nearly belong to him. Lowell's language is literary in the worst sense: it not only derives from books rather than from the spoken word but from older books, other men's thoughts and feelings, which he partially, but only partially, shared. It blunts his meanings almost always in his most serious poetry.

"Loving those roots that feed us from the past," as he said, Lowell did not, perhaps, actually love the *language* in which past poets had expressed themselves, but he could conceive of no other. Instead, in both theme and language, he indulged in the romantic gesture, struck the romantic stance, hoping perhaps that by using the language he might be infected by the feeling; then shifted to the clown's grimace to counteract the naivete of it. As he wrote in "Agassiz":

Well might I, as of old, appeal to you,
O mountains, woods and streams,

To help us mourn him, for ye loved him too;
But simpler moods befit our modern themes.

And simpler language, too. It is not only that Lowell uses words that carry with them meanings and feelings he does not really share, so that the world he pictures seems out of focus, not quite real or honest. Even his darkest doubts, even the probings into truth that most clearly demonstrate, in the abstract, his fundamental honesty, are conveyed in a language that blunts the edge of his awareness. We are almost tempted to say that Lowell read too much. In any case, he is certainly remembering Shakespeare and others rather than thinking of his own century's industrial and scientific revolution when he writes, in the Harvard Commemoration Ode:

With our laborious hiving
What men call treasure, and the gods call dross,
Life seems a jest of Fate's contriving,
Only secure in every one's conniving,
A long account of nothings paid with loss,
Where we poor puppets, jerked by unseen wires,
After our little hour of strut and rave,
With all our pasteboard passions and desires,
Loves, hates, ambitions, and immortal fires,
Are tossed pell-mell together in the grave.

Only a few years after Lowell wrote his last poems, Eliot would discover how to make highly original and expressive poems out of scraps and fragments taken from the older poets. One of the reasons he was able to make the method work for him was that he seems always to be using his fragments, not being used by them. He knew, and practiced, what Lowell only partially knew in theory and hardly at all in practice, that "words made magical by poets dead," as Lowell put it, lose their magic when the vision that produced them becomes only putatively held. Eliot seems always aware both of the distance that separates him from the older poets and of his kinship with them. The double awareness produces a distinct *tone* that makes his poems his own even when they are most crowded with echoes and allusions. Lowell, by contrast, fails most obviously in his lack of control of tone. Without Eliot's irony, he can only first echo and then criticize, retract; or affirm and deny at the same time, with the denial running like a sad, only half-acknowledged or even unacknowledged, undercurrent beneath the surface affirmation. Agreeing, for example, with Wordsworth's thought and borrowing some of his language, he writes, in "The Cathedral," that

> These virginal cognitions, gifts of morn,
> Ere life grow noisy, and slower-footed thought
> Can overtake the rapture of the sense,
> To thrust between ourselves and what we feel,
> Have something in them secretly divine.

But despite the language and the asserted agreement in thought, Lowell is *not* Wordsworth. He knows that "thought" already has overtaken the "virginal cognitions." The subjunctive mood of "grow" is no more than a gesture of loyalty requiring a suspension of thought. In effect, Lowell here is Prufrock longing to see mermaids, but without admitting that myth is myth. There is no irony here. How the cognitions can continue to contain the "divine" *after* thought has done its work seems to be a secret Lowell understands no more than the reader.

Sometimes Lowell's language fails in an opposite way. Instead of conveying too much, his words undercut or falsify a feeling we know, from other evidence, to be genuine. Thus for example his literary nationalism was, in theory, as deep as Emerson's or Whitman's: he thought the American poet ought to make use of American materials, and in his poems about New England back country he tried to practice what he preached. But when he writes, in "L'envoi: To the Muse," of his pursuit of the Muse in logging camps and across barroom floors, our suspicion that he does not really mean it (for to ask us to picture a Muse in a bar is to take neither the Muse nor the bar seriously) is deepened as he goes on to tell us how he has sought the goddess

> Through mountains, forests, open downs,
> Lakes, railroads, prairies, states, and towns.

There are no "downs" in this country. The word is as literary and derivative, as false in this context, as the metaphor that structures the whole poem is. A poet who really believed in the value of what Emerson had called "our incomparable materials" would not write this way, we say. But Lowell really did believe; he did not mean to make a mere joke of the whole idea. What he didn't believe was that he himself would ever find the inspiration, which in effect meant finding his own voice. Expressing his self-doubt, also in "L'envoi," he demonstrates by the manner of his expression one of the chief reasons for his failure:

> Whither? *Albeit* I follow fast,
> In all life's circuit I but *find,*
> Not where thou art, but where thou *wast,*
> Sweet beckoner more sweet than *wind!* (Italics added.)

If we could feel sure that Lowell knew what he was doing here, we might find the poeticisms an appropriate vehicle of a wry self-directed irony, but it seems pretty clear, when we look not just at isolated passages such as this but at the whole body of his poetry, that Lowell was only dimly and intermittently aware that, except in his dialect poems, he was writing in a dead language. Really believing, as his prose sometimes tells us effectively, that American experience ought to find its poetic expression, he found himself unable to hear the music in the sound of Whitman's hawk uttering its wild barbaric cry. If he had lived to know the harsh cadences of Frost's oven bird, he would have found no poetry in that voice either. He knew that the accents of the nightingale sounded false when he used them, but the only solution he could imagine was to make jokes or turn to the dialect of comic rustics.

That is why, apart from "Fritz Adam's Story" and a small handful of other poems, Lowell's work lives for us today chiefly in excerpts. The rest can be read only as document, interesting both to the student of nineteenth-century American culture and to the student of poetics who likes to puzzle over the reasons for the egregious failure of a talented, learned, and fluent man who said truly of himself that he *might* have been a poet. Would it have helped him to be what he wanted to be, we wonder finally, if he had been born either fifty years earlier or fifty years later, if he had not been suspended between a world he loved but could not quite believe and a world he understood but could not love?

JOHN GREENLEAF WHITTIER

Whittier's contemporaries loved and respected him and paid him great honor in his later years, but those whose literary opinions we have any reason to respect had no illusions about his being a great poet. They thought of him as a noble and lovable man whose verse gave unique expression to sentiments and ideas they valued.

At one time or another they noted most of his defects of artistry, and though we should want to phrase the list of his deficiencies differently, we should not be making any new discoveries if we were to note that his poetic ear was deficient, his moralizing often obtrusive, his language too often a jarring mixture of the rustic and the literary, his meters too often inappropriate to the subject, and so on.

All this and much more is too obvious to need rehearsing. I can see no need for any further debunking of Whittier's reputation as a poet. At the present it might almost be said that he *has* no reputation, but cultural changes alone may well be sufficient as an explanation for that. Instead of undertaking the too easy task of explaining why he is not worth reading, criticism might better address itself to the question of what lasting worth there is in the poems. Which of them still have the power to move us? What would be lost if he were to become completely unread, dropped even from the college anthologies? What reason is there, if any, for valuing Whittier as a *poet?*

Of course the mere asking of such questions implies that I think he does have some value. It seems to me that to lose touch with Whittier entirely would be to lose both a significant part of our national past and certain possibilities of present personal experience — to lose touch with a part of *ourselves,* in short.

But to keep in touch with the self while continuing to grow is often difficult, and never more so, critically, than with Whittier. No famous nineteenth-century American poet offers greater obstacles to a just evaluation today. None of the "schoolroom poets," except perhaps Longfellow in his several worst poems, is easier to ridicule. More so even than Longfellow's, Whittier's poetry is "old-fashioned," and old-fashioned precisely in the way recent criticism has taught us to consider inferior. If Brooks and Warren's *Understanding Poetry* and similar handbooks contain the whole truth about poetry, then we ought to be able to write off Whittier as a poet without even bothering to read him. Why read him when we already know that he is generally moralistic, sermonizing at almost every opportunity? When it is clear that he distrusts and often undercuts his own symbols; worse, that he distrusts *all* symbols and ultimately poetry itself, extending his Quaker preference for unmediated apprehension of Reality to all experience? Why read a poet who thought that "The outward symbols disappear/ For him whose inward sight is clear"?

Poetry for Whittier, as for the Puritans, is a concession to the flesh, an expedient of words and meters required only because man's spiritual sense is still so imperfect. "The world will have its idols,/ And flesh and sense their sign." In a fallen world, truth must be conveyed in the "trappings" of form, but poetry aspires to the "deepest of all mysteries, silence." A very old-fashioned idea! But doesn't it, in some sense? Can a poet say *all* in a poem? Do words exhaust our meanings? Are we quite sure that poetry does not, as Emerson said, aspire to express the inexpressible? Whitman and Dickinson held the same view.

Whittier's opinions of the work of other poets seldom imply any feeling for specifically *poetic* values. Though he paid his respects, usually rather perfunctorily, to older poetic masters whom he knew he could not hope to rival and spoke of himself as a rude and "untaught" versifier, the only really operative principle of literary judgment he had to work with was moral. Poetry for him was message. Valuing the message of hope he found in "A Psalm of Life," he once said it was "worth more than all the *dreams* of Shelley, and Keats, and Wordsworth." (Italics mine. He is not really comparing *poems,* here, not really making an aesthetic judgment, but comparing Longfellow's "vision" with the British poets' visions and attitudes, and preferring the American.) He thought very highly of the poems of Lydia Maria Child, Grace Greenwood, and Alice and Phoebe Cary, characterizing the last two as "richly gifted." He considered *Uncle Tom's Cabin* one of the "noblest" works of the century and wrote a tribute to "sweet Eva" beginning "Dry the tears for holy Eva,/ With the holy angels leave her." On the face of it, it would seem unlikely that a man with such taste would write any poetry worth reading today.

Likely or not, he did. Though he seems to have been incapable of distinguishing between the moral and the moralistic, his best antislavery poems are moral satire and invective, with nothing moralistic about them. Though he was capable at his worst of outrageous sentimentality, as "The Barefoot Boy" or "Barbara Frietchie" may remind us, there is nothing in the least sentimental about "Snowbound." Whittier was able to respond poetically to three areas of his experience. When he wrote about the demands made by the religious conscience, about memories of his own childhood, or about nature considered as symbolic revelation, he quite frequently wrote better than he knew, better than his theory or his taste should have permitted him to write.

On these subjects he could sometimes do more than set doctrine to meter or retell unimaginatively old legends. Where the three subjects overlap, as they quite often do in the later work, he sometimes embodied his meanings in images used symbolically and functionally to create a handful of better poems than any that the other schoolroom poets wrote. That a search through the massive collected edition reveals only a dozen or so such poems is precisely what we should have expected: The schoolroom poets are all minor poets, and one of the reasons why minor poets are not major poets is that they are not able to write very many good poems. But "Snowbound" alone would be more than sufficient to make a young poet's reputation today.

In general, the least readable of Whittier's poems are those he devoted to his "great cause," the abolition of slavery. Yet even his poems of reform deserve, at their best, to be read as *poems*. Denouncing slavery, they raise what we might be inclined to see as an archaic and long-since corrected evil to a level of universal meaning where it requires no effort on our part to see it as still *our* problem. Prompted by specific events or prepared for specific occasions, a number of these poems transcend their interest as historical documents to remind us powerfully of the timeless discrepancy between what we are and what we ought to be, between profession and deed, between our faith and our works.

On this last subject Whittier most often wrote at his best level in the pre-Civil War poems. Since for him conscience was the voice of God, his chief scorn was directed at those "clerical oppressors" who were either blind to the implications of their faith or actively perverted what seemed to him its clear meaning in their defense of an institution of which, as he noted, they were the beneficiaries. Though even on this subject Whittier's diction often fails, there are enough fine lines and passages to make it worth our while to reread occasionally such long unread poems as "Clerical Oppressors," "Letter from a Missionary of the Methodist Church South, in Kansas, to a Distinguished Politician," and "On a Prayer-Book, with its Frontispiece, Ary Scheffer's 'Christus Consolator,' Americanized by the Omission of the Black Man."

The better-known, because more often anthologized, poems

of reform like "Massachusetts to Virginia," "Ichabod," "The Haschish," "The Panorama," and "Laus Deo!" contain passages of some of the best invective verse in our literature. The voice in them is righteous but not self-righteous, angry but not shrill; not moralistic so much as prophetic in the great tradition. "Massachusetts to Virginia" is a merely sectional poem only to those who miss its moral meaning, and "Ichabod" is so enriched by its Biblical allusions that Daniel Webster, whom the poem attacks, becomes the type of any betrayer of any high cause.

Nevertheless, though a number of these early poems are too good to be totally forgotten, Whittier did most of his best work after the Civil War. Turning now chiefly to nature and childhood for his subjects, he became less suspicious of form and symbol. He had time now to read more, and though he read mostly prose, particularly in books about the Eastern religions and Eastern mysticism, with which his own thought had much in common, his poetic taste broadened and became more sensitive. Without giving up his belief that words could at best merely prepare us for silence, he grew to feel more and more that since words are a *necessary* evil, the poet has a *duty* to be as careful with them as he can. Poetry remained message for him in theory, but he grew more conscious of the necessity of indirection in the expression. More often, now, he achieved expressive form.

"Telling the Bees," for instance, is strengthened by Whittier's handling of visual imagery. In it, as in the greater "Snowbound," both black and white suggest death, and colors suggest life. With a reliance upon implication all too rare in his work, Whittier here makes both the imagery and the action dramatic. The speaker in the poem is one to whom things happen. He and the reader together share a gradual revelation.

The effect is rare in Whittier, but by no means limited to this one poem, as "The River Path" will illustrate. Here the speaker finally states explicitly the consolation he finds in nature, but not before he has experienced fully the darkness in which he has walked. The ending, with its support for the hope of immortality, gains force from the extended emphasis on "the damp, the chill, the gloom" in which, reading the poem, we too find ourselves immersed as we gaze with the speaker out of the darkness toward the light.

"Monadnock from Wachuset," often anthologized, has more point when it is read along with the poem with which Whittier paired it in his final arrangement of his poems, under the single title of "Mountain Pictures." The first poem, "Franconia from the Pemigewasset," finds the speaker gaining hope for his own and his country's life from the sight of the White Mountains standing out clearly against the sky in the morning after a night of storm. He hopes, at the end, that the "battle-storm" of the Civil War will pass away, leaving a greener earth and a fairer sky. Nature has provided a lesson in hope.

"Monadnock from Wachuset" finds the speaker once again gazing at a mountain, but now the time is sunset rather than morning and the vision more religious than political — though it is typical of Whittier not to make a sharp distinction between the two areas. The speaker and his companions are moved to feelings of awe by nature's beauty:

> I would I were a painter, for the sake
> Of a sweet picture, and of her who led,
> A fitting guide, with reverential tread,
> Into that mountain mystery. First a lake
> Tinted with sunset; next the wavy lines
> Of far receding hills; and yet more far,
> Monadnock lifting from his night of pines
> His rosy forehead to the evening star.

As twilight deepens they hear sounds coming from a farm lower down on the mountainside. "With home-life sounds the desert air was stirred." Descending from the peak, "soothed and pleased" by what they have seen, they stop to congratulate the farmer on the beautiful setting of his home. The farmer answers that, yes, it is beautiful, but he loves it for his mother's sake, "Who lived and died here in the peace of God." Pondering the "lesson of his words," the speaker and his companions come to realize the inadequacy of nature's consolation when man is left out of the picture. The painter has learned that landscape is not enough, because man is "more than his abode, — The inward life than Nature's raiment more."

Granted that the syntactic inversion here is awkward, as Whittier so often is, even in his best work. Nevertheless, if we can somehow get past the stylistic roughness, if we can respond at all to a voice that speaks to us honestly in accents half rustic, half bookish, but never urbane, we shall see that something interesting is being done here. The first poem of the pair has celebrated the beauty of nature and given thanks for the lessons it affords. Addressing nature directly, the speaker has hoped

> So shall my soul receive
> Haply the secret of your calm and strength,
> Your unforgotten beauty interfuse
> My common life . . .

The second poem begins, thematically, where the first ends. Nature is once again beautiful and inspiring, suggesting lessons of endurance and hope. The summits of Monadnock and Wachusett are still in the light as the climbers start the return journey down Wachusett's slopes. Overhead there is still light, with "A single level cloud-line" seeming to menace the darkness with "its golden spear," but they descend into a deepening twilight, broken only by the "shorn greenness" of the farm clearing. Golden sky, black woods, and green clearing form the elements of a picture that says through its images what the poem means before Whittier offers his explicit interpretation, beginning "We felt that man was more than his abode." Green is the color of hope. Whittier's hope, though often refreshed by such glimpses of the Transcendental as the view from the summit has provided, rested chiefly on the redeemed human will acting in community.

The two poems make a pair not only thematically but formally. The speaker's gaze in the first poem is upward out of darkness toward the light on the peak. In the second poem he moves downward into the darkness, carrying the memory of light with him, only to find a better, because more inward, light in the little clearing surrounded by the dark woods. The poems are complementary but not interchangeable. Their images of height and depth, light and darkness, morning and evening, and nature and man move to a climactic revelation.

Though he had his era's taste for the picturesque in nature, Whittier was no primitivist. He loved the sea, the mountains, and the rural countryside, but he repeatedly dissociated himself from what he once called the "cult of nature shaming man." It is at once a reflection of his essential sanity and an evidence of the role his religious faith played in his life that he should have been deeply responsive to "the sacramental mystery of the woods," seeing nature as God's handiwork, yet have remembered always that "sweeter than the song of birds/ Is the thankful voice." Our "common earth" is, he was sure, "a holy ground," but a simple "return to nature" solved neither moral nor religious problems for Whittier — and for him the moral and the religious were as central as they had been for the Puritans.

In the "Mountain Pictures" we have been looking at, nature provides epiphanies in the light on the peaks. But Whittier knew from personal experience that nature was not always so inspiring. No pantheist, he did not need to try to deny that nature was often dark and often silent. Unlike Emerson, he could find nature's revelation consoling and humanly meaningful only when extended and corrected by the Revelation in Scripture. His religious conservatism preserved the historic paradox of a God both within and beyond his creation. If God is transcendent as well as immanent, the voice of nature will never wholly suffice as revelation, even when we can hear it. The objects of nature were never more for Whittier than "attendant angels to the house of prayer." When he could hear no voice speaking to him in nature, he was too honest to pretend. He was left then with only a wordless faith and the inner voice that spoke of Duty. Some of the most moving passages in his poetry record his frustration as he tried to move from nature to God, only to discover that often "the hollow sky is sad with silentness."

In "Snowbound" nature speaks, but not to console. It speaks in the sound of the "mindless wind." Man is now not only "more" than his abode, as he was in "Monadnock from Wachuset," he is actively threatened by a hostile environment and brought to know his essential humanity by that threat. In the attitude it implies toward nature, "Snowbound" is closer to Stephen Crane than to most of Whittier's contemporaries. It is not only a fine poem; it is a document of considerable importance in nineteenth-century intellectual history.

"Snowbound" is surely the finest American pastoral poem before the pastorals of Frost. It is a true pastoral, not an idyl, despite Whittier's misleading subtitle. It pictures rural life under simplified conditions, not in order to idealize it but to find out what its meaning is for us. Comments on the poem have too often ignored the conclusion, with the unfortunate result that we have been taught to read the poem as an expression of simple nostalgia. There is nostalgia in the poem, to be sure, but the nostalgia exists in tension with judgment. Though we do not associate Whittier with complexity of feeling or subtlety of thought, in his greatest poem he expressed more meaning than his critics have been patient enough to grasp.

One approach to the poem that has the advantage of making clear why it should be called a pastoral is to compare it with another poem about a blizzard that is not a pastoral, Emerson's "The Snow-Storm," the first nine lines of which Whittier printed as an epigraph to his own poem, and which he echoes in several lines in "Snowbound." Emerson's nature mysticism is as clear in his poem as Whittier's Christian humanism is in his. Though a theist in his special way, Emerson is much closer to being a pantheist than Whittier. He sees the storm as offering a lesson in submission to nature. "Come see the north wind's masonry," he invites us, and then characterizes that masonry as "wild," "fanciful," "savage," and unordered — "nought care he/ For number or proportion." The world of the storm seems all the better for not being a *human* world.

As for the "friends shut out" by the storm, there is no mention of them after the opening lines. Nor is Emerson concerned with the experience of those shut *in,* the family sitting, like Whittier's, "Around the radiant fireplace, enclosed/ In a tumultuous privacy of storm." They are "enclosed," but not, so far as we know, in any way drawn together by the experience. The storm does not so much emphasize and clarify their human frailty, their mutual dependence, as purge them of it. The speaker's gaze in the poem is exclusively outward toward "the mad wind's night-work" as it creates "The frolic architecture of the snow" which man's art slowly and imperfectly imitates. Man ought to turn to nature for inspiration, and the wilder, the less human the nature he turns to, the better. The contrast with the view of nature offered in "Snowbound" could not be sharper.

In Whittier's poem nature clarifies human life by threatening it. Nature's *mindlessness* suggests to Whittier that man is *not* mindless, or loveless. Though he begins by describing the storm at length, his real concern is for people. The storm is important for him only as the occasion of the family's enforced companionship around the fire. More than two-thirds of the poem is taken up with the portraits of those present. More significantly, the poem culminates in the long religious meditation beginning "Clasp, Angel of the backward look," in which the "Flemish pictures of old days" that have been presented are offered as having more than sentimental value: They may touch the heart of the "worldling" and move him beyond his secularism, and they strengthen the speaker's resolution to continue to work for a better world. Emerson's poem teaches a lesson in "wildness," Whittier's in community.

If one of the functions of memory as it has been exercised in the poem is to make us see more clearly the full implications of the "green hills of life that slope to death," and so to deepen our faith beyond that of the worldlings, another is to remind us that the past provides resources that can help us do our duty in the present:

> I hear again the voice that bids
> The dreamer leave his dream midway
> For larger hopes and graver fears:
> Life greatens in these later years,
> The century's aloe flowers to-day!

That is, things we have long worked for have come to fruition, but the voice of conscience will not let us go on dreaming. When the storm was over there was work to do; now that it has been relived in memory, there is work of another kind to do. The final lesson nature has to teach us is the necessity of moral commitment.

This becomes clearer when we notice the changes in point of view as the poem proceeds. At first the voice is generalized and impersonal as the coming of the storm is objectively described. Then, on the first morning after the storm, as the father and the boys start to shovel the paths, the point of view of childhood becomes dominant and the whole experience becomes an exciting adventure. This is the only part of "Snowbound" that should remind us of Emerson's poem. Memory lets Whittier for the moment simply relive his childhood as though nothing has happened since: This is how it seemed *then.* The childish speaker looks outward, as Emerson's mature speaker had looked, and is similarly entranced by the "marvelous shapes" the snow has assumed. He is "well pleased" with this escape from the routine life of the household. For two verse paragraphs there are no references to nature as a threat. But then as these images return and we hear once again "the shrieking of the mindless wind," we become aware of a more mature point of view being counterpointed with the childish one. We are prepared thus for the conclusion, in which we discover that all this took place long ago in the speaker's youth; that all but one besides the speaker of those who gathered around the hearth are now dead; and that these memories should not be sentimentally dwelt upon but be put to use so that life may prevail over death.

The implications of the imagery are wholly consistent, throughout this very long poem, with such an interpretation of its meaning. In other poems Whittier had sometimes lamented nature's silence. Now nature seemed, as it spoke through the storm, to be *alien*. He describes it as "dark," "cheerless," "sad," "ominous," "a threat," "cold," "hard," "dreary," "bitter," and "gray." The images imply that it is also *blind* and *dead*.

Not that Whittier has changed his mind and given up his Quaker Christianity for naturalism; rather, he is writing as a *poet* of his memories of a specific event and of the particular face nature showed in that event. Looking out into the storm, the speaker saw a world previously "unknown"; he could see in it "nothing we could call our own." The snow obliterates all signs of those values that have given meaning to the speaker's life:

> No church-bell lent its Christian tone
> To the savage air, no social smoke
> Curled over woods of snow-hung oak.

Church and home gone: the same images Hawthorne chose to present to Hepzibah and Clifford at the end of the flight through the storm in *The House of the Seven Gables.* In their favorite images, Hawthorne and Whittier reveal themselves as more similar than we have realized. Of all the "schoolroom poets," Whittier is closest to Hawthorne — and to Frost.

Like Hawthorne's too is Whittier's emphasis on the "dead" nature outside as motivating a turn inward to the light and warmth of the fireside. Hawthorne many years before in "Night Sketches: Beneath an Umbrella" had explored a nature that revealed itself as a "black impenetrable nothingness," before returning to the hearth. For both writers the images of *circle* and the *hearth* counter the isolation induced by a feeling that human values may not be backed by nature. As Whittier puts it now, the "human tone" is wholly absent from this "solitude" made more intense

By dreary-voiced elements,
The shrieking of the mindless wind,
The moaning tree-boughs swaying blind,
And on the glass the unmeaning beat
Of ghostly finger-tips of sleet.

The face that nature is showing here is also like that which Melville made Ishmael and Ahab confront in Moby Dick — unmeaning, mindless, blind, blank, the huge white forehead of the whale, with no discernible features. Whittier almost certainly never read *Moby-Dick,* but his response in this poem to the threat posed by nature is essentially the same as Melville's and very different from Emerson's: instead of Melville's monkey rope and a squeeze of the hand, he offers images of circle, warmth, and color — images of life — to balance the cold meaninglessness. It is just because

Beyond the circle of our hearth
No welcome sound of toil or mirth
Unbound the spell, and testified
Of human life and thought outside

that the life *inside* gets its meanings clarified. If everything outside is "dead white" or "pitchy black," inside the human "circle" around the hearth all is "rosy," warmly lighted, meaningful, flowerlike; indeed, the light from the fire seems to make the whole room burst into bloom.

The contrast between life-imagery and death-imagery is maintained consistently throughout the poem, not simply in the initial description of the storm. Life is "unfading green," a "pleasant circle," characterized by "warmth and light" and "green hills"; death is imaged as snow on graves and the blackness of a "bitter night." By the time we are told, late in the poem, that death has now claimed all but one of those who made that human circle, we are thoroughly prepared for the meditation on the hope of reunion in another world.

The question has become, which of nature's several voices speaks the ultimate truth, the "mindless" voice or the voice that pronounces, at other times, what seems like a "benediction of the air." We cannot *know,* Whittier implies, we can only *hope* that at the foot of the green hill of life the "mournful cypresses" have "white amaranths" in bloom beneath them. We have stretched "the hands of memory forth/ To warm them at the wood-fire's blaze." The very intensity of the cold has made it the more necessary to seek and treasure warmth. Nowhere is Whittier closer to Hawthorne than in this expression of one of Hawthorne's commonest themes, in some of Hawthorne's favorite images. But Whittier's religious faith was firmer than Hawthorne's, and there is nothing guarded or ambiguous about the imagery of his conclusion. Faith, for him, restores the "circle" broken by time. The fragrance blown in the end from "unseen meadows" by a wind no longer cold and mindless was foretold in the beginning by the "circling race/ Of life-blood in the sharpened face." The meditation with which the poem concludes, far from being "tacked on," merely makes explicit what the images have been saying all along.

Whittier never wrote so well again, but "Snowbound" was no lucky accident. If we have understood, for example, the religious position expressed by the other poems, we are prepared for the way he paints his portraits of the people in this poem. As we might expect of a devout Quaker who, in "Haverhill," counseled his fellow-townsmen to

> Hold fast your Puritan heritage,
> But let the free thought of the age
> Its light and hope and sweetness add
> To the stern faith the fathers had,

he loves these people but he does not idealize or sentimentalize them.

His was no theoretic or "ideological" love for an idealized humanity, like Barlow's, but a tender concern for and loyalty to actual people in all their imperfection. He devoted his life to trying to do His will on earth, but he did not think the Kingdom had arrived yet or that the future would inevitably bring it into being through the effects of climate and soil. Though he rejected the Puritan dogma of total depravity — as he rejected all dogmas — he agreed with the Puritans that in the world as we know it, "guilt shapes the terror." It was an essentially Puritan insight that led him to picture the uncle in "Snowbound" as close to "Nature's heart," learned in the "mysteries" of the woods, yet, nonetheless, "strong only on his native grounds." The realism of the portraits is not surprising if we have heard Whittier say in other poems that man must learn "the lesson of endurance" and be "taught by suffering."

The Puritans banished Quakers or cut off their ears, but one approach to an understanding of the religious meaning of "Snowbound" is to think of Whittier as preserving the essentials of the historic faith by interpreting it in the light of later knowledge and a more sensitive conscience. No merely individual salvation could satisfy him while others, thought to be not Elect, were suffering. Rejecting dogma and ritual in favor of active commitment to others, he never moved to Comte's and Robert Ingersoll's "religion of humanity" but let his conscience be guided always by a faith adequately summarized in the New Testament's two Great Commandments. As he wrote in the poem he contributed to the celebration of the anniversary of the founding of Haverhill, his beloved native town,

> Earth shall be near to Heaven when all
> That severs man from man shall fall,
> For, here or there, salvation's plan
> Alone is love of God and man.

Too much aware of the darkness ever to become simply a secular humanist, he was yet more sensitive to the human plight of the whole family of man than the Puritans whose heritage he clung to had been. Refusing to call anyone heretical, reading widely in world religions, he yet was more faithful to "orthodoxy" than any of the nineteenth-century poets we have been considering. Translating it, he kept it alive. As he said of himself once,

> He reconciled as best he could
> Old faith and fancies new.

Uniting as it does the three subjects on which he could write best, memories of childhood, nature, and the demands of a religious conscience, "Snowbound" gave Whittier his best, perhaps his only perfect, chance to be a good poet without ceasing to be a good Quaker. It gave him a chance to utilize his best resources as a poet, his quite personal memories, and yet to raise them to national, if not universal, significance, just because he was fortunate enough to share the background of most Americans. "Snowbound" is replete with "metre-making" arguments. Its style could hardly be plainer, less embellished. It passes Emerson's test of the true American poem.

These were the poets most prized by the nineteenth century. Toward the end of the century their collected works in gilt-topped editions graced parlor tables all over the land. Meanwhile greater poets were writing or had written better poems that the age ignored. Emerson was prized as a sage, not as a poet. Whitman had only a small following, and Emily Dickinson was not publicly known at all. The discovery, a generation or so ago, of this strange state of affairs with its obvious injustices was followed by an impulse to turn everything upside down, to simply invert nineteenth-century popular standards. Melville, who had written *Moby-Dick,* had written poems that went unread: *He* should be elevated as a poet and Holmes forgotten. Dickinson had written some of the finest poems ever written by an American and had been discouraged from trying to publish them: The veneration accorded to Whittier must be absurd and the man neurotic.

Ages, like individuals, achieve their own identity in part by rejecting their parents. Our century has achieved its own somewhat unhappy self-hood by now and can afford to relax a little in its rejection of the century that brought it to birth. Almost every distinctively new feature of the poetry and criticism of the first half of our century was calculated to make it impossible for us to read nineteenth-century popular poets with pleasure or take them seriously. But now that "modern" poetry may be characterized as "Modernist" — a term intended to suggest that it is "dead," at least for the more creative young poets — we need to take a fresh look at the poets who have not been read sympathetically by readers of any sophistication for half a century. When we do, we find ourselves variously rewarded for our trouble.

We do not, of course, like them so well as their contemporaries did. The prejudices they bolster and the assumptions they never examine are, to a considerable extent, not ours. In any age it seems just not worth while to examine certain ideas: They seem either too obvious, or too much needed, to be taken other than as given. "The Psalm of Life" consoled an age that felt so desperately lost that *any* action, however unspecified its nature or direction, seemed better than inaction, which would give one time for thought — which, as Lowell said, was *always* sad. If we are not comforted by the poem, it is ultimately because we ask certain questions which the poem doesn't intend to answer. It is, I think, a poor poem for other reasons, but this is the chief reason why it does not console us.

But Longfellow also wrote *some* poems that do not raise questions they cannot answer. His age valued him too highly, of course, and he himself had very little idea of where his real strength as a poet lay. But even he, whose immense popularity and pervasive sentimentality make him epitomize the problem we have when we try to achieve a just estimate of all these poets, wrote sometimes in a way that should make us call him a genuine if minor poet.

No single reason for the failure of the "schoolroom poets" to achieve more than they did can, I think, be found. Certainly not, as we have recently been told, that they were too close to, reflected too directly, "popular" culture. Lowell's culture was deep, not popular, and Holmes's thought ranged far. Yet precisely these two of our five failed most often to achieve real distinction in their serious work. The theory seems to work best with Longfellow, who enjoyed his reputation as priest and philosopher and gave the people what they wanted — but *not* hypocritically or cynically, gave it because that was all he had to give. But the theory works not at all with Whittier who, without in any sense being a profound thinker or a man of really deep culture, still managed in his best work to avoid most of the cliches of his age.

Perhaps the reason why we must call them minor poets that comes closest to applying equally to all of them is that, by and large, in the bulk of their work — with some notable exceptions to be made for Lowell and Whittier — they failed to respond, except superficially, to the new experience of being American in the middle of the nineteenth century. Though they frequently wrote of American subjects and scenes, they did so, for the most part, in borrowed language and forms. They failed by the tests provided in Emerson's "The Poet": America was not a poem in *their* eyes, for even when they wrote about it, they generally wrote as though they were "poeticizing" an intrinsically unpoetic subject; they did not think that "thought makes everything fit for use"; they did not, generally, use "forms according to the life, and not according to the form" or believe that "it is not metres, but a metre-making argument, that makes a poem," or recognize "the instant dependence of form upon soul." Instead, they were content, for the most part, "to write poems from the fancy, at a safe distance from their own experience," not realizing that "the experience of each new age requires a new confession" and that the new world was waiting for its poet so that it might come to know itself.

By Emerson's standard these men were all — except, in the very best of his work, Whittier — "men of poetical talents, or of industry and skill in meter," but not "true" poets. Insofar as they failed to respond in depth either to themselves or to their time and place, they failed Emerson's test that makes "the value of genius to us" lie in "the veracity of its report."

Except, except. . . . There *is* no *single* reason for their lack of greater accomplishment, not even Emerson's Transcendental poetics. What we need to do now is to find out *what* they accomplished, not concentrate on trying to explain why they did not accomplish more. If all of them must now be rated below the level they were placed at in their own time, it fortunately no longer seems necessary to deface the portraits on the schoolroom wall.

PART TWO

Transcendental Dawn

CHAPTER III

Sursum Corda: The Poet as Friend and Aider

There comes Emerson. . . .
Whose prose is grand verse, while his verse, the Lord knows,
Is some of it pr— No, 't is not even prose;
— J. R. Lowell, in *A Fable for Critics,* 1848

John G. Whittier says that Ralph Waldo Emerson is the one American who is sure of being remembered a thousand years.
— From the "Personal" column of the
New York Tribune, Sept. 9, 1878, p. 4.

If there be a Spirit above that looks down and scans authors, here is one at least in whom It might be well pleased.
— Whitman, in 1881, four months
before Emerson's death

A search for perfect truths throws out a beauty more spiritual than sensuous. . . . If Emerson's manner is not always beautiful in accordance with accepted standards, why not accept a few other standards? . . . Though a great poet and prophet, [*Emerson*] *is greater, possibly, as an invader of the unknown — America's deepest explorer of the spiritual immensities. . . .*
— Charles Ives, in *Essays Before a Sonata,*
published in 1920

I suppose I have always thought I'd like to name in verse some day my four greatest Americans: George Washington, the general and statesman; Thomas Jefferson, the political thinker; Abraham Lincoln, the martyr and savior; and fourth, Ralph Waldo Emerson, the poet. I take these names because they are going around the world. They are not just local. Emerson's name has gone as a poetic philosopher or as a philosophical poet, my favorite kind of both.

I have friends it bothers when I am accused of being Emersonian, that is, a cheerful Monist, for whom evil does not

> *exist, or if it does exist, needn't last forever. Emerson quotes Burns as speaking to the Devil as if he could mend his ways. A melancholy dualism is the only soundness. The question is: is soundness of the essence?*
>
> — Robert Frost in 1959, "On Emerson."

RALPH WALDO EMERSON

EMERSON is our nineteenth-century poet most in need today of being rediscovered. We have not read him as he deserves to be read, for a long time now, not since the beginning of the Modernist era in literature, which defined itself by breaking with the nineteenth century, and particularly by rejecting anything that smacked of "idealism." I find it quite extraordinary that Oliver Wendell Holmes's chapter on the poetry in *Ralph Waldo Emerson,* his volume in the American Men of Letters Series, is still the most helpful survey of the whole subject.

A number of Emerson's finest poems have seldom or never been reprinted in selections or anthologies; and since no modern edition of his complete poems is available, this means that most readers, including, it would seem, the anthologists and literary historians, have never read them. Some of his most interesting poems are to be found only in the Appendix of the 1884 and the Centenary editions. Written early and sometimes left unfinished, these almost totally unread poems and fragments of poems are full of brilliant passages that often express Emerson's seminal insights more sharply and memorably than the poems he chose to publish in his two volumes, *Poems,* 1846, and *May-Day and Other Pieces,* 1867.

But it is not simply that some of Emerson's best poems and passages have remained virtually unknown and unnoticed for some fifty years now. The poems that are best-known because they have been reprinted most often should be reread with Charles Ives's "other standards" in mind rather than the standards that have dominated critical thinking about poetry for the last half-century.

How to begin? Matthew Arnold long ago decided that though Emerson ought to be valued as "the friend and aider of all who would live in the spirit," still it had to be admitted that Emerson was not only outside the ranks of "great" poets, he was not even a "legitimate" poet.[1] Most recent writers on Emerson's verse have tended to agree with the negative part at least of Arnold's judgment. As for the positive part, they have not generally thought that any aid could be found in the work of a Transcendental Idealist.

But Emerson's poetry ought to be reread and restudied today not just because we have not known how fine it often is, or why — though this would be reason enough, surely — but because it is an important part of the body of writing of Emerson the man and writer; and without understanding Emerson we cannot possibly begin to understand the later development of our poetry. No other poet, unless it be Whitman, has been so important as Emerson to later poets, including the greatest of them. And when the story of his impact on Whitman is better known, we may well come to decide that Whitman's twentieth-century followers are profoundly in Emerson's debt too, though they often do not know it, not knowing Emerson's work. I think we shall decide, when more is known about our literary history, that Yvor Winters was not wrong when he went behind Whitman to Emerson to locate the source of what he considered Hart Crane's romantic errors.

There are then not two distinct major "lines" in American poetry, as Leslie Fiedler has suggested, the one starting from Emerson and the one starting from Whitman, but three lines springing from the two figures, considered separately and together. There are those poets who have responded to Emerson but not, in an important way, to Whitman. There are others, chiefly in the twentieth century, who have responded to the aspects of Whitman that are farthest from Emerson, that distinguish him from Emerson. And there are those, chiefly in the present and very recent past, who have responded to both Whitman and Emerson, or else to precisely those aspects of Whitman that are most Emersonian.

Whitman himself and Dickinson, Robinson, and Frost are the chief of those who, as we shall see, would have written very differently, or perhaps not at all, without Emerson.[2] They define the direct Emersonian line.

The Whitman-minus-Emerson line was a phenomenon chiefly of the poetic renaissance of 1912 and after. In the 1920's and 1930's particularly there were poets whose Whitmanism had nothing clearly Transcendental or Emersonian about it. Carl Sandburg is perhaps the clearest example — until his latest work — but Ezra Pound is another.

The Emerson-Whitman line, broken in the later nineteenth and earlier twentieth centuries, may be traced in Hart Crane, Theodore Roethke, and a good many contemporary young poets like Denise Levertov, many of whom are not conscious of any debt to Emerson. Once or twice distilled, through Whitman and the late poems of William Carlos Williams, their kinship with Emerson is still recognizable if unavowed.

Without knowing Emerson, in short, we cannot understand our poetic history. But there is a larger, less "literary" reason than this for rediscovering him, now that the literary and philosophic preconceptions of the first half of our century no longer seem unquestionable. The reason is the one Arnold, once again, gave so long ago for valuing Emerson's presence, even if not his poetry — that he is "the friend and aider of all who would live in the spirit." We are ready at last, I think, to let Emerson speak to us, to discover his relevance to us.

The reason for our readiness is not hard to find. We no longer feel obliged to destroy the nineteenth century in order to achieve a literature of our own. We can see why Eliot had to make Emerson his symbol of a naive unawareness of evil in "Sweeney Erect," and why Pound was impelled to speak of "that messy, blurry, sentimentalistic nineteenth century." Until the fathers were destroyed, the great Modernists could not "make it new," more pertinently, could not write creatively at all. But for us, the destruction has long since been accomplished. Emerson and his contemporaries no longer pose any threat to our autonomy. Instead, we should like to know what it was that Emerson saw that made possible his famous smile. We are ready to read him as he wanted to be read.

Of the many recent signs of our readiness for Emerson, I shall mention only one, singling it out just because in some ways it may seem so surprising. Robert Penn Warren, ironist as poet and novelist and critic, whose fiction and poetry have so often emphasized the dangers inherent in an idealistic vision of life, has recently written a series of seven lyrics bearing the over-all title "Homage to Emerson, on Night Flight to New York." The poems speak of Emerson's largest significance for us.

Can we, in this dark time, the poems ask, can *we* find, as Emerson thought he did, a light not imagined or merely desired but "real"? Can we rediscover for ourselves what he seems to have known, "a way by which the process of living can become Truth"? Can we find in nature, which is to say in our total experience of the "not-me," any reason to smile, as Emerson did? Is there a way of *seeing* that will make it seem that irony is not the only honest poetic stance?

Emerson's essays lie open on the lap of the speaker in these poems, seeming to glow under the shaft of light cast by the reading lamp above the seat, a narrow beam that does not illuminate the "pressurized gloom" of the rest of the cabin or affect the darkness outside. "At 38,000 feet Emerson/ Is dead right." Which word, we wonder, should receive the chief emphasis when we read this, "dead" or "right"? Or should the stresses be equal?

Apart from the eccentric composer Charles Ives, it has been our poets who have thought most highly of Emerson's verse, not our scholars or critics, who have usually found it deplorably "unpoetic." It would seem a strange state of affairs if poets, including acknowledged great ones, could not be trusted to know good poetry when they read it.

Why is it that when we read our standard literary handbooks and histories we find Emerson's poetry given short shrift, as *The Oxford Companion to American Literature* does in its two sentences in a three-column article? Why is the poetry apologized for, or faintly praised, when no less sensitive and qualified readers of poetry than Whitman, Dickinson, Robinson, and Frost — to name only the greatest of Emerson's poetic admirers — have praised it and, Whitman excepted, have even paid it the immense compliment of rewriting it?

One reason for this anomaly is suggested by Matthew Arnold's use of the word "legitimate" to suggest his feeling that Emerson's verse was not properly "poetry" at all. Arnold had a clear idea of what poetry in the English language should be like. Emerson's verse did not fit the idea. It was not that Arnold's taste was excessively narrow. He liked the great English poets, particularly those of the seventeenth and nineteenth centuries, and even those he did not like so well he thought at least "legitimate." Pope might seem to him "a master of our prose," but most English poets, even the lesser ones, were he felt at least working within known poetic laws even if they were not Chaucers or Shakespeares or Miltons.

Arnold's difficulty with Emerson's verse, like Lowell's, was caused by the fact that it was not like the verse of any of the poets who provided the two with models for their judgments. Most clearly, it did not resemble the British poetry of its own time.

Between it and the verse of Tennyson, Browning, or Arnold himself, not to mention the lesser Victorians, there was an immense gap, as both Arnold and Lowell quite rightly saw.

Nor was it much closer, except on an abstractly thematic level, to the work of the great British Romantics. Arnold saw that Wordsworth and Emerson, for example, often wrote about the same things and expressed similar attitudes, but he was too sensitive to poetic values to fail to see that Emerson did not *write* like Wordsworth, even in those poems in which he was closest to him in idea and attitude. Still less, as Arnold could see, did Emerson's verse resemble that of Coleridge or Keats or Shelley. It must therefore exist, Arnold could only suppose, somewhere outside the area occupied by "legitimate" poetry.

If Arnold had said "British" instead of "legitimate," his judgment would have been more useful. Emerson stands at the beginning of an American poetic tradition that has diverged more and more widely through the years from the British tradition. Much of the best American poetry has been as different from British poetry as the greatest American fiction has been from British fiction. It has tended just as strongly toward the metaphysical (but not in the sense of that word that applies to Donne), the symbolic (but not in the sense in which we speak of "Symbolist" poetry), and the eschatological as American fictional "romances" have. It has treated the fabric and distinctions of the social order just as casually. At its best, it has generally centered its attention on searching out the possibilities of discovering ultimate meaning in individual experience, assuming no order as final except that discovered in the self and in the "not-me."

What are the typical American poems? Another, and better, list of examples might be named, but there would at least be nothing essentially misleading in naming as typical "Uriel," "Song of Myself," Dickinson's "Like Rain it Sounded Till it Curved," "The Man Against the Sky," "Kitty Hawk," "Sunday Morning," and "The Bridge." What they have in common, for present purposes at least, despite their stylistic and formal differences, is that none of them can be understood except in religious terms. They are all eschatological poems.

No less humanistic a critic than the late R. P. Blackmur once said that the poetry of Taylor, Whitman, Dickinson, Frost, Eliot, Stevens, and Robert Lowell "can be understood only if it is taken as religious." He was right, but his list might have been greatly extended. The same thing might be said, to be sure, of many British poets and poems, but not, I think, of so large a proportion of the best and most representative of them as is true of our poetry. As soon as there came to be a body of American poetry that differed markedly from British poetry, it became clear that American poets have tended to think of poetry as prophecy, not as the practice of an art whose rules were known, and not as a way of thinking about a fixed and known "reality."

By contrast, British poets — with the great Romantics, Yeats, Dylan Thomas, and some others as partial exceptions — have *tended* to think of poetry as an art, and to write within the accepted "rules" of the poetic art. It is no accident that our greatest and most typical American poets have been called eccentric, barbarous, "tasteless," and primitive by cultivated readers of poetry of their time. To the Americans, climbing "to Paradise, by the stairway of surprise" has seemed more important than conforming to civilized tradition. They have not expected to *be* here very long, so why bother much with the customs of the country?

Without seeing that Emerson was writing a different kind of poetry, guided by different purposes, from most of the poetry he was used to, Arnold could hardly have been expected to know what to do with Emerson's verse. But his difficulty did not end with his inability to "place" Emerson's poetry, in this very broad sense. His difficulty grew greater when he considered the American's poetic "style" even in the narrowest, most limited, sense of the word. By Arnold's standards, Emerson's style could hardly be said to *be* a style. Or if it was, it was not one proper to poetry. It was too declarative, too "thin," too "prosaic." Too often it seemed to consist of flat assertion. It seemed a style proper to a sage, not to a poet, or perhaps to a visionary preacher, but not to an artist.

Since, except for Taylor, whose work Arnold could not have known, Emerson is the first in the line of American poets who have given American poetry the features that distinguish it from British poetry, so far as it *is* distinguishable, Arnold can hardly be blamed for not recognizing Emerson's poetry as valuable or his style as one that a poet who thought of himself not as a singer but as a Namer and Sayer might appropriately use. But what of the scholars and critics of American literature in the past forty years or so, who are not British and whose standards are presumably not Arnold's, who have done no better than Arnold? Why have *we* seen so little to admire in Emerson's poetry?

In part, I suspect for Arnold's reason: Not knowing how to classify it, we have not known what to say about it. The poet reading another poet feels less need to classify. He can respond, enjoy, let the poem speak to him directly. He is less likely to have worked out ideas of legitimacy for the poetry of others, though he may be very clear in his mind about what is legitimate for himself in his own writing. The scholarly mind, by contrast with the poetic, suffers from a need first to classify, to "comprehend," before it can respond. This is one of the penalties of intellectualism, as Emerson pointed out.

The other reason why we have not only failed to appreciate Emerson's poetry adequately but frequently seem not even to have read much of it is that since American literature became an academic "field" of specialization, beginning in the 1920's, the philosophical assumptions of "naturalists" and "humanists," and the theological assumptions of the religiously "neo-orthodox," have made it extremely difficult to understand what Emerson was up to, or what value he could have, as a thinker. And since his is a "poetry of wisdom," or philosophical poetry, as Frost preferred to call it, a failure to find any wisdom in Emerson would leave his verses seeming very flat and dull indeed.

For those who first thought of themselves as "naturalists," then as "neo-naturalists" who had moved on beyond the reductionist attitudes satirized in Frost's "The White-tailed Hornet," and finally, today, as "humanists," Emerson's "Transcendentalism," his link with the "superstitions" and "mythical thinking" of the past, as they saw it, was the stumbling block. He sounded so often as though he were merely translating Jonathan Edwards or Edward Taylor into neo-Platonic terms! For those, on the other hand, who, beginning generally in the 1940's, thought in neo-orthodox Christian terms, Emerson seemed fatally naive about man's limitations and his capacity for evil. Warren puts this reaction most briefly and pertinently in his "Homage to Emerson . . .": "No sin. Not even error." What could be made of Emerson, then, by either group? How could a man who had written in the tradition of gnomic, oracular, aphoristic "wisdom poetry" be thought of as having accomplished anything, if his "wisdom poetry" was not wise?

Despite the philosophic and religious climate prevailing for the past several generations, Emerson's essays have survived in the academy somewhat better than his poetry because they are easier to see as "significant," even if not "wise." They are easier to relate and classify and subsume. Their rhetoric is recognizably related to Emerson's early experience in the pulpit, and their topics are often easily compared with similar topics treated by other writers, as *Representative Men* may be compared with Carlyle's *Heroes and Hero-Worship* (Emerson was more democratic in his attitudes in his book), or the theology of "The Divinity School Address" may be compared with that of the elder Channing (Emerson has moved a step or two, or maybe three, beyond the great Unitarian preacher in the march of "liberalizing" theology). We can, in short, *talk* about the essays more easily than about the poems without responding to Emerson's central meanings and purposes.

Since Emerson's philosophy, which drew readers in his own century to him so strongly, has been one of the chief reasons why his poetry has not been taken seriously in our time, it is perhaps a useful strategy today to back into the poetry through the essays. With Emerson, this procedure is less hard to justify than it would be with many poets.

Emerson developed his Transcendentalism as a way out of the early crisis caused by personal suffering and loss of faith in the Bible and in historic Christianity as he had received it. "Idealism," as he usually called it simply, was a way of finding meaning in life once again, when it had seemed for a time that there *was* no meaning. Aware of the threats to faith that we have seen occupying central places in the work of the "schoolroom poets," Emerson set about the task of supplying a substitute for the loss that saddened Longfellow and depressed Lowell. To one of his late poems, Lowell gave the title, "Credidimus Jovem Regnare," loosely, we used to believe that God governs. Years before, Emerson had taken it to be his special mission to show that, despite the loss of Biblical faith, God most assuredly still governs. He called one of his poems "Sursum Corda," lift up your hearts; the title points to the intention behind all his thinking.

The distinguishing characteristic of metaphysical idealism, historically considered, is its emphasis on "mind over matter," the proposition, variously expressed, that the knower somehow creates the known, that the conditions of perceiving determine the content of perception. But as Emerson tried to elaborate this proposition into a system, he found that his experience was too rich and various to be held by his thought. Refusing to suppress the contradictory insights, he found himself using words more and more loosely in an effort to express attitudinal meanings *no* doctrinal system could hold. Sacrificing consistency to new experience, logical coherence to growth, he contradicted himself more and more and did not care. Why should he, when his most important insight was that life always bursts the bonds of systematic thought? When the clearest implication of his "system" was that there could *be* no system?

At its deepest level of motivation, Emerson's thought was not philosophic — in the modern sense, in which the philosopher is characterized by his concern for careful thinking and precise use of words — but religious. That his effort was not so much to clarify the nature of reality as to enable men to live in it under the new and terrifying conditions that depressed Lowell may be deduced either by studying the life that issued in the thought or by analyzing the thought itself.

That is why Emerson could write that "give away" sentence in "Nature" about the "advantage" of idealism, which sounds to the modern reader so much like an admission that his system rests on "wishful thinking." ("The advantage of the ideal theory over the popular faith is this, that it presents the world in precisely that view which is most desirable to the mind.") That is probably the ultimate reason why he could remain unconcerned about his own inconsistency, which in the end means his own over-all lack of a purely philosophic, or systematically rational, clarity. It is not surprising that professional philosophers today ordinarily do not take Emerson seriously. We can hardly blame them for not knowing what to do with a philosopher who was at heart a preacher without a pulpit, a prophet announcing a new way of life, a mystic who had only rudimentary mystical experiences, and a poet in his prose as well as in his verse.

Emersonian Transcendentalism, like Existentialism, must be called a religious movement expressed in philosophic terms. It was an effort to get us all to dance "To the cadence of the whirling world/ Which dances round the sun," as Emerson put it in a poem not published during his lifetime. Or as he said in "The Transcendentalist," it was a revolt of the young men against the religious authority of the past, in the name not of irreligion but of a deeper and truer religion. All its other aspects — economic, political, literary — sprang from this central core of purpose. To let Emerson say it once again, Transcendentalism is what Faith becomes in "Unitarian and commercial times" — that is, in a culture which he saw as dryly rationalistic, moralistic, and utilitarian, a culture which, as Kierkegaard said of his own, professed faith but really had none. Rather than being faithless, as its opponents charged, Emerson felt that Transcendentalism might more fairly be accused of being a "Saturnalia or excess of Faith." To be sure, he had his tongue halfway in his cheek when he said this, for the Transcendental Saturnalia had been preceded, and motivated, by his own loss of faith in the miraculous and supernatural aspects of his *inherited* faith.[3] A son and inheritor of the Puritans, Emerson had first doubted all that the Puritan faith rested on, before he had found comfort in conceiving a different kind of loss of self from that envisaged by Edward Taylor.[4]

The rational justification for the Saturnalia was the conviction that "God IS, not WAS." Scholars who have commented on this statement lying at the center of Emerson's thought have too often taken it as simply a skeptical rejection of orthodoxy. But the statement affirms more than it denies. If on the one hand it means that we ought not to be bound by the limits of the religious experience of the past ("not *was*": which is to say, God is not to be identified exclusively with any of the ancient Scriptures; certainly not to be thought of as adequately revealed in the Biblical Revelation), it no less clearly means that God really *is,* exists, operates, reveals Himself, right *now,* to *us.* As he put the matter in 1836 in the "Introduction" to *Nature,*

> The foregoing generations beheld God and nature face to face; we, through their eyes. Why should not we also enjoy an original relation to the universe? Why should not we have a poetry and philosophy of insight and not of tradition, and a religion by revelation to us, and not the history of theirs?

What Emerson intends to say — and did sometimes say so magnificently — is that if the term "God" means to us only an ancient belief, then for us God is effectively dead. Revelation did not cease when the canon of Holy Writ was determined, nor are true reports of Him limited to one book. Revelation is continuous, universal, and unmediated. The God who exists and manifests Himself in "the eternal now" matters to us in ways we have not understood. The forms of ancient belief and ritual have lost their power; they conceal God from us instead of revealing Him. A God who only "was" cannot matter to us. "I draw from nature the lesson of an intimate divinity."

This is the core insight of Emerson's original Transcendentalism. As he grew older, he tried to deal more seriously with the philosophic difficulties that arose when one asserted immediate and continuous revelation to every man. Why was the relation between experience and reality not clearer? Why did so many men seem unaware of the revelation nature continuously offers? What part does *illusion* play in experience? By the time of *The Conduct of Life* Emerson's thought had grown more rationalistic, less intuitive, less mystical. But though he continually qualified, he never really renounced his early position.

If "God is, not was," then He must be present in our experience when we apprehend the transcendent aspects of experience. Experience, *our* experience, is all, and is sufficient. Logical proofs of God are as unavailing as dubious reports of ancient miracles. Truly apprehended, all experience is miraculous. *Apprehended,* not reasoned about. The "method of nature" is the method of "ecstasy." Experience of transcendence needs no logical proof and no scriptural authority; it is self-authenticating, as the *heart* knows. The truest knowledge is revealed only to the depths of our being but that does not mean, in Emerson's view, that it is wholly subjective, something we just imagine or wish or "make up." The revelations available to us in experience can come only if we "open" ourselves to experience, "unlock our human doors," as he said in "The Poet," and let the "tides of Being" flow through us.[5] Or as he put it in "The Method of Nature," ". . . all knowledge is assimilation to the object of knowledge." Though he agreed with the main thrust of Blake's conviction that "If the doors of perception were cleansed everything would appear to man as it is, infinite," Emerson anticipated Whitman in finding more need for "opening" than for "cleansing" the doors of the self. To find God in experience, he thought we had to learn how to *look* for Him.

Using vision as a metaphor for all sensuous experience, Emerson developed, unsystematically but fully, a *method* of transcendence. Seeing with transparent eyeballs, opening the doors of our being, we could see the eternal Beauty, the flowing Spirit, everywhere. Without using the term, Emerson gave directions for attaining, or preparing oneself to receive, what R. M. Bucke would later call "cosmic consciousness." Emerson's method of transcendence through a sharpened and expanded consciousness is related to the *via affirmativa* of the mystics, the "affirmation of images." This way to mystical awareness and union moves by means of the senses "through nature to God." Though its end is the same — vision of and union with the Absolute or All — its method is the reverse of that of the *via negativa,* the "negation of images," which moves downward into the darkness of the self instead of outward into the light of things.

Between Emerson's thought and Zen Buddhism there is also a close relation, though Emerson knew about Oriental religion only at second hand until after he had developed the essential core of his philosophy, and then only imperfectly.[6] But he knew about George Fox, the Quaker mystic, and Plotinus, and others; and he had read Henry Vaughan and other seventeenth-century writers influenced by Cambridge Platonism, and some of the Cambridge Platonists themselves. Perhaps the sentence that most strikingly reveals the central area of agreement between Emerson's thought and Zen is the one he placed third in the essay "Circles": "St. Augustine described the nature of God as a circle whose centre was everywhere, and its circumference nowhere." [7] To which he immediately added, "We are all our lifetime reading the copious sense of this first of forms."

But of course our "reading" will have to be direct and intuitive, a kind of *immersion,* if that which defines the circle as a circle, that is, its circumference, can be found "nowhere." The "centre" is equally, according to this definition, in the self and in all other selves and things. Emerson was attempting to clarify one of the implications of his metaphor when he wrote, later in the same essay, that from Idealism "We learn that God IS; that he is in me; and that all things are shadows of him." He knew, of course, that such a statement did not exhaust the manifold suggestions of his metaphoric definition of God. If it had, there would have been no need for the essay. And he probably also knew that the definition he misattributed to St. Augustine was a commonplace of Medieval mystics in the neo-Platonic tradition and was revived by the Cambridge Platonists, where it is likely

Emerson found it. As W. T. Stace has argued, the testimony of the mystics in East and West, past and present, is essentially the same.

The inconsistencies of Emerson's philosophic thought on these matters, particularly on just how we are to understand nature as symbol, need not now concern us, for we are not trying to evaluate him as a philosopher. (With most professional philosophers today having given up any claim to "wisdom," perhaps we ought not to think of him as a philosopher but as a "wisdom writer.") Though he was troubled by a recurring suspicion, fatal to his particular kind of Saturnalia of faith, that *all* experience may be illusion, he had an even deeper reason than that to be disturbed. His ability to experience nature as his theory told him he should grew less and less with the years, particularly after the death of his son Waldo in 1842. His faith had rested on the possibility of ecstatic revelations coming within and through experience, illuminations, epiphanies granted day by day. But if the illuminations did not come, then what? How could he go on being a Transcendentalist?

Gradually, almost imperceptibly, he modified his thinking in the direction of the sort of theistic evolutionary humanism we find in *The Conduct of Life* and in the late poem "The Adirondacks." Nature, which once had impressed him chiefly as an opportunity for illumination, now was redefined as "limitation," another word for "fate." The Over-Soul was now an emergent deity, and natural evil, which he had once called merely "privative" — that is, the absence of good, not ultimately Real in itself — was now the starting point for his thinking, as it is in "Fate." Opposing fate there was now thought, with its untested powers of creativeness, instead of illumination. Before this point in his development was reached, Emerson had written most of his poetry and those essays that present his most distinctive contribution to the life of the mind in America. The essays in *The Conduct of Life* are great in their own way, and they are important in the development of our poetry, as we shall see, but their importance is nothing like that of the earlier works. If we center our attention on them, we tend to see Emerson as another, and greater, Holmes, foreshadowing James's pragmatism and, through James, John Dewey's instrumentalism. This is a legitimate way of seeing Emerson, but this is not the man who put his personal stamp on American poetry to such a degree that we cannot imagine what it might have been like without him.

If we turn the comparison with James around, so that we see, not Emerson partially foreshadowing James, but James continuing, in such works as *Varieties of Religious Experience* and "Pragmatism and Religion," the chief thrust of early Emerson, we shall be in a better position to appreciate what Emerson meant to later poets. James's speech at the Concord Centenary celebration of Emerson's birth makes it perfectly clear that for him the Emerson who greatly mattered, the central Emerson, was the Emerson of the earlier writings.

The key passage in 1836 *Nature,* Emerson's attempt at a systematic presentation of the metaphysic of idealism, comes very early in the essay. It is the passage about the sudden illumination that occurred when he was "crossing a bare common, in snow puddles, at twilight, under a clouded sky." Suddenly he had found himself "glad to the brink of fear." Losing himself, becoming as it were "nothing" while "seeing" all, letting "the currents of the Universal Being circulate through" him, he knew himself as "part or parcel of God."

The loss of self was the "preparation" which brought immediate "assurance" of "grace," would be a way of describing this experience in the terms Emerson's Puritan forebears had used. Emerson preferred to say, "In the woods we return to reason and faith." Whitman, Dickinson, and Frost, among others, tested and retested Emerson's conviction in their nature poems.

The heart of "The Divinity School Address" lies in the idea of God's immanence. If God is immanent and the old Scriptures no longer speak to us, we shall have to learn to listen and look in a new way. "O taste and see, the Lord is good," wrote the Psalmist, not "listen to the voice of the ancient authorities." "Attentiveness and obedience," to use Thomas Mann's description of the religious attitude, are what we need if our lives are not to seem empty of meaning and reality. Emerson's idea of the *continuous* nature of revelation in his address to the Divinity School is essentially the same, surprising as it may seem, as Eliot's central meaning in *Four Quartets*: that it is possible to find in our own experience, if we do not close ourselves to its meaning, sufficient assurance that "the fire and the rose are one."

"The American Scholar" calls us to trust things, not words; to approach learning as though we had a life to live in which "learning" could play a vital role but was not the only value, or the only guide; to bring ideas to the test of action and action to the test of an eschatological vision. The attitudes Emerson expresses here have been re-expressed not only by Frost but by many other poets besides, including some very contemporary ones.

Similarly with "Self-Reliance," in which Emerson's central point is not that we do not need to rely on anyone or anything beyond ourselves but that in the last analysis there *is* nothing else to rely on, if our experience is to be our own and our decisions authentic. Unless we can love and trust ourselves, we shall not be able to love and trust anything or anyone, and shall be cut off from the springs of life.

Readers of the essays today are likely to find "The Over-Soul" one of the hardest to get into. In it Emerson is attempting to talk directly about his central religious convictions, to say as much as he could say abstractly about the relations of center to circumference, and his terms — "Unity," "Over-Soul," "One," "Law," "the Soul" — are not such as we find it easy to grasp. He is likely to speak more directly to us when he speaks metaphorically about the same subjects and relations, as he does in "Circles." But there are many passages in "The Over-Soul" in which, moving from abstractly discursive language to metaphor, Emerson puts his meanings in ways that many of our poets at least have understood, whether we can or not.

Here are two such passages, both of them relevant to the work of such poets as Thoreau and Very, Whitman and Dickinson, Hart Crane and Roethke. In the first, the image of "light" finally carries the meaning; in the second, the image of "seeing" and of being "invaded":

> . . . All goes to show that the soul in man is not an organ, but animates and exercises all the organs; is not a function, like the power of memory, of calculation, of comparison, but uses these as hands and feet; is not a faculty, but a light; is not the intellect or the will, but the master of the intellect and the will; is the background of our being, in which they lie, — an immensity not possessed and that cannot be possessed. From within or from behind, a light shines through us upon things and makes us aware that we are nothing, but the light is all.
>
> We distinguish the announcements of the soul, its manifestations of its own nature, by the term *Revelation*. These are always attended by the emotion of the sub-

> lime. For this communication is an influx of the Divine mind into our mind. It is an ebb of the individual rivulet before the flowing surges of the sea of life. Every distinct apprehension of this central commandment agitates men with awe and delight. A thrill passes through all men at the reception of new truth, or at the performance of a great action, which comes out of the heart of nature. In these communications the power to see is not separated from the will to do, but the insight proceeds from obedience, and the obedience proceeds from a joyful perception. Every moment when the individual feels himself invaded by it is memorable.

"The Poet" is not only one of Emerson's greatest essays — perhaps only "Circles" is likely to seem greater today — it is also the most important single critical document in the history of our poetry, more important even than Whitman's 1855 Preface to *Leaves of Grass,* which so often echoes and expands upon Emerson. Discussion of "The Poet" will be found in chapter VI, Whitman, because, as Emerson himself recognized, in many important ways Whitman was more nearly the new poet that Emerson called for in his essay than Emerson himself, in his own verse, was able to be.

But if it is clear enough that Whitman was not only a greater poet than Emerson but even a more "Emersonian" one, if we let the essay "The Poet" define Emerson's ideal, nevertheless to say so much is not to say that we know just how "minor," when compared with Whitman's, Emerson's poetic achievement was. The reader who comes with an open mind and heart to the complete poems is more likely to revise his estimate of Emerson upward than downward. The early, unfinished, or unpublished poems — unpublished during Emerson's lifetime, that is — in the Appendix of the 1884 edition, or in the still further "appended" "Poems of Youth and Early Manhood" of the Centenary edition, alone would justify such an upward revision. The canon needs to be revised by addition, not subtraction. Poems we have not read should become known and discussed. Often they turn out to be as interesting and memorable as "Water," to be found only in the Appendix of the two early editions. The first part of the poem suggests to me Frost's "Sand Dunes," the second part Eliot's "The Dry Salvages":

The water understands
Civilization well;
It wets my foot, but prettily,
It chills my life, but wittily,
It is not disconcerted,
It is not broken-hearted:
Well used, it decketh joy,
Adorneth, doubleth joy:
Ill used, it will destroy,
In perfect time and measure
With a face of golden pleasure
Elegantly destroy.

All day the waves assailed the rock,
I heard no church-bell chime,
The sea-beat scorns the minster clock
And breaks the glass of Time.

A good many of these poems were written very early in Emerson's career, before he had established himself by publishing *Nature,* before, that is, he had become a public figure with a public figure's responsibilities. He probably considered that some of them expressed his thought too outspokenly, would hurt too many people, and so did not publish them. "The Bohemian Hymn," with its extreme antinomianism, may be one such. Certainly it is an impressive poem, and perhaps the most succinct expression we have of the insights it contains:

In many forms we try
To utter God's infinity,
But the boundless hath no form,
And the Universal Friend
Doth as far transcend
An angel as a worm.
The great Idea baffles wit,
Language falters under it,

It leaves the learned in the lurch;
Nor art, nor power, nor toil can find
The measure of the eternal Mind,
Nor hymn, nor prayer, nor church.

Another such is "Limits," with its radical implications for humanistic moralists and its utterly plain, pared-down style:

Who knows this or that?
Hark in the wall to the rat:
Since the world was, he has gnawed;
Of his wisdom, of his fraud
What dost thou know?
In the wretched little beast
Is life and heart,
Child and parent,
Not without relation
To fruitful field and sun and moon.
What art thou? His wicked eye
Is cruel to thy cruelty.

The long work called "The Poet," made up of "Fragments on the Poet and the Poetic Gift" and "Fragments on Nature and Life," ought to be called one of the most important treatments of its subject in our verse. In it we see Emerson working out ideas that later found expression in the essay "The Poet," but it has more value than a mere rehearsal would have. Some of the fragments express Emerson's central insights better, with more bite and sharpness, than later published versions of the same ideas. Take for example these lines rejecting superficial Romanticism and calling for an insight deep enough to see the beauty in unlikely things and places:

Let me go wher'er I will,
I hear a sky-born music still:
It sounds from all things old,
It sounds from all things young,
From all that's fair, from all that's foul,
Peals out a cheerful song.

It is not only in the rose,
It is not only in the bird,
Not only where the rainbow glows,
Nor in the song of woman heard,
But in the darkest, meanest things
There alway, alway something sings.

'T is not in the high stars alone,
Nor in the cups of budding flowers,
Nor in the redbreast's mellow tone,
Nor in the bow that smiles in showers,
But in the mud and scum of things
There alway, alway something sings.[8]

Whitman and Cummings may be the first to come to mind as we read these lines, then perhaps Dickinson and Denise Levertov. Is it certain that any one of them has more compactly and memorably expressed Emerson's idea?

"Monadnoc" and "The Titmouse," published in *Poems* and *May-Day,* respectively, will be my final examples of poems the anthologists, for the most part, have not reprinted and which, with no modern edition of Emerson's complete poems available, readers generally have not known. Both poems deserve to be considered among the finest things Emerson ever wrote.[9] "Monadnoc" was a favorite of both Frost and Robinson, and I suspect Frost may have had "The Titmouse" in mind when he wrote "The Wood-Pile." More will be said about both of these poems later, in connection with Robinson and Frost.

Needless to say, "Monadnoc" and "The Titmouse," and the shorter "Water," "Limits," and "The Bohemian Hymn," do not exhaust the "discoveries" remaining to be made among the poems that are not well known. Nor are whole poems the only kinds of discoveries to be made. I think of single lines, or pairs of lines, in "The Poet" that are concentrated expressions of themes that have often preoccupied later poets, as are these lines from the description of Saadi, the ideal poet, especially the middle two of the four:

He felt the flame, the fanning wings,
Nor offered words till they were things,

Glad when the solid mountain swims
In music and uplifting hymns.

Reading these lines, we may think of the late Stevens, dissatisfied with metaphor and trope, or of Williams' lifelong attempt to reach the truth of *things* through his words; but the relevance of the passage is not limited to these two. The lines condense a theme important in our poetry throughout its history, in a way that only Emerson could.

There is certainly no need in the present state of affairs to dwell on Emerson's limitations as a poet. It is perfectly true, but too obvious to need expanded discussion, that Emerson only partially and intermittently wrote poems that could pass the test announced in his essay "The Poet." Emerson knew that too, as he knew most of what he needed to know. He hailed Whitman as the poet he had been waiting for.

"The world being thus put under the mind for verb and noun, the poet is he who can articulate it." Emerson worried about his capacity to "articulate" the world he saw. He worried about his tendency to write only in "sleepy generalizations," and about his inability, much of the time, to put together into *whole* poems his scattered and partial illuminations. Both self-criticisms were partially justified: they accurately describe the kinds of dissatisfaction *we* feel in a good deal of his verse. But neither criticism applies to his best poems, and both of them need to be qualified.

Though Emerson was very fond of seventeenth-century English poets, the only one of them whose style his own at all resembles is Ben Jonson. But since Jonson had no followers in British poetry after the eighteenth century, Emerson effectually cut himself off from later styles when he followed Jonson in writing aphoristic verse. He cut himself off from the possibility of comparison with the very poets whose work he himself most enjoyed — with Shakespeare and Herbert and Herrick, and the greater Romantics and Victorians. He ought to have anticipated Arnold's dilemma.

The virtues of Emerson's style when he is at his best, even in the most abstract, least imagistic poems, can more easily be seen if we compare him not with any English poet, not even Jonson, but, first, with the "plain" style of his New England Puritan forebears and then with the styles of Thoreau and Very. *The Bay*

Psalm Book and *The New England Primer* are at least as relevant to the styles of all three Transcendentalists as are any more "literary" sources. And Emerson's superiority to Thoreau and Very in the gnomic or aphoristic style is too clear to need demonstrating.

But this is not the whole story either. Not all of Emerson's verse is bare of the images the modern reader misses, though, to be sure, his verse at its most typical is more abstract than the poetry we have learned to like best. The very early poem "A Letter" will illustrate how Emerson sometimes found the right images — though to be sure he is not, in this poem, conveying an achieved insight but describing the purpose and nature of his quest:

> Dear brother, would you know the life,
> Please God, that I would lead?
> On the first wheels that quit this weary town
> Over yon western bridges I would ride
> And with a cheerful benison forsake
> Each street and spire and roof, incontinent.
> Then would I seek where God might guide my steps,
> Deep in a woodland tract, a sunny farm,
> Amid the mountain counties, Hants, Franklin, Berks,
> Where down the rock ravine a river roars,
> Even from a brook, and where old woods
> Not tamed and cleared cumber the ground
> With their centennial wrecks.
> Find me a slope where I can feel the sun
> And mark the rising of the early stars.
> There will I bring my books, — my household gods,
> The reliquaries of my dead saint, and dwell
> In the sweet odor of her memory.
> Then in the uncouth solitude unlock
> My stock of art, plant dials in the grass,
> Hang in the air a bright thermometer
> And aim a telescope at the inviolate sun.

Language, tone, and rhythms combine with the images here to announce Emerson's sense of the purpose and plan of his career.

He does not intend to become a primitive, ignoring modern knowledge, but he finds he must back off from the culture in which he finds himself before the books and instruments can be useful to him. Not surprisingly, the instrument he reserves for the climactic place in his poem is the telescope, which enlarges the power of *vision*.

Just one other example will have to do for many possible ones in this effort to suggest that it would be wrong to take Emerson's own worry about his too generalized style at face value. The poem "Compensation" is considerably more concrete and imagistic than the essay it condenses, though the essay, too, breaks into poetry again and again. Here are the opening lines of the poem:

The wings of Time are black and white,
Pied with morning and with night.
Mountain tall and ocean deep
Trembling balance duly keep.
In changing moon and tidal wave
Glows the feud of Want and Have.
Gauge of more and less through space,
Electric star or pencil plays,
The lonely Earth amid the balls
That hurry through the eternal halls,
A makeweight flying to the void,
Supplemental asteroid,
Or compensatory spark,
Shoots across the neutral Dark.

As for Emerson's other self-criticism, that he could not often make wholes out of his fragments, that, too, represents acute self-knowledge, but do we know yet how many "whole" poems he did manage to create? "Uriel" may not be "the greatest Western poem yet," as Frost called it, but it is surely a *whole* poem, and, I think, a great one. No more prophetic lines have been written by an American poet than

"Line in nature is not found;
Unit and universe are round;
In vain produced, all rays return;
Evil will bless, and ice will burn." [10]

As Frost once said to me in private conversation, these lines fully anticipate the *moral* meaning of Einstein. "Uriel" is the most impressive expression of our antinomian tradition. But "Hamatreya" too, though it mixes voices and verse forms, is no mere heap of unrelated fragments. It is, I should say, one of the triumphant expressions of the eschatological vision in our poetry, as well as a daring experiment, for its time, in metrical or prosodic freedom.

"Merlin," with its brilliant, often-quoted lines in the first part, *may* seem open to the charge of lack of wholeness; but how many of us have read both parts of the two-part poem, of which the anthologists have chosen to reprint only the first part, without indicating that it is an excerpt? "Merlin I" and "Merlin II," read together as one poem, as they were meant to be, seem to me to have a sufficient unity to hold together the brilliant quotable lines. I cannot think of many greater poems in our literature on the poet and his role than "Merlin" I and II.

Similarly, "Each and All" may well be our finest poetic expression of the concept of organic wholeness, as "Brahma," one of Frost's favorites, may be the most memorable brief statement of the antinomian and anticlerical strain in our poetry. "The Snowstorm," beloved by Dickinson, is surely one of Emerson's fully realized poems. In short, not only in some of his best-known and best-loved poems, of which "Bacchus" and "Threnody" may be the supreme examples, but in poems that have been seldom read in the past forty or more years, Emerson very often gave the lie to his own melancholy suspicion, and to the standard allegation of others, that his poems are jumbles of fragments. When his imagination worked at its best, he could and did bring his flashes of light together to make a steady beam.

If what I have just said about Emerson's poems seems more polemical than judicial in tone, and more appreciative than analytical in substance, the fault is, I like to think, not wholly my own. Chiefly, I have tried to clear away barriers and suggest possible rewards, in an attempt to get Emerson *read,* to get his work, and particularly his poetry, taken seriously — and in its own terms, not ours. Emerson, Whitman, and Dickinson seem to me the three great American poets of the nineteenth century. Few, I suppose, would quarrel with my last two choices, but Emerson has not been seen as belonging in the company of the others, not even as the least of the three.

True enough, he seems to be saying at times what the speaker in the opening poem of Warren's "Homage to Emerson" thinks he is saying, "No sin. Not even error" — a denial most of us would no doubt find contradicted by our experience. But that was not all he had to say, if indeed it is a fair summation of what he meant. His wisdom at its best is both unsystematic and partial. His poetry as well as his prose was, we might say, programmatic, designed, like Puritan verse, to save souls. Most of his verse might be described by the title Edward Taylor gave some of the best of his poems, "Preparatory Meditations."

Arnold was right, and right even from Emerson's own point of view, when he called Emerson "the friend and aider of all who would live in the spirit." Arnold's mistake was in supposing that poetry could not be "legitimately" controlled by such a purpose. Or perhaps he just read the poetry too carelessly, as his acknowledged failure to understand "The Titmouse" would suggest. In either case Arnold is in a large and distinguished company.

The company of those who in our time have been not just unaware of Emerson but positively repelled by him includes many moralistic humanists like Yvor Winters, who saw fit to blame Hart Crane's suicide on Emerson, and humanists of a more "scientific" cast, who suspect Transcendentalism of being just a watered-down version of Christianity, an unacceptable "myth," in short. It includes also many "neo-orthodox" Christians who find Emerson deficient in realism about our nature and our condition, and "neo-orthodox" Jews, who stress the importance of obedience to the Law revealed in the Hebrew Bible. It includes "New Critics" and old "Liberals," for different reasons of course. It includes conservatives of all stripes. It includes ideologues. It is a massive and heterogeneous company. Most of us in middle age today have been in it at one time or another.

For those young enough not to have participated in the "Modernism," literary or cultural, of the past half-century, the philosophy Emerson announced in *Nature* and assumed in all his best poetry may of course still be an insuperable barrier to sympathetic reading. But Emerson does not ask us to accept a particular philosophy, Idealism, though to be sure he found it useful himself and recommended it. What he tells us we must do, first of all, is to be true to our own feelings and to what we know. "Sursum Corda" — "Lift up your hearts," a phrase from the Prayerbook — ought, I should suppose, to speak to "all sorts and conditions of men," not least to the young in our time, who may not find "The Over-Soul" an easy concept to grasp but who value the authentic response and are, like Emerson himself, seekers after light:

Seek not the spirit, if it hide
Inexorable to thy zeal:
Trembler, do not whine and chide:
Art thou not also real?
Stoop not then to poor excuse;
Turn on the accuser roundly; say,
'Here am I, here will I abide
Forever to myself soothfast;
Go thou, sweet Heaven, or at thy pleasure stay!'
Already Heaven with thee its lot has cast,
For only it can absolutely deal.

CHAPTER IV

Ecstasy in Concord and Salem

Last night Henry Thoreau read me verses which pleased, if not by beauty of particular lines, yet by the honest truth, and by the length of flight and strength of wing; for most of our poets are only writers of lines or of epigrams. These of Henry's at least have rude strength, and we do not come to the bottom of the mine. Their fault is, that the gold does not yet flow pure, but is drossy and crude.

— Emerson, in his *Journal,* November 11, 1842

When Jones Very was in Concord, he said to me, "I always felt when I heard you speak or read your writings that you saw the truth better than others, yet I felt that your spirit was not quite right. It was as if a vein of colder air blew across me."

— Emerson, in his *Journal,* December 1841

. . . *The community in which we live will hardly bear to be told that every man should be open to ecstasy or a divine illumination, and his daily walk elevated by intercourse with the spiritual world.*

— Emerson, in "Man the Reformer"
1841 (the lecture)

HENRY DAVID THOREAU

WALKING on Cape Cod in 1849, Thoreau met and enjoyed talking to an old Wellfleet oysterman who interspersed all his remarks with quotations from the Bible, using them particularly to express, as Thoreau says, "a sense of his own nothingness." He would repeatedly exclaim, " 'I am a nothing. What I gather from my Bible is just this; that man is a poor good-for-nothing critter, and everything is just as God sees fit and disposes.' "

Pointedly, Thoreau did not respond to this pithy summation of the human condition; instead he simply asked the old man his name. With children, woodsmen, fishermen, Indians, and very old people — with people who could not possibly patronize him, as he felt Emerson did, with people who could not arouse his obsessive feeling of inferiority — Thoreau could be courteous and even gentle. The usual acerbity and the combativeness fell away and he showed another side of his nature from the one Emerson saw. He did not pursue the religious question with the old oysterman. If he had, he probably would have thought he had to express a sharp opposition to the central article in the old man's faith. On the level of opinion, at least, he certainly did *not* believe that he was "a nothing," though he might have been willing to agree that "everything is just as God sees fit and disposes." But Thoreau knew more than his opinions knew, as his Transcendental philosophy asserted, and as some of the best of his verse can show us.

A part of what he might have said to the old man in reply, if he had not judged any reply inappropriate, he had already said in one of his best poems, "Smoke," in which he concluded by addressing the clear light smoke of his wood fire thus:

> Go thou my incense upward from this hearth,
> And ask the gods to pardon this clear flame.

The flame of his fire was "clear" because his hearth contained no fatty "burnt offerings," to thicken the flame and darken the smoke, but only good seasoned wood. The "pardon" is ironical, almost sarcastic, in tone. The poem is Promethean, not Christian, in its general attitude. Neither repentance nor humility forms any part of its meaning. Clearly, the speaker in it does not think of himself as "a nothing."

Our first response to the poem may be to the "brag" in it. Henry is "crowing" too loud, as usual, we may say, without even the excuse that serves him in *Walden,* that he is doing it to wake his neighbors up. Yet, if there is a sense in which the poem approaches *hubris,* it is saved from being either a doctrinaire expression of Transcendental self-reliance or a neurotic assertion of self-sufficiency not only by the fact that the point of the last two lines — a feeling of self-sufficiency that asks no pardon — is expressed ironically rather than directly, but also by the imagery that precedes the last two lines. The poem is short enough to quote entire, and good enough to deserve it:

Light-wingèd Smoke, Icarian bird,
Melting thy pinions in thy upward flight,
Lark without song, and messenger of dawn,
Circling above the hamlets as thy nest;
Or else, departing dream, and shadowy form
Of midnight vision, gathering up thy skirts;
By night star-veiling, and by day
Darkening the light and blotting out the sun;
Go thou my incense upward from this hearth,
And ask the gods to pardon this clear flame.

The images here express a more complex meaning than any answer he might have made to the old oysterman about the need for self-reliance. They take us to the heart of that complicated set of tensions in Thoreau that gives his work its uniquely Thoreauvean flavor and much of its value. The smoke is Icarus, flying toward the sun, aspiring, not apologizing or cringing; but it is also Icarus falling, his pinions melted by the heat. It is a *promise* — of song and of dawn, a new and better day ("There is more day to dawn. The sun is but a morning star," Thoreau concluded in *Walden*); but it is also a dream departing, the dream of one who knows that Icarus fell. Though it soars *upward,* into the source of all light, yet it also sometimes *darkens* the light and even blots out the sun.

When therefore Thoreau asks the smoke of his fire to seek the pardon of the gods for his failure to offer sacrifice, he is not simply being sarcastic. The imperative amounts to a prayer that his clear flame may be found acceptable. If the poem is "pagan," it is also, no less so, "religious"; if it is Transcendental in its major note of confident self-assertion, it is also Existential in its minor note, which implicitly recognizes the ambiguities of dream and dreamer.

Unfortunately, most of Thoreau's poems are not on this level. Most of them are bare statements of opinion, rhymed doctrines, or poetry as artless prophecy omitting all those tensions that give his best work its unique tang — tensions between religious rebellion and defiance, and religious seeking; between self-assertion, and a nagging sense of worthlessness and fear of humiliation; between assertions of innocence and a feeling of guilt; between soaring aspirations and a recurrent sense of failure. More typical of the verse in its single-valued use of words, its doctrinal clarity, and its usual paucity of imagination would have been another reply he penned to the old oysterman's Puritan theology —

In Adam's fall
We sinned all.
In the new Adam's rise
We shall all reach the skies.

No sense here that Icarus' wings may melt, that the dream may *hide* the sun as it rises toward it. Here he answers the *New England Primer's* doctrine with a contrary doctrine — in verse of the same quality. Emerson was not wrong when he said that Thoreau's verses were "often rude and defective. . . . The thyme and marjoram are not yet honey."

If the occasion when Emerson made this judgment had not been a funeral sermon and thus necessarily a sort of eulogy, he might have said not "often" but "usually." Except in a small handful of poems, Thoreau was never at ease, never in full control of his medium, within the formal requirements of verse as he understood them. As with Melville, there is vastly more and better poetry, and even better rhythms, in his prose. The man whose best prose was constantly witty, metaphoric, and complexly evocative, wrote verse that for the most part is bare, abstract, univocal, literal, and almost completely unimaginative. "Time is but the stream I go a-fishing in," in *Walden,* begins a paragraph which rings changes on several related metaphors in a manner at once witty and profound, developing the theme Thoreau has been discussing and at the same time expressing his whole outlook with utmost economy. There is nothing quite so fine in even the best of the poems.

Instead, on a level above that of his revision of the *New England Primer* but still considerably below the best of *Walden,* he usually wrote like this:

I make ye an offer,
Ye gods, hear the scoffer,
The scheme will not hurt you,
If ye will find goodness, I will find virtue.

Though I am your creature,
And child of your nature,
I have pride still unbended. . . .

These lines too he might have used as a reply to the old oysterman — and the oysterman would have understood the reply sufficiently well. He knew what "scoffers" were, and he had his own views of those who relied on their own unaided virtue. Pride, he would have called it, as Thoreau did, but with a different evaluation. And there the matter would have stood, doctrine against doctrine in perfect opposition.

But even in this inferior poem Thoreau does not *quite* settle for so clear a choice. He moves toward his conclusion with a paradox:

And I swear by the rood,
I'll be slave to no God.

That is, he expresses his rebellion by swearing by the cross — a very religious gesture indeed for one who expressed so much contempt for all churches except that of his own mind. But Emerson said all that needs to be said about this matter:

> His habitual thought makes all his poetry a hymn to the cause of causes. . . . While he used in his writings a certain petulance of remark in reference to churches or churchmen, he was a person of a rare, tender and absolute religion.

Though much of his verse is hymn-like in a sense Emerson did *not* intend here — that is, it is only useful for a worshipper in the same church — now and then Thoreau wrote a poem almost worthy of himself as an artist. His early "Sic Vita," with its memories of George Herbert, is memorable, though a little awkward. It gives the lie to those who claim that Thoreau *always* bragged like chanticleer: In it he admits conflict and difficulty — "I am a parcel of vain strivings tied/ By a chance bond together." The confession seems not so surprising as it may before reflection when we remember that even in his role as chanticleer, he said he crowed not just for himself but for his neighbors too, to wake them up to a new faith and a new hope against the threat of meaninglessness and hopelessness, of which he judged them to be not aware. A sense of mission may stimulate a sense of one's inadequacy to the mission.

But "Inspiration," which translates traditional Protestant piety into the new Transcendental terms, is both a more typical and a better poem. As Emerson counseled, Thoreau waits for inspiration as their forebears had waited for the voice of the Holy Spirit. "The wit of man" comes by the grace of God, Emerson was saying in the years when Thoreau was writing his poems; and "I conceive a man as always spoken to from behind, and unable to turn his head and see the speaker." [1] Thoreau agrees: he *stoops* and *listens* and *gropes* for his inspiration:

> But if with bended neck I grope,
> Listening behind me for my wit,
> With faith superior to hope,
> More anxious to keep back than forward it —

if he did *this,* his verse, instead of being "weak and shallow," would achieve the timelessness that can result only when "soul" and "heart" are united and self-reliance becomes what it must be, God-reliance: "Time cannot bend the line which God hath writ."

There is a good deal of Biblical imagery in the poem — indeed, more than enough to satisfy the old oysterman of Wellfleet — and it is used to good advantage. In it, orthodoxy is transmuted but not wholly lost. If Thoreau looks with the eyes of faith, he will see beyond "learning's lore" and find out, as Emerson had counseled, how to "trust the love untold" which has brought him to this evening. The poem seems very un-Thoreauvean only if we accept the stereotyped notion of him as harping always on just one note, a notion that a reading of more of his work than *Walden* would quickly destroy. Just as *Cape Cod* shows an awareness of tragedy absent in *Walden,* so "Inspiration" shows him closer to the Puritans than he probably realized. The idea being expressed here Edward Taylor would have called the doctrine of Grace. Thoreau insists that neither his insights nor his verse can be forced by acts of will. The love that wooes him was not "bought" either by his worth or by his want, but if he submits and listens it will enable him to live *moments* who otherwise would live only *years,* knowing nothing but the emptiness of time.

Un-Thoreauvean? One of the chief reasons why his verse is of interest to us, even when the poems are, as we are likely to say, "not very good," even though he is generally so much greater an artist in his prose, is that it often brings us up sharply against the fact of his complexity. The man who wrote "Inspiration" also wrote, in prose, something that might seem not to have come from the same pen: "May I love and revere myself above all the gods that men have ever invented." Of course, anyone who is normally "self-reliant" will not need to *hope* that he may come to love and revere himself. As Emerson, once again, quite correctly said, "His biography is in his verses." Emerson did not say, but might have said with equal correctness, his *artistry* is mostly in his prose. The "I" of *Walden* is Henry's ideal self-image, a mythical personage, a creation of Thoreau's maturest art. The "I" of the poems is always Henry himself, who went to a good deal of trouble to try to be the perfect Transcendentalist but could achieve his ideal self-image only in a fiction.

Still, artless as they generally are, a few of the best poems may make us wish Thoreau had gone on longer with verse, instead of giving it up in the early 1840's for prose — not that we should want to lose the prose, of course. In his verse he really did bend his neck "and listen and grope," and once in a while the result comes through. "Winter Memories," one of his best poems and a very good poem indeed, will serve to illustrate. At least one of its lines strongly suggests Frost — "The upland pastures where the Johnswort grew." Elsewhere, in imagery and theme though not in phrasing, it suggests Emily Dickinson, as Thoreau's verse quite often does, usually without her brilliance. It takes an honorable place in the main line of New England poetry from Bryant to Frost.

To get at one of the chief ways in which it is interesting to us, I should like to quote the late Perry Miller, writing in *Consciousness in Concord* of the lost Journal. Thoreau, Miller tells us, could not afford to admit the threat of winter —

> Openly to admit that life in New England was in danger of extinction every January would be to concede that circumstances shape man's purpose — a concession which, as Thoreau explained to Isaiah Williams, no self-appreciating consciousness would allow.

But whatever he may have said to Isaiah Williams, the whole

effect of "Winter Memories" is to make just this admission — and "openly," too. What he remembers in the deprivation of winter — "High in my chamber in the frosty nights" — is the sights and sounds of summer that have been to him sudden epiphanies of a meaning not obvious or apparent to most men. The simplest experiences have been the vehicles of transcendence, as when he has "seen," as Hopkins would, later, "the furrows shine but late upturned." *Now* such moments of inspired seeing are only memories, but the memories will prove sufficient to last him through the winter, as they have been in past winters,

> When all the fields around lay bound and hoar
> Beneath a thick integument of snow.

Robert Frost, one might say without being merely whimsical, rewrote this poem many times, generally toning down or omitting entirely the implied Transcendental hope it contains. For Thoreau, the threat of meaninglessness was real, but he refused to admit, as Frost later felt he had to, that the world was permanently diminished. Winter for Thoreau was a *season* of the soul, a test of one's staying power which left hope still possible. The meaning of the poem is very close to that which he later expressed in *Cape Cod,* which begins with a shipwreck and a close inspection of the bodies, and later dwells on the stench of death on the shore where dead whales litter the beach. But though death is everywhere present, life is the last word. The work vibrates with vitality. Thoreau could agree neither with the old oysterman that man was "a nothing," nor with modern atheistic naturalists. Spurning churches and creeds, he outdid the orthodox in proclaiming that life will prevail over circumstances and time.

If he had been totally unaware of the threat of winter, he would not have needed to stress *endurance* as he did in "Inspiration," or to end the poem by affirming that the strength necessary for endurance would be supplied. In the cold season, if experiences of transcendence refused to come, *memories* could make possible the paradox expressed in the closing lines —

> So by God's cheap economy made rich
> To go upon my winter's task again.

The Thoreau we have generally known best, the Thoreau of the sharp combative opinions who, as Emerson said, seemed always to want a "fallacy to expose," always to need a sense of victory, ought, we suppose, to have *argued* with the Wellfleet oysterman, exposing the fallacies of the old man's simple orthodoxy. Instead, he just asked him his name. If we have read the best of Thoreau's verse attentively, we shall not be surprised that the two took to each other. Beneath the level of opinion, they understood each other very well. If the prose works have led us to value Thoreau, we shall want to read his early poetry too. We shall not be wholly disappointed by it.

JONES VERY

Thoreau's definition of himself as "a mystic, a transcendentalist, and a natural philosopher" would seem at first thought to fit Jones Very as well — at least if we take "natural philosopher" to mean lover and student of nature, as Thoreau meant it. For Very was certainly a mystic, he was accepted for a while by the Transcendentalists as one of them, and he was as much of a nature lover and student as Thoreau. Yet the description will finally not do. Emerson may have thought at first that he had found a disciple, but he had not, and as he moved away from his early Transcendentalism and Very deepened in his religious orthodoxy, the older man's enthusiasm for the brilliant young Harvard tutor waned. There had been misunderstanding on both sides from the very beginning. Though Very had attended meetings of the Transcendental Club in Emerson's home, he was with them but never really of them. Emerson at first thought him inspired and edited his poems for publication, but when Very tried to convert Emerson to his own Antinomian version of Christianity, Emerson was bored and annoyed. This was not what he had meant when he called for young men to feel and to live the doctrine announced in the Divinity School Address, that "God IS, not WAS."

Yet the misunderstanding was natural. Very took Emerson quite literally, submitting himself, he believed, completely to God's immediate presence and guidance; which is to say, perhaps, that he was "mad," as society judges madness. The voice of the Spirit was all: He struggled to achieve the will-lessness that would accompany that absolute trust that the older philosopher recommended. He went his own way, enduring misunderstanding and suspicion as he denounced the materialism and faithlessness of the times and proclaimed that he spoke what the Spirit within dictated.

He dared to be *absolutely* self-reliant because he really *believed* what Emerson had said, that self-reliance and God-reliance amount to the same thing.

But Very's relationship with Emerson can take us only part of the way into the work of a poet capable of writing

> 'Tis done the world has vanished Christ remains
> The only sure the only lasting trust.

(One of the things Emerson felt he had to do with Very's poetry when he edited it was to punctuate it.) The more Emerson found out what Very really believed, the less he liked what he found. Emerson had given up Christianity for what he called the "new thought" of a "Revolutionary age," saving only those elements in the inherited faith that seemed to him viable, saving them by translating them into new terms and concepts. Very, on the other hand, had incorporated some of the new thought into his belief — just as much of it as seemed to him to support his quite "orthodox" faith. In an essay that traduces Emerson and ends by overrating Very as a poet, Yvor Winters long ago wrote most of what needs to be said on this matter: Very's most important affinities are not with Emerson but with the Puritans and the early Quakers.

Still, Very was not simply an anachronism, as Winters' statement might seem to imply. Apart from his religious conservatism, he was distinctly a man of his own time, as a comparison with Hawthorne and Thoreau will suggest. His late sonnet on visiting the graves of the two men can give us the clue here. The poem is not a tribute so much as an expression of affinity. Though the relationship is not obvious, as is the more superficial one with Emerson, and may surprise us a little at first, it is not really hard to understand why Very felt the *presence* of the two men as he stood beside their graves and hoped to meet them again in Heaven.

Hawthorne had been the first important writer to recognize Very publicly, listing him in "A Virtuoso's Collection" along with Halleck, Bryant, Longfellow, and Lowell as the only American poets worthy of mention in 1842. Recognizing Very's obscurity, he implied that it could be accounted for by a deficiency in public taste: "a poet whose voice is scarcely heard among us by reason of its depth." Both were sons of Salem shipmasters; both men were orphaned at an early age. More pertinently, both were a little provincial, as Salem was provincial compared with Boston — or even with Concord, as Emerson was shaping it.

Both were conservative enough, and provincial enough, to think of themselves as Christians, in a time when it was unfashionable in intellectual circles to continue in the mode of what Emerson referred to unfavorably as "Hebraic" language and thought. Hawthorne was more skeptical, but perhaps Very only suppressed his doubts more firmly. Both were, as Very put it, "acquainted with grief" and let the acquaintance enter into the structure of their thinking, as a datum not to be ignored, the way Emerson seemed to try to ignore it. The poet often expressed himself in language we can only call "Hawthornesque" — for Hawthorne, the greater artist, had already made it his own. Thus in "The Grave-Yard" Very writes of the heart as "a secret cavern filled with death and sin." Both men believed, as Very said in "The Dead Elm," that evil is a real and subtle thing: We turn away from the grosser sins and think we are safe, but just as the soil sometimes contains poisons which kill the tree, so the soul finds evil "mixed with the very food on which it lives." If Very later read Hawthorne's "Rappaccini's Daughter," he must have responded to it more sympathetically than Emerson would have.

His affinity with Thoreau is less easily documented by quotation but is no less revealing. Their styles differ greatly, but the *men* were much alike. Both were "mother's boys" who could not bear the thought of leaving home. Both contrived, by some rather extreme renunciations, *not* to leave, to remain all their lives within the family circle. Both were provincial and felt inferior in company; neither would have been at home, as Emerson so very much was, in the Saturday Club. Both really *were* mystics — or at least so they convince us — whereas Emerson seems most of the time only to be recommending mysticism. Both sought a more intense and penetrating consciousness, a condition of being fully "awake," as Thoreau said in *Walden* and Very said in "Morning" and other poems.

Both men dared to be "different." Very at times seemed a little mad — seemed to have a strange light in his eyes — though whether his was a "higher" or a "lower" madness was not clear then and is not now; while Thoreau was very sane indeed, though his neighbors called *him* "queer" too. Both were irresponsible from any point of view that emphasizes community values. Hawthorne once noted that he found Very to be "vain," and Thoreau was certainly egocentric in principle if not always in practice; both were at any rate as overwhelmingly concerned with *personal* salvation as Edward Taylor had been.

Both loved nature and practiced a life-long communion with it, and both found God there. If Thoreau was careful to speak of this discovery in terms that could not possibly imply orthodoxy, while Very preferred to use language that always seems too orthodox and trinitarian for even a "Channing Unitarian," as he called himself, still their orientation was finally much the same: Both lived always in time with their gaze fixed on eternity. What Thoreau once said of himself and his writing might as well have been said by Very: "The other world is all my art . . ." — which is not *quite* true of Thoreau, but very nearly so, and almost entirely true of Very. Emerson, quoting this statement, comments in words that apply even more clearly to Very: "This was the muse and genius that ruled his opinions, conversation, studies, work and course of life."

Lowell noted in his copy of Very's *Essays and Poems,* the 1839 volume Emerson had edited, that "Some of the sonnets . . . are better poetry than has yet been published in America" — a statement that was perhaps just in 1840, when Lowell apparently wrote it. Just, that is, unless we take account of Poe, as Lowell apparently did not; and possibly even if we *do* remember Poe. For though Very is often simply dull, as Poe never is, and usually awkward, at his best he has a depth and complexity of meaning that Poe seldom or never achieved. "Some" of these sonnets, Lowell said; by reason of "depth," Hawthorne said. Neither comment was very wide of the mark.

But of course by 1840 very little of the best American poetry had yet been published. Very remains today an interesting minor poet. If he had been a better one, more imaginative and linguistically resourceful, he would remind us of Hopkins. As it is, generally only the themes of the two are similar — God shining out through nature, present everywhere even in the humblest circumstances and least "sacred" objects; man dependent on Him always, even as he moves and breathes. If he had been more witty and "metaphysical" in the literary sense, he would more often remind us of Edward Taylor. The *ideas* of the two are often indistinguishable, except when Very is writing directly about the objects of nature, when it becomes clear that *his* view of it is truly sacramental, while for Taylor nature is generally just illustrative.

Very seems to have had trouble meeting people, but his contacts with nature were true "meetings" in the sense which Martin Buber has given to the term. It was, unfortunately, generally quite true, as he wrote, that "Nature! my love for thee is deeper far/ Than strength of words, though spirit-born, can tell," yet now and then he found the words to suggest to us what nature meant to him. "The Columbine" was a favorite of his contemporaries and deserves to be better known today. In it his feeling for the flower is that of one created being for another. The sympathy does not seem affected or arch: He knows very well what dryness means and can say without coyness, "And here will drink with thirsty pores the rain." He does not suppose that the flower is "wiser far than human seer," as Emerson thought "the humble bee." He does not appropriate the flower as an illustration of a doctrine, or use it for any ends of his own. He simply accepts it as real, valuable, and alive, as *he* is. We are close here to St. Francis, and close to Thoreau, too; and, oddly enough, as it may seem, to a good many *haiku* poems and to one of the dominant characteristics of our own newest poetry, the poetry of the 1960's. Very's poetry anticipates thematically — though not of course formally — contemporary "objectivist" poetry: He moves toward the transcendent through the senses — without benefit of LSD.

Very's poetry is repetitious and very often bare of anything but the doctrines he wishes to express. Convinced that it was his role merely to listen to the Voice within and write down what he was "told" ("You hear not mine own words, but the teachings of the Holy Ghost," he once wrote), he was unwilling — or unable? — to try to perfect a style — to sacrifice, as it would seem to him, inspiration for the sake of mere effect. He was the living example of what Emerson, in "The Problem," had said must be true of any great artist: He wrote "in a sad sincerity:/ Himself from God he could not free." He thought he merely took dictation, now and then perhaps missing a word, but never letting "vain or shallow thought" affect what he was doing. The Holy Ghost, it would be possible to conclude, if we took Very on his own terms, often writes very awkwardly and dryly.

Yet when he found the words to make *us* hear what he heard and the images to enflesh the doctrines he believed, he wrote poems that have value beyond their use as devotional aids. Never a master of language and too often dependent on the time-worn verbal formulas of orthodox faith, so that much of his verse not labeled "hymns" *reads* like hymns, still, syntactical awkwardness and all, his very best poems remind us of the first-rate minds and best artists of his own time and foreshadow those of our time. They earn for him the right to take his place in the long line of American poets who, beginning with Edward Taylor, have defined the American style in poetry. Of his very best poems, this is *true,* we say; I had not realized how true. We feel ourselves in the presence of a first-rate mind and authentic experience.

For instance, "The Mind the Greatest Mystery." The mind in this poem is imaged first as a cavern, then as the sea. The inversions are awkward and the language perhaps too bare. Very does not conceive of himself as creating an effect, as Poe would, but of having something important to say and saying it as plainly as possible. He begins

> I threw a stone into a cavern deep,
> And listening heard it from the floor rebound;
> It could not from my thought its secret keep,
> Though hidden from the sight its depth I found,

and ends

> But when, from these, I turned to explore the mind,
> In vain or height or depth I sought to find.

Here at last, by a circuitous route, we come back to Emerson. The mind is immeasurable, and in the mysteries of both its depth and its height we find God. Very preached as Emerson once said Jesus did, *ab intra,* from within, as one *in-spired;* he preached both in Unitarian pulpits throughout New England and through the medium of poetry as the language best suited to the Spirit. Except in the specific content of his faith, he was everything Emerson said the poet should be. If in the end he reminds us more of Hawthorne and Thoreau and Edward Taylor and John Woolman, it is because he really *was* true to the Voice he heard within and not to the voices he heard, but would not follow, saying more fashionable things. Instead, like Taylor, he made of both his life and his work a long "preparatory meditation." Though he is often merely tediously devout, and though he speaks in a voice that seems always close to a stammer, Very is perhaps the American poet who most completely embodied the quality the Transcendentalists valued highest, absolute trust in the inward vision. As a result, his poems often bring to at least partially adequate expression insights not available to him in the literature and learning of his time. "The Dead," with its wasteland imagery, anticipated Eliot, as does "The Hand and Foot." "Soul-Sickness" anticipates Freud and contemporary psychiatry. "The Columbine" and other poems show his understanding of the possibility of an I-Thou relationship with nonhuman things, long before Buber.

To praise him in more "absolute" — that is, aesthetic — terms, by comparing his accomplishment with that of poets of his own time, I think we should remember his poems on the Fugitive Slave law and on the completion of the transcontinental telegraph as not only the best ever written by any poet on these subjects but as good reading today. His sonnet "On Visiting the Graves of Hawthorne and Thoreau" is surely better than Longfellow's on Hawthorne's funeral. "The New Man" and "The New World" *almost* express the inexpressible timeless dream of a new heaven and earth when time shall be at an end.

Not long after editing Very's poems, Emerson wrote, in "The Poet," that he found nothing "of any value in books excepting the transcendental and extraordinary." He went on to say, "If a man is inflamed and carried away by his thought, to that degree that he forgets the authors and the public and heeds only this one dream which holds him like an insanity, let me read his paper, and you may have all the arguments and histories and criticism." It seems likely that he was not thinking of Very when he wrote these words, but every specification in them would apply more perfectly to the work of the Salem mystic than to many of Emerson's own verses. What is generally missing in Very is only that "adequate expression" that Emerson took for granted as the gift of the poet.

CHAPTER V

Transcendental Despair

Mask thy wisdom with delight,
Toy with the bow, yet hit the white . . .
— Emerson, in "Fragments on the Poet and the Poetic Gift"

Good poetry seems so simple and natural a thing that when we meet it we wonder that all men are not always poets. Poetry is nothing but healthy speech. . . .
— Thoreau, in his *Journal,* November 30, 1841

Do I like Poe? At the start, for many years, not: but three or four years ago I got to reading him again, reading and liking, until at last — yes, now — I feel almost convinced that he is a star of considerable magnitude, if not a sun, in the literary firmament.
— Whitman in 1888, to Horace Traubel

EDGAR ALLAN POE

THE difficulty that arises when Poe is grouped with the Transcendentalists may be located most easily by letting William James summarize for us the gist of Emerson's thought, which supplies the central insight of American Transcendentalism. Speaking on the occasion of Concord's celebration of the centenary of its most famous writer's birth, James summed up Emerson's meaning this way:

> This is Emerson's revelation. . . . The point of any pen can be an epitome of reality; the commonest person's act, if genuinely actuated, can lay hold on eternity; . . . His life was one long conversation with the invisible divine, expressing itself through individuals and particulars.

Poe denied this "revelation" both in theory and in practice. Aspiring to the realm of what he called "Supernal" Beauty — not quite "supernatural" in the traditional religious sense, but certainly above or beyond or totally different from experienced nature — he found access to the Supernal possible only by destroying or negating the actual, by obliterating all "individuals and particulars." He found nothing in his waking experience that pointed toward the divine. If it is meaningful at all then to speak of "transcendence" in his work, it is only in the sense in which "to transcend" would be to destroy what is being transcended. But in the tradition of Western thought at least "destructive transcendence" is an oxymoron.

To "transcend," not only in Emerson's sense as James interpreted him but in the sense of the *via affirmativa* of mystical tradition, is not to negate or destroy but to affirm — to affirm as having dimensions of meaning and value not immediately perceived or commonly recognized. It is to affirm as more and not less significant and valuable than ordinary vision perceives it to be. To experience transcendence is always of course in some degree to move "through" or "beyond" the apparent objects or situation to God or the All or Spirit, through the "real" to the "Real"; but Emerson's early Transcendentalism does not intend to leave the "real" behind in this progress to the "Real." Whitman's way of looking at grass is Transcendental in this sense. As Whitman's work makes clear, the way of transcendence is dependent upon something like aesthetic vision, as opposed to utilitarian or analytical ways of "seeing": it looks long and hard, attending to the unique particularity of the object and only thus finding its meanings. To transcend is, ultimately, to see nature as symbol.

As symbol, not as sign. One glances at a sign only to find out where it is pointing. A sign is not important *in itself,* but only as a means to something totally other. A roadside sign pointing toward Boston is not in any sense, physically or otherwise, *like* Boston. The Puritan poets generally took nature as sign. If they had taken it as a symbol, they would presumably not have been so fond of the anagrammatic elegy, for the letters of a person's name are not intrinsically *like* the person to whom they are attached by accident or Providence. To find them significant is to assume that they are occult signs.

Insofar as Emerson was consistently Transcendental according either to his own explicit or James's implicit definition, he took nature as symbol. To be sure, even in his Transcendental poems he often transcended too quickly, did not look long enough at the object, as we may see in "Two Rivers," in which he does little more than make a bow toward the Musketaquit before ascending to the spiritual river. But this was a failure of art, perhaps also of temperament, not of intention. He did not *want* to disparage the Musketaquit but to find its transcendent significance and thus to affirm it fully, not just sensually. "I expand and live in the warm sun like melons," he wrote on another occasion, choosing an image suggestive of utter dependence to express his determination to avoid any implication of disparagement in his attitude toward nature as apprehended by the senses.

But of course part of the time, or perhaps with a part of himself at all times, he was simply not a Transcendentalist in this sense, not true to his own "revelation." Temperament, combined with Puritan habits of mind that he never really threw off despite his determination to do so, made him sometimes seem to be flatly denying the revelation he had begun by announcing. Thus when he defined God once as "dazzling, terrific, inaccessible," the definition was more Puritan than Transcendental, for if God is not immanent in nature but "inaccessible," then one cannot hold a "conversation with the invisible divine" by paying attention to its manifestations in "individuals and particulars."

As his experiences of ecstatic communion with nature, the inspired moments when he was ready to receive the epiphanies, grew rarer with the passing years, Emerson more frequently thought of nature not as symbol, or even as sign, but simply as illusion, *maya*. Appearance and Reality were perhaps totally discrete. The manifold unique particulars of experience only *seemed* to differ from one to another. The long discussion of Illusion in the essay "Experience," written after the death of his son Waldo, movingly displays the struggle going on within him at this time to keep his faith in the immanence of the divine and in the soul's ability to experience it. It came to seem to him, much of the time, that "All things . . ./ Deceive us/ seeming to be many things,/ And are but one . . ."

Here at last we come close to Poe by way of Emerson. If *this* is Transcendental poetry, then it makes sense to call Poe a Transcendentalist. For in these lines, and in many more like them, Emerson has just as surely negated experience in order to get at the "Real" as Poe ever did to reach the Supernal. For Emerson in this mood and for Poe always, actual waking experience simply has no intrinsic meaning. Life is a sort of dream, with only a dream's phantasmagoric substance. This is "denial of images" with a vengeance. So far as Poe's work may be classified metaphysically then, it belongs within the tradition of the *via negativa.*

But the usable truth of this last statement depends upon our understanding it in the most abstract sense, as a metaphysical generalization about possible attitudes toward nature and supernature. If it were taken to mean that Poe should therefore be thought of as a *mystic* in the tradition of the negation of images, it would be about as misleading as anything one could say about him. It is hard to think of any important American poet, unless perhaps it is Wallace Stevens, whom either a genuine mystic or one who credited the reports of the mystics without being one himself would be less likely to call a mystic. It was no accident or a merely personal prejudice that made Emerson call Poe "the jingle man," or that made Whitman late in life try hard to grant him some significance. Emerson and Whitman were well qualified to recognize the marks of Transcendental mysticism wherever they found them.

The mystic, whatever tradition he is in, affirmative or negative, "extrovertive" or "introvertive," as some students of the subject prefer to name the two traditions, claims to intuit or experience the Divine or the All, whether in and through nature or by emptying himself of everything natural. He thinks of mystical experience as attaining unusual vision, a sudden deepening and sharpening of perception, the dawning of a light. His metaphors all point in the same direction, toward the idea of union with or perception of something objectively "real," something he did not "invent," even though, as in Buddhist tradition and in Vedanta, all that is necessary for the perception of the primacy of Spirit may lie within him. Imagination does not *create* the object of mystical experience, in the mystic's view of the matter, though it may be a *means* to perception or union. The mystic, that is, does not think of himself as merely imagining, or dreaming, or projecting *out* of himself the Divine or the All.

Something "imagined," "dreamed," created by the poet's own mind, something *projected* is precisely what Supernal Beauty seems to be in Poe's poetry. Not for a moment can we take it seriously as a report on what truly is if only we could see it. Poe himself did not claim to be reporting on something existing independently of himself. That, finally, is why no mystic would ever recognize him as a mystic.

If Poe's work has no value as mystical report, neither has it any authentic religious value. The fact that "the things of this world" did not interest Poe does not make him "religious" as religion has been defined in the Judeo-Christian tradition. True, Christianity has sometimes been strongly "otherworldly" in its emphasis, particularly in the Middle Ages, and has always contained some otherworldly elements. But even at its most Gnostic and ascetic, Christianity has always thought that the other world has meaning for this world, even if this world is only a preparation for that one. Contemplation of the eternal, that is, has been thought to have moral and spiritual consequences of a sort that would help one to live better in time. That is because for the truly religious mind of whatever Western creed or doxy, whether Emerson's or St. Augustine's, Calvin's or Whitman's, God is not only ultimate Reality and ultimate Power but ultimate Goodness. Ultimate Goodness demands our goodness, which is not necessarily identical with "morality" in a sense which any particular society would approve. Paul's warning against worldliness in *Hebrews,* "For here have we no continuing city, but we seek one to come," has not been thought to be inconsistent with another Biblical pronouncement, "By their fruits shall you know them." "Vanity of vanities, saith the Preacher, vanity of vanities; all is vanity"; but also, "Let us hear the conclusion of the whole matter: Fear God, keep his commandments; for this is the whole duty of man."

Not to be interested in finding, or listening to, or obeying God, or in achieving righteousness, is, in Western tradition, not to be counted as religious. Neither Jews nor Christians have ever thought that Heaven could be dreamed into being or created by an assertion of the will. Even Neoplatonists, who did not think the experienced world really Real, thought it Real in proportion as it contained Spirit, and defined the ultimate Spiritual Reality in terms of both truth and goodness. But Poe was only interested in a Heaven that by his own definition as well as by the implications of his practice had nothing at all to do with either truth or goodness.

When Emerson in "The Transcendentalist" and again in "The Poet" said that the Transcendental poet ought to worship at the shrine of Beauty even more than at the shrines of Goodness and Truth, it might seem that he was calling for a poet like Poe. But the context makes it clear that he meant that man should worship Beauty because *true* Beauty, transcendentally perceived, *includes*

Goodness and Truth. He meant to say that Reality is, above all, Beautiful. He meant that the philosopher must take his cue from the artist and cultivate intransitive attention as a means of attaining revelation. He meant that he wanted a poetry that would be visionary, not moralistic. He meant what he had implied in "Each and All": "I yielded myself to the perfect whole."

It is not only that Poe was not interested in goodness or truth, or even, really, in beauty — that is, perceived, experienced beauty — but only in Supernal Beauty; he was not interested in "yielding" himself to anything, not even to Supernal Beauty. How could he be, when the Supernal Realm was his own, he made it, he projected it? His "angelic imagination," as Allen Tate once called it, was the source of all. It could *will* Reality. The philosophical theory he elaborated in *Eureka,* positing a dispersed and then, by the power of imagination, recondensed god, was made up late in life to provide a rationalization for attitudes and meanings that may be found in his work at all times, from *Al Aaraaf* on.

Poe had read his Coleridge, but not well. If we look beyond Concord to find out how to define Transcendentalism in such a way as to include Poe, we may call it simply "romantic idealism," that is, the philosophical expression of the European and American romantic movement. If we take this tack, another paradox very like the one we began with — Poe as a transcendentalist who does not transcend — emerges. For he carried certain aspects of romanticism to their logical extreme, and in doing so emptied romanticism of meaning. It is not surprising that the young neoromantic poets of our time do not look to Poe. They have no desire to replace the modernism they are rejecting with a poetry of infantile wish-fulfillment that makes romanticism look like escapism.

I am backing into Poe in this way because the problem of whether we can find any general meaning in his poetry, and if so how, seems to me to be acute. Two final paradoxes and we shall be through with preliminaries.

When we look at Poe's life, we find him thoroughly involved in the changing America of his time, but when we read the poetry we find it shedding very little light on the nature of that time. Yvor Winters' dismissal of Poe's poetry as bad verse springing from bad theory and reflecting all the bad taste of contemporary popular culture is too extreme an indictment, but as so often, Winters is merely grossly overstating a partial truth. The truth is that if we look at the poetry with the eye of the cultural historian, we find that it reflects more light than it sheds.

This becomes obvious when we compare Poe's work with that of his contemporaries, Emerson and Thoreau, or Hawthorne and Melville. Emerson chose Concord over Boston as his home because, as he tells us, it was quieter and closer to nature. Thoreau traveled widely, he once said, in Concord, but for a while he found even Concord too much for him and took to the woods. Hawthorne and Melville retreated, for a time, to the then remote Berkshires. All these men cultivated solitude and periodically disengaged themselves from society.

Yet we may turn to their work for an understanding of the *meaning* of their society. History does something to explain them to us, but they do more to explain history. Not so with Poe. Out of his hectic involvement with the life of his time in New York and other cities he created no poetry, and very little prose, that expresses either any deep concern with or any deep knowledge of the America of his day. His career suggests that the ivory tower, the haunted chamber, a whaling ship in the remote Pacific, the shores of Walden Pond, or a quiet piazza in the Berkshires may be better places than an editorial room for a romantic artist to ponder the meaning of life in his own or any age.

The final paradox has to do with Poe's reputation, past and present. Almost deified by the French and called "the greatest of American poets" by no less a poet than Yeats, Poe has remained for most Americans a high school favorite. The majority of the most respected American writers and critics have seen no reason to value his work highly. Emerson, usually so kind in his judgments, dismissed him contemptuously. Thoreau, Hawthorne, and Melville ignored him. Whitman, asked about him in extreme old age, decided on one occasion that he should be called one of the "electric lights" of literature, thus emphasizing both his novelty and his artificiality. One suspects Lowell of trying to see him in the best light possible — with Poe still living — when he said of him in "A Fable for Critics" that he was "three-fifths of him genius and two-fifths sheer fudge."

Poe was dead when Henry James recorded his opinion, so the novelist had no reason to temper his judgment with mercy. "An enthusiasm for Poe," he declared, "is the mark of a decidedly primitive stage of reflection." He wavered between "valueless" and "superficial" as the best adjectives to describe Poe's whole body of work. Eliot, trying to explain why the French liked Poe so well, decided that it was because the chief enthusiasts for him did not know English very well and so could read into him all their own meanings.

Two recent critical treatments of Poe's poetry betray a similar lack of real respect for it. Both, supposedly discussing it, actually change the subject and talk mostly about something else. Richard Wilbur in his Laurel Edition of the poetry, deciding that the poems are meaningful only when read in terms of the myth Poe elaborated in his prose, particularly in *Eureka,* gives more space to the prose than to the poetry. Roy Harvey Pearce in *The Continuity of American Poetry* devotes only three of his eleven pages on Poe to the poetry; for the rest, he implies an indirect defense of it by discussing the distrust of the imagination found in Scottish "common-sense" philosophy and in many sermons of the time.

We are of course glad that Poe did not distrust the imagination, but can nothing positive be said about his *poetry?* How imaginative is it? How meaningful? How good is it, really? In attempting to answer these questions, I shall proceed on the basis of three working assumptions without any further discussion of them. The first one is that we should simply accept the evaluation most American critics have reached of Poe as a minor poet whose work, even at its best, exists somewhere outside the main stream of the best American poetry — which means that we shall not further diminish his stature by looking for and not finding real greatness in his verse. Second, since minor poets write at best only a few poems that can still hold our attention after a hundred years, we ought to try to decide which poems these are, and why. Third, we should reject Poe's theory of poetry, both because it is a very crude poetics which, as Winters has correctly said, if followed consistently would be likely to produce only bad poetry, and because it is so clearly a rationalization of Poe's idiosyncracies, with very little relevance to the work of other poets of the time; rejecting it, we should insist that precisely Poe's kind of poetry makes it necessary to insist with Emerson that poetry is a kind of "saying" or "naming" which may be "song" but is not pure music.

If this is so, it is legitimate, indeed wholly proper, to ask what Poe's poems *say* to us that other poets have not said better.

Though Poe's kind of Transcendentalism seems empty by Concord standards, there may still be values and meanings in his work that the Concord men were unaware of or chose not to explore.

We may start by ruling out of consideration all those poems in which Poe appears to be not even trying to say anything but only to achieve an "effect" — to make us shiver or to bring tears. Poe's desired "effects" almost never come off, partly because his attempt to control the reader's response is so transparent, partly because the response he asks of us is so excessive. At their best, poems like "Ulalume" are too obvious; at their worst, vulgarly theatrical and emotionally dishonest.

But when Poe forgot about the theory he enunciated in "The Philosophy of Composition" and elsewhere, when he did *not* first decide the "effect" he wanted to get, then choose the "means," etc., he occasionally wrote well enough to deserve a mature reader's attention. His best poems say something still worth listening to on two subjects, poetry itself, and the life of fantasy and dream. Those poems that may be read as notes on what it feels like to be an artist, and those that bring us "notes from underground," are worth remembering.

"Sonnet — To Science," one of Poe's earliest poems, makes an interesting comment on the plight of the poet in a scientific age. Revealing Poe's conscious reason for turning away from outward experience to explore the inward realm of dream, it blames science for the disappearance of mystery and glory from the world. Science has destroyed myth, leaving the poet only "dull realities" for his subject. One of the reasons why the poem strikes us as a little superficial — quite apart from the neatness of Poe's science versus myth dichotomy — is that the poem does not mention, or even hint at, the less conscious but more compulsive reasons for the speaker's preference for "the summer dream" that science has taken from him. If the soul's winter is acknowledged as present reality, the longing for the lost summer dream would seem sentimental if the only reason for lamenting the loss is that reality is "dull." If there were deeper, more personal reasons than this, or if myth contained its own sort of truth which the truth of science had made unavailable to us, the lament would seem more inevitable. But only in later poems did Poe suggest such reasons.

Superficial or not, though, the poem is the first explicit statement in American poetry of a problem that is still with us, except insofar as the youngest poets have really gone beyond the "Modernism" of the first half of our century. What can poetry do, now that only science tells the truth? The fact that "Sonnet — To Science" was prescient in its statement of the problem is suggested by the extent to which it might be explicated in terms drawn from a book written a century later, I. A. Richards' *Science and Poetry*.

The too-simple positivism — science equals truth — on which the conflict in the poem rests may not satisfy us, and certainly suffers by comparison with Emerson's or Thoreau's thought on the subject, but in fairness to Poe we ought to remember that a very similar positivism not only is assumed in the first edition of Richards' book but provided the challenge which shaped the careers of many twentieth-century poets, Hart Crane and Wallace Stevens for example. Both of these poets began by assuming the validity of Poe's opposition between scientific truth and the dreaming imagination. Crane tried to create a new American myth to replace Poe's lost hamadryads, while Stevens tried to work out a philosophical resolution of the problem. Of the two, Crane was much closer to Poe, even to being driven, like Poe, to try to create a poetry so "pure" that it could not possibly conflict with science. But "reality" and "imagination" never ceased to define the limits of the poet's ultimate problem for Stevens, as they did for Poe in "Sonnet — To Science." (Fortunately, "realities" did not seem "dull" to Stevens.)

"Romance" shows us how well Poe could sometimes write when he combined talking about his art with talking about himself. The poem has something interesting to say and says it well. Explicitly, it contrasts the natural and joyous romanticism of childhood with the deeper, troubled romanticism of maturity. Implicitly, its development of this contrast reveals Poe's basic strategy as an artist, countering the threats posed by science and practicality, time and death, by diving into the depths of the self, into the waters of the unconscious. When this strategy is stated superficially, as Poe often stated it, it looks like mere escapism, a method of rejecting "dull realities" for make-believe, but here the images suggest that there is more to it than that.

Romance — from Poe's point of view, *all* good art — is imaged first as a "painted paroquet," then, in the second part of the poem, as a "condor." The pretty, exotic bird that teaches the child its alphabet and makes him feel at home in nature is replaced in mature years by the South American equivalent of both the American eagle and the vulture. The great bird of the Andes pictured on the coins of Chile and other South American countries is like Melville's Catskill eagle in *Moby Dick* in its ability to soar to "the very Heaven on high," but it has another characteristic the eagle lacks. Vultures feed upon carrion. As an image of the mature romantic imagination, the condor lives on death, eating the poet's own heart out. Mature romance, the poem says, is a desperate and fearful thing.

But even youthful romance is not mere exoticism. The "painted paroquet," though it only "parrots" a language destroyed in maturity by the condor's truths, is pictured as existing under water, "far down within some shadowy lake." Water is often a symbol of the unconscious or irrational in Poe's work, as it clearly is in the ending of "The Fall of the House of Usher." Here, working in contrast not with images of madness, as it does in the story, but with images of soaring and truth, it suggests not so much the irrational as the prerational. The complex image of the paroquet under the water of the lake condenses the ideas of innocence, security, and myth, lost when conscious reason has done its ambiguous work.

The condor is a nobler bird than the paroquet, but it is also *guilty*. It has dared to probe "forbidden things." Like Emerson's truth-speaking angel Uriel, the condor shakes the heavens with the truths it dares to imagine. The image suggests both ascent into knowledge and fall into sin.

If it seems that all these implications are no more than the standard ingredients of the romantic artist's conception of himself as a noble but guilty Prometheus, we should at least grant the freshness and condensation of Poe's version of the stereotype. The superiority of this poem to "Sonnet — To Science" results in large part from the way its images suggest a conflict more complex than that in the earlier poem. It repeats the theme of the destruction of the world of dream by truth, but now truth is not just scientific fact, it is imagination's *own* truth, gained when it becomes fully conscious of itself and the world. The final implication of the poem is that rationality and mature art are achieved at a frightful cost.

"To Helen" ("Helen, thy beauty") is also saved from banality by what Poe does in it with images that are more conventional than those in "Romance" but that cease to be conventional as Poe uses them. Superficially, "To Helen" has the appearance of an old-fashioned idealistic love poem combining traditional praise of the lady's beauty with the equally traditional theme that love can be redemptive. Thoughts of Helen's beauty transport the speaker at last into "regions which are Holy Land," an image that might suggest Beatrice's guiding Dante to a glimpse of the divine.

But a closer look at the poem suggests that thinking about Dante's praise of Beatrice as we read "To Helen" will mislead us. Poe's meaning is not traditional but novel. The poem's subject is not really Helen, or even Helen's beauty considered as an attribute of Helen, but Helen's beauty considered as an attribute of the speaker: "Helen, thy beauty is *to me* . . ." Though the speaker addresses Helen and praises her beauty in terms borrowed partly from the "religion of love," there is no suggestion anywhere in the poem that the speaker really *loves* Helen. What he "loves," one gathers, is the *feelings* produced in him by thoughts of her beauty. What opium or alcohol have done for some, contemplation of Helen's beauty does for Poe. "Helen" is the name the speaker gives to a datum in his awareness having the power to provoke in him certain sensations. "Helen" is wholly his own.

Exploring the nature of the feelings stimulated by Helen's beauty, the speaker uses images of security, inspiration, and faith. He first thinks of himself as a hero of myth dwelling against his will in an alien land. In this image he is a modern Ulysses nostalgic for his "native shore," a "weary, way-worn wanderer" on "desperate seas." Helen's beauty is the ship that will take him home. In the next stanza he becomes the artist and thinker whose intellectual home is Greece and Rome, which he is reminded of by Helen's "classic" face.

In the final stanza images of travel and of art become images of spiritual illumination, as the lamp in Helen's hand lights up a "Holy Land" for a spiritual quester who has found his true home at last in the Ideal, in the psyche itself. It is not quite clear whether the "Psyche" addressed in the last two lines is "Helen" or the speaker's own soul, but by this time it does not much matter. If Psyche is not literally his own imagination, at least her only interest for the speaker lies in her effect on him. In its egocentricity, the poem reminds us of some of Emerson's more clearly Transcendental comments on the spiritual uses of friendship. (Friends who make no demands upon us are excellent to have, for they stimulate our own best thoughts.)

"Israfel" is also suggestive of Emerson, this time of his

"Merlin." Like "To Helen," "Israfel" carries Emerson's guarded subjectivism to an extreme that makes us aware of all the possible objections to it, but the two poems about the ideal artist work with the same body of Transcendental ideas. Emerson, to be sure, does not say that "Our flowers are merely — flowers," and he clearly realizes that the poet must "mount" to Paradise, while the speaker in Poe's poem seems — unconvincingly — to believe he is already there.

But Emerson's ideal poet captures the same visionary, or supramundane, or "Supernal Beauty" that Israfel records, and he is just as divinely inspired as Poe's angelic singer. Both ideal poets are characterized by a certain wildness, by ecstasy, by a wisdom thought to be not inconsistent with passion. Emerson's figure of the poet as magician and Poe's of the poet as angel equally point toward the Platonic aspect of Transcendental theory, with the important difference of course that Poe's figure implies self-pity, while Emerson's figure implies only the poet's transcendence of ordinary logic and mundane rationality. (A man is not likely to think of himself as an angel unless he secretly thinks of himself as less than a man.)

In both poems, poetry is conceived in terms so widely overlapping with those of religion as to make it in effect a substitute for religion, though in Poe's poem, when the speaker enters openly in the last stanza to contrast himself with Israfel, we can only say that it *might* have been a substitute had the speaker existed under more fortunate circumstances. A comparison of the two poems, so similar in falling within what we recognize as the general categories of Transcendental thought about art, yet so different in the effect they have on us, has the two-fold advantage of showing why Poe ought to be called a Transcendentalist of some sort, and of exhibiting the degree to which his version of Transcendentalism always seems more like a desperate wish than an achieved and meaningful faith. The final effect of "Israfel" is that of pathos.

The pathos springs from an even deeper despair in "The City in the Sea" and "A Dream Within a Dream." Time in both poems brings only death, and death means annihilation, the reduction of being to nothingness. "The City in the Sea" pictures all men as equally damned, or doomed — it does not matter which, for in the end nothing matters. The city of man itself is destined to sink beneath the waters of oblivion, with all its inhabitants, "the good and the bad and the worst and the best." Life is a nightmare all the more terrible because the seas that engulf us are not stormy, or obviously threatening, but "hideously serene." We all sink without a sound, without even the possibility of a struggle.

Reading Poe as though he had moral or ethical meaning is almost always a mistake, and never more so than with "The City in the Sea." Unless we simply ignore the explicit and emphatic statement that "all," good and bad alike, are here, we cannot possibly interpret the sinking of the city as a punishment for sin. This city is no Sodom or Gomorrah but, explicitly, the city of *man*. Neither is there anything in the poem to suggest, as one interpretation would have it, that *artists* are exempted from the common fate. One suspects that such readings as these reflect an inability to believe or imagine that Poe could really be saying what he appears to be saying. But it would seem best to put aside any prejudice we have against expressions of total hopelessness and keep our eyes on the poem Poe actually wrote. That poem numbers all of us among the living dead. Every statement and every image in the poem seem to me to support such an interpretation. The concluding lines of the fourth verse-paragraph explicitly deny the possibility of any contact with a "Supernal" or transcendent Realm that would give life or value to the city of the dead:

> Along that wilderness of glass —
> No swellings tell that winds may be
> Upon some far-off happier sea —
> No heavings hint that winds have been
> On seas less hideously serene.

"A Dream Within a Dream" takes us even more quickly into the center of Poe's sensibility. It is a desperate poem, saved as a work of art from seeming hysterical in its despair only by the firmness of its structure. Though it is possible to read it as a condensed allegorical expression of the "philosophy" set forth in *Eureka,* as Richard Wilbur has done, to do so seems to me really to reduce its impact and relevance. Considered as an allegory, it is simply esoteric. Poe's journalistic attempt at metaphysics has no philosophical interest; to make the poem dependent on *Eureka* is in effect to belittle the poem by making it a document in Poe's biography.

In any case, reading the poem in terms of Poe's peculiar version of Neoplatonism does not so much change the *emotions* expressed as shift our attention from them to a set of dubiously relevant metaphysical ideas. If the speaker in the poem is really dreaming his private dream within God's dream, and if the dispersal of the grains of sand which he is unable to prevent will in some future age, in the second phase of universal process, be reversed, nevertheless, his response to his situation is horror. The recondensation of God by the power of imagination — if indeed this idea is in any way relevant to the poem; certainly it is not clearly *in* the poem — is no comfort to the speaker as he struggles to hold back the seconds that bring inevitable oblivion.

If we read the poem as complete in itself in its meaning, what we seem to have is a little drama in which the movement is from total despair to the possibility of some hope. There are two people in the poem, a speaker and a listener, and there is an implied argument. In the first stanza the speaker defends himself against the charge that he has not seen reality truly but has lost hope only because he has been living in a private dream. He answers, in effect, that living in a dream does not make him unique; rather, it unites him with all mankind. Like the narrator in the ending of Mark Twain's "The Mysterious Stranger," the speaker asserts that there is simply no way out of the dream: "*All* that we see or seem/ Is but a dream within a dream."

In the second stanza the speaker turns from defending his own dreaming by asserting the universality of dream, to contemplating his actual situation as *he* knows it. As the falling sand in an hourglass measures the passing moments, so the sand falling through the fingers of the man trying to grasp it measures the approach of oblivion. "O God! can I not save/ *One* from the pitiless wave?" is a cry of horror. Whether the sea is the mind of a dispersed God or only death, its wave is pitiless. Having now fully confronted his situation, the speaker changes his assertion of the first stanza into a question: "Is *all* that we see or seem/ But a dream within a dream?"

Poe's intention here is obscure, but it is possible to see an ambiguity, whether or not consciously intended. If we take "dream" in the poem always in its negative connotations, then the assertion of the first stanza that all is a dream is said in self-defense, but this defense crumbles when the speaker confronts the full implications of what he has said, leading to the final question. The matter is no longer closed. There may *be* some reason to believe that *something* is firm and real, and therefore some reason to hope.

If on the other hand we read "dream" with the panpsychism of *Eureka* in mind, the final lines of the second stanza seem to question the system itself. Confronted with the horror of the "pitiless wave" into which the grains of sand fall, the speaker wonders whether he has not at last found something "real," something which is not merely an idea, a dream. In this reading, there is no progression in the poem toward the possibility of hope, but only the breakup of an idealistic metaphysic when the speaker is faced with a fact he cannot easily fit into the system.

Though there is nothing in the poem that makes this second reading impossible, it is equally true to say that nothing in the poem requires it. Centrally, the poem seems to me to be about loss of hope, whether or not everything is a dream:

> You are not wrong, who deem
> That my days have been a dream;
> Yet if Hope has flown away
> In a night, or in a day,
> In a vision, or in none,
> Is it therefore the less *gone?*

Though it is one of the most enduring of Poe's poems in its expression of a universal emotion, the despair that comes when we contemplate time without hope, "A Dream Within a Dream" will not bear the weight of very much speculation. It is one of the ironies of Poe's life that he prided himself on being a "thinker," for his poetry is generally best when it most closely approaches the purely personal lyric. This is true both of the poems about the artist and of those that project the life of fantasy. Poe's mind had a certain keenness, but his thinking was obsessional to an unusual degree. He may have been able to solve cryptograms almost as well as he said, just as extreme paranoids may play bridge well, but he could not think objectively — that is, other than defensively — about any problem potentially more threatening than the problems offered by cryptograms.

That is certainly one of the reasons, if not the basic one, why he could not write a successful long poem, or a really complex one, or a philosophically interesting one — which is odd, if he was a "thinker," as he supposed he was. The more ambitious the effort, the more it failed. The poem of which he was proudest,

"The Raven," was meant to induce sadness, but its clumsy diction, inappropriate (often unintentionally funny) rhymes, and its mechanical form that overrides the content make it seem only grotesque. If it has any effect at all on a mature reader, the effect is very unlikely to be the one Poe intended.

Even in the handful of his best poems, both the ideas and the emotions are generally so simple that no great maturity, either intellectual or emotional, is required to appreciate them. In the poems in which he has the most to "say" to us, the poems on art, it is intensity, not complexity, of feeling that makes them memorable; of *feeling,* not thought. And of course what I have called his "notes from underground," his poems of fantasy, are all the better for being "senseless" in terms of rational paraphrase. The kind of meaning they have is the kind dreams have.

Poe's dreams were almost all bad dreams. The "bottomless vales," "caves," and "sad waters" of his poetry are nightmare images. Whether in literal dreaming or in waking fantasy, Poe could only imagine truly a world in ruins, characterized by "Mountains toppling evermore/ Into seas without a shore" and by "Lakes that endlessly outspread/ Their lone waters, lone and dead."

Death is at the center of Poe's dreaming poetry. His mountains are always toppling, his cities always sinking. No wonder he felt he could reach the ideal only by destroying the real. The instinctive movement of his psyche was not "upward" or "onward" *through* experience, the way of real transcendence, but downward and backward into the unconscious. His psychic development ended at a very early stage. Intending to affirm the reality of the transcendent Ideal, he made of Transcendentalism a doctrine of negation and despair. No wonder Emerson did not recognize their affinity.

PART THREE

The Transcendent Self

CHAPTER VI

Singing for Soul and Body

Two well-assorted travellers use
The highway, Eros and the Muse.
From the twins is nothing hidden,
To the pair is naught forbidden. . . .

— Emerson, in "Love and Thought"

We lie in the lap of immense intelligence, which makes us receivers of its truth and organs of its activity. . . . All things are made sacred by relation to it, — one as much as another. . . . in the universal miracle, petty and particular miracles disappear. . . . history is an impertinence and an injury, if it be anything more than a cheerful apologue or parable of my being and becoming.

Man is timid and apologetic; he is no longer upright; he dares not say "I think," "I am," but quotes some saint or sage. He is ashamed before the blade of grass or the blowing rose.

— Emerson, in "Self-Reliance"

I find it [Leaves of Grass] *the most extraordinary piece of wit and wisdom that America has yet contributed. . . . I give you joy of your free and brave thought. . . . I find incomparable things said incomparably well . . . I greet you at the beginning of a great career . . .* [*Your book*] *has the best merits, namely, of fortifying and encouraging.*

— Emerson to Whitman, July 21, 1855

"I seem to have various feelings about Emerson but I am always loyal at last. Emerson gratified me as a young man by what he did — he sometimes tantalized me as an old man by what he failed to do. You see, I both blaspheme and worship." I reminded him: "You once addressed Emerson as Master." He nodded his assent. "So I did — and master he was, for me, then. But I got my roots stronger in the earth — master would not do any more: no, not then: would no longer do." "And when you say your last word about Emerson — just before you shut up shop for good — what will it be?" He laughed mildly. "It will be loyal," he said " — after all the impatiences, loyal, loyal."

— Whitman and Horace Traubel,
July 31, 1888, in Traubel,
With Walt Whitman in Camden.

WALT WHITMAN

EMERSON would have had to read no farther than the first page or so of the strange anonymous book he received in the mail, sent him, he could only suppose, by the unknown author himself, to realize that the writer was expressing some of his own central thoughts, sometimes in the same images. Here was a man neither timid nor apologetic, who dared to say "I am," even "I celebrate myself." Here was a man unashamed before a blade of grass. The first lines he read in the 1855 edition, the opening lines of a poem finally called "Song of Myself," were these:

> I celebrate myself,
> And what I assume you shall assume,
> For every atom belonging to me as good belongs to you.
>
> I loafe and invite my soul,
> I lean and loafe at my ease. . . . observing a spear of
> summer grass.

Whether Emerson remembered, when he read these lines, the passage he had written in "Self-Reliance" about learning to live above time, like the blade of grass or the blowing rose, we cannot know. But if he did not yet recognize variants of his own images in the "lean and loafe" (he had said "we lie in the lap") or in the "observing a spear of summer grass" (he had offered a "blade of grass," as model for man), he would not have had to read much farther to sense how close the kinship between himself and this unknown poet was.

Not only in image and symbol but explicitly the poet was dissolving all miracles in the universal miracle, living wholly in the present where eternity is to be found, celebrating the "sanity and authority" of his soul. By the time Emerson had read to the forty-third line — "I and this mystery [the grass] here we stand" — he surely must have known that he was in the presence of a wholly like-minded poet.

In the passage from "Self-Reliance" which I have partially quoted as an epigraph, Emerson had fully stated the assumption that would make it not absurd for this unknown poet to "celebrate" himself. What Emerson puts abstractly, Whitman makes concrete, using himself as the example of one who has had contact with the "divine wisdom." Emerson's words are these:

> The relations of the soul to the divine spirit are so pure that it is profane to seek to interpose helps. It must be that when God speaketh he should communicate, not one thing, but all things; should fill the world with his voice; should scatter forth light, nature, time, souls, from the centre of the present thought; and new date and new create the whole. Whenever a mind is simple and receives a divine wisdom, old things pass away, — means, teachers, texts, temples fall; it lives now, and absorbs past and future into the present hour. All things are made sacred by relation to it, — one as much as another.

In what would later be numbered as section five of this opening poem in the first *Leaves of Grass* ("I mind how we lay in June," the "mystical experience" section), Whitman relates an instance of one "relation of the soul to the divine spirit." He then interprets the experience as bringing "the peace and joy and knowledge that pass all the art and argument of the earth."

In short, the unnamed poem Emerson read, that would later be called "Walt Whitman" and later still "Song of Myself," begins as a translation into concrete and personal terms of what Emerson had said about how to attain to "self-trust" in several paragraphs of "Self-Reliance." But Emerson, reading the poem, might have recognized not only his own generalizations in concrete rendering. He might have found superior analogues of some of his own images.

For Emerson was not always abstract. The paragraph that opens with "Man is timid and apologetic" continues this way:

> He is ashamed before the blade of grass or the blowing rose. These roses under my window make no reference to former roses or to better ones; they are for what they are; they exist with God to-day. There is no time to them. There is simply the rose; it is perfect in every moment of its existence. Before a leaf-bud has burst, its whole life acts; in the full-blown flower there is no more; in the leafless root there is no less. Its nature is satisfied and it satisfies nature in all moments alike. But man postpones or remembers; he does not live in the present, but with reverted eye laments the past, or, heedless of the riches that surround him, stands on tiptoe to fore-

> see the future. He cannot be happy and strong until he too lives with nature in the present, above time.

In his next paragraph Emerson draws the contrast between those who live in perfect trust in the eternal now like the grass and the rose and those whose knowledge of God is indirect, speculative, and based on the experience of someone else:

> This should be plain enough. Yet see what strong intellects dare not yet hear God himself unless he speak the phraseology of I know not what David, or Jeremiah, or Paul. We shall not always set so great a price on a few texts, on a few lives. We are like children who repeat by rote the sentences of grandames and tutors, and, as they grow older, of the men of talents and character they chance to see, — painfully recollecting the exact words they spoke; afterwards, when they come into the point of view which those had who uttered these sayings, they understand them and are willing to let the words go; for, at any time, they can use words as good when occasion comes. If we live truly, we shall see truly. It is as easy for the strong man to be strong, as it is for the weak to be weak. When we have new perception, we shall gladly disburden the memory of its hoarded treasures as old rubbish. When a man lives with God, his voice shall be as sweet as the murmur of the brook and the rustle of the corn.

Emerson must surely have seen, as he read Whitman's poem, a remarkable parallel between what he had written and what he was reading. For he found himself in the presence of a poet neither postponing nor remembering, claiming to have heard God without citing "the phraseology of . . . Paul," joyfully aware that everything about him was "sacred." He found the poet turning away from those who cite texts and going instead "to the bank by the wood" where he could "become undisguised and naked," like the grass itself or the rose. There, living "with nature in the present, above time," as he had recommended, the man whose verses he was reading claimed to know what the talkers in the rooms could not know:

I have heard what the talkers were talking. . . . the
    talk of the beginning and the end,
But I do not talk of the beginning or the end.

There was never any more inception than there is now,
Nor any more youth or age than there is now;
And will never be any more perfection than there is now,
Nor any more heaven or hell than there is now.

Emerson could not have found it surprising that a poet who claimed to know such things as these could turn from past humiliations and present worries as he turned from the "linguists and contenders." He must have found it "fortifying and encouraging" to read a poet who could celebrate himself despite "the sickness of one of my folks — or of myself. . . . or ill-doing. . . . or loss or lack of money. . . . or depressions or exaltations."

The man who had written that in mystical experience, all things are seen as "sacred . . . one as much as another," would not be expected to have difficulty understanding the "drift" of even such "shocking" lines as these:

Divine am I inside and out, and I make holy whatever
    I touch or am touch'd from;
The scent of these arm-pits is aroma finer than prayer,
This head is more than churches or bibles or creeds.

With Emerson too much out of favor during the past half-century or so to be read thoroughly and perceptively by those who write our literary history, and with Whitman scholars thrown off the track, or rendered cautious, by Whitman's own deliberate efforts to obscure the extent of his knowledge of and debt to Emerson, it is perhaps not really surprising that the most important literary relationship in our poetic history has only just now begun to be studied and analyzed in detail. Whitman's emphatic denial, in writing, that he knew Emerson's work before he published the first edition of *Leaves of Grass* has too often been taken at face value.

Whitman was going to hear Emerson lecture and reading the essays for some ten years or so before his own book appeared. He reviewed Emerson and quoted from him in articles he wrote for the newspapers he was working for. He carried the essays in his dinner-pail to read at noon while he was working as a carpenter building houses in Brooklyn. At the end of his life he was still reading and talking about him compulsively with Traubel. After his final visit with Emerson in Concord a few months before Emerson's death, he mystified Traubel by saying that he now knew that Emerson still loved him, that Emerson had given him a sign, but not in words. Now that at last he had achieved independence of the father, he could afford to forgive him everything and love him as he deserved.

The story of the personal relationship of the two men, recently told by Alvin Rosenfeld,[1] confirms the greatness, the magnanimity and openness and intelligence, of them both. It also makes it perfectly clear that Whitman's addressing Emerson as "Master" in his open letter replying to Emerson's wonderful letter of praise was no gesture of merely deferential politeness. It had been literally true, as he was once, much later, to admit, that he had been "simmering" and Emerson had brought him "to a boil."

He would not have needed to know Emerson's essays as well as he did by the time he started to write the poems of his first edition in order to have been brought to a boil. He could have known no more than the essay on "The Poet," for everything he needed was there. This is true not simply because the essay states nearly all the ideas Whitman was later to express in his poetry, or even because the essay recommends that the ideal poet should write in the *manner* of the author of *Leaves of Grass*. It is true because Emerson's idea of what a poet is and does was precisely the idea Whitman needed if he was to move beyond journalism and mediocre versifying.

He needed an idea that would allow him to begin as a poet where he *was,* with all his liabilities and his strength, and yet make it possible for him to move on toward the realization of his ideal self-image. A whole book has been written about "Walt Whitman's pose," showing that he was not the man he said he was. True; but he *became* the man he said he was. Roger Asselineau's title, *The Evolution of a Personality,* in which "evolution" should receive the chief stress, contains the clue we need both to get beyond discussion of Whitman's pose, or poses, and to begin to see how the man, the ideas, and the work are related.

In "The Poet" Emerson had said that the poet tells us "how it was with him," writing "his autobiography in colossal cipher." One of the reasons we are all better for his confession is that we *all* "study to utter our painful secret." Imaginative utterance of the "secret" is not simply purgative, Emerson stressed, it is creative, for the power of imagination is such that it creates a reality that would not otherwise exist. "The man is only half himself, the other half is his expression"; or, as Whitman would say, "Speech is the twin of my vision." The poet is the representative man; he speaks for *us*. The world is always waiting for its poet to say what has not been said and cannot even be known until the poet says it.

If Emerson was right, the journalist with the "painful secret" — his strong homosexual tendency — could turn his liability into an asset. If isolation was the common lot of man, intensified in the poet as representative man, his own isolation could be seen in a new light. The poet, Emerson had said, "is isolated among his contemporaries, by truth and by his art"; but if he confesses truly what is in him, his confession will serve for us all.

Poetic confession would allow him to translate his uniqueness into universality and at the same time to move toward his ideal of himself, to become that "other half" which was his expression. As Asselineau has shown, Whitman spent his life creating a self to fit the ideal self-image he announced in verse in 1855. Walter Whitman first imagined a "fictional" character, "Walt Whitman," then devoted himself to becoming that character.

The poetic confession gave the ideal a basis in truth. If the ideal had been announced without confession, if the poet had not been telling us how it *really* was with him, the ideal would have been the mere "pose" it has been called. But Emerson had stressed that the value to us of the poet's confession lies precisely in "the veracity of its report"; only thus, he said, could autobiography become universal symbol and the poet become at once our spokesman and our prophet. Emerson's formula for the poet called for absolute fidelity to fact as the means to a realization of the ideal.

Whitman was to discover that becoming Emerson's kind of poet enabled him finally to be the kind of man he wanted to be, strong, loving, courageous, secure, imperturbable, his feet "tenon'd and mortis'd in granite." Making art out of his life, he was able to make his life a work of art freely created. With so much at stake, he could afford to disregard literary niceties. "Who touches this book touches a man."

But he might also have said, of course, who touches this book touches an artist. For Emerson and Whitman, the man who suffers and the poet who creates are not distinct, as Eliot would later say, but united. The artist in words — the poet — is Man Naming. Naming is both a superior kind of Knowing and a superior kind of Doing. To give a name to a thing is to make it available to us, for the unnamed is the not yet known. The imagination, the gift that distinguishes the Namer from the Knower and the Doer, is thus constitutive of that part of reality that comes to consciousness. The artist is therefore creative in the deepest sense possible: He is man sharing with God or the Over-Soul in the act of creation. Responding to the "divine aura," he discloses a "reality" that for the rest of us did not exist before he named it. The artist is distinguished from other men not essentially by being a better technician in words, a "miglior fabbro" or greater artisan, but by being more of a *man* than most of us manage to be, which, as Emerson explained, means having a greater power both to receive and to impart. Allowing the suppressed to come to consciousness, drawing on "dream-power," and seeing all things freshly, not as the mind categorizes them or society catalogues them but as they are in themselves, he reattaches the parts to the whole, the many to the one, and thus sees, and makes *us* see, all things, even supposedly trivial or ugly things, as beautiful. Doing this, he enables us to grow toward larger circles of being. By the power of his imagination the poet can save us who "on the brink of the waters of life are miserably dying." Saving us, he also saves himself, though he may have to endure the jeers of the world. He becomes in the end the earth's only true landlord, he for whom the rain falls as Beauty, who finds all conditions opportune, none ignoble.

That Whitman derived his idea of his role as a poet primarily from Emerson will some day I believe be known and accepted, but that was not all he got from Emerson, though of course it would be more than enough. One of the most puzzling lines in "Song of Myself" can give us the clue here. Section forty-six in the Deathbed Edition opens with lines that read like this in the 1855 edition:

> I know I have the best of time and space — and that I
> was never measured, and never will be measured.

I tramp a perpetual journey,
My signs are a rain-proof coat and good shoes and a staff
cut from the woods;
No friend of mine takes his ease in my chair,
I have no chair, nor church nor philosophy;
I lead no man to a dinner-table or library or exchange,
But each man and each woman of you I lead upon a
knoll,
My left hand hooks you round the waist,
My right hand points to landscapes of continents, and a
plain public road.

Why should a "rain-proof coat" be the first of the "signs" of the true poet? There is no indication in the lines that precede or follow this passage that the poet tramping his perpetual journey is encountering bad weather — that rain is falling on him.

The idea of the poet as *homo viator,* man on the road, is, of course, all through Emerson; it is one of the chief ways, he thought, in which the poet *represents* us. But only in the ending of "The Poet" is the idea expressed in images that combine the metaphor of the *journey* with the metaphor of *rain.* Emerson's peroration to his essay concludes with these remarks on the true poet's reward for all his "renunciations and apprenticeships." I have added the italics.

> . . . The world is full of renunciations and apprenticeships, and this is thine; *thou must pass for a fool and a churl* for a long season. This is the screen and sheath in which Pan has protected his well-beloved flower, and *thou shalt be known only to thine own, and they shall console thee with tenderest love.* And thou shalt not be able to rehearse the names of thy friends in thy verse, for *an old shame* before *the holy ideal.* And this is the reward; that the ideal shall be real to thee, and *the impressions of the actual world shall fall like summer rain,* copious, but not troublesome to thy invulnerable essence. Thou shalt have the whole land for thy park and manor, the sea for thy bath and navigation, without tax and without envy; the woods and the rivers thou shalt own,

> and thou shalt possess that wherein others are only tenants and boarders. Thou true land-lord! sea-lord! air-lord! Wherever snow falls or water flows or birds fly, wherever day and night meet in twilight, wherever the blue heaven is hung by clouds or sown with stars, wherever are forms with transparent boundaries, wherever are outlets into celestial space, wherever is danger, and awe, and love, — there is *Beauty, plenteous as rain, shed for thee,* and though thou *shouldst walk the world over,* thou shalt not be able to find a condition inopportune or ignoble.

It is not hard to imagine how this passage would have struck Whitman, with his consciousness of his "peculiarity" and his life-long interest in the "signs" by which friends might know each other. (Emerson had spoken earlier in the essay of the "signs" by which we might know the true poet.) Rain would be a hardship for an ordinary walker on the open road, but for Whitman with his rain-proof coat the hardship would be transformed into "Beauty" and power. An "old shame" could not keep him from knowing that his "essence" was "invulnerable."

The point is that Whitman is thinking of himself in the opening lines of section forty-six as *the* Emersonian poet, not just as a poet who accepts the general outlines of the ideal poet Emerson had described — an ideal widespread of course in the Romantic movement, an ideal that, in its most general outlines, Whitman might have found in a dozen places, or simply have picked up because it was "in the air," was common property. With his special situation, with his sense of his "shame," he could find himself justified, and not only justified, exalted, in the ending of Emerson's "The Poet."

That he undoubtedly read this passage with partially different meanings in mind from those Emerson had meant to express is what we should expect. Just so he seems to have read the "Friendship" essay, with its metaphors that could be read as intended to convey hints of manly love between friends. The point, once again, was that he thought he had found in Emerson not just a sage but a kindred spirit, true friend, a "Camerado" indeed. Late in life he repeatedly told Traubel that he knew Emerson loved him.[2]

So he would follow in detail the friend's directions for becoming a true poet. Hence the catalogues. Hence the "receiving" and "imparting." Hence the "metre-making argument"—the "free verse." Hence the constant "naming." No single prescription by Emerson in "The Poet" for the poet's *manner* of writing is ignored or overlooked in the first edition of *Leaves of Grass.*

But this is another story just now beginning to be studied and understood, another book indeed. For present purposes it will be sufficient to say that what I consider our greatest single critical essay was profoundly influential on the man who may well be our greatest poet. Along with the other essays by Emerson, it made it possible for Whitman to *become* a poet.

Much of what is hardest for us to take in Whitman often consists of flat, literal, simplified journalistic restatement of what in Emerson's prose is essentially not statement at all but poetic metaphor. In many of the declarative passages in his early poems, Whitman seems to be not so much restating as caricaturing Emerson, putting Emerson's ideas in the worst light possible, as though an uneducated journalist with political interests were trying to paraphrase a subtle metaphysician whom he did not quite understand. "Omnes! Omnes! . . . I say there is in fact no evil." Or "Americanos! conquerors! marches humanitarian!/ Foremost! century marches! Libertad! masses!"

But the late Randall Jarrell has said perhaps as much as needs to be said about this aspect of Whitman, so far as critical evaluation of it is concerned:

> I have said so little about Whitman's faults [in an essay devoted to enthusiastic appreciation] because they are so plain: baby critics who have barely learned to complain of the lack of ambiguity in *Peter Rabbit* can tell you all that is wrong with *Leaves of Grass.*

All that needs to be added to this is that a great deal of "what is wrong" turns out to be the rhetoric of Emersonian doctrine so badly stated as almost to justify Leslie Fiedler's speaking of Whitman's "absurd ideas." For a single illustration—when so many are possible, one should be enough—compare the passage in the essay "The Poet" culminating in "America is a poem in our eyes" with Whitman's lines, just quoted, beginning "Americanos!" Both passages express the same idea—Whitman says he will elicit the poetry inherent in our land by making chants of Ohio, Indiana, Illinois, etc.—but Whitman's way of saying it makes the idea seem more than a little absurd.

But it is not true, it seems to me, to say, as Fiedler goes on to say in the same passage, that all of Whitman's ideas "fall away" when we really appreciate his poetry. Quite apart from the passages of bad rhetoric, even if we were to cut them all out of the work, leaving only the fully imagined passages and poems, the best of the poetry that would remain would imply—not state, *imply*—the whole body of Emerson's Transcendental doctrine. And to call Transcendentalism itself essentially absurd, no matter *how* stated or implied, seems to me not so much to make an intelligible judgment as to indulge in a hostile gesture.

To make what might easily become a long story as short as possible, Whitman's poetry rests on the vision Emerson first articulated—which does not mean, of course, that we would ever mistake a Whitman poem for an Emerson poem. Whitman's intention, like Emerson's, is to affirm "Life," just *because* that affirmation seems difficult. He does so by turning from custom and received belief to the individual and to nature as the repositories of true values. To elicit the unseen or hidden values, he relies on the imagination, which is able to see fact as symbol. His work preserves the Emersonian paradox. The poet's imagination is creative, but its creation is also a discovery. The poet's way of seeing allows him a glimpse of the "Real." If this were not so, Whitman insists just as strongly as Emerson, the poet could not *save* us, as he can and must. Before the poet can be a true Namer, he must be a true Seer. The value of his vision to us lies in the veracity of its report.

The sense in which Whitman was truer to the original impulse of Transcendentalism than Emerson sometimes was emerges when we consider that he was never tempted to obliterate the actual to get at the real. Late in life, when his vigor and imagination were waning, the "impressions of the actual world," as Emerson had put it, fell on him less copiously; but even in the flattest, least imaginative, of his late poems Whitman never ceased to assert in *theory* that nature is symbolic revelation. He never took back the thematic program he announced at the beginning: "Materialism first and last imbuing."

To "imbue" materialism with meaning, purpose, spirit—in the context he did not need to explain "imbuing"—is to do what

Emerson had first called for, to see the "Ideal" not somewhere beyond, in another realm, but *in* the actual; it is to take "things" seriously just because they are not "mere" things but vehicles, symbols, epiphanies. Whitman sometimes expressed this as a paradox: "I will make the poems of materials, for I think they are to be the most spiritual poems. . . . Because having look'd at the objects of the universe, I find there is no one nor any particle of one but has reference to the soul." "Materials," "objects"—these words point to the concrete factual "givenness" of the "materials" he intends to "imbue." Through them, through "things" perceived in all their particularity, he will, as James would later say Emerson had done, hold a lifelong "conversation with the invisible divine."

His differences from Emerson, so far as they have to do with ideas, so far as they are manifest rather than latent, are mostly implicit in the poetry, not stated, certainly never stressed *as* differences, but they have a great deal to do with the impression the poetry makes on us. Whitman is more personalistic, less pantheistic than Emerson. He was also more "honest" in facing the "reality" of natural evil, or pain, despite his most strenuous denials of it as metaphysically ultimate. Even his flat-footed "I say there is in fact no evil" seems, when we read it in context, easier to take seriously than Emerson's private admission that he had never been able to make evil "seem real" to himself, as though he had struggled to achieve an insight not granted him. It was so "real" to Whitman that he felt compelled to deny it any *metaphysical* reality as loudly as he could. Finally, he was more open than Emerson to *others,* just as he was more responsive to the solidity of *things,* of nature. This greater openness to the "not me" was not inconsistent with his being more of a Transcendental mystic than Emerson. Transcendental illuminations, as Emerson in theory knew and said so often, demand just such openness.

In the passage I have drawn upon for a characterization of Whitman's ideas as "absurd," Leslie Fiedler argues that it is not only the *ideas* that must be discarded if we are to read the poetry with pleasure:

> He has survived his images, and at last the outlived posturing, the absurd ideas, the rhetoric borrowed and

> misunderstood fall away, until only the poetry remains, and the poet, anonymous in the end as they were in the beginning.

Fiedler's response to the poetry here is genuine and sensitive, personal and passionate. Whitman would probably have liked this statement, for he too responded to literature as though it mattered, discarding all that seemed to him not to matter. Perhaps many of us will have to discard everything in his poetry except the purely lyric expressions of what Fiedler calls Whitman's two great themes, love and death. To some extent criticism must always, no doubt, amount to remaking writers in our own image. One of the signs that a poem is great is that it permits each of us to see in it something of our own, responding to it without sharing all the ideas and values of the author.

But is it really necessary to judge the bulk of Whitman's work so dated and provincial that, if we are to enjoy it, we must reduce it to a core of pure anonymous emotion that Whitman would not have recognized as containing either his full intention or his final achievement? It is doubtful, for one thing, that "ideas" and "poetry" can be so sharply separated as Fiedler seems to imply. It is even more doubtful that Whitman's poetry can survive if we totally reject his "images." To speak of his "posturing" is to come close to repeating the failure of both understanding and sympathy that produced Esther Shepard's *Walt Whitman's Pose,* a book right in many details but totally misleading in its general effect. Finally, neither the poetry nor the poet should be thought of as "anonymous": universal, yes, but by no means anonymous. To make Whitman, of all poets, "faceless" is to misunderstand, I believe, the whole drift of his work. If we do this, isolated lines and passages, and perhaps even a few whole poems, may survive, but Whitman as a major poet will have been lost or destroyed.

Whitman is the poet of the self, but not merely of the self that loves and dies, the "naturalistic" self.[3] We sometimes seem to forget that it is not "Song of Myself" but *Leaves of Grass* as a whole that, in the Deathbed edition, opens with "One's-self I sing, a simple separate person." Whitman is our greatest exponent of the individual conceived as containing the possibility of self-transcendence, or growth beyond the determined and known. Like Emerson before him, he refuses to place a limit on the self's possibilities. There is no known circumference, Emerson had said, to the self-evolving circle that we are, not even death itself. The known, rationalistically empiric self was never, for either Emerson or Whitman, the whole self. William James would later acknowledge the same idea of unlimited transcendence as central among his own "overbeliefs." As he put it in "Pragmatism and Religion," "I firmly disbelieve, myself, that our [known, measurable, "scientific"] human experience is the highest form of experience extant in the universe." Unless we conceive the self that is affirmed in Whitman's work in some such terms as these, his affirmation becomes ridiculous. "Walt Whitman" as the major symbol in his own poems is the indestructible human individual, fully aware, as a modern man, of death, yet knowing himself in some sense "immortal" nonetheless, living in time but not contained by it, constituted by the chemistry of a particular ancestry living in a particular place, yet not the creature of space either; a mystery of incarnation, not contained between his hat and his boots, a "body overflowed with life," as Emerson, once again, had put it.

"Who touches this book touches a man": the point is not that the book contains biology or history rather than poetry, but that the man himself is symbol. Such a man as we find in the book can be (as Walter Whitman much of the time was not, and as *we* mostly are not) imperturbable, "aplomb in the midst of irrational things," because he believes that *all* selves are ultimate and indestructible. He says he "knows," and will make us believe, as he does, that it is "lucky to be born," and "just as lucky to die." Finding irreducible value — "Beauty," Emerson had called it — in all things, even in beetles rolling balls of dung, even in the pimply prostitute, he is able, without forcing his feelings, to find "the earth good and the stars good, and their adjuncts all good." Yet he believes that he himself, and every man with him, is more than earth:

> I am not an earth nor an adjunct of an earth,
> I am the mate and companion of people, all just as
> immortal and fathomless as myself,
> (They do not know how immortal, but I know.)

This is Whitman's way of conceiving the transcendent self who, having confronted "night, storms, hunger, ridicule, accidents, rebuffs," yet knows himself "master of all." One way to state the greatness of Whitman's achievement as a poet is to say that, to some of us at least, he makes this incredible claim seem valid. I say "incredible" not on the basis of any philosophic or theological presupposition, so far as I am aware, but simply existentially, because we too, having confronted all this, do *not* as a rule find ourselves "master" of all; much less pertinently, we may find it "incredible" because we know, if we have studied his life, or even read his poems closely enough, that Whitman himself was very far from always being "imperturbable." We know that he brought his affirmations out of the depths of his anxieties.

But why this should make us talk about his "posturing" I cannot imagine. It ought rather to make the symbol "Walt Whitman" seem more universal, richer in its power to evoke response in us than any mere doctrinal statement of belief could possibly be. Where else would the affirmation of meaning beyond the empirically perceived situation come from if not from anxiety? Do naturalists who dispose of Whitman's religious faith in a phrase suppose that they alone are exempt from a recognition of our powerlessness and nothingness, the "central paranoia," as some psychoanalysts have put it? It has always been true, both psychologically and theologically, that growth proceeds, and life is affirmed, by an act of faith, which may also be an act of response. "Credo quia absurdam" is a statement not limited in its relevance to a type of early Medieval theology.

This does not of course mean that we as readers must "accept," doctrinally, as articles of our own faith, all that Whitman believed. But it does mean that we must either be able to entertain his faith imaginatively, not dismissing it on doctrinal grounds as absurd or childish or even necessarily unintelligent, or else be content to adopt one or the other of two choices: to value him only for his occasional felicities, or to create a "Whitman" of our own. Criticism which is content with the first alternative is parochial; criticism content with the latter is so subjective as to look more like an exercise in self-therapy than an act of reflection.

For there can be no question about Whitman's intention. It is fully — though, to be sure, unevenly — expressed artistically in every aspect of his book, from the design of the lettering on the green cover he prepared for his first edition, to the arrangement of the contents of the Deathbed Edition. Whitman meant it to be clear that the whole book, and not just one section of the opening poem, was "out of the hopeful green stuff woven." In the first edition an untitled poem later to be called "Poem of Walt Whitman, an American" and later still "Song of Myself" opened the volume, and "Great Are the Myths" closed it. The first line in the first edition of the book was, "I celebrate myself" and the last, "Sure as the stars return again after they merge in the light, death is as great as life." Clearly, the self here being celebrated believes it is "going somewhere," as a very late poem puts it.

No wonder Thoreau said that reading the second edition had done him "more good than any reading for a long time." Like Whitman, Thoreau too was consciously in search of valid reasons for hope. He remembered best, he said in the same letter to Harrison Blake, "the poem of Walt Whitman, an American, and the Sun-Down poem"—by which he must have meant "Crossing Brooklyn Ferry." Unlike many modern Whitman critics, Thoreau was prepared to respond to Whitman's fundamental meanings.

Though he found "two or three pieces in the book . . . disagreeable, to say the least," yet, "after whatever deductions," it sounded to him "very brave and American." He did not believe "that all the sermons, so called, that have been preached in this land put together are equal to it for preaching." As for the author, he thought "we ought to rejoice greatly in him . . . He is awfully good." As Emerson was to say in a few years in his funeral address, Thoreau was a very good reader. Modern criticism could do no better than start at the level of perception Thoreau attained. Rejoicing greatly in Whitman after deductions that will not amount to excisions of his central meaning, we might then try to find out how and where it is truest to say that he is "awfully good."

Whitman wrote best when he wrote of all three of his central preoccupations at once. Death and love and transcendence are inseparably mingled in all his greatest poems. On any one of the themes separately considered, he sometimes wrote well, but never at a level comparable with the best parts of "Song of Myself" or "Lilacs."

I have said that Whitman's ideas, in particular his Emersonian Transcendentalism, are all implicit in his best poems. But that does not make him a "poet of ideas." When thoughts of love and death led him to write poems specifically on religion, for example, the result was seldom more than competent and much of the time, especially in his last years, very flat and poor. "Chanting the Square Deific" is one of the best of his religious poems, but to compare it with section six of "Song of Myself," "A Child said

What is the Grass?" is to reduce it from a poem to a mere idea, an interesting idea to be sure, but still an idea in verse, not a great poem. "To Him That Was Crucified," a poem that those who care for Whitman are likely to respond to, illustrates the same point: it states a sentiment and an idea and contains one striking line — "I do not sound your name, but I understand you" — but no one would think of it as giving us Whitman at his best.

So too with the poems on love treated in isolation from death and transcendence. I think we ought to be glad Whitman wrote the "Children of Adam" and "Calamus" poems, and even more glad that he refused to respond to pressures to remove them from his book for the sake of his contemporary reputation, but I doubt that they have ever been very widely read or very much enjoyed. To read them as little allegories of "ideal" love, as James Miller has suggested, is to destroy whatever value they have as poems of *experience*. In general, the poems in "Calamus" are more truly felt and imagined than those in "Children of Adam," but most readers today find them not "shocking" or "immoral" but embarrassing and boring. Only "Of the Terrible Doubt of Appearances" strikes me as really memorable among these poems.

Whitman almost never, until very late in life, wrote on death without writing on love and transcendence at the same time. The very late "Life" and "Going Somewhere" sufficiently illustrate what happened when he did. The "struggling soul of man," resolute, undiscouraged, finds everywhere, even in science, reasons to believe that life is an endless march in which "the world, the race, the soul," everything, is "surely going somewhere." These and other late poems of the same sort, affirming a faith at once evolutionary and Transcendental, are "good Whitman" in doctrine and point of view, and reminders that the sick old man never lost his courage even in great adversity, but they are not very good poems.

Very much better in the same vein is "To Think of Time," one of the poems first published in 1855. Perceptive readers of the first edition might have found in this poem the challenge that produced the unqualified affirmations in "Song of Myself." Death is the primary fact here, as it had been for Emerson, the threat that must somehow be dealt with if we are to continue to "take interest" in life:

> Have you guess'd you yourself would not continue?
> Have you dreaded these earth-beetles?
> . . . .

> Not a day passes, not a minute or second without a
> corpse.
>
> . . . .
>
> Slow-moving and black lines creep over the whole earth
> — they never cease — they are the burial lines. . . .

After "a reminiscence of the vulgar fate" in section four — the life and death of a wagon-driver — the poem moves directly to its affirmation:

> What will be will be well, for what is is well,
> To take interest is well, and not to take interest
> [that is, after death] shall be well.

For although the dead take no interest in the living, we are not to think of them as lost or destroyed. "You are not thrown to the winds," for the individual person is the key to the "real": "It is not to diffuse you that you were born of your mother and father, it is to identify you . . ."

Explicitly, the implications of a naturalistic vision — such as that in the main body of "Thanatopsis," for example — are denied:

> If all came but to ashes of dung,
> If maggots and rats ended us, then Alarum! for we are
> betray'd,
> Then indeed suspicion of death.
> Do you suspect death? If I were to suspect death I
> should die now,
> Do you think I could walk pleasantly and well-suited
> toward annihilation?

Rather than "suspecting" death, the poet says he has "dream'd that we are not to be changed so much, nor the law of us changed . . ." In lines that Edward Taylor would not have felt required to modify for doctrinal orthodoxy, the poet states the essence of his "dream":

> And I have dream'd that the purpose and essence of the
> known life, the transient,
> Is to form and decide identity for the unknown life, the
> permanent.

But Taylor would have been shocked, I suppose, by what immediately follows — or at least would have felt that Whitman had betrayed the faith by making it too easy and too inclusive. Taylor might have quoted Scripture — "Strait is the gate, and narrow the way . . ." — when he went on to read, "I swear I think now that every thing without exception has an eternal soul! . . . I swear I think there is nothing but immortality." Clearly, this man Whitman, who had begun his affirmation so promisingly, from Taylor's point of view, did not believe in Hell. Looked at from a traditional Christian perspective, he combined two heresies with a remnant of orthodoxy: His version of salvation was both Unitarian and Universalist.

That he thus anticipated the merger of these churches in our century would presumably not have made Taylor any happier with what he read. If Stoddard was to be condemned for admitting people too freely to Holy Communion, how much more so Whitman, who admitted *everything,* all men and all nature, to ultimate blessedness. What meaning could there be in the idea of Election if *all* were Elect? This new poet seemed to be proclaiming justification by faith, not by works, but the faith was not in Christ but in the ultimate goodness of all reality, empiric and nonempiric, what is in time and what is beyond time. Was *this* where Taylor's cherished Protestantism would end?

From a more distant, less Christian, view than Taylor's, it might seem that the really significant difference between the faith of the two poets could be better described in philosophic than in theological or creedal terms. Whitman's faith in a reality that transcended logic and the senses did nothing to belittle or denigrate the world of experience. His affirmation minimizes the dichotomy between nature and Heaven, this life and the life to come, the real and the Real. He finds the Now significant because it is penetrated and permeated by the Eternal; which is only another way of saying that he was not a Puritan but a true Transcendentalist. Interestingly enough — to return to a theological perspective for a moment — some contemporary theologians might find Whitman's "orthodoxy" on this matter greater than Taylor's.

I have given so much time to this poem, which no one else has ever claimed as one of Whitman's best, though it seems to me so, because parts of it put so baldly the rationale of Whitman's celebration of the self, himself and every self, and of life in all its variety and promise. Unless one were to argue that it is untypical

— and such an argument could not be maintained if all the evidence were honestly faced — it shows us how misleading it is to speak of Whitman as "secularizing" the faith of the fathers, as making a clean break with the past by turning his attention to "this world." "To Think of Time" is not only not a "secular" poem, it is an explicitly and emphatically antisecular poem. That which is "in" time — the "secular" — is not less but more meaningful, the poem says, *because* its dimensions extend beyond time into the Eternal. Except for the missing specifically Christian interpretation of incarnation, which separates Whitman from Eliot as, in a different way, it separates him from Taylor, the argument of the poem is very close to that in *Four Quartets*: Only in time can time be redeemed, but the meaning of time is found only when our experience ceases to be adequately described by the meaning we usually assign to "secular."

What such a faith might mean for living *in* time — that is, its "secular" implications — Whitman did not leave us to guess. "O Living Always, Always Dying," which first appeared in the 1860 edition, is one of the best brief expressions of the personal and psychic thrust of his faith. It is short enough to quote entire, and good enough in its own right to deserve full quotation:

> O living always, always dying!
> O the burials of me past and present,
> O me while I stride ahead, material, visible, imperious
> as ever;
> O me, what I was for years, now dead, (I lament not, I
> am content;)
> O to disengage myself from those corpses of me, which I
> turn and look at where I cast them,
> To pass on, (O living, always living!) and leave the
> corpses behind.

That the poem has reference to facts in Whitman's life that are known or that may some day be known — the "selves" he was trying to outgrow; that it invites a reading in psychiatric terms designed to elicit the laws of human growth; and that it is not about some unknown entity called "the soul" but about the "material, visible" Walt Whitman — these facts, and they are certainly facts, do not in any way make it improper to call this a "religious" poem, religious precisely in the sense made clear in "To Think of Time." That this faith, as more abstractly proclaimed in the earlier poem and more concretely and personally applied in the later one, is at the heart of all Whitman had to say as a poet should be too clear to need further illustration. Whether we like the faith or not, or can agree with it, is not the point. If it had always been kept in mind we might have been spared some of the more absurdly subjective and unhistorical interpretations of Whitman, and particularly of "Song of Myself," that in recent years have become a massive barrier to understanding.

This is not the occasion to attempt a detailed analysis of any of Whitman's best poems, among which I should want to include "Song of Myself," — perhaps America's greatest poem — "The Sleepers," "Song of the Open Road," "Crossing Brooklyn Ferry," "Out of the Cradle Endlessly Rocking," "When Lilacs Last in the Dooryard Bloom'd," and a number of short poems, particularly "There Was a Child Went Forth," "Cavalry Crossing a Ford," "When I Heard the Learn'd Astronomer," and "A Sight in Camp in the Daybreak Gray and Dim." Each of the longer great poems deserves, and will eventually get, a chapter or book to itself. Since that is impossible in the present work, I shall conclude with some comments intended, hopefully, to be suggestive of fruitful ways in which Whitman could be approached. The remarks that follow will focus on what I take to be the problematical or controversial areas in contemporary Whitman criticism.

"There Was a Child Went Forth," which first appeared in the 1855 edition, deserves more notice than it has received, both as a fine poem and as an epitome of Whitman's philosophic stance, his Transcendentalism.[4] Moving outward from the home to the shore and from infancy to maturity, the speaker in the poem also moves from unquestioning acceptance, to doubt, to reaffirmation of life and goodness. Another way of putting it is to say that the poem moves toward and through the birth of consciousness, with the alienation this brings, and beyond pure conscious rationality to reunion and reintegration.

The poem begins very simply:

> There was a child went forth every day,
> And the first object he look'd upon, that object he
>   became,
> And that object became part of him. . . .

To put it in abstract language, the child is formed by nature, constituted by his environment (as we read in "Song of Myself," "form'd from this soil, this air,/ Born here of parents born here from parents the same, and their parents the same"), yet also "contains" nature — the objects that become "part of him." No simple environmentalism but a two-way process of reception and creation is suggested here. The possibility of transcendence, and the shadow of future doubt, are already implicit in the opening lines.

But these are mere undercurrents in the first part of the poem. Predominantly, until the crucial break in the middle of the last section, the attitude is "realistic" and "accepting." (As Emerson had said in "The Poet," the poet is the representative man who speaks for us by virtue of his greater power to "receive and impart.") Whitman takes the world of Appearance more seriously than Emerson, as a comparison of this poem with the Master's "Two Rivers" would show. With loving attention the speaker here details his experiences as he "goes forth" in time and space. When he reaches an awareness of the role of his parents in his development, he is mature, ready for thought. The reality has not been ideal: The mother with her clean cap and gown, "a wholesome odor falling off her person and clothes as she walks by," is balanced by the father, "strong, self-sufficient, manly, mean, anger'd, unjust,/ The blow, the quick loud word, the tight bargain, the crafty lure." But all this, even the father, is accepted as partaking of "reality," and loved with an "affection that will not be gainsay'd."

In the middle of the line that climaxes the statement of the affection, the attachment felt in the "yearning and swelling heart," suddenly, with no more separation than a comma can provide, comes the doubt: "the sense of what is real, the thought if after all it should prove unreal,/ The doubts of day-time and the doubts of night-time, the curious whether and how,/ Whether that which appears so is so, or is it all flashes and specks?" The "doubt of appearances" proves "terrible" here, as it would more explicitly in 1860 in the poem titled with those words: terrible because however imperfect this "reality" was, however far from the Real, it was at least "real" in a sense that *preceded* the metaphysical question, real both as the "given" and as the loved.

But supposing, as Emerson sometimes seemed to be saying, this world of the apparently real were merely phenomenal, not noumenal, the creation indeed of the poet's own mind? ("The Universe is the externization of the soul.") If the "objects" — note the solidity, the firmness of the word — if the objects of the child's experience were only, in Emerson's sense, a "part of him," perhaps not really real at all except as he perceived them, then what about the affection that could not be gainsaid, whatever metaphysics might say? Was the heart directing its love to phantasms of the imagination, to "flashes and specks"?

This doubt apparently did not much trouble Emerson. He insisted that he loved nature even though he knew it was not metaphysically "Real." Far from troubling Poe, the idea of the unsubstantial character of the world of sense delighted him as evidence of the power of his "angelic imagination." But it troubled Whitman: He was not willing to settle for "another world" if such a choice involved denigrating this one.

After a further cataloguing of loved items of experience that will be denied reality if that which appears is *not* so, the speaker moves through the streets of the city westward toward the river as the sun is setting. Looking across the water toward "the horizon's edge," he literally "sees" less and less. The sights of the city, along with those of the home, have fallen away. He is left at last with only the sense of smell, a primitive, prerational sense. What he smells is good, as the smell of his mother had been: "the fragrance of salt marsh and shore mud." In the darkness, then, when he can no longer *see,* he recovers his initial sense of wholeness and meaning. As sight gives way to insight — Emerson would have said to "intuition" — he moves beyond the doubts that threatened him, so that he may end his poem with a fully earned reaffirmation of his experience:

> The horizon's edge, the flying sea-crow, the fragrance of
> salt marsh and shore mud,
> These became part of that child who went forth every
> day, and who now goes, and will always go forth
> every day.

As he said elsewhere, growth, which necessarily involves self-transcendence, remains possible because "Logic and sermons never convince,/ The damp of the night drives deeper into my soul." That the process by which Whitman reached the certainty that the faith of the child was true despite later doubts, that the objects of his love were *not* just flashes and specks, and that he would always go forth — that the psychic aspects of this process could be given an explanation in psychiatric terms, an "explanation" no doubt centering on the relation of Whitman and his mother, is obvious, but not, as I see it, relevant to literary criticism. All history, not just poetry, is open to psychiatric explanation, but psychiatrists are as much conditioned by history as the rest of us are.

The idea that we are the first to know about unconscious motivation is one of our more disabling superstitions. Applied to writers like Whitman, its chief effect is to protect us from being forced to reorganize our ideas by remaining open to what they have to say to us. It was William James who pointed out that the manifestations of the religious life "frequently connect themselves with the subconscious part of our existence." But he also went on to write, in his next chapter (the italics are his), that

> As I have elsewhere written, the most interesting and valuable things about a man are usually his over-beliefs.
>
> Disregarding the over-beliefs, and confining ourselves to what is common and generic, we have in *the fact that the conscious person is continuous with a wider self through which saving experiences come,* a positive content of religious experience which, it seems to me, *is literally and objectively true as far as it goes.*

To turn from fruitless argument about whether the affirmation in the poem is "valid" or merely revelatory of the mechanisms of Whitman's personality, we may at least say that the affirmation is earned in the poem. The movement in the poem has several aspects, all of which complement and reinforce one another: from home to immediate surroundings (the lilacs in the yard), to more remote surroundings (the city), and finally to that which surrounds and encloses us all, the dark waters of the river; from childhood to maturity and finally to death; from "objects" to parents to other people, and finally to a fully realized sense of the self; from morning to night; from innocence to doubt to a newly won, an *achieved,* innocence; from security to insecurity to a deeper, autonomous security; from nature as all, to nature as a momentary flash in the darkness, to nature as illumination, but an illumination that can be perceived only from the vantage point of the darkness. Finding transcendent values in the givenness of concrete experience, the poem expresses the central and original meaning of Emerson's gospel.

"The Sleepers" is not, as it has been called, a dreaming poem — the speaker is awake, contemplating sleepers — but it draws deeply upon that "dream power" that Emerson had known was available to the poet, and it illustrates another insight of the master's, that "A beauty not explicable is dearer than a beauty which we can see the end of." It is not likely that anyone will claim to "see the end of" the beauty of this poem, but it might be well for criticism to make a start toward understanding it by noting the interrelationships of its images of night, mother, sea, and the beautiful dying swimmer. This poem seems to me one of the least consciously controlled of Whitman's poems and one of the most beautiful. In it he speaks, as Emerson said, "somewhat wildly" — and most truly. No poem of his more fully confirms, not Emerson's philosophy, but Emerson's conception of the way the poet should work. But to speak of the poem as an "illustration" of something is somehow absurd, even if true: "The Sleepers" is simply one of the great poems in the language.

What it "means" is not translatable, but in the affirmation of its closing lines we can see some of the elements we identified in "There Was a Child Went Forth":

> I will stop only a time with the night, and rise betimes,
> I will duly pass the day O my mother, and duly return to
> you.

"Song of Myself" is probably the greatest long poem in American literature, unless that place should be reserved for "Lilacs." But unlike the later poem, it is also extremely uneven poetically, incoherent logically (that is to say, seemingly without rational structure and progress), and in places "tasteless." The chief reason it does not invite parody is that in it Whitman at times seems to be parodying himself. No wonder it has been so often misunderstood by those critics who have not ignored it.

It is not of course "comic drama," as one of the best-known interpretations would have it. When Whitman said things that strike us as funny, like "Divine am I inside and out," he was not making jokes. It is not "epic," as another widely read interpreter would have it, not even in a nontraditional sense, not even as "an American equivalent of an epic." For if the comparison with the epic mode is to have any meaning at all, surely we cannot empty "epic" of all significance except that of "a long poem with large intentions." An "epic" tells a story of heroes or mythic prototypes and tells it objectively. "Song of Myself" tells no story, has only the speaker as a "character," and is wholly subjective. To call this a new kind of "epic" takes us a good way into the mind of the critic but not very far into the poem, for whatever epiclike qualities "Song of Myself" has are not central to its purpose and meaning. Though Whitman was probably conscious that he was echoing Virgil when he opened his poem by saying that he would "celebrate" and "sing" himself, as Virgil had "sung" arms and the man, an interpretation which took this echo to be a sufficient clue to the poem to follow would end by making the poem an expression of secular humanism, as some readers would like to have it be, but as it most assuredly was not intended to be.

It is not quite "inverted mysticism," either, as James Miller, one of Whitman's more sympathetic contemporary critics, would have it. We are nearer the center of the poem here, but not close enough. "Song of Myself" is a mystical poem, but mystical in the Transcendental manner: It reaches its vision of union with the divine by the *via affirmativa,* short-cutting the journey of the more traditional Christian mystics by affirming the goodness of the created world from the very beginning, not simply at the end, after having turned away from it.

Miller's analysis, it is true, does more to explain certain puzzling passages and apparent transitions than any other yet offered, but the final effect of juxtaposing the medieval mystic way as described by Evelyn Underhill's *Mysticism* with Whitman's way is, it seems to me, to diminish the poem, both by devaluating a part of its richness and by making Whitman's way look like a deviation from an agreed-upon standard. Mysticism did not end with the Middle Ages, nor is it confined to Christianity, or indeed to any of the higher religions. I do not find Asselineau's "body mysticism" a very fortunate phrase, but certainly it is nearer the mark than "inverted" mysticism. "Erotic mysticism" would seem to me to be better yet. Only if we have not yet learned Whitman's "lesson" do we need to assume that there is anything "pseudo" about mysticism which depends upon erotic experience.

"Song of Myself" is, as Thoreau implied when he characterized its author, both very brave and very American. It is "brave" in the way its speaker unlocks at all costs his human doors, laying himself open to ridicule; brave in the way the poem pushes its truth to the point of absurdity to test its validity; most of all, perhaps, brave in daring to transform embarrassing deviation into a source of strength and faith.

It is "American" in all sorts of ways too obvious to mention, but chiefly in a way which must not be obvious, for it has generally escaped notice; I mean in the way in which it brings together freely and creatively the most diverse strains from the past to create an image of man facing the future. Not that the poem is a mere amalgam — though Whitman did of course want to speak for *all* men — but that it is as open in its meanings as it is in its form, and so loses very little of the best of the past, even though its attention is, or seems to be, centered wholly on the future.

More concerned with receptivity than with consistency, with growth than with maintaining an already established identity, it is, one would like to be able to say, a very *pragmatic* poem, if "pragmatic" had not picked up too many negative connotations since James's day. But whether "pragmatic" or not, it turns out that the "modern man" celebrated in the poem shares Taylor's awareness of death and his faith in God, but also Barlow's confidence in science and his sense of the promise of a better life to come in the new land; shares also Thoreau's sense of the need for waiting and his cultivation of consciousness, and Emerson's belief that the world is the body and blood of Spirit and that the self must daily transcend itself.

Denying all creeds, yet affirming the intent of all, saying in effect as Blake had that *all* religions are "true," heretical therefore from the point of view of *everybody's* "doxy," denying the validity for the individual self of *any* doxy not discovered by and for oneself, yet affirming, religiously, the value of every *self* beyond fact and circumstance and time, this "Walt Whitman," symbol of "the modern man," is finally even better than Thoreau thought. He is not only "brave" and "American" but universal. At its deepest level of meaning and impact, this most provincial of poems really is, as Whitman wanted it to be, timeless and placeless, composed of "the thoughts of all men."

What we learn about Whitman's point of view from "Song of Myself" prepares us for the very much later — the post-Civil War, indeed — "A Sight in Camp in the Daybreak Gray and Dim." This is one of Whitman's finest short poems, typical in its sensibility and ideas, untypical of the bulk of the best work in the tightness of its formal organization, and yet again typical of the tendency of the later poems to move toward an "Aristotelean" organization — to have a "beginning, middle, and end" in the more than merely spatial or temporal sense, and to move logically, not rhapsodically. The early poems tend to be "unorganized," from a logical point of view, to have, as we are likely to say, no discernible structure, but to be imaginatively rich. Most of the later ones tend to be "better organized," or at least organized in ways we can recognize more readily, but also to be, with the passing years, less and less imaginative. Here in 1865 we have a poem that has both imaginative vigor and formal organization. It belongs to Whitman's last period of greatness, among the poems he published in 1865 and 1866. Formally and thematically, it should be compared with "Lilacs."

"A Sight in Camp" consists of four verse paragraphs, the first introducing the scene, each of the others introducing one of three dead soldiers lying on stretchers outside a hospital tent. The first corpse is that of an old man, with gray hair and "flesh all sunken." The speaker wonders who he "is." The second form is that of a boy "with cheeks yet blooming" who hardly appears to be dead. Again the speaker wonders who he "is." The third form he thinks he recognizes: The face is that of a man neither old nor young, neither "gray" nor "blooming" but "beautiful yellow-white ivory":

> Young man I think I know you — I think this face is the
> face of the Christ himself,
> Dead and divine and brother of all, and here again he lies.

As Whitman had said five years before in "To Him That Was Crucified," "I do not sound your name, but I understand you." If any evidence were needed that this was not an idle boast, "A Sight in Camp" would provide it. "Dead and divine and brother": "dead" and "brother" would have offended orthodox trinitarians as an apparently flat denial of the Resurrection, and thus of the "divinity" of Jesus; "divine" would have offended Emerson as superstitious and excessively "Hebraic."

To Whitman the whole phrase, "dead and divine and brother," seemed not an oxymoron but a paradox, what is called, in discussions of faith, a "mystery." The falling rhythm of the last line, and especially of the three iambs, suggests that there is no tentativeness in the three-fold description; rather, finality. No one of the three attributes is less "meant" than another, even though the series builds toward "brother," suggesting Christ's role as *avatar.*

There is no need to debate the question of whether "Lilacs" or "Song of Myself" is Whitman's greatest poem, since the answer would have more to do with personality than with rational judgment. How much do we value order, how much spontaneity? How "classical" or "romantic" are we by temperament? Surely "Lilacs" is Whitman's most fully formed and finished long poem of great imaginative energy. The images in "The Sleepers" are more elusive and perhaps more evocative just because they are less open to rational explication. The best sections of "Song of Myself" are more intense, imagistic, and original. But a reader who inclines in any degree toward "formalism" might well find "Lilacs" a better example of Allen Tate's definition of poetry as "the art of apprehending and concentrating our experience in the mysterious limitations of form." "Lilacs" has the kind of "form" that can be rationally discerned and discussed.

Symbolically, the poem moves from its opening "trinity" of lilac and star and "thought of him I love" to its final trinity of "lilac and star and bird." In between, the progress of the poet from grief to acceptance is delayed by the "black murk" first mentioned in section two, and advanced by the song of the hermit thrush in section fourteen. The reluctance of the poet to listen to the bird he knows is singing, and his final readiness to listen only after he has both fully experienced his grief and tried to find reassurance everywhere else but in the swamp where the bird is — this movement of hesitation, false starts, retreat, and promise to listen "soon" gives the poem a dramatic interest that has not been sufficiently noted by its critics. And not only the prosody but the drama is structured in terms of a "trinity." Three times the poet becomes aware of the song and three times he turns away as not yet ready to listen.

Delicately, the shape and sound of the verse repeat the tripleness of the symbols and the dramatic movement. The six lines of the opening section are spaced as three and three. Rhythmically, they move toward the regular iambic trimeter of the sixth line, "And thought of him I love." Often, but not regularly or obtrusively, this triple rhythm recurs throughout the body of the poem (seven of the fourteen sections before the final one end with lines of three stresses, or of three and three with a pause between) until in the final lines it breaks out in triumphant release and dominates everything —

> Lilac and star and bird twined with the chant of my soul,
> There in the fragrant pines and the cedars dusk and dim.

Surely there is no better example than this in our literature of what Emerson had meant by organic form, or "metre-making argument." Whitman was suspicious both by temperament and by belief of the "restrictions," the limitations, of form. He thought, with Emerson, that it was of the nature of the imagination "to flow and not to freeze." But in "Lilacs" the form proves not a limitation accepted and worked within, but an emergent, a discovery of the meaning of the materials, a not necessarily final resting place.

It will not do I think to subject the symbols of the poem to too rigorous an explication. The poem being of the kind it is, any gain in abstract clarity would be likely to be accompanied by a diminution of power. Still, it should do no harm to the poem to note what Whitman himself has so strongly emphasized, that the lilac has "heart-shaped leaves of rich green" (the phrase is repeated without change three lines after it is first used), combining suggestions of love and hope; that the "song of the bleeding throat" comes from a singer "bashful and tender," "solitary," "withdrawn," whose song is "limitless out of the dusk" — reminding us of the ending of "There Was a Child Went Forth"; and that *only* the song "from deep secluded recesses" saying "Come lovely and soothing death" can free the poet from his initial grief and despair.

The hermit thrush may seem at first glance to foreshadow Philomel, the mythic nightingale of Eliot's early poems, but second thought persuades us that it is really much more like the wood thrush in Eliot's later "Marina," for Philomel sang of a "public" faith now lost, while the wood thrush sang, as the hermit thrush does in Whitman's poem, out of fog and the scent of pine, of a faith wholly internalized.

After "Lilacs," Whitman wrote no more truly great poems. "Passage to India," though grand in design, is, in too many of its sections, more conceptualized than imagined, failing right at the center, in its effort to show us how "the unseen is proved by the seen," so that its conclusion, announcing a "passage to more than India" seems unsupported. The mystical experience recorded in "Song of Myself" is only wished for here — "Bathe me O God in thee" — and the safety achieved in the earlier poem is not so much experienced as believed —

> O my brave soul!
> O farther farther sail!
> O daring joy, but safe! are they not all the seas of God?
> O farther, farther, farther sail!

Reading these lines, we are likely either to admire the man who wrote them, or to agree with the conception of an open-ended but not humanly meaningless world they imply, or both. What we are not likely to do is to be deeply and secretly moved by them. Hart Crane's rewriting of the poem in "The Bridge" may move us more, but without Whitman there would have been no "Bridge."

Whitman is great enough, and more than great enough, to survive his failures, as he survives his absurdities. He is the archetypal American poet, and I think the greatest we have yet had.

CHAPTER VII

Proud Ephemeral

Nature centres into balls,
And her proud ephemerals,
Fast to surface and outside,
Scan the profile of the sphere;
Knew they what that signified,
A new genesis were here.
— Emerson, in "Circles"

EMILY DICKINSON

To Emerson's way of thinking, the profile of a sphere implies a center. The essay "Circles," of which the poem "Circles," prefixed to it, is a partial condensation, begins with the eye, "the first circle," moves outward to the horizon, which is a segment of the spherical earth, and then back to the center to define it in the third sentence of the essay: "St. Augustine described the nature of God as a circle whose centre was everywhere, and its circumference nowhere." That one may realize the presence of God everywhere, anywhere, in all experience, is the unstated Emersonian conviction underlying the poem. *This* is what would make a new birth possible, if nature's proud ephemerals only knew it. It seemed to Emerson that man's situation was at once precarious and immensely hopeful.

Emily Dickinson made it her business as a poet to scan the profile of the sphere, but the harder she scanned it, the less she thought she knew what it signified. Perhaps the profile of the sphere, when fully understood, would turn out to be a "purposeless circumference," an emblem not of birth but of death. Perhaps at the center there was only an emptiness and a silence. Perhaps man could not bear what was signified. More remote from the mystical tradition than Emerson, she devoted herself to attempting to define what Emerson had said was intrinsically undefinable. If Emerson's faith, which rested ultimately on a *way* of "seeing," was only partially and theoretically available to her, at least she knew what it *felt* like to be, as she put it, "a speck upon a ball," a proud ephemeral clinging precariously to nowhere. Preferring the more imagistic word "evanescent" to Emerson's "ephemeral" as a description of the dying self, she spent a lifetime exploring the ambiguities latent in Emerson's paradoxical combination of "ephemeral" with "proud."

Her personal situation and her psychic necessities joined forces with her religious and philosophic heritage to make the experience of living in constant awareness of the coming of death, and the imaginative realization of dying as the climactic experience of living, become the subjects that increasingly preoccupied her and that give her verse its special quality. Like Pain and Bradstreet and Taylor before her, she seldom lost sight of the grave. They would have agreed perfectly with the definition she offered her Norcross cousins in a letter of 1863: "Life is death we're lengthy at, death the hinge to life." Death and Immortality became the chief speakers in a poetic debate she carried on with herself on the subject of the evanescence, or the possible permanence, of life and love.

But of course it is not necessary to go back to the Puritan poets of the seventeenth century, of whom she so often and so sharply reminds us, to find an analogue for her sensibility. The Puritan mind was still intact in Amherst, and not unknown even in Concord, however contemptuously Emerson might ignore its presence and the truths it witnessed to. Emerson's own Aunt Mary Moody Emerson had ridden through Concord on a donkey dressed in her shroud. She had made the shroud herself and had worn it daily as an outer garment, to remind herself, and perhaps others, of mortality. Her idiosyncrasy seemed to Emerson, who was fond of her and felt indebted, a charming example of a self-reliant willingness to follow "whim." If Dickinson had known Aunt Mary, surely she would have understood better than Emerson why one might thus choose to try to get in the habit of the tomb. She herself in the end chose to wear only white, a color that contained as many ambiguities for her as it had for Melville in his explication of "The Whiteness of the Whale."

But Emerson was perceptive about his Aunt Mary in one respect: she did not really share the attitudes of the new age he was helping to initiate; she was old-fashioned and in the end rather out of touch. But there was nothing old-fashioned about Dickinson. However she might share a style of life, created as a symbolic gesture, with Emerson's aunt, her mind was thoroughly contemporary. Comparisons with the Puritans, or even with Emerson's eccentric relative, will prove thoroughly misleading if they suggest that she ought to be thought of as typical of an earlier age rather than her own. Her seclusion was not from books or ideas. Intellectually, she was a woman of her time with an extremely intelligent and well-stocked mind. Alice James's *Diary* provides a closer analogue to her literary situation than Anne Bradstreet's *Tenth Muse.*

The sister of Henry James and William James was eighteen years younger than Emily Dickinson, but she died only six years later. In 1889, already an invalid for years and knowing she had not long to live, she turned from keeping a commonplace book to keeping a personal diary. Her motive for the change she put down as her first entry: "I think that if I get into the habit of writing a bit about what happens, or rather doesn't happen, I may lose a little of the sense of loneliness and desolation which abides with me." In the entries that follow, "Life is reduced," in the words of Leon Edel in the Introduction, "largely to the simple existential fact — as it was for her. . . . The claim of life against the claim of death — this is the assertion of every page . . ." Reading it after her death, brother Henry thought it constituted "a new claim for the family renown."

That she had hoped for this result is nowhere explicit but may be guessed not only from the care with which she dictated revisions in her final entries, after she was too weak to write, but from the definition of genius she quoted inaccurately from brother William's *Psychology,* a definition she could not fail to see as encouraging to the literary ambition of a dying woman keeping a diary: "William says in his *Psychology*: 'Genius, in truth, is little more than the faculty of perceiving in an unhabitual way.' This seems to the sisterly mind, or heart rather, more felicitous than the long-accustomed 'infinite capacity for taking pains' . . ."

Looking at life from the perspective of death, reducing all issues finally to "the claim of life against the claim of death" — such a way of perceiving was no longer common in the last half of the nineteenth century, as it had been among the Puritans. It tended to be characteristic now only of invalids or the very elderly. It was not, as William James was soon to put it, "healthy-minded." (But as James also said, a little later, "Even prisons and sickrooms have their special revelations.") Whether healthy-minded (whatever that means) or not, in Dickinson's poems, as in Alice

James's *Diary,* it produced an awareness that broke through the habits, proprieties, and utilities that normally protect us from too sharp a realization of experience. Knowing herself a proud ephemeral, as Emerson had put it, the poet scanned both the "profile of the sphere," the circumference of reality, and its minutest irregularities, searching for a revelation of meaning that would make a "new genesis" possible. She saw all things freshly, as though for the first, and the last, time. The "genius" of Dickinson's poetry, that which gives it both its uniqueness and its value, rests finally on an unhabitual way of perceiving, an angle of vision that found both formal and thematic expression.

The religious heritage bequeathed her by her family and Amherst, actively inculcated by her father and identified with him by his daughter, is made quaintly clear for us in a sampler Emily embroidered when she was fifteen. It begins,

> Jesus Permit Thy Gracious Name to stand
> As the First efforts of an infants hand

and ends with the petition that He may write His name upon her heart, just as (she implies) she has embroidered it on this sampler. If this were unidentified, we might suppose it to have been written by one of the versifiers of the seventeenth century. This is poetry conceived as an extension of the function of prayer, as an aid to right feeling and the practice of the devout life, and as wit's offering to the milder Son of the angry Father in Heaven.

Edward Dickinson, "Squire Dickinson," Emily's earthly father, was both a respected leader in Amherst society and one of the chief pillars of its religious orthodoxy. "Orthodoxy" in the Amherst in which Emily matured had a very clear and definite meaning. Not until after 1850 were there any churches in town besides the Congregational one that Edward Dickinson helped to lead, and Congregationalism as Amherst knew it was trinitarian, Bible-centered, dogmatically articulate, and concerned chiefly with individual salvation in a life after death. To be "religious" in this village society was to experience a conviction of salvation, to become an active member of the church, and to profess publicly faith in its dogmas.

To be uncertain of any of the dogmas, in a church that held to "justification by faith through grace" and that defined faith not as a motion of the heart but as giving assent to certain propositions, was to give proof that one was not one of the Saints, the Elect, who would be saved. Emily began by not being certain she could believe the dogmas and ended by being certain she couldn't. With no other options open to her but the choice of belief or unbelief, until she learned of the existence of other possibilities through her reading, she chose unbelief as more honest. But rejecting belief in the dogmas of the faith did not, could not, mean for her becoming indifferent to the questions the dogmas purported to answer. Instead, the "faith of the fathers," as Amherst knew it, became the antagonist in terms of which she defined her own position. As late as 1862, more than a dozen years after she had discovered Emerson and other outlets in the New Thought for her religious emotions, Amherst's way of defining the issues of faith and unfaith was still assumed in her statement to T. W. Higginson about her family: "They are religious — except me."

Those who were "religious" guarded their faith fiercely, knowing it to be threatened from all sides by mid-century currents of thought. With Amherst's rural isolation disappearing, "the latest infidelity" centered in Concord could not be kept out, though the young could be cautioned against it. A tutor at the college was specific: "Leave . . . Emerson alone," he warned. And not only of course Emerson, but all those who seemed to the faithful to be more concerned with "this world" than with the world to come. Like earlier Puritans, the faithful had to engage in battle on two fronts at once — against secularism as well as against new heretical faiths. The way the Puritan quality of mind lingered in Amherst despite all that had been happening elsewhere in the world for the past century is succinctly and amusingly revealed in a word Emily used in a letter to her brother Austin late in 1851. The whole family had just come home from meeting, and now "Father and Mother sit in state in the sitting room perusing such papers only, as they are well assured have nothing carnal in them." Brother Austin could be expected to understand; he would smile with her at their parents' fear of "the world, the flesh, and the devil" embodied for them in all things "carnal."

A year before, early in 1850, she had not been amused. Writing a school friend in a mood of earnest doubt, she speaks of how she hears the faithful talk of Jesus as their refuge and guide, then asks, "Will you tell me if it be he?" While "they" talk of Jesus, she listens and wonders, and reads Emerson's essays. For Christ-

Emerson for more than a decade. Almost certainly she had already read "Intellect" in *Essays* First Series, in which Emerson had spoken directly to her condition:

> God offers to every mind its choice between truth and repose. Take which you please, — you can never have both. Between these, as a pendulum, man oscillates. He in whom the love of repose predominates will accept the first creed, the first philosophy, the first political party he meets, — most likely his father's. . . . He in whom the love of truth predominates will keep himself aloof from all moorings, and afloat.

The poet's rejection of orthodoxy was now complete, but the language in which she conveys her rejection is drawn from the Bible and the church. Religious options have multiplied in the Dickinson family and she has chosen Transcendentalism as the faith associated in her mind with the "immortal colors." From now on the Bible will continue to be her favorite reading and the chief source of her language and images, but for revelation she will turn to "The Revelation of the Book/ Whose Genesis was June." With her father's faith rejected, she has found a wider God and a new way of asserting the claim of life against death. As she would put it a dozen years later:

> Somewhere upon the general Earth
> Itself exist Today —
> The Magic passive but extant
> That consecrated me —
>
> Indifferent Seasons doubtless play
> Where I for right to be —
> Would pay each Atom that I am
> But Immortality —
>
> Reserving that but just to prove
> Another Date of Thee —
> Oh God of Width, do not for us
> Curtail Eternity!

But now, in 1859, the sense of what she had lost was acute. Having telescoped the religious history of a century, Edwards to Emerson, into a decade, she went on "trudging to Eden, looking backward," to use a figure she once applied to David Copperfield. The belief was gone, but not the legacy of feeling:

> "Houses" — so the Wise Men tell me —
> "Mansions"! Mansions must be warm!
> Mansions cannot let the tears in,
> Mansions must exclude the storm!
>
> "Many Mansions," by "his Father,"
> I don't know him; snugly built!
> Could the Children find the way there —
> Some, would even trudge tonight!

Emily Dickinson could be said to have had two fathers and to have been deeply attached to both of them, though they pulled her in opposite directions. Emerson was as powerful an influence on her as he was on Whitman, and the evidence of her debt to him is just as clear. Her nineteenth-century readers could see this and said so, but recent scholars, beginning with George F. Whicher, have either denied it, as he did, or have only partially understood it. The fact that until Albert J. Gelpi's work on her sources came out in 1965 no scholar or critic had come even fairly close to estimating Emerson's importance to her is eloquent testimony to the disfavor in which Emerson has been held in recent years. As the Johnson indexes show, the Bible was her chief literary resource, Shakespeare next, then Emerson — this on the basis of a simple (and incomplete) numerical count of her allusions. The first two would have been the same for most writers of her period — Melville, for instance — but Emerson was in a different category. His impact on her, counterpointed against that of Edward Dickinson, was what, more than anything else, gave her work its special quality.

What Emerson meant to her is apparent not so much in the *number* of her references to him, despite his position in this respect right after the Bible and Shakespeare, as in the *nature* of them — in their tone, in the contexts in which they appear, and in the uses to which they are put. For the most part, she didn't need to quote him: He had been too thoroughly digested for that. But when she did quote, it was from memory, inaccurately, and in a kind of private shorthand language. Even without considering, for a moment, the poems, which provide all the evidence one would need to show that Emerson was essential to her, we can find in the letters alone very strong evidence that Emerson meant very much more to her than any of the writers or works she named to Higginson except the Bible.

"I had a letter," she wrote one of her former Amherst Academy teachers in 1850, " — and Ralph Emerson's Poems — a beautiful copy — from Newton the other day. I should love to read you them both — they are very pleasant to me." Her "pleasant" we may take as a typical New Englandism. A quarter of a century later she would be more explicit about what Emerson meant to her. Consoling the wife of her "preceptor" Higginson in a time of illness, she wrote, "I wish you were strong like me. I am bringing a little Granite Book you can lean upon." The book was the latest edition of *Representative Men,* just out for the Christmas trade in 1876. Dickinson knew what it meant to lean on Emerson. He had given her strength, and now, in friendship, she wanted to share this spiritual resource with Mrs. Higginson. Her "granite" may have been an allusion to the many uses of "rock" in the New Testament to mean Peter or the church. Emerson was her rock, in the shelter of which she had built her own church with its congregation of one. Implicitly she was declaring that the resources *she* leaned on were not two but three: To the consolations offered by Nature and the Bible she now added Emerson.

Higginson, with his usual obtuseness, thought this letter and gift a delicious joke. Writing his sister about a party he had attended at which the hosts improvised a game, he was in high good humor:

> The Woolseys were bright as usual & wrote some funny things for different guests — one imaginary letter to me from my partially cracked poetess at Amherst, who writes to me and signs 'Your scholar.' (N.B. She writes to Mary now and sent her Emerson's 'Representative Men' as 'a little granite book, for you to lean on'). . . .

Time has turned Higginson's delicious little joke around so that it is on him, not on the poet who had turned to him for help when she could find none in Amherst, and had given him her confidence, which we now see him betraying by making her a laughing-stock among his friends. Once more he had missed the point, as he always would, only this time he had missed it emotionally as well as intellectually. Dickinson's gift came from the heart, out of sympathy kept active by her own anguish. Friends in trouble or sorrow were constantly on her mind. Letters intended to console account for a considerable part of her correspondence, particularly in the later years. Sometimes she copied out a verse or two from the Bible and sent the quotation with a flower, without comment. Friends would know what was intended. Higginson had seen so much of her verse by this time, and read so many of her letters, that he might have been expected to know, too, even though his letter reveals that she was mistaken in thinking him a friend to be trusted.

Emerson remained a major resource to the end, despite her awareness of the criticisms that might be made of his early doctrines, criticisms that in fact he himself partly made and partly implied in *The Conduct of Life,* especially in the essay "Fate," which she almost certainly drew upon for several poems.[1] Two years before her death she copied "Tumultuous privacy of storm," her favorite line in a favorite poem, "The Snowstorm," onto a separate sheet of stationery and enclosed it, without comment, in a letter of her sister Lavinia's to Mrs. Todd. Less than a year before her death, writing to Mrs. Todd herself this time, thinking of the rewards of a trip to Europe, from which Mrs. Todd had just returned, she wrote, "The Honey you went so far to seek, I trust too you obtain." This made her think of Emerson, so she started a new paragraph: "Though was there not an 'Humbler' Bee?" And then another: "I will sail by thee alone, thou animated Torrid Zone."

The naturalness and casualness of this, the quotation inaccurately done from memory, the unconscious improvement in Emerson's line — for "sail by" is certainly better than Emerson's more abstract "follow" — these facts about the *quality* of this allusion are more important than the fact that it counts for only one more reference in an index. It is just the sort of allusion one would expect if Emerson had been so thoroughly absorbed, had become so permanent a part of the furniture of her mind, that she could draw upon him merely to make a casual letter move. When she was deliberately being "literary," or trying to suggest the breadth of her reading, she did not refer to Emerson — or, generally, to the Bible either. Emerson and the Bible were not literary but personal resources, as a study of the allusions in her letters makes very clear. The question to be asked in any study of the effect of her reading on her is not the quantitative one that can be answered by counting references to each writer or book, but the question of when and how, under what circumstances, writing to what types of people, she refers to her several chief literary resources.

Except in answer to his direct question about her reading, she never referred to the Bible, or borrowed its language, in writing Higginson, for example. Why not? Because he was not the sort of person to whom a Biblical reference would have meant much. (Of course, to him *no* sort of reference meant much, but Dickinson was either unaware, or pretended to be unaware, of that.) He would, she knew, not have thought any better of his "scholar" because of it. The Bible she saved for real friends and relatives, those she loved and trusted. But sometimes, instead of the Bible, she chose Emerson in these letters in which she was not trying to put her best foot forward. Writing, for example, a mere thank-you note for a gift of bulbs, she might draw on Emerson again to help her express how much they meant to her:

> I have long been a Lunatic on Bulbs, though screened by my friends, as Lunacy on any theme is better undivulged, but Emerson's intimacy with his "Bee" only immortalized him — .

"Lunatic" she may have been by the standards of a Higginson, but she was sane enough to have kept her sense of humor in her attitude toward both herself and Emerson. Emerson the inspirer and consoler, the great defender of the soul's right to live by its dream of truth and power, was he perhaps an Innocent? When he lectured in Amherst in 1857, she did not go to hear him but wrote a note to Sue, who did go and was enchanted: "It must have been as if he had come from where dreams are born!" Even in 1857 this would have been a slightly ambiguous compliment from her pen, for she was beginning to explore some of the conflicts between fact and dream, between truth and wish. Chiefly, though, at this time she meant to affirm the truth of Emerson's kind of dreaming against the falsehood of her family's faith.

Nearly a quarter of a century after her comment on Emerson's Amherst lecture she wrote to Higginson a comment that implies that she has now definitely located the early Emerson who had meant so much to her in the 1850's, among the Innocents slaughtered by time and fact, at the same time implying a continuing affectionate loyalty to him:

"With the Kingdom of Heaven on his knee, could Mr. Emerson hesitate?

" 'Suffer little Children' — ."

When Emerson died in 1882, just four years before her own death, she noted the fact in a letter to her close friend Judge Lord in such a way as to leave no doubt at all about how she continued to feel about him: "My Philadelphia [Charles Wadsworth] has passed from Earth, and the Ralph Waldo Emerson — whose name my Father's Law Student [Newton], taught me, has touched the secret Spring. Which Earth are we in?"

In one elegiac sentence she has included four of those she had loved and lost — her father most of all of course, and Newton and Wadsworth, both of whom had "taught" her, and Emerson — "the" Emerson, that special one, who, through his books, had taught her most of all in the critical period of her early maturity. Much that he had taught her in the beginning, she had discarded or reinterpreted by this time, as he too had by 1860, but not the independence, the valor, and the integrity that, as she believed, he had both exemplified and inculcated.

From Emerson, Dickinson got not only a religious alternative to late Calvinism but a conception of the proper role of the poet. He gave her in fact not only the general conception but the image through which the imagination could grasp it, and even the very word she normally used to suggest the image. And there is no need to try to guess *where* she found the word, the image, and the conception in his works. She found them all in the essay "Circles," in which Emerson drew out the implications of the poem with which this chapter opened.

Even from the cryptic little poem she might have got the image. To make it one's business to "Scan the profile of the sphere," as (the poem implies) one must if he is to find a "new genesis," is to study "circumference." But the word itself is not in the poem, and what the whole image means is only implied, so that if the poem were all Emerson had written about circles, we should be left wondering whether or not he was behind Dickinson's statement to Higginson in her second letter, "My Business is Circumference." The idea implied by the image is certainly Emersonian, but perhaps, as Whicher was correct in saying, such ideas were all around, so that one could hardly avoid contact with them. We might suppose that it was simply "Emersonian" but not from Emerson directly, like her statement in a later letter to Higginson which paraphrases an Emersonian idea that was such common property that no "source" need be sought:

> I was thinking, today — as I noticed, that the
> "Supernatural," was only the Natural, disclosed —
>
> Not "Revelation" — 'tis — that waits,
> But our unfurnished eyes — .

But with the essay open before us we need wonder no more.

The compactness of Dickinson's statement of the nature of her "business" as poet left Higginson, as he confessed later in an article that presents him in the best light possible, "somewhat bewildered." But if he had opened "Circles" and read it through, he might have caught a glimmering of what she meant. To be sure, Emerson's first paragraph is constructed of aphorisms almost as cryptic as Dickinson's statement:

> The eye is the first circle; the horizon which it forms is the second; and throughout nature this primary figure is repeated without end. It is the highest emblem in the cipher of the world. St. Augustine described the nature of God as a circle whose centre was everywhere and its circumference nowhere. We are all our lifetime reading the copious sense of this first of forms. . . . Our life is an apprenticeship to the truth, that around every circle another can be drawn; that there is no end in nature, but every end is a beginning; that there is always another dawn risen on mid-noon, and under every deep a lower deep opens.

The rest of the essay expands and clarifies these intuitions and applies them to various aspects of experience. But even in this first paragraph a more imaginative and intelligent reader than Higginson could find a number of suggestions for an interpretation of "circumference." To be concerned with the "highest emblem" might mean to be searching for God as "everywhere" — immanent — and "nowhere" — transcendent, not within time and space, and so in no "place" at all, not even in "Heaven." Or it might mean seeking ultimate reality in the confidence that it could be found within oneself. Or entering on a quest for the ineffable, the circle with no conceivable limit or circumference, the deep beyond all deeps. Or searching for a beginning, another dawn, a rebirth to be found in endings, the life contained in death.

The key words in the rest of the essay, repeated, in Emerson's usual fashion, over and over in different contexts, are "growth," "valor," "possibility," "revelation," "imagination," and, of course, "circles" and "circumference." The key ideas revolve around the delusiveness of the safety supposedly provided by any dogma, the superiority of new truth to old, the law that the only alternative to continued personal and intellectual growth is death, the superiority of the possible over the actual in a reality whose limits are shrouded in mystery, the imagination as the key to growth, poetry as the supreme embodiment of imagination and so the best aid to the soul's growth, and the superiority of action to comprehension, since only in action conceived in faith and guided by imagination can the truth be apprehended and the soul grow. All the ideas in the essay revolve around its call for self-transcendence.

The essay is a sufficient basis in itself for an explication not just of what Dickinson meant by "circumference" in her statement to Higginson but of several dozens of her poems, and not only those that contain the word "circumference" or one of her synonyms for it — "disk," "wheel," "arc," "Possibility," and so on, but poems on growth, valor, risk, and other subjects, in which neither the word for, nor an implied image of, a circle appears. Many of her poems that have been found most obscure cease to be obscure when put beside a sentence or passage from "Circles." I shall give just one example, hoping not to be guilty of laboriously explaining the obvious.

Emerson had written that the soul's growth toward unknown circles of being and knowing ("There is no circumference to us") required *valor,* the courage to listen to "the revelation of the new hour," but that, difficult though it was, it would be granted the "quick and strong" soul responsive to the "Omnipresence" of "the eternal generator" of circles, the soul grasped by experience and grasping it by the method of "abandonment." Dickinson compressed all this into four lines that have puzzled many of her readers:

Circumference thou Bride of Awe
Possessing thou shalt be
Possessed by every hallowed Knight
That dares to covet thee.

Emerson ends the essay with praise for enthusiasm, abandonment, a spiritual counterpart of the "dreams and drunkenness" produced by "opium and alcohol," an idea he had already expressed in "The Humble-Bee" and elsewhere and would soon include in "The Poet," an idea behind a number of Dickinson's poems. I shall also quote a part of a paragraph just before the end of the essay, in which Higginson might have found the answer to another passage that must have puzzled him in one of her first letters. Emerson writes:

> Life is a series of surprises. We do not guess to-day the mood, the pleasure, the power of to-morrow, when we are building up our being. Of lower states, of acts of routine and sense, we can tell somewhat; but the masterpieces of God, the total growths and universal movements of the soul, he hideth; they are incalculable. I can know that truth is divine and helpful; but how it shall help me I can have no guess, *for so to be* is the sole inlet of *so to know*. [Emerson's emphasis.]

In the letter to Higginson shortly before the one in which she defined her business as circumference, she apologizes for fatiguing him with details of her personal life and then, with an apparent incoherence that must have increased his bewilderment, says, "I would like to learn — Could you tell me how to grow — or it is unconveyed — like melody — or witchcraft?" If she hoped he would recognize the allusion and reply appropriately, she was overestimating him. But more likely, she didn't expect an answer: She was trying to stimulate his interest in her by asking a question she knew the answer to very well — much better than he, as it turned out.

She knew that the secret of growth could not be conveyed because she knew her Emerson. He had said that God kept it hidden, that it was incalculable — like melody or witchcraft, she added to his thought. And she knew too that it ought not to have been necessary, at a time when Emerson's reputation was at its highest point, to state explicitly the connection between wanting to *learn* and asking for the secret of *growth.* To one who knew his Emerson, the connection surely was sufficiently clear: the growth of the soul, he had said, was the only way to apprehend, and bear, new truths which the smaller or less valorous soul would find unbearable.

Immediately before telling Higginson that she wanted to *learn,* she had been telling him about her family, how her mother "did not care for thought" and her father was "too busy to notice what we do." This emphasis on her separation from her family led her to speak of her difference with them in religious matters. Her father, she said, "buys me many books — but begs me not to read them — because he fears they joggle the mind. They are religious — except me — and address an Eclipse, every morning — whom they call their 'Father.' "

To perceive herself as not "religious," in any sense that her family could accept, to realize that the faith they lived by was no longer available to her, yet not to be able even to guess how her newly perceived truth would be helpful to her, she found of course very painful, just *how* painful a reading of her early poems and letters makes abundantly clear. It required all her valor to stand erect as Emerson had said in the same essay the strong soul must, now that her father's God was in eclipse for her. Yet she *did* stand, tautly erect, now and later. Not knowing where her safety lay, or whether there was any safety, she stood, preferring, as Emerson had counseled, truth to her past perception of truth, determined to learn and grow, to "draw a new circle" that would let her being expand — though she ended her letter by confessing that her size felt small to her.

If we keep in mind Emerson's argument in "Circles," the progression of her thought in this seemingly incoherent letter is clear enough. She was saying in effect that she accepted the challenge and the risk of growth. She felt there was no need to say whether she meant growth as a person or growth as a poet, for it was just as inconceivable to her as it was to Emerson that the two could be separately considered. To grow as a person would be to grow as a poet, and to grow in poetic vision would be to get the "platform," as he had said, needed for viewing her present life and the "purchase" by which she might move it. To explore *circumference* would be at once to explore her own unknown limits and to explore the mysteries of life and death, of Immortality and the Possible, of finite existence immersed in the infinite; to explore these mysteries by means of intuition and poetic imagination, the only way, she was sure, they could profitably be explored. There is a terrible pathos in her asking this kind of help from Higginson, who not only was inadequate to teach her anything about growing, as either poet or person, but who never even understood, then or later, what question it was she was asking him.

Her most succinct poem relating to the theme of circumference suggests the answer she worked out for herself when she got no help from Higginson. She does not use the word now, though she uses one of Emerson's synonyms that she made her own, "the Possible"; and she is not, this time, trying to define the undefinable. Instead, she is making a note on methods and means of approach to the limitless, on *growth* or self-transcendence as it would be understood by a poet whose business was circumference. All the conceptual counters she is playing with here may be found in the essay — valor or heroism, action, illumination (as contrasted with mere understanding), the Possible, the imagination:

The gleam of an heroic Act
Such strange illumination
The Possible's slow fuse is lit
By the Imagination.

This is not just vaguely Emersonian, it is straight out of "Circles," and nothing in addition to that essay is needed to explicate it. But it is not one of her richest poems. Her best work was usually done when the lines of her dual heritage drew together and crossed, with the tension between them quickened at the point of crossing. In "A Route of Evanescence" both parts of her heritage and all three of her favorite "books" — the Bible, Shakespeare, and Emerson — are drawn upon and imaginatively fused:

A Route of Evanescence
With a revolving Wheel —
A Resonance of Emerald —
A Rush of Cochineal —

And every Blossom on the Bush
Adjusts its tumbled Head —
The mail from Tunis, probably,
An easy Morning's Ride —

The hummingbird that disappears almost before it is seen brings news of what Emerson, in "Circles," called "the Unattainable, the flying Perfect, around which the hands of man can never meet." But its very evanescence, the fact that it cannot be grasped by the intellect but only glimpsed, suggests the existence of larger circles or wheels. Its wings beat so rapidly that they are not seen separately as wings, only as a circular blur, like a segment of a revolving wheel, which only the imagination can complete. Even its colors, emerald and cochineal (red) are revelations: They are the colors of the throne of God as described in the book of Revelation, 4:3.

The message brought ("probably") by the visitor to the garden who disappears so quickly that his presence is known chiefly by its effect on the flowers, *may* be from "the Queen of Tunis," who, in Shakespeare's "The Tempest" (II, 1, 246–248) is said to dwell "ten leagues beyond man's life." If so, he is bringing news from beyond the grave ("When Cogs — stop — that's Circumference — / The Ultimate — of Wheels"), news of realities we can never really *see* or *know,* but that the poet, who imaginatively completes the circle suggested by unseen wings, can make available to our imaginations. Where the plain man would have seen only a spot of bright color and a blur, the poet has seen an illimitable circumference.[2] This is what she thought was the true business of the poet. As she had put it some fifteen years earlier, "Poets light but Lamps — / Themselves — go out — / . . . . Disseminating . . . / Circumference."

Critics who wish to find a single meaning in Dickinson's work — the "real" or "deeper" meaning they usually call it — need only select the poems that "prove" their point and ignore the rest. Is she a poet of faith, resting her faith on an Emersonian intuition? We have "I never saw a moor" and many others like it to prove the point. Does she reject all faith for empirical observation? We have

"Faith" is a fine invention
When Gentlemen can *see* —
But *Microscopes* are prudent
In an Emergency

in which, probably inspired by the passage discussing man's inventiveness in Emerson's "Fate," she uses the Biblical metaphor of *seeing with the eyes of faith* to suggest that those who — like herself presumably — don't *have* faith had better turn to some other means of seeing. The poem might be used to introduce a great many in which she asks, in effect, what is the *evidence?*

Is she a "modern," "one of us," a humanistic naturalist like Wallace Stevens, as a whole book has argued? Then cite this:

The Props assist the House
Until the House is built
And then the Props withdraw
And adequate, erect,
The House support itself
And cease to recollect
The augur and the Carpenter —
Just such a retrospect
Hath the perfected Life —
A past of Plank and Nail
And slowness — then the Scaffolds drop
Affirming it a Soul.

Here she seems to be saying not just that she is getting along fine without faith — the "Props" — but that, as Nietzsche was saying at the same time, the death of God is necessary for the achievement of true selfhood. This rejection of "props" prepares us for the rejection of "balm" in a poem Johnson places on the same page of *The Complete Poems*:

Ourselves we do inter with sweet derision.
The channel of the dust who once achieves
Invalidates the balm of that religion
That doubts as fervently as it believes.

If it were argued that because Johnson tentatively assigns the two poems I have just quoted to 1869, the "humanism" they express was the point of view toward which she was moving, after having lost first her father's faith and then Emerson's, what should we say about "And with what body do they come?" which belongs to 1880? The poem affirms faith in immortality:

> "And with what body do they come?" —
> Then they *do* come — Rejoice!
> What Door — What Hour — Run — run — My Soul!
> Illuminate the House!

Based on First Corinthians, 15:35–36 ("But some man will say, How are the dead raised up? and with what body do they come? Thou fool, that which thou sowest is not quickened, except it die.") this poem was sent in a letter to Perez Cowan, Dickinson's favorite "Cousin Peter," to console him for the death of a daughter. Must we suppose that the poet didn't really "mean" this poem, that her desire to console was stronger than her honesty, so that she knew herself to be writing merely comforting nonsense?

To answer that no poet ever "means" his poems, that as an artist-craftsman he simply uses ideas and points of view for the sake of making poems, and that *this* is his "business," will not do when we are discussing Dickinson any more than when we are discussing Emerson or Thoreau or Whitman. For all of them, poetry is a form of, or a means to, illumination, and the poet is a seer or visionary first of all, and only secondarily, *if* at all, a "craftsman," an "artificer." Fantastic distortions result when we view romantic poets through the lens of Eliot's "impersonal" theory of art. The question "*Did* she mean it?" or "*How* did she mean it?" is not at all an irrelevant response when we read "And with what body do they come?" after reading "Ourselves we do inter with sweet derision." Dickinson's conception of poetry is clearly enough expressed in a good many poems that offer no difficulties of interpretation — "This was a Poet," "I would not paint — a picture," "I found the words to every thought," "To pile like Thunder to its close," and "I dwell in Possibility," for example. The view is familiar, and she never qualifies or complicates it: The artist's concern is with the ineffable, and his poems are revelations of truth, the kind of truth only the imagination can glimpse.

We are left, then, with Dickinson's lack of consistency in belief as a problem. There are three considerations that may help us to reduce the size of the problem. The first involves considering once again her Emersonian heritage; the second, considering the correspondents being addressed in the case of the poems she enclosed in letters; the third, looking for signs of *growth* in her work.

Two poems will take us quickly into the first, the Emersonian, consideration. In the first, she writes a comment on Emerson's "Days": the real reason why we get only "herbs and apples," the practical gifts, instead of "stars, and sky that holds them all," is not, as Emerson had implied, that we *choose* wrongly, but that Nature *gives* us no choice, will not let us inside the show, *keeps* its meanings to itself:

> Dew — is the Freshet in the Grass —
> 'Tis many a tiny Mill
> Turns unperceived beneath our feet
> And Artisan lies still —
>
> We spy the Forests and the Hills
> The Tents to Nature's Show
> Mistake the Outside for the in
> And mention what we saw
>
> Could Commentators on the Sign
> Of Nature's Caravan
> Obtain "Admission" as a Child
> Some Wednesday Afternoon.

But two poems later in the Johnson edition we read this, which is in effect a comment on the comment:

> My Cocoon tightens — Colors teaze —
> I'm feeling for the Air —
> A dim capacity for Wings
> Demeans the Dress I wear —
>
> A power of butterfly must be —
> The Aptitude to fly

Meadows of Majesty concedes
And easy Sweeps of Sky —

So I must baffle at the Hint
And cipher at the Sign
And make much blunder, if at last
I take the clue divine —

What this says in effect is that we are not necessarily forever to be kept outside. We may "take the clue divine" and come to read nature's Signs correctly, if we have an "Aptitude to fly." In another mood now, the poet blames herself, where before she had blamed the nature of things. Emerson could have told her — did tell her — that responding intuitively to nature's meanings was not at all like doing algebra, so that to "cipher at the Sign" would be a sure way of remaining outside the mystery. The two poems belong together as parts of a dialogue. In the second the faithful self answers the skeptical self, saying, as Prufrock would say much later, that she too much debates these matters. Emerson would have approved the second poem as much as he would have deplored the first.

The problem of "consistency" tends to disappear when we look at her poems this way. They are interdependent, a body of work, no one of them attempting to present "the whole Truth," not aiming at general "truth" abstractly considered at all indeed, not attempting, even in their entirety, *as* a body of work, to construct a "philosophy," but recording movements of the mind responding to "the revelation of the new hour." Once again Alice James's *Diary* is a helpful analogue. Dickinson's poems were *her* diary. Both women were interested in creating a record of what it felt like to live day by day awaiting death. Both felt the sharpest obligation to truth, but the truth they were interested in was the truth of *experience*. One could experience ideas as well as things. One watched ideas go through the mind, watched emotions forming, watched even the debate one carried on with oneself. One might think of Dickinson's poems as a record of a continuous dialogue between parts of herself, aspects of her mind, segments of her complex heritage; except that there are not just the two speakers required by dialogue but always a third, a watcher and listener, amused or dismayed, aware of the limitations of what can be conveyed by words, superior to all dialogue. This ultimate self watches the self writing in the diary or engaging in poetic debate. This self is absolute.

Lad of Athens, faithful be
To Thyself,
And Mystery —
All the rest is Perjury —

The "lad of Athens" is probably Dionysius the Areopagite, of whom we read in Acts 17:34 that he was one of those converted by Paul's preaching on Mars Hill in Athens. Prior to his conversion, he was presumably also one of those whom Paul accused of worshipping a "God Unknown." The poem, which Johnson tentatively dates only a few years before the poet's death, tells us how well she understood what Emerson had meant by "self-reliance" and how much the idea continued to mean to her to the end. The self to which one must be faithful was deeper than the rational or the believing self, deeper than all proof and all argument, a self, as he had said, with no known or knowable circumference. Not to rely on *this* self would be to refuse all ultimate responsibility. *This* self might entertain any sort of argument, consider any sort of evidence, face any fact, and remain, as Whitman put it, "imperturbable." No merely logical contradiction could embarrass it.

The poem also tells us what Emerson had meant by his warning against a "foolish consistency." The thrust of his aphorism is against our superficial selves, our social and conventional and worldly selves, which he fears may prevent our being true to the deeper self. The thrust is against the claim of propositional reason to be the arbiter of truth, against the kind of concern for logical consistency that would prevent us from changing our minds, once we had become committed to a proposition, against being imprisoned in our own categories. If in fact as he said "there is no circumference to us," then the only consistency that matters might better be called by another name, perhaps integrity. Emerson's warning is in effect a plea, a plea for openness, for growth, for never closing the circle.

"Philosophic" consistency would not be expected of a poet who held such ideas as these. Even when she argued against him, Dickinson was true to Emerson's principles. *Everything* is perjury that does not spring from faithfulness to the self that transcends all argument and all knowing.

The second consideration bearing upon her inconsistency, the poems enclosed in letters, may be treated more briefly. Naturally enough, and quite properly, the poet enclosed in her letters poems appropriate to the correspondent and the occasion. She sent "Faith is a fine invention" to Mrs. Samuel Bowles, who was a very "liberal" Protestant, while "And with what body do they come?" was enclosed in a letter to Perez Cowan, a rather orthodox trinitarian minister. Just as she addressed her Norcross cousins, in her letters, in very different terms from those she used in addressing the Bowleses, so she enclosed different sorts of poems in her letters to her different correspondents. No doubt when she composed a poem for the occasion, she was influenced by sympathetic consideration of the views of the intended recipient.

But if the preceding discussion of the effect of her Emersonian heritage is valid, this fact — her tendency to respond to people in their own terms, and so to select, or to write, poems for inclusion in letters to them that would speak to them — this fact by no means implies any degree of "insincerity" on her part, nor does it support the view of those who would make her a "technician" unconcerned with ideas, as certain post-Eliot poets might be said to be. Simply, she was capable of entertaining, and taking seriously, various points of view, including even contradictory ones. But she was also exceptionally sensitive to the responses of *people*.

If her only consistency was the consistency of growth, we ought to be able to say something about the direction of that growth, perhaps even discern its stages. Until recently, this was impossible, but now that we have Johnson's editions of the letters and the poems, most of them dated, we can at least make a start. But it will have to be a very tentative start, partly because I shall have to assume the correctness of Johnson's dating of letters and poems, but even more because the subject is large enough, and complex enough, for a book that has yet to be written. A "perhaps" should be understood as preceding all the major assertions in what follows.

Reading all the poems at one time, so that one has them more or less in mind all at once, has resulted, in this reader, in several preliminary impressions. Apart from the love poems and occasional poems — saying goodbye to a friend, writing a thank-you note in verse — the majority of her poems may be classified as relating to one of three subjects on which she was always debating within herself. She debated with her father on the subject of the validity of his faith, she debated with Emerson on the validity of *his,* and she debated with both of them, her *two* fathers as it were, on the question of whether there could be any valid faith at all, as they both thought.

Logically, she had won the debate with her father at least as early as 1859, but the debate continued for many years, for her victory was of the mind only, not the heart, and she found herself drawn back again and again to questions she had already resolved. Some of her finest poems on this subject date from as late as the early 1870's. Meanwhile the debate with Emerson had begun in the early 1860's, at a time when personal crises made her feel that pain and limitation ought to be given a central place in any description of experience, not ignored or mentioned only as an afterthought in what she came to feel was Emerson's way in his early essays. Sometimes, in these years, she drew upon late Emerson to rebut the Emerson who had freed her from her father's faith, as in "I had not minded — Walls," which takes note of "limitation" in images drawn from "Fate" in *The Conduct of Life.* By 1875 she had made all the criticisms of Emerson's early doctrines she was ever to make. "Unto the Whole — how add?" was so devastating a critique of the master's Transcendental faith considered as a *religion* that it left nothing more to be said; and for once she said nothing more in this vein. Though some of her later poems might have been written by Emerson himself, it is the Emerson of *The Conduct of Life* that we find in them, not the Emerson of the Transcendental dawn.

The third subject of the inner dialogue recorded in her poems, the debate in which her skeptical self opposed both her "fathers," began in the early 1860's, reached its peak in the late sixties and early seventies, and then was dropped entirely. Among the poems dated by Johnson in the years from 1879 on until her death in 1886, not one of them returns to the question of whether *any* sort of religious faith is possible for one both informed and honest with himself. "Faith" in these last poems comes to be thought of as a "venture" of the soul with no expectation of "proof" from either a sacred book or the sign language of nature. Whereas both her father and Emerson had thought that their very different faiths had rested on some sort of revelation, divine or natural, and would have agreed that without revelation there could *be* no faith, Dickinson came to believe that far from being required by anything we could "know" about a reality outside ourselves, faith was simply a "first necessity" of our being, resting on nothing but need.

Redefining faith as commitment in the manner of later Existentialists was agonizingly difficult. Against both of her "fathers" she had urged lack of evidence, an insufficiency of revelation. Increasingly in the 1860's she had found God faceless and nature silent, until by 1868 she could announce, "That odd old man is dead a year," and in the following year anticipate Frost's "Design," in its picture of a universe in which, if there is any "design," any teleology, it is a "design of darkness" too dark for us to penetrate; or else, it may be, of a universe in which the apparent last word that evil has is real and final as well as apparent ("Physiognomy"); or, if neither of these surmises is true, then at least it must be said that the God who saves some and damns others has not revealed his intentions ("Himself himself inform"):

> A Spider sewed at Night
> Without a Light
> Upon an Arc of White.
>
> If Ruff it was of Dame
> Or Shroud of Gnome
> Himself himself inform.
>
> Of Immortality
> His Strategy
> Was Physiognomy.

In the same year she had written what is perhaps her most despairing poem, beginning "The Frost of Death was on the Pane" and concluding

> We hated Death and hated Life
> And nowhere was to go
> Than Sea and continent there is
> A larger — it is Woe.

It was out of such despair as this that her redefinition of faith came, and with it, a new acceptance of life as tragic but not necessarily meaningless. The new definition is best expressed in an early poem, written at a time when she already knew theoretically what her heart could not yet accept:

> Faith is the Pierless Bridge
> Supporting what We see
> Unto the Scene that We do not —
> Too slender for the eye
>
> It bears the Soul as bold
> As it were rocked in Steel
> With Arms of Steel at either side —
> It joins — behind the Vail
>
> To what, could We presume
> The Bridge would cease to be
> To Our far, vacillating Feet
> A first Necessity.

When in the years after 1879 she returned to the subject of the nature of faith itself, she reaffirmed the definition she had first achieved at a time when it could not help her. A little poem of 1881 will serve as an example of many similar ones:

> Not seeing, still we know —
> Not knowing, guess —
> Not guessing, smile and hide
> And half caress —
>
> And quake — and turn away,
> Seraphic fear —
> Is Eden's innuendo
> "If you dare"?

Her new "proveless" faith did not cancel anything she knew. It left her as aware as ever of "transport's instability" (contra Emerson), of the impossibility of imagining "costumeless consciousness" (contra her father and personal immortality), aware of what it meant to "cling to nowhere" waiting for the "Crash of nothing." Yet it did have two effects. More often now she returns to Emersonian sentiments like those of "A Route of Evanescence," which dates from this period. Emerson might have written

Estranged from Beauty — none can be —
For Beauty is Infinity —
And power to be finite ceased
Before Identity was leased.

Or this:

No matter where the Saints abide,
They make their Circuit fair
Behold how great a Firmament
Accompanies a Star.

The other effect was on the tone of her references to the Bible. Though she still thought it as a whole "an Antique Volume — / Written by faded Men/ At the suggestion of Holy Spectres," more often now she wrote of Christ sympathetically —

Obtaining but our own Extent
In whatsoever Realm —
'Twas Christ's own personal Expanse
That bore him from the Tomb —

or with gentle humor —

The Savior must have been
A docile Gentleman —
To come so far so cold a Day
For little Fellowmen —

The Road to Bethlehem
Since He and I were Boys
Was leveled, but for that 'twould be
A rugged billion Miles — .

More often now the *example* of Christ seemed relevant to her:

How brittle are the Piers
On which our Faith doth tread —
No Bridge below doth totter so —

Yet none hath such a Crowd.

It is as old as God —
Indeed — 'twas built by him —
He sent his Son to test the Plank,
And he pronounced it firm.

Her finest expression of what Christ had come to mean to her would probably have pleased even her father, if he had still been alive to read it and she had shown it to him. Remembering the petition with which her early sampler had ended, we may decide that in her last years, the name of Christ *was* written on her heart, whether she could see all the letters or not:[3]

The Road was lit with Moon and star —
The Trees were bright and still —
Descried I — by the distant Light
A Traveller on a Hill —
To magic Perpendiculars
Ascending, though Terrene —
Unknown his shimmering ultimate —
But he indorsed the sheen —

So she arrived at the simple, almost doctrineless, but existentially meaningful faith she expressed most succinctly two years before her death:

Though the great Waters sleep,
That they are still the Deep,
We cannot doubt —
No vacillating God
Ignited this Abode
To put it out — .

The development I have been tracing through the poems is apparent simply from an inspection of the poems themselves, without considering any external evidence. But the letters tell the same story, often using some of the same phrases. For instance, writing of the death of her mother some two years before she wrote the poem just quoted, she says:

She slipped from our fingers like a flake gathered by the wind, and is now part of the drift called "the infinite."

We don't know where she is, though so many tell us.

I believe we shall in some manner be cherished by our Maker — that the One who gave us this remarkable earth has the power still farther to surprise that which He has caused. Beyond that all is silence. . . .

Writing a friend at Christmas the same year (1882), to thank her for a Christmas gift, she epitomizes most of what I have been saying about the growth of her mind as I have traced it through the poems. This letter was written when her own griefs and losses were piling up faster and faster, when her own health was precarious and her death not far off, but in it we may see the familiar dialogic play of a keen and restless mind, the familiar valor, the old gallant attempt to strengthen another perhaps less strong, the old movement of the mind between Emerson and the Bible, with the difference that now they no longer seem to conflict and she has at last made her peace with them both:

To Mrs. J. G. Holland *after Christmas 1882*

Sweet Sister.

The lovely recollection — the thought of those that cannot "taste" — of one to whose faint Bed all Boons were brought before revealed, made the sweet Package mighty — It came so long it knows the way and almost comes itself, like Nature's faithful Blossoms whom no one summons but themselves, Magics of Constancy —

The Fiction of "Santa Claus" always reminds me of the reply to my early question of "Who made the Bible" — "Holy Men moved by the Holy Ghost," and though I have now ceased my investigations, the Solution is insufficient —

Santa Claus, though, *illustrates* — Revelation

But a Book is only the Heart's Portrait — every Page a Pulse —

Thank you for the protecting words — The petit Shepherd would find us but a startled Flock, not an unloving one —

Remember me to your Possessions, in whom I have a tender claim, and take sweet care of the small Life, fervor has made great — deathless as Emerson's "Squirrel" —

Vinnie gives her love and will write, if a Lady goes away who is calling here — Maggie prized your remembrance — Austin seldom calls — I am glad you were glad to see him — He visits rarely as Gabriel —

Lovingly,
Emily —

The last words she put to paper compress the themes of a lifetime and suggest that the valor and the ability to love that had enabled her to live with doubt and to grow did not leave her at the end:

To Higginson, who was ill *early May 1886*
Deity — does He live now?
My friend — does he breathe?

To Her Norcross Cousins *May 1886*
Little Cousins,
Called back.
Emily.

Dickinson has often been thought of as deprived and weakened by the narrowness of Amherst culture, by the emotional ties that bound her so closely to her family and her home, by the inner necessities that confined her first to house and garden and finally to her room. There is a sense in which it is quite true that she *was* deprived — of personal contact with other artists of comparable stature, even of contact with minds equal to hers and concerned with the same problems. Except in her reading, she was isolated from the best thought and the best minds of the time. None of her correspondents, with the possible exception of Helen Hunt Jackson, was capable of meeting her on her own intellectual level. But it has not often been seen how she managed to turn her deprivation into a source of strength.

I suspect we ought to think of the obtuseness and conventionalism that kept Higginson from recognizing the quality of her work as fortunate, for if he had been able to understand her and help her to get published, she might have been drawn to his kind of vapid idealism and bland moralism. As it was, she had no temptation to write in any way other than to please herself and her ideal reader. Higginson was incapable of corrupting her by drawing her out of her isolation into his own world of borrowed feelings and second-rate ideas.

When, after her death, he had been reluctantly persuaded to edit some of her poems for publication, first-rate minds immediately began to recognize her for one of themselves. The comment Alice James entered in her *Diary* upon reading the poems shortly after their publication is very much to the point:

> It is reassuring to hear the English pronouncement that Emily Dickinson is fifth-rate, they have such a capacity for missing quality; the robust evades them equally with the subtle. Her being sicklied o'er with T. W. Higginson makes one quake lest there be a latent flaw which escapes one's vision — but what tomes of philosophy *resumes* the cheap farce or expresses the highest point of view of the aspiring soul more completely than the following —
>
> How dreary to be somebody
> How public, like a frog
> To tell your name the livelong day
> To an admiring bog!

Dickinson at times would have liked to endure for a while the dreariness of being "somebody," but she found no way of reaching the "admiring bog" — for even Higginson, though his mind was sufficiently boggy, was not *admiring*. Failure, then, partly endured, partly sought, condemned her to be what she was and make do with what she had. What she had culturally was a uniquely fortunate dual heritage that condensed for her the poetic and spiritual resources of past and present and that, by eliminating the peripheral and the merely timely, kept her work in the main stream of the great tradition in American poetry. If one were forced to choose just one poet to illuminate the nature and quality of American poetry as a whole, to define its continuing preoccupations, its characteristic themes and images, its diction and its style — even to suggest the kinds of subjects and concerns typically *absent* in it — one ought to choose Dickinson.

There are very few important American poets either before or after her whose work is not suggested somewhere in hers, whose images she did not try out, whose insights she did not recapitulate, criticize, or anticipate. She not only bridged the gap between Edward Taylor and Emerson, she bridged the one between Emerson and Frost — and even, more rarely but distinctly enough — between Emerson and Eliot and Stevens. All this came as her special sensibility responded to her limited experience, and responded chiefly in terms of the Bible, Shakespeare, and Emerson. She would have been poorer without Shakespeare, but the Bible and Emerson, their conflict and their coherence, were what chiefly shaped her ideas, her language, her sensibility, and even her choice of verse forms.

The "common meter" which is the basis for almost all her work she adopted from the hymns she was hearing in "meeting" every Sunday. That the meter and stanzaic form of most of the older hymns was the same as that of the traditional folk ballads and the commonest nursery rhymes was a positive advantage from the Emersonian point of view that was hers by the time she reached poetic maturity. To write in this simplest and most "natural" of forms, the form chosen by Samuel Johnson when he extemporized a quatrain to illustrate for Boswell his idea that the mere presence of verse does not guarantee the presence of poetry —

> I put my hat upon my head
> And walked into the Strand,
> And there I met another man
> Whose hat was in his hand — .

to write in this form would ensure that, whatever her verse might be like, it would not be that mere "tinkling of piano strings" that Emerson had condemned. In *this* form she would have to *say* something, or the result would be nothing at all.

Her earliest poem, apart from the sampler, is her verse Valentine of 1850. It begins like this:

> Awake ye muses nine, sing me a strain divine,
> Unwind the solemn twine, and tie my Valentine!

If she had only gone on like *this,* Higginson would have realized that she was writing *poetry.* But the voice here is not her own. Prosody and language, along with ideas drawn from her early reading of Emerson, are being used for merely humorous effect. For serious poetry, for poetry that could convey "the noiseless noise in the garden" that she listened for and wanted to make others hear, for the news conveyed in her "letter to the world," she would have to find a form of her own, as Emerson had said so emphatically and repeatedly. If she wanted to be a "true poet," and not just a person "of poetical talents, or of industry and skill in metre," he had said, she would have to find a way of making the "argument" create the "metre."

It was no accident that she turned to the form preferred by writers of hymns and ballads and nursery rhymes — a form debased in our time to being used in advertising jingles — and used it as freely as she felt the occasion demanded. It was a children's form — and she thought of herself increasingly, after she was twenty, as a little girl — or sometimes as a little boy, a little tippler, or even a little gnome. It had the great advantage of not being a "literary" form — though Wigglesworth had used it, and Bryant occasionally, and Emerson often. It suggested to her not literature but life — her own, for in it the most important things had been said. She might have heard sung a hymn new in her youth but written in the old form:

> There is a green hill far away
> Without a city wall,
> Where our dear Lord was crucified
> Who died to save us all.

But whether she heard this one or not does not matter, for Watts's *Christian Psalmody* and his *Psalms, Hymns, and Spiritual Songs,* both part of her father's library and used in her church, were full of both this meter, and its variations, and this *thought,* and *its* variations. (The edition edited by Samuel Worcester, available to her both at church and at home, also contained the suggestion for her use of dashes, on which so much foolishness has got into print. Worcester explained his frequent use of dashes in his versions of Watts's hymns by saying that "The dash is intended to denote an expressive suspension.") If now in the first flush of her revolt against her father's religion she chose to deny the thought, how better deny it than in the form in which the thought was most commonly expressed, a form that would not seem to be a real poetic "form" at all but simply a *vehicle* for thought? The chief problem created by such a choice might be to keep the poems from sounding too much like

Mary had a little lamb,
Its fleece was white as snow,
And everywhere that Mary went,
The lamb was sure to go

but that could be prevented by deliberate roughening of meter, by using slant rhymes or none, by breaking up the stanza, or by doing all three at once. This form and the variations of it — listed and named by Watts — not only provided the pattern for almost all of her early poems, but was used without need for any significant alteration in most of the greatest poems of her late maturity, such as "A Route of Evanescence," "A single Clover Plank," "The Road was lit with Moon and Star," " 'And with what body do they come'," "Glass was the Street — in tinsel Peril," "My life closed twice before its close," and many others.

The advantage the form had for her of which she was *conscious* is made clear in a poem short enough, and interesting enough, to bear partial repetition:

The murmuring of Bees, has ceased
But murmuring of some
Posterior, prophetic,
Has simultaneous come.
The lower metres of the Year
When Nature's laugh is done
The Revelations of the Book
Whose Genesis was June.
Appropriate Creatures to her change
The Typic Mother sends
As Accent fades to interval
With separating Friends

Till what we speculate, has been
And thoughts we will not show
More intimate with us become
Than Persons, that we know.

The poem is richer of course than a mere comment on form, on choice of "meters," but something about that choice is surely *one* of the things it is saying. "Lower" and more "natural" meters are appropriate to the time; when the murmuring of bees is heard no more in reality, it had better not be heard in too melodious verse. Here, as so often, she foreshadows both Frost and Stevens, particularly the former's "Oven Bird" and the latter's "Sad Strains of a Gay Waltz." Her meters were one of her strategies for dealing with a world she anticipated both of them in seeing as "diminished," as Frost would put it. As *she* had put it in an earlier poem, poets in her time had to learn to sing "a few prosaic days," after the bright autumnal colors were gone and before the snow came. How better to do this than in the commonest and plainest of forms?

One of her late poems will illustrate what she learned to do with a form associated chiefly in her mind with doggerel and jingles — how she created a new poetic intensity of suggestion in a form recommended to her chiefly by its prosaic, almost its antipoetic quality. There are no murmurings of bees in the following poem, dating from about 1872, but the "music" of idea that has found its form:

Like Rain it sounded till it curved
And then I knew 'twas Wind —
It walked as wet as any Wave
But swept as dry as sand —
When it had pushed itself away
To some remotest Plain
A coming as of Hosts was heard
That was indeed the Rain —
It filled the Wells, it pleased the Pools
It warbled in the Road —
It pulled the spigot from the Hills

And let the Floods abroad —
It loosened acres, lifted seas
The sites of Centres stirred
Then like Elijah rode away
Upon a Wheel of Cloud.

The Bible and Emerson unite here, the Bible supplying imagery that is finally interpreted in Emersonian terms that alter but do not cancel the Biblical meanings. Is it then a Biblical poem or a Transcendental one? The answer of course is that it is both and it is neither. It springs from an amalgamation of her two heritages that by this time was peculiarly her own.

The Biblical sources are I Kings, Chapters 17 and 18; II Kings, 2:1, II Kings, 2:11; and Ezekiel, Chapter 1. The passages in first and second Kings tell of Elijah, who recalled his people to the worship of the true God. Behind the poem is the drought, recorded in I Kings, with which the Lord punished the Israelites for their apostasy. During the course of the drought, Elijah performed a miracle of resurrection:

> And he stretched himself upon the child three times, and cried unto the Lord, and said, O Lord my God, I pray thee, let this child's soul come into him again.
>
> And the Lord heard the voice of Elijah; and the soul of the child came into him again, and he revived.
>
> — I Kings, 17:21–22

Having asked the people how long they would "halt . . . between two opinions" and having mocked them for worshipping Baal, Elijah rebuilt the broken altar, "and it came to pass . . . that the heaven was black with clouds and wind, and there was a great rain" (I Kings, 18:45). Second Kings provides the image of a "whirlwind," and of a chariot of fire, drawn by horses of fire, in which the Lord carried Elijah up into heaven — the image utilized in the last two lines of the poem. But the vision of God in the first chapter of Ezekiel is perhaps the most crucial of the three Biblical sources. Here again we have a whirlwind, but this time it does not carry the prophet away, but brings him a vision: "out of the midst thereof came the likeness of four living creatures. And this was their appearance; they had the likeness of a man."

These creatures of dream with their multiple faces and wings but their "likeness of a man" appeared to be carried in, or perhaps to be synonymous with, a mystic vehicle composed of nothing but wheels: "and their appearance and their work was as it were a wheel in the middle of a wheel"; "for the spirit of the living creature was in the wheels":

> And when they went, I heard the noise of their wings, like the noise of great waters, as the voice of the Almighty, the voice of speech, as the noise of an host. . . .
>
> And above the firmament . . . was the likeness of a throne . . . and upon the likeness of the throne was the likeness as the appearance of a man. . . .
>
> As the appearance of the bow that is in the cloud in the day of rain, so was the appearance of the brightness round about. This was the appearance of the likeness of the glory of the Lord. And when I saw it, I fell upon my face, and I heard a voice of one that spake.
>
> And he said unto me, Son of man, stand upon thy feet, and I will speak unto thee.
>
> — Ezekiel 1:24–28: 2:1

This vision of Ezekiel's has often been interpreted, as it was by Blake, as a vision of man lifted up into god-likeness. If this is the way Dickinson read it, as I suspect, then the Lord's command, stand upon thy feet, conforms exactly to Emerson's advice and is a part of the meaning of the poem. And the Biblical image also matches Emerson's image of spiritual growth; for in "Circles" he had written that only "the force of the individual soul" determined "the extent to which this generation of circles, wheel without wheel," could go. Just two final notes and I shall leave the matter of sources. The sea in Dickinson's poems is almost always, and certainly here, death, which would make "lifted" seas consistent with the resurrection imagery of the Biblical sources (Revelation, 21:1,4: "a new heaven and a new earth . . . no more sea . . . no more death."); and the "Centres" whose sites are stirred should be interpreted, I think, as an allusion to that definition of God that Dickinson had got from Emerson — as a being whose center was everywhere and circumference nowhere.

If we recall how Emerson had defined reality as "a system of concentric circles," and how often Dickinson used the image of the wheel to suggest what she called, with Emerson, "circumference," we may perhaps interpret the "Wheel of Cloud" as the ultimate of circumference. But whatever the poem means, it is clear that it could not have been written at all if either part of the poet's heritage had been missing. It might be described as a Biblical poem containing its own Emersonian gloss.

If, by concentrating so exclusively on Emerson and the Bible as essential to the special quality and special achievement of her work, I have by this time created the impression that Emerson and the Bible were all she knew, that impression was far from intended. She read constantly and penetratingly. Hawthorne, for instance, was probably second only to Emerson among those who shaped her imagination, important enough to her at any rate to prompt her once to think of herself as Hepzibah, that forlorn old maid; important enough to provide the source of "I heard a Fly buzz — when I died — ." [4] Forgetting about her art for the moment, we may say that the quality of her *thought* alone would put this somewhat hysterical woman in a class with the best minds of her age.

Take for example her criticisms of Emerson. Apart from differences of temperament and situation which made her say of the Master in effect just what Melville scribbled in the margin of one of Emerson's essays, that this man must never have experienced a toothache, some of her criticisms of the early philosophy considered as a substitute for her father's religion anticipated by a quarter of a century the criticism that William James would make in *The Varieties of Religious Experience*. When, in his "Conclusion," James turned from his discussion of what seemed to him, speaking as a scientist and philosopher, *verifiable* statements about religious experience, and began, brave spirit that he was, to offer his own "over-beliefs" — that is, beliefs beyond the available *evidence* — he told his audience why, despite his inability to accept any religious orthodoxy, he preferred to continue to use the word "God" rather than to follow Emerson's example and say something like "Over-Soul" or "eternal generator of circles." "God," he wrote,

> is the natural appellation, for us Christians at least, for the supreme reality, so I will call this higher part of the universe by the name of God. . . . [In doing so, he

> said he was only following] the instinctive belief of mankind: God is real since he produces real effects. [Then, as a footnote to the first of these sentences, he added:] Transcendentalists are fond of the term "Over-soul," but as a rule they use it in an intellectualist sense, as meaning only a medium of communion. "God" is a causal agent as well as a medium of communion, and that is the aspect which I wish to emphasize. [Then, in the "Postscript," footnoting the sentence, "Both instinctively and for logical reasons, I find it hard to believe that principles can exist which make no difference in facts," he thinks again of Transcendentalism as his best example:]
>
> Transcendental idealism, of course, insists that its ideal world makes *this* difference, that facts *exist.* We owe it to the Absolute that we have a world of fact at all. "A world" of fact! — that exactly is the trouble. An entire world is the smallest unit with which the Absolute can work, whereas to our finite minds work for the better ought to be done within this world, setting in at single points. Our difficulties and our ideals are all piecemeal affairs, but the Absolute can do no piecework for us; so that all the interests which our poor souls compass raise their heads too late. We should have spoken earlier, prayed for another world absolutely, before this world was born. It is strange, I have heard a friend say, to see this blind corner into which Christian thought has worked itself at last, with its God who can raise no particular weight whatever, who can help us with no private burden, and who is on the side of our enemies as much as he is on our own. Odd evolution from the God of David's psalms!

There is also a very close parallel between the poet's thoughts and the scientist-philosopher's on what might be meant if one called the self "transcendent," as he did, or simply assumed transcendence without using the word, as she did. James might be paraphrasing a dozen Dickinson poems when, in his "Conclusion" to *Varieties,* he first states his conviction, then adds his "over-belief" on the dimensions of the self:

> The reason [why the "scientific attitude" is "shallow" when used to explain away religion] is that, so long as we deal with the cosmic and the general, we deal only with the symbols of reality, but *as soon as we deal with private and personal phenomena as such, we deal with realities in the completest sense of the term. . . .* [Italics James's. And now the over-belief.] The further limits of our being plunge, it seems to me, into an altogether other dimension of existence from the sensible and merely "understandable" world. Name it the mystical region, or the supernatural region, whichever you choose.

I shall cite as a last example of the sophistication of the thinking of this secluded and tortured woman a comment by Henry James the novelist on the question of "Immortality," a word that occupies so prominent a place in all her poetry. Since the James family has been drawn upon so often already in this discussion, in my effort to counter the currently prominent, and I fear growing, notion that Dickinson ought to be thought of either as a quaint provincial, or as a compulsive neurotic, in her thinking about time and death and religious faith as required by belief in the transcendence of the self, no one will be surprised.

Over and over in her last years, we recall, Dickinson had said that the *evidence* available to her, lacking as she did any such mystical experience as Whitman had had,[5] was insufficient to support any definite religious belief on the subject at all, so that all she had to go on was her "uncertain certainty," her "guess" or "surmise," and her willed commitment to the Possible. As she said in one poem, "Of Death I try to think like this." To "try" to think is to be aware of the whole extent of the problem.

In the conclusion of the essay "Is There a Life After Death?" which he contributed in 1910 to a volume called *In After Days, Thoughts on the Future Life,* James, who was no more a philosopher than she, not only reached something very like her conclusion but reached it by a similar route. The poet's *trying* to think he put as *liking* to think, a change of wording which, in the context of such a discussion, amounted to no change at all in attitude and assumption. We cannot know, he wrote, how we *ought* to think about such matters, but

> If I am talking, at all events, of what I "like" to think, I may, in short, say all: I like to think it open to me to establish speculative and imaginative connections, to take up conceived presumptions and pledges, that have for me all the air of not being decently able to escape redeeming themselves. And when once such a mental relation to the question as that begins to hover and settle, who shall say over what fields of experience, past and current, and what immensities of perception and yearning, it shall *not* spread the protection of its wings? No, no, no — I reach beyond the laboratory-brain.

The essay as a whole makes clear what is only slightly implied in this brief segment of the conclusion, that James is anticipating the thinking of two modern Existentialist theologians, Martin Buber and, especially, Gabriel Marcel, with his category of "fidelity." This is of course not surprising to anyone who knows the quality of James's mind. The point is that Dickinson had thought the same way thirty years earlier.

PART FOUR

Doubts, Dilutions, Strategies

CHAPTER VIII

Some Lesser Figures

But Nature whistled with all her winds,
Did as she pleased and went her way.
— Emerson, in "Fragments"

The running battle of the star and clod
Shall run forever — if there be no God.
— Melville, in *Clarel*

J. G. HOLLAND

WHEN Charles Dudley Warner was putting together his *Library of the World's Best Literature,* which appeared in thirty large volumes in 1897, naturally he didn't include Whitman, who was thought to be morally suspect and perhaps not even a real poet, or Emily Dickinson, though her work was in print after 1890. He did, though, allot six pages to Dr. J. G. Holland, Dickinson's friend, the poet, editor, and novelist who helped to found, and later edited, *Scribner's Monthly.* Six pages were not many to be sure, but they were enough for a generous biographical and critical sketch and four poems. For a poet who had two different collected editions of his poems published in his lifetime to be represented by a smaller number of poems than this would have seemed an injustice; but to be included in the work at all was of course a signal honor. It meant recognition as one of the world's greatest writers of all time.

Mrs. Holland corresponded quite regularly with Dickinson, who sometimes included copies of her poems in her letters. Dr. Holland, during his years as an editor of *The Springfield Republican,* saw to it, very possibly as a favor to his wife, that the paper published a few of the strange woman's verses, suitably edited. By 1873, when he published *his* anthology, the *Illustrated Library of Favorite Song,* his paper had actually printed five of her poems. But since they could hardly be described as anybody's "favorite song" — surely not his; privately, he thought them "not poetry" — he did not include Dickinson among the American writers.

His own verse, for which there was so strong and dependable a demand, was recognizably poetry and not something else. The sentiments in it were recognizable, too. They were Emersonian, but without the sage's obscurity or the jagged corners and rough edges of his ideas and diction and meter; Emersonian in theme with the added advantage of being clear and melodious. "Intimations," from *The Marble Prophecy and Other Poems,* 1872, is a fair example of how the good doctor could render Emerson clearer and make him *sing:*

Ah! soul of mine! Ah! soul of mine!
  Thy sluggish senses are but bars
  That stand between thee and the stars,
And shut thee from the world divine.

A later stanza makes the same idea clearer yet, and adds several others:

Nay, God is here, couldst thou but see;
  All things of beauty are of Him;
  And heaven, that holds the cherubim,
As lovingly embraces thee!

Holland's verse is typical enough of the kind of poetry recognized and applauded by the representative literary figures of the post-Civil War period so that there is no need to sample other popular poets of the time like Bayard Taylor, E. C. Stedman, and Madison Cawein. Emerson had written a generation before that his age was retrospective, and no doubt it was in some degree, but to nothing like the degree that characterized the last forty years of the century. Retrospection, nostalgia, and an intense yearning for escape became dominant attitudes and emotions as the romantic impulse dwindled into sentimentalism. Holland and others might go on uttering hopeful sentiments about God's immanence, but their tone shows that they found it harder and harder to believe. God might in some sense — no, must, somehow — be "here," but *romance* was surely elsewhere — in the Orient (Bayard Taylor), or the Wild West (Bret Harte), or the world as it was before the late War (the "local colorists" in fiction, the "female poets"). Not here and now, at any rate, in a time and place in which almost everything the fathers had believed and felt had come to seem to be a Problem.

Apart from Whitman and Dickinson, the best poetry of the period was written by the older figures whose careers had been shaped long before the War. The period from 1860 to 1890 was the heyday of the "schoolroom poets," not only because they had had time to build their reputations but because (again excepting Whitman and Dickinson) none of the younger poets was clearly better — or indeed, in most cases, half so good. Whittier, Longfellow, and Lowell were all doing some of their best work during these years. Whittier's "Snowbound" is probably the finest poem of the period — except again for the poems by our two exceptions — though it too reflects the nostalgia that characterized the age. The world's bright colors seemed to be fading. The area in which the imagination could move freely seemed to be shrinking. It was not clear what one could or should make of so seriously diminished a set of circumstances.

Most of the best of the new poets seemed then, and still seem today, very minor when compared not just with Whitman and Dickinson, but with Whittier and the others of his generation.

HERMAN MELVILLE

Melville, for example, published four volumes of verse between 1866 and 1891 — or five, unless we count the two volumes of *Clarel* as one — but none of his verse even remotely approaches the imaginative vigor or the rhythmic effects of his "poetry" in *Moby-Dick.* He has been called a major poet by two such different distinguished critics as Matthiessen and Randall Jarell, a judgment that strikes me as chiefly valuable for the way it illustrates the occasional fallibility of even the finest critics. It is easy enough to admire *Melville* so much that the admiration carries over to everything he wrote. But a gifted prose writer is not necessarily a poet of any distinction, no matter how firm his thought may be, even if it seems to us to have the quality of "fine hammered steel."

Melville never found a voice for his poetry. Or rather, the voice that speaks is not the voice of anyone alive, and it is not speaking to anyone in particular, not even to itself. It is a voice neither colloquial nor literary, a voice such as we have never heard, even with the mind's ear. It is a voice chilled, benumbed, all emotion frozen out of it or repressed too deep to show. Its rhythms are broken and jagged; it alternately jogs along with the meter and abruptly departs from it entirely to get a thought expressed. The sound of it is neither "the sound of sense," as Robert Frost would later call what he tried to achieve by taking natural speech units and working with them in traditional verse patterns; nor yet the kind of poetic "music" in which Poe and Lanier specialized, in which sound takes precedence over "sense."

In the representative passage from *Clarel* that follows, we hear first the narrator, then the most sympathetic character in the poem, the one whose ideas are most like Melville's own:

> Considerate uncommitted eyes
> Charged with things manifold and wise,
> Rolfe turned upon good Derwent here;
> Then charged: "Fall back we must. Yon mule
> With pannier: Come, in stream we'll cool
> The wine ere quaffing. — Muleteer!"

The best thing that could be said about such a style as this is that it sounds like Browning indulging in self-parody. We notice that both the narrator and Rolfe speak their sentences backward. Only when, in the first two lines, the narrator is admiring himself in the guise of Rolfe, does the verse come alive at all as *verse*. The trochaic opening of the second line, followed by the three regular iambs achieved without departure from normal word order, makes this one of the rare readable lines in this immensely long and almost completely unreadable poem. The third line returns to the jogtrot, achieving its regularity without forcing the language into any absurdities, simply by the addition of the wholly unnecessary "good" before "Derwent." (Derwent, the reader knows by this time, is not "good" in any way; and if "good" is ironic, then the irony is wasted because otiose. No, "good" is there for the sake of the meter.) The last three lines are simply grotesque. No one could possibly be imagined who would speak this way. "In stream" is not English, but not any other language either. The archaic literary "ere" and "quaffing" are inappropriate to the supposed character of Rolfe and to the dramatic situation. The inversions can only be for one purpose, to make possible the A-B-B-A rhymes. This is amateur poetry written by a man with no ear for speech and only the most abstract sense of the reality of his own characters.

Melville himself referred to the poem in 1884, in what was perhaps a moment of insight, as "a metrical affair, a pilgrimage or what not, of several thousand lines, eminently adapted for unpopularity." This seems a fair enough description, especially the "metrical affair" and the "pilgrimage or what not" phrases, though the "several" thousand lines *ought* to be "around nineteen thousand." In the Constable edition of the works, the poem occupies two large volumes totaling 630 pages, with an average of about thirty lines to a page. In both length and obsessive quality, the American poem it can best be compared with is Taylor's "Metrical History of Christianity." Of the two, if I had to read one again, I would choose Taylor's as at least interesting, in a gruesome sort of way, in places.

Except in very rare passages, whatever virtues *Clarel* has have nothing at all to do with the fact that its words march along in meter. There are a good many interesting ideas in it about history and society, and what seems to have been intended as the final meaning is, abstractly considered, "good Melville." Clarel, the pilgrim to the Holy Land in search of faith, must carry his cross like the rest of us, even though his pilgrimage has disclosed to him chiefly the fraudulence of piety. Melville would later express the same general idea more concisely in a poem he included in *Timoleon,* his final volume of verse. "The Enthusiast" has as its epigraph, "Though he slay me yet will I trust in him," and as its final lines,

> Walk through the cloud to meet the pall,
> Though light forsake thee, never fall
> From fealty to light.

One can imagine this idea becoming rather exciting — Clarel as another White Jacket searching for maturity of faith beyond mere innocence — but in *Clarel* Melville manages to make it seem banal. In the last glimpse we get of Clarel, he is mingling with a crowd moving along the street in Jerusalem called the *Via Crucis*:

> In varied forms of fate they wend —
> Or man or animal, 'tis one:

Cross-bearers all, alike they tend
And follow, slowly follow on.

So much for the crowd. Now we see Clarel moving along with the rest and hear him talking to himself. He is pondering, apparently, on the irony that appears when we think at the same time of the Atlantic cable, just completed, and of tombstones:

Wending, he murmurs in low tone:
"They wire the world — far under sea
They talk; but never comes to me
A message from beneath the stone."

The four "books" into which the poem is divided have place names for titles. Within each book the sections have titles that suggest Melville's indecision about his purpose in the poem. Sometimes they are tourists' guidebook headings — "The Sepulchre," "David's Well," "Of the Crusaders." Sometimes they seem to be sermon topics — "Of the Wickedness of the World." Sometimes they focus on the "characters" (I put the word in quotes because they are all merely pasteboard figures), sometimes on brief narrative interruptions of the interminable debate. What did Melville think he was doing here? Writing a philosophical poem spiced with a little action and some names of characters to represent different points of view? Taking us on a guided tour of the Holy Land, with brief lectures on its history and longer ones on theology? I doubt that he could have answered any such questions. He was not well, and he was writing to combine escape and self-therapy.

Even on the thematic level of its most general meanings, the poem is deeply incoherent. Christianity is dead, but science offers no substitute. Each man must carry his cross, but why, or where to, is not clear; perhaps it is only fate that makes him do it. When Clarel arrives at the object of his pilgrimage and sees the towers of Jerusalem, he thinks of the blankness and whiteness of the Arctic poles: "Thy blank, blank towers, Jerusalem." The Seeker has apparently found, to quote MacLeish's "End of the World," "nothing, nothing, nothing — nothing at all." But if this is so, then the narrator's advice to Clarel in the Epilogue surprises us. We cannot tell quite what to make of its apparent affirmations:

Yea, ape and angel, strife and old debate —
The harps of heaven and the dreary gongs of hell;
Science the feud can only aggravate —
No umpire she between the chimes and knell:
The running battle of the star and clod
Shall run forever — if there be no God.

. . . .

But through such strange illusions have they passed
Who in life's pilgrimage have baffled striven —
Even death may prove unreal at the last,
And stoics be astounded into heaven.

Then keep thy heart, though yet but ill-resigned —
Clarel, thy heart, the issues there but mind;
That like the crocus budding through the snow —
That like a swimmer rising from the deep —

. . . .

Emerge thou mayst from the last whelming sea,
And prove that death but routs life into victory.

The chief problem here is that nothing earlier in the poem has prepared us to believe that Clarel *will* be successful in his search for something more than the Arctic blankness he saw in Jerusalem's towers, or that there is any likelihood of his rising from the last whelming sea. He has seemed too dispirited at the end even to search further for any sort of newness of life. The resurrection images of the final lines come to the reader as a complete surprise. Reading them, we wonder whether we have missed something that would serve as a basis for this final burst of hope. If we compare Melville's final affirmations with Tennyson's in "In Memoriam," we get an insight into what is perhaps the chief reason why the English poem is great and the American one at best a noble failure. The two poems have much in common thematically. For both poets, nature, "red in tooth and claw," as Tennyson put it, reveals only death. For both poets, the visible world comes to seem to consist of nothing but "strange illusions"; as Tennyson put it, paralleling a number of passages in *Clarel,*

The hills are shadows, and they flow
    From form to form, and nothing stands;
    They melt like mist, the solid lands,
Like clouds they shape themselves and go.

For both poets, nothing that we can know offers any ground at all for religious faith or trust, any hope for any sort of resurrection, no matter how conceived. Yet Tennyson's affirmations of trust at the end have been prepared for so thoroughly that they come to us as no surprise. For one thing, he prepared us for them in his opening section (which he wrote last, to be sure) —

Strong Son of God, immortal Love,
Whom we, that have not seen thy face,
By faith, and faith alone, embrace,
Believing where we cannot prove. . . .

Much of the imagery of the sections that follow in the poem is consistent with — indeed, constitutes a continual reminder and reinforcement of — the existential faith stated in the beginning. Images of light and dark, of crying in the night, of hands that stretch forth, and many others, in effect *develop* the opening's "We have but faith; we cannot know." Despite the fact that the poem was written at intervals over a period of many years, it is internally coherent. As a result, we know very well what *Tennyson* means at the end, whether we have been moved to any sort of agreement or not.

By contrast, Melville's final burst of faith is touching but, in the context of the poem, deeply obscure. The only thing that is really clear about these lines is that suddenly the verse itself has become much firmer and more controlled, less awkward, less halting, less cold. Though the inversions of word order continue, they are suddenly less forced, as are the rhymes. There is eloquence here, an emotion at last, some lovely images, and even several fine whole lines. What happened to raise this dreary "metrical affair" suddenly into poetry at the very end?

Clarel was Melville's most ambitious poem, and by all odds his worst, but his other three volumes are generally only a little better. If the author of *Moby-Dick* had not written them, they would now be unknown — except to specialists in minor American nineteenth-century poets and to antiquarians. Though here and there we can find in them a successful whole poem, and memorable lines and phrases are fairly frequent, for the most part they are painful to read. Except for a few images and now and then an idea, we would not be likely, even in the half a dozen or so best of the short poems, to guess that the author of *Typee* and *Moby-Dick* had written them. They are cold, passionless, detached, written by a man in mourning — for himself first of all, then for the whole world. In the best of them, like "The Portent" and "The Maldive Shark," intellect alone turns the trick, giving them the kind of interest Puritan anagrams had. What did Melville mean by this? Is this detail symbolic? Should this image be read as we read it in *Moby-Dick*?

I shall try to illustrate with one of the best poems in *John Marr and Other Sailors*. There has been general agreement that "The Maldive Shark" exhibits Melville at his best level as a poet:

> About the Shark, phlegmatical one,
> Pale sot of the Maldive sea,
> The sleek little pilot-fish, azure and slim,
> How alert in attendance be.
> From his saw-pit of mouth, from his charnel of maw,
> They have nothing of harm to dread,
> But liquidly glide on his ghastly flank
> Or before his Gorgonian head;
> Or lurk in the port of serrated teeth
> In white triple tiers of glittering gates,
> And there find a haven when peril's abroad,
> An asylum in jaws of the Fates!
> They are friends; and friendly they guide him to prey,
> Yet never partake of the treat —
> Eyes and brains to the dotard lethargic and dull,
> Pale ravener of horrible meat.

When we think of Flask's sermon to the sharks in *Moby-Dick,* and the cook's soliloquy, does this poem not shrink to a pale restatement? In the prose there is nothing like the awkward "How alert in attendance be," where the inversion and the choice of verb form are so obviously dictated by the need for a rhyme. In the prose treatment, the emotion is implicit throughout, but kept from being excessive by the control afforded by a high-spirited humor. In the poem, the emotion appears only in the last line, and even then partly because we know what "paleness" meant to Melville. This poem was written by a man who has himself been turned to stone by a glimpse of the Gorgonian head.

In his Preface to *Battle-Pieces and Aspects of the War,* Melville made a remark that suggests that he achieved a partial insight into what was wrong with his poetry. "I seem," he wrote of these poems of portent and commemoration, "I seem, in most of these verses, to have but placed a harp in a window, and noted the contrasted airs which wayward winds have played upon the strings." That is, he had remained a detached observer of something *out there,* a war and its countless dead. He had "*but* placed . . . and *noted* . . ." There is of course nothing intrinsically wrong with a poet's maintaining distance from his material — provided it is the right material and he is the right poet to remain distant from it. Some of Stevens' greatest triumphs are of this kind.

But Melville's genius had been quite different from so impersonal a mode as we see in Stevens and the early Eliot. He had written greatly because he had been totally involved. He had speculated passionately and *felt* metaphysically. He had identified so fully with his characters that he was unable to untangle some of the skeins of meaning in *Moby-Dick* — for that would have required taking sides, and he could not, for he himself was not just Ishmael, he was Ahab too — and Queequeg, the innocent and noble savage, and even, with some part of himself, Starbuck, pathetic in his unspeculative integrity and in the doom imposed upon him by forces he could not fight. *Moby-Dick* is passionately alive in every sentence, ambiguous to the end, vibrant with emotion even in the "Cetology" chapters, written by a man wholly committed to life and to his own insights and feelings. Mrs. Hawthorne's pictures of Melville in the Hawthorne home in Lenox, as he told, and acted out, some of his experiences in the South Seas, and Melville's surviving letters to Hawthorne, tell the same story. To the delight of the whole family, Melville had made his tales so vivid that he created illusions in the spectators. Could it be, Mrs. Hawthorne wondered, that that stick he had thrashed about with so violently was only *imaginary?*

But now, as he wrote about the Civil War, he made the actuality of it seem "imaginary" — because he wrote as a man infinitely remote, totally uninvolved, "noting" (not even "listening," which would be the sensuous response to a wind-harp's sounds) *noting* the "contrasted airs" played by "wayward winds." [1] The whole story of what happened to this romantic artist, whose distinctive power had rested on the way the range of his sympathies and the depth of his involvement united with the dartings of an eagerly speculative mind, is implicit in that one word "noting." "Wind-harps," also called "Aeolian harps," appeal to the sensibilities, not to the mind of an observer who can no longer allow himself to feel. As Emerson had written in his "Maiden Speech of the Aeolian Harp,"

> For gentle harp to gentle hearts
> The secret of the world imparts.

Melville's use of the wind-harp image in his Preface has nothing to do with any secrets of the heart or of the world, or with the secret affinity between the heart and the world. It is simply his way of saying that there is nothing deeply personal about these poems. He was right, unfortunately; there is not. They are as cold as ice and as dead as the deaths they intend to commemorate. When Hawthorne last saw Melville, in Liverpool in 1856, when the latter was on his way to the Holy Land in search of health and faith, he noted in his Journal, after describing Melville's depression, that his friend seemed to have "made up his mind to be annihilated." I suspect that the process of psychic annihilation was already far along by that time, if not indeed almost complete. At any rate, the poems Melville began to write several years after his return from his pilgrimage were written as though from beyond the grave.

SIDNEY LANIER

Sidney Lanier, it seems to be universally conceded, was the best of the poets produced by the South in the last half of the century, as Poe was the region's foremost poet in the first half. But it might be more expressive to turn this statement around and say that he was the least bad of them. Henry Timrod and P. H. Hayne are the other two in this regional category, and their work is so bathetic that to call Lanier's *better* is not to say anything absolutely positive. Why the South in the nineteenth century could not produce more and better poets, when it produced more than its share of fine writers in the twentieth, is a question that only a philosopher of culture who was also an experienced literary historian and literary critic should attempt to answer, and I know of no one with all these qualifications.

Lanier was a florid romantic, a musician, and a man who suffered from poverty and tuberculosis during much of his short life. His poetry is full of intense feelings about Nature and God; of elaborately euphonious patterns of sound, including sounds that are intended to remind us of the sounds of musical instruments; and of personal bravery. But the feelings tend to float freely around in a misty atmosphere, unanchored to any palpable earth; the sound patterns have little relation to what Eliot would later call the only "music" proper to poetry; and the bravery is felt only as a quality of the man, not as a quality of the verse.

How standard and unanchored the feelings are can be illustrated by two brief passages from what is acknowledged by Lanier's admirers to be his best, and is certainly his most famous poem, "The Marshes of Glynn." The first passage describes the marshes and prepares us for the second:

> Glooms of the live-oaks, beautiful-braided and woven
> With intricate shades of the vines that myriad-cloven
>   Clamber the forks of the multiform boughs, —
>   Emerald twilights, —
>   Virginal shy lights,
> Wrought of the leaves to allure to the whisper of vows,
> When lovers pace timidly down through the green
>   colonnades
>   Of the dim sweet woods, of the dear dark woods,
>   Of the heavenly woods and glades,
> That run to the radiant marginal sand-beach within
>   The wide sea-marshes of Glynn.

Shortly after this we learn why the woods have been called "dim" and "sweet" and "dear" and "dark": They provide "Cells for the passionate pleasure of prayer to the soul that grieves." They provide refuge from "the scythe of time and the trowel of trade." In the marshes, the speaker tells us, "belief overmasters doubt. and I know that I know." It will no doubt seem terribly crass and unfeeling to note that the poem does not tell us, in this passage or anywhere else, very much about how the marshes support and strengthen the speaker's religious faith.

Late in the poem the speaker resolves to remain close to God, as he has felt himself close while in the marshes. Like Bryant before him, he finds an analogy for his situation in the behavior of a waterfowl. Wishing to be like "the catholic man who hath mightily won/ God out of knowledge and good out of infinite pain/ And sight out of blindness and purity out of a stain," he decides to imitate the marsh-hen:

> As the marsh-hen secretly builds on the watery sod,
> Behold I will build me a nest on the greatness of God;
> I will fly in the greatness of God as the marsh-hen flies
> In the freedom that fills all the space 'twixt the marsh
> and the skies;
> By so many roots as the marsh-grass sends in the sod
> I will heartily lay me a-hold on the greatness of God;
> Oh, like to the greatness of God is the greatness within
> The range of the marshes, the liberal marshes of Glynn.

When Emerson had found God in his experience, in moments of exceptional and unpredictable readiness, as in the moment he describes in *Nature* when he crossed the bare muddy Common on a dark day late in winter and suddenly felt "glad to the brink of fear" with the epiphany he had experienced at that unlikely time and place, he had understood the experience as made possible by a rare inward harmony and alertness — body-sense, instinct, emotion, conscience, intellect, imagination, all working together. He had felt himself suddenly *one* with nature, and through nature with God, because he had been one with himself. Perfect wholeness was the condition of such an experience and of the insights it yielded. The scene itself did not have to be especially beautiful or sublime, vast, dim, or ethereal. And the God Emerson found this way was not the God of the New Testament.

But Lanier was hoping to move "through Nature to God" — to use the title of John Fiske's popular book of the period — without keeping, as Emerson had counseled, *all* his "faculties alert." There is a good deal of emotion in his poem, and a good deal of imagination, of a sort, but no suggestion of a bodily or instinctive response to the sensuous or tactile quality of the marshes, and only the flimsiest sort of analogies to represent intellection. A marsh is water and mud and grasses and sand; but the sand on the beach never gets into Lanier's shoes or blows in his eyes. Instead, it is seen only at a distance, and not *felt* at all. It is presented as what he knows is on the beach, and would know, even if he had never seen a beach; and the beach itself as it curves away into the distance reminds him of "a silver-wrought garment that clings to and follows the firm sweet limbs of a girl."

By this time we are pretty far from the sandiness of sand. We may perversely wonder whether the garment made of it ever irritated the sweet limbs of the girl. Unhelpfully, the parody words of "Red Wing" come to mind, only to be pushed back out of the way so that we may look again, for the last time, at the beach along the edge of the marshes, to see if it ever becomes really *sandy*. But no. In the next lines we find it

> Vanishing, swerving, evermore curving again into sight,
> Softly the sand-beach wavers away to a dim gray looping
> of light.

As for intellection, Lanier seems not to realize, what Emerson had realized so long before, that to take nature as a sufficient revelation of God required among other things keeping oneself open to the possibility of having to redefine what one *meant* by "God." When Lanier writes that the vast spatial extent of the marshes is like the greatness of God, he seems not to realize that his analogy could be manipulated in various ways. "Natural theology" generally convinces only the already convinced. "If design govern in a thing so small," then the open-minded thinker ought to consider not just the apparently Providential way in which the marsh seems planned for marsh-hens to build their nests on, but the predators that find the marsh-hens Providentially provided for them as food. One could as easily infer from the marsh, as it exists in Lanier's poem, a "design of darkness to appall" as one could a loving personal God. Somewhat more easily perhaps. The diminished, wistful ghost of Bishop Paley, that great rationalistic theologian of the beginning of the century, hovers over the poem, holding in one spectral hand the "evidences of the existence and attributes of the Deity, collected from the appearances of nature." Lanier writes as though Emerson, Thoreau, Hawthorne, and Melville, in their several ways, had not made it impossible for the thoughtful late-nineteenth-century poet to be completely satisfied by the good bishop's version of the argument from design.[2]

Lanier wrote several poems that most modern readers are likely to enjoy more than they do "The Marshes of Glynn" — the beautifully restrained and quiet "A Ballad of Trees and the Master," for instance — but the effort for which he is best-known in the literary histories, his attempt to unify the arts of music and poetry, was misguided from the start. In "The Symphony," in which he tried to imitate the sounds of several of the instruments of a symphony orchestra (he himself played the flute in the Baltimore Symphony, as well as teaching at Johns Hopkins), sound and sense fight it out with no decisive victory. And surely, without the title and the several clues thrown out in the poem to guide our reading, we would never guess that we were supposed to be listening to the sounds of flutes, violins, and so on.

In *The Science of English Verse* Lanier tried to provide a theoretical basis for such practice by proposing a system of prosody analogous to musical notation. The best that can be said for the book is that it makes a courageous attempt to do what Lanier was not equipped by either temperament or study to do — to explore the whole history of English verse and deduce from it the laws that govern what he calls "tune" in poetry.

There is of course no "tune," that is, no melodic line as we find it in music, in poetry, so that no matter how learned Lanier had been, no matter how incisively clear-thinking a scholar he might have been, he could not possibly have succeeded in his effort. Poetry has "tone" (of voice), and, depending on the way the reader responds to its ideas and emotions, irregular risings and fallings of pitch and volume, but it never has anything that, even speaking loosely, could be called "tune." It has rhythms, determined by partly schematic, partly elocutionary, and partly linguistic factors, but nothing really comparable to the $3/4$ time or $6/8$ time of music. It has "overtones" (of meaning) but not the complex harmonic effects of music. The word "music," we now know, has various meanings, and Lanier's misguided effort depends for its plausibility very heavily on assuming that all these meanings are somehow the same meaning. But as Eliot, among others, has said, the "music" of poetry is a radically different kind of "music" from the "music" of music. If that were not so, then the most "musical" poetry ought to be composed in sounds that were not words, that had no *semantic* value. Fortunately, no American poet, with the exception of John Gould Fletcher in his last pathetic period, has yet been influenced by Lanier, either by his theory or by his practice. I say "fortunately" not just because the theory is unsound and Lanier's practice not such as any later poet, up to now at least, could imitate successfully, but even more because if it were *possible* to apply the theory to the creation of an actual poem, the result would be such very poor and thin and uninteresting "music" — like whistling the Brandenburg Concerto, or playing Handel's Water Music on a Jew's harp.

STEPHEN CRANE

The farther we get from the period that valued J. G. Holland above Emily Dickinson and Bayard Taylor above Walt Whitman, the clearer it becomes that Stephen Crane is the most interesting of the new poets of the later nineteenth century in America. If we must continue to think of him as "minor," it is more because he wrote so little, within so narrow a range of subject and sensibility, and so little of what he did write represents him at his best, than because his *best* cannot stand comparison with the work of greater poets.

He published just two slender volumes of verse before he died in 1900 at the age of twenty-eight, but a dozen or so of his poems are not adequately praised by saying that they are the most memorable and distinctive poems written in America in the 1890's. If Hemingway's mention of Crane in *The Green Hills of Africa* as one of the three "good" writers before himself in America — the other two being Henry James and Mark Twain — is clearly idiosyncratic and irresponsible when read as an objective evaluation, as it is presented, rather than as a statement of personal preference and affinity, yet it still remains true that many of the finest artists and critics of the recent past have found Crane a "good," and often a brilliant, writer. A significant test of a writer's quality is the quality of the minds he attracts.

Hemingway was thinking, almost certainly, of Crane's fiction, not of his verse, when he thus singled him out, but judging from his own early work in verse, he might well have said the same thing of Crane the poet. His "Neo-Thomist Poem" might have been written by Crane, though not by Crane at his best.

The Lord is my shepherd, I shall not
want him for long.

Here we see the same effort at compression, the same stripping away of all that might be thought of as traditionally "poetic," and the same rejection of ancestral pieties that we find in most of Crane's best-known poems. Whether the result is "poetry" or not need not trouble us for the moment. The line from Crane to Hemingway is as clear and direct in *verse* as we have long assumed it to be in fiction.

There was a tradition *behind* Crane, as well as one stretching before him to the present. Daniel Hoffman in his very fine critical study of Crane's poetry tells us that the two important *direct* influences on Crane were Ambrose Bierce and Olive Schreiner, not, as so many critics have surmised, Whitman and Dickinson; but his kind of verse had been called for, and in some degree even foreshadowed in practice, in the tradition which Emerson had initiated long before. In "The Poet," which Crane very probably never read, the chief American critic had said things that, taken on the level of practical advice, with the metaphysical context ignored, Crane might have used to justify his own practice. The "argument" should be primary, the "finish of the verses" secondary, Emerson had said; and "the value of genius to us is in the veracity of its report." Less guardedly, with a greater appearance of aesthetic naivety, Crane would make the idea that "The nearer a writer gets to life the greater he becomes as an artist" the center of his artistic credo. Even in his more traditionally structured poems, in which he departed from the "free verse" for which he is best known, there is never any suggestion of that "tinkling of piano strings" that Emerson had warned against in "Merlin."

Whitman in his 1855 Preface to *Leaves of Grass* had gone on record to the same effect — though once again, it is likely that Crane did not know it. "Who troubles himself about his ornaments or fluency is lost. . . . The art of art, the glory of expression and the sunshine of the light of letters is simplicity. . . . Most works are most beautiful without ornament. . . . The fluency and ornaments of the finest poems . . . are not independent but dependent."

Crane might have been following such advice when he wrote

some of the early poems included in *Black Riders and Other Lines*; for instance number XLVII:

"Think as I think," said a man,
"Or you are abominably wicked;
You are a toad."

And after I had thought of it,
I said, "I will, then, be a toad."

Certainly the "argument" is primary here, the "finish of the verses" secondary; the poem does without "ornament" entirely, including the "ornament" of meter and rhyme; and whatever "fluency" there is, is from within, is "dependent." The line division seems dictated primarily by the movement of the thought, so much so indeed that if the poem were printed as prose it would probably not be suspected that it was intended as stripped-down verse. Only the division into two verse-paragraphs, a visual device which throws the poem's chief emphasis on "toad" as the word is used by both speakers and produces the effect of rhyme, gives the little narrative a dimension that would be less apparent in a prose printing.

Poem LXVI of *Black Riders* shows Crane composing "in the sequence of the musical phrase," as Pound would later word the Imagist determination to avoid traditional syllabic-accentual prosody. And the cadences seem to grow, as Emerson had said poetic form should, from the thought, "a thought so passionate and alive, that, like the spirit of a plant or an animal, it has an architecture of its own, and adorns nature with a new thing" —

If I should cast off this tattered coat,
And go free into the mighty sky;
If I should find nothing there
But a vast blue,
Echoless, ignorant —
What then?

Here the cadences are strong enough to survive a prose printing, but the division into lines enhances their effect.

By comparison, a typical late Whitman poem is much more regularly rhythmic (tending toward iambic measure, and with five stresses in each line) and considerably less pointed, less compressed, less witty as *statement* than Crane's "Think as I think," and less shaped from within outward than "If I should cast off." Here, for example, is "Life and Death," a representative late Whitman poem:

> The two old, simple problems ever intertwined,
> Close home, elusive, present, baffled, grappled.
> By each successive age insoluble, pass'd on,
> To ours today — and we pass on the same.

Of the three poems, Whitman's is certainly the most "poetic" in the traditional sense: The order of the words and the division into lines are controlled in it by something other than the prose "sense" of them, by the demands of something beyond "what" is being said. The reader would *hear* it as verse, even if it were printed as prose. On the other hand, apart from its falling rhythms and its alliterative effects underscoring the meaning of the last two lines, Whitman's poem seems flatly unimaginative and somewhat redundant. Both of Crane's poems are better *prose* than "Life and Death," but in the first of them only an enhancement of the wit, and in the second only an emphasis on the movement of the cadences, justifies the *verse* printing. Of Whitman's poem, we might properly ask, Is it "good" poetry? Of Crane's two poems, simply, Are they "poetry"? (Reasonable answers might be "No" to the first question and "Yes" to the second, but neither answer is so obvious as to make the question not worth asking.) Is there no limit to how *free* verse can be and still deserve to be called "verse"? If the characteristic American style in poetry exhibits a strong tendency toward "plainness," how "plain" can a poem be and still move us?

A poem better known because more frequently chosen by anthologists exhibits Crane writing in such a way that nothing at all besides the placement of the words on the page gives any hint that the lines are meant as "verse":

> A man said to the universe:
> "Sir, I exist!"
> "However," replied the universe,
> "The fact has not created in me
> A sense of obligation."

Here neither wit nor cadence governs the division into lines. Here we have not even Marianne Moore's arrangement of the words in a visual pattern designed to bring out the "light rhymes," ordinarily not noticed in prose, to give this status as "verse." Since this is from Crane's second volume, it becomes doubtful that we should talk about any steady development in the *form* of his verse, for between the last two poems just quoted lay many experiments in richer, more evocative, and more traditional forms. Nevertheless, "A man said to the universe" is a fair specimen of a considerable part of Crane's work, and its bare, spare, ascetic quality, the length to which it goes to avoid the appearance of being "poetic," seems to me to represent an impoverishment of poetry. The *thought* is the only thing that matters in Crane's poem. When Dickinson similarly relied on abstraction and personification in her more gnomic verses, she had the hymn meters at the back of her mind to play her words against.

But Crane's work is not always so thinly assertive. Anthologists have done him a great disservice by choosing to reprint chiefly his most strikingly "original" poems — "original" in their contrast with the more traditional poetry of the age, especially with the work of the more learned poets; "original" too in the extent of their repudiation of the resources of poetic language; "original" finally in their unqualified expression of the new "naturalism." But the poems that may be so described are not generally Crane's best, as Daniel Hoffman has so convincingly shown. If Crane's work does not exhibit a steady development, at least it is not so much all of a piece as those who know only a few of his poems have supposed.

In much of his best work Crane's repudiation of the traditionally poetic is less extreme than it is in "A man said to the universe." He sometimes shapes his lines to regular stanzas, he sometimes uses refrains, he often employs Biblical parallelism in a somewhat Whitmanesque manner, and now and then he even makes sparing use of internal rhyme. His rhythms do not tend toward the kind of regularity that makes it profitable to count syllables, as Whitman's often tend to do in his later work, but in his finest poems the *stresses* do come regularly, as they do in speech uttered under the pressure of strong emotion. The final stanza from "The Blue Battalions" will illustrate:

The clang of swords is Thy wisdom,
The wounded make gestures like Thy Son's;
The feet of mad horses is one part —
Ay another is the hand of a mother on the brow of a youth.
  Then, swift as they charge through a shadow,
  The men of the new battalions,
      Blue battalions —
  God lead them high, God lead them far,
  God lead them far, God lead them high,
  These new battalions,
        The blue battalions.

With great emotional intensity and with a compression of meaning that is his hallmark, Crane explored a narrow range of feeling and themes. The old label "naturalist" of the literary historians is only partly applicable to the ideas and attitudes we find equally in his verse and his fiction. In the less than a decade of his development Crane moved in several directions, trying out various, sometimes logically incompatible, attitudes and stances. John Berryman has examined this aspect of Crane in Freudian terms, and Daniel Hoffman has looked for an explanation in Crane's divided religious heritage of frontier Methodism on his mother's side and liberal Protestantism with an ethical emphasis on his father's.

The two types of explanation are not necessarily incompatible. They both tend to make more understandable the philosophic confusion so common in Crane's work, especially in his longer fictions. A writer who could in *Maggie,* his most nearly consistent naturalistic novel, at once develop as his chief theme the idea that we are the products of our environment, the helpless puppets of "forces," and at the same time blame the clergyman Maggie meets on the street for not being a Good Samaritan and helping her, and blame also, with scornful sarcasm, Maggie's mother for having *produced* the environment that produced Maggie, was not clear in his mind about what he meant by environmental determinism. (He was clear in his *heart,* though — in effect the book is a plea for love toward all the Maggies of the world.)

One of the reasons why I think that, apart from "The Open

Boat" and perhaps several other stories, we might well prefer the verse to the fiction is that in it Crane's philosophic confusions generally are not apparent in any one poem. Different poems are incompatible, thematically, with each other, but that only adds interest to the body of work as a whole as a kind of *distillation* of the thought of the 1890's: It does not weaken any particular poem. "The Blue Battalions" ends with a prayer to God for the men in blue, while "Blustering God" ends in Promethean or Ahabian defiance, but both represent aspects of Crane's sensibility we can understand and sympathize with, and both are fine poems. Remembering Dickinson, we find it not hard to understand how a poet could pray to "God" in "Blue Battalions" but reject someone else's (in this case, Crane's mother's) "God" in "Blustering God":

> I fear You not.
> No, not if the blow
> Is as the lightning blasting a tree.
> I fear You not, puffing braggart.

There were only a few things Crane was sure of in all his work, and he expressed them over and over in both his weakest and his strongest poems. He was sure he could not accept the church, any church, or expect it to tell us anything *true* about God:

> You tell me this is God?
> I tell you this is a printed list,
> A burning candle, and an ass.

He was sure that the God who has not revealed himself in the message proclaimed by the churches is not revealed by nature either. Nature seemed to him clearly indifferent to man's fate, alien to his needs and longings; as Frost would soon say as a gloss to his early poem "Stars," "There is no oversight of human affairs."

Sometimes it seemed to him that all animate nature cried out together with man for succor; that all the voices of life, equally the "unknown appeals of brutes" and "the screams of cut trees," were joining together in a despairing and incoherent cry of suffering toward God, or toward the stars. ("All nature groaneth and travaileth together," Paul had once written, as Crane, with his years of enforced Bible study, almost certainly knew.) What the theologians have called "the problem of evil" — Job's problem — is everywhere present in Crane's work, early and late, providing one of the strongest connecting links between poems otherwise thematically inconsistent with each other.

He was sure, finally, that he preferred to accept man's sinful condition as an unalterable fact, and then to try to make it the basis for brotherhood — that he preferred this to any attempt to extirpate it for the sake of achieving a godliness that would get one "saved." Here he reminds us of Hawthorne, with his "brotherhood of guilt," and Dickinson, with her gibes at the "elect," who chose safety in their alabaster tombs over experience; though, typically, his *thought* on these subjects was much less sophisticated than that of either of them. If man was sinful, he asked in effect over and over, who had *made* him so? The Christian answer he was familiar with seemed to him both incredible and cruelly unjust.

Toward the end of the decade he seems to have been moving away from his partial and spasmodic "naturalism" toward a position that might be called a kind of heroic humanism with theistic overtones but with no communication possible between God and man. Man must accept responsibility for his fate and find the courage within him to act in freedom and in readiness to sacrifice himself for others. Man is small, weak, almost helpless, almost overwhelmed; but if he dares to act as a man and not a thing, he can become human. (If this begins to sound as though I were describing not Crane but Camus or Sartre or Hemingway, the reader may take this as a clue to what it was in Crane that so strongly attracted Hemingway and so many others in the present century.)

Still, the humanity that man might thus achieve was, for Crane at the end of his life, an insufficient counter to despair, if God did not exist or could not in any way be reached. Or at least so we would have to conclude from the lines he carefully placed last in *War Is Kind*. The poem begins,

> A spirit sped
> Through spaces of the night;
> And as he sped, he called,
> "God! God!"

and ends with the seeker dead, after having been driven, "mad in denial," to scream, "Ah, there is no God!"

As Daniel Hoffman has pointed out, the seeker in the poem both is and is not Crane himself. The theme of "faith desperately sought and not found" had run through many earlier poems and may be taken as Crane's sense of his own situation. But Crane was not, certainly not at this period in his life, "mad in denial." His position, rather, could be described in the famous epigram of the Existentialist philosopher Heidegger: "I do not deny God's existence but I affirm his absence." And perhaps even His apparent absence, Crane may have thought, is the result of man's "blindness"; so, at least, a number of earlier poems suggested. Or perhaps He is known only through his *wrath,* never through *mercy.* Immediately after the seeker in the last poem in *War Is Kind* denies God,

> A swift hand,
> A sword from the sky,
> Smote him,
> And he was dead.

At any rate, one thing is clear in this ambiguous poem: Crane's usual irony is absent from these concluding lines, so that the question of the fate of a seeker who was *not* driven mad is left open.

Crane's emotional range and freedom are limited, and his themes equally so. Irony is his commonest tone, and fear and a sense of intense loneliness are the feelings that tend to remain with us from the poems after we have put them down. His love poems, marked both by the intensity of their yearning and by the privacy of their symbols, seem to me, with a very few exceptions, less impressive than his poems on the themes I have just been discussing. His technical virtuosity in his best poems exceeds in range and inventiveness the stock of emotions and ideas he had to work with — as perhaps one ought to expect to be the case with so young a writer, so gifted.

Crane's poetry is just as "original" as it has commonly been called, but not for the reasons commonly given. It is original chiefly because it speaks to us in a fresh, unmistakably personal, wholly honest voice about old themes experienced afresh by one almost innocent of both literature and history. What results is a kind of compressed and distilled recapitulation, in a *style* essentially American, if Emerson is to be trusted, of some of the major themes of American poetry and fiction up to 1900. No doubt it was an advantage to Crane — Eliot's argument in "Tradition and the Individual Talent" notwithstanding — that he did not know it had mostly been done before — all but the way he *felt* his themes, and the personal voice in which he spoke to us of them. If he was not the first to note God's silence and nature's blankness, to feel man's helplessness and his isolation, to concern himself with the problem of evil and the difficulty of attaining truth, not the first to realize that the argument from the evidences of design in nature might as easily lead to the idea of God's malevolence as to His benevolence, and not the first either to do all this in a style deliberately plain, yet he *was* the first to go so far toward making Emerson's criterion of "veracity" his overriding concern, and the first after Whitman to achieve forms that might really be described as "organic," growing from within outward. If this were not distinction enough, the critic who wished to argue that placing Crane among the "lesser" poets, as I have done, is unfair to him, could point to the purity and intensity of his expression of a feeling that links his sensibility with ours, the feeling that the universe is experienced first and most immediately as hostile, threatening, a wild and lonely place in which the outcome of man's effort to preserve his identity is desperately uncertain.[3]

WILLIAM VAUGHN MOODY

When we turn from Stephen Crane to William Vaughn Moody, we find ourselves faced immediately with the question of the relation of the poet to traditional culture, especially to the accumulated body of European poetry behind him. Crane, it would not be much of an exaggeration to say, *had* no culture, was largely unconscious of any relation his own work might bear to what had gone before. He read little, and that little mostly in contemporary works long since forgotten. He seems not even to have been aware of the scientific and philosophic developments that were disturbing Robinson in the 1890's and shaping the verse of his more learned contemporaries like Moody and Stickney. Except for the Bible and Bierce and Schreiner, Crane really *had* no "literary" resources. As it happened, his kind of verse had not been written better before, but if it had been, he would not have known it.

The classic conservative statement of the question posed by juxtaposing Crane and Moody is of course Eliot's "Tradition and the Individual Talent," with its argument that the poet can only be "original" in a good sense when he is aware of all the great work of the past and thinks of it as existing in a moment of time, while he serves as a conductor for the altered sensibility of his own age. The sharpest attack on such assumptions came from Karl Shapiro a few years ago in his *In Defense of Ignorance,* with its violent assault on the "culture" poets, the "poets of the library."

Eliot's and Shapiro's ideas will occupy us later. For the moment, their significance lies only in this: that if we follow Eliot's argument, Moody ought to have been a better poet than Crane — unless we are content to say that Moody simply lacked "individual talent"; but then we are in effect avoiding the question at issue by falling back on something unknown and probably unknowable. The question at issue is whether a rich cultural heritage is intrinsically and necessarily an advantage to a poet. If it is, then it follows that Moody ought to have written better than Crane. His *History of English Literature,* written in collaboration with Robert Morss Lovett, was a splendidly learned and tasteful performance, so much so that it remained the best work of its kind for many years. As for contemporary poetic and cultural developments, Moody made a point of keeping abreast of them. When he went from Harvard to join the faculty at the new University of Chicago, it seemed that at last we might have a scholar-poet. But it was not his untimely death that kept him from fulfilling this expectation. What he *did* write before his career was cut short is very much inferior to what Crane was writing in the same years.

Moody had everything, it would seem, that we ought to like in a poet, not just his thorough acquaintance with poetic tradition. He had intelligence and taste and a sophisticated awareness of the Urgent Questions of his time. He was a liberal with an active social conscience, as we may see in his poem on one of our earlier adventures in Imperialism — "On a Soldier Fallen in the Philippines." While Crane was somewhat guiltily expressing his rebellion against his family's Methodism by smoking cigarettes and becoming the friend and defender of prostitutes, Moody was pondering *Faust* and considering the necessity for Promethean poems in an age of scientific triumph. While Crane was compulsively writing love poems in which the beloved's *arms* seemed to be what chiefly attracted him, Moody was demonstrating his sanity and poise in everything he did, both scholarly and poetic. He had both a feeling for nature and a hope for culture. His humanism was broadly inclusive and tolerant.

But in his best poem, which is also his most famous one, "Gloucester Moors," he was unable to put all these bits and pieces of himself and his heritage together to create a coherent, or moving, or meaningful work of art. Perhaps no comparably famous American poem is more of a jumble of unrelated and undeveloped ideas and feelings, or a better illustration of what Eliot meant by his phrase "the dissociation of sensibility," or splitting apart of thought and feeling.

The poem opens with the speaker on the shore, sitting or reclining presumably, and noticing the beauty of nature around him. The opening lines are readable and pleasant enough. Though the language and versification are wholly traditional, the imagery seems fresh, perhaps partly because of the speaker's cool detachment from the scene he carefully describes:

> A mile behind is Gloucester town
> Where the fishing fleets put in,
> A mile ahead the land dips down
> And the woods and farms begin.
> Here, where the moors stretch free
> In the high blue afternoon,
> Are the marching sun and talking sea,
> And the racing winds that wheel and flee
> On the flying heels of June.

In the next stanza the speaker turns his gaze to what is close at hand:

> Jill-o'er-the-ground is purple blue,
> Blue is the quaker-maid,
> The wild geranium holds its dew
> Long in the boulder's shade.

In the following stanza he lifts his eyes from the ground to follow the flights of land and sea birds, including the gulls who fly seaward. Of the ten identically rhymed stanzas in the poem, these first three have moved coherently, first inward and downward, then outward and upward. We are likely to feel when we get this far that something interesting is going to happen in the poem. The various promises of meaning contained in Bryant's verse, but never developed by him, seem about to be given their names by the Namer.

But abruptly the speaker turns from evocative description to stating his thoughts about the fate of the world. The spaciousness of sea and sky surrounding his little spot of earth have made him think of the interstellar space through which the earth itself moves:

> This earth is not the steadfast place
> We landsmen build upon;
> From deep to deep she varies pace,
> And while she comes is gone.

Anticipating what Archibald MacLeish would later call his "sense of infinity," the speaker in the poem feels the motion of the earth as he would the motion of a ship:

> Beneath my feet I feel
> Her smooth bulk heave and dip;
> . . . .
> Like a gallant, gallant ship.

After a stanza that develops this analogy between the earth and a ship (the clouds are sails, the sun a masthead light, and so on), the speaker turns to the thoughts prompted by his situation and his analogy. Is the world, considered as a ship, going anywhere? Or is the world, nature, simply blind and meaningless?

> God, dear God! Does she know her port,
> Though she goes so far about?
> Or blind astray, does she make her sport
> To brazen and chance it out?

As if this question were not profound enough for one short poem that started out as nature description, as if this analogy were not already sufficiently complicated for one poem to develop, the speaker drops (right in the middle of a stanza) the religious or metaphysical question he has been asking — the question of "teleology," or purposive direction — and starts to describe the ship's crew. It turns out, naturally, that they are just like the people on the "ship of earth," some "gorged at mess" in the cabin, some before the mast, some down in the hold under a battened hatch, these last uttering "cries too sad to be told."

At this point the speaker has apparently had enough of his own analogy, for he turns back to contemplating the forgotten flowers around him, repeating the lines about the jill-o'er-the-ground and the quaker-maid. Nature has ceased to offer an analogy for the world and has become a means of escape, an answer to the speaker's wish

> To be out of the moiling street
> With its swelter and its sin!

Yet the terrible problems suggested by the earth-as-ship will not be pushed aside for long —

> Who has given to me this sweet,
> And given my brother dust to eat?
> And when will his wage come in?

By this time the modern reader, used to taking the implications of images in poetry seriously, may well feel confused. The much-emphasized blue of the quaker-maid has proved to be merely decorative, or just "pretty," like the flower. The local scene, that at first seemed to be expanding into all time and space, has contracted into a secluded retreat from nasty problems of social injustice. The sea, which has always suggested the great mysteries of beginning and end, has been forgotten once it set the ship of the world rocking. The land-sea imagery that Melville had done so much with in *Moby-Dick* has similarly dropped out of sight, and the metaphoric question of whether "the ship of the world" is making for any port, or just drifting around, has contracted to the question of whether, or when, we shall achieve "democracy."

Every image, every symbol, every metaphor has been forgotten, or pushed aside as "too sad to be told," or else diminished to something less unpleasant to contemplate. Without any apparent recognition of what he is doing to his own symbolic structure, Moody ends his poem with three parallel questions, implying that they are really all the *same* question. He asks first (recalling, apparently, the earlier metaphor),

But thou, vast outbound ship of souls,
What harbor town for thee?

Then immediately, with mythic overtones of Acheron and the river Styx — for the sea has "shores," a river, "banks":

What shapes, when thy arriving tolls,
Shall crowd the banks to see?

(The shades of those departed earlier, obviously, one answers.) Then the question he seems to be *really* interested in:

Shall all the happy shipmates then
Stand singing brotherly?

Stephen Crane, without having read any of the writers Moody is remembering in this poem, might have told him that he was confusing several different orders of questions. "Gloucester Moors" is full of pretty images and deep thoughts — including some the poet prefers not to contemplate too long — and full too of reminiscences of Wordsworth and Shelley, Melville's *Moby-Dick,* and Darwin's *Origin of Species.* The sentiments in the poem are admirable. Most of us certainly hope we shall achieve justice and democracy as soon as possible, the sooner the better. But "Gloucester Moors" is not saved as a poem, even for the most sympathetic reader, by the promise of its opening stanzas or by the "idealism" of its later sentiments. It remains both a very incoherent work and a typical product of the well-educated poets of the end of the century, of the years when Robinson and Frost were learning their craft, and learning, too, to adjust their attitudes to a time that seemed unpropitious for the production of great poetry — unless, like Stephen Crane, one were "protected" as it were from the age by ignorance.

FREDERICK GODDARD TUCKERMAN

Our impression that the later years of the nineteenth century were very bad times for the poet is strengthened when we look from the middling poets we have been considering to the least of those who can be taken at all seriously today. I am not referring now to those temporarily popular poets, many of whom held editorial positions or in other ways partly produced and partly reflected the taste of the age, the Stoddards and Stedmans and Hollands and Bayard Taylors of the period. It may be that a time will come when they will be rediscovered and read with pleasure once more, as our grandfathers or great-grandfathers read them; but the sensibility of such an age would have to be so very different from ours that it is impossible even to imagine its features. It is not clear that the temporarily popular poets of any period are really worse or better than those of any other period, but for *us* at least most of the poets the late nineteenth century liked best are better forgotten.

The exceptions, who can be read with pleasure even while we hold to our reservations, are not many. Chiefly, it seems to me, they are Frederick Goddard Tuckerman and Trumbull Stickney. The first had, in his most original poems, only a single theme and a single tone, the second wrote no more than half a dozen poems at most that retain real interest today; but each of them achieved enough to deserve to be read once at least and to be retained somewhere in a corner of our memory.

Tuckerman seems likely to remain, what he has been for the past century, a poet overpraised by those with special biases, unjustly ignored by most, continually "rediscovered" and then forgotten again. When he sent copies of his 1860 *Poems,* privately printed in England, to many of the most distinguished writers of the time, Emerson and Hawthorne both found something to praise in their letters of acknowledgment, though both, obviously, were being as kind as they could, letting him down gently. Jones Very, who had been Tuckerman's tutor at Harvard, commented on a few of his former student's untypical poems with real warmth. By 1864 Tuckerman had enough prestige to warrant an American edition by Ticknor and Fields, the distinguished Boston publishers.

By his death in 1873 he had been completely forgotten. Only the local newspaper carried any notice of his death, and even to that paper he was known only as a wealthy recluse who had graduated from Harvard and studied law but never practiced any profession, and as an "excellent scholar," who had written "several fine poems." Yet a generation later an obscure anthologist in New York "discovered" him and Walter Prichard Eaton, who saw the two sonnets included in the proposed but unpublished anthology, wrote an essay about him in 1909. Witter Bynner saw the essay and finally brought out his edition of Tuckerman's *Sonnets* in 1931. Benet and Pearson included him in their widely used, and influential, *Oxford Anthology of American Literature* in the late 1930's. But later anthologists have not followed their lead. When Tuckerman's hitherto unpublished long ode, "The Cricket," was published in 1950, Yvor Winters, who had long before recommended that Tuckerman be looked into, told the readers of the *avant garde Hudson Review* that the poem was "one of the greatest meditations on death to be written since the 17th century" and also — even more surprisingly, since not very many "meditations on death" have been written in any century — "probably the greatest single American poem of the 19th century." In 1962, Edmund Wilson discussed Tuckerman respectfully in *Patriotic Gore*.

Early in 1965 Tuckerman's *Complete Poems* were published, edited with an Introduction by N. Scott Momaday, with a Critical Foreword by Yvor Winters. It would appear that at last Tuckerman had been *really* "discovered," past all possibility of being "forgotten" again.

But Tuckerman's merits are said, by both Winters and Momaday, to depend on our rejecting, indeed on our despising, Emerson, and Romanticism generally; and I suspect that there are many besides myself who will think that if this is really true, it is too high a price to have to pay merely to find another American poet worth reading. As Winters puts it in his new piece, Tuckerman was "one of the three most remarkable American poets of the nineteenth century. The others were Jones Very (1813–80) and Emily Dickinson (1830–86)." So far, one might *possibly* follow him: Very was "remarkable," in the most literal sense of the word, and so, in a different way, was Dickinson. After all, "remarkable" need not involve any value judgment. But immediately after this it becomes clear that for Winters "remarkable" is indeed a normative word, and very positively so: "Emerson had talent, which was badly damaged by foolish thinking. . . . Of Poe and Whitman, the less said the better." Winters' catalogue of nineteenth-century poets is complete at this point. (He mentions, and dismisses, Bryant in the clause I have omitted.) What all this clearly implies is that Tuckerman appeals strongly to critics who have a long history of eccentric opinions.

The editor in his Introduction follows the Winters line more guardedly. "If Tuckerman," he says in his concluding paragraph,

> is to emerge completely in our literature, he had best be revealed for the right reasons. There are two in particular. First, he stands in historical opposition to the mainstream of nineteenth-century American Romanticism. That fact ought now to account for his renown. . . . Second, Tuckerman's poems are valuable in their own right. They are the best possessions of a man whose vision is keen and whose judgment is sound.

(We may ignore the editor's second reason, since he offers no evidence at all for it apart from what he presents in his first reason.)

As an example of a man whose "vision" was *not* "keen" ("vision" here means simply *eyesight*), the editor cites Emerson: Tuckerman, he says, "perceived in much greater detail" than Emerson, offering us indeed "*point-blank* descriptions of nature," along with the sound judgment that nature's details are in fact *meaningless:* "Where Emerson found realized in nature the transcendent spirit of the universe, Tuckerman saw only a various and inscrutable mask." Emerson is also the editor's example of a man who did not have Tuckerman's "sound" judgment. Emerson, he tells us, held that

> Intuition is superior to intellection. The Emersonian thesis is clear: communion with nature is possible only through the repudiation of reason. But the repudiation of reason is also the repudiation of maturity. . . .

So far as I can see, Tuckerman's "discoverers" and promoters have so far offered us no valid reasons at all for not forgetting him completely. But, oddly enough, there *is* one: Tuckerman wrote quite a large number of very good lines, a fair number of passages that can stand repeated reading, and a few good whole poems. His friend Tennyson was certainly his chief inspiration. He was a "Victorian," which is to say, British, poet — for "Victorian" is a term that has no meaning in the writing of our best nineteenth-century writers; it may be used only for the unimaginative imitators. Unless one thinks it important that Tuckerman mentions a number of peculiarly American botanical species in his descriptive poems, he is not even, in any important sense, an "American" poet despite his family connections with long-settled families and his almost lifelong residence in Greenfield, Massachusetts. And he is not a romantic poet, either. His fame, whatever it finally turns out to be, must rest on the fact that he is the best example in American poetry of how every item in the Romantic faith became for the English Victorians a Problem. This is what Winters and Momaday really mean when they say or imply that Tuckerman's "judgment" was too "sound" to permit him to be a "Romantic." That neither of them has the faintest conception of what Emerson's real meaning was I shall not argue; what I would say if I did should by now be too obvious.

Tuckerman was a doubting, despairing, grief-stricken Episcopalian. Tennyson had written at great length in "In Memoriam" about the necessity of "believing where we cannot know." Tuckerman thought this impossible. His first sonnet, first series (there are five) ends with the line he intends as an answer to Tennyson: "God were not God, whom knowledge cannot know." His second sonnet in the series starts,

> Wherefore, with this belief held like a blade,
> Gathering my strength and purpose still and slow,
> I wait, resolved to carry it to the heart
> Of that dark doubt in one collected blow. . . .

But nature, he discovers, reveals nothing, unless it be simply death. Experience, it appears, is mostly, perhaps entirely, illusion; and behind the illusion there is nothing. Reason is impotent to find any "reasons," but faith which ignores "reason" is meaningless. No wonder we encounter a good deal of imagery in the sonnets that seems to foreshadow later "wasteland" imagery:

> But not for him those golden calms succeed
> Who while the day is high and glory reigns
> Sees it go by, as the dim pampas plain,
> Hoary with salt and gray with bitter weed,
> Sees the vault blacken, feels the dark wind strain,
> Hears the dry thunder roll, and knows no rain.

"The Cricket," Tuckerman's best poem except for the "Sonnets," is good enough to replace some poem of equal length commonly anthologized from the poets of the period, especially from the "late Romanticists" who followed the letter but doubted the spirit, Timrod or Hayne for example. It is heavily padded, but here and there despair and frustration rise to a certain eloquence, as they do in the concluding lines, cited by Winters to prove that this poem is not only "the greatest poem in English of the century" but superior to a distinguished poem of another century — "a greater poem than Wallace Stevens's 'Sunday Morning' ":

> It matters not. Behold! the autumn goes,
>   The shadow grows,
> The moments take hold of eternity;
> Even while we stop to wrangle or repine
>   Our lives are gone —
>   Like thinnest mist,
> Like yon escaping color in the tree;
> Rejoice! rejoice! whilst yet the hours exist —
> Rejoice or mourn, and let the world swing on
> Unmoved by cricket song of thee or me.

"The Cricket" is indeed a "remarkable" poem in American poetry; that is, it ought to be noticed or "remarked," and of course read. As a poet, Tuckerman is less ill-at-ease in verse than Melville, though Melville's several best poems can stand comparison with Tuckerman's. Certainly Tuckerman ought to be considered a better poet than the much more famous Moody. Further than this I am not certain we ought to go.

TRUMBULL STICKNEY

The poetry of Trumbull Stickney has been overpraised, though in different, and less absurd, ways, and for different reasons — by friends who knew him and mourned his early death, and by Modernist critics and poets who saw in a few of his poems very strong anticipations of their own wasteland images and themes. He wrote perhaps half-a-dozen or so memorable poems, but if we look into his two volumes of verse to find other poems like "Mnemosyne" or "In the Past," we find very few that seem to have been written by the same poet. "In the Past" looks back to Poe and at the same time anticipates the published parts of Allen Tate's poem in progress, "The Buried Lake." Playing with images of a secret life hidden under or within images of death, it reads rather like an academic exercise in imitating the very early Eliot, Tate, the early Warren, *et al.* — an imitation written, of course, before there was anything to imitate. After a Poe-esque first stanza ("The City in the Sea"), the poem moves through "a void space and dry" to the paradox of hours that "lag dead in the air/ With a sense of coming eternity" (Eliot's "Preludes," Tate's "Ode to the Confederate Dead"). There are tracks of snakes to be seen (Warren, Tate) but "no star shines" (Robinson, "Credo"). Nevertheless, despite the unremitting darkness,

> The heart is alive of the boatman there:
> That boatman am I.

In "Mnemosyne" the "remembered" country is called "cold," "empty," "lonely," and "dark." Set apart formally as well as thematically, so that there can be no conjunction of the two, are images of light and sun, love and singing, and natural life and hope. The poem that has moved through irony and paradox ends in alienation and despair, overtly expressed:

> But that I knew these places are my own,
> I'd ask how came such wretchedness to cumber
> The earth, and I to people it alone.
>
> It rains across the country I remember.

With only occasional lapses, the language in the poem is the kind of virile, direct, idiomatic language called for, and practiced, earlier, by Emerson, and later, by Pound and Eliot. We have moved worlds — *poetic* worlds — away from Tuckerman in about the space of a generation, and, more remarkably, away from Moody too, in no time at all. But not from Crane, though of course the sensibility that informs the language of Stickney and Crane is very different — Harvard, rather than Lafayette and Syracuse. Crane's language is that of a man *speaking* to us, and *saying* something, not just writing poems: much closer to the language Emerson himself had practiced, and advised, whenever he turned his mind briefly to questions of technique.

But what the sensitive reader who is not himself a poet but is concerned with poetry as something that makes a difference in life may remember better than the language, is what the language "says": the autumnal atmosphere, the disappearance of all light, the loss of hope, the life that must be buried and hidden if it is to survive at all. No wonder Robinson and Frost, already writing, and knowing more than Stephen Crane did of what Stickney knew, spent a good deal of ingenuity in their early work in an effort to keep the sources of their hope hidden.

CHAPTER IX

The Idealist *in Extremis*

Miniver Cheevy, child of scorn,
Grew lean while he assailed the seasons;
He wept that he was ever born,
And he had reasons.
— Robinson, in "Miniver Cheevy"

Robinson is perhaps the greatest master of the speculative or conjectural approach to the writing of poetry.
— James Dickey, in his Introduction to *Selected Poems of E.A.R.*

EDWIN ARLINGTON ROBINSON

WHEN Emily Dickinson died in 1886, Robinson was in high school in Gardiner, Maine, already experimenting with verse forms. Ten years later, he published his first volume. The two poets were separated in time by only thirty-nine years, a long generation, and in space by the distance between Amherst and Gardiner, which even under the travel conditions of that day was not very great. Yet reading their verse, one might suppose that the two had been born aeons and worlds apart, so much that was vital to both of them had happened in the thirty-nine years between their birth dates.

Dickinson had grown up at a time when even in a college town in the Connecticut valley, Christianity, in the form of late Calvinist dogmatics, had seemed powerful enough to challenge, and Mr. Emerson of Boston and Concord just the man to challenge it. Robinson grew up at a time when even in a small town in Maine, if the town had an educated professional class, as Gardiner had, Christianity in any of its historic forms was coming to seem unworthy of the attention of thinking people, and Emerson, though greatly honored as a sage, seemed not to be addressing himself to current problems. So far as he was an active influence now, it was chiefly through Mary Baker Eddy, who had found in his Idealism the inspiration for her system of Christian Science, which was spreading rapidly though without touching the most highly educated. To them it was apparent that any religious belief at all, including Emerson's, had been revealed as wishful thinking by the facts uncovered by science. In what the new president of Cornell University called the "History of the Warfare of Science with Theology in Christendom," science had definitely won what appeared to be a final victory; and in the less heralded warfare of science with Transcendentalism, victory seemed almost as certain. When nature was viewed in "the light of day," mystic intuitions had a way of evaporating even for John Burroughs, who loved nature as much as any man could.

Scientific naturalism in the 1890's — a philosophy already so remote from us today that we must exercise all our powers of historical imagination to recreate it — had no room in its strictly defined view of reality for anything miraculous, whether "the miraculous" meant Biblical miracles or Emerson's "natural supernaturalism," his strategy of making God chiefly immanent. It had no room for intuition either, or for nature as symbolic revelation, or for Emerson's idea of the self as transcendent of time and place. The new philosophy conceived both man and nature on the model of machines. Anything Transcendental must be either unreal or completely unknowable — which would perhaps amount to the same thing.

Robinson's name for this new philosophy was simply "materialism." By that word he meant to include both what is sometimes called "mechanism," the idea that reality, human and nonhuman alike, is best compared to a machine, which has neither freedom nor spontaneity; and also what is called, in a more limited sense than his, "materialism," which is the view that reality, all that is, consists exclusively of what can be weighed and measured. From this point of view, anything that cannot be stated in quantitative terms and reduced to law is unreal. Clearly, this point of view made Emerson seem no less naive than Luther or Calvin or St. Paul — perhaps more so indeed.

It was the British Darwinian Herbert Spencer, who is taken seriously by no present-day philosopher I know of, who first broke the bad news to Robinson that what the science of the time could deal with was all there *was* to be dealt with. Like Hamlin Garland and Theodore Dreiser and many other Americans of the period, Robinson felt that however unpleasant the new doctrine might be, simple honesty, respect for *facts,* required that he accept it. If it seemed to render life meaningless by denying reality to everything qualitative, including all the values by which man had always thought his life could acquire meaning, perhaps we should acknowledge that life *is* meaningless. "Life was something before you came to Spencer," Robinson wrote a friend in 1890. But two years later, while a special student at Harvard from 1891 to 1893, he found himself reading some Emerson, during a mastoid attack, "in order to drive the pain away." Not surprisingly, in view of the position from which he approached them, he felt that he got very little out of the essays on "Friendship" and "Love."

From Josiah Royce's expounding of Absolute Idealism he got even less, indeed "absolutely nothing," he once wrote a friend. He took to writing letters in class while the irrelevant lectures went on. But toward William James he found himself unable to maintain his lofty indifference. James challenged him harder and evoked a fine scorn of both the man and his ideas. Precisely what it was about James's ideas that Robinson didn't like, his letters do not make clear, except in one respect: James's thinking was incompatible with Spencerian monistic naturalism.[1]

Robinson decided that the reason this "metaphysical funny man" with his "spiritual vulgarity" talked the way he did was that he had either not read, or had not understood, Spencer. In 1898, five years after he had left Harvard as a student, he was still expressing his fierce contempt for James. Years later, at the MacDowell Colony, he surprised a friend and fellow colonist by coming in to breakfast one day and without any warning, or any relevance to anything that had been said, launching into a vehement denunciation and clever parody of James and several others among his Harvard professors as "stuffed shirts" and pretenders who had had nothing to teach him. This outburst was so unlike Robinson, who was generally so quiet, retiring, and kindly in his judgments, that the friend remembered the incident vividly. We can only suppose that Robinson must have spent one of many sleepless nights brooding on the matter, to have had to get it off his chest at breakfast this way.

Throughout the 1890's Robinson wavered between the fierce loyalty to Spencer that made him reject Royce and James, and an increasingly warm response to Emerson, to whom he returned in the middle of the decade, after his mother's death, under the influence of a Christian Science friend. Beset by grief and loss — his father, his mother, and his older brother Dean all died in the

1890's — and often ill himself, he desperately sought consolation wherever he might find it. He went back to Carlyle, whom he had read before going to college, and decided now that *Sartor Resartus* and Christianity, Jesus and "illuminated commonsense," all pointed in the same direction, toward "a denial of the existence of matter as anything but a manifestation of thought." Shortly after his mother's death in 1896 he announced that he was "very glad to be able to stand up and say that I am an idealist. Perhaps idealism is the philosophy of desperation, but I do not think so." Rereading St. John's Gospel in the light of his new idealism, he found it making sense to him for the first time.

During a period of trouble with his eyes, he had a friend read to him.

> . . . J. and I are reading up (J. is reading and I am listening) on Oriental Religions. I have been interested to find out that Christianity is in reality nothing more than Buddhism humanized; and that Nirvana and Heaven are from the idealist's point of view — which is to me the only point of view — pretty much the same thing. . . .
>
> I have just read Emerson on "The Oversoul." If you do not know it, for heaven's sake get hold of it.

His "conversion" to a really firm faith in what he took to be the core of meaning common to the teachings of Jesus, Buddhism, Carlyle, and Emerson was short-lived, but for a while it seemed to him to make him better able to endure life's torture chamber. "How long do you think a man can live in hell?" he asked a friend in 1897. No one, he thought, could be happy in such an age as his, when "the whole trend of popular thought" was "in the wrong direction." But he was strong enough now, perhaps, he thought, with the help of his new philosophy, to get along without happiness, to endure the results of having been born at the wrong time. Now that he was assured that light *could* be found by those not self-blinded, he could afford to joke at times about an age that was proud of its materialism:

> The age is all right, material progress is all right, Herbert Spencer is all right, hell is all right. These things are temporal necessities, but they are damned

> uninteresting to one who can get a glimpse of the real light through the clouds of time.

But hell was not always so easy to dismiss. When the glimpses of the light were slow in coming, Robinson more and more found his best help in Emerson.

Returning to him again and again all through the 1890's, he kept finding new depths of meaning he had formerly missed. When he came to *The Conduct of Life* in 1899, he confessed to a friend "with burning shame" that this was a *first* reading. He decided that he liked this late Emerson better than the Emerson of the essays: Here there was more "humanity and humor," less contrast with his own "diabolical system." This was the book, he now realized, that one ought to start with. It revived his faith in Emerson's wisdom. But as time went on and the first effects of his conversion wore off, he began to value the poetry more and the prose less, until at last, late in life, he could say to a friend at the MacDowell Colony:

> Emerson wrote some of the purest poetry we have in America — though not a great deal of it. The trouble is, nobody reads it. And most people don't know it exists. They get side-tracked to "Self-Reliance" or "The Oversoul."

But it was not as a "pure" poet that Emerson had first attracted Robinson, or even as a poet at all, but as a consoler and strengthener. In Robinson's later public comments on Emerson, we may find something of the same innocent covering of tracks that may be seen in *The Torrent and the Night Before* and *The Children of the Night.* Emerson's influence is apparent in both books, particularly — much more than has been realized — in the later one, but Emerson's name never appears in either one. There are poetic tributes to Zola, Crabbe, Thomas Hood, Hardy, Calderon, Verlaine, and Whitman, but none to Emerson. Why not?

When these books came out in 1896 and 1897, Robinson had not yet begun to respond to Emerson as a writer like himself to whom one might pay literary tribute. Emerson was the "sage" who had been of incalculable help to him in time of trouble, not an artist from whom one might learn something about how to write. Despite the later high praise of Emerson as poet, it is doubtful that Robinson ever did learn anything about the poet's craft from him, more's the pity. At any rate it is very clear that Emerson the priest and prophet was not, in the 1890's, a part of Robinson's "literary" experience at all, but his chief secret spiritual resource.

Increasingly, Robinson found it embarrassing to acknowledge publicly this particular source of consolation. It must have come to him fairly early — I should guess by 1902, the date of *Captain Craig,* though I have found no evidence in the letters to substantiate this guess — it must have occurred to him that if William James were vulnerable to the charge that his thought ignored Spencer's naturalism, Emerson's philosophy was even more vulnerable. All his life Robinson continued to read books of popular science and scientific philosophy, and the trends he observed therein, though he might think them "all wrong," yet left him more and more on the defensive. Those with better minds than his, he observed, were all, or so it seemed to him, becoming mechanistic naturalists. His early Harvard and Gardiner friend, Lawrence J. Henderson, teaching biological chemistry at Harvard, was not alone in reducing life to "nothing but" a physiochemical mechanism. This was what science seemed to have discovered by its rigorous methods of truth-seeking. How was a mere poet, who could claim neither mystic revelation nor competence in philosophy, to answer? Surely not by saying, "But I have read Emerson, and he intuited divinity everywhere."

So far as I have been able to discover, it was not until 1916, when he was nearly fifty, that Robinson could bring himself to pay any sort of *public* tribute to Emerson. In that year he told Joyce Kilmer in an interview that he considered Emerson our greatest American poet, and thought that his best things, fragments usually rather than whole poems, were as great as anything ever written anywhere in any language. His praise thus exceeded even that of Frost, who would later call "Uriel" the "greatest *Western*" — that is, American — "poem yet."

It is not surprising that this tribute of one poet to another says nothing about Emerson's usefulness to Robinson in his struggle with materialism, even though Robinson would soon publish "The Man Against the Sky," the whole point of which was to reject materialism. But that he had not completely reversed himself on Emerson, and would indeed never really do so, is suggested not only by his last poems, but, more explicitly, by one of his last letters. Writing from the hospital bed where he was dying of cancer to a young correspondent who was in difficulty, he repeated Dickinson's gesture of sharing a source of her own strength with Mrs. Higginson by sending her a volume of Emerson. "Perhaps Emerson will help," he wrote his young correspondent.

Emerson's influence on the poetry increases perceptibly through Robinson's first three volumes, then drops off after *Captain Craig,* finally to return to prominence in the last two long poems. If the preceding account, drawn from letters and other sources of information external to the poetry, is sound, this is what we should expect to find, providing just one more piece of external evidence is added.

Late in his life Robinson was much cheered by the new climate of scientific philosophy that began to be apparent in some quarters in the middle and later 1920's. Reading the British astrophysicists Eddington and Jeans, who were Platonists and religious in tone, Robinson was encouraged to hope once more that his implicit Transcendentalism would not in the end prove utterly indefensible. There was, he decided in 1933, a new "non-theological" religion on the way, to be "revealed" by science when we had the wits to see it. To an age when churches were only buildings and theology had lost all meaning, the coming religion would bring fresh hope and a renewed faith in the transcendent self. This new confidence of Robinson's lies behind the affirmations he intended to make in *Amaranth* and *King Jasper.*

But to return to the beginning of the career. Emerson's presence is not very obvious in *The Torrent and the Night Before,* or very important, but it is perceptible in at least four of the poems, and perhaps in others. What chiefly dominates the book, of course, is the sense of loss and grief, but Emerson provides a contrapuntal theme. To begin where one might not expect to find him, the sonnet in praise of Zola shows Robinson thinking in Emersonian terms about a naturalist of whom he knew little. He had read, he later confessed, only one book by Zola before writing the poem, and he had apparently not grasped the philosophic intention of *that* one. If Zola had been able to read the sonnet, he would no doubt have wondered whether the author's use of his name as the title were not a mistake; for in the poem he is praised not for anything he had said in *The Experimental Novel* he wanted to accomplish, but rather for penetrating through appearances to "the human heart/ Of God" and thus helping us all to find and cherish "the divine heart of man" — the two hearts being really, it is implied, the same heart. The doctrine assumed here is very good Emersonianism but very bad naturalism of the Zola variety.

There is a good deal in "The Children of the Night" that is straight out of Emerson, which may be one of the reasons why the poem was later omitted from the *Collected Poems.* Such Emersonian counsels as

> So let us in ourselves revere
> The Self which is the Universe!

sound like Robinson only in the smoothness of their meter. "Credo," which tells us more about what Robinson would like to believe, or hopes some day to believe, than about anything he actually does believe, almost certainly gets the suggestions for its images of music and light and darkness from Emerson's "The Poet" — the poem, not the essay — as these pairs of lines partially suggest:

"The Poet":

> I see the coming light,
> I see the scattered gleams,
> Aloft, beneath, on left and right
> The stars' own ether beams.

"Credo":

> I cannot find my way: there is no star
> In all the shrouded heavens anywhere;
> . . . .
> I know the far-sent message of the years,
> I feel the coming glory of the Light!

The important substitutions in Robinson's poem are in the verbs: In place of Emerson's concrete and positive "I *see* . . . I *see* . . . ether *beams,*" we have the negatives of Robinson's first two lines (he does *not* see, there *is no* star), followed by affirmatives entirely different from Emerson's, affirmatives that have little to say about *present experience.* For the "know" is equivalent to "know about" or "have heard about" the message from the past; and the light in the last line is still not *seen,* not experienced directly, only "felt," and even so not felt as *light* but felt as "glory." So that in effect this poem whose title says "I believe" contains neither belief nor experience from which belief might proceed, but only memory and hope. The poem suggests the predicament of an Emerson born too late, into a wrong world, as a child of the night who cannot honestly and simply assert, "I see."

But "Two Sonnets" makes Emerson's relation to this early poetry of Robinson's still clearer. The two poems are meant to be read together, and together they take off from a line in "Monadnoc," one of Emerson's greatest poems and one of Robinson's favorites, even this early, no doubt partly because the concluding lines of the poem affirm, in a manner more rare in Emerson's poetry than in his prose, his belief in the permanence of individual life. The mountain, Emerson writes, shames us at times, and humbles us always, but also, for those capable of seeing its meanings, enlarges and purifies our faith:

> Mute orator! well skilled to plead,
> And send conviction without phrase,
> Thou dost succor and remede
> The shortness of our days,
> And promise, on thy Founder's truth,
> Long morrow to this mortal youth.

While still searching for a way to accommodate himself to his mother's death, in the interval between the publication of his first volume in 1896 and his second in 1897, Robinson, writing a friend about his grief, misquoted, without identifying them, two earlier lines from Emerson's poem: "For the world was made in order, and the atoms march in time," he wrote. Emerson had written

> For the world was built in order,
> And the atoms march in tune,

by his last word suggesting the *melodiousness* of reality, an image which the immediately following lines take up and extend.

The first of Robinson's "Two Sonnets" comments on the conclusion of "Monadnoc," saying, in effect, yes, man *is* immortal, but immortality carries with it no memory of our earthly existence. We must not, the sonnet concludes, "cherish, in the life that is to come,/ The scattered features of dead friends again." The poem never says, but its tone suggests, that the reason is that life is too painful to be remembered.

The second sonnet is a comment on the earlier lines that Robinson misquoted in his letter. Just as the first one had said "Yes, *but*" to Emerson's belief that nature's revelations had as their ultimate implication man's immortality, so this sonnet too says "Yes, *but*" to Emerson's vision of cosmic harmony. Robinson accepts the vision but devotes his poem to stating the *difficulty* of attaining it. It is perhaps, he thinks, too demanding a vision for most of us. "Never until our souls are strong enough," the sonnet begins, "To plunge into the crater of the Scheme," not until we are morally and intellectually reborn somehow, "are we to get/ Where atoms and the ages are one stuff." We shall not be able to know how "the cursed waste/ Of life" — his mother's early death, for instance — is consistent with "the beneficence divine" that manifests itself in starlight and sunlight and "soul-shine" — not, that is, "Till we have drunk . . . / The mead of Thought's prophetic endlessness."

The two sonnets are not likely to strike most of us today as very good poems, partly because their very involved obscurities can hardly be unraveled unless we have Emerson's "Monadnoc" in mind, but unravel all too easily if we do, leaving the poems to be compared with Emerson's much greater one — a comparison wholly to Emerson's benefit. So I shall spend no more time on them, except the time it takes to say that Robinson's translation of Emerson's lines as implying a *place* "where atoms and the ages are one stuff" seems to fit in, in a curious way, with the particular form of his misquotation of the second line, his changing "tune" to "time." At any rate, Robinson's version in the sonnet omits much of both the poetry and the theology of Emerson's concrete and imagistic lines and strikes me as a very cloudy image indeed, if it *is* an image and not rather a vague concept.

As a result of Robinson's intensive, grief-motivated rereading of Emerson in late 1896 and early 1897, his second volume, *The Children of the Night,* is markedly more Emersonian than his first. For the most part, the contents of the two volumes are the same, but two poems in the first volume were dropped in the second, and a number of new ones were added. The longest, and thematically the most important, of the additions was a series of meditative poems called simply "Octaves," twenty-five of them in all. They have a single subject, Robinson's attempt to come to terms with Emerson. They state Robinson's agreement in theory with the one he calls now "the master," and at the same time sometimes merely imply and again explicitly state his inability to feel the way the "master," who is never named, felt: "Truth neither shakes/ Nor wavers; but the world shakes, and we shriek."

The speaker in the "Octaves" makes a central theme out of his awareness that he cannot measure up to the standards set by Emerson. He can *admire* the faith of the master, but not really, he fears, *hold* it. The first Octave will have to be a sufficient illustration of this theme which runs throughout the series:

> We thrill too strangely at the master's touch;
> We shrink too sadly from the larger self
> Which for its own completeness agitates
> And undermines us; we do not feel —
> We dare not feel it yet — the splendid shame
> Of uncreated failure; we forget,
> The while we groan, that God's accomplishment
> Is always and unfailingly at hand.

Emersonian terms, or Robinson's equivalents of them, are used throughout what is in effect a twenty-five-part dialogue between the two, but Emerson's *meaning,* as rendered here to be contrasted with the speaker's own difficulty in attaining belief, is never quite the same as what Emerson meant. Throughout the poems we get terms and phrases like "All-Soul," "Truth" considered as "divine, transitional, transcendent," and the "Real" in contrast with the merely actual of "this life"; yet the speaker quite clearly is thinking of the master's system as a defensive *retreat* from a discredited orthodoxy, while Emerson himself, as we have seen, thought of Transcendentalism as a recovery of original religious insights. Emerson had worked out his point of view, as he saw it, not as a substitute for a faith rendered philosophically obsolete by Darwin and Spencer but in part at least in reaction against the cold and increasingly practical moralism of the Unitarian movement, and in part as a way of mastering his own special and personal impotence and dread. As he saw it, after he had worked out his new ideas, Unitarianism, with its emphasis on reason and morality, was a church without a religion. The vital element in any real religion consisted of direct response to God within, in religious *experience* in short. Pondering what he ought to do with his life now that he was out of the Unitarian ministry, he went to the White Mountains to meditate and read, particularly to read, and read about, George Fox, the Quaker mystic. Fox had lived his life as though he knew that "God IS, not WAS." This, Emerson decided, was the only knowledge that was wholly essential.

This mystical and antinomian core of Transcendentalism, the elements that later led Emerson to declare that the movement ought to be described as "a Saturnalia of faith," could never be inferred from anything in Robinson's "Octaves." The "master" is a wise man who knows how important it is to believe in the Soul, and finds fewer obstacles to doing so than the speaker in the poems. Recalling the delight Robinson experienced several years after writing the "Octaves" when he first discovered *The Conduct of Life,* we can see that he was prepared to prefer the late Emerson, the theistic humanist, prepared before he ever read him. This late Emerson, he said, had more "humanity" and "humor": precisely, and less commitment to mystic experience. The late Emerson was something like an oriental sage, but a sage who had given up Zen's concentration on the immediate perception of being in depth. The late Emerson was less confident than he once had been that experience was equivalent to revelation. No wonder Robinson felt greater kinship with him. The wonder is that the Emerson we meet in "Octaves" is already old before Robinson had any way of knowing from his reading what Emerson would become. Robinson seems to have arrived at his interpretation by subtracting from Transcendentalism the elements that were meaningless to him in terms of his own experience. What was left after all the subtractions was a sort of stoical idealism.

The two "Octaves" that state the most unequivocal agreement with Emerson were, significantly, omitted from the *Collected Poems.* They are on art, and the role of the poet, and there is nothing at all in them which is not Emersonian — though there is much in Emerson that is not in *them.* For several years Robinson felt that on this subject he had no differences with the master. But as he began to see that metaphysics and aesthetics are not unrelated, I think he became embarrassed by the explicit Emersonianism of these two "Octaves" and so took them out of his works. They remind us of another poem he decided not to include in his collected works, his tribute to Walt Whitman, beginning

The master-songs are ended, and the man
That sang them is a name. And so is God
A name; and so is love, and life, and death,

and continuing to lament the fact that "We do not hear him very much to-day" for "His piercing and eternal cadence rings/ Too pure for us." Years later, Robinson said he had "never gotten much" out of Whitman — as we might guess by the extreme generality of the poem that praises him — but why write the tribute, then? It is possible, of course, that the older Robinson simply *forgot* one of his early enthusiasms. But it seems to me much more likely that the late statement was accurate, and that the poetic tribute was written in response neither to Whitman's actual works, nor to the actual man, but to Whitman thought of as a symbol of a secure Emersonian faith. If this is so, the decision not to collect the poem would suggest the waning of Robinson's own faith.

Emerson's impact on Robinson's work is clearest and most pervasive in *Captain Craig,* Robinson's third volume, which appeared five years after *The Children of the Night* and reflected the intensive rereading of Emerson that Robinson was doing in 1899 and 1900. That *this* should be the volume in which Robinson most carefully covered his tracks is one of the things that makes the work interesting to the literary historian.

A single example of careful track-covering will illustrate. Among the poems Robinson added to this volume, in addition to the long title poem, were two that he called, in print, "The Sage" and "Erasmus." But who, we might wonder, is the "sage" referred to? Reading the letters, we need not wonder long. "I am trying to do something with my Emerson and Erasmus sonnets," he wrote a friend in 1900. No sonnet in either *Captain Craig* or the *Collected Poems* is called "Emerson," but the evidence makes it clear that the two poems he was referring to in the letter are the ones called, both in *Captain Craig* and later in *Collected Poems,* "The Sage" and "Erasmus." What he was apparently doing with them was revising them to make them a pair in which each would provide a comment on the other.

In the first of the two as we now have them, the sage is praised for having preserved for us "the mintage of Eternity" by going "back to fierce wisdom and the Orient." The sage himself, "previsioned of the madness and the mean," has found the Truth hidden within "Love's inner shrine" without being "scarred," as the Orient has been, by his contact with "the Unseen." He remains "unfevered and serene" because he was "foreguarded" when he went "back to the perilous gates of Truth."

This seems a curious, and perhaps inept, way to praise Emerson — until we remember that Robinson is now thinking of the Emerson who wrote *The Conduct of Life,* discovered by Robinson while he was working on this volume. The author of *this* book might well be described as "unfevered and serene."

The subjects of the two poems have much in common as Robinson describes them. Both are men of religious vision who came into conflict with religious authority. The unnamed sage of the first poem is praised for having gone *"back"* (which is very much emphasized, both the second and the third lines starting "Back to"), back to an older and fiercer revelation, while Erasmus in the second poem is praised for looking *forward* to the world's need for more than the medieval "crusts" of divinity. One sage recovers what had been lost, the other anticipates a need; both were called heretics by the conservative. The two poems read together seem to imply that both recovery and reform are necessary for the proper guarding of the "mintage of Eternity."

But why in a pair of poems about two sages is one sage left anonymous while the other is named? With no direct evidence available of what went on in Robinson's mind beyond that in the poems themselves, I think it is still possible to guess. It was too late, in 1900, to be seeming to affirm Emersonian idealism, even Robinson's guarded late-Emerson variety. If one should be called upon to stand up and explain what he meant by equating the power of the Unseen with the rending of the curtain guarding the inner shrine in Love's temple, what could he possibly say? How explain what "Eternity" meant to a friend like Henderson? Better not to try, and so better not to encourage such questions.

The second sonnet of the pair would make it clear whose thought was being drawn on in both poems even if we did not have the external evidence identifying the sage as Emerson. The octave of the sonnet describes Erasmus in such a way as to imply that his humanistic awareness of "the man within the monk" frightened a Church that had lost touch with both man and God into charging him with "recreance" and "heresy." The sestet both makes this implication explicit and reveals that the literary model of a rebel against religious authority that Robinson *really* has in mind in describing Erasmus is not, as we might expect if the poem had been written by Emerson or Melville, Prometheus, but Emerson's own Uriel:

> And when he made so perilously bold
> As to be scattered forth in black and white,
> Good fathers looked askance at him and rolled
> Their inward eyes in anguish and affright;
> There were some of them did shake at what was told,
> And they shook best who knew that he was right.

Emerson, we recall, had ended "Uriel" by having all "truth-speaking things" in Nature confirm Uriel's radically humanistic, anti-authoritarian, and antinomian words, so that

> . . . a blush tinged the upper sky,
> And the gods shook, they knew not why.

In Robinson's poem the "Good fathers" of the church are granted more insight than Emerson was willing to credit the old gods with; they *know* why, and shake all the more because they know: "And they shook best who knew that he was right."

"Erasmus" makes a typically Robinsonian comment on the sage who wrote "Uriel." Emersonian in sympathy though he was, the younger poet could not accept Emerson's wholly antinomian conclusions, just because he lacked faith in the religious basis of antinomianism. Unless the rebellious soul is really in contact with God, his denial of society's norms *ought* to be called seditious and subversive, as it always is. But suppose there *is* no God, or suppose there is no way of knowing anything about Him, as Herbert Spencer had said? Then antinomianism would seem to be only irresponsible idiosyncrasy.

Furthermore, though Robinson could go along with Emerson in describing himself as an "endless seeker," he could not at all agree with the way Emerson ended his description of himself, "with no past at my back." Despite his intellectual skepticism — "wavering commitment" might be a better description of it — Robinson now and all through his life was very much tied to the past. As he saw it, it was not that the past lacked insight into reality, but that such insights were denied to *us,* and there was no use our pretending to have them. "Erasmus" comments on the Reformation from a *Protestant* point of view, but there is nothing in it of the radical antinomianism of Emerson's poem. Robinson's affinity with Emerson was tempered both by his almost equally strong affinity with Hawthorne, and by his sense that Transcendentalism was no longer really possible as a philosophy or as a way of life.

In the title poem of the volume, "Captain Craig," Robinson creates an aged Emerson whom he puts to tests more severe, as he supposes, than any that Emerson had faced, in order to watch the results. The Captain is dying and dependent on the charity of "five or six" young people who come to his room to hear him talk. One of the five or six, the speaker in the poem, is the most sympathetic, indeed even a kind of "secret disciple" like the Nicodemus of John's Gospel that Robinson would write about later; but even he cannot fail to recognize, sadly, that for all his immense courtesy, serenity, and benevolence, the Captain is something of a crank. Certainly his unqualified claim to be speaking with the voice of God would seem monstrous egotism in anyone less completely benevolent or less truly modest, in his person if not his philosophy.

But perhaps more important than his courtesy and his benevolence in keeping him from seeming a mere madman is his sense of humor. To ease the embarrassment caused by his being at once the host and instructor of his young friends, and the grateful recipient of their charity, the Captain "makes game" of them, humorously overstating on one occasion the fundamental conviction by which he has lived:

> "You are the resurrection and the life,"
> He said, "and I the hymn the Brahmin sings,"

thus claiming for them identity with Christ and for himself identity with Brahma, as pictured in Emerson's poem of that title.

Thus the Captain passes every test but one to which he and his philosophy are put. His actions — whatever "actions" a bedridden, dying mendicant is capable of — are the proof of his words — for *him,* but perhaps for him only. For all his magnificent talk, he never reveals the secret of his confidence. That it is not simply the result of well-being and success is clear to all his listeners, but what *is* its source? There is a curious cloudiness about all the Captain's attempts to explain. He states at one time or another almost every major Emersonian doctrine — except the one on which they all ultimately rested, the mystical doctrine of "the way up," the soul's ascension to God through Nature as the intuition and the imagination read Nature as a symbolic language. Clearly, the Captain's firm belief that the ultimate pattern of the universe is love has allowed him to preserve his serenity, but how are the five or six to know that his belief is true? The one test he does *not* pass, because he never even recognizes its existence, is the purely abstract and intellectual one, the "evidential" one: How do we *know?*

The "I" of the poem, the "secret disciple," seems to have a glimmering of how the Captain knows, but he never attempts to reduce his understanding to words. Is it his sense that the Captain's words are *true* that makes him listen so intently and sympathetically while the others cough and doze? Or could it be that the tie between them was not their sharing a knowledge hidden from the others but simple gratitude? Explaining the Captain's superiority to a sense of sin and the need for repentance — the soul's mumps, as Emerson had said — the speaker defines the Captain's self-chosen role this way:

> No penitential shame for what had come,
> No virtuous regret for what had been, —
> But rather a joy to find it in his life
> To be an outcast usher of the soul
> For such as had good courage of the Sun
> To pattern Love.

This would remind us of the way Matthew Arnold had just characterized Emerson in his American lecture on him — as "the friend and aider of those who would live in the spirit" — except for the "outcast" before "usher of the soul." An "outcast" is one without status. Captain Craig himself can hardly be called an outcast, unless every prophet and sage who rejects the norms of his society, including its idea of what constitutes success, should be so called. "Things are in the saddle and ride mankind," Emerson had said, thus rejecting his society's practical materialism; but Emerson was no outcast.

I suspect the word is used by the "I" of the poem to describe the Captain because the sage who had meant so much to Robinson several years before had been, as a *philosopher,* cast out by the naturalism of the time, deprived of philosophical status. If this is true, then the unexplained sympathy of the speaker with the Captain rests not on secret knowledge but on secret gratitude. The basis of the gratitude could not be explained without the speaker himself suffering loss of status. Robinson's decision to remove Emerson's name from the sonnet praising him shows that he was becoming sensitive to the charge of being an Emersonian. The charge would be, in 1902, in the eyes of his friend Henderson and many others, almost equivalent to being called a frustrated Romantic, or a wishfully-thinking Idealist, or even a mystagogue. Surely Robinson is speaking partly for himself, or at least about what he feared *might* have happened to him had he not covered his tracks so well, when he has the "I" of "Captain Craig" say that as a result of his championship of the Captain,

> They loaded me with titles of odd form
> And unexemplified significance,
> Like "Bellows-mender to Prince Aeolus,"
> "Pipe-filler to the Hoboscholiast,"
> "Bread-fruit for the Non-Doing," with one more
> That I remember, and a dozen more
> That I forget.

I can't help wondering whether the "one more" remembered but not divulged may not have included the name of Emerson. At any rate, after *Captain Craig,* which could never have been written without Emerson, Robinson stopped writing his friends about Emerson's philosophy as a resource — until that last letter written from his deathbed. The reason, I suspect, was not any nervous compulsion to hide a "source" but a growing recognition that Emerson was no longer really useful to him as a resource. The darkness had seemed to be lifting, but now it closed in again. There *must* be a Purpose and a Law, as he was soon to write, but he now realized that Emerson, inspiring example though he remained, could not tell him *why* there "must." What I have called the covering of tracks certainly occurred, but the motive for it was partly Robinson's lack of confidence in his own thinking and partly a disillusion with the "master" considered as Sage. Hereafter the debt would be paid by tributes to Emerson the *poet.*

*

With relatively few exceptions, Robinson's best later poems contain no suggestion of his debt to Emerson. Even when they include muted suggestions of ideas that might be Emersonian, or at least vaguely Transcendental, the *tone* is as completely un-Emersonian as it is possible to imagine any tone being. As Robert Frost said in his Introduction to *King Jasper,* Robinson, in his best work at least, is the poet of "immedicable grief," whose theme — his real theme, whatever his intention — is "unhappiness itself." Though Robinson would not have thought this a fair or perceptive description of his work — and it does omit a number of fine poems — there is a sense in which Frost's characterization of the work ought to be thought of as a primary insight, needing to be qualified in a number of ways but not reversed.

The tone and atmosphere of Robinson's work as a whole are epitomized in the concluding lines of one of the poems first published in *The Children of the Night,* "The Clerks":

> What comes of all your visions and your fears?
> Poets and kings are but the clerks of Time,
> Tiering the same dull webs of discontent,
> Clipping the same sad alnage of the years.

A comparison of Emerson's "Monadnoc" with Robinson's much briefer and simpler "Monadnock Through the Trees" would be a better way — because fairer to Robinson — of getting at the same point, his prevailing tone. Emerson's poem does not simply acknowledge, it strongly emphasizes, the mountain's *enduring* quality compared with man's brief span of life, and its indifference to the little men who live in its shadow; yet Emerson's tone is confident and positive, and the concluding lines affirm, as we have seen, the centrality and permanence not only of life but of the individual. When Robinson looked at the same mountain from Peterborough, he saw its pyramid as the shape of death and its "calm" endurance — the quality that Emerson had stressed — dwarfing and diminishing life. The resulting poem amounts to an elegy for all mankind:

> Before there was in Egypt any sound
> Of those who reared a more prodigious means
> For the self-heavy sleep of kings and queens
> Than hitherto had mocked the most renowned, —

Unvisioned here and waiting to be found,
Alone, amid remote and older scenes,
You loomed above ancestral evergreens
Before there were the first of us around.

And when the last of us, if we know how,
See farther from ourselves than we do now,
Assured with other sight than heretofore
That we have done our mortal best and worst, —
Your calm will be the same as when the first
Assyrians went howling south to war.

The elegiac effect of "Monadnock Through the Trees" is conveyed more briefly and more poignantly in one of Robinson's most memorable short poems, "The Dark Hills":

Dark hills at evening in the west,
Where sunset hovers like a sound
Of golden horns that sang to rest
Old bones of warriors under ground,
Far now from all the bannered ways
Where flash the legions of the sun,
You fade — as if the last of days
Were fading, and all wars were done.

Robinson was quite right, of course, in his feeling that the First World War, in the background of the poem, the "war to end war," would not be the last of wars, that days would go on fading and the wars never be done, but it is not as sad prognostication that the poem is chiefly impressive. The lines express a grief too pure to be lightened by any merely historical change, an "immedicable" grief, as Frost said. Life itself, the poem implies, is like a war in which defeat is inevitable; with or without the wars of nations, we are all of us Rolands fighting a doomed rear-guard action in a narrow pass, only for us there are no "golden horns" to sing us under ground.[2]

That Robinson himself would have denied — *did* deny, repeatedly — that any such statement as this was a fair summary of his *belief,* is not to the point. This is the way he tended to *feel* about life. Against the feeling, he could oppose only a set of beliefs for which he could find almost no support. The result was that a good many of his poems are weakened by the incompatibility of their emotional tone and their explicit statements of belief. It is not at all surprising that Robinson's first reviewer found the atmosphere of *The Torrent and the Night Before* to be like that of a "prison-house." He was anticipating Frost's reaction to all the later work — and not only Frost's, but that of what seems to be the majority of Robinson's critics. He was responding to a palpable atmosphere, to the work as *poetry,* in short, rather than to the many direct expressions of Emersonian idealism sprinkled through it.

This disparity between sensibility and belief that runs through so much of his work, particularly that part of it which attempts in any degree to be philosophical, probably has more to do with the preference of most readers for the early Tilbury Town portraits than any other factor. In the best of these studies of failure and alienation, the art is marvelously controlled. In the very best, there is a strong identification between the character in the poem and Robinson himself, or someone closely identified with him, leading to a balance Robinson could not always maintain between pity and humor. "Mr. Flood's Party" clearly reflects Robinson's own experience with liquor consumed in vast quantities as an anodyne, and "Eros Turannos," which may well be Robinson's greatest short poem, clearly reflects his hopeless and tragic love for the incredibly beautiful Emma, brother Herman's wife.[3] But "Miniver Cheevy" is probably the most instructive example of a subject that permitted Robinson to write at his best level in the Tilbury Town poems.

Miniver is the archetypal frustrated romantic idealist, born in the wrong time for idealism. He is close enough to being Robinson himself so that Robinson can smile at him and let the pathos remain unspoken.

> Miniver Cheevy, child of scorn,
> Grew lean while he assailed the seasons.
> He wept that he was ever born,
> And he had reasons.

Here and throughout the poem the relation between what Miniver knows and what the speaker knows is subtle and effective. Miniver wept and the poet does not weep, but not because he thinks there are no *reasons* to weep. Robinson knew too much about the reasons for an idealist to weep to permit him to make Miniver a mere butt of humor. Apart from his intellectual reasons, which I have already said enough about, there were more personal and emotional ones that are relevant to any discussion of Robinson's identification with Miniver Cheevy. Robinson was born the third son of a family whose hearts were so set on having a daughter this time that they had made no provision for the name of an unwanted son. For more than six months the boy remained unnamed, until strangers at a summer resort, feeling that he ought to be granted an identity beyond that of simply "the baby," put slips of paper with male first names written on them into a hat and chose someone to draw one out. The man who drew out the slip with "Edwin" written on it happened to live in Arlington, Massachusetts, which seemed to provide the easiest choice for a second name; and so by an "accident of fate," we have a poet named Edwin Arlington Robinson. Robinson hated the name and thought of himself as a child of scorn — and he had reasons.

> Miniver sighed for what was not,
> 	And dreamed, and rested from his labors;
> He dreamed of Thebes and Camelot,
> 	And Priam's neighbors.
>
> Miniver mourned the ripe renown
> 	That made so many a name so fragrant;
> He mourned Romance, now on the town,
> 	And Art, a vagrant.

Like Miniver too, Robinson "dreamed of Camelot" — and wrote three very long, and very tedious, Arthurian poems in which the "dreaming" is compulsive and unrecognized. But in "Miniver Cheevy" the dreaming is compulsive only for Miniver, not for the poet. Who would *not* turn to the past for his values if he lived in an age when the "facts" of coldly objective knowledge seemed to leave no room for any "ideal" values and when a "mere poet" who made no money was considered a failure by Tilbury Town's standards? For Romance to be "on the town" meant for it to be the object of the township's charity, in the poor farm or on home relief; in either case the object not only of "charity" but of the scorn that would accompany it. "Vagrants" — tramps — would sometimes spend a few days or weeks "on the town" before wandering on. The connection between Miniver and Emerson comes through Captain Craig, who was also described as a "vagrant" and was also the object of charity; for the penniless philosopher of the earlier poem was not, as critics have so often said, Robinson himself but Emerson *in extremis.*

Miniver scorned the gold he sought,
  But sore annoyed was he without it;
Miniver thought, and thought, and thought,
  And thought about it.

Miniver Cheevy, born too late,
  Scratched his head and kept on thinking;
Miniver coughed, and called it fate,
  And kept on drinking.

But unlike the Captain, Miniver *is* Robinson, or at least that part of Robinson that Robinson recognized as being Romantic and Idealistic. He too had "thought, and thought, and thought,/ And thought about it," without arriving at any conclusions definite enough to be stated very clearly, even to himself. He too had resented his poverty while condemning practical materialism and popular notions of success. He too had "called it fate" and for many years "kept on drinking." A good deal of the time he was almost as convinced as Miniver that he had been "born too late."

It should be unnecessary to say that such a lining-up of the parallels between Robinson and his character is no substitute for a close critical analysis of the ways in which the poem works. My purpose in calling attention to the analogy is two-fold: first, to illustrate the earlier generalization that Robinson wrote at his best level in the Tilbury Town poems when he wrote about a projection of an aspect of himself; and second, to prepare the way for a further conclusion, namely, that the side of himself that Robinson could stand off from and smile at was the *believing* side, never the deeper self that felt only the grief. So that the lack of any *direct* expression of his Transcendentalism in most of his best poems — "Captain Craig" excepted — does not mean that his debt to Emerson is confined to a few early minor works. Emerson remained indirectly useful to his art even while he failed the man. When Robinson finally got to the point where he could be amused at beliefs that had once seemed capable of saving him from despair, he transformed frustrations into some of our finest poems.

The tragedy of Robinson's career was his failure to develop beyond the level of achievement he reached very early — in *Captain Craig* in 1902, and for short poems, in *The Man Against the Sky* in 1916. It is doubtful that he ever again wrote so fine a long poem as "Isaac and Archibald," in the *Captain Craig* volume, which strikes me as much greater than the long character studies of back-country New Englanders that Robert Frost would shortly do. And the title poem of the volume seems to me very much better than the infrequent and generally slighting comment on it would lead one to expect. As for the short poems, surely he never excelled "Miniver Cheevy" in *The Town Down River* in 1910, unless it was in "Hillcrest" or "Eros Turannos" in *The Man Against the Sky*. The general opinion that the very long poems on which he spent most of his time after 1916 are for the most part quite unreadable needs a little qualifying but is not basically mistaken. Why did Robinson fail to develop?

The worst of the long poems are undoubtedly the Arthurian legends and the earlier long narratives of modern life. Most of them have patches of good writing, to be sure. Robinson himself thought he had never written better than in the concluding lines of *Tristram,* and it is true that in them he does bring grief and despair to quintessential expression. But in general the combined prolixity and obscurity of these poems make them not worth reading or rereading. Words at this point in his career seem to have become a way of blotting out time with Robinson, as though he were not writing poems but playing solitaire and hoping the game might last as long as possible. He is using words in these poems not to reveal but to delay or obscure meaning.

The only conspicuous exceptions to this statement in the period between *The Man Against the Sky* and *Cavender's House* in 1929 are the Biblical poems, "The Three Taverns" and "Lazarus," both included in *The Three Taverns* in 1920. Just why these are so very much better than the other long poems of the period is still anybody's guess. Of course, they are not so long as the others, for one thing. But their superiority is not simply negative. My own guess is that Robinson's sympathies were more fully engaged here and his imagination stirred, but it is also true that the Biblical stories he expanded seemed to him to contain their own meanings, so that he was not under the necessity of philosophizing, an activity that he was now incapable of, as almost every new long poem made clearer. The *narrative* structure had been supplied in the Arthurian tales, to be sure, but not the *meaning*. When he returned to Biblical narrative in *Nicodemus* in 1932, he produced another of his best long poems.

Now he had something like the special advantage he had had in "Miniver Cheevy," the advantage of combined sympathetic identification and distance that had enabled him in that poem to understand Miniver as Miniver understood himself, yet also smile as one who knew more than Miniver. For increasingly in these last years Robinson himself was a sort of "secret disciple" like Nicodemus, who visited Jesus at night to ask how a man might be born again. But his discipleship was not to an orthodox Christ so much as to a blend of Emerson, Christ, and Buddha. So that in this poem not only the narrative (as in the Arthurian poems) but the meaning and the point of view were *supplied* him.

The partial recovery of control that occurred in the last half dozen years of Robinson's life amounted to a kind of return to what he had tried to do in prose drama in *Van Zorn* and *The Porcupine* in 1914 and 1915. So far as it is possible to tell from reading Robinson's critics and the literary historians, no one appears to have read these plays for the past fifty years, but they are very much more worth reading than most of the long poems that pad the *Collected Poems* to its forbidding length of 1488 pages of small print. Whether they are "good theater" or not I will not even try to guess, but certainly they are good reading.

Van Zorn: A Comedy in Three Acts seems to me the less credible of the two, but even it has its points. Adapting itself to the conventions of drawing-room comedy of the time, it strongly anticipates Eliot's *The Cocktail Party* in its reliance on a wise and mysterious benefactor who brings about a cure of souls partly by helping the lost children to discover what they are and want and partly by events he arranges to have happen. The only important difference between Eliot's psychiatrist and Robinson's "Flying Dutchman" Van Zorn is that the psychiatrist is part of a group of the enlightened who work with him closely, a church in short, while Van Zorn works entirely alone. This is what should be expected from the differing theological backgrounds of the two plays. Eliot's play is explicitly Christian, Robinson's vaguely oriental, or at least a sort of amalgam of Christianity and Buddhism.

The hero who is turned to the light and given a second birth by the influence of the redemptive Van Zorn is sometimes jokingly called Phoebus Apollo, or light and wisdom, and sometimes "Old Hundred," — "Praise God from whom all blessings flow . . . Praise Father, Son, and Holy Ghost," the hymn adapted from the one hundredth Psalm. In either case, he has some sort of special relation to God — or *is* God. As wisdom and light, he is the God within, frustrated, suffering, "drinking too much"; as "Old Hundred" he is a sort of Christ-figure. When he gives up drinking, he says he has been "born again" and is said by others to be "illuminated"; and after this there is a good deal of play on *light,* once again anticipating *The Cocktail Party.*

Van Zorn himself is called a "fatalist" and said to have an "Oriental" way with him — unusual, surely, in a Dutch millionaire. He is also said to have "mirrors" into which he can look, so that perhaps the wisdom he helps the others to attain is really self-knowledge, which would be a way to salvation close enough to Buddhism to justify the "Oriental" epithet. The universal compassion and feeling for destiny that emerge from the play as felt rather than from stated themes are also of course oriental — which fact does not prevent them from being at the same time gifts to Robinson from Emerson, who himself in middle and later years was much attracted to the Orient.

The Porcupine even more clearly looks back to Emerson and the "oriental reading" Robinson did in the 1890's, and just as clearly points forward to Eliot's later plays. In its use of a redemptive character with the power to change people's lives, it suggests *The Cocktail Party,* as *Van Zorn* does, but in its concern with the relation of self-knowledge to vocation, it looks toward Eliot's *The Confidential Clerk.* In its emphasis on growth beyond one's earlier "self," it suggests Eliot's "Fare forward, voyager," of *The Four Quartets.* Larry, the redemptive character, says at one point,

> Yes, Rachel, that's just about what we are — children. The best and the worst, the wisest and the silliest of us — children. Tumbling, blundering, groping children,

> — getting our heads bumped and our fingers burned, and making ourselves generally uncomfortable. But all this needn't keep us from growing, or from looking now and then as if we had not committed the unpardonable sin in being born.

I think we may see in *The Porcupine's* theme of growth or death — the one who is called "the porcupine" develops protective quills, refuses to grow, and ends by suicide — some remnant of Robinson's legacy from Emerson, though there is nothing specifically Emersonian in the language of the play. But whether there is any actual influence of Emerson on the play or not, is not really the point. Like *Van Zorn* it gives us a Robinson writing clearly and coherently, interestingly and pointedly, of the elements of his faith that, woven together, gave him whatever hope he had. With no attempt to reason systematically, as he would soon try to do in "The Man Against the Sky," these two plays taken together give us a much better idea of what his "philosophy" came to be than the poem does. Of the poem, he once wrote an inquirer that he considered it his best statement of his "philosophy — as you choose to call it." Both the aesthetic failure of the poem itself and the qualification attached to this statement about it suggest the failure of the long semiphilosophical narratives that were soon to follow.

In *Amaranth* and *King Jasper,* his last two poems, the writing becomes clearer than it had been for years, the prolixity diminishes, and the stories *move.* The themes are the by now familiar ones of finding the true self and the true vocation, the danger and the promise of growth, and the search for the light. In both we meet again the wise guide, the disseminator of true knowledge, who makes one know oneself, the semisupernatural teacher. In both, the end sought is the wisdom that makes it possible for us to accept change and to grow. It is hard to say whether the two poems should be called more Buddhist or more Emersonian.

Amaranth is completely Hawthornesque in its form, and chiefly Emersonian I should say, though also oriental, in its meaning. A dream-allegory of life in a hell of illusion where there is no knowledge of the true self, it ends for Fargo — who will, we guess, go far — in an awakening that brings new hope and a burst of light —

While he spoke,
The world around him flamed amazingly
With light that comforted and startled him
With joy, and with ineffable release.
There was a picture of unrolling moments
In a full morning light. . . .

King Jasper glances at the social problems of revolution in the 1930's, with unyielding Capitalism and destructive Communism apparently equally to be deplored; but its real center is the problem of change and growth once again. Zoë, whom Robinson defined for an inquirer as not life but knowledge, is the life-giving wisdom that comes to those who maintain their contact with the eternities. Robinson hints allegorically, but with sufficient clarity so that one would have thought that the inquirer would not have needed to inquire, she is to be thought of as one of the daughters of Proteus, the Old Man of the Sea. She comes into the castle of the industrial magnate, the "King" of the present world, offering freedom and new life, but neither the King nor his Queen is able to face newness, and in the end, after they have committed suicide and their son, who has understood and loved her, has been destroyed by the materialist revolutionary, Zoë is alone with her secret and saving knowledge. Despite the suicide and slaughter of all the ordinary human characters in the poem, the ending is intended, I think, to express a hope that others may find and love Zoë.

One difference between these two long poems and the earlier ones is their frank use of allegory. Most of the earlier ones, even in the Arthurian cycle, were "realistic" without seeming "real." Another difference is the greater hopefulness of them, especially of *Amaranth*. But what strikes me as the really significant difference is that in them Robinson is no longer just maundering, piling up distinctions without a difference or making affirmations that affirm nothing more solid than that affirmations are much to be desired. The poems have their defects, to be sure, some of which are implied in the preceding summaries, but the defects are not crippling. The poems deserve a better fate than to go unread, as they have for so many years. Like the plays, that have gone unread even longer, they give us a Robinson who has something worth saying, who knows what it is, and who goes about saying it with sufficient power and relevance to our interests to make it well worth our time to read them.

There are many ways to tell the story of Robinson's career. To approach him chiefly through a study of his relations with Emerson, as I have just done, is of course simply one of them. Some years ago I told the same story more briefly from the vantage point of Robinson's knowledge of science and scientific philosophy, its effect on him, and his attempts to refute some of its implications. The conclusions I arrived at then were not strikingly different from those that have emerged in my writing this time. It seemed from that earlier vantage point that Robinson was damaged as a poet, kept from developing his special gifts as he might have, by his excessive preoccupation with the "materialism" of science, which forced a man with no gifts for abstract thought to try to be a poetic philosopher.

The story should be told some time from the standpoint of Robinson's relations with *both* of his favorite American writers, who were also Dickinson's — Hawthorne and Emerson. His responses to the two were very different, especially in the formative years of his career. His first response to Emerson, as we have seen, was to a sage who might provide comfort in time of trouble, and at no time does his early interpretation of the sage seem particularly acute. He seems at first not really to have confronted the problem of epistemology, the problem created by the fact that the metaphysic of Idealism rested upon a theory of how and what we *know*. He at first appears to have tried to accept Idealism without accepting the theory of knowledge that supported it.

Some degree of awareness of the difficulty of this maneuver must have been present to Robinson even from the beginning, though, for his attempt to find support for Emersonian Idealism in Eastern religion was essentially an attempt to fill in what seemed to him a gap in Emerson, to give Emerson's thought the foundation it seemed to him to lack. Thus when in "The Sage" he describes Emerson as having developed his philosophy by going back to ancient oriental truth for his wisdom, he is being inaccurate about Emerson historically, and certainly misinterpreting the early Transcendental Emerson; but he is also instinctively repeating Emerson's own development, for Emerson himself, as the ecstatic moments of awareness came less and less frequently, leaned increasingly on the support he found in oriental religion. What both the late Emerson and Robinson tended to omit in their response to oriental teaching was the element best represented in Zen Buddhism, the concentration on full awareness of the concrete actual event or object — the *actual* perceived in such depth as to reveal the indwelling eternal spirit. Thus once again Robinson tended to miss the way of *knowing* on which the conclusions rested, as he had when he drew on Emerson.

The Emerson of Robinson's plays and late poems is an evolutionary theist who makes no mystical claims, who only calls for continued growth or self-transcendence, for the superiority of individual over societal claims, and for acceptance of one's destiny. Here it seems to me Robinson's understanding of the later Emerson who had appealed to him *was* acute. Emerson so interpreted is a very substantial figure, however far he may be from the more exciting Emerson of the early poems and lectures. The substantial quality of his thought accounts for a considerable part of the value of Robinson's plays and latest long poems.

Robinson responded to Hawthorne surely and acutely from the very beginning, not as a sage but as an artist. His kinship with the older writer was temperamental, not philosophic, a shared response of the whole sensibility to experience, not the satisfaction of a need for belief. The only thing he missed in his aesthetic response to Hawthorne was the "light" that Hawthorne wanted to affirm, and sometimes did affirm, more or less successfully. But if, as it seems to me, Hawthorne himself felt the darkness of experience more strongly and instinctively than he felt the light, then it is not surprising that Robinson, responding as an artist to an artist, should have sensed primarily the "blackness" there that Melville had noted long before. Robinson found in Hawthorne a great writer who was a kindred spirit.

Unfortunately, in *Amaranth,* where Hawthorne's presence is most apparent, it is the Hawthorne of the allegorical sketches like "The Great Carbuncle" and "The Christmas Banquet," not the Hawthorne of the less abstract tales, who is primarily evident. *Cavender's House* is less obviously Hawthornesque but the Hawthorne we find in it is better Hawthorne. The house is an image of the mind, and as Cavender explores its dark rooms, searching for he knows not what, he confronts his own deeper self, its guilt primarily, but its innocence too. The two themes of the poem, that the answers to our most urgent questions cannot be given us from outside ourselves but must be found within, and that when we stand in the darkness we are better able to see the light, are good Hawthorne as well as good Robinson. *Cavender's House* is one of the more rewarding of the long poems.

Robinson was much closer in his style, everywhere in his work, to Hawthorne than to Emerson. He seldom *sounds* like Emerson, but very often like Hawthorne. His preference for traditional meters and stanzaic forms, his diction, and especially his hesitant, tentative rhythms, draw him as close, perhaps, to Hawthorne as verse can ever come to prose. Both artists were men with the strongest feeling for ancient pieties and traditional verities; both had an instinctive sense that the more everything changed, the more it was the same; both felt shut out from the warmth of life by conditions within them, for which they blamed sometimes fate and sometimes themselves.

All this and more that is so important in Robinson's work has necessarily received scant recognition in a treatment in which Emerson has provided the focus. But not everything can be said at once. The focus provided by Emerson has had the advantage, as I hope, of throwing more light on two matters that seem to me greatly in need of being lighted up than an approach to Robinson through Hawthorne would have. The first of these is Robinson's place in the *tradition* of American poetry, the question, for instance, of where he stands in relation to Dickinson and Frost. The second is the problem created by his failure to develop, as Dickinson did and Frost would, when his literary resources were so much like hers and when he shared with Frost a major debt to Emerson. From this point of view the primary question is not how he succeeded — on *this,* Hawthorne could throw much light — but why he failed as much as he did.

Perhaps he himself pointed toward the answer when he thought of himself as born in the wrong time — the wrong time at any rate for a man of sensibility who was inclined to be an Emersonian Idealist.

CHAPTER X

The Strategic Retreat

Sleep lingers all our lifetime about our eyes, as night hovers all day in the boughs of the fir-tree.

— Emerson, in "Experience"

The question that he frames in all but words
Is what to make of a diminished thing.

— Frost, in "The Oven Bird"

Emerson was an Abominable Snowman of the top-lofty peaks. But what a poet he was in prose and verse.

— Robert Frost, in a letter to Lawrance Thompson, 1959

ROBERT FROST

WHEN a poet who has occupied an eminent position dies, especially if his career is so long that he was writing before most of his commentators were born, so that he seems like a permanent part of the literary scene, there is likely to be a spate of re-evaluations. If the poet has won great honors and been widely acclaimed, the general trend of the re-evaluations is almost certain to be downward. So with Robert Frost, who was of Robinson's generation. He attained personal and poetic maturity before the revolution of "modernism" set in, lived and wrote through and beyond it, and died early in 1963 as a sort of semiofficial poet laureate.

Comment since his death has tended to follow one or the other of two quite different approaches to conclusions that have in common a scaled-down estimate. If the critic likes Frost and wants to save him as a major poet from being destroyed by the inanities and duplicities of the popular image Frost himself labored to create, he is likely to discover that Frost wrote some of the darkest poems ever written by any American. He will find the genuine Frost in the poems that yield most fully to a discovered "design of darkness." Irving Howe, writing a valedictory piece shortly after the poet's death, put this conclusion most succinctly. Much of Frost's work, he decided, will not live, especially the "wisdom" poems and the attempts at various affirmations, but:

> The best of his poems are neither indulgences in homely philosophy nor wanderings in romanticism. If anything, they are antipathetic to the notion that the universe is inherently good or delightful or hospitable to our needs. The symbols they establish in relation to the natural world are not, as in transcendentalist poetry, tokens of benevolence. These lyrics speak of the hardness and recalcitrance of the natural world; of its absolute indifference to our needs and its refusal to lend itself to an allegory of affection; of the certainty of physical dissolution; but also of the refreshment that can be found through a brief submission to the alienness of nature, always provided one recognizes the need to move on, not stopping for rest but remaining locked, alone, in consciousness.

This is penetrating. Without a shift of ground to a different vantage point from that implied in the way Mr. Howe uses "romanticism" and "transcendentalist" as though they equated with wish and illusion and so were in the sharpest contrast with fact and reality, I do not see how we could seriously challenge this summary of the meanings of a great many of the poems that seem to come from the deepest part of the poet's sensibility. And even if we *do* shift to other assumptions, the darkness of much of the poetry, perhaps the best of it, will remain to be responded to and dealt with. As evaluation put in the form of description, this is excellent; but taken at face value, as description, it will not do. It leaves too much of the poetry, including some very good poetry, out of account, and it simplifies too much the largest meanings even of those poems it intends to describe.

Less sympathetic critics are more likely, now that the career is complete, to take a long look at the whole body of work, relate it to the nineteenth-century tradition of which it is clearly a part, and find in it a diminution and diminishment of that tradition. Frost is an Emersonian, we are told, but an Emersonian with no faith in the Soul, so that "self-reliance" becomes in him mere stubbornness and idiosyncrasy resting on a willful narrowing of the sympathies. Lacking a coherent view of nature, he is unable to tell us why he finds it so important. He keeps hinting that he has some secret source of strength, but he refuses to let anyone else in on the secret. In him Transcendental vision is reduced to canniness and the Emersonian metaphysic of growth to a shrewdly calculated strategy aimed at survival. Fundamentally, it is fear of experience that produces the typical Frostian shrug of the shoulders, the wisecrack, the undercutting change of tone that comes at the end of so many of Frost's poems. Even "Design," we remember, ends with a line that invites us to deny, if we wish, that the pattern of images has revealed any important meaning — *"If* design govern in a thing so small."

So compressed a summary of the views of an apparently growing number of unsympathetic critics does not of course do justice to any one of them, but surely it is impossible simply to deny that important features of Frost's poetry are here being described, or at any rate glanced at. Some years ago I wrote about this aspect of Frost under the title "The Strategic Retreat." Someone then wrote that I had condemned Frost for being "cowardly" in his fear of commitment, his "spiritual drifting," as Yvor Winters long ago called it. But a *strategic* retreat, in the military language from which the phrase is borrowed, has nothing to do with either cowardice or courage. Morally, the term is perfectly neutral. A general makes a strategic retreat in order to win a later battle, or to get into a position to win the whole war. The move is an action dictated by the practical intelligence. If the military metaphor has any validity for the conditions of the individual's life — and surely in the world of Frost's poetry at least it does — then we may say that the person who never shrewdly retreats to prepare for another engagement is simply a fool.

If we want to understand a poet we must begin by granting him his world. It is never exactly our world, but in proportion to his greatness, we shall find that the circles of his experience overlap with ours. But the condition of discovering this, as the Romantics quite correctly said, is a condition of the heart, "sympathy" as Hawthorne put it, not the attainment of a "correct" philosophy or a "correct" set of critical principles. Doctrines and dogmas have their uses, even in criticism, but their uses are more likely to come late than early in the critical act.

*

Frost's world gets its special characteristics from its unique combination of closeness to and distance from Emerson's world. If we will attend closely to a bird poem by each poet, we shall find both the closeness and the distance. Emerson's "The Titmouse" is too long to be quoted entire, but here is its opening verse-paragraph:

> You shall not be overbold
> When you deal with arctic cold,
> As late I found my lukewarm blood
> Chilled wading in the snow-choked wood.
> How should I fight? my foeman fine
> Has million arms to one of mine:
> East, west, for aid I looked in vain,
> East, west, north, south, are his domain.
> Miles off, three dangerous miles, is home;
> Must borrow his winds who there would come.
> Up and away for life! be fleet! —
> The frost-king ties my fumbling feet,
> Sings in my ears, my hands are stones,
> Curdles the blood to the marble bones,
> Tugs at the heart-strings, numbs the sense,
> And hems in life with narrowing fence.
> Well, in this broad bed lie and sleep, —
> The punctual stars will vigil keep, —
> Embalmed by purifying cold;
> The winds shall sing their dead-march old,
> The snow is no ignoble shroud,
> The moon thy mourner, and the cloud.

Except for the rhythms, which in Frost would be iambic, the first two lines might well have been written by Frost. The *sense* of them he *did* write, over and over again. And the question in the fifth line, "How should I fight?" was the chief question behind Frost's work throughout his career. The home miles off, the numbed senses, the desire for sleep, the equation of sleep and death — all this and more suggests the later poet's "Stopping by Woods on a Snowy Evening."

But at this point in the poem, with "fate" — Emerson's name for all that is alien and threatening — with fate "coming fast," the poet hears the "cheerful cry" of the titmouse, "a saucy note/ Out of sound heart and merry throat." The bird is bright, active, and unafraid—a rare "nature note" [1] in Emerson, a nice use of a bit of ornithology, for the actual titmouse is noted for its curiosity and friendliness, its lack of fear of people. *It* is not numbed or made drowsy by the cold:

> Here was this atom in full breath,
> Hurling defiance at vast death;
> This scrap of valor just for play
> Fronts the north-wind in waistcoat gray.

The speaker wonders what the bird's secret is, and decides to listen and learn how to endure the cold:

> What fire burns in that little chest
> So frolic, stout and self-possest?
> Henceforth I wear no stripe but thine;
> Ashes and jet all hues outshine.

The song of the bird teaches the poet that "the soul, if stout within,/ Can arm impregnably the skin," which the poet takes to mean putting away anxiety and trusting in Providence.

Unfortunately, after some wonderful imagery and many fine lines, the poem ends with a rather shrill preachment on the necessity of valor:

> I, who dreamed not when I came here
> To find the antidote of fear,
> Now hear thee say in Roman key,
> *Paean! Veni, vidi, vici.*

The "oven bird" of Frost's poem with that title is small, gray, and inconspicuous, like the titmouse. Like the titmouse, too, its song may be heard when other birds are silent or departed, heard when conditions seem inauspicious for birdsong. Its popular name is "teacher bird," from the sound of its song, which is a loud, harsh, ringing *tea-cher, tea-cher,* with the second syllable somewhat more strongly accented than the first. Like the titmouse, finally, the bird has a lesson to teach the poet. But the lesson it teaches suggests not so much an act of faith as a practical maneuver:

> There is a singer everyone has heard,
> Loud, a mid-summer and a mid-wood bird,
> Who makes the solid tree trunks sound again.
> He says that leaves are old and that for flowers
> Mid-summer is to spring as one to ten.
> He says the early petal-fall is past
> When pear and cherry bloom went down in showers
> On sunny days a moment overcast;
> And comes that other fall we name the fall.
> He says the highway dust is over all.
> The bird would cease and be as other birds
> But that he knows in singing not to sing.
> The question that he frames in all but words
> Is what to make of a diminished thing.

Frost's bird has learned to *make-do,* to adjust and adapt in order to endure and keep on singing. Though the leaves are old in mid-wood and flowers are few, at least *there,* in solitude, he will find less highway dust to mute what colors remain. His harsh song — characterized in the poem only as "loud," with a reliance upon the reader's knowledge of nature that is typical of Frost — is not beautiful, but to the speaker in the poem it is certainly better than no song at all, and under the circumstances it is remarkable. His maneuver is shrewd and tough. He has stepped back from the ideal, lowered his expectations, taken on a protective coloring, roughened his song — in order to preserve *something* from the general wreckage.

If we return for a moment to "The Titmouse" and note two lines I have not yet quoted, we shall find both the similarity and the difference between the two lessons epitomized. The lines are the final climactic ones in the poet's translation of the "sense" of the bird's song:

> And polar frost my frame defied,
> Made of the air that blows outside.

The syntax of the first line involves an inversion of normal word order that Frost would not have permitted himself. "My frame" is the subject of the sentence; it defies the polar frost — by the power of soul, the two preceding lines tell us. The defiant frame is "made of" the polar air it defies; so that in effect nature rises above, transcends, itself when the soul is valorous enough, and faithful enough, to admit its complete involvement in nature. Nature without soul is fate, and fate is inimical, but the soul that opens itself to nature and fate without loss of faith will surely triumph. The titmouse really *sings* when he sings. He says "vici," "I have conquered." Emerson's "nature note" here — for a bird's bones *are* hollow and filled with air — works wonderfully to express his theme. The bird has done more than just "immerse" himself in "the destructive element"; he has taken the destructive element *into* himself.

The oven bird itemizes the several aspects of diminishment, then ends by propounding a question to which the answer is implied in his tone: To the poet or singer as a man, he says, toughen up, lower your expectations, endure; to the man as singer, he says, roughen your verse, avoid any suggestion of romanticism or idealism in image or diction, let the tone indicate your awareness of the failure of spring's promises. Both the bird and the poet in this poem find themselves standing over against nature in a posture of defense. And the poet is aware that the worst is yet to come, for the fall that has not yet come has already been foreshadowed by the fall of the petals from the trees in spring. If this poem were all that Frost had written, Howe's statement of the meaning of nature in Frost's work would be fully adequate. For here, certainly, the aspects of nature that are noticed are not "tokens of benevolence"; nature itself, the poem implies, is indifferent to the needs of oven bird and poet alike; time brings only diminishment and loss, a movement from "a moment overcast" to final darkness.

But it is interesting to note how the critic's statement arrives at a kind of fairness to Frost by way of a caricature of "transcendentalist" poetry. If we assume for the moment that "The Titmouse" and "The Oven Bird" are typical products of the two poets, then we should have to say that it was Emerson, not Frost, who most explicitly and unequivocally recognized that nature outside the self is threatening; and Emerson, not Frost, who counseled "submission to the alienness" — though not just a "brief" submission, or a submission merely for "refreshment," but a total submission for the sake of victory. Emerson's way is analogous to the mystic's way; Frost's, to the maneuvering of a general or a chess player. The two poets were responding to the same threat, the threat posed by "fate," or nature objectively seen as soulless, without value, purpose, or meaning. It is not really necessary to invent a naive Transcendentalist who never existed in order to find a way to praise Frost.

In a great many of Frost's poems, particularly in those published before his wife's death in 1938 — that is, up through *A Further Range* — we find ourselves in a diminished version of an Emersonian world. The familiar Emersonian emphases are here — the concentration on the individual searching for himself and for meaning, on nature as a resource, on immediate experience as a way to some kind of truth. But the mood is autumnal, the tone ironic or noncommittal, and the very categories of thought that are being played with have been scaled down in size. Emerson's "Woodnotes" for instance becomes Frost's "The Need of Being Versed in Country Things." The advantage gained from acquaintance with nature, Frost's poem says, is that it allows us to penetrate the illusion that nature cares for the burned house and deserted farm, allows us to realize that for the phoebes now nesting in the barn, "there was nothing really sad" about the scene the human observer finds so desolating:

> One had to be versed in country things
> Not to believe the phoebes wept.

Early and late, Emerson thought he knew *that* already, even without going to nature. Early, in his creative and purely Transcendental period, he might have wanted to ask Frost a question if he had read this poem. Granted that this insight achieved by the purely intellective function of the soul, by the understanding, is true, how may the integral soul put this truth together with other, no less indubitable, truths, so that it will become a part of a *vision* of this place, the burned house, the deserted barn, the phoebes, and all, including the observer? Is there a way of experiencing this scene so that we may feel joy as well as fear, an increased sense of selfhood, rather than the loneliness and alienation you seem to me to have expressed in your poem?

The scaling-down process that occurs between Emerson and Frost may be seen again in two poems having something to do with nature as revelation. In "For Once, Then, Something" the speaker tells of his having knelt at the curbs of wells — old-fashioned dug wells — to look down and see what he could see in the watery depths. Generally, he saw only a reflection of himself on the water, looking very godlike against the "summer heaven"; but once, *just* once, he thought he caught a glimpse of something other than himself, something beneath what had always before been the impenetrable surface, "something white, uncertain,/ Something more of the depths — and then I lost it." Now he no longer knows whether he really saw anything or not, or, if he did, what it was. "What was that whiteness?/ Truth? A pebble of quartz? For once, then, something."

The Emersonian search continues in this poem, but the skeptical mind finds no definite conclusion warranted from the one uncertain epiphany. Perhaps, though, as the speaker in the poem admits, the reason he didn't see more was that he knelt "Always wrong to the light." Where would the fault lie then? In himself? In his fate? No point in speculating on that. Something less than vision would have to do. "Dust of Snow" records a moment of awareness that was granted, not achieved — as the poet had tried to achieve vision by kneeling at the well — a perception or experience too modest to be called a vision, yet that brought a sustaining satisfaction. The poem is short enough to quote entire:

> The way a crow
> Shook down on me
> The dust of snow
> From a hemlock tree
>
> Has given my heart
> A change of mood
> And saved some part
> Of a day I had rued.

Since we are talking about the diminishment of Emerson's world in Frost, I shall note that aspect first. The experience described has only changed a "mood," something quite irrational, so that in effect the poem makes no claim for any intuitive *meaning* gained from the experience. Anyway, it has saved only "some part of a day," a very modest claim for its value, surely. But there is another way to read the poem which makes it good Emerson — and I suspect Emerson would have liked it. The blackness of the crow and the almost-blackness of the hemlock against the whiteness of the snow add up, to be sure, to a lovely picture; but the poem does not say that it was the picture, looked at by a detached observer, that partly saved a bad day. It was the *way* it happened, and the way the speaker was drawn into the process or event, that saved something. And it was no usual or ordinary event. Crows are highly unlikely to let a person get so close as to be under or near the very tree in which they are perched, so near that the snow brushed from the branches by their flight falls on the walker. It must have been the surprise of the experience, perhaps even being startled into momentary fear, that contributed to the joy that changed the mood. For once, momentarily but without any element of possible self-deception, the speaker has been let *inside* nature's tent, to paraphrase Emily Dickinson's poem on how she was kept *outside* nature's show. "Canis Major" says much the same thing, though it says it less meaningfully and less convincingly.

A final example of diminishment, of the many more that one could dwell on if one wished to: Emerson had defined poetry as vision, and as therefore essential to the soul's growth. It contains, potentially, he thought, all the wisdom the soul needs, and this regardless of what doctrines it may imply. It affords us "a platform whence we may command a view of our present life, a purchase by which we may move it." Poetry for Emerson is essentially a revolutionary force. . . . In sharp contrast with this, Frost wavered most of his life between viewing poetry as a personal performance — of which I shall have something more to say later — and seeing it as "a momentary stay against confusion." The shift to negative terms again is what counts here: not a force *toward* something, but a "stay" *against* something. A "stay" is a check, a hindrance, a restraint; something that holds one *from,* that stops movement. And if confusion is momentarily checked or prevented by a poem, what then? Then for the moment we are not swept away, we endure. To make any greater claim for poetry, or for us, would open us to the charge that we had been taken in by romantic illusions. The poet who has learned the oven bird's lesson well enough, at least need not fear that.

*

But to be content to stop at this point, with Frost supposedly fully "explained" as a "diminished" Emerson, one would have to want to destroy him. To seem to be the whole truth about Frost's work, this approach must concentrate chiefly on the early poems, ignoring or denying all signs of development in the later work; and it must also ignore, or classify as inferior and so not worthy of being taken seriously, all those poems that express aspects of Emerson's outlook *without* diminishment. And there are a good many such.

To be sure, as with Dickinson, so with Frost, most of the poems that seem most perfectly Emersonian are less impressive, less likely to be among the poems Frost will finally be remembered by, than the dark lyrics like "Stopping by Woods" or "Desert Places" or "Spring Pools." Still, this is a relative judgment, and some of the Emersonian poems are very fine in their way. Indeed, I should say that the best of them make Emerson's points for him in ways that Emerson himself would have recognized as superior to the "sleepy generalities" that are too commonly all one finds in a great deal of the verse he chose to publish.

The illustrative poems here are Emerson's "Two Rivers" and Frost's "Mowing." The former makes a mere bow to the actual river, then turns impatiently to the Transcendental river. The latter treats the factual details of mowing with a scythe lovingly — perhaps too lovingly, as though there were to be more implication finally than there is — and then hints at meanings that transcend the facts unimaginatively seen: "The fact is the sweetest dream that labor knows." Emerson's point exactly: that "dream" is not "off there" somewhere, in another realm, but is to be experienced *within* nature, in what we usually experience as "only" fact. Frost's poem, one might argue, makes its Transcendental point more subtly and convincingly than Emerson's; but it might also be felt to make it *defensively*.

Two poems that Frost paired in *West-Running Brook* may stand for all the others that restate Emersonian themes without either reducing them or adding any very important new philosophic dimensions to them. In "Sand Dunes," man and nature are at odds; the purposes of the one are not the "purposes" — if any — of the other. Nature, in the form of sand dunes, remains a constant threat to what men have built, to the "fisher town" that represents their precariously achieved civilization. In the end she will overwhelm the town and "bury in solid sand/ The men she could not drown." Still, nature cannot cut off "mind," which knows how to turn to advantage all threats and losses:

> Men left her a ship to sink:
> They can leave her a hut as well;
> And be but more free to think
> For the one more cast-off shell.

Early Emerson would probably have said "soul" where Frost said "mind," but otherwise he would have liked the poem, with its theme of triumph through submission and relinquishment of all that is unessential and merely material. This, after all, is much like the theme he had developed in "The Titmouse." The bird had triumphed by building its frame of the very air that threatened it. But even closer to "Sand Dunes" than the poem is the essay "Fate" in *The Conduct of Life*, which could have supplied Frost with both his ideas and his images—and probably did.[2]

"Canis Major," which faces "Sand Dunes" in all editions, celebrates a moment when a man alone does not feel himself at odds with nature, but joyously united with it. Looking at the stars, particularly at the constellation called Canis Major, "the larger dog," containing Sirius, the Dog Star, the solitary speaker sees it as vital, alive — the constellation, it seems to him, "gives a leap" and "dances." He knows himself poor in comparison, but the recognition of kinship makes consideration of size and power unimportant. Nature seems not, in this moment, to be alien:

> I'm a poor underdog,
> But tonight I will bark
> With the great Overdog
> That romps through the dark.

Not a great poem, surely, but how Emersonian in its thrust! The humorous tone that makes the affirmation seem casual is the only conspicuously non-Emersonian feature. (Here the poet seems closer to Thoreau, as he quite often does, even when he is most Emersonian in outlook.) In his 1836 essay "Nature," Emerson had written,

> To go into solitude, a man needs to retire as much from his chamber as from society. . . . But if a man would be alone, let him look at the stars. The rays that come from those heavenly worlds will separate between him and what he touches. One might think the atmosphere was made transparent with this design, to give man, in the heavenly bodies, the perpetual presence of the sublime. . . . If the stars should appear one night in a thousand years, how would men believe and adore; and preserve for many generations the remembrance of the city of God which had been shown!

And now Frost, in the two paired poems, accepts Emerson's assumptions about nature and civilization, and solace and solitude, drawing back only from committing himself to words and ideas that Emerson could use without embarrassment but that would be out of character for Frost — "the sublime," "believe and adore," "God." (That *privately* he was more committed to Emerson's *full* meaning than he cared to have his poems admit, his letters make clear; but that is another story.)

There is so much of Emerson in Frost that it would seem very curious that it has not been more widely noticed — were it not for two considerations: Frost's masking proclivities, and the fact that most readers of Frost today, including some of his best-known critics, "know" Emerson only at second hand, know only somebody's idea of Emerson, or an essay or two read many years ago. When Frost called "Uriel" "the greatest Western poem yet" in *A Masque of Reason* in 1945, it should have been clear enough to anyone who remembered "Uriel," from the line he paraphrased, what poem he was referring to without his having to name it, but the critics were puzzled; one of them wondered whether or not it was the *Divine Comedy* he had in mind. The lines in which he makes the evaluation of Emerson's poem go like this:

> . . . .
> The serpent's tail stuck down the serpent's throat,
> Which is the symbol of eternity
> And also of the way all things come round,
> Or of how rays return upon themselves,
> To quote the greatest Western poem yet.

The lines being paraphrased in "Uriel" tell us that Uriel:

With a look that solved the sphere,
And stirred the devils everywhere,
Gave his sentiment divine
Against the being of a line.
"Line in nature is not found;
Unit and universe are round;
In vain produced, all rays return;
Evil will bless, and ice will burn."

Since during an afternoon I spent with Frost in his Ripton cabin in 1939 or 1940, we had discussed Emerson, and I had heard him quote these very lines from "Uriel," declare that they contained the essence of all modern knowledge, including Einstein's relativity, and end by calling the poem "the greatest Western poem yet," I was not puzzled by any obscurity in the lines in *A Masque of Reason.* My point is not that any external evidence *ought* to have been needed to show what poem was meant, but that in fact it *was* needed, and that the *fact* that it was, reveals something, or several things, about recent literary history.

Whether Frost's "Fire and Ice" takes off from the same passage in "Uriel" I cannot be sure, but it seems to me very possible. Toward the end of his life Frost wrote to Lawrance Thompson,

> I trust my philosophy still bothers you a little. It bothers me. You should have heard me talking the other night about Uriel your class in American Literature wouldn't let you talk to them about. One or another of us will fathom me sooner or later. Did Trilling have something the other night? I was a little bothered by him but chiefly because I didn't hear very well. . . . At least he seemed to see that I am as strong on badness as I am on goodness. Emerson's defect was that he was of the great tradition of Monists. He could see the "good of evil born" but he couldn't bring himself to say the evil of good born. . . .

The quotation, "the good of evil born," is from the last lines of "Uriel" —

Or out of the good of evil born,
Came Uriel's voice of cherub scorn,
And a blush tinged the upper sky,
And the gods shook, they knew not why.

"Fire and Ice" notes that what we generally take as good may produce evil, as well as the other way around, Emerson's way. Combining a humorous comment on the identity for practical purposes of the Biblical and the (then) scientific views of how the world will end, in a final holocaust or in a freezing out as the sun cools, with the observation that hatred and desire may have the same destructive effect, the poem seems to glance at Emerson's paradox that "ice will burn":

Some say the world will end in fire,
Some say in ice.
From what I've tasted of desire
I hold with those who favor fire.
But if it had to perish twice,
I think I know enough of hate
To say that for destruction ice
Is also great
And would suffice.

With Emerson so often in Frost's mind early and late, it is not surprising that there are echoes of Emerson everywhere in the work, even in poems that as a whole are non-Emersonian, or even anti-Emersonian, in general intent and effect. "The Tuft of Flowers," for example, would not make us think of Emerson, I should say, despite its concern with and feeling for the natural world—would not, that is, except for two lines, which make explicit the moral of the poem.

"Men work together," I told him from the heart,
"Whether they work together or apart."

Emerson had said as much in "Each and All," in "Friendship" (both the poem and the essay), and in many other places. In the poem he had said that the absent friend made possible for him "a daily sunrise" by the example of his nobleness. In Frost's poem, the absent fellow worker who has spared the tuft of flowers in his mowing brings "a message from the dawn." (In both Frost and Emerson we often get the impression that men work together *better* when they are apart, and that those friends are best to have whom one seldom or never sees.)

So far I have cited only poems in which we may see some kind of echo of Emerson, some turn of phrase or twist of thought that makes it possible to name specific works by the two writers that ought to be compared for similarity and difference. That there are many more not yet identified may be assumed. But this is work yet to be done. Now I should like to end by mentioning two poems that do not sound in the least like Emerson, or seem to be stating his ideas, but that nevertheless do restate his themes in a new key.

"The Wood-Pile" ought never to remind us of Emerson in any purely "poetic" way — as a pattern of sound, as a pattern of images, as an exercise in control of tone. But when we turn away from the poem itself and think about its meaning quite abstractly, we find ourselves suddenly confronted with the ghost of Emerson again. The bird in the poem, unlike Emerson's titmouse, does not exhibit largeness of soul or valor. Instead, he is a nervous, frightened, "careful" little bird who takes everything as personal, sees threats where none are intended, and allows "his little fear" to carry him off. The "lesson" is taught the speaker by the split cord of maple left to rot in the woods, not by the bird, except as *he* teaches in *reverse.* Instead of being taken in and used for firewood, to heat a country house, the woodpile has been simply forgotten or abandoned, presumably by "Someone who lived in turning to fresh tasks" — by an Emersonian hero of growth, in short. Such a one as this, the anxious little bird's opposite, would be happy enough to forget his labors of the past and leave the wood

> To warm the frozen swamp as best it could
> With the slow smokeless burning of decay

secure in the knowledge that "decay," from the point of view of the sciences of nature, is an oxidation, a slow sort of "burning." No wonder Yvor Winters, who has spent so much of his energy hating Emerson, found in this poem evidence of an Emersonian sort of "spiritual drifting." But it might better be seen as paralleling that aspect of Emerson that reminds us of Eastern philosophy and religion, or of the Western doctrine of "justification by faith."

A poem with even less apparent connection with Emerson — for after all "The Wood-Pile" at least paralleled "The Titmouse" in its images of a winter walk in the woods, and an instructive bird — will do best for my last example. "The Bear" not only does not *sound* in the least like Emerson, it does not contain a single image or phrase that, taken out of context, might remind one of anything specific in Emerson's prose or verse. Yet it is nevertheless a thoroughly Emersonian poem thematically.

The free, or wild, bear with which the poem opens moves through nature in the condition of a "lover." Her first act is to "kiss goodbye" to chokecherries and start on her cross-country trip. Since her relation with nature is an "original" one, she can, like the man who left his woodpile to rot, afford to leave a lock of hair on the barbed wire and feel none the worse for the loss, any more than she regrets the chokecherries left behind in her progress. "Such is the uncaged progress of the bear."

But *our* relation to nature is not so direct, so spontaneous, or so happy. We approach it not as lovers but as thinkers, and not even as "original" thinkers:

> The world has room to make a bear feel free;
> The universe seems cramped to you and me.
> Man acts more like the poor bear in a cage
> That all day fights a nervous inward rage,
> His mood rejecting all his mind suggests.

As we "think," or do what we call thinking, we sway back and forth between telescope and microscope, in scientific philosophy, or between two Greeks — Plato and Aristotle — in metaphysics, without ever seeming to come any closer to feeling at home in the world. The caged bear is *our* model:

> He sits back on his fundamental butt
> With lifted snout and eyes (if any) shut,
> (He almost looks religious but he's not),
> And back and forth he sways from cheek to cheek,
> At one extreme agreeing with one Greek,
> At the other agreeing with another Greek

Which may be thought, but only so to speak.
A baggy figure, equally pathetic
When sedentary and when peripatetic.

"The Bear" has sometimes been blamed for making a sneering rejection of both science and philosophy, of "rationality" in short; but it seems to me it would be better to think of it as a plea for an Emersonian kind of free intelligence which is not simply "understanding"—a plea for "the growth of the soul," in Emerson's terms. It makes this plea, to be sure, in a joking tone, and partly by laughing at the vacuity of "thought" that stays always at one remove at least from experience; but the final point of the poem is that there is no real necessity for us to be "caged" by the logic of science and philosophy, especially not by the categories of "dead men's thoughts," to use Emerson's words. We could, if we would only open all our faculties to integral experience, break out of the cage and be as free, and feel as much at home in the world, as the uncaged bear.

Or as Emerson put it in *Nature*:

> The foregoing generations beheld God and nature face to face; we, through their eyes. Why should not we also enjoy an original relation to the universe? . . . Why should we grope among the dry bones of the past? . . . The sun shines today also. . . . Every man's condition is a solution in hieroglyphic to those inquiries he would put. He acts it as life, before he apprehends it as truth.

The free bear experiences nature "face to face"; the caged bear, through instruments, or through the ideas of "foregoing generations." To sway back and forth between Plato and Aristotle is not very different from groping among dry bones. (Emerson: "Every thought is also a prison. . . . For it is the inert effort of each thought, having formed itself into a circular wave of circumstance [into a kind of cage, in short] . . . to heap itself on that ridge, and to solidify and hem in the life. But if the soul is quick and strong, it bursts over that boundary. . . .") The free bear also reminds us of Emerson's description of himself as an "endless seeker, with no past" at his back; for the course she sets out on when she makes her cross-country cannot be clearly charted. Insofar as the free bear is a model for man, her way of knowing is a way first of all of *being* and *doing:* she "knows" organically, *"so to know."*) Neither the quantifiable knowledge of science nor the logical distinctions of philosophy can contain her. The poem is good enough Emerson to remind us of Whitman's "Song of the Open Road" and of the later Eliot's "Fare forward, voyager."

In his *Selected Letters of Robert Frost,* Lawrance Thompson writes this introductory note to one of Frost's letters to Louis Untermeyer, written in 1920:

> This letter suggests a conflict in the marriage of RF and Elinor Miriam Frost: the sharp contrast between their religious views. RF regarded his wife's atheistical denials in a defensively light and jocose manner; but they troubled him deeply. He had heard her make such denials repeatedly, starting soon after the death of their first child on 8 July 1900. (See hints in "Home Burial.") In later years, as she experienced other painful losses, she became more skeptical, more intensively bitter.
>
> For a brief time around 1900, RF was inclined to similar notions; the poem "Stars" (published in *A Boy's Will* with the gloss, "There is no oversight of human affairs") was written that year. But he did not maintain that attitude long. Even while his recurrent moods of skepticism and denial gave picturesque colorings to his heretical beliefs, he came to express profound religious affirmations with more and more frequency.

Since Frost has been repeatedly praised for being an agnostic, a naturalist, and even, most recently, a "materialist," I shall let Thompson speak to this point once again. The paragraph that follows, from the editor's Introduction to the letters, summarizes all the biographical evidence on the poet's religious attitude. If the reader finds the gist of this statement hard to square with his understanding of some of the poems, I hope he may stay relaxed and read on. An attempt at an explanation will be forthcoming in due time:

> How did Frost ever bear up under the devastating griefs and heartbreaks caused by all those untimely

> deaths? A good answer was given by a clergyman who, knowing the poet well, called him "a Job in our time." Many of the later letters give new pertinence to that analogy. Like Job, our puritanical poet seemed to find his most bitter sorrows and doubts made bearable by his capacity to accept loss and pain as mysterious trials administered by an inscrutable and yet benevolent deity. Even the most secular of Frost's friends felt that to differ with him concerning this assumption which gave him consolation desperately needed, would have been an act of cruelty. A deep religious faith had been nurtured in Frost by his mother during his childhood, and although he subjected different aspects of this faith to severe challenge, mockery, and skepticism, he never rejected it for long. Partly from shyness and partly from a desire to express his non-conformist religious independence by uttering heresies, he often encouraged misunderstandings; and strangers cited his apparent blasphemies as evidences that Frost was an atheist. He never was. But his curiously Greek-Roman-Scotch-Yankee temperament responded with sympathetic vigor to the Aeschylean proverb that God helps those who help themselves — particularly in the task of discovering how to survive and how to go on living in this world after each new loss might temporarily injure the desire to survive.

Since anyone who wants to know the evidence on which this summary of Frost's religious attitudes rests may find it by turning to the letters, I shall say no more about this matter of his stubborn religious faith. But it might be well to listen to Frost himself, for a moment, speaking about *another* aspect of himself to friends, in his letters.

To Thomas B. Mosher in 1913: "You are not going to make the mistake that Pound makes of assuming that my simplicity is that of the untutored child. I am not undesigning."

To Louis Untermeyer in 1915: (After discussing the way friends may say what they please to each other, including "fooling" — hiding rather than revealing the truth, with a kind of verbal love-play): "The beauty of enmity is in insecurity; the beauty of friendship is in security." And then:

> Even here I am only fooling my way along as I was in the poems in The Atlantic (particularly in The Road Not Taken) as I was in what I said about Spoon River. I trust my meaning is not too hidden in any of these places. I can't help my way of coming at things.

To John T. Bartlett in 1927:

> . . . My isnt it a chill to hear how those youngsters of yours are coming up? If they are that old how old must I be? Tell them easy does it. They must be fine children who can be appealed to. You cant so much as grow in this world without affecting somebody to tears. People had better be careful how they grow. There is something invidious about the way the young grow. I'd like to tease them. They look as if they could take care of themselves. I probably couldnt baffle them very much at my crypticest. Never mind I can baffle some people.

To Sidney Cox in 1932: "I have written to keep the over curious out of the secret places of my mind both in my verse and in my letters to such as you."

Clearly, the stance revealed in these statements is that of a man on guard, defensive and aggressive at once. As Thompson has put it, "How to express one's self and how to defend one's self became two inseparable themes for him." Thompson relates this to Frost's psychological situation — to recurrent suicidal impulses, to violent outbursts of rage, to "persistent feelings of guilt." But a psychological explanation of this sort does not mean — and in this case I assume is not intended to mean — that less personal factors did not play their part too in creating the characteristic defensive posture, or that the posture itself would not find expression in other ways than the merely personal. What kind of style, in the largest sense of the word, would we expect of an artist who as a person thought of the problem of expression always in terms of the problem of self-defense? I shall let Frost himself speak, indirectly, to this question, and then we shall be done with preliminaries. He is writing to Louis Untermeyer in 1924:

> Since I last saw you I have come to the conclusion that style in prose or verse is that which indicates how the writer takes himself and what he is saying. . . . I am not satisfied to let it go with the aphorism that the style is the man. The man's ideas would be some element then of his style. So would his deeds. But I would narrow the definition. His deeds are his deeds; his ideas are his ideas. His style is the way he carries himself toward his ideas and deeds. Mind you if he is down-spirited it will be all he can do to have the ideas without the carriage. The style is out of his superfluity. It is the mind skating circles round itself as it moves forward. Emerson had one of the noblest least egotistical of styles. By comparison with it Thoreau's was conceited, Whitman's bumptious. Carlyle's way of taking himself simply infuriates me. Longfellow took himself with the gentlest twinkle.

The question framed by the oven bird "in all but words" was "what to make of a diminished thing." The development of Frost's style from "My Butterfly," his first published poem, with its overt romanticism, to the great dark lyrics of his maturity, to the gnomic affirmations of his later years, gives us the answer the poet worked out for himself, partly by design, partly unconsciously.

Emersonian of sorts though he was on so many matters, Frost felt obliged to take the totally non-Emersonian tack of working out his own version of the "impersonal" view of art that Pound and Eliot had popularized by the time Frost began to be widely recognized. Very early in his career Frost saw that Emerson's idea of poetry as a kind of prophetic confession in which the poet speaks to and for *all* men by putting into words the vision *he* has had would no longer do — not for him, not in *this* time, at least. Frost had written as though Eliot's idea were true that the man who suffers and the artist who creates are totally separate, long before he put the idea into words in a letter to Sidney Cox in 1932 — the same letter in which we hear the "secret places of the mind." Protesting Cox's attempt to relate the man he knew to the poet he read, he wrote:

> The objective idea is all I ever cared about. Most of my ideas occur in verse. . . . I keep to a minimum of such stuff [personalities] in any poets life and works. . . . To be too subjective with what an artist has managed to make objective is to come on him presumptuously and render ungraceful what he in pain of his life had faith he had made graceful.

To keep his verse objective and graceful, the poet would give his verse the sound of *sense,* and speak through a variety of masks — the mask of the literate back-country farmer, the mask of the detached observer of his own emotions, the mask of the tough realist who knows too much to be taken in by any romanticisms, and then, in the latter third or so of the career, the mask of the shrewd, wisely cynical, but at the same time cherishing, sage. These were Frost's equivalents of the Prufrockian mask of the early Eliot.

What all these masks — or, to use the fashionable critical jargon, the several *personae* in the poetry — have in common is the refusal of the speaker either to be "found out," or to be "taken in." Humor could serve both purposes. Except for the humor in "The Bear," which gets broader and broader toward the end, as the speaker turns his scorn on science and rationalistic philosophy, the poem would really *commit* Frost to an Emersonian position. The jokes keep the commitment a secret from all, perhaps, but the knowing few. Or a sudden shift of tone would do as well — a sudden playfulness, an unexpected touch of whimsy, as we see it in the "Let them think twice" line in "Spring Pools." Or the simple use of a pronoun that would separate the speaker from the objects of his observation, as in "Neither Out Far Nor in Deep":

> They cannot look out far.
> They cannot look in deep.
> But when was that ever a bar
> To any watch they keep?

Why not "any watch *we* keep"? Does the poem ridicule those who search endlessly for answers where there are none to be found? Would it be better to turn one's back on the sea and look only at the land, to be content with the secular? Or is there another alternative, perhaps looking at the "wetter ground" where "the water comes ashore" and there are reflections? If one knows enough about Frost's life and opinions outside the poetry, he may well, I think, decide that this last possibility represents the way Frost himself would read the poem. It would then be another expression of his Emersonianism: nature reflects the eternal when one knows how to see, and where to look.

But if this is the *intended* meaning, the religious affirmation the poem makes when read this way is certainly made most guardedly, so guardedly in fact that one cannot feel sure, from evidence within the poem, that he is not overreading, or misreading. The only thing that is really clear about the poem is its detached observation of the curious persistence with which men "turn their back on the land" and look toward the sea. If there is a commitment behind the poem, the mask of detachment keeps it well hidden from the "over curious."

Late in life, when the recognition for which he had had to wait so long, so very long, had become world-wide fame with a large admixture of adulation, Frost dropped his masks more and more frequently. There was no longer the need to guard the secrets of the heart when everywhere he was recognized as *the* American poet, and more than a poet, the embodiment of the best in the American character and a sage of the first rank. His last volume, *In The Clearing,* dispenses with masks entirely. He had no need for them any more.

Meanwhile, from *West-Running Brook* (1928) onward, what Frost was *against* had become clearer and clearer. He was against scientific positivism or "scientism" ("The Bear," "The White-Tailed Hornet," "At Woodward's Gardens"), against philosophic rationalism ("It's knowing what to do with things that counts"), against naturalism as a philosophy, especially in its reductive forms with its "downward comparisons" ("The White-Tailed Hornet"). He was against the directions society was taking in the 1930's — against liberals and planners and New Dealers of all stripes. Modern society was a kind of hell ("In Dives' Dive") in which both the true artist and the sensitive man could endure only by exploring to the limit the possibilities of disaffiliation and disengagement ("One Step Backward Taken").

Frost's conservative — "reactionary" would be the more accurate term if it did not carry for most people so heavy a load of disapproval — his conservative views on social, political, and economic matters were even more pronouncedly conservative in private than in the verse, but a good many of the poems written between 1930 and 1950 speak out clearly enough ("Build Soil," "On Our Sympathy with the Under Dog," "An Equalizer," "On Taking from the Top to Broaden the Base," "The Planners"). While none of those I have cited, or the many others like them, is among the great poems, those who think of themselves as "liberal" ought to try to resist the temptation to use these poems to belittle Frost. It is worth remembering, for one thing, that Frost's individualism, which so often is hard to distinguish from heartlessness, has a long tradition behind it. Emerson's "New England Reformers," for instance, starts off sympathetically enough, but by the end it has neatly pulled the rug out from under the reformers. Are we quite *sure* that we can have a redeemed society without a majority of redeemed individuals?

It ought to be remembered, too, that just a few years before Frost began to be open about the "backward" steps he was taking, Eliot had announced, with an air of bravado, a really giant stride backward — back to Royalism, Anglo-Catholicism, and Classicism. At the same time, Pound, even more contemptuous of Roosevelt and liberalism than Frost was, was searching for true values in Provençal poetry and the ancient Chinese classics; and he would soon announce that he found the ancient virtues embodied equally in Jefferson and Mussolini. Meanwhile Hemingway was writing of "the stench of comrades," and the Southern Agrarians were announcing *their* disaffiliation from the national culture, and they and their literary descendants were producing some of the finest writing of the time. "Reaction" is called for when what is being reacted against is bad enough, and "conservatism" is essential when what is being conserved is worth the sacrifices necessary to conserve it. Frost's social sympathies remained very rudimentary to the end, so that most of his poetic editorials on social topics strike me as more peevish than wise; but I am not alone in suspecting that in years to come the threat to the individual's possibilities of self-realization that Frost saw in contemporary social trends will appear more and more real.

About 1947, when both *Steeple Bush* and *A Masque of Mercy* were published, Frost began, as I have said, to do without the protection of a mask more and more frequently when writing on his personal commitments. There had been, much earlier than this, occasional poems in which the mask was almost dropped, like "Sitting by a Bush in Broad Sunlight," with only its lightness of tone to guard against the danger of its being called a "religious" poem; or "Not All There," which would seem quite noncommittal except for the way in which the title of the whole poem gets its meaning only from the second quatrain. But such relatively clear poems of positive commitment had been rare.

Now they became very much more common. The final passage of *A Masque of Mercy* will serve as a striking example of many similar droppings of the mask. Assigned to a sympathetic character, Paul, the passage is straightforward and serious:

> We have to stay afraid deep in our souls
> Our sacrifice, the best we have to offer,
> And not our worst nor second best, our best,
> Our very best, our lives laid down like Jonah's,
> Our lives laid down in war and peace, may not
> Be found acceptable in Heaven's sight.
> And that they may be is the only prayer
> Worth praying.

Another sympathetic character in the masque has the last word after this:

> Let the lost millions pray it in the dark!
> . . . .
> We both have lacked the courage in the heart
> To overcome the fear within the soul
> And go ahead to any accomplishment.
> Courage is what it takes and takes the more of
> Because the deeper fear is so eternal.
> . . . .
> Nothing can make injustice just but mercy.

Compare Paul's speech with this, from a letter written in the year in which *A Masque of Mercy* was published:

> My fear of God has settled down into a deep inward fear that my best offering may not prove acceptable in

> his sight. I'll tell you most about it in another world. My approach to the New Testament is rather through Jerewsalem than through Rome and Canterbury.

Or this, written six years later to his friend Rabbi Victor E. Reickert, in whose Temple Frost had given a talk in 1946, and with whom he had often discussed the Bible, particularly the Book of Job:

> Do you want to tell me where in the Bible if at all the idea occurs as a prayer that our sacrifice whether of ourselves or our property may be acceptable in His sight? Have I been making this up out of nothing? You know how I am about chapter and verse — somewhat irresponsible some would say.

In the last decade of his life Frost moved closer to the New Testament in his religious thinking. Now, far from wishing to hide the light he had found in the clearing, he took pains to give it the greatest prominence. The passage celebrating incarnation as a law alike of religion and art — indeed of all human ventures — is printed twice in *In The Clearing,* once in the poem "Kitty Hawk," of which it is a part, and once, earlier, on a separate page following the dedication and preceding the table of contents, as a "Frontispiece," as it is called in the table of contents. This passage, the poet is now going out of his way to insist, should be taken as the clue to the whole volume, and to the symbolism of its title, with its allusion to the first poem in his first volume, "Into My Own," in which the boy goes into the dark woods to find his identity:

> But God's own descent
> Into flesh was meant
> As a demonstration
> That the supreme merit
> Lay in risking spirit
> In substantiation.
> Spirit enters flesh
> And for all it's worth
> Charges into earth

In birth after birth
Ever fresh and fresh.
We may take the view
That its derring-do
Thought of in the large
Is one mighty charge
On our human part
Of the soul's ethereal
Into the material.

Compare this with a letter written shortly before his death:

> I'm mighty glad you like this poem for Christmas ["The Prophets Really Prophesy as Mystics . . ."]. Why will the quidnuncs always be hoping for a salvation man will never have from anyone but God? I was just saying today how Christ posed Himself the whole problem and died for it. How can we be just in a world that needs mercy and merciful in a world that needs justice. We study and study the four biographies of Him and are left still somewhat puzzled in our daily lives. Marking students in a kind of mockery and laughing it off.

A number of years before he had become as unguarded as this about his religious beliefs, he had begun openly defending the will to believe, on strictly pragmatic grounds. In the "Four Beliefs," printed at Dartmouth as a prose pamphlet in 1944, the first belief, in *yourself,* which is also a means of *creating* the self believed in, is worded in such a way as to throw some light on Frost's need for masks: "One is the self-belief, which is a knowledge you don't want to tell other people about because you cannot prove that you know. You are saying nothing about it till you see." The "national" belief makes explicit the pragmatic reasoning behind *all* the beliefs: "And the national belief we enter into socially with each other to bring on the future of the country . . ." Likewise of a work of art, it may be said that the artist has "believed the thing into existence," complete with meanings he did not foresee but that are his own after his faith has brought them into being. And then, climactically:

> And finally there is the relation we enter into with God to believe the future in. That by which we believe the future in is our belief in God.

Though I have no external evidence that Frost was reading William James during these last years, internal evidence in "Four Beliefs" and elsewhere makes it seem very likely. "Four Beliefs" reads like a combined digest and application of James's *The Will to Believe* and "Pragmatism and Religion," from the second of which I shall quote only one of the concluding sentences: "The various over-beliefs [beliefs beyond the evidence] of men, their several faith-ventures [such as the belief that "higher powers exist and are at work to save the world"] *are in fact what are needed to bring the evidence in*." (Italics mine.)

Frost's shift of emphasis from skepticism to belief in his poems and public statements was accompanied by a parallel shift in his conception of poetry. In his early years he had tended to think of it as a "personal performance." It should not surprise us that a man who was not recognized in his field until he was forty should come to think of the practice of his art in terms of personal triumph or failure. The poet who makes a practice of reading poetry aloud before large audiences *must* of course be a "performer"; especially a poet who has suffered from neglect for so many years.

But by the time of "The Figure a Poem Makes" in 1939 he was blending Emersonian terms like "revelation" and "wisdom" with such apparently Modernist ideas as that the initial image predestines the final outcome of the poem, controlling every movement in it. But the concession to newer fashions of thought were not so much a masking as they were an adaptation of Emersonian thinking to the new situation. Emerson had spoken of the artist as building better than he knew, and Frost spoke of the "outcome" of the poem as "unforeseen" but "predestined." Emerson had spoken of the poem as surprising even the poet himself, and Frost wrote that "the initial delight is in the surprise of remembering something I didn't know I knew." Emerson had counseled the poet, in "Merlin's Song," to

> Mask thy wisdom with delight,
> Toy with the bow, yet hit the white

and Frost — was he remembering Emerson's words, or had he now forgotten where they came from? — gave as his central definition of the figure a poem makes, "It begins in delight and ends in wisdom."

The "wisdom" horrified some of the New Critics, but the "delight" pleased them. Frost's critical theory at this point was an exercise in attaining "the middleness of the road." It was still somewhat defensive: How could a poet who continued to think of poetry in Emersonian terms keep from sounding naive in the age of Eliot and I. A. Richards? He could be cryptic, and he could blend divergent notions skillfully together. The first "open" tribute to Emerson, even then without *naming* him, would not come until 1945, in *A Masque of Reason.*

But there was nothing cryptic about the statement to Harvey Breit in an interview in 1956, reported in Breit's *The Writer Observed.* Frost told Breit he had things to say to young poets, and that what he chiefly had to say was this:

> One thing I care about, and I wish young people could care about it, is taking poetry as the first form of understanding. If poetry isn't understanding all, the whole world, then it isn't worth anything.

Which would seem to make his own character studies in *North of Boston* and *Mountain Interval* not "worth anything," for whatever the "truth" is that they convey, it is certainly considerably less than "all." Of course, Frost was thinking of poetry as a whole here, not of individual poems. Still, since the nature of poetry as a whole must bear some relation to particular poems, it is clear that there has been a considerable shift of emphasis since "The Figure a Poem Makes." Except that he would have found some other word to use in place of "understanding" — bearing in mind the Coleridgean distinction between the "understanding" and the "reason" — Emerson might have made such a statement as this to the interviewer. The statement represents Frost's increased confidence and consequent willingness to commit himself openly to his deepest beliefs.

Yet even in the last college lecture he gave before his death, he still mingled disclosure and hiding in his characteristic way. The talk is of special interest for several reasons, particularly for the use to which the Bible is put, and the evidence it affords of

Frost's debt to Thoreau. Speaking in a relaxed and friendly setting to the students of his own college, Dartmouth, almost exactly two months before his death, Frost took as his topic "Extravagance."

He began by calling attention to the extravagance of the universe itself:

> I was thinking of the extravagance of the universe. What an *extravagant* universe it is. . . . How stirring it is, the sun and everything. Take a telescope and look as far as you will. How much of a universe was wasted just to produce puny us. . . .

Then, implying the poet's obligation to follow the moods and insights of the moment, with no attempt at doctrinal consistency ("The poet . . . resigns himself to his mood," Emerson had said.), Frost defined the extravagance of poetry by suggesting that the poet is always, in effect, saying, "It sometimes seems as if."

Following a comment on the extravagance of the thought in one of his own recent poems, Frost continued:

> And my extravagance would go on from there to say that people think that life is a *result* of certain atoms coming together, instead of being the *cause* that brings the atoms together. There's something to be said about that in the utter, utter extravagant way.

"The universe is the externization of the soul," had been Emerson's way of putting the same thought.

A little later, Frost quoted the lines on the Incarnation from "Kitty Hawk" that he had used as a "Frontispiece" in *In The Clearing,* then commented, "That's a whole philosophy. To the very limit, you know." This led into a discussion of the Bible's justification of "extravagance":

> Some people can't go with you. Let 'em drop; let 'em fall off. Let the wolves take 'em.
>
> In the Bible twice it says — and I quote that in a poem somewhere, I think; yes — twice it says, 'these things are said in parables . . .' — said in this way I'm talking to you about: extravagance said in parable, . . . so the wrong people won't understand them and so get saved.

From the Bible it was no long step to Matthew Arnold:

> It's thoroughly undemocratic, very superior — as when Matthew Arnold says, in a whole sonnet, only those who've given everything and strained every nerve "mount, and that hardly, to eternal life."

For emphasis, Frost then repeated the quotation from Arnold twice again.

Near the end of the talk, the Frostian strategy was acknowledged without apology. Speaking of the "literary criticism" contained in his poems — "*in* them," he repeated for emphasis — Frost confessed, "And yet I wouldn't admit it. I try to hide it."

It seems to me very likely that the idea for the topic and title of this talk resulted from the poet's late rereading of Thoreau. The long paragraph celebrating "extravagance" in the "Conclusion" of *Walden* might well have inspired Frost's meditation on the word — as a kind of "exposition of the text," in the manner of Biblical commentators. Thoreau begins with a thought often in Frost's mind in his last years, "It is a ridiculous demand which England and America make, that you shall speak so that they can understand you," and concludes with a sentence that might be taken as the expression of the central theme of Frost's talk: "The words which express our faith and piety are not definite; yet they are significant and fragrant like frankincense to superior natures." The whole paragraph would have struck Frost as a wonderful justification of his life-long propensity for "fooling," hiding, masking; in short, for revealing his "faith and piety" — in an age hostile to piety — only to those "superior natures" who deserved to be saved.

Not long before he gave the talk, Frost visited for the last time the Abernethy Collection in the Middlebury College Library. After looking around in the room housing the collection of his own works, he paused before the nearby notable Thoreau collection. After a few moments of silence, he turned to the Curator of the Collection and said, "You know, I have come to think he was a greater one than Emerson, after all." [3]

Explaining, in 1942, why he had selected sixteen of his poems for Whit Burnett's *This Is My Best,* Frost wrote that he had enjoyed looking over his work to select these poems. "The interest, the pastime, was to learn if there had been any divinity shaping my ends and I had been building better than I knew." The unacknowledged quotation from Emerson's "The Problem" continues the development toward open acknowledgment of a primary resource that I have been tracing. The difference between this and the kind of use Frost had made of Emerson only a few years before in "The Figure a Poem Makes" marks another increase of confidence. Emerson, we recall, had written of the medieval builder that he

> Wrought in a sad sincerity;
> Himself from God he could not free;
> He builded better than he knew; —
> The conscious stone to beauty grew.

Frost had tended to think that in order to be a successful instrument of Providence, it was necessary to be "designing." He had been "designing" in both senses of a deeply ambiguous word. Now he was more and more dropping the sense that points toward concealment of real intention.

He "designed" *In The Clearing,* which he expected to be his last book and which was in fact published only a few months before his death, to give shape to a career, much as Whitman had worked over the "Deathbed Edition" of his *Leaves* — but more successfully, I should say, than Whitman had. We have had occasion to note the significance of the title and the "frontispiece," but this volume lifts the whole career to conscious form in other ways as well. The work is so thoroughly a "designed" summary, recapitulation, and justification, that only a long discussion could bring out *all* the ways in which it summarizes, recapitulates, and defensively reinterprets the career. I shall mention just two points that seem to me of the greatest importance as Frost's own comments on, and interpretation of, his life work. (The volume contains several of Frost's best poems, which of course deserve study in their own right, not just as comment on something else. "A Cabin in the Clearing" and "The Draft Horse" particularly are as fine as any poems Frost ever wrote.)

First, he says in effect: *the career might have been more Emersonian, had fate permitted.* Using the image of flight much as Hart Crane had used it — or attempted to use it — in the "Cape Hatteras" section of *The Bridge,* Frost in "Kitty Hawk" ("A

Skylark . . . in Three-Beat Phrases") writes that the "flight" that *should* have been his own had he not been "out of sorts with Fate" *would* have taken him "Into the unknown,/ Into the sublime . . ."

Second: he says, just as Emerson had, that *the central problem for man remains the individual's problem, not society's problem, for every society is certain to decay:*

> As a confirmed astronomer
> I'm always for a better sky.
> (I don't care how the world gets by.)

The real problem for man is the question of identity: If we ever find out *who* we are, we shall be in a position to start to find out *where* we are.

To those of his critics who see this position, and the career as a whole, as escape or retreat, Frost has, in this work, two answers. In "Escapist — Never" he answers the first charge by saying his career has been not a flight but a seeking:

> Any who seek him seek in him the seeker.
> His life is a pursuit of a pursuit forever.
> It is the future that creates his present.
> All is an interminable chain of longing.

(Emerson too had defined himself as a "seeker" — and also as "an endless experimenter, with no past" at his back. The "future that creates the present" is essentially Emerson as interpreted by William James. Regarding the "interminable chain of longing," Emerson had pictured the "worm" as "mounting through the spires of form.")

To the charge that he has "retreated," the poet answers, in the poem placed significantly as the last one in the book, that the retreat has been only *strategic.* Significantly, too, the poem has no title, but its first line amounts to a kind of summary of a whole life, as seen from within: "In winter in the woods alone." The oven bird long ago had endured *summer's* dust and foreseen the winter — and had adjusted his song accordingly.

> In winter in the woods alone
> Against the trees I go.

I mark a maple for my own
And lay the maple low.

At four o'clock I shoulder axe
And in the afterglow
I link a line of shadowy tracks
Across the tinted snow.

I see for Nature no defeat
In one tree's overthrow
Or for myself in my retreat
For yet another blow.

The "justification" of the "retreat" is that it was needed for survival of both the man and the artist. I can't think of a better justification. Since the maneuver was successful, we have a body of poetry that belongs with the best ever written by any American, a body of work perhaps as permanent as, and certainly very much like, Emily Dickinson's. Frost must have been hard to live with, but he was tough and crafty, and he and his talent endured. We are the richer for the poems he forged in pain and loss and fear — and in determination to survive. In an age hostile to almost all that he most deeply believed and felt, he not only continued to write but won outstanding success, first with the anthologists who reflected the public taste, then at last, at the end of a very long and very difficult life, even with critics of the left, who found a *part* of his work "great" despite his politics; and with New Critics of the right, who thought "masks" essential in poetry and found his use of them admirable *poetically*. Both left and right, of course, deplored his "Emersonianism," which, as a poet hoping to be as tough and enduring as an oven bird, he had long hidden and disguised as best he could.

PART FIVE

The Revolution of Modernism: Image

Science and Poetry: Imagism

. . . If you demand on the one hand,
the raw material of poetry in
all its rawness and
that which is on the other hand
genuine, you are interested in poetry.
— Marianne Moore, 1921

To me, at that time, a poem was an image, the picture was the important thing.
— William Carlos Williams, 1958

Pollock's blobs of paint squeezed out
with design! Pure from the tube.
Nothing else is real.
— William Carlos Williams, 1958

MODERNISM in American poetry could be said to have begun in 1911, when Eliot wrote "Portrait of a Lady." A more public kind of calculation — since that poem was not published until several years later — might set the date at 1914, the year of the first Imagist anthology. The latest date one could choose would be 1917, when Eliot's *Prufrock and Other Observations* appeared. Poets and critics who had missed the significance of the Imagist anthologies did not miss the significance of this. Modernism quickly became the dominant school in American poetry, and remained so for almost thirty years.

It was so genuinely the cutting edge of literary advance, the new poetry for a new age consciously in revolt against the past — "For the experience of each new age requires a new confession, and the world seems always waiting for its poet," as Emerson said — that careers were made and careers ruined by the decisions of poets to join or oppose the new movement. The reputations of poets like Robinson and Frost, with already established styles, were seriously damaged. Frost's lifelong defensiveness is partly accounted for by the fact that he was in his early forties and just beginning to achieve recognition, after more than twenty years of writing, when Eliot's *Prufrock* made Frost's kind of writing seem as out-dated as that of the late Victorians. To endure at all, as a poet of the kind he already was and could only remain, Frost had to become tougher and more devious than ever. And he had to spend a great deal of his energy denying, and trying to prove by what he wrote, that he was not an "escapist."

For modernism seemed to most of our best minds, both critical and creative, the only honest and sensitive way a poet could write — and feel — in the new age. It seemed, and I suspect in a sense it was, the only way of writing that represented a fully *conscious* response to the radically altered social and cultural conditions of the early years of this century. A school of criticism — the "New" Criticism — arose to explain and defend the new poetry, and to provide it a rationale which would guarantee its being seen not as one way of writing but *the* way of writing, the way in which all good poets in all ages had always written. Poets like Hart Crane who began late in the second decade of this century did not suppose there was any other way a modern poet *could* write.

But Modernism is now dead, and has been for some time. Almost exactly thirty years after writing "Portrait of a Lady," which contained every quality essential to Modernism, Eliot announced its demise in the passage on style in "East Coker" in 1940. Most younger poets who began to write in the 1940's significantly modified the still dominant Modernist tradition in one way or another — Robert Lowell by returning to strict syllabic-accentual meters, for example — but only a few were really in rebellion. They were still making personal adjustments in an accepted stye. With poets beginning their work in the 1950's, rebellion was the norm. Most of our younger poets in the 1960's no longer feel any need to rebel. With some curious exceptions whom they sometimes venerate — Pound and Williams chiefly, for very different reasons — they write almost as though the revolution of Modernism had never occurred. Their affinities are with poets long out of fashion, with Whitman for instance. Though they find much to admire in Stevens, they cannot write in his manner. Poets who continue to think of the great Modernist poets as "the enemy" are generally over fifty.

So far as the public could know, with Eliot's earliest work still unpublished, the Imagist movement initiated Modernism. As a poetic "school," Imagism was at once, paradoxically, short-lived, and in its emphasis on concreteness, the most lasting feature of

Modernist poetry. Insignificant in the number of memorable poems it produced that really exemplify its principles, it yet had an enormous influence which in some respects is still discernible today.

It was in 1912, Pound has told us, that he and H. D. and the British poet Richard Aldington decided that they were agreed on the following principles:

1. Direct treatment of the "thing," whether subjective or objective.
2. To use absolutely no word that does not contribute to the presentation.
3. As regarding rhythm: to compose in the sequence of the musical phrase, not in the sequence of the metronome.[1]

Two years later Pound attempted to illustrate the kind of writing such principles would produce by editing an anthology he called *Des Imagistes.* Then, for reasons partly having to do with personalities and partly related to his own changing ideas of where poetry should go, he broke with the "movement" and relinquished the leadership of it to that "demon saleswoman," as Eliot somewhat later called her, Amy Lowell. He began to speak of Imagism contemptuously as "Amygism," a set of principles not broadly enough conceived to hold a developing poet.

Pound's "Amygism" resulted in three more anthologies, all called *Some Imagist Poets* and edited by the movement's new leader in 1915, 1916, and 1917. Then the publication of Eliot's *Prufrock and Other Observations* in 1917 effectively put an end, for young poets, to Imagism as a movement, by incorporating all that was meaningful in Imagist principles while at the same time relating the image to human experience of the image — by relating neutral "facts" to human values. "Prufrock" seemed no less "objective" than the Imagists wished to be, but quite clearly it could not be described as just a "picture."

Pound, by far the most intelligent and crafty of the Imagists, gave the best definition of the only part of the Imagist credo that made the movement distinctive — its concentration on the *image,* clearly and precisely rendered. He did it the simplest way, by defining what he meant by the word "image." "An 'Image,' " he wrote in the first of many attempts to locate what he continued to take to be the basic unit of poetry, "is that which presents an intellectual and emotional complex in an instant of time. I use the term 'complex' rather in the technical sense employed by the newer psychologists such as Hart."

When Pound made this statement, Bernard Hart was not just "newer," he was newest. And when we look into his work, we find that Pound was not really using "complex" as Hart used it at all, but only bluffing as usual — though his definition of the image *does* translate something of the spirit of Hart into poetic strategy. A British psychologist, Hart published *The Psychology of Insanity* in 1912, just before Pound offered his definition. Hart proved himself a little more than abreast of the times by acknowledging indebtedness for specific ideas to the then almost unknown Professor Freud of Vienna. To balance this, he also proved himself solidly embedded in the late nineteenth century by crediting his general approach and methodology to Karl Pearson, author of *The Grammar of Science,* whose book remained the classic statement of scientific mechanism and materialism until one of the major modern philosophers, Alfred North Whitehead, enunciated the definitive answer to it in one of "the books that changed our minds," *Science and the Modern World,* in 1925.

Hart began his definition of a "complex" by stating his basic assumption:

> Before we endeavour to discover the causes underlying morbid psychological phenomena we must be convinced that our quest is reasonable, we must firmly believe that such causes exist. This belief involves the adoption of psychological determinism — the doctrine that in the psychical world, as in the world of matter, every event must have a cause. Provided that the necessary antecedents are present, then the result will inevitably follow; and if we see the result, then we know that certain definite causes must have combined in order to produce it. Chance has no more part in psychology than it has in physics. Every thought which flits through the mind, however casual or irrelevant it may seem to be, is the only thought which can possibly result from the various mental processes which preceded it.

A few pages later, he came to the definition itself:

> Complexes, then, are causes which determine the behaviour of the conscious stream, and the action which they exert upon consciousness may be regarded as the psychological analogue of the conception of "force" in physics. They are not, of course, constantly active, but only become so under certain conditions. These conditions consist in the presence of a "stimulus," occurring whenever one or more of the ideas belonging to a complex is roused to activity, either by some external event, or by processes of association occurring within the mind itself. . . . So soon as this necessary stimulation has occurred, the complex immediately tends to exert its effect upon consciousness. The effect consists normally in the introduction into consciousness of ideas, emotions, and trains of activity belonging to the complex. Of the ideas, arguments, etc., presented to the individual, those which are in harmony with the complex are reinforced, whereas those not so in harmony tend to be inhibited and to lose their cogency.
>
> The mode of thought produced in this manner by the activity of a complex is quite different from that occurring in genuine logical thinking.

The "technical sense" in which Pound said he used the word *complex* should now be sufficiently clear. Lumping together what Hart distinguished as the cause (the "complex" itself) and the effect (the resulting "trains of activity" in the consciousness), Pound has hinted at a definition of the Imagist's proper subject which is much broader than that implied in his first principle, "direct treatment of the 'thing.'" What did it matter if Pound had seized upon a word that Hart had used to describe a complicated set of "proclivities" which, working together, could be said to "cause" our "stream of consciousness" and had used it as though it meant the "effect," that is, as Hart said, the "ideas, emotions, and trains of activity" produced by the "complex" itself? The important thing was that Pound had gained a "scientific" authority for his definition, and that he had thought with the same *model* in mind that Hart had had in mind. Both talked about human conscious experience in terms of the model of a machine, in which "forces" are exerted and produce inevitable results.

Imagism, it would now appear, need not be limited to *description* — that is, to describing the external "stimulus" which activated the "complex," which activated the resultant "trains of activity." If an Imagist is a poet who devotes himself to presenting images, as Pound has now defined them, he may write a genuine Imagist poem by presenting, in such a way as to give an effect of simultaneity, a mental "stimulus" and the resulting mental processes that make up its "effects"; provided that in doing so he writes in a manner consistent with the implications of the scientific abstractions, "cause" and "effect," understood in terms of the model of a machine. As Pound said a year later, in 1913, "The arts, literature, poesy, are a science, just as chemistry is a science . . . . The arts give us a great percentage of the lasting and unassailable data regarding the nature of man. . . . No science save the arts will give us the requisite data for learning in what ways men differ."

That is to say, the poet, writing as a scientist collecting "data," is to present an experience not as though *he had it,* but as though it just *happened to him,* as a brick might fall on his head or sand blow in his eyes. So far as his imagery is visual, he must write as though vision were not purposive, not selective, not *active,* but a passive inflow of something "out there," the way images are imprinted on the film or plate in a camera. If his images are not limited to the visual, if they include various affective responses as well as external stimuli, so that the camera metaphor becomes inadequate, then the ideal model becomes a chemist watching chemical "forces" produce chains of chemical "effects" in a laboratory. For the Imagist, the "laboratory" would be his own sensibility. Imagist poetics grew out of scientific positivism.

All this is implicit in Pound's early definition of the image, with its reference to Hart. But of course most of the Imagists had not thought so hard about poetic theory as Pound had, or if, like the British Imagist poet and philosopher T. E. Hulme, they *had* thought about it, they had done so in different terms, with different interests. Hulme would probably have flatly denied it if asked whether he was taking his cue from technology or the sciences. All he wanted to do, he repeatedly said, was to destroy liberalism and Romanticism; but this, he realized, meant getting rid of the Romantic or transcendental *person* and the associated concept of *personality.* Hulme's "classic" and authoritarian ideals coincided nicely with the "objective" kind of poetry Pound wanted and was explaining by use of a "scientific" term.

But Hulme, though influential in several ways, most of them disastrous, did not speak for many of those we call Imagists. For them, Imagism had no philosophic underpinning of which they were aware and contained no philosophic implications. It was just an anti-Romantic and anti-Victorian, a "clear" and "hard" and "unillusioned" way of writing, the poetry of the "real," in short. "Free verse," most of them thought, was normally desirable if one wanted to avoid both the sound and the sense of the illusioned fathers, but even Amy Lowell, who elaborated Pound's three principles into six without saying anything new, said it was only desirable, not essential; and if she had been a clearer thinker she might have gone on to say that it could not be used to distinguish Imagism from other kinds of poetry. Indeed, of the six Imagist principles she promulgated in *Some Imagist Poets,* only the fourth — "to present an image. . . . [to] render particulars exactly" — is even approximately adequate as an attempt to state a *distinguishing* principle. The others — "freedom in the choice of subject," and use of "common speech" and the "*exact* word" are typical — are either ideals common to many poets in several periods or warnings that few poets of any school would wish to disregard.

Amy Lowell's fifth principle will serve to illustrate how difficult it is to find out from self-proclaimed Imagists what Imagism was. Her principle calls for poetry that is "hard and clear, never blurred nor indefinite." Poe and the French Symbolists often strove for "blurred or indefinite" effects, so the statement apparently tells us that Imagist poetry should not be like theirs. But most poetry that is judged good could not be described as "blurred" or "indefinite," in any ordinary meaning of those words, so the statement does not take us very far. And if "clear" means something more than "understandable," as presumably it does, what does it mean? And what would "hard" poetry be? If there is any precise meaning in this principle, it must lie *behind* the words, not in them.

Partly hidden, partly revealed by Amy Lowell's pronouncements were the two ideas that emerge when we interpret Pound's first principle in the light of all that we have seen implied in his definition of the image. These two ideas are sufficient without any additions to separate Imagism from other poetic movements. They are such curious notions that, once we have pondered them, we are no longer surprised that it is hard to find very many poems that deserve to be called "pure" Imagist poems by the test they offer. The two hard-core Imagist ideas are these: first, the idea that the poet's work is essentially the *recording* of *observation,* with "observation" conceived as a completely objective, nonpurposive process; and second, the idea that the poem should present what is being observed, the "thing," "directly," which we are now in a position to understand as meaning "without interpretation or comment" of the poet as person. The poet should present, in short, as Miss Moore said, "the raw material of poetry in all its rawness."

These two ideas imply a third, which characterized not just Imagism but Modernist poetry in general. If the personality of the poet is irrelevant to his work, and his strictly poetic function is limited to neutral observation, what is there left for him to do, besides *versify* — and versifying in *free* verse is really not difficult. He can design, as Marianne Moore would say, imaginary gardens for real toads — imaginative shapes for the facts his poetry will be made up of. This, it was supposed, would require not insight or vision, passion or pity, but simply and exclusively *craftsmanship.* The poet, as Amy Lowell said in a preface, is exactly like a carpenter: he has a *skill.* She might better have said, exactly like the popular notion of a scientist writing up a report of an experiment. The poet sets up an experiment in his sensibility, watches what happens, then writes it up. Therein lies the skill, the craft.

All three of these ideas — that the poet is a recorder of observations, that he must not intervene in the process of recording, and that his contribution is limited to the technical skill with which he records — that is to say, the skill with which he designs a "setting" for the "raw materials of poetry" — were better put by Eliot in his first book of essays in 1917 than they had yet been, or ever would be, by Pound. Choosing an analogy from chemistry, Eliot explained his desire for impersonal poetry by elaborating his famous catalyst theory. The poet's mind, he said, is like the filament of platinum that, when it is immersed in two elements, causes the creation of a third without being itself in any way affected. Remaining totally inert, inactive, it still, simply by *being there,* brings about the creation of the third element — the poem, one understands. Poetry, Eliot continued, has nothing to do with the poet as *person.* The man who writes the poetry has only his skill. He *intends* nothing, *chooses* nothing, is *responsible* for nothing. Poetry is not an expression of personality but an escape from personality.

Eliot's "impersonal" theory of poetry might better have been called "antipersonal." Resting on an intense revolt against Romanticism, it could draw upon some apparently "obvious" evidence to make its case: A great many artists have been "bad" men; what society calls "good" men do not necessarily produce "good" art. "Man" and "artist," then, must be entirely separate. The man, the *person,* has his life and insights and personality; but if he happens also to be an artist, all these are irrelevant to his work and final value as a poet. The poet is not, as Emerson had said, man functioning as Namer and Sayer, but someone who has learned or invented certain techniques. The New Critics would later insist that "paraphrase," the attempt of the *reader* to render the poem personal once more, to relate it to himself, to his interests and purposes and grasp of meaning, was "heresy." The poem should be left as it was created, an artifact like a curiously carved jewel.

Randall Jarrell made one of the most perceptive comments on this Imagist-Impersonal theory. Discussing what he called the "odd climate of poetic opinion" that was Williams' Imagist background, he said that in Imagist theory, "The subject of poetry . . . changed from the actions of men to the reactions of poets." This is true and fine, but insufficient. For poets are also, whether they like it or not, persons, precisely as Emerson and Whitman said. And persons, insofar as they are sane, are *not* mere passive "receptors" or automatic "reactors."

To consider the poet as simply a neutral *observer* of a train of mental and emotional events that take place within him as a result of a stimulus, a passive watcher of something that happens to him, is effectively to separate the poet from his own experience. The *self* that experience "happens to," then, has been emptied of content; and the experience that simply "happens" has been emptied of meaning. As Erik Erikson has recently reminded us in *Insight and Responsibility,* those we call "insane" exhibit a conspicuous lack of the two qualities embodied in his title, and those who are most creative exhibit them very conspicuously.

The idea of man implicit in such poetic theory is the materialist one that he is like the Pavlovian dog whose mouth waters when a bell rings. Whether we call Imagist-Impersonal poetic theory "Behaviorist," or "mechanist-materialist," or "positivist," it is clear that this earliest poetics of Modernism was not philosophically neutral. The poets generally talked only about "craft," to be sure; this poem was thought to be "expert," that one not "expert." But behind the talk about techniques lay a new conception of man — as a "thing" like the " 'things,' whether subjective or objective," that Pound had insisted the poet should write about.

Eliot gradually, over a number of years, gave up this theory, but Pound never did. Instead, Pound sought refuge in ever more obscure allusions to justify it as he translated it into what he came to call "the ideogramic method." In the last several years of his life, Williams decided to add another book to *Paterson* because the critics had decided that Book IV, the final book as he had projected the poem, was not "expert." History plays many jokes. Nothing in *Paterson* is "expert" by any accepted standard of *expertise.* What his friendliest critics disliked about *Paterson Book IV* was its seeming betrayal of Williams' own ideals of freedom and growth.

What Imagist-Impersonal poetic theory amounts to in the end is a translation into poetic terms of what may be called positivistic "scientism" and this in turn amounts to an ultimate denial of responsibility. Emerson faced the same crisis of knowledge versus faith and knew better how to handle it. Frost had earlier faced the problem and adopted a strategy better than that of the Imagists for dealing with the "diminished thing" presented the poet by modern knowledge. Imagism was the first phase of a literary movement characterized ultimately by themes of alienation, by insistence on denial of responsibility, by the preference for the "anti-hero" — Prufrock, Senlin — and finally, when philosophy and theology, as popularly known, had caught up with Pound's early poetics, by despair and emptiness. Imagism is the poetic equivalent of fictional naturalism.

"You are all suffering from nothing," Gertrude Stein told a group of Modernist writers in the 1920's, thus perhaps inspiring Hemingway to write one of his greatest short stories, "A Clean, Well-Lighted Place," which, with magnificent economy, explores all the meanings of suffering from a perception of *nada,* nothing. This is of course getting ahead of our story of the Imagists. But that life and all the values that keep it going, both immanent and transcendent, are really "nothing," was already implied by a poetic theory which in its earliest forms assumed that man had neither insight nor responsibility.

The best-known Imagist poem, kept alive by anthologists and literary historians chiefly to illustrate what Imagist poems ought to be like, is Pound's "In a Station of the Metro." It is very short, and very simple — and would long since have been forgotten if it were not so convenient and brief an illustration of all three Imagist principles as enunciated by Pound:

> The apparition of these faces in the crowd;
> Petals on a wet, black bough.

Tested by each of Pound's three principles, the poem is found to be a faithful example of the Imagist credo. It treats directly, without comment or interpretation, both an "objective" and a "subjective" "thing" — the faces, and what *perceiving* them causes to happen in the mind of the poet; or, as the psychologist Hart would have put it, the stimulus and the inevitable mental response. It would of course not be fair to this poem, but it would be fair to a poet who wrote a good many such poems, to ask why the speaker never moved close enough to the faces to see them as the faces of *people,* of individuals, not merely as blobs of white against a black background in static arrangement. The people behind these faces were going somewhere, as we would never guess from the poem.

But to move on to the other two Imagist principles: The poem obviously does not waste words, and it is not written in syllabic feet; so that it passes these tests, too. But of course Whitman's "A Sight in Camp" also does not waste any words, and is not written in syllabic feet, so that these two principles tell us nothing about whether this is an Imagist poem or not. What does tell us something is the difference in the way the speakers in the two poems look at the faces they see.

The faces in Whitman's poem literally are those of dead men, but the speaker in the poem moves close, looks at each face in its full particularity and potential expressiveness, recognizes the faces as belonging to men like himself, and tells us what they mean to him. As a result, he "brings them to life" for himself and the reader, and, in a deeper sense, at the same time wills their lives for themselves, independently of any purposes of his. The one thing the faces are not, in the end, is "apparitions" existing only in and for his experience. Thus, though "A Sight in Camp" is short and pictorial, though it is composed almost entirely of images, and though it is in free verse, it is not in any sense an "Imagist" poem. The dead soldiers in Whitman's poem are not viewed as objects of his experience, *data* in the mind, to be observed and recorded.

Compared with Pound's poem, the anthologists' other favorite illustration of the practice of Imagism is both a more attractive and interesting poem and considerably less "pure" as an example. Williams' "The Red Wheel Barrow" treats "things," but treats them as though the speaker *is* and the reader *ought* to be related to the things because they contain intrinsic values. Instead of "treats," it might better be said that the poem "celebrates" "things." In doing so, it moves beyond Imagism to Williams' "philosophy" of "realism," his insistence that by paying the closest attention to the "thinginess" of things, we find value, not just neutral, external "fact."

The poem begins by saying, "So much depends" on the two precise images that follow, of red wheelbarrow glazed with rain and of white chickens beside it. It does not tell us *what* "depends" on these objects, but by the precision of detail with which they are described it gives us the clue we need. If we are to live in the "real" world, Williams in effect is saying, and not move into the transcendent realm of meaning too quickly, as Emerson did in "Two Rivers," we must pay the closest, most loving attention to what both the thoroughly "practical" and the thoroughly "transcendental" man might call "insignificant" details. We must look long, carefully, and lovingly at the details of the world if we are to see their beauty and their meaning. Images are important because they contain intrinsic meaning and value.

This poem does not fit Pound's first principle of Imagism nearly so well as "In a Station of the Metro," especially if that principle is interpreted in the light of Pound's definition of the image. There is no suggestion of determinism in Williams' poem, or of the alienation of the observer from his own observations, or, finally, of an "impersonal" art. Indeed, the poem begins with, and is totally dependent on, a forbidden "comment" or interpretation. A *mind* is at work here, not a chemical reaction. Williams, we would conclude on the basis of this sample, was either no Imagist at all, even early in his career, even though he himself thought he was, if we use the term *Imagism* strictly; or the best of the Imagists, if we use the term very loosely, ignoring Pound's principles and definitions and making it mean only a kind of poetry that emphasizes the concreteness and particularity of experience, and does so at the expense of *interpretation* of experience. Insofar as Imagism implies something like the dispassionate and objective observation supposedly characteristic of the scientist in his laboratory, no poet could well be farther from the Imagist ideal than Williams. He wrote always as the completely involved and wholly committed man, even when he wrote most simply of "things." What he said late in life describes even his early "Imagist" practice: "I have always had a feeling of identity with nature, but not assertive; I have always believed in keeping myself out of the picture. When I spoke of flowers, I *was* a flower . . ." But of *this* kind of "Imagism," more later.

Meanwhile, not to leave the impression that Pound's two-line poem is the only real example of pure Imagism one can find, we may note a few other poems that qualify for the label. Pound himself wrote very few if any other poems that stay within the limitations of the principles of 1912, though his *Cantos* rest ultimately on Imagist principles and he continued to define and redifine the image and continued, too, to write about both people and his own ideas as though they were *things* out there somewhere. But H. D., "the perfect imagist" as she is always called, wrote a good many poems that qualify as "Imagist," early in her career, and Eliot in his earliest period wrote some of the finest pure Imagist poems ever written. "Morning at the Window," for instance, expressing total alienation, is not only an impressive poem but a much more instructive example than "The Red Wheel Barrow" of Imagist ideas about poetry. The prose-poem "Hysteria," again, is perfect of its kind, as a careful, precise, alienated observation both of a woman laughing and of the effect this "stimulus" has on the emotions of the speaker-observer. He says of himself that he was "becoming involved," but the "involvement" was not with a person, only with teeth and shaking breasts and laughter itself. In the end the speaker concentrated his attention "with careful subtlety" in an attempt to avoid being swept along by what Hart had described as a compulsive "activity" within him, "quite different from that occurring in genuine logical thinking" — and quite different too,

I might add, from anything having to do with a personal relation between the laughing woman and the fascinated, cold, almost helpless, unsympathetic, and finally, despite his visceral reactions, personally *uninvolved* observer.

Imagism is the defensive-imitative poetic response to the antihumanistic and antipersonal implications of nineteenth- and early twentieth-century scientific philosophy — its mechanism and materialism, in short. (Not all those called "Imagists" *were* Imagists in *this* sense, to be sure. But there are always many who follow a fashion without knowing what it means.) For a mechanist, a *machine* offers the best model of reality. For a materialist, *things* are more real than persons or thoughts or processes. Thoughts themselves are best understood on the model of *things,* as we have seen Hart argue. And as a famous Cyberneticist recently said, to talk about the Soul is to talk about an imaginary "ghost in the machine." For the attitude that accepts these supposed implications of scientific knowledge and adds to them positivism, the notion that only scientific method gives any valid knowledge of external or objective reality, I use the word "scientism." (As far as I have been able to find out, this complex of ideas is no longer characteristic of most respected professional philosophers, and perhaps never characterized any of the great ones; but the truth of that statement depends on which ones are thought to be great.)

If there had been no "scientism," there would have been no Imagism. Imagism is the poetic equivalent not only of fictional naturalism but of that curious phenomenon, Semantics. In 1923, C. K. Ogden and I. A. Richards began the movement with *The Meaning of Meaning,* which examined the possibilities of "meaning" from an extreme nominalist and extreme positivist point of view. Language, they decided, could be divided into two uses, true symbolization and emotive uses. In true symbolization, words refer to "things in the external world"; only to this usage could the words "true" or "false" be applied. Certain simple types of *events,* such as a match bursting into flame after being struck, are considered, the authors say, for the sake of convenience, to be "things" — that is, they are concrete, localized, tangible, publicly verifiable. Less easily located or measured phenomena are dubiously "true" or "false": "such apparent symbols [i.e., words pointing to things or events] as 'character,' 'relation,' 'property,' 'concept,' etc. . . .

[must be understood] as standing for nothing beyond (indirectly) the individuals to which the alleged character would be applicable."

Ogden and Richards are quite careful to qualify their meanings. Their positivism is insistent but not entirely crude. Later semanticists were more jaunty in dismissing all reality but the reality of "things." In 1938, S. I. Hayakawa in his best-selling *Language in Action* proposed, as an infallible test of whether we were talking "sense" or "non-sense," that we simply cover our mouth with one hand and point to the *object* we were talking about with the other. Failing to find an *object* to point to, we could know that what we were saying was only "emotive." To the extent that Hayakawa's word "object," for the "referent" to which statements that make "sense" refer, is more narrow than Ogden and Richards' "thing," the later Semantics was more precisely and explicitly materialistic in its assumptions. "Meaning" applies to "objects"; all else is mere emotionalism. Science is the activity that tells us the truth about objects.

What should poets write about, then? "No ideas but in things," Williams decided, and kept repeating all his life, while writing "Tracts" to teach his fellow-townsmen how to conduct a funeral, defending "early martyrs," and protesting against moralistic conventions.

When Richards wrote his *Science and Poetry* in 1926, his purpose was to show that though poetry is not concerned with "truth," which is the realm properly assigned to science, yet its "pseudo-statements" still have value for us even in an age of science. Asking, "How is our estimate of poetry going to be affected by science?" he answered that once our true situation was properly understood, a new defense of poetry would be possible. The novelty of our situation resulted, he thought, from the fact that "Suddenly, not long ago . . . [man] began to get genuine knowledge on a large scale — knowledge, that is to say, purified from the influences of his wishes or his fears." This flood of verifiable knowledge had already fundamentally altered every part of the intellectual climate, but its importance for poetry lay chiefly in one of its effects:

> The central dominant change may be described as the *Neutralization of Nature,* the transference from the

> Magical View of the world to the scientific, a change so great that it is perhaps only paralleled historically by the change, from whatever adumbration of a world-picture preceded the Magical View, to the Magical View itself. By the Magical View I mean, roughly, the belief in a world of Spirits and Powers which control events, and which can be evoked and, to some extent, controlled themselves by human practices. The belief in Inspiration and the beliefs underlying Ritual are representative parts of this view. It has been decaying slowly for some 300 years, but its definite overthrow has taken place only in the last 70. Vestiges and survivals of it prompt and direct a great part of our daily affairs, but it is no longer the world-picture which an informed mind most easily accepts. There is some evidence that Poetry, together with the other Arts, arose with this Magical View. It is a possibility to be seriously considered that Poetry may pass away with it.

But poetry would not pass away, Richards felt sure, for it was needed to "organize" our attitudes and emotions. Once its statements were recognized as the "pseudo-statements" they were, they could be very useful "as a means of ordering, controlling and consolidating" experience — for the "dawning science" of the mind had shown that experience was not chiefly a matter of reason or intelligence, and anyway the truth discovered by science would remain largely irrelevant to actual living even if we were more rational than we are.

Richards' chief concern was to defend traditional and post-Imagist poetry, with *The Waste Land* as his main example of the latter, not Imagism, which he knew had been given up by the poets he most respected, like Eliot. But if there had been an Imagist around still looking for a rationale for his practice, he could have found it perfectly articulated in *Science and Poetry*. For the pure Imagist poem does not require for its defense even Richards' ingenious (and as he later admitted, mistaken) justification of "pseudo-statement": it starts from an acceptance of the "neutralization of nature" and makes no claim to any sort of truth that needs verification. It says only, "This is the way the 'thing' looked — smelt, felt, sounded, etc. — to *me,* and this is what it made me think of or feel." Its images are not symbols, for it knows that nature is not a "picture-language," as Emerson had thought it.

A less intelligent positivistic critic than Richards, but one equally devoted to scientism, several years later made an even better case for Imagism as "demanded" by science — not being confused, as Richards was, by partially understanding *The Waste Land.* Max Eastman's *The Literary Mind, Its Place in an Age of Science* was already somewhat outdated by 1931, when it came out, but in its attack on the vulnerable "literary [i.e., 'Victorian,' or prescientific] mind," it spoke for many at the time. The trouble with the literary mind, Eastman thought, was that science had changed all that the literary mind believed in. There was not even, as we would be told much later by a mind much like Eastman's, though not so generous, "two cultures"; there was only one, and poets could not participate in it, unless. . . .

Like Richards' *Science and Poetry,* Eastman's *The Literary Mind* begins with a chapter on "The March of Science" (who could stop a "march," or even break its rhythm to get a question in?). This rhetorically effective chapter is followed by chapters entitled "Literature on the Defensive," "Literature in Retreat," "Toward a Science of Literature," and "The Future of Literature." This last is unexpectedly hopeful. Addressing himself to the problem posed by Matthew Arnold's essay on the subject, "Literature and Science," Eastman concludes, "You might sum it up by saying that science, having displaced magic and religion and abstract philosophy as a source of help and guidance, is now successfully attacking 'literature.' " Nevertheless, he thought, the success of science will not be complete if poets have the good sense to concede to science what is science's proper domain, truth, and stick to their last:

> Once we realize that poetry and the poetic element in literature is made out of the immediate qualities of experience, and that the knowledge *about* experience which comes to us from books is literature only if it comes mingled with these qualities or conveyed by them — then we are in a position to distinguish literature from science and from directions for playing pingpong or oiling a Ford motor, and arrive at some considered judgment of what is happening to it in this extraordinary age.

> Literature is becoming more and more deeply differentiated from science; it is becoming differentiated from science in wider and wider spheres. Science is steadily and sharply advancing into all those fields in which the art of poetry and poetic prose has flourished. . . .
>
> And so in every sphere of life into which science advances, no matter how tentatively and with a groping instrument, in some form or other the distinction is immediately set up between the various ways in which things may be experienced and the valid conception of them in their practically important relations. What had been "literature" — an amateur commixion of experience with interpretation — falls apart into a more universally reliable interpretation on the one hand and a more individual and abandoned experience on the other.

Imagists, including Pound long after he had ceased to call himself an Imagist, have often claimed the support of oriental poetry as a precedent or model for their own. Several of them, again including Pound, also have paid tribute to Whitman as a kind of immature and naive but nonetheless in some unspecified sense genuine poetic ancestor. But if the central core of meaning in Imagist theory is what it would appear to be from the evidence so far examined, both relationships ought to turn out to be very superficial. I shall let an Imagist who explicitly acknowledged both "debts" serve as a test case for all the others.

Amy Lowell opened her *Pictures of the Floating World* in 1919 with an epigraph from Whitman's poem "With Antecedents." He was, we are apparently meant to infer, *her* antecedent. The first section of her book, however, is made up of poems derived from her other source, oriental poetry — "Lacquer Prints," which, she tells us, were inspired by Japanese *haiku* poems, and "Chinoiseries." I shall take up the contents of the volume in reverse order, following the lead given by the epigraph rather than that given by the "Foreword." The fact that the bulk of the volume is devoted to the nonoriental "Planes of Personality" (221 of the volume's 257 pages, to be exact) would seem to justify this procedure.

"Planes of Personality," following the epigraph from Whitman, strikes one as a very Whitmanesque title. It is followed by others equally inspired, it would seem, by "the good grey poet." The subsections of "Planes of Personality" are "Two Speak Together," "Eyes, and Ears, and Walking," "As Toward One's Self," "Plummets to Circumstance," "As Toward War," and, finally, "As Toward Immortality." Whitman was certainly concerned with all these subjects and might be imagined as having used these phrases as titles of some of his poems.

But the poems so introduced could be called Whitmanesque only if anything written in "free verse" — unrhymed, or irregularly rhymed, cadenced lines — must remind us of Whitman. Whitman's meanings are noticeably absent, except when they are implied by being reversed. The first poem in the section called "As Toward One's Self," for instance, "In a Time of Dearth," begins this way —

> Before me,
> On either side of me,
> I see sand.
> If I turn the corner of my house
> I see sand.
> Long — brown —
> Lines and levels of flat
> Sand.

After a several page development that culminates in

> But I only see sand,
> Sand lying dead in the sun,
> Lines and lines of sand,
> Sand

the poem concludes with this verse-paragraph:

> I will paste newspapers over the windows to shut out the
> sand,
> I will fit them into one another, and fasten the corners.
> Then I will strike matches
> And read of politics, and murders, and festivals,
> Three years old.

But I shall not see the sand any more
And I can read
While my matches last.

Only if we think most abstractly about the general, paraphrasable situation, paying as little attention to the expression of it as may be, will we think that the speaker here is Walt in the Waste Land. It is not only that if he had found himself in this sandy place, it would not have *remained* a waste land for him very long, but that every quality of his mind and of his verse is being denied. The inspiration here, despite the epigraph and the headings, is not Whitman but Eliot, and a particular poem of Eliot's at that, his "Portrait of a Lady." Not just the tone but even the situation of the speaker in Eliot's poem is being echoed. Eliot had written

You will see me any morning in the park
Reading the comics and the sporting page.
Particularly I remark
An English countess goes upon the stage.
A Greek was murdered at a Polish dance,
Another bank defaulter has confessed.

Eliot's poem had been published four years before Lowell's in *Poetry* magazine, and again, in book form, two years before, in *Prufrock and Other Observations,* and must have made a deep impression on her, though when she came to treat Eliot several years later in her *A Critical Fable,* she damned its author for his expatriation and his cold-blooded intellectuality.

There is almost as little of the intention and effect of *haiku* poetry in the opening section as there is of Whitman in the rest of the book. The *haiku* in its mature form, after Basho, rests upon and implies Zen Buddhism. Its images are not conceived as presenting a "complex," in Pound's and Hart's sense, in which a "thing" external to the self starts an involuntary "chain" of subjective association. Instead, the "things" cease to be *objects out there* and become a *part* of the self — as in Whitman at his best, as in Emerson by intention — until the distinction between *thing* and *self* disappears and a sense of the unity of all being comes in its place.[2]

Here are three examples, as translated by Peter Beilenson. I choose these three because they all treat winter cold.

Cold first winter rain . . .
    Poor monkey, you too
    Could use
A little woven cape
        — *Basho*

Tea-water, chilly
    Waiting while we
    Watched the snow . . .
Froze itself a hat
        — *Sokan*

Winter rain darkens
    Lichened letters
    On the grave . . .
And my old sadness
        — *Roka*

Now here are two on similar subjects by Amy Lowell: In "The Pond"

Cold, wet leaves
Floating on moss-coloured water,
And the croaking of frogs —
Cracked bell-notes in the twilight.

And again in "Desolation"

Under the plum-blossoms are nightingales;
But the sea is hidden in an egg-white mist,
And they are silent.

Amy Lowell's "oriental" poems are not really oriental at all, but fairly "pure" specimens of Imagism. They record details of nature succinctly and offer either no comment or interpretation, or only an implied one. (The bell that is like the frogs' croaking is "cracked"; the nightingales, despite what Eliot had said, are *silent.*) She "observes" these details, "records" them in a manner "hard" and "clear," and hints that she concludes from them that man and nature are totally at odds. What she sees in nature makes her just *sad.* More than anything else they express her alienation. Nothing in the poems suggests Basho's identification with the monkey, Sokan's with tea-water, or Roka's with those long dead. The spirit of Amy Lowell's poems is Western, twentieth-century, and more nearly out of Pound by Eliot than out of Zen by *haiku.* Pound came closer to oriental poetry, as we shall see, though not very close except when he was translating.

Some Imagists

As for the future, Les Imagistes . . . *have that in their keeping.*

— Ezra Pound, in Ripostes, 1912

The point de repère *usually and conveniently taken, as the starting-point of modern poetry, is the group denominated 'imagist' in London about 1910.*

— T. S. Eliot, in "American Literature and the American Language"

AMY LOWELL

AMY LOWELL played an important part in the "Poetic Renaissance" that lasted for a little more than a decade after 1912. Her books were often reprinted and frequently won high praise from eminent critics. With her wealth, her flamboyant personality, her big black cigar, and her flair for organizing and promoting, she seemed for a time to be a major force in the new poetry.

Now and then she wrote a memorable poem, usually — except for the "oriental" poems — in a manner that could hardly be called Imagist. "Meeting-House Hill," surely one of her best, is more Symbolist than Imagist. "Patterns," her best-remembered poem, and a good one, makes an explicit protest against Puritan inhibitions and society's repressive conventions. "Lilacs" is moving in places, when her feeling for the past of her native region comes out most clearly. This *home* feeling for New England is perhaps the only *genuine* feeling in her work; the rest appear to be borrowed, except the spite, which is seen chiefly in her prose and her unsigned *Critical Fable.*

This last poem is one of her more interesting productions. Adopting the matter and meter of her famous ancestor, she redoes his "Fable for Critics" for 1922. A good deal of the poem today seems rather pointless, and certainly the attempt at vernacular humor is less successful than that of the earlier "Fable"; but there are some evidences of shrewdness in its judgments as well as much that was conventional critical opinion in advanced literary circles in 1922.

The two most striking evidences of critical acumen, and they are important, are the remarks on the unacknowledged and then unrecognized "madness" of the characters in Frost's *North of Boston,* and the inclusion of Wallace Stevens, who had not yet published a single book, as the last of the twenty-one poets discussed. The outstanding example of critical *misjudgment* is in the quick and easy way Pound and Eliot are written off as expatriates who have nothing but learning to their credit, and in Pound's case sham learning at that. At this point the poem approaches the nativism and anti-intellectualism of the first American review of *The Waste Land,* in which the anonymous reviewer decided that the poem must have been intended as a hoax. Though she does not quite come out and say so, Lowell makes it clear by tone, arrangement, and the assignment of relative amounts of space, that she prefers fourteen of her twenty-one figures, especially native voices like Sandburg, Masters, and Lindsay, to either Pound or Eliot, who had lost their western and midwestern accents. In view of the amount of borrowing from Eliot to be found in her work, this seems odd, but she was not the only poet to dislike Eliot while learning from him. Pound's remarks on "Amygism" would have been sufficient cause for the way she treats him.

JOHN GOULD FLETCHER

Two of those she discusses, John Gould Fletcher and H. D., were in Pound's original Imagist anthology. With help from Amy Lowell, Fletcher had achieved considerable contemporary fame with his *Irradiations,* 1915, and *Goblins and Pagodas,* 1916. The "Irradiations" are short descriptive mood-poems written largely in late romantic language, more openly personal — "self-centered" might be a better word — than Imagist poems generally were supposed to be —

> I am like a drop of rose-flushed rain
> Clinging to crimson petals of love.

"Sand and Spray (A Sea Symphony)" develops moods through the "objective correlatives" of a storm, sailboats, the tide, and so on. All the moods turn out to be finally the *same* mood — a desuetude of spirit. In the still more famous (at the time) "color symphonies," the identical process is repeated: all the colors, at first apparently taken seriously, quickly get reduced to one color, a dull gray. We may think for a while that the real greenness, the "greenness of green" as Williams might have said, will last —

> I am a glittering raindrop
> Hugged close by the cool rhododendron.
> I am a daisy starring
> The exquisite curves of the close-cropped turf.

But no, before we know it the green has darkened to black or faded to gray —

> Now let the black tops of the pine-trees break like a
> spent wave,
> Against the grey sky:
> These are tombs and memorials and temples and altars
> sun-kindled for me.

The whiteness of "White Symphony" shows greater staying-power, but that is because Fletcher "sees" whiteness, as Melville had before him, as "the visible absence of color":

> Blue, clogged with purple,
> Mists uncoil themselves:
> Sparkling to the horizon,
> I see the snow alone.

Attempting to explain his method in the Preface to *Goblins and Pagodas,* Fletcher asks his reader to imagine a book lying on the poet's desk and to imagine, further, that the poet is about to write a poem about the book. How will he go about it? He will not, Fletcher says, analyze and criticize it, as a Victorian poet would. He will not simply describe it, as a "realist" poet would. Rather, he says,

> I should select out of my life the important events connected with my ownership of this book, and strive to write of them in terms of the volume itself, both as regards subject-matter and appearance. In other words, I should link up my personality and the personality of the book, and make each a part of the other. In this way I

> should strive to evoke a soul out of this piece of inanimate matter, a something characteristic and structural inherent in this inorganic form which is friendly to me and responds to my mood.
>
> This method is not new, although it has not often been used in Occidental countries. Professor Fenollosa, in his book on Chinese and Japanese art, states that it was universally employed by the Chinese artists and poets of the Sung period in the eleventh century A.D. He calls this doctrine of the interdependence of man and inanimate nature, the cardinal doctrine of Zen Buddhism. The Zen Buddhists evolved it from the still earlier Taoist philosophy, which undoubtedly inspired Li Po and the other great Chinese poets of the seventh and eighth centuries A.D.

Clearly, Fletcher is at least as far from understanding oriental art and Zen Buddhist teaching as Amy Lowell was. As we have seen in her case, when examining the *haiku* form she claimed to be following and recreating for Westerners, *haiku* poems do not "endeavor" to "link up" two things that remain separate; they imaginatively *realize identity*. The *haiku* poet does not "strive" to "evoke a soul" out of a "piece of matter" (this phrase alone would be sufficient to reveal the vast distances between Fletcher and Zen); and especially not to do so just in order that the (imagined? invented?) "soul" may be "friendly" to *him* and respond to *his* mood. Fletcher is describing, not the poetic method of Zen, as he supposes, but a sort of solipsistic romanticism.

Even when, in the next paragraph, he comes closer to the reality of what he is describing ("the doctrine of the interdependence of man and inanimate nature," attributed to Fenollosa), he is almost as far away as ever. "Interdependence" suggests precisely the kind of Western *analytical* distinction (two abstractions, related in a third abstraction) that the practitioner of Zen wants to break down. It is just this kind of thinking that, according to Zen, *prevents* the experience of identity or union. If instead of "interdependence" Fletcher had said "interpenetration," it would be easier to believe that he had a real grasp of what he was talking about. As one student of Zen Buddhism has expressed the idea of "interpenetration":

> Having reached the state of *satori,* we become aware that *everything* in all this world about us, all other living and non-living things . . . are part of Absolute Being — and are thus essentially holy. Mountains and rocks, trees and grass-blades, elephants and microbes, all share equally in the Eternal. . . . We are all a part of Absolute Being, and we are all a part of each other.

But of course immediate realization of interpenetration was not what Fletcher really wanted. Though he knew differently, he wanted to imagine, for the sake of creating poems, that nature conceived as "the other," was yet friendly and responsive to his moods. But no amount of "striving" to imitate the "method" he had read about in Fenollosa could persuade him that nature was *really* friendly. The blurred focus of his poems is apparent also in the prose of his attempt to explain himself. "Evoke," for instance, in "evoke a soul out of this piece of inanimate matter," is ambiguously used. It ought to mean "call forth what is already there." But if "matter" has a "soul," why call matter "inanimate," which means precisely "soul-less," or why even call it "matter," since if it *has* a "soul" to be called forth, and is therefore really "animate," then it is no more, and no less, "matter" than we are?

All the distinctions Fletcher is making in the passage, the whole thought-process indeed, is Western, rationalistic, and unconsciously materialistic. Fletcher does not for a minute, either as poet or as man, take seriously the "souls" he says he is striving to "evoke" in nature. And even if he did, he would still be worlds of thought away from the teaching of Zen, which, however hard it may be to describe in Western words and concepts, can at least be negatively characterized as *not* being a technique for "using" nature to mirror *our* moods.

What Fletcher missed, was what Amy Lowell missed, the religious *meaning* of Zen, which gives the art forms that derive from and express it *their* meaning. Zen has been described as "pantheistic mysticism" and also as "immanentist mysticism." Whether "mysticism" is the right word in these descriptions is, to be sure, debatable, but even if we were to substitute for it a phrase like "religious feeling," it would still be necessary to say that Fletcher missed the ultimate meaning of the method he so much admired.

Much later, when he was past his creative period, Fletcher showed a firmer grasp of Eastern art and thought, but in 1916 he had only a very limited understanding of the art forms he admired.

To suggest what he and the others missed, here are five of the 112 ways given by Shiva in answer to Devi's question: How may we enter the "life beyond form pervading forms," "the beneficence," as Emerson sometimes described the "Over-Soul"? To these I add one more *haiku* poem.

> Feel the consciousness of each person as your own consciousness. So, leaving aside concern for self, *become each being.*
>
> In rain during a black night, enter that *blackness* as the form of forms.
>
> See *as if for the first time* a beauteous person or an ordinary object.
>
> Feel your substance, bones, flesh, blood, saturated with *cosmic essence.*
>
> Imagine spirit simultaneously within and around you until the entire universe *spiritualizes.*
>
> . . . .
>
> Dewdrop, let me cleanse
> In your brief
> Sweet waters . . .
> These dark hands of life.
>
> *Haiku* poem by Basho

H. D.

To say that Hilda Doolittle (Mrs. Richard Aldington), H. D. as she preferred to sign her work, was by far the best poet among the Americans included in Pound's *Des Imagistes* is at once to say too much and too little. It is to say too much because to anyone who has even just dipped into the works of all of them — H. D., Fletcher, and Amy Lowell — it is too obvious to need saying that she towers over the other two like a mature sugar maple over the undergrowth of moosewood and hobblebush, which do not have it in them to grow very tall, no matter how long they survive. It is to say too little because the comparison is fundamentally inapt; sugar maple, and moosewood or striped maple, are both of the *genus acer,* to be sure, but no useful conclusions are likely to emerge from a comparison of *acer saccharum* with *acer pennsylvanicum.* We can take H. D.'s measure only by comparing her with the major poets of the twentieth century, or at least with those in some sort of second category, like Aiken or MacLeish or Ransom.

The label "the perfect Imagist" was applied early and still continues in use, even though it describes — so far as it is apt at all — considerably less than half of her work.[1] As she has said, objecting to the label,

> However, I don't know that labels matter very much. One writes the kind of poetry one likes. Other people put labels on it. Imagism was something that was important for poets learning their craft early in this century. But after learning his craft, the poet will find his true direction.

Even her earliest, most clearly Imagistic poems usually transcend the limitation of Pound's "instant of time" definition. ("Heat," which does not, is perhaps so often anthologized just for this reason.) If there is a feeling of stasis in them, and I think there is, it results not from anything so abstract as a "principle" but from a *feeling* of being caught in a time when all meanings are gone and so any movement would be directionless, any *growth* impossible. It is not, for H. D., as it had been for Robinson, that we find ourselves "the children of the night," groping in darkness. H. D.'s poems are filled with light, but a light too brilliant to be endured. At "Mid-day,"

> The light beats upon me.
> I am startled —
> a split leaf crackles on the paved floor —
> I am anguished — defeated.
> . . . .
> My thoughts tear me,
> I dread their fever.

The living poplar "is bright on the hill"; it is "deep-rooted among trees." But the sight of it does little for the observer:

O poplar, you are great
among the hill-stones,
while I perish on the path
among the crevices of the rocks.

"Sea Gods" opens with a rare explicit statement of the reason for this situation:

They say there is no hope —
sand — drift — rocks — rubble of the sea —
the broken hulk of a ship,
hung with shreds of rope,
pallid under the cracked pitch.

they say there is no hope
to conjure you —

"They" say this, but the speaker is not ready to accept what they say. She will search for meaning, first through immersion in the concrete, then through realizing the community of mankind through time as that is suggested by the mythic extensions of archetypal images. Allusions to Greek myth allow the mind to move back and forth through time between past and present. But still, in her *Collected Poems* of 1925, the poet never implies a future, except as the image of *waiting* implies a readiness for whatever may come: within "the dead peace/ of heart and brain worn out,/ you must wait,/ alert, alert, alert."

It does great violence to H. D.'s earlier poems to quote lines out of context this way. Her poems are characterized by their wholeness, their delicacy of suggestion, and by the almost complete absence in the best of the early work of explicit statements of theme or idea. Nothing that I have quoted yet gives the least idea of why these poems are so poignant and powerful. But perhaps a few such violations are pardonable for the sake of getting at the feelings that ultimately give these poems their shape and contribute to their peculiar reticence.

The poet is still waiting in *The Walls Do Not Fall,* but now she knows much more clearly what she is waiting for, and so the waiting no longer need be limited to a passive alertness of the senses. The spirit is *moving* now, searching, no longer waiting without hope. At the time of her beginning,

Evil was active in the land,
Good was impoverished and sad;

. . . .

but gods always face two-ways,
so let us search the old highways

for the true-rune, the right-spell,
recover old values. . . .

These prosy lines from a deliberately prosy poem show both a changed style and a changed attitude behind it. Assuming Spirit — that Spirit spoken of by all the faiths, "Creator/ Fosterer, Begetter, the Same-forever/ in the papyrus-swamp,/ in the Judean meadow" — the poet can now "profit by every calamity":

for I know how the Lord God
is about to manifest, when I,

the industrious worm,
spin my own shroud.

The poet now takes her stand alongside Emerson — though I do not mean to suggest that she was conscious of how closely she now paralleled the sage's thought — in affirming that "Dream,/ Vision" are the begetters of "thought and idea," and are "beyond" what they beget. All gods are the same god, but that does not mean that every worshipper is wrong and He is wholly unknown:

Now it appears very clear
that the Holy Ghost,
childhood's mysterious enigma,
is the Dream.

The "Dream" in these lines is ambiguously Freudian and idealist-transcendental, but Emerson would have found nothing obscure in the poet's request to be taken "home" "where the mantis/ prays on the river-reed" and "where the grasshopper says/ *Amen, Amen, Amen.*" "Osiris," we are told, equates with "O-sire-is," as we can see when we have uncovered the "cankerous growths/ in present-day philosophy,/ in an endeavor to make ready,/ as it were, the patient for the Healer." "Our awareness leaves us defenceless," so that the prayer we need most to pray is "Grant us strength to endure/ a little longer," in the hope that we may be given the ability to apprehend the presence of "the eternal generator of circles," to use Emerson's words for the Godhead, everywhere, even in the most unlikely places:

> *Sirius:*
> *what mystery is this?*
>
> where heat breaks and cracks
> the sand-waste,
> you are a mist
> of snow: white, little flowers.

Here we are close not only to Emerson, and to that strain in Christian history which finds its best symbol in St. Francis, but also to Zen Buddhism. Close to all these — but H. D.'s meaning is her own, growing with perfect integrity out of her whole career. "They" had said that there was no hope in the sandy waste land, but she has discovered for herself, with some help from Freud, late but not too late, that the "invasion of the over-soul into a cup/ too brittle, a jar too circumscribed" both increases the difficulty of our role as "voyagers, discoverers" and makes the voyage worth while.

Emerson, and Whitman too, might also have liked the thirty-ninth poem (the poems are untitled), which is brief enough to quote entire:

> We have had too much consecration,
> too little affirmation,
> too much: but this, this, this
> has been proved heretical,
> too little: I know, I feel
> the meaning that words hide;
> they are anagrams, cryptograms,
> little boxes, conditioned
> to hatch butterflies . . .

The Walls Do Not Fall not only gives expression to a new faith and expresses it in a new style; it comments on the style which has been given up as no longer appropriate. In doing so, it not only acknowledges that Imagism as a way of writing grew from a way of believing, or not believing; it bids farewell to Modernism as a whole, in all its post-Imagist phases. The opening lines of poem thirty-two describe the "worn-out poetical fashion" Eliot had renounced in "East Coker" several years earlier.

> Depth of the sub-conscious spews forth
> too many incongruent monsters
>
> and fixed indigestible matter
> such as shell, pearl; imagery
>
> done to death; perilous ascent,
> ridiculous descent; rhyme, jingle,
>
> overworked assonance, nonsense,
> juxtaposition of words for words' sake,
>
> without meaning, undefined; imposition,
> deception, indecisive weather-vane;
>
> disagreeable, inconsequent syllables,
> too malleable, too brittle,
>
> over-sensitive, under-definitive,
> clash of opposites, fight of emotion
>
> and sterile invention —
> you find all this?

H. D.'s long poems after *The Walls Do Not Fall* continue explorations of the world of myth begun in that volume. *Tribute to the Angels* (1945), *Flowering of the Rod* (1946), and *By Avon River* (1949), almost unknown to readers of American poetry, are notable experiments in finding a style that can express the contemporary consciousness. These journeys of discovery, guided by her metaphysical quest — her "wish to make real to myself what is most real" — led her at last, by way of *Tribute to Freud* and her novel *Bid Me to Live,* to her last long poem, *Helen in Egypt* (1961), which develops the theme that the fighting and dying at Troy was for an illusion; the reality was elsewhere.

Mixing prose and verse, and narrative, dramatic, and lyric modes, the poem brings to a fitting close the career of "the perfect Imagist," whose work, early and late, had outrun the understanding of literary critics and historians with a penchant for labeling.

H. D.'s journey from the barren land where the light was so insufferable that it made her seek shelter in the crevices of rocks was of course the typic journey of her generation. She made it at her own speed, in her own way, seeming not to move at all for several decades but arriving, late, as at a station on the way, at a cracked and crazy-angled house where there was shadow as well as light and where, though "we know no rule of procedure," still the walls do not fall, we "do not know why." At the end, in *Helen in Egypt,* she was still searching the many meanings of "the question that has no answer," pondering "the ultimate experience, *La Mort, L'Amour,*" and exploring, as Emerson had before her, the meanings of the image of the wheel, or circle, that brings the "ever-recurring 'eternal moment.' " The notes she made in her journey, in her poems, compose one of the really distinguished bodies of work of this century.

MARIANNE MOORE

Though H. D. is usually singled out as "the" Imagist, that distinction, such as it is, ought rather to go to Marianne Moore. Until the publication of her *What Are Years?* in 1941, no poet more persistently devoted himself to writing poems that exemplify the poetic ideal suggested either by Pound's definition of the image — "an intellectual and emotional complex in an instant of time" — or by his idea that the arts, especially poetry, give us "data" from which we may draw conclusions about the nature of man. If Miss Moore has ignored the philosophic implications of Pound's use of "complex," she has not missed the point of his drive toward the antipoetic, his definition of poetry as a "science," in short, his effort to defend poetry in terms derived from the "real" world of "fact." In most of her early work she seems determined to be the "pure" poet, the completely antiromantic poet, and the poet of the most rigorous determination to keep poetry free from that "emotional slither" that Pound had condemned, to keep it free by concentrating exclusively on "direct" treatment of the "thing."

Her *Selected Poems* of 1935 reads like the work of someone

who has lived among books so long that she has almost come to hate them — all but a few favorites — and is determined not to become "bookish" herself, at the cost of whatever narrowing of interests. Or it reads like the work of an editor of a magazine (as she was for years — *The Dial*) who has seen, and rejected, so much bad poetry, so much "self-expressive," pretentious, poorly controlled, vaguely romantic poetry, that she has almost come to dislike poetry too, unless it is "hard," "clear," cold, exact, and "literal." Her admission that, "In fact, the only reason I know for calling my work poetry at all is that there is no other category in which to put it" exhibits both her customary modesty and her fine perceptiveness. Miss Moore's description of herself as a "literalist of the imagination," an oxymoronic phrase she picked up in Yeats's essay "William Blake and the Imagination," derives from the same repudiations. Her work in *Selected Poems* illustrates one possible strategy of survival for poetry in an age when fashionable critics kept wondering out loud whether poetry had any function in an age of science.

Surely no one could find anything "unscientific" or transcendental in *Selected Poems.* Eliot, writing an Introduction to lend his prestige to the volume, classified the poetry — or "most of it," as he said — as "descriptive." What "descriptive" poetry written by a poet who had made Miss Moore's repudiations would be like is suggested in the most often quoted and best remembered poem in the book — a poem not in itself Imagist or descriptive — "Poetry." This dry catalogue of the poet's likes and dislikes begins with an enormous repudiation — of all that is not "genuine," and what is "genuine" is defined, apparently, by the examples of hands, eyes, hair — the "things" Pound had said that Imagists write about.

> I, too, dislike it: there are things that are important
> beyond all this fiddle.
> Reading it, however, with a perfect contempt for it,
> one discovers in
> it after all, a place for the genuine.
> Hands that can grasp, eyes
> that can dilate, hair that can rise
> if it must, these things are important not because a

high-sounding interpretation can be put upon them but
because they are
useful. . . .

The poet who wants to write "genuine" poetry should not, we are told, "discriminate against 'business documents and school-books' " as supposedly unimaginative. These are, after all, data, "facts," which, as Pound had said, it is the business of poetry to give us. The role of the imagination in the poem is limited to the shaping of "facts" into a sort of ordered structure: genuine poems "present for inspection, 'imaginary gardens with real toads in them.' " Those who do not ask *this* from poetry are not interested in poetry, we are told flatly, but in something else presumably, something not "genuine." Perhaps not even Pound has more sharply denied any cognitive function to the imagination. We may think of Williams' "No ideas but in things" as similarly positivistic and anti-idealist, but though it is also meant to aim a blow at "high-sounding interpretation" and transcendental nonsense, it at least leaves the poet free to find the "ideas" in "things," while Miss Moore's definition of genuine poetry leaves him only the craftsmanlike function of shifting the "real toads" around to make some sort of pattern. No more stringently self-denying definition of poetry has ever been made by an American poet.

No wonder Eliot in his Introduction could only praise the author for being exactly the reverse of the "true poet" of Emerson's definition. Here, Eliot implied, was a poet concerned *only* with techniques. It was his opinion that "Miss Moore's poems form part of the small body of durable poetry written in our time," but the reasons he gives for this judgment seem hardly adequate to support it. For one thing, he says, the poet "had taken to heart the repeated reminder of Mr. Pound: that poetry should be as well written as prose." This perhaps explains his earlier statement that he considers Miss Moore "one of those few who have done the language some service in my lifetime." But apart from writing as "well" as though she were writing prose, and doing an unspecified service to the English language, Eliot can think of only one thing that makes these poems "durable": they prove to him that this poet is "the greatest living master . . . of the *light* rhyme."

I find it difficult, myself, reading this, to remember three things that I believe to be true, that Eliot was a great poet, that he was serious here, and that his remark was not intended to destroy Miss Moore's reputation. Surely not many would care to debate the proposition that when any art comes to be exclusively concerned with techniques, and spends all its energies elaborating and refining them, it is decadent.

Actually, a number of the best poems in the collection escape the unintended derogations of Eliot's praise. Most of them are exceptions to his label "descriptive," also, though one of the very best of them, "The Fish," is "description" that sends the mind on to interpretation. "The Steeple-Jack" and "The Labours of Hercules," two of the most memorable, anticipate the style of the later volumes by turning from "the raw material of poetry," as that is defined in "Poetry," to comment, opinion, and interpretation — though the interpretations are generally not "high-sounding."

Typically, the poems in this volume achieve Miss Moore's idea of the "genuine" in poetry by even more stringent denials of traditional poetic resources than we find in the ones I have called the best of them. In their sound, they go further than Pound's third principle of Imagism, avoiding not only metrical feet ("the sequence of the metronome") but *any* kind of accentual pattern ("the musical phrase"). Attempts have been made to reduce this "syllabic" but "non-accentual" verse to a system; but the fact of the matter seems to be that the nature of the language is such that nothing distinguishes, or can distinguish, the sound of verse in English from the sound of prose but some kind of pattern of recurrent *stress.*

Since the poems have neither meter nor cadence, their line division is in effect purely subjective and arbitrary, "governed," if that is the word, only by the writer's desire to highlight, or to play down, certain rhymes that pass unnoticed in ordinary prose, or by syllable-count, or by both. Some of the lines are quoted, with scrupulous quotation marks, from newspapers and books, unaltered except for arrangement on the page. But it is not only rhythm or cadence, and the line as a unit of sound, that have been repudiated in this verse. The poet makes every effort to play down, or make to seem casual and inconsequential, the *sense,* too. Incoherence, or what is carefully made to *seem* incoherence, is the hallmark of these poems made up of prose statement arranged on the page in such a way as to bring out light rhymes and assonances:

Literature is a phase of life. If
  one is afraid of it, the situation is irremediable; if
one approaches it familiarly . . .

This is the opening of "Picking and Choosing." It reads like the beginning of a Victorian essay. We hear the "light rhyme" of the two "if's," and we are made more aware of the parallelism of the two clauses than we might be; but essentially the technique here functions in the service of prose statement. But *as* prose statement the poem that follows these lines has very little to say to us. It says that one likes critics who are "right," not attempting to enlighten us about how one can be sure to be right except by referring to someone's description of a dog who was apparently *really* on the scent of something. If this means that good critics must be gifted with "good taste" or sound instinct, the observation seems hardly worth puzzling out.

I suspect that the poems that will prove most "durable," to use Eliot's word, were mostly written *after* Eliot made his comment. "What Are Years?," "Nevertheless," and "In Distrust of Merits" offer their praise of fortitude and tolerance in a style from which the defensive mannerisms of the earlier poems have to a considerable extent dropped away. The last of these especially sounds very unlike a work of the poet Eliot praised, and equally unlike the ideal poet described by the poet herself in "Poetry." Lamenting our own social and personal betrayals of the ideals for which the Second World War was supposedly fought, and memorializing the dead of the war, again and again the poet breaks into song, and very "traditional," even Presbyterian, song at that, though untraditionally arranged on the page. "O/ quiet form upon the dust, I cannot/ look and yet I must." "Beauty is everlasting/ and dust is for a time."

The poet's own final comment on the subject of the poem, her "interpretation," is surely as "high-sounding" as any aphorism Emerson ever wrote into his poetry. But "The Wood Weasel" and "Elephants," from *Nevertheless,* which are also, I think, poems that will last, are more typical of the bulk of the work. Transcending Pound's or anyone's definition of Imagism, they also escape the limitations of the poet's own definition of the "genuine" in poetry. In these and her other best poems Marianne Moore shows us how observation can become vision.

CHAPTER XIII

In the American Grain

The greatest poverty is not to live
In a physical world. . . .

— Wallace Stevens, in "Esthétique du Mal"

In spite of their faults . . . poets like Whitman and Williams have about them something more valuable than any faultlessness: a wonderful largeness, a quantitative and qualitative generosity.

— Randall Jarrell in 1949

Much that Williams said about the American idiom is not really borne out in his poetry because much of it rises way above the American idiom as it is commonly used. It's a kind of high language.

— Denise Levertov in 1965

WILLIAM CARLOS WILLIAMS

THE first paradox that strikes us when we look back at the whole poetic career of Dr. William Carlos Williams of Rutherford, New Jersey, pediatrician, poet, novelist, playwright, and essayist, is that the voice we hear in the poetry is almost always wholly romantic, as Wallace Stevens said more than thirty years ago; but when the poet tells us what he intends, and what he thinks poetry is, the formulas he falls back on are generally as antiromantic as Eliot's and Pound's. The second paradox is that the man behind the voice we hear in the poetry, as we come to know him through his autobiography, his letters, and his comments on his own career, is likely to strike us as characterized chiefly by his simplicity, honesty, and openness; yet he produced a body of poetic work and poetic opinion so complex, various, and self-contradictory that no single generalization about it is valid for all of it. A third paradox is that this poet whose most sympathetic critics — including R. P. Blackmur, Wallace Stevens again, and, especially, Randall Jarrell — do not think him a clear abstract thinker, prided himself particularly on his role as a *theorist* of poetry. He wrote a critic on one occasion, "I think you fail sufficiently to take into consideration my role as a theorist," and added that only by approaching his work through his "theory of the poem" could the critic achieve a just estimate of it.

When all the paradoxes are added up, we see that even the *method* of paradox fails to do justice to the man and the work at once. But to live with Williams' work, all of it, for any considerable time is to come to feel a unity which partially defies any simple formulation into statement.

That is why Randall Jarrell's Introduction to the 1949 *Selected Poems* remains the best short criticism ever written on Williams. Jarrell begins and ends with the qualities of the man one senses within the poems, ignores the man's *opinions* — except as he glances at them by saying that "He is even less logical than the average good poet — he is an 'intellectual' in neither the good nor the bad sense of the word . . ." — and so, with a critical procedure as thoroughly anti-Modernist ("New Critical") as it could well be, ends by accomplishing for this Modernist poet what he thinks is "the most important thing that criticism can do for a contemporary poet," which is "to establish that atmosphere of interested respect which gets his poems a reasonably careful reading . . ."

> That Williams' poems are honest, exact, and original, that some of them are really *good* poems, seems to me obvious. But in concluding I had rather mention something even more obvious: their generosity and sympathy, their moral and human attractiveness.

To which we want to say only yes, emphatically.

But if one's purpose is not just to get the poet a careful reading but to try to locate his place in the developing traditions of American poetry, the paradoxes of man and work cannot be so quickly brushed aside. It is perfectly true, as Jarrell implies, that Williams' constant pronouncements on poetry and poetics are almost never of such a quality as would force us to take them seriously, but it is also true, I think, that the intellectual innocence and confusion they exhibit show in a good many of the poems, though not in the best of them, and so must be considered in any picture of the *whole* career, with its failures and its successes. Williams was a hard-working practicing physician all his life. He wrote a great deal, often very fast, in the evenings. He read very little — there was not time to, for one thing, and I suspect not much inclination to. And if ability to handle abstractions is taken as *the* mark of intelligence, then he was also very much less "intelligent" than Stevens or Eliot or Pound, or perhaps than any modern poet with comparable fame and achievement.

Williams is the classic American example of a poet who wrote better than he knew. (An entire book on Williams has been written to disabuse us all of this old idea, but I remain unconvinced. It will not do to pass over jumbled and self-contradictory ideas as "seeming paradoxes.") He could never resolve in his mind what it was he was trying to do as a poet. In the essay "How to Write" he sounds like a latter-day Emerson: The poet must tap the "primitive profundity of the personality," draw on dream, allow his "genius" to speak out of "the rhythmic ebb and flow of the mysterious life process," and let the words simply *come,* only later, and then sparingly, expunging and correcting. Good poems are made from "the released personality" of the poet, "written with his deepest mind." All this in 1936. Yet as late as *I Wanted to Write a Poem* in 1958, when he was in his middle seventies, he was still repeating the early Modernist formulas of his youth: A poem is an artifact that is "made — *made,* mind you"; it is simply a "machine" that works or doesn't work; it is perfectly self-enclosed; it is not "about" anything and has no subject but the words it is made of; it is an "object" like any other object in nature; the *only* test of the value of the poetic artifact is the "expertness" with which it has been made; and so on and on.

To the end of his life he mingled with such opinions as these others fundamentally incompatible, continuing to speak of his poetry as expressing *himself,* his personality, as aimed above all at capturing truth and reality, as a continuation of Whitman's "theme," as founded on and expressive of his relation to a *particular* locality, as re-expressing old verities in new form, and as a means of celebrating and promoting the dominance of light over darkness and life over death — in short, as having a subject or subjects, expressing truth about a reality outside the poem, and having a moral purpose.

So far as the root of Williams' confusion was not psychic, it may be found in his mixed feelings of loyalty and antagonism toward Pound and Eliot and his feeling for his mother. Pound, a college classmate and life-long friend, had launched him as a poet, writing an introductory note for the six poems he got published for his friend in *The Poetry Review* in England in 1912. ("Mr. Williams may write some very good poetry.") But Pound had not only launched him; he had *taught* him. As Williams put it in *I Wanted to Write a Poem,* for him, "Before meeting Ezra Pound is like B.C. and A.D." Williams had started by imitating Keats. By the time he showed a group of poems to Pound, he had moved on to Whitman, but Pound put an end to that phase:

> Pound got me to read *Longinus on the Sublime,* but it meant little to me. The books that influenced me were my own discoveries. I knew Palgrave's *Golden Treasury* by heart, and Shakespeare and the romantic poets I've mentioned. The copybook poems, my secret life, the poems I was writing before I met Pound, were what I can only describe as free verse, formless, after Whitman.

Pound, in Williams' own words, "arranged for the publication" of Williams' first commercially published volume, *The Tempers,* in 1913. (The earlier volume, a privately printed pamphlet, *Poems,* 1909, can hardly be said to have been "published.") Williams' fourth regularly published book, *Kora in Hell,* 1920, was partly inspired by a book Pound had left in the Williams house. "I am indebted to Pound for the title," Williams has said. "We had talked about Kora, the Greek parallel of Persephone, the legend of Springtime captured and taken to Hades . . . and I felt I was on my way to Hell (but I didn't go very far)."

About this time Williams says he threw away "Portrait of the Author" "because I thought it was sentimental and I was afraid I was imitating Pound." (Is Pound's work then sentimental? Or is there an "also" to be understood before the second clause? Statements of this kind are the rule, not the exception, in Williams' prose.) Nearly forty years later Williams opened his comment on *A Dog and the Fever: Translated by William Carlos Williams and Raquel Helene Williams,* 1954, this way: "This book, another one that Ezra Pound dropped into the house, offered a challenge to my mother and myself"—and closed it this way:

> I had also found a piece [needed to make enough material for a volume] about my mother, her childhood, so

> I made it into the true story of our work together on the translation. I was interested in this, didn't care anything about style. Perhaps this is the way to do certain things. Ezra Pound was tickled, thought it the best piece of prose I'd ever written.

There is much more of this kind of indirect revelation of what Pound meant to Williams, but perhaps enough has been said to make it clear that Williams was understating the case when, speaking of the poems written in the period after the publication of *The Tempers,* he said that they "were more or less influenced by my meeting with Pound." His mother and Pound were the two paramount influences on Williams as a poet, and the two influences, working at different levels of consciousness, pulled him in different directions.

He identified his mother, as he himself has said, with all that was romantic, free, heroic, rebellious, in short, with the self he wanted to become. Jewish and Spanish, preferring to speak Spanish in the home, she seemed an exile in industrial northern New Jersey:

> I was conscious of my mother's influence all through this time of writing [the early years, after meeting Pound], her ordeal as a woman and as a foreigner in this country. I've always held her as a mythical figure. . . . Her interest in art became my interest in art. I was personifying her, her detachment from the world of Rutherford. She seemed an heroic figure, a poetic ideal. I didn't especially admire her; I was attached to her. I had not yet [in his late twenties] established any sort of independent spirit.
>
> Ezra found an old copy of lyrical poems, out of Spanish Romantic Literature, and knowing that Spanish was spoken in my home, gave them to me. [Williams began to translate the poems but never completed the book.] I've always determined to go back to it someday; Spanish still seems to me synonymous with romantic.

How curiously the mother and Ezra move in and out together in all these memories recorded in old age, linked private symbols as it were of romance and "realism," freedom and authority, impulse and discipline, the unconscious and the conscious. It was the mother who chiefly shaped the man, but Ezra who chiefly shaped the poet's consciously held ideas about poetry. No wonder Williams spent a lifetime uttering opinions that flatly contradicted his other opinions and often denied or betrayed the poetry he had written out of his deepest impulses. After Pound's instruction had "taken," how could he think of himself as a romantic poet? There is really no need to puzzle over what it was about Stevens' deeply respectful and penetrating Preface to Williams' 1934 *Collected Poems* that offended Williams. Stevens *began* wrong, from Williams' point of view:

> There are so many things to say about him. The first is that he is a romantic poet. This will horrify him. Yet the proof is everywhere.

It did horrify him. The Preface was never reprinted, and Williams preferred not to talk about it.

Twice in his life Williams felt his poetic career terribly threatened — perhaps, he felt at the time, destroyed — once by Eliot, with Pound cast in a minor part, and then again, years later, by a situation in which Pound was a chief actor and Eliot had a walk-on part. Both situations serve to point up Williams' dilemma, which he became partially conscious of only in the very last years of his life — how to *be* in fact a "romantic" poet while accepting, and generally trying to write in terms of, an antiromantic, and implicitly behavioristic, theory of poetry; or how to be true to mother, his self-image, and Ezra, all at the same time.

This is the way Williams describes the first setback in his *Autobiography:*

> These were the years just before the great catastrophe to our letters — the appearance of T. S. Eliot's *The Waste Land*. . . . Our work staggered to a halt for a moment under the blast of Eliot's genius which gave the poem back to the academics. We did not know how to answer him. . . .
>
> Then out of the blue *The Dial* brought out *The Waste Land* and all our hilarity ended. It wiped out our world as if an atom bomb had been dropped upon it and our brave sallies into the unknown were turned to dust.

> To me especially it struck like a sardonic bullet. I felt at once that it had set me back twenty years, and I'm sure it did. Critically Eliot returned us to the classroom just at the moment when I felt that we were on the point of an escape to matters much closer to the essence of a new art form itself—rooted in the locality which should give it fruit. I knew at once that in certain ways I was most defeated.
>
> Eliot had turned his back on the possibility of reviving my world. . . . I had to watch him carry my world off with him, the fool, to the enemy.

Thus the defeat was recalled in 1948. A decade later Williams remembered his sense of defeat as having occurred earlier; all the details are different now, but the feeling is the same:

> When I was halfway through the Prologue [to *Kora in Hell*], "Prufrock" appeared. I had a violent feeling that Eliot had betrayed what I believed in. He was looking backward; I was looking forward. He was a conformist, with wit, learning which I did not possess. . . . I felt he had rejected America and I refused to be rejected and so my reaction was violent. . . . It was a shock to me that he was so tremendously successful; my contemporaries flocked to him—away from what I wanted. It forced me to be successful.

The second setback was the direct result of Pound's receiving the Bollingen Prize for publishing the best book of poems in 1948—*The Pisan Cantos*—while confined in St. Elizabeth's Hospital as insane. Pound had been charged with treason in connection with broadcasts for Mussolini while we were at war with Italy; the successful insanity plea of his lawyers had kept him from facing a charge that in wartime carried a death penalty. The prize had been awarded by the Fellows of the Library of Congress, a fact that made it seem to some that the government's left hand did not know what its right hand was doing. Eliot was one of the Fellows who awarded the Prize. Williams kept up his friendship with Pound while Pound was confined. Now we may let Williams and his wife continue the story:

It was just at this time that I received the appointment for the Chair of Poetry at the Library of Congress. I had had a stroke at the time, not a bad one, but crippling for a brief period. Floss wrote them, and they said to take my time. When I was well enough to take care of the duties in Washington — I was anxious to live up to the obligations of this honor — they didn't want me. A release from *The New York Post* Home News of August 4, 1949, more or less tells the story:

> A congressional move to reorganize or abolish the fellows of the Library of Congress was revealed today in the continuing controversy over the award of a poetry prize to Ezra Pound . . . Javits (Rep.) pointed out that the Ezra Pound clique among the library fellows has been strengthened by the appointment of William Carlos Williams as a member.

"What the whole mess did was drive Bill into a serious mental depression," Mrs. Williams said. "I am convinced if Bill had gone down as he was able to do, he would have been as he is now. Coming after the stroke, it was too much; it set him back tragically, kept him from poetry and communication with the world for years."

Until Williams' biography is written, or his letters all published, or both, we shall not know many things we should like to know about this second blow that affected him so terribly. (He says he wrote his *Autobiography* as "therapy," and, reading it, one can see how working off his resentments and frustrations may have been good for him.) At any rate, this incident, in which he suffered from being associated with a man he had learned so much from and felt so deeply indebted to, seems to have had a good effect on him after he had recovered from the shock. His chief new poems after this, *Journey to Love,* "Asphodel, That Greeny Flower," and *Paterson, Book V,* show him much more sure of himself and his intentions. *Paterson, Book IV,* is the last Poundish poem he ever wrote. In the end, his mother won out. He left uncompleted the book he planned to write about her, and the projected *Paterson, Book VI,* but the last item recorded in *I Wanted to Write a Poem* seems to suggest a good deal about the difficulties and the achievements of a career: "*From My Notes About My Mother.* Excerpts from a book in progress." The poet himself I should say was "in progress" at the end.

Williams thought of himself, and in a sense was, a "naturalist" and a "realist." He often spoke of his poetry as having been shaped by his "scientific" training. He despised "religionists and statists and all those who want the past to stay as it is for their benefit — mostly pecuniary." For most of his life after he had met Pound and been taught how "messy, blurry, sentimentalistic" the nineteenth century was, he spoke slightingly of Whitman, reversing himself on this only after Randall Jarrell had taught him that it was all right to have been impressed by Whitman once and to have continued to be like Whitman without knowing it.

Furthermore, quite apart from whether he really *was* a sort of modern Whitman or not, as Jarrell suggested — and I think he was — it is clear from the references he made to the older writer throughout his life that he really knew very little about Whitman. Perhaps he had, as he said late in life, read *Leaves of Grass* when very young, but nothing he ever said about it suggests that, if so, he had *understood* what he read. When we follow his references to Whitman through the years we find a pattern emerging. For many years, there are only occasional references, and those brief and slighting, to Whitman as a predecessor from whom there was not much to learn because after "Song of Myself" his verse became looser and looser, more and more formless. (Since in fact the opposite is true, this makes it clear that Williams was not speaking from first-hand acquaintance with Whitman's whole book.) Then, in the English Institute talk in the late 1940's, for which Williams obviously made intensive preparation, he reversed himself. Speaking of the formal structural qualities of some of the later poems like "Lilacs," he felt that the increasingly formal organization of such poems was a defect and offered no model for us. In this talk he reduced the *meaning* of *Leaves of Grass* to "democracy," an interpretation that suggests strongly that he still, even after preparing so carefully for this talk before scholars, had only the most elementary idea of all that Whitman and he had in common.

What is quickly learned is quickly forgotten. A few years later, and continuing to the end of his life, Williams returned to his old manner of referring to Whitman. In *I Wanted to Write a Poem* his last words on the subject suggest the same misconceptions, the same lack of real acquaintance with the poetry, that we find in the allusions of thirty and forty years before, the only difference being the slightly defensive tone that has appeared. With Whitman now greatly in favor — with those who were his own best defenders and interpreters — he was eager at last to pay tribute. He had been influenced, he said, to adopt free verse by reading the "opening lines" of "Song of Myself." All the evidence suggests that so long as we are talking not of parallels or traditions but of actual direct influence, this statement of Williams' is perfectly adequate. I strongly suspect that not only the "influence" but the early reading did in fact stop with the opening lines of "Song of Myself." By the time Williams read a few of the later poems with some care, and looked into the prose and some of the scholarship, in preparation for his talk to the English Institute, he was far beyond the stage of his own development when he could be influenced by any other poet. No wonder he found himself confused, and not wholly pleased, when his friendliest critics placed him in the Whitman tradition. How *could* a poet who thought of himself as writing "pure" poetry, as the abstractionists in painting created "pure" paintings, feel any deep kinship with Whitman as an *artist?*

Williams' favorite answer, after lectures when questioners asked him what he meant by certain passages or poems, consisted of repeating the story of the rich woman at the Daniel Gallery who, about to buy an expensive painting, paused for a moment, "walked away from it, approached it and said, finally, 'But Mr. Hartpence, what is all that down in this left hand lower corner?'

"Hartpence came up close and carefully inspected the area mentioned. Then, after further consideration, 'That, Madam,' said he, 'is paint.' "

Or as he put it once more clearly to the students at the University of Oregon, most poets — except for himself and a few others — had never made

> the progression from the sentiment, the thought (philosophy) or the concept to the poem itself — from the concern with Hamlet to *Hamlet,* the play. That was the secret meaning inside the term "transition" during the years when the painters following Cezanne began to talk

> of sheer paint: a picture a matter of pigments upon a piece of cloth stretched on a frame. I told them the Hartpence story.

Emphasizing "the poem itself" was, of course, exactly what the "New Critics," taught by Eliot's "autotelic" theory, had all along been trying to get us to do. By the time Williams made this defiantly Modernist speech, New Critical theory had long since reached the textbook stage, and it would have been a very unsophisticated student who didn't know that "the poem itself" was best "analyzed" without regard to personal or historical context, that it would be naive to ask what a poem "meant," and that a poem could no more be said to be "about" anything than an abstract painting could be said to "picture" anything. The Hartpence story again, and New Critical warnings against "the heresy of paraphrase."

The curious thing about this University of Oregon story is that Williams apparently was so uninformed about the state of affairs in the Academy that he did not realize, first, that the New Critics, for whom he had the greatest scorn, had already triumphed there; and second, that the doctrines he was claiming as radical had not only reached the handbook stage but were in fact precisely the doctrines of those he considered "the enemy," the despised "academic critics." It was of course the farthest thing from his *intention* to agree with them; for the most part they had ignored his work or treated it slightingly, and he suspected them, with considerable justice in most cases, of belonging in the Eliot or "enemy" camp.

But of course "intention" is a word we use — and perhaps ordinarily must use — loosely, without specifying exactly what kind or level of intention we mean, or how we would go about finding out what kind of intention was operative in a given instance. To say that "intention" operates at various levels of the mind, some of them inaccessible to critics, some inaccessible to the intender himself, is a truism that will remain true. It would be fair to say that Williams "intended" to write "pure" poetry; that he also "intended" to defend and celebrate the native and the local; that he "intended" to write poems in which the only thing that mattered about them, or that critics should attend to, was the "expertness" with which he handled "the variable foot";

and that he "intended," despite repeated denials, to affirm the beauty and interest of the commonplace, the supposedly ugly, the apparently trivial, the outcast and outlawed and despised.

The deepest impression we are likely to carry away from his work is that it "intends" to affirm, and at its best succeeds in affirming, the intrinsic values of life itself, here and now and with no need to be "twice born." Except for Whitman's religious views and his Transcendental metaphysics, most of what William James said about Whitman could be said about Williams. He was in the Whitman tradition, very deeply so, even if he didn't, with a part of his mind, "intend" to be. Attracted to him at the beginning, then warned off by Pound, he was closer to him in the end than he knew. If Whitman, writing just as he did, had insisted that his poems should be thought of as "sheer words" and that his work should be judged entirely on the ground of *technique,* the two poets would of course be still closer together. But they are close enough as it is, without having to invent a different Whitman. "Who touches this book touches a man" is very nearly as apt a comment on Williams' poems as it is on *Leaves of Grass.*

Williams' best poems, from *Al Que Quiere!* in 1917 on to the end of his life, and increasingly so in the last ten years, are squarely within the Whitman tradition. Stevens' remark that they are distinguished by the tension in them between romantic feeling and a determination to confront reality could equally well have been made of Whitman's best work, especially "Song of Myself." As the youthful Whitman accepted what he called "materialism," but then "imbued" it with spirit, so Williams, determined to be a "realist," looked long and hard at *things* — and found in them the source and sufficient basis for dream.

"Gulls," for instance, one of the earliest of the good poems, "says," among other things, that the *harsh* cries of the gulls make a better hymn for Williams than the hymns he hears sung in the churches, hymns evoking "some great protector" and outraging "true music." (True music, as Emerson would have said, must be more *natural* and less afraid.) Still, the speaker is not angry with his townspeople, for (in Whitmanesque accents),

> You see, it is not necessary for us to leap at each other,
> and, as I told you, in the end
> the gulls moved seaward very quietly.

"By the Road to the Contagious Hospital," which Williams once called merely a "picture," says, or "means," or suggests through its total symbolic structure, that "realism" as Williams conceives it means finding the promise of life, and the struggle toward it, in the most unlikely places, where most of us would not think to look. "One by one objects are defined," and as they are defined, we sense the quickening of life. The poem ends with a paradox: the "rooted" things have to "grip down" before they can come up into the light and air. "Awaken," the last word in the poem, toward which all the details move, gets its power chiefly from the fact that all the *difficulties* of awakening have been faced. This "picture" poem, then, is "about" something—about how to find signs of *life* in an urban waste land.

The people in the poems similarly "awaken" as Williams treats them. Often they are first seen at a distance, as "objects" like the white faces in Pound's "Metro" poem. But then the poet moves closer and picks out the individual features, or the people stir, come alive, and the point of view shifts; seen in motion, they are known as "people," *not* "things." "Fine Work with Pitch and Copper" will illustrate. At first, while the workmen on the roof are resting during lunch hour, they look "like the sacks/ of sifted stone," like "objects" in a still life, in short. But then they go to work again and suddenly it becomes clear to the observer that they are *persons* like himself, precariously in control of the material they work with:

> One still chewing
> picks up a copper strip
> and runs his eye along it.

Williams himself said that this poem was intended to be about himself and poetry, and of course that is the most obvious way to read it. The workmen are artists, working with "things" as tangible as pitch and copper, and skillfully making them serve their purposes. But the poem also says something about the nature of man as we find him in Williams' poems: the *model* in terms of which we should conceive him is not a "thing," and not a "machine" that "reacts," but an *artist* who acts, shapes, creates, moves toward goals.

The alienation of the poet from his material and from himself implicit in early Imagist theory and exhibited in the early work of

Eliot and in all the work of Pound is almost never found in Williams' work except when he fails most badly, which is usually when he writes a poem he has "thought out." Most commonly, the relational and empathic meanings of the work are merely implicit, but now and then, especially in the later poems, they become explicit. "A Unison," for instance, one of Williams' greatest triumphs, could hardly be more open in its affirmation of the values of man and nature, of life and reality. But "affirmation" is not quite the word for it. The poem "affirms" by *being* a celebration, a kind of religious rite. Nature is "sacred" and "undying," and also the "reality" that humbles man:

> . . . And there it is
> and we can't shift it or change
> it or parse it or alter it.

But when we approach it religiously, we find it "singing," providing indeed for properly attuned ears

> . . . A certainty of music!
> a unison and a dance, joined
> at this death's festival.

At the end, even the stones come alive for the speaker and contribute to the melody and the dance:

> Stones, stones of a difference
> joining the others at pace. Hear!
> Hear the unison of their voices. . . .

The suspension points after the last line are Williams' own: The singing goes on; the dance continues, turning death's festival into life's festival. Probably no more thoroughly Emersonian poem, in spirit and theme and attitude, has been written by any twentieth-century American poet. Thematically, it parallels both Emerson's "Monadnoc" and his "The Titmouse"; imagistically, it is closer to his prose than to his poetry, especially to certain passages in *Nature,* "Circles," "The Intellect," and "The Over-Soul." Williams would probably not have been pleased by having it pointed out, but it is also thematically parallel with several passages in *Four Quartets,* particularly the ending of "The Dry Salvages." That it is also one of Williams' best poems tells us something about the tradition in which he belongs when he writes from his deeper mind and not from his efforts at thinking.

Paterson IV, intended as the final book in Williams' epic celebration of the local and the actual, might be cited as an exception to much that I have been saying, but it is an interesting and revealing exception. Here for once Williams seems not to like his people or his scenes; the implicit theme is one of decline and degeneration. Even Williams' most enthusiastic and sympathetic followers did not like the poem. Williams was hurt by their reaction and began planning new books of *Paterson* to correct the impressions he had left in Book IV.

The poem reflects the mood of discouragement and depression that afflicted Williams in the late 1940's, for one thing. For another, the plan of the poem was dictated by the original design for *Paterson* as a whole: to begin at the headwaters of the Passaic River and move down, in space to the mouth, in time to the present. The river at its mouth is extremely polluted by the industrial cities along its banks. This is a *fact:* what could a poet who wanted to be true to fact always, *do* when this fact was raised to symbol, what could he do but write like the early Eliot ("Burbank with a Baedekker, Bleistein with a Cigar") or like Pound ("Hugh Selwyn Mauberley"), noting evidences everywhere of "tawdry cheapness" and perversion and blight?

Asked about the poem in 1958, Williams responded at length and with some bitterness. I shall quote the whole reply because only by reading all of it can we see why it is that Williams always did his best work when he did not "think it out," when both the theme and the form were discovered in the course of the poem itself. In what follows, we shall find Williams falling back on the old Imagist ideas of Pound (a poet merely "*sees . . . reacts*") in an attempt to explain and justify himself:

> [Randall Jarrell] didn't react at all to Book Four—couldn't take the identification of the filthy river with the perversion of the characters at the close of the fourth section of the poem. It was typical of him that he lost track of the poem as a poem and became identified with the characters. I was getting up closer to the city, approaching the mouth of the river, identified with the mouth of the Hudson . . . the Passaic enters into Newark Bay. If you are going to write realistically of

> the conception of filth in the world, it can't be pretty. What goes on with people isn't pretty. With the approach to the city, international character began to enter the innocent river and pervert it; sexual perversions, such things that every metropolis when you get to know it houses. Certain human elements can't take the gaff, have to become perverts to satisfy certain longings. When human beings herd together, have to face each other, they are very likely to go crooked. What in the world is an artist to do? He is not a moralist. He *sees* things, reacts to them, must take them into consideration. Therefore when the river reaches pollution, which my river comes to face in Book Four, I had to take the characters and show them graphically. My critics, Randall Jarrell among them — and Marianne Moore had the same reaction — felt that Book Four was less expert than the earlier parts of the poem.

It would not be fair to Williams to quote this if it were not thoroughly typical of him when he tried to handle ideas, and if, also, I had not already tried to make a case for the greatness of his poetry when he was not *thinking,* and were not about to try to strengthen and extend that case. A statement could hardly misrepresent Williams' basic attitudes and feelings more completely if it were made up by an enemy and attributed to him. It shows us why we must *not* approach his poetry by way of his work as a "theoretician."

The statement might have been made by Pound if he had first suffered a loss of his intelligence and his ability to phrase ideas incisively. To be concerned with the largest implications of a poem, including its moral implications, it says, is to lose sight of it as a poem, which is not supposed to *have* any implications. (Why then had Williams written so many poems like "Tract" — "I will teach you my townspeople . . . ," — and "Yachts," which Williams once explained as a protest against conditions during the Great Depression?) When "international" character enters the innocent American scene, perversion begins. (This is an innocently nativist version of Eliot's and Pound's idea of the perversion of *culture* by rootless cosmopolitan types, or "international bankers.") People in cities "are very likely to go crooked." (Perhaps; but this sounds more like the Southern Agrarians whom Williams thought he despised, or like Frost at his most agrarian conservative, than like Williams in his best poetry; compare "Beautiful Thing.") "My critics felt" that this poem was less "expert." (It is highly unlikely that that was what they felt, whatever they may have said. They probably felt that it was an unpleasant and untypical and wholly inappropriate ending of a poem that had begun in a mood of celebration.) . . . Is the poet *responsible* for the poem he creates or is he not?

Fortunately, Williams' career did not end on this note. What Williams had to say to us that is worth hearing, he could say only in his poetry (sometimes too, but not often, in his fiction), never in his expository prose. During the final decade of his life he wrote some of his very best work; and what *it* says is in a very different vein from what the comment just quoted says, and in conflict, too, with other opinions he had most cherished.

He had always said, for instance, that he despised "religionists" as much as he despised "statists." But what "religionist" (a negatively loaded word) would want to differ with the way "Deep Religious Faith" opens?

> Past death
>   past rainy days
>   or the distraction
> of lady's-smocks all silver-white;
>   beyond the remote borders
>   of poetry itself
> if it does not drive us,
>   it is vain.

"Asphodel, That Greeny Flower" is one of his last poems and surely one of his greatest. In it he writes as though he had never thought of himself as an Imagist and Pound's definition of the image were completely irrelevant to his work — as indeed it generally had been, to most of his *best* work, though not to his critical opinions. Reading it, we think not of Imagism but of some of our greatest poets. Reading "secure/ by grace of the imagination,/ safe in its care," we think of Stevens. Reading "If a man die/ it is because death/ has first/ possessed his imagination," we think of the later Eliot. We think too of the Emerson of "Bacchus" and the Whitman who wrote "There Was a Child Went Forth" as we read Williams' description of the daffodil, perennial harbinger of seasonal rebirth:

> Asphodel
> has no odor
> save to the imagination
> But it too
> celebrates the light.
> It is late
> but an odor
> as from our wedding
> has revived for me
> and begun again to penetrate
> into all crevices
> of my world.

PART SIX

The Revolution of Modernism: Idea

CHAPTER XIV

Ideogram, or the Method of Science

It was due more to Ezra Pound than to any other person that "the revolution" was on.

— Harriet Monroe

That importance may finally have consisted more in his critical stimulus and instigation than in his own work. . . .

— F. O. Matthiessen [Speaking of Pound's "important role in the poetic renaissance"]

Much of the permanence *of Mr. Pound's criticism is due simply to his having seen so clearly what needed to be said at a particular time; his occupation with his own moment and its needs. . . .*

— T. S. Eliot

Life wd. have been (in my case) much less interesting if I had waited till Joyce, Lewis, Eliot, D. H. Lawrence, etc. complied with what my taste was in 1908.

— Ezra Pound, in 1931

EZRA POUND

It is one thing to perceive that Modernist poetry is part of an historical movement that is over with, so far as continuing to provide a model for young poets is concerned. It is quite another to write the *history* of the movement with accuracy, fairness, and a decent balance of sympathy and perspective. We are too close to it, too many of the facts that we should know will not be known until the definitive biographies of the chief Modernist poets are written, and the poets themselves are so largely responsible for the poetic and cultural landscape *we* inhabit that we can be neutral about them only by remaining uncommitted not only about where poetry is or ought to be going but about who we are and where we want to go.

Many of the youngest poets acknowledge greater kinship with

Williams than with Pound, Eliot, or Stevens; and naturally so, for a good many of them have rediscovered Whitman, and see Williams as a Whitmanite, and some of them have turned to Zen, and find Williams often writing almost as though he too were a Zen poet. Others among them, especially some of those exploring the "deep image," profess to find in Pound the master whose work must be searched for clues to a new metric for our times. Among academic critics, on the other hand, Stevens is generally *the* poet today. Eliot for the time being is *out;* one demonstrates one's superior taste by showing oneself aware of his flaws and weaknesses.

This is just the sort of price one would expect the "literary dictator" of an age to have to pay, posthumously, in the age immediately following. To the more hot-headed among the rebels against Modernism, Eliot seems the source and quintessential expression of all that is loathsome and threatening. Poor Pound they can often forgive, for perhaps he was insane, and anyway, no one of great consequence has been influenced by his ideas; but Eliot they cannot afford to forgive. As Karl Shapiro has put it in his passionate attack on Modernism, *In Defense of Ignorance* (1960), Eliot remains the real enemy to be destroyed just because he was so much more intelligent and successful a poet than Pound:

> My own sympathies are much more with Pound than with Eliot; and this is the case with William Carlos Williams also, who is revolted by Pound but who is always ready to go bail for him. . . . I hope that this essay will help remove Pound from the position of prominence in which Eliot has placed him. . . .
>
> I would like to close with an apology and a summary. The apology is for continuing to hammer away at Eliot. This is tiring, I know, but it is the crux of the matter. I will continue to deal with Eliot wherever he rears his critical influence, and that unfortunately is practically everywhere. I have no apologies for my remarks about Pound himself because I consider him an effect rather than a cause. Actually, I have been gentle with Pound. . . .

If Shapiro spoke only for himself, he could be dismissed as a critic — not as a poet — while cooler heads got on with the job of writing the story of Modernism as seen in the work of the chief

Modernist poets, writing it as fairly and objectively, yet sympathetically, as possible. But Shapiro is not alone in feeling rage when he thinks of Eliot; he has merely been more willing to expose himself and his ideas to criticism than most of those who think as he does. Though it would not be difficult to point out the many ways in which his book is unfair, inaccurate, and even grossly uninformed in places, as criticism, doing so would not necessarily invalidate the point he wants to make: that the reputations of the Modernist writers of the recent past must be destroyed to make it possible for the younger poets to succeed with a very different kind of poetry. *In Defense of Ignorance* is an inverted manifesto.

Over and over those who have known Pound best have defined his central impulse as that of a *teacher*. His first pupil was William Carlos Williams, when Williams was twenty-one and Pound only eighteen at the University of Pennsylvania. Williams wrote excitedly to his mother to tell her how much he was learning from his young friend, whose egotism and arrogance he said he recognized but did not resent. A few years later Pound arranged Eliot's first regular publication outside *The Harvard Advocate,* suggested revisions in some of his poems, and continued to promote him in every way possible, until the protégé was more famous and influential than the master, after which Eliot did everything he could to repay the debt. It has been said that Eliot was chiefly responsible for the decision to grant Pound the Bollingen Prize for the *Pisan Cantos* in 1949, while Pound was awaiting trial for treason. Neither Williams nor Eliot ever gave Pound up — to their credit as men, I should say.

Pound "taught" and promoted many others besides Williams and Eliot, of course, including young poets unknown to him who wrote to ask his help or advice. A large part of his energy over the years has gone into a voluminous correspondence aimed largely at attempting to influence the course of modern poetry. In the early years especially, he cultivated friends and used them without apology to get done what he thought must be done, at first to save poetry from Romanticism and Idealism, later to make his influence felt toward saving "a botched civilization." Ideas were useless, he thought, unless they got into *action.* The statement of Harriet Monroe, quoted as a motto to this chapter, seems to me not much exaggerated. But Pound's impact in the early years of the century came chiefly from his "teaching" and promotional activities, and from the influence of those who were loyal to him as a man and benefactor, not, it must be insisted, from the example of his own poetry.

His first book, *A Lume Spento,* was published in 1908. The following year two more came out, *Personae of Ezra Pound*, and *Exultations of Ezra Pound.* But none of the poems in these, and only a couple in the next several volumes, could be considered examples of Modernist poetry. Most of them are late-Romantic, out of the 1890's chiefly, with imitations of Browning's abruptness and hearty tone, and signs that Pound had been studying the Provençal troubadours. With the possible exception of "Portrait d'une Femme," which appeared in *Ripostes* in 1912, none of these early poems really prepares us for the "credo" Pound stated in 1917:

> As to Twentieth century poetry, and the poetry which I expect to see written during the next decade or so, it will, I think, move against poppy-cock, it will be harder and saner, it will be what Mr. Hewlett calls "nearer the bone." It will be as much like granite as it can be, its force will lie in its truth, its interpretative power (of course, poetic force does always rest there); I mean it will not try to seem forcible by rhetorical din, and luxurious riot. We will have fewer painted adjectives impeding the shock and stroke of it. At least for myself, I want it so, austere, direct, free from emotional slither.

Though the latter part of this statement might seem an apt description of the best of Emerson's poems, and would surely have been accepted by Emerson as a restatement of his ideal, in its technical aspects, there is an immense gap between it and most of Pound's own poems of these early years. While preaching and teaching revolution, Pound continued for long to write not very memorable pre-Modernist poems. It was chiefly in his "translations," particularly the Chinese poems in *Cathay,* 1915, and "Homage to Sextus Propertius," 1918 and 1919, that he found his own mature voice. (The quotes are around "translations" because after they were attacked by scholars as inaccurate, Pound stopped calling them "translations." Perhaps the best term for them is "adaptations," or "creative translations." [1]) Not until 1920, when *Hugh Selwyn Mauberley* appeared, with its echoes of "The Love Song of J. Alfred Prufrock," did Pound *regularly* write in his mature manner. As a poet, Pound developed slowly, far more slowly than Eliot, whose apprentice poems are all in the *Harvard Advocate,* the work of a precocious undergraduate.

When Conrad Aiken introduced Eliot to Pound in 1914, hoping that Pound would be willing to help his friend get published, Eliot had with him the manuscripts of several of his most famous early poems, including "Portrait of a Lady," "Preludes," and "The Love Song of J. Alfred Prufrock." Pound, who was European editor of Harriet Monroe's Chicago *Poetry,* was immediately impressed, both by the man and by the poems, and succeeded in placing "Prufrock" in *Poetry,* where it appeared in June 1915. Other poems of Eliot's rapidly got into the magazines, and in 1917 *Prufrock and Other Observations* came out. A considerable part of its contents had been written a half dozen or more years before this, the earliest in 1910–1911. In view of the fact that it has so often been repeated that Pound produced or "created" Eliot as a poet, it is well to keep these dates in mind. No doubt each influenced the other in some degree, but it is important to remember that the Eliot that Pound "discovered" and helped get published had reached his poetic maturity some years before they ever met.

Even the "Mauberley" poems often fall short of the ideal Pound had been preaching for years. In 1915, for instance, one of his definitions had so impressed a visitor that she never forgot it: "A work of art is the honest reproduction of a concrete image. Imagination is the faculty which finds out all about this image, and never the revelation of the feelings aroused by it." By such a standard, how should we judge these stanzas from Mauberley"? —

> The tea-rose tea-gown, etc.
> Supplants the mousseline of Cos,
> The pianola "replaces"
> Sappho's barbitos.
>
> Christ follows Dionysus,
> Phallic and ambrosial
> Make way for macerations;
> Caliban casts out Ariel.
>
> All things are a flowing,
> Sage Heracleitus says;

But a tawdry cheapness
Shall outlast our days.

. . . .

Faun's flesh is not to us,
Nor the saint's vision.
We have the press for wafer;
Franchise for circumcision.

All men, in law, are equals.
Free of Pisistratus,
We choose a knave or an eunuch
To rule over us.

How much "honest reproduction" of concrete images is there here? If imagination is "never the revelation of the feelings" aroused by an image, but always a way of finding out "all about" the image, must we judge most of these lines unimaginative?

Or would it be fairer to judge them not by the 1915 statement but by the 1917 credo — to the effect that the force of poetry lies in its "truth, its interpretative power"? If we do so, it would seem that the lines will not come off much better. The theme of the decline of civilization is merely asserted, not made meaningful. If newspapers and the right to vote are examples of deterioration when compared with the religious rites of circumcision and the Holy Communion ("wafer"), by what logic are they comparable? Only if the poem presented a religious ideal, as Henry Adams had in his images of the Virgin and the dynamo, and then balanced it against the secular society of the franchise and the newspaper, could there possibly be any content in these comparisons. Since it is clear that the speaker's nostalgia for a better age is not for the substance, the meaning, suggested by his examples, the lines say no more than "I hate democracy and contemporary culture." Of course it is all right for a poet to dislike democracy, or any other form of government or social system for that matter; but we want to know *why*. Like almost all of Pound's "original" poems — that is, in all but his adaptations of the work of other poets — "Mauberley" is intellectually empty.

The *Cantos,* his immensely long "history of the world," as he once called them, are what Pound must finally stand or fall by as an original poet — though his creative translations may well contain his best verse. The *Cantos* are extremely uneven — uneven between groups of *Cantos,* between individual *Cantos,* and within single *Cantos.* It is doubtful that anyone, even the critics who write about them most enthusiastically, has ever read them all straight through, without any skipping. Large sections of them are indeed, in a quite literal sense, unreadable — toward the end, in the "Rock Drill" *Cantos,* intentionally so, apparently, being arranged on the page in such a way as to suggest not poetry, which exists in time, but sculpture, which exists in space.

Pound has always held that he was too far ahead of his time to be understood; that not until his revolutionary "ideogramic," or "ideogramatic," method is understood will the *Cantos* be appreciated. But though the poems themselves are often opaque, the method they are meant to illustrate is not in the least difficult to understand. It is simply an expansion of the implications of Pound's early definitions of Imagism, undergirded now, given support but not essentially changed, by Pound's discovery of oriental poetry and by an explicit "scientific" rationale in place of the implicit one of the early Imagist definitions. When other poets moved on beyond Imagism, Pound held fast to his ideas. He merely found new words for them and new "evidence" of their truth. Pound's psychic growth stopped, I should say, not much later than 1920.

If there is a danger that poetry may not survive in an age of science, then a good strategy for one who wanted to protect poetry might be to stop talking about "images" and talk instead about what science deals with, that is, about "facts" or "objects." This Pound began to do a few years before he wrote the earliest *Cantos.* Concentration on concrete "fact" had been implied in the Imagist platforms, of course, but making this implication explicit had the positive advantage of calling attention to the idea that the poet could be just as "scientific" in his way as the biologist. To be sure, an "image" might be defined as the verbal equivalent of a "fact" or "datum," but the word "image" tended to carry with it a suggestion that the datum should be simple and sensuous, like a blue sky or white faces on a wet black bough. Since we get our experience at least as much — in Pound's case surely *more* — from "culture," especially from written records, as we do from "nature," why not expand the idea of the "image" to include the whole history of the world, all the actual, concrete, known *facts,* and present them without comment, letting them "speak for themselves," as the Imagists had wanted to let their sensuous images do?

Images "speak for themselves" best when two images are placed side by side — or, since poetry is fundamentally a temporal, not a spatial art — one after the other in such a way that we feel their congruence or contrast, and the mind starts working from *there.* Those who are acquainted with Japanese *haiku* poetry, or with the other artistic expressions of Zen Buddhism, may well decide at this point that the "ideogramatic method" is identical with Japanese *haiku* poetry. And this is in fact what Pound at first believed.

Pound discovered oriental poetry in 1912, when he read Ernest Fenollosa's newly published *Epochs of Chinese and Japanese Art.* In his 1914 essay on Vorticism he appealed to the example of Japanese poetry as preceding and justifying his own, particularly his "In a Station of the Metro," which he called a "hokku-like sentence," that is, in it two images are juxtaposed. That *haiku* are an artistic expression of Zen Buddhism, Pound understood no more than did Amy Lowell.[2]

After 1916 Pound seldom used the term *image.* "Imagism," after all, went out of fashion rather quickly, partly because after Eliot's *Prufrock* in 1917 there was no longer any point in it. But the new words Pound began to use in place of "image" — "thing," "object," "fact," all, as he said, to be treated by means of the "ideogramatic method" — these new words do not indicate any fundamental change of approach to poetic theory as a result of his contact with oriental poetry. Rather they suggest Pound's gradual movement away from his late-nineteenth-century poetic models and his growing concern to have poetry catch up with the novel. He had been introduced to Russian fictional realism, had equated this with fictional naturalism, and as a result decided that poetry ought to catch up with fiction, ought to become more "scientific." I shall let W. T. Stace explain what "scientific" would mean in terms of Pound's frame of reference at the time:

> According to Auguste Comte . . . human knowledge necessarily passes through three stages, which he calls the theological, the metaphysical, and the positive. In the theological stage men explain events by gods or spirits. In the metaphysical stage they explain them by "abstract forces, personified abstractions." The essence

> of a metaphysical idea, in Comte's opinion, is that it is the idea of something *which cannot be observed.*
>
> . . . .
>
> In the third or positive stage of knowledge all explanation is given in terms of what can be observed, and what is in principle unobservable is dismissed as metaphysical. The positive stage is the stage of science which, when fully attained, abolishes both metaphysics and theology. In the golden age of the future which the triumph of science is to usher in, nothing will be considered knowledge unless it is science.
>
> . . . .
>
> In art and literature, I believe, the same tendencies can be observed. What is that realism which became fashionable with Zola and his followers and is still alive? The novelist's function as conceived by the realists is simply to describe, exactly and in detail, *what happens* in human affairs. He must not take sides with his characters, with the good or the bad. He must not praise or condemn. He must not see in what happens any significance or meaning, certainly not the interpretation of human life as permeated by any world-purpose. Hence the world which he depicts is the brute fact world of Hume where everything which happens does so without any reason, futilely, senselessly. It is also the artistic counterpart of the "descriptive" theory of science.
>
> In art criticism, and in philosophies of art, the romantic view that beauty is the shining of spirit through matter is anathema. All current theories of art are naturalistic.

History makes strange bedfellows. The influences that fused to produce the "ideogramatic method" seem now almost totally disparate, but the time was right in the second decade of this century for Pound to understand them as all meaning the same thing, all pointing in the same direction. Scientific positivism formed the cutting edge of the new thought. People better read in fiction than Pound confounded Tolstoi and Dostoevsky, on the one hand, and Zola and Dreiser on the other. With Zen Buddhism virtually unknown in the West until nearly a half-century later, and with other varieties of oriental thought and religion only imperfectly understood, Fenollosa's description of *haiku* poems in terms that made it easy for Pound to equate them with "Imagism" as the West understood it seemed plausible enough. Fenollosa missed the meaning of Japanese art before Pound did. In particular, his understanding of the Chinese written character as an "ideogram," that is, a simplified and condensed *picture,* or graphic imitation, served Pound's needs and purposes at the time. Oriental literature, Pound was led by his reading of Fenollosa to believe, was more "scientific" than Western writing, for it presented "things" even in the very *shape* of its characters, without passing them through an intermediary realm of human purposes, ideas, or feelings. "Hokku," as Fenollosa and Pound called them, were in effect, they thought, "copies" of things, imitated in written characters that demanded a minimum of intervention by the artist in the processes of nature. "Hokku" were thus, for Pound, the closest approximation in literature to the achievement of a truly scientific poetry.

The fact that modern linguistic scholarship has shown that Fenollosa was often mistaken in his ideas about Chinese script, the grammar of the Chinese language, and much else besides, is not really to the point. Pound seized on Fenollosa because he found there just what he needed at the time. Oriental poetry, he seemed to have discovered, was "Imagistic," and the Chinese written language was so close to "the thing itself" that it too was "Imagistic," partaking of, not talking about, "reality." In oriental literature he seemed to have found a way of preserving the core of meaning of his Imagist statement of 1912 while still going beyond mere *description.* By simply "juxtaposing images," which he now understood as arranging replicas of reality, he could "mean," he could write poetry the force of which would lie, in his own view at least, "in its truth, its interpretative power," without the poet's assuming any responsibility for its implied judgments, he could even attempt to reform society, without falling back on the discredited romantic notion of the poet as a "seer."

Fenollosa's ideas about oriental art and Chinese language recommended themselves to Pound with special force because Fenollosa himself had explicitly proposed them as "scientific." Such an approach to the subject would naturally appeal to a man who had turned to Hart's *Psychology of Insanity* for a definition of the poetic image. Fenollosa, who was as suspicious of metaphysics (which he usually called "logic") as Pound was, wrote that the virtue of the Chinese language was its utter concreteness; everything in it was specific and particular, not abstract or general or logically philosophic. Then he added:

> In diction and in grammatical form science is utterly opposed to logic. Primitive men who created language agreed with science and not with logic. . . . Poetry agrees with science and not with logic.

With so clear a warrant from his "source," no wonder Pound wrote in *A B C of Reading,* "Abstract arguments didn't get man rapidly forward, or rapidly extend the borders of knowledge," and followed this with "THE IDEOGRAMIC METHOD OR THE METHOD OF SCIENCE," all in very large capitals.

No one should have been surprised by Pound's equating the "ideogramic" method with "scientific" method. When he wrote this in 1934, he had been using analogies drawn from science to describe poetry for more than twenty years. He had turned as a matter of course to science to describe what he was trying to do for language, and to science again to explain why poetry should not deal either in "logic" or in explicit value judgments of any sort. The poet, he had explained over and over, could be just as important as the scientist if only he kept his language "efficient" and the "objects" in his poetry concrete, specific, carefully observed, and free from his own interpretation. He opened *A B C of Reading* by saying "We live in an age of science and abundance" and quickly went on to say, in his second paragraph:

> The proper METHOD for studying poetry and good letters is the method of contemporary biologists, that is careful first-hand examination of the matter, and continual COMPARISON of one "slide" or specimen with another.

Then, after telling the "anecdote of Agassiz and the fish," which suggests that the essence of science is careful *observation* leading to *description,* with imagination, hypothesis, creative thinking, construction, and experiment quite unnecessary, he had gone on, on his second page, to this:

> By this method modern science has arisen, not on the narrow edge of medieval logic suspended in a vacuum.
>
> "Science does not consist in inventing a number of more or less abstract entities corresponding to the number of things you wish to find out,"
>
> says a French commentator on Einstein. I don't know whether that clumsy translation of a long french sentence is clear to the general reader.
>
> The first definite assertion of the applicability of scientific method to literary criticism is found in Ernest Fenollosa's "Essay on the Chinese Written Character."

Shortly after this in the book we come to the heading "LABORATORY CONDITIONS," then a little later, "Good writers are those who keep the language efficient. That is to say, keep it accurate, keep it clear" (just the way scientists do, presumably). Then, "IF YOU WERE STUDYING CHEMISTRY"— and so on and so on.

Four years later, in *Guide to Kulchur,* as the English edition was entitled (or just *Culture,* as it was called in this country), Pound was even more impatient with the public's continued failure to understand his "method":

> If so lately as the week before last one of the brighter scholars still professed ignorance of the meaning of "ideogramic" I must try once again to define that term, necessary to the said student if he still wishes to follow me or my meaning.

So he "tried" again, writing seven arrogant and incoherent pages without ever once beginning a sentence with the words, "The ideogramic method *is,*" or in any other way attempting to say explicitly what meaning we should give to "ideogramic." The poet, one gathers, should be like a scientist, clear, precise, direct, exact, and so on, but the prose writer, or at least Pound as a prose writer, need not be. Pound's prose, especially after about 1930, is an incoherent jumble of maxims, slogans, vituperative irrelevancies, and hints at secret knowledge. Its chief tactics are evasion and attack, and its characteristic tone one of contempt for his readers.

But he did start out by saying *this* — without bothering to explain what bearing it had on the meaning of "ideogramic":

> Ernest Fenollosa attacked, quite rightly, a great weakness in western ratiocination. He pointed out that the material sciences, biology, chemistry, examined collections of fact, phenomena, specimens, and gathered general equations of real knowledge from them, even though the observed data had no syllogistic connection one with another.

After more pages of threats, boasts ("I have a certain knowledge") and mystifications ("I offer another axis of reference: the difference between maritime and agrarian usury . . ."), he ended his effort at "definition" by saying:

> In our time Al Einstein scandalized the professing philosophists by saying, with truth, that his theories of relativity had no philosophic bearing.
>
> (Pause here for reflection.)

This is Pound's final attempt at definition of his celebrated method, and of course all that he has said here constitutes a series of gestures of aggressive evasion. For many years he had said, in effect, you are all stupid not to see the plain truth; but he had always refused to attempt to tell us what the plain truth *is* that we don't see. And no wonder, for to have done so would have been to expose the emptiness, the lack of intelligence, of a method which turns naive scientific empiricism into poetic theory — as with some part of his mind Pound must have known, or he would not have been so violent and aggressive. (As he said of an unsympathetic poetic critic of his political ideas, "I'll split his face with my fists.") Though a number of Pound's critics have expressed awed admiration for the profundity of his poetic theory, it is noteworthy that no major poet among his contemporaries, with the lone exception of Williams, was impressed. None thought so simplisticly about the problems Pound solved with such apparent ease.

If one felt compelled to see the "ideogramatic method" in the best light possible — an effort which would require ignoring the crucial question of why the poet *arranges* the chunks of reality the way he does — it would have to be seen as a proposal that we get at the truth of history by *sampling,* without any controls or any announced guarantees of objectivity. In effect, it asks us simply to trust the poet to know — as we, he keeps telling us, don't know — what samples are fairly representative, and when the possibilities of sampling have been exhausted. The reasoning behind the method is circular. Because certain principles are true, the poet is therefore being "objective" when he selects documents to prove their truth. Since history is cyclical, and the present era represents the dying phase of a civilization, and usurers, especially International Bankers, who are mostly Jews, have killed it, and war and vulgarity are the products of this "usurocracy," therefore the facts of world history that Pound has put before us in the *Cantos* may be allowed to "speak for themselves," without need of comment by the poet. We are reminded of Zola's argument in *The Experimental Novel* that the novelist should be absolutely objective, like the scientist, and simply record without personal intervention those facts that "prove" that man is the same as a stone or a simple chemical element; that the novelist should, in short, remain completely uninvolved and uncommitted while "proving" materialist and mechanist principles. (But at least, we may say, Zola's *heart* was in the right place, and his novels do not really illustrate the theory he propounded.)

Such a "method" as Pound proposed could only produce a good poem if the writer's ideas and his sensibility existed in quite separate compartments, so that when he wrote as a poet his ideas were irrelevant to his work (the case of Williams) and when he struggled to enunciate theory, he betrayed his own creative work (the case of Zola). But Pound, unfortunately, is not that kind of writer. He tells us in prose that Jefferson and Mussolini were alike, and in the *Cantos* that Hitler was the victim of the Jews. He wrote the editor of the *Boston Evening Transcript* in 1915, in answer to the paper's mistaken statement that Robert Frost had won acceptance "unheralded, unintroduced, untrumpeted" (actually, Pound *had* "heralded," etc., Frost), "Now seriously, . . . your (?negro) reviewer might acquaint himself. . . ." [3] and while detained in Saint Elizabeth's hospital more than thirty years later, he took comfort in the constant visits of his disciple John Kasper, the militant racist. Pound's life, his ideas, and the intentions behind his poetry are all cut from the same cloth.

The *Cantos* are longer than "Song of Myself," which might have been a good title for them, in one sense — for despite Pound's claims for their objectivity, they are in fact highly subjective. They are more ambitious in scope than Taylor's "Metrical History" or Melville's *Clarel.* But despite some brilliant passages and the relative success of a few whole *Cantos,* especially the early ones, when we think of them as the parts of a single immense poem, we can only judge that poem as less successful than any of those it competes with in length — except possibly Taylor's, which it reminds us of in its obsessiveness, its moral insensitivity, and its unreadableness.

The *Cantos* are a poem about history, *literal* history, not mythic history, the same history the historian tries to recreate and understand; but no professional historian has ever thought that they do anything at all, in any way, to illuminate his subject. They are full of obscure facts and figures and quotations, but no responsible historian supposes that the documents and artifacts that make up his evidence have "self-evident" meaning. Whatever may be the case with a short Imagist poem, *history* cannot be responsibly treated in this fashion. The appearance of objectivity in the poem is wholly misleading. What the ideogramatic method, as it is operationally defined in the *Cantos,* means, in effect, is that the assumptions that guide the selection and control the treatment of the historical material are simply never acknowledged. The *Cantos* are a didactic poem. Of a didactic poem we have a right to expect that the content of its teaching will strike us as wisdom, and the manner of its teaching will be humanly responsible. We do not want to be "manipulated" by poets any more than by the "hidden persuaders."

The *Cantos* are a poem about the history of the world in which there are no people, only the names of people and allusions to them — and the typing of them as "good" or "bad." Even some of Pound's staunchest admirers and most loyal beneficiaries have admitted this deficiency in the poem — though without going on to draw the conclusion it suggests, which would be that a poem about history that does not show us *people* acting and suffering fails at the very center. Even Eliot said that the Inferno Pound presents in the *Cantos* "is a Hell for the *other people,* the people we read about in the newspapers, not for oneself and one's friends." And Yeats once said of Pound's treatment of the villains in the *Cantos* that he presents them as "malignants with inexplicable characters and motives, grotesque figures out of a child's book of beasts." The poet whose best-known slogan was "MAKE IT NEW!" would have written better perhaps if he had been more concerned with attempting to "make it human."

It could be argued, of course, that the *Cantos* are in the main stream of American long poems. Like Taylor's "Metrical History," Barlow's *Columbiad,* Melville's *Clarel,* and Williams' *Paterson,* they take history as their subject and attempt to reinterpret it to find a clue to the meaning of present experience. Like "Song of Myself," they dare to write the poet's autobiography — or at least the record of his reading and his response to it — "in colossal cipher, or into universality," as Emerson advised; they do this in fact, whatever Pound claimed about their "scientific" objectivity. Like both "Song of Myself" and Williams' *Paterson,* they make poetry out of supposedly antipoetic or nonpoetic materials, they heap up masses of detail, and, again as Emerson advised, let the fact create the form.

All this is interesting and may suggest that we have not thought enough about the peculiarly *American* quality of the *Cantos,* their place in a long tradition. But what *readers* of poetry are likely to carry away from any extended attempt to read the *Cantos* is not so much an impression of their centrality in the tradition of American long poems, or their exemplification of some of Emerson's poetic theories and Whitman's practices, as it is an impression of what they have said to him, their "interpretative power," when they have said anything to him at all. And what they have said, after all the crackpot monetary and historical ideas have been forgotten, their "truth," is that earlier ages and other cultures were nobler, more heroic. They always invert Emerson's and Whitman's deepest meanings even when they seem to be closest to Transcendental poetics.

Alienation from both the social and the natural worlds, an alienation that finds expression as an intense and all-pervasive nostalgia for a better time and place, is at once the structuring principle and the latent meaning of the *Cantos* as a whole. I suspect that a good many readers of poetry today besides myself find themselves bored by poems the chief meaning of which is nostalgia.

Two claims that have been made for Pound by his friends and

admirers need to be further examined. The first concerns his reputed "discovery" of oriental literature, the second his celebrated craftsmanship as a poet. Both claims need qualification.

His discovery of oriental writing through Fenollosa was good for Pound, no doubt, in seeming to offer him a way of moving beyond "Amygism" without basically altering his ideas; and no doubt his enthusiasm prompted others to look into the subject, Amy Lowell and John Gould Fletcher for example. Presumably this ought to be counted as a "good thing," even though the net results in their writing are not impressive.

But that part of Pound's prose which is most directly related to his discovery does no service to Western understanding of oriental literature. When, at Fenollosa's widow's request, he completed the translations and notes Fenollosa had left unfinished, and wrote an introduction for *Certain Noble Plays of Japan,* published in 1916 (currently called *The Classic Noh Theatre of Japan*), he showed, characteristically, a failure to grasp what the plays are about, their religious dimension, in short. They were, he decided, "more Shinto than Buddhist," and should be listened to "as though you were listening to music." Of Fenollosa's undeveloped note, "Buddhism, growing popularity of Chinese music," he could, not very surprisingly, make nothing at all. On the basis of this volume and the claims Pound himself made about it, he has become, for typical Modernist critics, a "scholarly" authority on *No* plays. *No* plays are one of the art forms in which Zen Buddhism got expressed, but one would never guess it from reading Pound's book.

So that when Eliot says, "Pound is the inventor of Chinese poetry for our time," we wonder what he meant. If only that Pound's *Cathay* was published before Fletcher and Amy Lowell exploited oriental subjects, then the statement is merely factual and accurate enough. But "inventor"? And for *whose* time? Is Eliot being intentionally guarded in his praise here? At any rate, if we change "inventor" to "discoverer," then it becomes clear that *No* plays and *haiku* poems were not "discovered" — in any depth of understanding — by either Fenollosa or Pound. Both of them in effect assimilated oriental art forms to the categories of modern Western "scientific" thought, which is to say, they noted the *form* but missed its *meaning.* Without "knowing" what Fenollosa and Pound knew, Emerson had come much closer to understanding

Eastern religion than either of the later men did. If he had been able to read *haiku,* he would have understood them too.

All Poundians and many poets and readers who could not be so described, particularly some of the young poets of today, hail his "craftsmanship," but I shall let Eliot make the claim, partly because of Eliot's critical authority, partly because he puts it in such a way as to lay bare one of the assumptions on which one form of the claim rests. Writing for the issue of *Poetry* magazine that paid tribute to Pound after his arrest for treason, Eliot said:

> I find nothing to abate in my introduction to a volume of Pound's *Selected Poems* . . . except that I should now speak more respectfully of Whitman. . . . If I am doubtful about some of the *Cantos,* it is not that I find any poetic decline in them. . . . In the *Cantos* there is an increasing defect of communication. . . . But the craftsman . . . has never failed. There is nobody living who can write like this. . . .

To begin at the end of this passage and work back, if "write" in "write like this" carries its normal meaning of "create poems," then we should have to say that there must be very few poets living today, except Pound himself, who would *want* to "write like this"—that is, as Pound writes in the *Cantos.* But of course "write" as Eliot uses the word does not really mean "create poems"; it means, rather, something like "shape the prosody of a line," or perhaps, more generally, just "exhibit craftsmanship." The first clue that "write" carries only this very special and limited meaning (so that the apparently unlimited praise is really severely qualified) comes in the second sentence that I have quoted: Eliot is "doubtful" about some of the *Cantos,* but he finds no "poetic" decline in them. In another context he had commented on the way the *Cantos* created a Hell for other people, implying a moral or ethical deficiency in them. Now he speaks of a "defect of communication" and calls some of them, in a sentence I have omitted for the sake of brevity from the quotation above, "opaque." He says they read, to him, as if the author were "irritated" with his readers. Nevertheless, despite all this, their "poetic" value for him, he says, is unblemished.

What could "poetic" mean in such a judgment? It must imply,

when used this way, not only the old form-content dichotomy (that is, the sometimes vicious, sometimes silly ideas in the *Cantos* do not affect the poem's "poetic" value) but another one, a dichotomy between "technique" as prosodic power and "technique" as the power to design and carry through the shaping of a whole poem, with all the problems and difficulties that implies. In a very long poem on history, a poet faces problems that cannot be solved merely by his possession of a good "ear." Even if every line in the *Cantos* were to be admitted as demonstrating unequaled mastery of prosody, the *poem* might still be a failure.

To this kind of nonsense did Eliot's admirable loyalty to Pound, combined with his — and Pound's — inadequate understanding of poetic *creativity,* bring him. Poe had sometimes claimed that the sound, the "music," of poetry was all that mattered, and Eliot, in "From Poe to Valery," had denied it, suggesting Poe's theory was primitive. But now we find him praising Pound in terms that Poe, in some of his moods, might have used; poetry has nothing to do with anything except an undefined "taste," for aesthetic experience is completely different from all other experience, the product of the Aesthetic Faculty.

Perhaps, of course, Eliot was consciously using double-talk because of the occasion: An old friend, who had greatly helped him years ago, was under indictment for treason, attacked fiercely in the press for his racism and fascism, of doubtful sanity, and needing *his* help now. He would give him the highest possible praise without really committing himself to saying any more than that Pound was a good technician. Perhaps. But the narrow aestheticism implied by the terms of the praise had already, many years before, been implied by the "poet as catalyst" analogy in *The Sacred Wood,* just as it was in Pound's 1912 definition of the image. Both definitions split apart poet and man, denying any relationship of responsibility between the two; both reduce the meaning of "poet" to "technician"; both are mechanistic theories; both are aimed at "saving" poetry in an age dominated by scientific ways of thinking by defining poetry in "scientific" terms. So Eliot need *not* have been conscious of any double-talk in his praise of Pound. But double-talk it seems to me to have been, of a peculiarly obfuscating kind.

Ezra Pound has a splendid ear for the sound of spoken language and has set a good example in his metrics. Numerous passages and many lines in the *Cantos* are memorably phrased. His creative translations will probably be read for a long time; unlike most of the *Cantos,* they are better to read than to read about. But many a less celebrated poet of our century has written a larger body of poetry we want to read and reread. Perhaps future generations will honor Pound as a poet's poet, a resource for young poets searching, as they continually must, for a way to "make it new."

CHAPTER XV

Myth and Memory

[Poetry] aims . . . at the reformation of the poet, as prayer does. In the grand cases — as, in our century, Yeats and Eliot — it enables the poet gradually, again and again, to become almost another man; but something of the sort happens, on a small scale, a freeing, with the creation of every real poem.

— John Berryman

The life of a man is a self-evolving circle, which, from a ring imperceptibly small, rushes on all sides outwards to new and larger circles, and that without end. . . . The continual effort to raise himself above himself, to work a pitch above his last height, betrays itself in a man's relations. . . . Literature is a point outside of our hodiernal circle, through which a new one may be described. The use of literature is to afford us a platform whence we may command a view of our present life, a purchase by which we may move it.

— Emerson, in "Circles"

There is no doubt that naturalism, with its corollary of the futility of human life, has brought despair into the world. It is the root cause of the modern spiritual malaise. . . . the spiritual darkness of the modern mind has its source in the scientific view of the world.

— W. T. Stace

THOMAS STEARNS ELIOT

PERHAPS the quickest way to get at the fundamental difference between the poetry of Pound and that of Eliot, a difference that comes to seem greater as the years go by, is to examine their responses to scientific naturalism. Discussions of the two poets usually center on what they share — their common rejection of the trend of our culture toward religious and cultural pluralism, secularism, and technology; their common nostalgia for apparently more heroic and ordered ages; their search for moral or religious authority. Eliot's description of contemporary Europe in his early review of Joyce's *Ulysses* might well have been written by Pound — the present scene, Eliot thought, presented only an "immense panorama of futility and anarchy."

All this and much more they shared in their early days, including expatriation in London, a common mid-western or far-western origin, a fondness for Henry James, and a penchant for expressing their willful disaffiliation by their dress and manner. But one thing they did not share even then, and as the years went on it became more and more apparent that this difference between them was crucial. Their reactions to scientific naturalism did more than anything else to determine the different directions their careers took, and the ways in which their poetry developed, or failed to develop.

Though it was not until 1934 that Pound opened his *A B C of Reading* with the flat declaration: "We live in an age of science," thus echoing the words of I. A. Richards and Max Eastman, among others, his earliest statements on poetry, as we have seen in the discussion of Imagism, imply that he is assuming the idea without feeling any need to say it. It is this unstated assumption that lies behind his contemptuous dismissal of all romanticisms and idealisms as unsuitable for the new age. To those in the void at the center of the Vortex, it seemed clear that nineteenth-century poetry was full of metaphysical and theological meanings that amounted to no more than "emotional slither." The first step a writer would have to take, if he were successfully to "MAKE IT NEW," would be to learn to present things and facts objectively. Pound's literary ideal was shaped by his response to scientific naturalism long before he explicitly equated "the ideogramic method" with "the method of science."

Literary naturalism as we find it in fiction has a number of characteristics, some of them self-contradictory, some of them essential, and some accidental — the tendency of the fictional naturalists to use naturalism for social uplift, for example. Pound's poetic naturalism, in theory at least, was simpler and purer. It centered on the positivistic element in scientific naturalism, on the naturalist's idea of what can be known, and how. There are of course various kinds and degrees of Positivism, from that of Comte in the nineteenth century to the far more sophisticated doctrines of the Vienna school of "logical positivists" who influenced the thought of Richards in his *Science and Poetry* period. Pound's version is not elaborated, so it is hard to know just where it ought to be placed, but the very simplicity of it reminds us of the early Positivism of Comte. That is to say, knowledge is progressive, moving upward from the *theological* (primitive, ridiculous), to the *metaphysical* (civilized, misguided), to the *positively scientific* (true, good, useful).

To assume that we are living in Comte's "third stage," as Pound in effect always has, is not only to dismiss metaphysics and theology, it is to dismiss along with them the areas of experience they spring from and talk about — man's *inwardness,* his "soul" if you will, his freedom, his responsibility, his intuitions of *purpose* in himself, in others, and, perhaps, in nature. (For the benefit of any reader who distrusts philosophy as much as Pound does, perhaps I should say that Conrad Aiken was our first *poet* to make such matters as these clear. He is a contemporary of Pound's, but saner, wiser, and more humane.) Pound's repudiation of metaphysics and theology in his statements is paralleled by the implications of the form of the *Cantos.*

Of the many ways in which the *Cantos* reflect Pound's Positivism in their form, the way the historical characters are treated is perhaps both the most obvious and the most damaging to the poem. Yeats's comment on how Pound treats those he sees as the villains of history, whose "characters and motives" he makes seem "inexplicable," went straight to the heart of the matter, but it says nothing of why these people seem to come from "a child's book of beasts." They are grotesque caricatures because "the method of science" — the kind of science Pound was acquainted with at any rate — has no way of getting at the subjective aspects of experience, and so must omit what man feels to be distinctively *human* about himself. To conceive of people without assuming that they have purposes and motives and the capacity for self-transcendence is to conceive of them as *things,* and thus to render their actions finally inexplicable. The *Cantos* rest on and imply scientific determinism, or mechanism.

W. T. Stace has written:

> Scientific explanation and mechanical explanation are one and the same thing. A fact is explained scientifically when its cause is given. It comes to the same thing to say that it is explained by being shown to be a particular case of a general principle or law. Science is thus wholly mechanistic. And this has not been altered by recent

> scientific advances. For any explanation is mechanical which is in terms of causes or laws and not in terms of purposes. And recent physics does not explain events by means of purposes.

A leading American psychologist of the years when Pound was "explaining" his ideogramic method, John B. Watson, was brash enough to spell out in some detail what the philosopher's generalization would amount to in more specific terms:

> The behaviorist began his own formulation of the problem of psychology by sweeping aside all medieval conceptions. He dropped from his scientific vocabulary all subjective terms such as sensation, perception, image, desire, purpose, and even thinking and emotion as they were originally defined. . . . We need nothing to explain behavior but the ordinary laws of physics and chemistry. . . . The behaviorist makes no mystery of thinking. He holds that thinking is behavior, is motor organization, just like tennis, playing golf, or any other form of muscular activity. . . . In one sweeping assumption after another, the behaviorist threw out the concepts both of mind and of consciousness, calling them carryovers from the church dogmas of the Middle Ages. The behaviorists told the introspectionists that consciousness was just a masquerade for the soul.

Appropriately, it seems to me, Watson, who carried the brunt of the "battle of Behaviorism" against admitting the evidence gained from introspection, but who made no significant contribution to the advance of psychological knowledge, left the laboratory for a later career as an advertising executive, a role ideally suited to one who believed that people are *things* to be manipulated.

Not every philosopher, of course, would agree with Stace that a purely scientific procedure must automatically rule out teleology — purpose — but most of them would agree that at least up to now it has done so. It is hard to find a philosopher today who would not agree with Eliot's statement of many years ago, "A purely 'scientific' philosophy ends by denying what we know to be true," though there are those who argue that this will not be so when we get better knowledge. Be that as it may, it was the widespread sense of the condition Eliot's comment points to that brought about the Existentialist movement in philosophy. Existentialists, whether atheistic or theistic, begin and end with all that Watson ruled out as medieval, which is another way of saying they begin with man's inwardness, with *experience* in short — with sensations and perceptions, desires and purposes, with remembering and thinking and planning.

Naturalism, conceived as Stace conceives it and as Watson illustrated it, would of course deny any validity to Berryman's analogy between poetry and prayer. It would even more clearly reduce to nonsense Emerson's idea that life is a "self-evolving circle" in which growth toward the unpredictable, or self-transcendence, is the *central* fact of life. It just as clearly denies any cognitive function to literature by which it may make available to us new circles of reality, and a "purchase" by which we may grow into those larger circles.

Though he does not have a philosophic mind, Pound was in some degree aware of all this. His response was not philosophic but historical: He searched past literature and history for examples of cultures in which men acted with dignity and purpose, believed in moral law, and exemplified in their own actions and characters virtues which science could never validate. There is a real point to Hugh Kenner's calling the *Cantos* an "effort" at "moral definition," even though that effort does not succeed, and even though the work contains ideas and attitudes that I should have to call profoundly *im*moral.

Perhaps the most profound reason why it does not succeed is that it finally rests upon nothing but a desperate nostalgia for better times. The "circumcision" and "wafer" references in "Mauberley" again: a yearning for the values of a religious society, while denying the validity of the beliefs on which that society rested, the beliefs that gave it its reason for being that particular kind of society, with those particular rites. The way Pound missed the religious significance of the *No* plays he translated and edited, and the *haiku* poetry he liked so well, makes it unnecessary to speculate very long on why the *Cantos,* despite some patches of brilliant style, are an unreadable failure. Their subject is the interpretation of history, but they have nothing to tell us about it which is worth hearing. The interpretation of history is a philosophic problem, as Henry Adams knew, but Pound was incapable of dealing with what he distrusted. No amount of technical brilliance can save a poem that is empty at the center.

Eliot responded to the naturalistic challenge more philosophically. There is no need to accept all his ideas, or all his attitudes, or be committed to the faith he finally found, in order to see that his reaction was an attempt to get at the *roots* of the trouble. He and Stevens, from very different points of view, saw what the real issues were, and worked on from there. He shared Pound's nostalgia for the past, but he was not content to rest in nostalgia. He searched for a set of beliefs that would *not* "deny what we know to be true." Though the aesthetic theory he expressed in the early essays is Positivistic, the poems are anti-Positivistic, and implicitly religious, long before Eliot came to the point of publicly accepting Christian orthodoxy.

The purpose of the poet's search was to find a way out of the same "spiritual darkness of the modern mind" that had oppressed Robinson and Frost. With his philosophic training — he completed his doctoral thesis on Bradley but did not take his degree — Eliot felt that there could be no way out short of denying philosophic naturalism in all of its aspects and beginning all over again on different assumptions. Humanism, though preferable to naturalism, was not enough; it could not defend itself rationally. With nothing like Emerson's or Whitman's mystical experiences available to him, the young poet turned back to the supernaturalist orthodoxy Emerson had rejected. Yeats created a spiritualistic myth of his own, Pound sought an accommodation with naturalism in the *Tao,* Stevens tried to be content with a merely "fictive" order; Eliot accepted the religion of his forefathers.

Given Eliot's temperament and family history, the influences he had been exposed to in his education, and the historic situation as we have seen it developing, some such about-face as Eliot made was predictable and, for the man and the poet, desirable, whether it seems to us today philosophically "possible" or not. In the years when Eliot was experimenting with various kinds of reaction, Robinson was coming to a creative dead end and turning away from the problem by writing Arthurian romances. Frost was guarding his secret resources so well that his readers never suspected them. Eliot, in contrast with both of them, sought ways to keep his life and his work, and his thought and his emotions, unified, not split up as, in different ways, both Robinson's and Frost's were. His return to orthodoxy made it possible. His poetry benefited as a result.

Williams, sensing the direction in which Eliot's journey was taking him and feeling his own career threatened, called Eliot, in *Kora in Hell* in 1920, "archbishop of procurers to a lecherous antiquity." I suspect that Williams, if he were alive today, would be unhappy about the way his followers have resurrected and are using this characterization. American poetry has room for an Eliot and a Williams too. Late Williams and late Eliot approached each other, coming from opposite directions. Between Williams' "A Unison" and "Asphodel, That Greeny Flower," and Eliot's "The Dry Salvages" there are all kinds of differences — of temperament, tone, style — but all three poems are closer in meaning to Whitman's "Lilacs" than they are to the early work of either poet. There are various routes by which a poet may make his *Journey to Love,* as Williams titled one of his last poems. Only religious or philosophic bigots would call one way legitimate, the other way illegitimate.

In suggesting that Eliot's philosophic thinking, which distinguished him from Pound, made his poetry better, I am not intending to suggest that poetry is always better if it reflects a systematic and coherent philosophy or theology. There *may* be some kind of ultimate truth in that idea, but if so I do not understand it, and I am not now interested in arguing it. What I do mean to suggest, in part, is that when poetry pretends to offer a "criticism of life," as Eliot's usually does and Pound's *Cantos* most emphatically do, then the criticisms it offers must strike us as containing wisdom, which is not the same as "correct doctrine." Writing from their very different points of view, Eliot and Stevens both pass this test. Williams, the least philosophic of these three, passes it in the best of the poems to which it would be relevant to apply it. Except in rare passages, Pound does not. Passages like the often-admired "Pull down thy vanity" lines in *Canto LXXXI* are too rare, and too much intermixed with dross.

An even sharper contrast between Eliot and Pound emerges when we examine their capacity for growth. It should be obvious, though it apparently is not to some of our younger poet-critics, that Eliot's career exhibits continual re-formations of the poet, and so of the poetry, continual efforts to "raise himself above himself," using poetry as the "purchase" by which he could move his life; and that Pound's career exhibits nothing of the kind. This is the point of the epigraphs from Berryman and Emerson with which this discussion began.

Eliot's advice in "The Dry Salvages," "Fare forward, voyagers!" would have seemed ironic as a motto for his career in 1927, but now that the career is complete, it is seen to be appropriate. The shape of the career as a whole begins to look more like a journey-quest than like a pilgrimage. True, Eliot as pilgrim went back to Little Gidding to pray and meditate where Nicholas Ferrar had; but Little Gidding sent him on. *The Elder Statesman* (1958) shows us a poet still on the move.

Eliot's paternal grandfather had come west to St. Louis to found that city's First Unitarian Church, and later to found also Washington University. A product of Harvard Divinity School, which, in the years since Emerson had shocked it with his "Divinity School Address," had come around to Emerson's way of thinking, the grandfather brought with him to the West both New England's new liberal Christianity and its old faith in education. Several centuries earlier, the Eliots had moved west to New England from the ancestral village of East Coker in old England.

The first phase of the poet's personal journey reversed the direction family history had taken. He came east to Harvard, where he was graduated in 1910 and took a year of graduate work, studying the philosophy of a late nineteenth-century antinaturalist, F. H. Bradley, and doing a little teaching. Then to Germany for further study, then to London, where he settled in and became a British subject and a member of the Anglican Church in 1927. Using the occasion to dramatize the extent of his revolt against the "normalcy" of the period, he announced with an air of bravado that he was a Classicist in literature, a Royalist in politics, and an Anglo-Catholic in religion. To most of his friends and associates, and to even more of the intellectuals of the time who were neither poets nor expatriates, all three positions seemed equally "impossible." The poet had turned back to a time before "the wrong turning" was made, the "turning" that produced the culture Adams had symbolized by the dynamo. At this stage in his journey he seemed more like one in flight than a true pilgrim. Only his religion, though it too was "reactionary," differentiated him from the many artists of the time who were flirting with more practicable versions of authoritarian philosophy and social organization than Royalism.

It was his religion that kept him on the move. As he struggled to understand its values and make them really his own, actually to "believe" what he had announced himself as believing, he found himself moving in a direction his 1927 announcement would not have enabled anyone to predict. Psychologists sometimes distinguish between values and beliefs nominally held and those "internalized." "Ash Wednesday," "The Journey of the Magi," and "A Song for Simeon" record the difficulties and disappointments of a modern mind attempting to "internalize" Christian orthodoxy. "Marina" records a moment when the faith was only a kind of dream, but if so, it was still the battered ship that would take the dreamer forward in his journey.

Less than ten years after the reactionary announcement of 1927, the poet began writing *Four Quartets,* a record of the growth of a poet's mind that reminds us in several respects of Wordsworth's *The Prelude.* The central theme of these meditations on time and eternity, the meaning of the reports of the mystics and the meaning of living "in passage," is that time and nature are not empty of meaning, so that belief simply on authority, in the medieval way, is *not* necessary. There is the Incarnation to show that God is immanent as well as transcendent; and there are many lesser incarnations. Nature *does* grant epiphanies of transcendental meaning to those prepared to receive them. "The way up" of the immanentist or Nature mystic and "the way down," or inward, of the medieval mystics, lead to the same still point. Emerson and the Unitarian grandfather would have rejoiced, even though they would have thought that the *Quartets* were a little too respectful toward the more orthodox "way down."

Four Quartets is a great poem and *The Elder Statesman* is not a great play, but Emerson and the grandfather might have liked the play even better because of what it *means.* In it they would have found the poet who had condemned Emerson by name in "Sweeney Erect" for not being aware of the bestiality and sordidness of ordinary ("fallen") human nature, saying that "human love" is an analogue of and preparation for "divine love"; that without it we cannot face the selves we are and grow toward new selves inhabiting larger circles of reality; so that, if anything can, love will save us. "Original sin" seems to have been forgotten. Thematically, the play overlaps with Whitman's "Of the Terrible Doubt of Appearances," in which his doubts were put at rest, and "curiously answer'd," though he remained unable to "answer" logically, by his "dear friends." The nineteenth century, it would seem, was not, after all, wholly wrong in the directions it took, as Eliot had said earlier, both as poet and critic.

In 1959, in an interview reported in *The Paris Review,* Eliot was asked, "I have heard that you consider that your poetry belongs in the tradition of American literature. Could you tell us why?" To which the poet replied: "I'd say that my poetry has obviously more in common with my distinguished contemporaries in America, than with anything written in my generation in England. That I'm sure of." It had required a long journey to reach a point not far from where we might suppose he could have started, had conditions in 1910 been different from what they were. But they were not different, and to attempt to prescribe the conditions of growth for another man is to indulge in dogmatism. The one thing that is certain about the poet's more than one step backward taken is that the poetry itself shows us how we ought to interpret the steps. As with Frost, so with Eliot, but more obviously, the backward steps were taken not in flight but in seeking.

Eliot's journey-quest — "the quest for salvation" — is not simply to be *inferred* from the poems; a good deal of the time it is the subject of them. Once we have noticed how visible the poet is behind the *personae,* it becomes clear that describing the poet's journey in metaphysical terms, as I have just done, gives us only about half the truth. The other half is the personal search for integration and fulfillment, the search for a new *self* to hold the new beliefs and experience the believed-in-values. From this point of view the word "redemption" is more appropriate than "salvation"; for the old self cannot be "saved" so long as it cannot love. And it cannot love so long as it *objectifies* all its experience. How can this self be re-formed, redeemed?

That question, and not the revealed emptiness of the lady, is the real subject of "Portrait of a Lady," the earliest of the major poems. The contrast with Pound's "Portrait d'une Femme" is instructive in this connection. Pound gives us a straightforward description of a woman whose mind is a "Sargasso Sea," full of "oddments of all things" without any real center, "nothing that's quite . . . [her] own." Readers have differed on whether the poem should be read as unqualified satire or as satire touched by pity, but whichever may be the case, the speaker himself in no sense at all suggests any question about his own judgment of his subject. He has painted, we are to believe, an "objective" portrait of an empty, and perhaps pitiable, woman who is an object of the speaker's experience.

Williams also wrote a "Portrait of a Lady" which is helpful in placing Eliot's. Though a good deal briefer than Pound's, Williams' poem is at once more complex, and a much more interesting poem. Essentially it is a debate between the romantic and the realistic sides of the *speaker* over how to interpret a woman's beauty. The romantic self has the first and the last word, but the assertive tone of the last line, "I said petals from an apple tree," implies that the debate will go on beyond this poem, endlessly. Beauty that suggests transcendence can always be redefined by the realist asking for precise definitions in such a way as to omit the transcendence. The woman's body suggests the romantic images of sky and shore to the speaker, but he is not content to let these go undefined. He wants to know what they *mean:* "Which shore? . . . Which shore?" (Ellipses Williams'.) The music of the poem, including the effect of its irregular division into lines, wonderfully supports and deepens the poem's thematic question: How shall we look at beauty? What is it, after all?

Williams' poem is so much briefer than Eliot's that a comparison of the two cannot be very meaningful, but it is clear at any rate that the two poems are much more alike than either of them is like Pound's. Eliot's poem has in common with Pound's only the pathetic emptiness of the woman. There the likeness ends. Like Williams' speaker, the speaker in Eliot's poem wonders how he should "see" and think about the woman. She has embarrassed him by her revelations and advances, put him "in the wrong." Would he have the right to smile if she were to die before his return from abroad? Why does he *feel* nothing but embarrassment? Granted that he could not respond to her as a lover, as she would have liked, might there not have been some way of responding to her as a human being? As we read the poem, the center of interest shifts from the subject suggested by the title to the self-revelation of the speaker. He has totally *objectivized* the woman, pinned her like an insect for study; in doing so he reveals, finally, more about himself than about her. The poem might have been called, from this point of view, "Portrait of an Incipient Prufrock."

There are a good many clues in the poem that suggest that this is the way it should be read. Perhaps the clearest of them is the allusion to Matthew Arnold's "The Buried Life," with its theme of isolation. Arnold had asked, "Are even lovers powerless to reveal/ To one another what indeed they feel?" The speaker in the poem is not a "lover," though he has had love offered him. The woman is sentimental: she has both felt and revealed more than the circumstances warranted. Like the realistic speaker in Williams' poem, the speaker here has insisted on seeing the "reality" with perfect clarity. In the room dimly lighted by candlelight, he still sees.

But most clearly of all, at the end, he sees himself, and what he sees he does not like. He has understood the woman perfectly objectively, but what does his doing so reveal about *him?* Would he be able to love a woman younger and less sentimental? How are poetry and the personality of the poet related? This question is also raised by "La Figlia che Piange," the weeping girl. As *artist,* the speaker in this poem appreciates the romantic beauty of the parting scene; he would even like to rearrange it a little to make it still more touching and dramatic. But as a man he is not involved; the girl and the scene are simply aesthetic objects of his own. But, also as a man, he feels guilty because he is not "involved." When the artist portrays ideal beauty, is he actually betraying real values? What is the relation between art and belief, or art and commitment? If the Prufrockian speaker yearns for ideal beauty such as he finds in art but cannot respond to *actual* beauty, is the beauty — are all the ideal values — a *lie?*

In the ending of "Sweeney Among the Nightingales" there is the phrase, "their liquid siftings," referring to the nightingales that "sang within the bloody wood." The phrase is ambiguous in meaning. Only the speaker in the poem knows about the nightingales of Greek myth, and only *he* has heard them singing near the convent, suggesting to him the resurrection myth of Philomel, who was changed by the gods into a nightingale after being raped and murdered. Is the poet, then, the "singer," the guardian of religious values in the sordid naturalistic world Sweeney inhabits? This would seem to be implied if the "liquid siftings" are taken to be the song of the nightingales.

But the phrase also suggests, particularly when we read "stain" in the next line, the liquid excrement of the birds. Is the poet's nostalgia merely a sickness, his art the product of neurosis? The voice in this poem sounds very like the ones we hear in "Portrait" and "Prufrock," and the sensitive young man and the sensitive middle-aged one are both "sick" — and know it. Is the artist who cannot accept the world described by scientific naturalism simply *sick?*

To the extent that a person retains insight, he is not sick beyond hope of recovery — beyond hope of re-formation or growth. Eliot's several poems in which the irony is directed against himself are evidence both that the *personae* of the early poems represent partial self-portraits, and that the poet has resources that the Prufrock-figure does not have. In "Mélange Adultère de Tout," for example, we can read a detailed summary of the nonpoetic side of the career so far, including the various jobs held, the moving about from country to country, and the discrepancy between the practical activities and the romantic ideals, all done in a tone of amused self-satire. The speaker in the poem finds his subject slightly ridiculous. About this time Eliot was holding a small job in a bank and ostentatiously adopting the banker's uniform of bowler hat and tightly rolled umbrella. But while trying to look the part of the little businessman, he dreamed of mermaids and the burning shores of Mozambique. He has told us that he wrote this and the other French poems as "exercises" at a time when he feared he had "dried up" as a poet. In them the impersonal mask is dropped, and the disguised self-criticism of "Portrait of a Lady" becomes an inhibiting self-doubt.

In "Mr. Eliot's Sunday Morning Service" the difficulties of the would-be worshipper who *knows* too much and *sees* too clearly to feel anything are the real objects of the satire, not the pimply ushers or Sweeney at home taking a bath. The way Mr. Eliot spends his Sunday mornings in church is amusing to both Mr. Eliot and the reader. The poem is self-satire, and its "Mr. Eliot" has precisely the characteristics of the Prufrock figure in the several poems. The unnamed speaker in the two early Sweeney poems is here named, and his name is Eliot.

The speaker in "Dans le Restaurant" is not named, but I think we are justified in connecting him with the Prufrock side of the poet. In the poem a waiter tells of a youthful sex experience in which he was frightened away from a little girl, "having gone only half-way." The speaker feels the greatest contempt for and repugnance toward the waiter, who is dirty and nasty. He wonders "By what right do you have experiences like mine?" The poem prepares us for the scene with the hyacinth girl in *The Waste Land* and suggests why Prufrock wonders if he dares to eat a peach — a traditional sexual symbol.

The Prufrockian inability to love and inability to believe, and so to act, fills out the details of the pattern of metaphysical search described earlier. The two perspectives are simply different ways of viewing the same personal journey. When they are thought of as complementary, they make it seem not surprising that the failure of the inhabitants of the city of the spiritually dead described in *The Waste Land* should be ascribed most insistently to sexual causes, and that sexual failure should be connected with alienation; and not surprising either that these failures should be expressible in religious terms as the lack of ability to believe, and to hope, and to love — Paul's "faith, hope, and charity." The way the psychic and the theological, or metaphysical, are seen as complementary and interdependent may be the profoundest insight in the poem. If it is not, then it is because the bold equation the poem makes between the truths of all religious myths should have that distinction instead.

If myth contains truth about experience that scientific methods can never get at, then the "mythical method" in poetry is justified. In his review of Joyce's *Ulysses* in 1922, Eliot defined the mythic method as that of presenting "a continuous parallel between contemporaneity and antiquity," and credited Joyce with discovering it. Eliot himself had used it in two poems that appeared in his 1920 volume, *Poems,* in its simplest form in "Sweeney Erect" and in a very complex manipulation in "Sweeney Among the Nightingales." He may have gotten the idea for writing this way when he read the early chapters of *Ulysses* in 1917. If so — and it seems probable — then those like Shapiro who are now so angrily damning Eliot for his "method of the library" should damn Joyce instead.

After *The Waste Land* Eliot never used the mythical method again. It had served him well there to express his feeling (which may or may not have come to conscious thought) that sex and religion are intricately interwoven — for the Holy Grail, or cup, and the Knight's lance, of the Grail legends, were transparently sexual symbols — and his growing conviction that myth was a kind of knowing, and that in it would be found the only possible answer to the negations of scientific naturalism.

I have said so much about the poet's ideas and capacity for personal and poetic growth, and so little about the poems themselves, especially the major ones, for several reasons. For one thing, Eliot's best known poems have been analyzed and explicated to death, so that it is almost impossible to say anything about them without repeating what a half a dozen critics have said and quarreling with a half a dozen others. For another, the growing chorus of rejection of Eliot, especially when it comes from young poets whose work one may like, is an embarrassment that partially shapes one's strategy. I do not wish to join the chorus, yet it is clear that Eliot *was* very wrong about many things, especially in his prose. I have therefore emphasized precisely those aspects of his career in which he seems to me most defensible.

If I have said little about his *craft,* it is for a different reason. Without his craftsmanship, he would have remained a minor poet, to be sure; that *ideas alone,* no matter how timely or interesting or "true," do not make a *poet* is too obvious, and has been too much repeated for the past half-century, to need any further emphasis. But when we look at poetry from the point of view of a *reader,* we see that once the ideas and feelings in a poem come to seem unreal or unimportant to us, or even such as ought to be positively resisted, then the "craft" with which and through which they are expressed comes to seem unimpressive, or even a positive annoyance. To be what Eliot called Marianne Moore, the greatest living master of the light rhyme, in short, is not necessarily to be a poet of any consequence to *readers* of poetry, though perhaps other poets may profit by seeing how the trick is turned.

Eliot was a master craftsman, but those who don't like his ideas and attitudes and don't share his emotions feel that they must resist him all the harder for this, much as one would resist the very eloquent spokesman for racism or war. No one enjoys being manipulated, by a poet, an advertiser, a spell-binding political orator, or anyone else, particularly if he thinks he knows in advance that the attitudes and purposes of the manipulator are not his own. As James Dickey has put it recently, "Oddly enough, it is only in poems wherein we forget that our feelings have been deliberately evoked that poetry as an art justifies itself. One thing is certain: If the reader does not, through the writing, gain a new, intimate, and vital perspective on his own life as a human being, there is no poem at all. . . ."

Precisely. Or as Williams once said, in the discussion after a talk, "Unfortunately, Eliot *is* a great master of technique, but I can't read him with any pleasure." For Williams, Eliot's craftsmanship was unfortunate because it was dedicated to purposes Williams did not like and expressed ideas and emotions he could not share. In a critical climate in which Williams' attitude toward the Old Possum who doubled as the Aged Eagle is widespread and likely to grow, it will not advance Eliot's reputation as a poet to point out that only a very clever technician in verse would have thought of describing the typist's "love affair" in *The Waste Land* in hidden disintegrating sonnets. "April is the cruellest month" has proved a very memorable line, but those who for one reason or another think April is *not* cruel would prefer to forget it themselves and are likely to wish Eliot had not said it so well.

Except in the three poems in which he used the mythical method, which very well illustrate the theory of poetry put forth in "Tradition and the Individual Talent," as Stanley Edgar Hyman has brilliantly demonstrated, there is generally a wide discrepancy between Eliot's prose and his verse. There is nothing even remotely "classic" about the verse, for example, in any of that word's several possible meanings, even in the early years in which Eliot was recommending "classic" poetry in his essays and calling himself a "classicist." The doctrinal authority of the church is irrelevant to "Ash Wednesday," which moves us precisely because the voice we hear in it is not that of a bishop proclaiming doctrines but that of a would-be believer suffering from fluctuations in his faith. For a last illustration, the doctrines "behind" *Four Quartets* are Anglo-Catholic, which is to say, in philosophic terms, essentialist; but the poem itself can be better explicated in the terms provided by the religious Existentialists than it can be by Catholic dogma, which it does not contradict, but does not depend on for its effect, either. Eliot's dogmas are in his prose, not in his poetry.

The poems helped to bring an age to self-awareness — and so, in a sense, to create the age they reflected and expressed. But they also transcend the age, as they transcend the dogmas of Eliot's prose. They named what had been nameless — and so only dimly known — and what they named, they brought to consciousness.

Only by misreading could Karl Shapiro turn "Portrait of a Lady" to his purposes, to bolster his case against a poet he admittedly hates. Less angry and biased readers — readers who have no reason to feel threatened by Eliot — will continue to see that poem for the magnificent achievement in testing points of view it is. A bored and weary sophistication is no longer a fashionable pose among young intellectuals, but so long as there remains any reason for a thoughtful and sensitive person to feel emptiness and alienation, "Prufrock" will continue to speak to us. Every age is in some degree, when we look at it from the vantage point of high expectation, a waste land, where love fails and hope dwindles, and the springs of growth seem to have dried up.

The best poems of any period survive radical shifts in taste and point of view, but criticism is more vulnerable. Eliot was the period's most influential critic by far; whole schools of practicing critics took their cue from his most undeveloped metaphors, his off-handed observations, his hinted preferences. But a new generation is irritated and thrown off by the tone, which combines the pontifical and the casual; and the opinions and points of view themselves now seem wrong a good deal of the time, as indeed Eliot confessed they did to *him* in his later years. The critical pieces most likely to last — again, as he himself said — are the early essays in which he expressed his appreciation for poets he found helpful to him in shaping his own poetry, plus several essays on general theory, like "Tradition and the Individual Talent" and "The Music of Poetry." The later essays are wiser but less original.

Eliot's social ideas in *Thoughts After Lambeth, The Idea of a Christian Society,* and *Notes Towards the Definition of Culture* were idiosyncratic, and to many readers deplorable in the completeness of their reaction against contemporary trends, even when these books were written. Like a good many others of his generation, Eliot flirted with the Right for some years, and these works of his, and others too, express the depth of his repugnance for the modern world.[1] Yet, though there is some hostility in them, and some callousness too, chiefly they are the expressions of a wholly committed man doing his best to think through problems that are hard for us now to imagine as ever having existed. But poets are not often great social thinkers, and Eliot is no exception.

None of the plays achieves the perfection in its own kind that the poems do in theirs. They are obviously the work of an intelligent mind and more or less interesting, and as a body of work important in the history of modern poetic drama, but they are not important as *poetry* — were not intended to be. *Murder in the Cathedral,* Eliot's first experiment in the drama, is something of an exception to this statement; but Eliot decided that the poetry in it would be a distraction on the stage in a play about the modern world. He wrote his later plays in verse so muted and prosy that it is of little interest as poetry.

It is the poetry that will last, even though young poets will probably find it too, like the criticism, a positive hindrance to their own efforts for some years yet to come. Eliot's early and most influential poetry may be thought of as lending support to his Impersonal theory of the poet's relation to his art; and that theory seems to many today besides Shapiro monstrously wrong. It is perhaps Eliot, in both theory and practice, more than any other single poet or critic, who is responsible for the condition noted by James Dickey, that "belief in the value of one's personality has all but disappeared from our verse." Naturally it has, in the aftermath of a poetic period in which from Imagist theory on through the Ideogramic method and the Impersonal and Autotelic theory of art, the poet as *person* was denied any responsible role in his poetry.

Yet there is a sense in which Eliot's career as a poet might serve as a model even for those who think as Dickey does, that Eliot's Autotelic theory ends by making the poet "a kind of monster" with a bag of tricks by which he manipulates our emotions. Counting out the "born" poet and writing only of the "poet of the second birth," who is trying to *learn* to be a poet, and a better one, Dickey writes,

> The poet of the Second Birth must strive all his life to become, in Pierre-Jean Jouve's luminous phrase, "master of a superior secret." The secret does not, of course, reside in a complete originality, which does not and could not exist. It dwells, rather, in the development of personality, with its unique weight of experience and memory, as a writing instrument and in the ability to give literary influence a new dimension which has the quality of this personality as informing principle. The Second Birth is largely a matter of self-criticism and

> endless experiment, presided over by an unwavering effort to ascertain what is most satisfying to the poet's self as it develops, or as it remains more clearly what it has always been.

Dickey might be describing Eliot himself, here, though that was surely far from his intention. Eliot's early theory and early manner caught on and helped to create an age in poetry, but he himself left early Modernists behind to turn to other manners, other theories, other tasks. His own personality did develop, and, despite his theory, it is the "informing principle" of his work at all times. "Self-criticism and endless experiment" characterize his career. Behind the masks of the early work, and in the undisguised personal voice of the later poems, we sense a man who was not always wise, or always charitable, and who felt impelled to react against the spirit of the age in many ways that no longer seem necessary, but who was immensely intelligent, very sensitive, and continuously self-critical, so that he remained capable of growth. Daring, in flat contradiction of his earliest theory, to write his autobiography into colossal cipher, he told us how it was with him, and we are all the richer in his fortune.

CHAPTER XVI

The Idea of Order: Fictive Music

The primary word I-Thou can only be spoken with the whole being.

— Martin Buber, in *I and Thou*

The poet is the sayer, the namer, and represents beauty. He is a sovereign, and stands on the centre.

— Emerson, in "The Poet"

After one has abandoned a belief in God, poetry is that essence which takes its place as life's redemption.

— Stevens, in *Opus Posthumous*

All existence for a man turned away from the eternal is but a vast mime under the mask of the absurd. Creation is the great mime.

— Camus

WALLACE STEVENS

FROM reading much of the contemporary criticism of Wallace Stevens, or criticism of other poets in which Stevens serves the critic as a model, one imagines an unstated argument underlying the aesthetic discriminations. Stevens, so the argument would run, is the modern poet *par excellence* because, apart from his magnificent linguistic and architectonic resourcefulness, he alone completely refused to resort to the consolations of myth or the irrational to make his life easier to live or his poetry easier to write. He alone, then, is the completely honest, the completely modern poet, writing out of a full and unqualified acceptance of the naturalistic philosophy made obligatory for us by modern scientific knowledge. All the others, even Williams, allowed feeling and wish to enter into their thinking at some point and so proved untrue to what we *know* by the strictest kind of knowing.

Though the key terms of our imaginary argument are all loaded with philosophic preconceptions, and though the singling out of

Stevens for this kind of praise does injustice to his contemporaries, most obviously to Aiken and Williams, still the general intention of the argument serves to disclose a truth about Stevens and his work. He thought of himself as poetry's "harmonious skeptic," and of his work as the "fictive music" such a poet makes to counter the wholly unmusical chaos of reality. He became, eventually, dissatisfied with metaphor and symbol, and the fictive music created from them, and listened for a music from the sun itself; but the general drift of our imagined argument does not much distort Stevens' own understanding of his position and his role during the greater part of his career.

Stevens saw himself as the poet of "reality," a term which at first in his work suggests that which in fact *is,* as contrasted with what is wished for or imagined; then, and more characteristically, the unordered, the chaotic, the formless and meaningless; then, chiefly in the late works, the void, the nothingness; and finally, tentatively, the inhuman but not meaningless flow and mixture of being and nothingness. Most of his best, and best-known, poems imply the second and third of the understandings of "reality" just listed. In either case, whether nature outside man's consciousness is unordered and therefore without meaning or whether it is ultimately just nothing at all, the void, if reason — philosophy — can find no "reasons," no order, outside ourselves, then the imagination will have to satisfy our need for order. An imagined or "fictive" order will have to suffice.

On such considerations as these Stevens rested the tremendous claims he made for the poetic imagination and poetry itself. Poetry seemed to him to have, as he once put it, "a role of the utmost seriousness . . . a spiritual role." This was so because "After one has abandoned a belief in god, poetry is that essence which takes its place as life's redemption."

When he is theorizing about poetry, Stevens sometimes sounds like the Existentialist philosophers, particularly Heidegger and Sartre. "We are conceived in our conceits" has an unmistakable Existentialist ring. "Life's nonsense pierces us with strange relation" includes Existential overtones of the Absurd. We may think of Nietzsche and Sartre when we read, in *Opus Posthumous* (1957), that "in an age of disbelief, when the gods have come to an end, when we think of them as the aesthetic projections of a time that has passed, men turn to a fundamental glory of their own and from that create a style of bearing themselves in reality."

But despite the Existentialist ring of these statements and many others like them, Stevens' outlook is not really very close to that of the Existentialists. The antidote to nothingness he offers is purely aesthetic, contemplative, and solitary. Existential engagement, commitment, the possibility of discovering meaning in action and relation, such ideas as these are foreign to his way of thinking. When, late in life, he modified some of his earlier positions on the nature and role of poetry, and thus necessarily on the relations between imagination and reality, he moved still farther from Sartre. But even before his final phase, the analogy with Existentialism will not take us very far toward understanding him. The vaguely Existentialist flavor of "The poet presents the mind in the act of defending us against itself," for instance, is much less apparent in the extended statement of the same idea: "In an age of disbelief, or, what is the same thing, in a time that is largely humanistic, . . . it is for the poet to supply the satisfactions of belief, in his measure and in his style." "Satisfactions"? Here Stevens sounds less like Sartre than he does like Santayana, who seems to have influenced him considerably and to whom he wrote a poetic tribute. Santayana understood religion as a kind of poetry. Stevens took poetry to be a substitute for religion.

The title of Stevens' first volume, *Harmonium,* implies a wry acknowledgment that the poet feels himself out of tune with the times, perhaps even by instinct a Romantic. The "harmonium" is an old-fashioned reed organ, a contrivance suitable for playing a waltz or a hymn perhaps, but as unsuited to produce tones that would suggest the sounds of nature, of "reality," as it is to produce more complex music. The harmonium may be thought of as Stevens' ironic and self-deprecating first choice for his special instrument, as the aeolian harp was Emerson's. It suggests that melody is man-made, precariously achieved, not produced by the wind blowing in the window from outside. The last poem in *Harmonium* is an address "To the Roaring Wind," which, in our sleep, seems to be seeking a syllable, but to our waking intelligence says nothing. There is, in short, no melody, no order, no "meaning" in the sounds of the wind outside.

But if that is so, poem after poem in the volume asks, how are we to understand the relation between disordered reality and the harmonious products of the imagination? The poets lie too much, Nietzsche had said, echoing Plato, but no such simple denunciation of poetry will satisfy Stevens. Still, if it is to be asserted that poems are more than pleasant momentary escapes from an unpleasant reality, in what sense are they more than this? Are not all poets, past and present, more than a little absurd in claiming so much for the imagination?

Whatever may be the answer to this question, at least it is clear that the romantic poets of the past have falsified reality. Where is the meaning they have pretended to discover? "Alas! Have all the barbers lived in vain,/ That not one curl in nature has survived?" The poets of the past have actually betrayed the imagination by claiming too much for it. Poets who would rhyme "catarrhs" with "guitars" are not to be trusted. If the claim for poetry and the imagination is to be made at all today, it must be made by poets with cold minds, who, looking at nature, will see "Nothing that is not there and the nothing that is." The modern poet, just because he treasures the imagination and its works, must accept reality as it is, which is to say, as meaningless. The modern poet must be a realist.

In a tribute to another realist poet, Stevens states explicitly the philosophic assumptions underlying his ideas about poetry. "Nuances of a Theme by Williams" begins with the lines from Williams, "It's a strange courage/ you give me, ancient star:/ Shine alone in the sunrise/ toward which you lend no part!" then goes on to expand their meaning:

> Shine alone, shine nakedly, shine like bronze,
> that reflects neither my face nor any inner part
> of my being, shine like fire, that mirrors nothing.

Stevens asks the star to resist man's efforts to anthropomorphize nature: "Lend no part to any humanity that suffuses/ You in its own light," he asks. Nonetheless, the realist poet, as in "A Quiet Normal Life," can create a light of his own:

> There was no fury in transcendent forms.
> But his actual candle blazed with artifice.

The style, the manner, the voice we hear in the early poetry are all designed to make the largest possible claim for "artifice," for poetry and the imagination, while protecting the poet from the charge of claiming too much. Stevens' wit often serves the same purpose as Frost's humor: it is a defensive maneuver that puts the reader in the wrong if he takes the poet too seriously. Thus in

"Earthy Anecdote," for instance, the *manner* of the poem effectively blocks any attempts to put possibly embarrassing philosophical questions to the poet. The firecat is the imagination subduing the clattering bucks of reality, forcing them into the circular forms of art. Everything in the poem works to prevent our asking the relevant question for philosophical aesthetics: In what sense does the making of a poem alter anything outside the poem? The poem is orderly, but is disorderly *reality,* as Stevens conceives it, changed, or defied, or escaped from, or what?

Similarly, in "The Plot Against the Giant," the girls who "check," "abash," and finally "undo" giant reality, using odors, colors, and sounds to lure him to his destruction, have "conquered" brute meaningless fact, not outside the poem but *in* the poem; that the poem exists shows that chaos can be ordered. But whether this aesthetic affirmation has any implications for metaphysics, the tone of the poem forbids us to ask. "Words alone are certain good," Stevens once said and often seems to have felt in the early years of his career.

But that he was not content to rest in aestheticism is clear as early as "The Comedian as the Letter C," which he once called his "antimythological poem." Perhaps the most serious and important effort to deal directly with the question, What can poetry do in an age of science? in our poetry of this century, "The Comedian" comes very close to ending in the conclusion that William James said even Pyrrhonistic skepticism itself left standing, that the only thing we can really know is that the consciousness of the moment exists. Very close to this, I said; but, in terms of what can only be called *hope,* not quite to this conclusion. For Crispin, the barber-valet-poet, recognizing his absurdity and the hopelessness of finding Truth, still preserved his "integrity," and in doing so suggested the possibility of a development in Stevens' thought that came about only very much later: "He gripped more closely the essential prose"—that is, truth, reality—"As being, in a world so falsified,/ The one integrity for him . . ." Crispin ends, that is, by becoming a "realist" poet; but with this difference, that he leaves open the possibility that at some time in the future the "prose" truth "to which all poems were incident" might wear a different aspect, one which would seem less inimical to the values of poetry. In literal truth, he decided, lay his only integrity, "unless/ That prose should wear a poem's guise at last." The line foreshadows the new way of putting his problem that we find in Stevens' late poem

"The Rock." Stevens's own integrity as man and poet is suggested by the many years he endured the despair implicit in "The Comedian" while continuing to nourish the hope that prose truth might wear a different guise at last.

Throughout *Harmonium,* the truth Stevens desired is contrasted principally with religion, which is understood as man's principal illusion. Reared in an orthodox Christian family, Stevens gave up his childhood faith early but never forgot it. "Romantic," "idealistic," "religious," and "illusory" or "fictive" formed for him a cluster of meanings so largely overlapping as to be at times almost interchangeable. The strength of desire for belief sharpened the militancy of his skepticism. That is one of the reasons why "Sunday Morning" is as great a poem as it is. There is passionate longing in it for what has been lost and must continue to be denied. The longing is not, of course, for the woman's Christian beliefs as such, but for something they represent to the speaker, some lost security perhaps. The poem is at once naturalistic in its ideas and religious in its feelings. The woman's dreams of "Dominion of the blood and sepulchre" are denied by the argument of the poem, but the speaker who argues away the woman's faith shows himself capable of experiencing religious emotions. The woman is essentially a device to make clear the separation between dreaming and thinking. Her presence in the poem gives the appearance of dramatic form to what in effect is an interior monologue, a debate within the speaker between aspects of himself. The rational mind wins the argument, but the man finds no exhilaration in his victory. Despite its denial of what it takes to be the supernatural and transcendental, "Sunday Morning" is the product of a religious imagination.

In the volumes after *Harmonium* Stevens tried to develop further his ideas on the relation of imagination to reality, or the role of the poet in a scientific age. What did it *mean,* he asked in poem after poem, to say, as he had in both prose and verse, that poetry could be a "redemptive" force? How could a music recognized as "fictive" create for men "a style of bearing themselves in reality"? The poems in Stevens' second volume, *Ideas of Order,* restate, often more abstractly, formulations of the problems and the answers that had already appeared in *Harmonium.* "Sad Strains of a Gay Waltz" promises that soon "some harmonious skeptic" will unite reality and the imagination in a "skeptical music" that will include both motion and shadows. Meanwhile, "The epic of disbelief/ Blares oftener and soon, will soon be constant," and

> There is order in neither sea nor sun.
> The shapes have lost their glistening.
> There are these sudden mobs of men.

In the most famous, and perhaps greatest, poem in the volume, "The Idea of Order at Key West," Stevens explores the old problem in the old terms by way of a new example, a girl singing beside the sea. How did the "order" of the song arise from the "disorder" of reality, if the girl herself is a part of nature?

> Whose spirit is this? we said, because we knew
> It was the spirit that we sought and knew
> That we should ask this often as she sang.

Between the sound of the sea and the sound of the song, there seemed to be no real relationship:

> The sea was not a mask. No more was she.
> The song and water were not medleyed sound . . .

Nature is *not* a symbolic language; nature does not reveal spirit. The beauty of the girl's song is her creation alone: "She was the single artificer of the world/ In which she sang." How then could the effect have been to "master" the night and "portion out" the sea? Can a momentary subjective impression of beauty, even if we are wholly caught up in it, change the way things *are?* The sea, reality, the poem says, is what it is, and what it is, is not in any sense melodic or harmonious. "Reality" is alien not only to song but to the girl and to us.

Nevertheless, though the terms of the dichotomy have not changed from what they had been in Stevens' earliest poems, the mood has changed. Crispin, to be sure, had allowed for the possibility that prose truth might approach poetic truth at last; but his tone in making the concession seems to imply that the possibility of this ever happening is slight and the significance, if it should happen, trifling. What the speaker is meditating on at the end of "The Idea of Order" is no mere conceptual possibility but something desired, an even more significant, or revealing, song than the girl's, a song made of

Words of the fragrant portals, dimly-starred,
And of ourselves and of our origins,
In ghostlier demarcations, keener sounds.

In Stevens' next volume, *Parts of a World,* the key poem of the volume, so far as Stevens' development is concerned, is "The Poems of Our Climate." Here Stevens bids farewell to "Florida," that is, to hedonism and aestheticism, to putting great value on the colors and sounds and shapes of things simply for the *pleasure* they can give. In effect, this poem means that Stevens is renouncing his role as a "connoisseur of chaos." We need "more," this poem says, "than a world of white and snowy scents," more than the aesthetic pleasures one may enjoy while retaining "a mind of winter." But the poem also restates the view of "Sunday Morning," that "The imperfect is our paradise," and insists that whatever the "more" may be, it must not be "mythic," that is, not religious. Perhaps we shall have to be content, the speaker in the poem concludes, with whatever pleasures there are in thought itself, in meditation considered as an end in itself. There are, after all, the "pleasures" of "the never-resting mind."

"Pleasures" and "never-resting" tell us how to place the poem in the story of Stevens' slow growth from reluctant hedonist to skeptical listener for sounds of the eternal within the real. "Pleasures" reminds us of the "satisfactions" of belief, and "never-resting" reminds us that Stevens had never, even in his earliest period, been "satisfied" by any "satisfactions" that were not ultimately more than "satisfying," whether those "satisfactions" might be aesthetic or religious. As another poem in the volume puts it, the task of the modern poet with a "never-resting" mind is to find out "what will suffice" to keep us alive and growing in understanding.

The majority of those who care for Stevens have found a noticeable decline in his late work, with some readers placing the beginning of the decline immediately after *Harmonium* and some at various later points, but none later than *Parts of a World.* The decline seems to me to be less noticeable than it has sometimes been said to be; yet, so far as the number of completely memorable poems in each new volume is concerned, it seems real enough. For a decade or so around the 1940's, Stevens appears to have been marking time. The reason, I suspect, lay in his increasing preoccupation with his great problem. When he turned away from the problem, as he did for instance in "Idiom of the Hero" and "Girl in the Nightgown," he could still write as powerfully as ever. But too often now he skirted the edge of the problem in poems that were weaker versions of poems in *Harmonium,* or attacked it directly in poems that substituted a pseudo logic for feeling and perception.

It is not surprising that Stevens spent some years repeating himself when we consider that the problem he was increasingly dedicated to thinking out was insoluble. All he could do was restate it and keep on restating it. "Imagination" meant for him all that was valuable, good, alive, formed or ordered, and meaningful. Reality, by this time in his career, meant the void, the unthinkable nothingness. So far as it had any qualities at all, they were wholly negative: whatever was not formed, not ordered, not beautiful, not valuable, and not meaningful, was "real." But to compare a mere negation, an "excluder," as contemporary linguistic philosophers call it, with something that has positive, definable qualities, is to set up a problem to which there can, by definition, be no philosophic solution. The terms in which Stevens conceived his problem made it a pseudoproblem. One may talk profitably about the relations between being and nothingness, or imagination and logic, or imagination and the world, but not about the relation between imagination and "nothing."

There is perhaps another reason too why Stevens' development involved him in a long pause between his initial statements of his problem and his final tentative suggestions for a solution. One of the lessons to be learned from American poetry as we have surveyed it, and equally from contemporary philosophy, is that, since the eighteenth century at least, no final or religious meanings will emerge when experience is approached in purely intellectualistic terms. The agony of most of the "schoolroom poets" alone, if there were no other evidence, ought to convince us of that. In our culture, whatever may be true of earlier or other cultures, "pure knowledge" has seemed to the poets, and to most of the philosophers, to suggest or validate no ultimate values at all.

A number of philosophers of our time believe this is true not just for modern Western history but always and everywhere. Gabriel Marcel and Martin Buber, for instance, would agree with an idea suggested by Emerson much earlier, that when people and things become for us, or for anyone, anywhere, simply "objects of knowledge," they immediately start evaporating, shrinking, thinning out to nothingness, entering the void. As Buber once put it, using the word "spirit" to include both what Stevens called "mind" and what he called "imagination,"

> The spirit is never independently effective in life in itself alone, but in relation to the world: possessing power that permeates the world of *It,* transforming it. The spirit is truly "in its own realm" if it can confront the world that is unlocked to it, give itself to this world, and in its relation with it save both itself and the world.

Emerson had implied this way of viewing the relation of "imagination" to "reality" when he defined the poetic gift as a very high kind of seeing, which "becomes" what it sees. One of the reasons why we should be grateful for the advance of modern psychoanalytic knowledge is that it has shown us, convincingly, that our moral and emotional natures are as significantly related to our ability to recognize "truth" as are our purely cognitive abilities.

In short, there are, when the problem is considered in purely intellectual terms, not just "thirteen ways of looking at a blackbird" but probably an infinite number, depending on an unknown and perhaps unknowable number of factors, including the particular spot in space and time from which the uninvolved consciousness looks. If one *likes* blackbirds, on the other hand, or feels any sort of "interpenetration of being" with whatever contains any evidence of being, then the number of ways of looking is considerably reduced.

As the years went by, Stevens became more and more locked in the solitary consciousness, more and more an observer of an unreal "reality" conceived as "out there." The possibility first announced in "The Comedian," that "prose" reality might some day be seen to have some of the qualities of "poetry" persisted, but its realization seemed for many years ever less probable.

Two poems included in *Parts of a World* will illustrate what is meant both by the logical difficulties inherent in the problem of the relation of imagination and reality as Stevens stated it, and by the sometimes harmful effects on his poetry of his intellectualizing and objectifying tendencies. The poem called "Study of Two Pears" takes the form of a dialogue between the side of the speaker's mind that insists on reality and the side that speaks for imagination. "Realism" says the pears are simply what they *are:* "They resemble nothing else." Imagination notes their colors and forms. In the end the speaker himself, who contains and can criticize both attitudes, tries to mediate between the two by allowing that the "shadows" of the pears are "blobs on the green cloth," but the pears *themselves* are still what they are. To the realistic poet, they ". . . are not seen/ As the observer wills."

The poem means both more and less than that the imagination should discipline itself by letting a concern for fact restrain its flights of fancy. It means more because its opposition is between the pears as observed and the pears as they are in themselves, when unobserved. But Stevens could discover no logical way to make any progress toward solving an opposition like this.

The poem also means less than it says it does. Since what the reader knows about the pears in the poem is given almost entirely by the precise observations assigned in the poem to the imagination, there is no point in the speaker's turning, in the final stanza, from the pears themselves to their shadows, or in his warning against seeing them as one wills. It is precisely the "imagination" that *has* "seen" the pears. The only positive statement assigned to the "literal" or "scientific" mind is that "They are round/ Tapering toward the top." The conclusion of the poem is thus doctrinaire.

"The Glass of Water" will illustrate the extent to which in these years the sensible world for Stevens was becoming assimilated to the void. A glass of water would seem to be a concrete and tangible object, but no —

> That the glass would melt in heat,
> That the water would freeze in cold,
> Shows that this object is merely a state,
> One of many, between two poles. . . .

The speaker concludes with the observation that ". . . Among the dogs and dung,/ One would continue to contend with one's ideas."

The implication is that if so "real" and solid an object as a glass of water is merely a "state," then the politicians and others who appear in the later part of the poem are merely "states" too, mere figments of thought. One is reminded of the way a famous astrophysicist of the period, Sir Arthur Eddington, explained, in his Introduction to *The Nature of the Physical World,* that the table on which he was writing *appeared* to be solid, brown, and so on, but that *knowledge* revealed it as nothing but atoms moving in space, and the atoms as only electrons moving in space, and the electrons . . . and so on. Nothing solid or brown was there at all. The scientist concluded from this that the seeming, or phenomenal, world is a thought in the mind of a mathematical God. Without Eddington's religious presuppositions, Stevens was left with the void. As one of his notes in "Adagia" puts it, "Reality is a vacuum." The idea does not seem to be one that would be likely to contribute to a poet's growth.

Stevens did not always, of course, find the experienced world empty of reality, as we may see even in *Parts of a World,* from which I have selected my illustrations of a tendency that could be more widely illustrated in both this and later volumes. "Idiom of the Hero" and "Girl in a Nightgown" in *Parts of a World,* as I have said, have no direct bearing on Stevens' great theme and would not at all illustrate the tendency I have posited. Both poems indeed turn away from the theme, the first of them explicitly— "This chaos will not be ended,/ The red and the blue house blended . . ." "Girl in a Nightgown" is even less argumentative about philosophical matters and an even richer and more memorable poem, far more so surely than "Connoisseur of Chaos" on the facing page in *Collected Poems* in which we are dropped back again into theses and countertheses.

But though Stevens' volumes of the 1940's offer many examples of fine poems that do not illustrate his tendency, especially during this period, to objectivize and intellectualize the substance and value out of experience, it was not until the 1950's, in the last years of his life, that we find him moving very significantly and consistently beyond the position by the middle of the 1930's, in *Ideas of Order. The Auroras of Autumn* and *The Rock* contain much that is simply good late Stevens, but a half dozen or more of these late poems introduce a decisively new note. I shall let three of them serve as examples of the direction Stevens' thought and experience seem to have been taking in the last years of his life.

"Metaphor as Degeneration" shows so clearly a movement beyond the position Stevens had reached in "The Idea of Order at Key West" that it is surprising that it has been so seldom mentioned in discussions of Stevens' "ideas of order." Unlike many of the late philosophical poems, this one is rich in images, even while it argues that man cannot imagine ultimate reality without distorting it. Metaphors do *not* tell the truth, it says. Nevertheless, "being" — which philosophers usually write as "Being" — is as real as nonbeing, or death and nothingness — the "chaos" of the earlier poems.

"Being" in this poem is not merely imagined or projected by *us,* is not "fictive," is not merely aesthetic. It is — in a way the poem *says* cannot be said but *is* "said" in this poem — it is "experienceable" in some sense, in the farthest reaches of experience, in what Philip Wheelwright called "threshold experience." "Being" for Stevens is "The swarthy water/ That flows round the earth and through the skies,/ Twisting among the universal spaces . . ." "River noises" are the images by which we know this water, which also appears, at times, as a "blown sheen — or is it air?" The conflict in the poem is no longer the one we expect in Stevens, between imagination and reality, but a new one, for him, between being and nonbeing, both of them available to imagination and thought and experience.

"The Rock," the title poem of Stevens' last volume, returns to the discursive and argumentative late manner and is perhaps for that reason alone less impressive than "Metaphor as Degeneration." Nevertheless, if not as powerful, it is just as clear an example of Stevens' new way of conceiving his great theme. Reversing the earlier assertion of "the domination of black," denying the earlier conviction that outside the mind, in "reality," there was finally only "nothing," the void, he now writes,

> It is an illusion that we were ever alive,
> Lived in the houses of mothers, arranged ourselves
> By our own motions in a freedom of air.
>
> . . . .
>
> Even our shadows, their shadows, no longer remain.
> The lives these lived in the mind are at an end.
> They never were . . . The sounds of the guitar
>
> Were not and are not. Absurd. The words spoken
> Were not and are not. It is not to be believed.

Apparently granted a new "birth of sight," the poet now defines the poem not as an artifact but as an "icon," and finds evidence of "the figuration of blessedness" in leaves ("the lilacs came and bloomed"), in the icon, and in man himself.

In the third section of the poem, "Forms of the Rock in a Night-Hymn," Stevens writes in a vein that is closer to late Emerson than anything he had ever written before. "The rock is the gray particular of man's life," the section begins, and continues, "The rock is the stern particular of the air . . ." This is in effect what Emerson had meant by "fate" in the essay of that title in *Conduct of Life*. What Emerson had meant by "illusions" in the earlier essay "Experience," which foreshadows some of the themes of *Conduct of Life,* is the subject of the middle part of the final section of "The Rock." [1]

The concluding lines of "The Rock," though, suggest Whitman more than they do Emerson. They celebrate Being as "That in which space itself is contained." Except for the strictness of the prosody, they could almost be imagined as coming from any of a number of Whitman's poems, perhaps especially "The Sleepers":

> . . . . the things illumined
>
> By day, night and that which night illumines,
> Night and its midnight-minting fragrances,
> Night's hymn of the rock, as in a vivid sleep.

The fact that Stevens wished the new insights and attitudes he had expressed in "The Rock" to be taken as his last word on the problem he had treated for so many years is suggested by his arrangement of the *Collected Poems.* Just as Frost placed last in his final volume "In winter in the woods alone," which echoes and comments on "Into My Own," the first poem in his *Complete Poems,* so Stevens gave final position to "Not Ideas About the Thing But the Thing Itself," his most explicit reversal of his earlier view. Thus *Collected Poems* opens with "Earthy Anecdote," suggesting that imagination forces chaotic reality into the circular forms of art, and closes with a poem that finds "choral rings" surrounding the sun itself. There would be no need for the imagination to "plot" against giant reality if circles were not fictive but real. The poem suggests a new idea of order and a new role for the imagination, a distinctly Emersonian role at last.

"At the earliest ending of winter,/ In March," the speaker hears the first bird of the morning, singing before sunrise. The sound is only a "scrawny cry . . . in the early March wind" and at first the speaker takes it for no more than "a sound in his mind." But it was no fictive music he was hearing, no product of "the vast ventriloquism" of dream. It came from outside, from reality itself, as "the sun was coming from outside":

> That scrawny cry — it was
> A chorister whose c preceded the choir.
> It was part of the colossal sun,
>
> Surrounded by its choral rings,
> Still far away. It was like
> A new knowledge of reality.

CHAPTER XVII

Sic Transit Gloria: Six Famous Poets

We do not, with sufficient plainness, or sufficient profoundness, address ourselves to life, nor dare we chant our own times and social circumstance. . . . We have yet had no genius in America, with tyrannous eye, which knew the value of our incomparable materials, and saw, in the barbarism and materialism of the times, another carnival of the same gods whose picture he so much admires in Homer; then in the middle age; then in Calvinism. Banks and tariffs, the newspaper and caucus, Methodism and Unitarianism, are flat and dull to dull people, but rest on the same foundations of wonder as the town of Troy, and the temple of Delphos, and are as swiftly passing away.

— Emerson, in "The Poet"

The impulse of the new verse [*of the 1920's*] *seems to abide in the poets, all Westerners, who trumpeted, as if in obedience to Emerson and Whitman, America's common moods.*

— Stanley T. Williams, in
American Literature, 1933

LITERARY historians of the "New Poetry" movement of the second and third decades of this century have often started their story with the founding of *Poetry: A Magazine of Verse* by Harriet Monroe in Chicago in 1912, and then gone on from there, keeping their eyes on the early issues of the magazine, struggling to bring some kind of order out of the multifarious and undigestible facts before them. Trying to discern the defining characteristics of the movement, they have found themselves faced with the impossible task of generalizing about poets who had nothing in common but their "newness."

Within a year and a half or so of its first issue of October 1912, *Poetry* had published the work of Ezra Pound and Grace Hazard Conkling; William Vaughn Moody and H.D.; Tagore and John Gould Fletcher; Vachel Lindsay and Robert Frost; Amy Lowell and Carl Sandburg. By 1915 it had added Wallace Stevens and T. S. Eliot to its roster. Having started from the perspective provided by *Poetry,* our poetic historians have asked: What do all these poets have in common?

With the distance afforded by the passage of half a century, it would appear now that the only answer that would not do violence to some of the evidence would be "not much." We can learn more about the characteristics of the poetry that dominated the first half of our century by looking long at the work of Pound, Eliot, Stevens, and Williams than we are likely to by any survey, no matter how prolonged, of the early years of *Poetry* magazine.

Between its founding and about 1920, the magazine championed "free verse" and Imagism. Perhaps it was fortunate, in the long run, that Miss Monroe had only a vague notion of what her two causes entailed; for if she had been clearer in her mind about them, she might not have welcomed to her magazine's pages so many poets who were neither Imagists nor writers of "free" verse. Her own taste was strongly for the simple, direct, and native in poetry, but she let Pound bludgeon her into publishing Eliot, and, at Pound's urging again, gave Frost his first American publication in an important national magazine. She managed to pay her contributors, and she was hospitable to unpublished writers. Her magazine did more for poetry than we would be led to expect if we knew only her autobiography, *A Poet's Life,* or her own slender volume of verse. *The Difference and Other Poems* is the only book of poetry I have ever seen that both opens and closes with a photograph of the author, who looks very distinguished in both poses. In between the handsome portraits there is some very undistinguished verse.

As a native Chicagoan who was proud of her city and hopeful that it might become a center for the arts, Miss Monroe was especially on the lookout for mid-western talent. Vachel Lindsay, Edgar Lee Masters, and Carl Sandburg, all from Illinois, seemed for a while, not only to her but to others like Amy Lowell, who ranked them in her *A Critical Fable* just after Frost and Robinson and just before herself, to justify her regionalist expectations. That the first two of them have almost completely ceased to be read by people under fifty, and that the third has come to be known chiefly as a folklorist, ballad-singer, and biographer of Lincoln, is the kind of historical irony that makes critics and editors apprehensive about recognizing new talent.

VACHEL LINDSAY

Vachel Lindsay might really have been what he has been called, a "folk poet," if the conditions for true folk poetry had existed in this country in the first third of the century. Again, if he had had more intelligence and self-restraint, it might not have been merely a wry joke to call him, as Peter Viereck has, "the Dante of the Fundamentalists." If self-criticism had been possible for him, he might have created more than an occasional poem capable of reminding us of Blake and Emerson and Whitman.

In a confused and thoroughly subintellectual way, Lindsay tried to re-express for mid-America in the twentieth century the visionary romantic affirmations of these three. His Disciplies of Christ (Campbellite) religious background gave him millennial hopes. He had been touched by Swedenborg, through friends in Springfield. Curiously, several of the influences on him paralleled those that affected Blake and Emerson. As an art student in Chicago, Lindsay had made copious notes on Blake and had tried, he tells us, to learn to draw like him. When we glance through the final edition of his *Collected Poems,* with its endpaper drawings of the "Village Improvement Parade," its "mystic" "Map of the Universe," and its insistence that we study certain drawings and poems for their hidden meanings, we see a Blakean influence that Lindsay never adequately acknowledged. Reading the poems, we find frequent verbal echoes as well as thematic parallels in poems on children, the poor, and the immanent divinity. But more often than not, Blake's visions seem ludicrous in Lindsay's version. Mysticism has been vulgarized to mystagoguery when a poet can speak so easily of "mystic Springfield" and say that "Swedenborg should be rewritten in Hollywood."

Emerson and Whitman are the only American poets mentioned in Lindsay's "Litany of Heroes"—

> Then let us seek out shining Emerson,
> Teacher of Whitman, and better priest of man,
> The self-reliant granite American,

but Lindsay's work does not make it entirely clear how much or how well he knew their writings. In the first of his "Three Poems About Mark Twain," he contrasts them both with the "genius of the stream" whom one cannot dodge:

All praise to Emerson and Whitman, yet
The best they have to say, their sons forget.

Still, no poet in this century wrote more as though he had not forgotten Emerson's advice in "The Poet" to write about the "poem" of America. With Whitmanic inclusiveness, Lindsay sang the praises of Johnny Appleseed and John L. Sullivan; General William Booth and Lincoln; liberal Governor Altgeld of Illinois and William Jennings Bryan; Jane Addams and Theodore Roosevelt; Pocahontas and the bronco that would not be broken. And once at least, in one of his best poems, he must have been remembering Emerson's very words about the carnival of the gods, Troy, and the "foundations of wonder." "Kalamazoo" opens with the fine lines,

Once, in the city of Kalamazoo,
The gods went walking, two and two,

but soon appears to be breaking down into sentimentality and gaucherie:

For in Kalamazoo in a cottage apart
Lived the girl with the innocent heart.
Thenceforth the city of Kalamazoo
Was the envied, intimate chum of the sun,

only to rise to authentic expression again as the humor and the wonder are played off against each other, almost as though Lindsay were adding a note to Emerson's comment on the Troys of America, saying that one need not be solemn about seeing beauty and romance in the awkward. The girl with "the innocent heart," which was perhaps not so innocent after all, his Helen,

. . . made great poets of wolf-eyed men —
The dear queen-bee of Kalamazoo,
With her crystal wings and her honey heart.
We fought for her favors a year and a day
(Oh, the bones of the dead, the Oshkosh dead,
That were scattered along her pathway red!)
And then, in her harum-scarum way,

She left with a passing traveller-man —
With a singing Irishman
Went to Japan.

. . . .

Who burned this city of Kalamazoo —
Love-town Troy-town Kalamazoo?

Lindsay did not often write so well. When the subject was closer to him, he was likely to fall back on flat assertions like those with which "Johnny Appleseed's Hymn to the Sun" opens —

Christ the dew in the clod,
  Christ the sap in the trees,
Christ the light in the waterfall,
  Christ the soul of the sun. . . .

In general, the Johnny Appleseed poems are among Lindsay's best, but simply to assert the idea of immanence this way is to leave a good many readers unpersuaded. Jones Very would no doubt have liked the lines, since they say what he had said, often more strikingly. But it is not hard to imagine Pound's reaction.

With an almost complete incapacity for self-criticism, Lindsay was capable of writing not simply flat lines but whole poems we can only call bathetic and absurd. The *Collected Poems* is full of verse that is embarrassing to read — if one sees any merit at all in Lindsay. One example will speak for all. "A Rhyme About an Electrical Advertising Sign" could be called Emersonian in its perceiving the "foundations of wonder" on which the then novel product of technology rests; or Whitmanic in "singing the strong light works of engineers"; it might be noted that it states one of the chief themes in Hart Crane's "The Bridge." But noting how central it is, thematically, in the native romantic tradition cannot save it as a poem. Lindsay's millennial expectations seem only naive when applied to this subject, so that a cynical rejoinder is likely to be the reader's only response to its vision of spiritual progress without pain. Very soon now, the poem says, the newly invented signs will cease to advertise men's collars and new fashions for "shame-weary girls," and will help us ascend to the divine — perhaps by advertising church services?

The signs in the street and the signs in the skies
Shall make a new Zodiac, guiding the wise,
And Broadway make one with that marvellous stair
That is climbed by the rainbow-clad spirits of prayer.

When *this* happens, one assumes that the ladder of spiritual contemplation will have been made plain and easy for the masses.

When we have read this and a good many other poems equally bad, and when we have noted that "The Congo" is absurd if it is read as its subtitle directs us to read it, as a "study" of the Negro race, and that the syncopated rhythms of both "The Congo" and "General Booth" get tiresome before the poems end — when we have noted all this and more that is damaging to what little reputation Lindsay still has, we are likely to conclude that he ought to be totally forgotten.

But we should be wrong. This poet who pleased patriotic critics like Amy Lowell by being so unmistakably grass-roots American, progressive, liberal, and wholesome — all in contrast with the attitudes of expatriates like Pound and Eliot — actually wrote quite a few fine poems and dozens of memorable ones. The Johnny Appleseed poems are worth reading once at least, and several other celebrations of the land and its people are unsurpassed of their kind — "The Golden Whales of California," "Abraham Lincoln Walks at Midnight," "The Eagle That Is Forgotten," for instance. "The Leaden Eyed" expresses Lindsay's thoroughly democratic sympathies far more effectively than "Why I Voted the Socialist Ticket." There are even moving passages in "Bryan, Bryan, Bryan, Bryan," in which the naive Populism is rendered as the memory of what it was like to be sixteen and in love and a Democrat in 1896 in Springfield. The best of Lindsay is worth saving.

EDGAR LEE MASTERS

That cannot be so definitely said about another poet immensely popular for a few years, whom Amy Lowell ranked higher than Pound or Eliot or Stevens. Edgar Lee Masters has more recently been called a "one book" poet, but it begins to appear that that too is an exaggeration. Reading his work along with that of Vachel Lindsay and the early work of Carl Sandburg, all of whom were enthusiastically welcomed by most of the "best critics" in the country at the time, we get a fresh insight into the excuse the

American cultural scene offered for Pound's inveterate rage and Eliot's gesture of disaffiliation. *Spoon River Anthology* became in 1915 that rare phenomenon, a book of poetry that is a "best seller," and remained so for several years, while Frost and Williams were still having difficulty getting published.

Lindsay's life ended badly, in bitterness, insanity, and finally suicide, but his verse at least was full of exuberance. Masters' work was almost as depressed from the beginning as the man himself became in his later years. The sketches of the inhabitants of Spoon River include some of people who found satisfaction in their lives, to be sure, but neither Masters nor his readers could identify with them enough to remember them. As in Sherwood Anderson's fictional counterpart of *Spoon River, Winesburg, Ohio,* published just three years later, repression, frustration, and eventual defeat seem to be the rule in the community, and the elegiac tone is unbroken even in the sections that tell of characters like Lucinda Matlock, who *says* she loved life, but protests too much in saying it.

Symptomatically, Father Malloy is not allowed to speak for himself as the others do who lie in the cemetery on the hill. Buried in "holy ground" — the separate Roman Catholic cemetery — he is said to have "believed in the joy of life." He "did not seem to be ashamed of the flesh," and he "faced life as it is." The speaker in Father Malloy's section thinks of Father Malloy as "Siding with us who would rescue Spoon River/ From the coldness and the dreariness of village morality." But the speaker cannot imagine what the priest would *say* if he spoke for himself; the faith that produced his joy and his healthy moral realism remains a total mystery.

In the "Father Malloy" section we come to understand the double focus of the whole poem. Implicitly, two different, and conflicting, general meanings emerge from this work that avowedly offers us only a realistic cross-section view of village life. Self-consciously, Masters is contributing his bit to the "revolt from the village" and the repudiation of lingering "Puritanism," a revolt that would continue to gain momentum for at least the next ten years, especially in works of fiction. From this point of view, Father Malloy offers the model for the better life. But at the same time, more or less unconsciously, Masters is saying, less explicitly but with more feeling, that the real enemy is not Puritan morality but "the nature of things," which to a thinking person made impossible the faith that sustained Father Malloy and Lucinda Matlock, who speaks as from Heaven. If life without the religious faith of these two is simply depressing, and if faith is impossible even to imagine except in Catholic priests and women who died long ago at ninety-six, then it would seem that the achieved meaning of the book is not that we ought to leave the village and cease being Puritans but that life's woe is irremediable.

In his Introduction to Robinson's *King Jasper,* Frost would later praise Robinson for having treated "immedicable" woes, "griefs" instead of merely "grievances." Masters and Robinson have in common a kind of grayness of tone. But there is an important difference between them: Robinson fully understood how "immedicable" the griefs that concerned him were, while it is not clear from *Spoon River Anthology* whether Masters did or not. It seems rather more likely that he didn't know exactly what he *did* mean, or what he intended, in the poem.

Though he had written a good many verses in formal meters before *Spoon River,* this first — and, as it turned out, last — great success spurred Masters on to rapid production. In the following year he brought out two more books of poems, *Songs and Satires* and *The Great Valley.* Not one poem in either book gives us any clue to the success of *Spoon River,* but a good many of them point to the unmentioned source of that poem's depressed tone. "Terminus," for example, in *Songs and Satires,* makes no secret of what the real source of the depression is:

> There is a void the agèd world
> Throws over the spent heart. . . .

If the metaphor seems mixed here, the *idea* is clear enough. Later in the poem we get a specific statement of what makes the heart empty and the sky "hollow." If we recall that Christ spoke of himself as a vine, the reason for the void in the heart is sufficiently plain:

> Oh, heart of man and heart of woman,
> Thirsting for blood of the vine,
> Life waits till the heart has lived too much
> And then pours in new wine!

In *The Great Valley* we find a more impressive, because better written, clue to the unacknowledged meaning of *Spoon River.*

In the long dramatic poem "The Gospel of Mark," in which Mark speaks to a younger disciple, the negative language and the agonized tone of Mark's final words remind us of many passages in similar poems by Robinson:

> No, it cannot be.
> Man's soul, the chiefest flower of all we know,
> Is not the toy of Malice or of Sport.
> It is not set apart to be betrayed,
> Or gulled to its undoing, left to dash
> Its hopeless head against this rock's exception,
> No water for its thirst, no life to feed it,
> No law to guide it. . . .
> . . . .
> Go write what I have told you, come what will
> I'm going to the catacombs to pray.

Masters explained the title of his next book of verse, in 1918, this way, in his dedication to William Marion Reedy: "I call this book 'Toward the Gulf,' a title importing a continuation of the attempts of Spoon River and The Great Valley to mirror the age and the country in which we live." Taking Masters at his word, we turn to one of the sketches in the book:

> Louise was a nymphomaniac.
> She was married twice.
> Both husbands fled from her insatiable embraces.
> At thirty-two she became a woman on a telephone list,
> Subject to be called,
> And for two years ran through a daily orgy of sex,
> When blindness came on her, as it came on her father
> before her,
> And she became a Christian Scientist,
> And led an exemplary life.

It is clear that Louise had a lot of hard luck, except for those two fortunate years when she could combine her vocation and her avocation, but it is not clear just what aspects of the age and the country her story mirrors. Could it be the rising divorce rate, or the rapid growth of the Christian Science Society, during those years?

The title of Masters' book of 1919, *Starved Rock,* could have been explicated with the same statement he made about *Toward the Gulf,* and in his very long *Domesday Book* of 1920 he returned to the formula of *Spoon River,* except that he now used blank verse instead of free verse. After this came many books, including *The New Spoon River* in 1924. Masters died in 1950, fifteen years after his last work, a study of Vachel Lindsay. His life is as sad a story as any he told in his verse. A few of the original *Spoon River* sketches are worth keeping in the anthologies to represent the short-lived attempt at "realism" in poetry, but nothing else by Masters is really worth reading. Lindsay originally was, and Sandburg eventually became, better poets.

CARL SANDBURG

Even if there had never been any New Critics to denigrate it, Sandburg's early work, with the exception of several short poems, would surely have been recognized by this time for what it was, an expression of the times that came as close to being subliterary as the work of any American poet of comparable reputation ever has. It is much more difficult, today, to understand why *this* poetry was once so greatly admired than it is to think ourselves back into the situation in which Whittier's poems were read with pleasure. However much we may approve of Sandburg's humanitarian and socialist views, and his efforts to write poetry in which "democratic" and "realistic" would amount to the same thing, we are likely to find the poetry itself, when we actually *read* it, more remote than Tuckerman's. Much of it reads like the worst of Whitman, if Whitman had had only ideology to guide him.

"I Am the People, the Mob," from the "Other Days (1900–1910)" section of *Chicago Poems* (1916), is typical. It begins, "I am the people — the mob — the crowd — the mass," and ends with these two "lines":

> When I, the People, learn to remember, when I, the People, use the lessons of yesterday and no longer forget who robbed me last year, who played me for a fool — then there will be no speaker in all the world say the name:

"The People," with any fleck of a sneer in his voice
or any far-off smile of derision.
The mob — the crowd — the mass — will arrive then.

If there is anything here to lift this above the level of socialist political oratory, it is difficult to see what it is. The outlook being expressed is no more and no less difficult to take seriously than Lindsay's Populism or Whitman's radical democracy and nationalism, though Sandburg looks for revolution to accomplish what they thought evolution would do. The trouble with these verses is that neither in terms of metrics nor in terms of imaginative use of language nor in any other way do we feel in them the presence of a "shaping spirit" doing anything to vivify the abstractions. If the poem calls forth *any* response from us, it will be a purely political one: Some people hope for, and some dread, revolution. If we do neither, we are likely to feel nothing at all. We turn the pages looking for a better poem.

Better ones are hard to find, but there are a few. "Fog" and "Nocturne in a Deserted Brickyard" are the poems most often anthologized, and they do seem less unimaginative than the rest, but Amy Lowell and a dozen other minor poets of the time wrote as memorably. "Chicago" is probably the poem for which the volume will ultimately be remembered, if it is remembered at all. The poem was praised at the time for being just as raw, violent, and unformed as its subject, for its "realism," in short. "The crude violence of the poem is the violence of the city itself," readers were told. The naturalistic aesthetic common at the time placed a high value on direct imitation. Art should be a replica. "Chicago" is full of the "raw material of poetry in all its rawness" that Marianne Moore would soon call the distinguishing mark of genuine poetry. But if the "toads" were "real" enough, there seems to be no "imaginary garden."

Sandburg's early work is full of things that remind us of other poets at the time, nearly always to Sandburg's disadvantage. "Prufrock," for example, which had appeared in *Poetry* the year before *Chicago Poems* was published, identified fog with a cat. The metaphor gains meaning and force in Eliot's poem from its context, including Prufrock's fear of the "animal" side of his nature and his ambivalent use of other animal images. Sandburg makes the identification the substance of the whole poem in "Fog." Lacking any context, his metaphor seems relatively pointless: Like cats, fogs come silently.

Pound's work supplies another parallel. The primitivism of his "Salutation," which contrasts the "thoroughly smug and thoroughly uncomfortable" with the happy "fishermen picnicking in the sun" in the company of their "untidy families," is suggested by Sandburg's "Happiness," which concludes that happiness is reserved for "a crowd of Hungarians under the trees with their women and children and a keg of beer and an accordion." But Pound's last line lifts "Salutation" far above "Happiness": "And the fish swim in the lake and do not even own clothing." We think of the healthy exuberance of the young Whitman, wishing to turn and live with the animals. Sandburg's poem makes us think only of our abstract objections to an abstract primitivism.

The poems in the next volume, *Cornhuskers,* in 1918, are generally less shapeless. Sandburg feels no need, now that life in small towns and on the farm, and memories of prairie scenes, have taken the place of Chicago as the subject, to make the poems "sprawl like the city." It is partly no doubt for this reason, and partly because memory has now replaced political preachment, that there are more realized poems in the volume. "Loam," "Godwing Moth," "Cool Tombs," and "Grass" all come from *Cornhuskers.* Still, when Sandburg writes on subjects others have treated, his inferiority is generally clear, as a comparison of his "Buffalo Bill" with Cummings' "Buffalo Bill's" illustrates. Sandburg's poem expresses simple nostalgia for the lost world of the child, to whom Buffalo Bill was the embodiment of romance. Cummings' poem does this too, but adds a witty adult question about how genuine that romance was, and then, with its suggestion of an equation between Buffalo Bill and Christ, enlarges the question still further. Are all such "romantic" figures the creations simply of wish?

After almost half a century of devoting his energies chiefly to things other than his own poetry, Sandburg published his best volume of verse in 1963. *Honey and Salt* would be a remarkable achievement for any poet, but for a poet in his middle eighties who gained his fame with "Chicago," it is extraordinary. The poems no longer demand to be classified as tough or tender, violent or sentimental. There is in them the mellowness and wisdom of age, which we should like to feel we could expect of very aged poets, but hardly dare to; and there is much more. This volume reminds us of the development of Williams in his last decade, both in sound and in sense. The lines now are much more strongly cadenced, yet still "free." The sound of "the American idiom," as Williams called it, is in fact more evident here than in the earlier, more "realistic," verse. And the sense is as different as the sound from what the early work prepared us to expect. The old reliance on ideology has been replaced by a concern for actual people and their actual experience and actual needs, without any loss in the strength of the vision of the family of man. (A few years before *Honey and Salt,* Sandburg did the captions for that wonderful book of photographs which had *The Family of Man* for its title.) The old tendency to fall back from ideology into pure sentimentalism is gone, too, without any loss of the genuine, controlled and meaningful, tenderness that was the chief distinction of the best early poems. In its place, we find a mature romantic imagination manifesting itself chiefly through sympathetic identification with all forms of life.

This is as different as it could be from the identification of the speaker's *interests* with those of "the mass — the mob" that we find in the early poems, and different also from the sentimental celebrations of corn and Buffalo Bill. Some of these late poems come very close to the spirit of Zen — a possibility always latent in the early poems, but never actualized there. "Foxgloves" will illustrate:

> Your heart was handed over
> to the foxgloves one hot summer afternoon.
> The snowsilk buds nodded and hung drowsy.
> So the stalks believed
> As they held those buds above.
> In deep wells of white
> The dark fox fingers go in these gloves.
> In a slow fold of summer
> Your heart was handed over in a curve
> from bud to bloom.

The new tendency to *meet* man and nature, instead of trying to manipulate them "for their own good," in the case of man, or submit to them, in the case of nature, leads to an explicitly religious consciousness in these poems — again, always implicit in Sandburg's early work, but in conflict, there, with both political ideology and his notion of "reality." In *Honey and Salt* we are reminded of Frost's late stress on the incarnational idea: In these poems, God is "no gentleman"; he "gets dirty running the universe." But his immanence does not now lead the poet to the vaguely suggested pantheism of the early poems. God is the Creator, and so transcendent, as well as immanent, a point very much emphasized in the climactic passage of the longest, and last, poem in the book, "Timesweep."

Our chief impression from this volume is likely to be that Sandburg has at last grown up to something like the level of his prototype, Whitman. His early work, in contrast, generally sounded either like the worst of Whitman, the lines we wish Whitman had left out of "Song of Myself" and "Starting From Paumanok," or like an unsuccessful adaptation of the Whitman whose chief preoccupations were love and death. In the more than half a century between the earliest poems in the Chicago volume and these last poems, Sandburg discovered in depth the meaning of the tradition in which he had always tried to work. Perhaps the years devoted to study of Lincoln, and the further years of collecting and singing American folksongs and ballads, helped. At any rate, line after line, and a good many whole poems, now remind us of the Whitman we value: "The personal idiom of a corn shock satisfies me. . . . The light of the sun ran through the line/ of the water and struck where the moss on/ a stone was green. . . . Sheet white egg faces, strong and sad gorilla/ mugs, meet yourselves, meet each other." Whitman would have felt, I like to think, that Sandburg's career justified him in the end. At any rate, he might have noted that there was no theme and no effect in *Honey and Salt* that he had not already suggested somewhere. Which would be a way of praising Sandburg, not of damning him. Whitman's vision has not been easy to recover in our century.[1]

For anyone who still enjoys contemplating the ironies of history and the fickleness of literary fortune, the careers of the three best-liked women poets of the 1920's and early 1930's could be an interesting subject of study. Sara Teasdale, Elinor Wylie, and Edna St. Vincent Millay were thought great by many who were themselves thought great, and are now nearly forgotten, except by a few of those who were young when they were young. When we set them against Emily Dickinson, who was not only almost unknown during her lifetime but rejected by those few who knew her work, the irony deepens. Those of us old enough to have a little Latin are likely to find themselves pondering on *ubi sunt* and *sic transit gloria mundi* themes.

The spectacle of three such similar poets suffering similar fates ought to be instructive, we are likely to feel. But how? There is a good deal that is calculated to induce melancholy, both in their work and in their lives, but very little to be learned, it would seem; not even the lesson that bad poets are sometimes temporarily popular with those who should know better; for they were not "bad" poets, just minor ones with the bad luck to be born in a revolutionary time which they were only partly prepared to understand. The one lesson that emerges from their examples with any clarity, we are likely to feel we do not need, having already learned it from such poets as J. R. Lowell and Moody: that a poet who borrows language and feeling from the Romantics, without being able to think as the Romantics did, is not likely to produce great poetry.

SARA TEASDALE

Between 1907 and 1933 Sara Teasdale published eight books of verse. After her first two slender volumes, devoted mostly to character studies, the rest is all of a piece, with one tone (elegiac), one overarching theme whatever the subject (the inevitability of loss and despair), and several related subjects, chiefly love, beauty (of nature, mostly), death, and the necessity of cultivating courage. The sense of life that dominates her poetry, giving it just one tone no matter what the subject, even when the poem means to affirm a momentary joy or triumph, is explicitly stated in her address "To an Aeolian Harp," the instrument that Emerson and Melville had written about:

> The winds have grown articulate in thee,
> And voice again the wail of ancient woe
> That smote upon the winds of long ago;
> The cries of Trojan women as they flee,
> The quivering moan of pale Andromache,
> Now lifted loud with pain and now brought low.
> It is the soul of sorrow that we know,
> As in a shell the soul of all the sea.

Memories of a lost faith dominate all the work, once again, whatever the subject. In "The Inn of Earth" memory and loss combine to create the subject, privation. The first of the five stanzas sets the pattern for the rest:

I came to the crowded Inn of Earth,
 And called for a cup of wine,
But the Host went by with averted eye
 From a thirst as keen as mine.

Privation enforced calls forth willed renunciation. Voicing a simplified version of Stevens' mighty theme, Teasdale sought refuge in poetry from her "spirit's gray defeat," her "pulse's flagging beat" and her "hopes that turned to sand,"

For with my singing I can make
A refuge for my spirit's sake,
A house of shining words to be
My fragile immortality.

Beauty found in experience would do, would *have* to do, if the poems didn't come. It would distract one from thinking of "Atoms as old as stars,/ Mutation on mutation,/ Millions and millions of cells/ Dividing," and other similarly depressing subjects. ". . . Forever/ Seek for Beauty, she only/ Fights with man against Death!" If only one could *really* love "all lovely things," then one might sing "as children sing/ Fitting tunes to everything,/ Loving life for its own sake."

Again and again Teasdale makes the claim that she actually *does* love all lovely things and love life for its own sake, but the brittleness of the affirmation is not only revealed by the rest of her poetry, it is exposed even in the affirmation itself, though not with the effect of intended irony. The poet says she has "*tried* to take" (my italics) the "stings" of "all lovely things" lightly, "with gay unembittered lips"; she has, she says, been "careless" if her "heart must break." Beauty "stings" of course because it is not permanent, perhaps not even "real." One thinks of Cummings' satirical poem on this theme that was so common in the 1920's, particularly in the work of the women poets — "Poem, or Beauty hurts Mr. Vinal." "Spare us from beauty," Teasdale, Wylie, and Millay all cried out over and over, in between statements that only beauty mattered. "Spend all you have for loveliness" might have been written by any of the three; Teasdale wrote it. Do so, she said, even though it hurts almost beyond bearing.

Teasdale writes often, in her later volumes, on another theme that both Frost and Stevens had made their own — not that she seems in any way indebted to them. I mean the "One must have a mind of winter" theme. Since everything, most especially the fleeting quality of beauty and love, makes the poet think of "The clock running down,/ Snow banking the door" ("Winter Night Song"); and since she can only picture her life as a tune that "climbs. . . ./ High over time, high even over doubt" but then, having climbed so high, "pauses/ And faltering blindly down the air, goes out," she spends a good deal of time renouncing every hope and insisting that she has "ceased to fear," as once she feared, "The last complete reunion with the earth." She will find peace when the rooftops are "crowned with snow," once she has become "cold with song."

The words ring hollow today, though they didn't seem to do so to many in her generation. She seems to have had no resources to fall back on except the determination of the agonized consciousness to create a "music of stillness" out of the "dream" of the "lonely mind." But she knew the music was only fictive, and therefore not sufficient. Even when she most earnestly asserts its supremacy, she does not convince, either herself or us. Only in her last volume, *Strange Victory,* when she had stopped trying to convince anyone of anything, when she had stopped hoping she could move beyond tragedy, did she begin to write in a way that does not seem embarrassing. Now she perceived that the "long tragic play" of life is "acted best when not a single tear/ Falls" and "when the mind, and not the heart, holds sway." For *her* poetry, this was a discovery worth making. *Strange Victory* is a very slender volume containing just twenty-two short lyrics, but it not only contains Teasdale's best work, it is a book any poet might be glad to have written. Perhaps half the poems in it are free from any pretense or any affectation, which had been her ruling vices. But the strange victory she had gained after her hope was lost, though it was salutary for her art, did not suffice the woman. Having at last learned to write well, she committed suicide in 1933.

ELINOR WYLIE

Expressing very similar attitudes, developing often the same themes, in a style derived, like Teasdale's, from the English Romantics, particularly from Shelley, Elinor Wylie created more poems that are still good to read. The several best of them, especially "Wild Peaches" and "Innocent Landscape," are very good. Wylie's spirit was tougher than Teasdale's had been before *Strange Victory,* and her mind clearer.

But what we are likely to notice first, as we read through her collected poems, is the similarity of the two. Among poets less gifted than the major figures of the age, the number of possible reactions to "the modern temper" was severely limited. Thus Wylie, echoing Teasdale, writes often of the advantages of a cold mind and of the heart's strategies of survival with a minimum of sustenance. In her best-known poem, "Let No Charitable Hope," she writes, "I live by squeezing from a stone/ The little nourishment I get." She is preoccupied always with erecting defenses against both "love's violence" and the knowledge of impending doom. Hearing continuously "the end of everything" approaching with a sound "insane, insistent," she seeks out ways to "be fugitive awhile from tears" and finds one of them in listening to a "Viennese Waltz":

> Now falling, falling, feather after feather,
> The music spreads a softness on the ground;
> Now for an instant we are held together
> Hidden within a swinging mist of sound.

So sad have the strains of a gay waltz become to ears attuned to "Doomsday" sounds. "Malicious verity" has touched everything, even Beauty and Love.

Often, reading poems like "Viennese Waltz," we wish for the astringencies of Marianne Moore or the intellectual firmness of Dickinson. This is a reaction especially hard to avoid when the poet attempts affirmations of self-sufficiency after the example of Emerson and Shelley. "Address to My Soul" begins,

> My soul, be not disturbed
> By planetary war;
> Remain securely orbed
> In this contracted star.
> Fear not, pathetic flame;
> Your sustenance is doubt:
> Glassed in translucent dream
> They cannot snuff you out.

"They" floats freely in the sentence, not needing to be attached to anything; readers of the period knew well enough who the enemies of the soul were. The "chaos" and "void" and "dissolving star" mentioned later in the poem were understood before being named as the reasons why the soul must try to "be brave." And the poem's concluding advice to the soul could also be anticipated: "Five-petalled flame, be cold."

Shelley has been drawn upon here to help Wylie make her affirmation ("Life, like a dome of many-colored glass, stains the white radiance of eternity"), and Emerson, with his confidence in the "singular" soul's ability to move through its "predestined arc." (One wonders why the poet never acknowledged her debt to Emerson as she did that to Shelley, calling herself once "a woman by an archangel befriended," with Shelley in the angelic role; and on another occasion spreading "A Red Carpet for Shelley.") But the use made of both older poets is ultimately superficial. Something has been borrowed from the superstructure of their vision, but the foundations have been omitted — both the pantheism suggested by Shelley's "white radiance of eternity," and Emerson's faith in the Soul, and in growth, in process.

Sometimes Wylie's debt to Emerson is more specific than that to Shelley. When it is, her way of contracting his meaning becomes, unfortunately, even clearer. "Beauty," for instance, draws from both "Each and All" and "The Rhodora," but what it omits from Emerson's poems and what it adds to them makes apparent the thinness of Wylie's romanticism. Emerson had said that "Beauty is its own excuse for being," which becomes Wylie's initial injunction, "Say not of Beauty she is good,/ Or aught but beautiful." Emerson had warned that the bride would diminish from "fairy" to "gentle wife" when caged in marriage, as a "bird from the woodlands" would cease to sing in captivity. Wylie expressed this by saying that beauty must be left "innocent and wild": "Enshrine her and she dies."

What she has omitted is the Emersonian vision that gives his maxims their meaning. He had concluded "The Rhodora" by saying that "The selfsame Power that brought me there brought you," which is to say, both flower and observer are directly related to, and derive their meaning from, the Over-Soul, and from this relationship get their relationship to each other. In "Each and All," he had discovered the organic unity of being which made futile all efforts to separate truth and beauty for the purpose of analysis. The speaker "yielded" himself "to the perfect whole," secure in the faith that nature was "Full of light and of deity." The beauty of every concrete aspect of being derives from, and is symbolic of, unconditioned Being. Thus it is that beauty needs no practical ("humanistic") justification, that it cannot be analyzed or controlled, that it disappears when separated, and that it can only be intuited in submission to the "perfect Whole." These are some of the meanings underlying and giving shape to Emerson's two poems.

Naturally enough, such Transcendental faith was impossible for Wylie. When she borrowed from Emerson, she could not borrow *this*. But to paraphrase Emerson's conclusions without supplying any substitute for the rejected religious vision on which they ultimately rested was to diminish the Transcendental to the merely sentimental.

Wylie's other borrowings from Emerson are similar. In "The Eagle and the Mole" she sounds very Emersonian, though she is probably also remembering Blake, when she counsels the soul to "Avoid the reeking herd" and "The huddled warmth of crowds," but what the eagle will gain, except possibly blindness, when he "stares into the sun," or what the mole will discover in his "intercourse/ With roots of trees and stones,/ With rivers at their source," the poem does not say or in any way suggest. Similarly, in "Let No Charitable Hope," the poet who lives, as she puts it, by squeezing her nourishment from a stone, says she looks on time without fear as

> In masks outrageous and austere
> The years go by in single file.

The metaphor is adapted from Emerson's "Days," in which the days march by the speaker "single in an endless file," but there is no relation in *meaning* between Emerson's poem and Wylie's.

It is hardly surprising, therefore, that her best poems are those in which she seems most remote from either Emerson or Shelley. Her sense of man's plight in a meaningless universe was her own, not borrowed and not wished for. From it came the "mind of winter" poems that are generally her best. "Innocent Landscape," for instance, notes that though the "reverential" trees look "like saints," yet

Here is no virtue; here is nothing blessèd
  Save this foredoomed suspension of the end;
Faith is the blossom, but the fruit is cursèd;
  Go hence, for it is useless to pretend.

"Wild Peaches" is her finest poem. In it she manages to make the familiar "mind of winter" theme seem fresh and compelling. For one thing, the personal approach, with its "I" and "we," suits her talent better than the bardic tone of her more openly "philosophic" poems. The poem means more than her other poems partly because it seems not to be *trying* to say so much, merely to be saying "I hate," and "I love"; and partly because its texture is richer than is common in her work.

The poem consists of four sonnets so closely linked that in effect they are stanzas in a single poem. The first three describe a kind of return to an unfallen Eden on "the Eastern Shore" reached by "a river-boat from Baltimore":

We'll live among wild peach trees, miles from town,
You'll wear a coonskin cap, and I a gown
Homespun, dyed butternut's dark gold colour.

There the two will "swim in milk and honey," and find "All seasons sweet, but Autumn best of all"; there the squirrels will fall to the hunter "like fruit" and the "autumn frosts will lie upon the grass/ Like bloom on grapes." The spring in that mild climate will begin "before the winter's over," and with it the months that are like "brimming cornucopias" spilling out their gifts of nature's richness.

The poem succeeds as well as it does partly because the picture in the first three stanzas of a friendly and fruitful earth is so concrete. We see and smell and taste lovely things until the senses are cloyed and we are ready for the last stanza's renunciation, its turn to the bareness and whiteness of a real winter:

Down to the Puritan marrow of my bones
There's something in this richness that I hate.
I love the look, austere, immaculate,
Of landscapes drawn in pearly monotones.
There's something in my very blood that owns

Bare hills, cold silver on a sky of slate,
A thread of water, churned to milky spate
Streaming through slanted pastures fenced with stones.

The reason — never stated, fortunately — for the speaker's preference for the bare winter New England landscape to the friendlier Eastern Shore of Maryland is that it is more "real." Innocence has been lost for good, and nature as a whole is *not* friendly, however fertile Maryland soil may be. The "Puritan" sensibility responds to severity. Looking at the seasons of man's life, it sees that spring is "briefer than apple-blossom's breath" and summer is "much too beautiful to stay." Its own seasons are

Swift autumn, like a bonfire of leaves,
And sleepy winter, like the sleep of death.

Sara Teasdale had not yet written so well as this, and Elinor Wylie, who died young in 1928, would not again. Edna St. Vincent Millay, the youngest of the three, would come close to it only at the very beginning of her career, but for a while in the 1920's and 1930's she was more famous than either of the others.

EDNA ST. VINCENT MILLAY

When Elizabeth Atkins published the first book on Millay in 1936, she began her Introduction with a disarmingly modest paragraph in which there are, nevertheless, certain certainties:

> Continually in England and America one hears the question, "Who is our finest living poet?" God help me, I think I know the answer. But I am in no mood to divulge it, for I am pacific and vulnerable, and it is terrifying to be set upon by a mob of militant believers in divers other poets. This book grows out of the safer question, "Who is our most popular and representative poet?" At that question the most disputatious roomful calms into agreement in an instant. Everyone recognizes that Edna St. Vincent Millay represents our time to itself, much as Tennyson represented the period of Victoria to itself, or Byron the period of Romanticism. She is the only living poet who is casually quoted in philosophical

> treatises and in moving-picture magazines, in churches and in night clubs, in the rural schools of Oregon and in the Sorbonne of Paris. It is this character of Edna St. Vincent Millay as our representative-at-large — the incarnation of our *Zeitgeist* — which has set me wondering.

So large a claim, which the author was by no means alone in making, sets *us* to wondering, too. If it is really true that Millay was the incarnation of the *Zeitgeist,* what a melancholy time to have lived in! But then, we reflect, *whose Zeitgeist,* or whose interpretation of the *Zeitgeist?* May we not learn more about the age by reading "Prufrock" or "The Waste Land," or by thinking hard about all the implications of "The Comedian as the Letter C"? But perhaps it might be objected that Eliot and Stevens, like major artists in any age, were not so much simply reflecting the age as taking its measure prior to deciding what their own role in it should be.

Only two years after she had been celebrated as our "most . . . representative" living poet by Miss Atkins, Millay was wondering rather bitterly why she had not received the Pulitzer Prize for her work since 1923, while Robinson and Frost had received it several times each. Writing another "traditional" poet — that is, not "Modernist," as I have let the Imagists, and Pound, Eliot, and Stevens define the term — Arthur Davison Ficke, she said that in considering those who ought to have been honored but had not, she had thought first of Elinor Wylie, then of Ficke himself, then of Robinson Jeffers, then of herself. She supposed that Wylie had never received it because "she had left her husband and her child to run off to Europe with a married man." Concerning Ficke, she thought of his resignation from his position as curator of Japanese prints at Harvard and of "all the circumstances attending the resignation." Concerning her own failure to get the prize, she was sure she knew the answer. She had been arrested and taken to jail for carrying a placard up and down before the State House in Boston protesting the execution of Sacco and Vanzetti. Robinson and Frost, on the other hand, had apparently led "blameless" lives, she supposed, "both sexual and political," which would be a sufficient explanation of their getting the prize again and again.

Or perhaps, she thought on other occasions, there was another reason for her declining fame, more important, finally, than anything in her private life. After the affair of the Bollingen Prize award to Pound in 1949, which had the effect on Williams of sending him into a temporary breakdown, she read Robert Hillyer's *Saturday Review of Literature* attacks on Eliot and Pound, and on the Committee for awarding the Prize to Pound, and thought the articles "brilliant and truly witty." Perhaps, as Hillyer had proposed, both Eliot and Pound were in effect conspirators, both of them enemies of direct, simple, sensuous, and intelligible poetry, Pound an enemy of the state as well. Perhaps *this* was why her fame had suffered. Writing her publisher, she said she had produced, after reading the Hillyer articles, "a satire in verse against T. S. Eliot."

In her last years she spent much time looking for a demon to blame for her frustration. If she had been able to think about the matter more calmly and self-critically, she might have hit upon another explanation: She had probably never written so well again as she had in the poem which first brought her fame, *Renascence,* which she completed in 1912 when she was twenty and published in 1917. *Renascence* is a romantic poem about an experience of "Cosmic consciousness," to use Bucke's phrase. The tone is excited, girlish, and naively ejaculatory, as why should it not be when a Maine seacoast girl of less than twenty (she held the poem and revised it for several years, then sent it out for the Lyric Year contest in 1912) had had such an experience? If the tone were cooler, more "modern," we should suspect the whole business of having been "thought up" to make a poem. Its emotions seem genuine, unforced.

The events narrated in *Renascence* fit the classic accounts of mystical vision. If we are to understand the poem, prior to evaluating it, we must do so in terms supplied by such writers on mysticism as Underhill and Bucke, James and Stace. Point by point, for instance, the speaker's report on the "meaning" of the illumination parallels Whitman's in "Song of Myself" — the same sense of the identity of all being, of the unity of life and death and time and eternity, of the ultimate "rightness" of what *is,* coming after an experience of the death of self. All this and more would make it easier to read this poem in terms of Underhill's schematization of mystical experience than James Miller found it to be with "Song of Myself." To say this is not, obviously, to suggest that there would be any *other* point in comparing the two poems as works of art. It is only to say that insofar as the subject of "Song of Myself" is mystical experience, the subjects of the two poems overlap. Even more clearly, the poem states the central meaning of *satori,* "enlightenment," in Zen.

> In this condition [*satori*] we lose our sense of Self, and know ourselves to be part of the great Oneness of all. Knowing ourselves to be part of Absolute Being, our ego and our problems of ego — sin, pain, poverty, fear — all dissolve.

The importance of this observation is that until we have noted what a poem is *about,* we are not in a position to say anything else about it, including anything about the form it takes.

Although it is written in the idiom of the Romantic poetry of the preceding century, *Renascence* is remarkably free from any suggestions of specific literary indebtedness to nineteenth-century writers. Parallels might be found with religious poets like Henry Vaughan and Thomas Traherne, but if Millay had any specific models in mind, they are certainly not evident in the poem. To be sure, the final twelve lines devoted to explicit interpretation of the experience express ideas that sound like those we have seen in Emerson, Whitman, and Dickinson, but in each case, it is the *idea* rather than the expression of it that reminds us of the older poets, who had, or believed in, or at least knew about, mystical experience. The parallels with certain passages in "Song of Myself" are especially striking.

The sensitive, intense, visionary country girl from Maine never fulfilled the early promise of *Renascence.* Her later attempts to affirm meaning sounded increasingly hollow as the years went by. Vassar and Greenwich Village in the 1920's undid her, perhaps, making her distrust the veracity of her own experience. At any rate, whatever the cause, all her affirmations came to have a quality of shrillness. More and more she sought moments of intense experience, but if she found them, the poetic result does not suggest that they brought any illumination. Her assertions that all was well with her came to seem to rest partly upon the necessities of rhyme and partly upon the felt *need* to cheer herself and others. She insisted that the candle she was burning at both ends gave "a lovely light," but "lovely" or not, the light did nothing to dispel her anguish.

She tried to settle for simple endurance, discovering that "Life must go on," though, as she said, she forgot just why. She was tortured by the spectacle of April coming "like an idiot" who babbled and strewed flowers. More and more often she felt herself "lost in whistling space" and sensed "anonymous death" in the "bubbling bowl" of the sun.

Toward the end of her life, she tried devoting her poetry to good causes to fill the emptiness within her, writing for instance a "Poem and Prayer for an Invading Army" to be read over the radio by Ronald Coleman on the Second World War's D-Day, but afterward she blamed herself for writing "propaganda" instead of poetry. Her love poems had always been rather fevered and brittle. Now, in her last years, tired and ill, she began to wish only for peace. She hoped that others might hope, as she once had.

She was not sure what had happened to deprive her of "the sure song" she could no longer sing. Her many admirers wondered too and were no more sure of the answer than she was.

CHAPTER XVIII

Melodies of Chaos

The state of modern thought is that every single item in this general doctrine ["the grand doctrine of Nature as a self-sufficient, meaningless complex of facts . . . the doctrine of the autonomy of physical science . . . the doctrine . . . I am denying"] is denied, but that the general conclusions from the doctrine as a whole are tenaciously retained . . . a dead Nature can give no reasons. All ultimate reasons are in terms of aim at value. A dead Nature aims at nothing.

— Alfred North Whitehead, in *Nature and Life,* 1934

ROBINSON JEFFERS

WHEN Robinson Jeffers chose the poems he wished to include in his 1938 *Selected Poetry,* he omitted everything in his first two books of verse, published in 1912 and 1916. *That* decision, he said without explanation, had been easy. When we turn back to them, already knowing his later poetry, we can see why in 1938 he decided to let them stay out of print. Love lyrics and "nature appreciations" in the Romantic tradition, they were conventional, for the time, in both form and theme, sentimental, and thoroughly undistinguished.

Jeffers tells us in his Foreword that he had discovered Nietzsche's "The poets lie too much" even before he wrote these early volumes, but that Nietzsche's meaning had not sunk in. When it did, Jeffers made a fresh beginning as a poet. "I decided not to tell lies in verse." It became evident to him

> that poetry — if it was to survive at all — must reclaim some of the power and reality that it was so hastily surrendering to prose. . . . It must reclaim substance and sense, and physical and psychological reality. This feeling . . . led me to write narrative poetry, and to draw subjects from contemporary life; to present aspects of life that modern poetry had generally avoided; and to attempt the expression of philosophic and scientific ideas in verse.

Reclaiming "power and reality . . . substance and sense" is, of course, what major poets are always trying to do, and minor ones too in times of poetic transition. It would be difficult to find any poet who didn't think he was concerned with some kind of "reality" and was making some kind of "sense." The only interesting question is *what* kind.

Jeffers decided, as Stevens was deciding during the same period, that only the "things" dealt with by the natural sciences were "real." With his training as a medical student interpreted through his reading of Nietzsche and Schopenhauer, he came to feel that the cadaver in the dissection room was more real than the living person it had been, more real too than those still alive, purposefully dissecting it. "Nature" was all, and man clearly was in many respects — the peculiarly *human* respects — a most "unnatural" being. Consciousness, he decided, was a temporary and inexplicable accident, perhaps a kind of "sickness," or at any rate an aberration, of matter. The farther one got from the human, the closer one came to reality. Thus hawks were more real than people, and stones than hawks.

If this summary of Jeffers' views begins to sound like a hostile parody, we may restore our confidence in the possibility of a man's actually thinking this way by setting this "naturalism," for a moment, over against Emerson's idealism. Starting from the "knowing process" rather than the "thing known," Emerson had found that the nearer we approach the "soul," the closer we are to "reality." Warning us not to think of the soul as an "organ" or a "function" or "faculty," or even as "intellect" or "will" or a combination of the two, he turned to metaphor as the best way of pointing toward what he meant: The soul is "the background of our being, in which [intellect and will and all] lie, — an immensity not possessed and that cannot be possessed. From within or from behind, a light shines through us upon things, and makes us aware that we are nothing, but the light is all." The light that was within because it was first outside he sometimes called the Over-Soul: "Within man is the soul of the whole; the wise silence; the universal beauty . . . that overpowering reality which confutes our tricks and talents. . . ."

What Jeffers finally came to call his "Inhumanism" has more in common with Emerson's philosophy than we would suppose, more than would appear if we simply contrasted idealism and materialism as metaphysical opposites. For both poets, reality is "overpowering," confuting our "tricks and talents." For both, the "universal beauty" is more impressive than the little triumphs of man's intellect or will. For both, abiding reality is "not possessed and cannot be possessed." Both, in short, oppose the kind of humanism that makes man the measure. Nature, for both, is where we must look if we are to find reality. Nature refutes man's deluded self-conceit. "Seen from this height, they [men] are shrunk to insect size," Jeffers noted in "Apology for Bad Dreams." Emerson would not have put it quite that way, but he often said very similar things, in "Monadnoc," for instance.

For both poets, the stimulus to thought was the experience and the spectacle of suffering, of cruelty and evil and loss and death. Out of his anguish of spirit and his sense of his own powerlessness, Emerson created his Transcendental Idealism, which in effect said that Reality was the very opposite of what he *felt* and *seemed* to know. It could be intuited only in moments of extraordinary insight, which could not be commanded or produced at will. Out of *his* anguish, Jeffers worked out a thoroughgoing denial of the significance, the "reality" if you will, of all humanity, of *people* like himself, and of all their dreams and wishes and values. His reality is defined by its power to obliterate all merely human knowledge and desire, and all *personal* experience, not merely the intuitive. Was Emerson thinking wishfully, and Jeffers more objectively? As the later poet's most sympathetic recent interpreter has put it, Jeffers' system of thought is "a rationalism based ultimately on a scientifically objective view of life"; his position "is essentially a materialism which yields from time to time to an idealism." His "yieldings," we are told, are his concessions to wish; his basic position is independent of wish.

Emerson as a poet seldom writes well when he writes as a moralist. A moralist ought to be something of a humanist; and what has been called, not very helpfully for present purposes, Emerson's "religious humanism" turns out to be more religious than humanistic. He was actually not much interested in what we generally mean by "morality," that is, the *mores* of the tribe. He generally writes well when he writes of how we *know* anything at all, especially how we are to recognize and accept our identity and our destiny. Jeffers, similarly, seldom writes well when he writes of *people* — never when he writes of ordinary, "sane" people — for he starts by assuming that *people* are not ultimately "real." Their actual experience therefore does not interest him, except as it provides the materials for allegorizing his philosophy. When he writes well, his subject is nature, or man's fate viewed from nature's perspective.

Jeffers' best poems find a kind of dignity in man's inevitable defeat. "To the Stone-Cutters" has been widely admired:

> Stone-cutters fighting time with marble, you
> foredefeated
> Challengers of oblivion
> Eat cynical earnings, knowing rock splits, records fall
> down,
> The square-limbed Roman letters
> Scale in the thaws, wear in the rain. The poet as well
> Builds his monument mockingly;
> For man will be blotted out, the blithe earth die, the
> brave sun
> Die blind and blacken to the heart:
> Yet stones have stood for a thousand years, and pained
> thoughts found
> The honey of peace in old poems.

In a similar vein, "Boats in a Fog" develops the thought that "it is bitter earnestness/ That makes beauty; the mind/ Knows, grown adult." *What* the mind knows is that love leads only to delusion, and so to perversion. In his poem of advice to his sons, "Shine, Perishing Republic," the poet cautions against any sort of attachment to anything human — and that of course means not just individual people but nations, civilizations, cultures, anything at the "center" of man's efforts and experiences. The poem succeeds so far as it does by not "philosophizing" the materialist metaphysic underlying this view, by simply saying, in effect: Remember, nature is more permanent than man; an injunction which is taken to justify the advice in the concluding lines:

> And boys, be in nothing so moderate as in love
> of man, a clever servant, insufferable master.
> There is the trap that catches noblest spirits, that
> caught — they say — God, when he walked on earth.

All of Jeffers' best poems are short, and all of them develop aspects of his single real theme, his desperate effort to teach the heart not to love. "The Treasure" combines ideas and feelings that may be found, put finally to a different use, in Emerson, Whitman, and the Hebrew prophets, combines them in order to celebrate the "peace" to be found in death. Not the "flash of activity" that is life, all life, but the "enormous repose after, the enormous repose before" should be the object of our desire, our "treasure." The poem redoes "Thanatopsis" (without that poem's tacked-on conclusion) in modern idiom, building its hymn to death out of the materials of historical geology and astronomy, chiefly. There is dignity in its lines:

> Mountains, a moment's earth-waves rising and hollowing;
> the earth too's an ephemerid; the stars —
> Short-lived as grass the stars quicken in the nebula
> and dry in their summer, they spiral
> Blind up space, scattered black seeds of a future;
> nothing lives long, the whole sky's
> Recurrences tick the seconds of the hours of the ages
> of the gulf before birth, and the gulf
> After death is like dated: . . . .
>
> . . . .
> Surely you never have dreamed the incredible depths
> were prologue and epilogue merely
> To the surface play in the sun, the instant of life,
> what is called life? I fancy
> That silence is the thing, ...

Deeper than the "scientific" rationale of Jeffers' "inhumanism" is his Ahabian rebellion against the God of his clergyman father. Summarizing the "ways of God" in the fourth section of "Apology for Bad Dreams," he writes:

> He brays humanity in a mortar to bring the savor
> From the bruised root: a man having bad dreams, who
> invents victims, is only the ape of that God.

It is surprising to find the word "God" appearing so often in the poems of so militant a "materialist," but "God" wanders on and off the stage of the poems like the drunken ghost of a hated, but never quite to be escaped, father. If we follow the suggestion of Radcliffe Squires and think of Jeffers as a modern Lucretius, or philosophic poet of Nature, "scientifically" conceived, we might go on to compare his "God" with the gods of Lucretius. Like them, Jeffers' God is capricious, unconcerned, and irrelevant. Unlike them, though, He does have one function whenever He appears; He is useful for attaching ultimate blame to. What kind of a God, Jeffers keeps asking, would it be that would make *this* kind of world?

At this point in his philosophizing, Jeffers usually becomes incoherent. Often, as in the final lines of "Apology for Bad Dreams," "God" is rejected for being cruel, affirmed for being real, as cruelty is real, and finally denied any existence at all, all in the same passage:

> I have seen these ways of God: I know of no reason
> For fire and change and torture and the old returnings.
> He being sufficient might be still. I think they
>   admit no reason; they are the ways of my love.
> Unmeasured power, incredible passion, enormous craft;
>   no thought apparent but burns darkly
> Smothered with its own smoke in the human brain-vault:
>   no thought outside: a certain measure in phenomena:
> The fountains of the boiling stars, the flowers on the
>   foreland, the ever-returning roses of dawn.

The bulk of Jeffers' work is in the long narratives that are seldom read any more, that are not even easily available for the most part. These are allegorical poems with a superficially "realistic" surface. The violence in them has often been called meaningless sensationalism, but it would be hard to get further from the truth. The poems are obsessive, to be sure, but *meaningful* at the same time, as obsessions can be meaningful. Incest in them stands for man's love of man; to love one's own kind is in effect to love within the human family, hence incestuous. Incest leads to perversions, mass murder, and finally to nameless and all-pervasive horrors, like those in a nightmare that are at once real and indefinable.

"Roan Stallion," the shortest of the long narratives, is also the best. Though it is weakened by several long passages of overt philosophizing, the tale it tells of a woman crazed with desire committing sodomy with a horse, then shooting the object of her love after it has killed her husband, has a kind of power I can only call "religious," in the same sense in which Diana Trilling has called the violence of Norman Mailer's fiction "religious." For once, Jeffers has sympathy for one of his characters — the woman. It helps, also, in a curious way, that he keeps his philosophizing separate from the narrative, so that it interferes only sporadically. The reader, as a result — this reader, anyway — is able to identify, in part at least, with this driven, desperate creature, the "type," for Jeffers, of mankind.

As for the philosophy, it is the expected. "Humanity is the start of the race; I say/ Humanity is the mould to break away from . . ." This is so because of "vision that fools him/ Out of his limits, desire that fools him out of his limits, unnatural crime, inhuman science . . . Useless intelligence of far stars." God, "not in a man's shape," listens to the praises sung him by breaking atoms, and approves; he "laces the suns with planets/ The heart of the atom with electrons":

> what is humanity in this cosmos? For him, the last
> Least taint of a trace in the dregs of the solution . . .
> the atom to be split.

Perhaps so. But in that case, why even bother to tell the woman's terrible story? The poem has worked to persuade us that both she and the stallion are worth our concern, but the philosophic narrator tells us in his sections that they are not. As Jeffers puts it in another poem, "Pain and pleasure are not to be thought/ Important enough to require balancing. . . . Such discords/ In the passionate terms of human experience are not resolved, nor worth it."

I have spoken so far only of the poems that seem to me to be the best of Jeffers' work. I have said little about Jeffers' technique because it seems to me that to approach them from that angle is inevitably to start noting limitations, and I have wanted to "save" a part of Jeffers, even perhaps to rescue the best of his work from the near-oblivion in which it currently rests. His verse very seldom has the musical felicity that often charms us in Pound or Stevens. It has none of the inevitability of phrase that makes Eliot's lines stick in the memory. It has only that power which Jeffers' imagining of evil and nothingness gives it in a language in itself undistinguished, but fired, at its best, by passionate brooding honesty and thwarted love, that come through the cumulative effect of whole lines and groups of lines.

When the poems move us deeply, they do so because they convey an antisecular, antihumanist vision of nature as power and beauty. To the best of Jeffers, the philosophy (electrons are more "real" than people, death more "real" than life) is irrelevant. Regardless of what the "real" is, man's life is short and bound to end badly; the tragic view never wants for evidence. Jeffers is agreeing with his father's theology, and with Anne Bradstreet and Edward Taylor, when he writes, in "The Caged Eagle's Death Dream," that "life was more than its functions/ And accidents, more important than its pains and pleasures . . ." When he adds, in the next line, that it is "A torch to burn in with pride," he is leaving the Puritans for Nietzsche and Melville's Ahab; and when he adds to this, "a necessary/ Ecstasy in the run of the cold substance," he has moved beyond Ahab too, into ontology. The first part, the Puritan part, is prosy here, but not always so in his poetry. The second part comes in a fine tragic metaphor. Both of these feelings are at the center of all that is best in Jeffers.

About the third part, the ontology, or theory of the "real," the less said the better. Since Kant, "naive realism," as the philosophers sometimes call it, which in effect means equating words and things, ignoring *what* we know about *how* we know, has been impossible to hold, epistemologically. Jeffers' materialism rests upon a naive epistemology. This is the ultimate reason, I think, why readers have found the poems in which Jeffers philosophizes most earnestly and lengthily, as he does in "Margrave," bathetic; this, and not the question of the dubious taste of writing about a man by talking about the electrons and molecules that are supposed to account for him.

Whatever his philosophy told him, and it told him many contradictory things, Jeffers' real concern was with nature as the "beautiful Necessity," to use a phrase from Emerson. So far as he was concerned at all with doomed man, he was concerned with that part of him, "the ghost in the machine," as Norbert Wiener has called the soul, which might learn to love something utterly nonpersonal and nonhuman: nature itself, which as Emerson said is not possessed and cannot be possessed, which denies our every request and reduces to nothing all that we initiate. If Jeffers had been able to accept his father's religion, he would presumably have restored the inherited Calvinism to its pristine rigor.

CONRAD AIKEN

Two poets more different from each other than Robinson Jeffers and Conrad Aiken would be hard to find, though they were within two years of being the same age, were preoccupied with the same great question, of what meaning or value life could have in a universe "dedicated to death," and wrote poetry that is always just about to become abstract philosophy. Aiken's early "symphonies" and "preludes" are not allegories as Jeffers' long narratives are, but they are just as abstractly conceived. Aiken gives them the appearance of dramatic poems, but they are not even as dramatic as morality plays, for in them *every* character is Everyman. And Aiken's "burden of grief" springs from the same source, so far as its source lies in conscious thought, as Jeffers'.

There the comparison ends. There is no misanthropy in Aiken's work, no movement toward "inhumanism," and no tendency to deny the multifariousness of human experience in order to make experience fit a doctrine. Aiken's mind is not monolithic, and his continuous preoccupation with a single theme through many years and many volumes is not obsessive. When his work suggests the work of others, it makes us think of Stevens and, particularly, of Eliot, never of Jeffers.

Aiken never *sounds* like Stevens, early or late. The similarity of the two exists only on the thematic level, or — what amounts to the same thing in the end — in shared symbolic images. An example would be Aiken's frequent use of winter and snow, as in the opening lines of "Preludes for Memnon":

> Winter for a moment takes the mind; the snow
> Falls past the arclight. . . .
> . . . .
> Winter is there, outside, is here in me:
> Drapes the planets with snow, deepens the ice on the
> moon,
> Darkens the darkness that was already darkness.
> The mind too has its snows. . . .

This is not crisp enough, the writer is not distant enough from his images, for it to *sound* much like Stevens, but thematically it is close to "The Snow Man": "One must have a mind of winter."

Unlike Stevens, Aiken does not develop toward more and more abstract forms of writing. The opposite, rather, is true, as he discovers, in the late work, the "intelligible forms" implicit in experience, the various melodies in the chaos. *Sheepfold Hill* (1958) is the work of a poet of advanced age, but the poems in it are no less sensuous in their texture, and more concrete in their approach to people and their experience in time, than the earliest poems Aiken has cared to preserve. In his late work, Aiken is much closer to the late Eliot than he is to Stevens. But he no longer *sounds* like Eliot, as he did so often, and so strikingly, in the early work. Now he *thinks* like him, and often *feels* like him. The two began at the same point and developed by utterly different routes to final positions curiously similar. Aiken's 1953 rearrangement of much of his early work under the general heading "The Divine Pilgrim" suggests that he would find no inappropriateness in having the metaphor of the pilgrimage applied to his career. Following his own hint, then, we might say that the pilgrimages that Aiken and Eliot began at Harvard first diverged and then converged. Contemporary Little Gidding and historic Sheepfold Hill are closer together in the world of the mind than their separation by an ocean in space would suggest.

It would be drastically simplifying the facts of Aiken's development, but I think not essentially distorting them, to say that the mature work begins with the feelings expressed in the final lines of the title poem of his second volume, *Turns and Movies,* in 1916, and "ends," as of now, with their opposites in "The Crystal," in *Sheepfold Hill.* The 1916 lines present the musing of a lover:

> But some day one of us, grown half possessed
> With pain unbearable, will walk away
> Into the emptiness of time he came from,
> Saying no word, since there's no word to say.

The pain begins in the perception of time's emptiness and ends in the isolation of the lovers from each other. The contrast with the situation in "The Crystal" is immense. In the late poem the poet, speaking as himself, pays homage to Pythagoras, who made basic discoveries in mathematics and taught the transmigration of souls.

To the poet meditating on Sheepfold Hill, this means that he found the immanent *logos* or word that would bring the chaos of nature into intelligible form in the mind; and that, in his transmigration doctrine, he was moving in the same direction in his thinking about man, finding identity when there seemed to be only separation, drawing into communion the living and the dead. In both areas, he found ways of connecting the Many and the One. Praising him, the poet writes lines that suggest specific passages in both Eliot's "Burnt Norton" and Emerson's "The Over-Soul" (the essay):

> . . . What does not your hand
> turn up or over, living or inanimate,
> large or small, that does not signal
> the miracle of interconnectedness
> the beams meeting and crossing in the eye and the mind
> as also in the sun? How can you set end to it
> where is no ending and no beginning
> save in the one that becomes the many, the many
> that compose the one? How shall we praise the forms?

The poem ends with a rite, and with feelings, that suggest Eliot's *The Cocktail Party*:

> The cocktails sparkle, are an oblation.
> We pour for the gods, and will always,
> you there, we here, and the others who follow,
> pour thus in communion. Separate in time,
> and yet not separate. Making oblation
> in a single moment of consciousness
> to the endless forever-together.
> This night
> we all set sail for the west.

The similarity of Aiken's early work to Eliot's of the same period is often much more striking than this late example from "The Crystal." Passages in which we may feel the resemblance are so numerous, and demand analysis from so many different points of view, that they call for an extended treatment they have never received. Since they are crucial to an understanding of Aiken's development, I shall give just a couple of examples. Thus on the first page of *Collected Poems* we read:

After the movie, when the lights come up,
He takes her powdered hand behind the wings;
She, all in yellow, like a buttercup,
Lifts her white face, yearns up to him, and clings;
. . . .
She was a waitress in a restaurant,
He picked her up and taught her how to dance.
Love-phrases that he whispered her still haunt.
She feels his arms, lifts an appealing glance,
But knows he spent last evening with Zudora;
And knows that certain changes are before her.

The brilliant spotlight circles them around,
Flashing the spangles on her weighted dress.
He mimics wooing her, without a sound,
Flatters her with a smoothly smiled caress.
He fears that she will some day queer his act;
Feeling her anger. He will quit her soon.

This is so close, metrically, and in tone and diction, to the description of the seduction of the typist in *The Waste Land,* that the same poet might have written both passages:

The time is now propitious, as he guesses,
The meal is ended, she is bored and tired,
Endeavours to engage her in caresses
Which still are unreproved, if undesired.
Flushed and decided, he assaults at once;
Exploring hands encounter no defence;
His vanity requires no response,
And makes a welcome of indifference.

Several years after "Prufrock" appeared in *Poetry,* Aiken created his own version of Prufrock and called him Senlin. If parts of Senlin's monologue were inserted in "Prufrock," no great disruption would result:

It is morning, Senlin says, and in the morning
When the light drips through the shutters like the dew,
I arise, I face the sunrise,
And do the things my fathers learned to do.
Stars in the purple dusk above the rooftops
Pale in a saffron mist and seem to die,
And I myself on a swiftly tilting planet
Stand before a glass and tie my tie.

. . . .

It is morning, Senlin says, and in the morning
Should I not pause in the light to remember god?
Upright and firm I stand on a star unstable,
He is immense and lonely as a cloud.
I will dedicate this moment before my mirror
To him alone, for him I will comb my hair.
Accept these humble offerings, cloud of silence!
I will think of you as I descend the stair.

No "great" disruption, I said. There would be a small one, and it would signalize a crucial difference between the two poets, a difference that would become more important with the passage of time. The two lines in the first passage beginning "Stars in the purple dusk" are "romantic" in a way Eliot would not have approved. He would surely have cut "purple" before "dusk" and "saffron" before "mist" — or Pound would have done it for him, if these lines had appeared in *The Waste Land.* Aiken in these lines is responding to nature's *beauty* even while he is conceiving nature as meaningless. (A few lines after this he has Senlin think of himself as inhabiting "a whistling void.") Eliot came to respond to nature positively, as he does in "Marina," only *after* he had thought his way through to a *belief* in its value as "creation." Aiken responded as though to creation while *believing* only in nature's meaninglessness. Aiken is a more sensuous poet, and a more naturally romantic one, than Eliot, as is fitting in one who has come to feel so strongly united with the grandfather who was president of the Free Religious Association and who worked for "a peace convention of religions, a worship/ purified of myth and of dogma," as we are told in "Hallowe'en" in *Sheepfold Hill.*

But before the feeling of identity with the grandfather could get into the substance of his poetry, the poet had a journey lasting many years to make. The "foul seeds/ Laid by the intellect in the simple heart" had to be endured as foul until the salting made them clean again; they could not be wished away or plucked out. "The intellect," in the early years of Aiken's work, was synonymous with its product, materialistic naturalism. Teaching us "the chemistry of the sunset," modern knowledge seemed to be describing only "the iterations of the meaningless." Aiken's assessment of the situation of the modern intellectual did not differ in any significant way from Eliot's, though his response to that situation was different.

Preludes for Memnon is subtitled "Preludes to Attitude." An "attitude" is a stance, a posture, a bearing. Sane attitudes are related to truth, are a way of taking a stand, or preparing to take one, in terms of what we know. But what *do* we know? In *Preludes for Memnon* Aiken's skepticism allows for no answers at all of a sort that seem to the poet humanly relevant. If we know nothing, all attitudes are equally appropriate. We exist in a void, and if at times we think we hear

> The deep void swarming with wings and sound of wings
> The winnowing of chaos, the aliveness
> Of depth and depth and depth dedicated to death,

even this discovery is not certain, is only a way of trying to imagine reality; for the flower and the frost that kills it are one, together making a single "bright ambiguous syllable/ Of which the meaning is both no and yes."

We are locked in our own minds, with no way out. "Seeking the ding-an-sich" brings only despair. Poetry is little help. Thinking to trust it, we come face to face with "the maddening fact:/ If poetry says it, it must speak with a symbol." But symbols are only our own thoughts again, or the creation of our thought; they are not knowledge. And so we are dead at last without ever having known anything, having only imagined, perhaps — but what else could we imagine? — that "Space is our face and time our death/ two poles of doom." For the grief brought by such imagining of the obliteration of the personal, there is "no message of assuagement," only "the whisper/ Of time to space," with none alive to hear.

Between *Preludes for Memnon* and the poems in *Sheepfold Hill* there is a very great distance in outlook and sensibility, but no sudden shift of attitude, no conversion or change of mind or heart. In *Time in the Rock,* which appeared only five years after *Memnon,* there is a new note:

> O patience, let us be patient and discern
> in this lost leaf all that can be discerned;
> and let us learn, from this sad violence learn,
> all that in midst of violence can be learned.

The shift is in part a turning from the known to the knowing, from listening outward to "the soulless whisper of sun and moon and tree" to listening inward, to try to find out *why* the tree's whispers seem "soulless," as they had seemed in *The Charnel Rose.* In effect, this is a turning from nature to mind:

> Timeless. The morning is not deep as thought.
> Spaceless. The noon is not as deep as dream.
> Formless. The night is not as deep as death.
> And I defer the notion of the infinite,
> the thought of you, the thought of morning,
> idea of evening, idea of noon.

Another aspect of the new emphasis in *Time in the Rock* would seem, on the surface, to run counter to what I have just described as a shift of attention from nature to mind, or from the content to the process of consciousness. This second note of newness might be described as an increasingly "psychological" approach to mind. The older sciences of nature have been displaced in the poet's imagination by the newer "science of the soul," with its tendency to cast doubt upon the older, positivistic, rationalism. From one point of view, this new emphasis amounts to a deepening of skepticism — "What the hands touch is true. . . . What the mind touches is a ghost." But what the hand touches is not molecules or laws of physics but actual textures and shapes. So that what results from the thought that what the hand touches is "true" is not "materialism" but an increased concern with "aesthetic" perception.

To be concerned with perception, with *lived* experience in all its concreteness, is, for a poet at least, to break free from doctrinal naturalism — or perhaps any *ism* except "Existentialism," which denies all *isms.* It is to cease taking the world as an object of thought, and to try instead to "meet" it, as Buber would say, on equal terms. So that in effect Aiken's deepening skepticism leads to an opening of possibilities for fresh thought, new interpretations. Aiken is closer, in *Time in the Rock,* to the "radical empiricism" of James than he had been in any of the earlier poems. Now he is ready to apprehend without preconceptions "the flower's simplicity," to "lie open to all comers," to let the "other" speak its secret in "the lifelong season of meeting."

In the sequel to *Time in the Rock,* called *And in the Human Heart,* five years later, Aiken begins to sound, in the *mind's* ear, though not in the literal one, like late Williams. Section XV, for instance:

> Snowflake on asphodel, clear ice on rose
> frost over thistledown, the instant death
> that speaks Time's judgment, turning verse to prose,
> or withering June to blackness in a breath —
>
> . . . .
>
> snowflake on asphodel — how clear, how bright
> the blue burns through the melting star! how brave
> the dying flower, and the snow how light
> that on the dying flower makes his grave!
> Snow's death on dying flower, yet both immortal —
> love, these are you and I — enter this portal.

If we are quite close here, not stylistically, certainly not metrically, but in attitude and emotion, to the Williams of "A Unison" and "Asphodel, That Greeny Flower," we are only a little less close to the basic attitudes, and even some of the images, of Emerson's "Titmouse." Aiken was ready now for the ritual celebration of transcendence that is the burden of *Sheepfold Hill.*

The old convictions remain what they were, so long as they are primary intuitions and not derivations of simply "the modern temper" in knowledge. The poet is no longer concerned with "the vile atom" of "positive" knowledge, but with the tragedy of life in time that remains what it always was before atoms were thought of. The summation of wisdom in the early "Blues for Ruby Matrix,"

for what is wisdom, wisdom is only this —
history of the world in a deathbed kiss

has not been repudiated, but the "only" in the first line no longer receives all the stress. Our condition of "not knowing" remains, too, though "The Crystal" in *Sheepfold Hill* puts the condition in a significantly different context of meaning:

. . . So the page turns
always in the middle of a sentence, the beginning of a
  meaning;
the poem breaks in two. So the prayer, the invocation,
and the revelation, are suspended in our lives,
suspended as in a thought.

But now the poet can write without embarrassment and without the irony so often used in the earlier poems to hide it,

. . . We invoke,
and what is life but an invocation,
the shore beyond the vortex, the light beyond the dark,
the number beneath the name. . . .

Or this:

All life
is ritual, or becomes so. . . .
. . . Each action, no matter how simple,
is precious in itself, as part of the devotion,
our devotion to life. . . .

But most surprisingly of all, if we have ignored the poet's gradual development and are thinking of him still as Senlin, this:

Design shines implicit in the blind moment
of self-forgetful perception: belief is steadfast
in the putting forth of a hand, as in the first
wingbeat, or extension of a claw; the law
unfolding and infolding forever.

"Surprising," for here we are very close indeed both to Zen and to Emerson.

In the second poem in the volume, "Hallowe'en," the poet entertains the spirits of all the dead, particularly that of his ministerial grandfather, who was, he makes a point of telling us in the volume's prefatory Note, "a friend of Emerson." The poem concludes with lines that suggest that the grandson too might have been a friend of Emerson. The grandfather who "interpreted the wonders of god"

> is himself dissolved and interpreted.
> Rest: be at peace. It suffices to know and to rest.
> For the singers, in rest, shall stand as a river
> whose source is unending forever.

"Hallowe'en" is one of our great contemporary religious poems. Aiken has always been a poet on the move, his work always "work-in-progress." It is critical heresy to say so, but I find him more interesting as a "philosophic poet" than Stevens, who increasingly wrote his poems to illustrate his theories, and seems seldom to have lost himself in perception. Stevens, to be sure, had a wider range of stylistic effects at his command, and produced a larger number of wholly memorable poems. But Aiken has been a poet of singular integrity and fine intelligence. His work has never been sufficiently honored.

ARCHIBALD MACLEISH

Archibald MacLeish is our poetic weathercock. A glance at his work in any decade will tell us which way the wind of thought and feeling and poetic fashion was blowing. Jeffers' work, by contrast, fitted the mood of the times only in the late 1920's and early 1930's; after that he continued to write in the same way, growing increasingly remote from all but a handful of readers. Aiken has never really been popular. Early in his career he was overshadowed by Eliot, whom he so often resembled. By the middle of the 1930's, he was coming to seem old-fashioned. The growth to be seen in *Sheepfold Hill* is a growth from within, accomplished entirely in the poet's own terms.

MacLeish has participated in every movement, learned from every poetic "generation" (with a new "generation" coming every decade or so), and never seemed even slightly old-fashioned or out of touch. Yet to many it seems less a capacity for growth than a responsiveness to external weather that keeps the poet always on the move. MacLeish has grown old gracefully, but it is not clear that his work of recent years, though wiser surely, is any better than the work that quickly brought him fame in the 1920's. With considerable lyrical talent, he has yet written only a handful of poems likely to be long remembered, out of the many that seemed unforgettable in the years in which they appeared.

The Pot of Earth in 1925 began with an epigraph from Frazer's *The Golden Bough* describing the gardens of Adonis, the dying god. Its first part is called "The Sowing of the Dead Corn" and as we might expect is full of echoes of *The Waste Land,* in both sound and sense, especially of the poem's first section, "The Burial of the Dead." Part Two of the poem is called "The Shallow Grass"; the sense of the title is clarified early in the section:

> I tell you the generations
> Of man are a ripple of thin fire burning
> Over a meadow, breeding out of itself
> Itself, a momentary incandescence
> . . . .
> I tell you we are the shape of a word in the air
> Uttered from silence behind us into silence
> Far beyond, ...

The most noticeable echoes in this section are of the closing lines of the low-life scene in *The Waste Land*'s "A Game of Chess";

> They said, Good Luck! Good Luck! What a handsome
> couple!
> Isn't she lovely though! He can't keep his
> Hands off of her. Ripe as a peach she is. Good Luck!
> Good-bye, Good-bye —

The Pot of Earth could be called accomplished, but highly derivative, poetry.

MacLeish's best early work was done in the last half of the 1920's, particularly in "Einstein" and in *New Found Land,* which contained the famous "You, Andrew Marvell." In all the best of these poems the poet's imagination is dominated by a sense of the immensities of time and space. What we have in them, in effect, is an imaginative evocation of the unimaginable space-time cosmos being revealed by astrophysics. It is the distinction of these poems that in them MacLeish defined an area of sensibility and made it his own. Perhaps only Aiken expressed so memorably man's new sense of living in "a four-dimensional space-time continuum," in a world neither solid nor stable; rather, as a popular interpreter of Einstein has put it, "insubstantial, impalpable, and enigmatic."

The vistas of space-time in these poems have something of the same effect on the experienced world that the vision of heaven had for the Puritan poets; both visions tend to empty the perceived world of content. Reality is elsewhere, or in another, unperceivable, dimension. What the poet perceives is not a world but the "reverberations of a world/ Beating in waves against him"; he senses himself as "hollow" in a continuum of hollowness. Following the lead of contemporary scientists, who mostly assumed that the cosmos knew no life except for the improbable accident that had occurred on Earth, the poet associates contemporary knowledge with the certainty that death is the only reality, always and everywhere. Life's texture, like the texture of heard music, is inexplicable, its notes dissolved to silence:

> So then there is no speech that can resolve
> Their texture to clear thought and enter them.
>
> The Virgin of Chartres whose bleaching bones still wear
> The sapphires of her glory knew a word —
> That now is three round letters like the three
> Round empty staring punctures in a skull.

"Einstein" is an "original" poem precisely to the degree that it demands, for explication, not, like *The Pot of Earth,* some other poem by Eliot, or any poem by anyone, but the scientific theory of the time, as appropriated by the poetic imagination. Eddington and Jeans, Bertrand Russell and philosophic interpreters of Einstein, are more important for explicating the poem's images and ideas than anything in poetic tradition. Russell, for example, defined the mind as "a spot in space," and MacLeish appropriates whatever is meaningful in the notion this way:

> He lies upon his bed
> Exerting on Arcturus and the moon

Forces proportional inversely to
The squares of their remoteness and conceives
The universe.

Though a good many of MacLeish's poems of this period ought to be read with a book like Lincoln Barnett's *The Universe and Dr. Einstein* open beside the poems, the very best of them are less dependent on technical knowledge. In "You, Andrew Marvell," for instance, in which time is imagined as the movement of shadow around the earth, nothing more recondite in the way of knowledge or experience is demanded of the reader than that he know about — or, preferably, have experienced — the way the sharply edged shadow of the earth's own surface may be seen moving up the slopes in mountain country on an evening at sunset. Looking westward and downward from a sunlit peak, we may watch the darkness moving up the slope to engulf us. Looking eastward toward a higher range, we may watch it rising to engulf others. The way the shadow moves suggests, as MacLeish makes it do in the poem, the rising of water. The image of "flooding" in the third stanza is suggested again by "go under" as a description of evening's coming to Spain; together, they make the experience into a kind of death by drowning.

Another of MacLeish's best poems of this period, "The End of the World," resembles "You, Andrew Marvell" in the way it makes the void imaginable without drawing on astrophysical theory, relying instead on the development of a single image. Its succinct and memorable expression of the attempt, so common in the poetry of the time, to imagine "nothing," Hemingway's *nada,* Stevens' "the nothing" that *is* there, depends for its success largely on the *pace* with which it moves through the very palpable objects and events under the "big-top," the circus tent, with Ralph the lion "engaged in biting/ The neck of Madame Sossman," until the "pall" of the sky is "revealed" in the last line and all the activity ends as the performers and spectators look upward, when the tent blows away, at the sudden blackness "Of nothing, nothing, nothing — nothing at all." The light rhymes have helped the poem rush along to the end of its single sentence, broken into two periodic parts at the end of the octave. Structurally a Shakespearean sonnet, "The End of the World" is as untraditional, as much an expression of the thought and sensibility of the 1920's, as Aiken's *Preludes.*

In 1932 MacLeish won a Pulitzer Prize for *Conquistador,* which occupies more than a hundred pages at the end of his first, and still most distinguished, collection, *Poems, 1924–1933.* Out of Pound's *Cantos* in its style and general plan and out of Eliot's *The Waste Land* in its attitudes and its notes, this poem, written as the author tells us in 1928, 1929, and 1931, epitomizes and brings to a full stop the poetic fashions of the preceding decade. Highly mannered, with its constant colons implying both that everything equals everything else and that nothing means anything, it draws upon a historical text describing the conquest of Mexico to picture a New World wasteland. The poem was hailed by eminent reviewers as "one of the great tales of the world," "the most eloquent saga-poem of this generation," and "perhaps the most perfect piece of sustained poetry that anyone has written in America in recent years." Today it reads like an exercise designed to test the theory of poetry MacLeish had announced in "Ars Poetica," that "a poem should not mean but be" — that is, be concrete, specific, dense with precise images. Except for Pound's later Cantos, *Conquistador* was the last long poem written in this style by MacLeish or by anyone else.

In the 1930's, a new spirit was abroad. The Great Depression and the rise of new totalitarian governments in Europe gave social problems an urgency that they had not seemed to have in the 1920's. MacLeish, responding to the new climate, was prominent among the many artists who turned from the ultimate metaphysical subjects of the 1920's to the more immediate problems involved in making democracy work here and now, in America.

Roosevelt was elected in 1932 and installed in 1933, the year MacLeish published *Frescoes For Mr. Rockefeller's City,* which could have been used as a campaign poem if it had come out a year earlier. Who owns America, these poems wanted to know. Mister Harriman, who built railroads? Who is responsible for betraying Jefferson's dream and promise?

Frescoes established MacLeish as both a responsive and a responsible poet, liberal in the best tradition, patriotic, concerned, practical. Writing against Fascists in poems and in plays designed for radio performance, he also dissociated himself from the Communists, as in "Speech to those who say Comrade." His 1936 volume of verse was called *Public Speech,* a title which aptly described his new poetry. Late in the decade, with the Spanish revolution over and the Second World War approaching, he caused a sensation in literary circles by his essay denouncing artists who were not contributing their art to the cause of freedom and democracy; they were "The Irresponsibles." But very little of his poetry of this period, or of the following decade, when he became preoccupied with American history, has survived the events that gave rise to it.

In the 1950's the wars were still going on, but the poet turned again. Writing once more, after a twenty-year interruption, in the "private speech" of a lyric poet, he disavowed not only the ideological abstractions that had preoccupied him in his political period, but the scientific abstractions that had stirred his imagination in the late 1920's. Now, reversing the advice he had given in "The Irresponsibles," he urged a new "Theory of Poetry" on all poets:

> Know the world by heart
> Or never know it!
> Let the pedant stand apart —
> Nothing he can name will show it:
> Also him of intellectual art.
> None know it
> Till they know the world by heart.
>
> Take heart then, poet!

Now he praises those who write about the lasting questions and "impose on the confused, fortuitous/ Flowing away of the world, Form." His "Reasons for Music," dedicated to Wallace Stevens, closes with stanzas that Stevens himself probably would not have found unworthy, and might have written:

> Why do we labor at the poem?
> Out of the turbulence of the sea,
> Flower by brittle flower, rises
> The coral reef that calms the water.
>
> Generations of the dying
> Fix the sea's dissolving salts
> In stone, still trees, their branches immovable,
> Meaning
>   the movement of the sea.

The new poet MacLeish has become in this, his fourth phase,

writes "Songs for Eve," in form derived from nursery rhyme, children's singing-games, and hymns, expressing a tolerant humanistic naturalism, sometimes with slightly religious overtones — "Our human part is to redeem the god/ Drowned in this time of space, this space/ That time encloses." We must "read these faces, figures, flowers" for their immanent meanings, he tells us, or else "everything vanishes." Wordsworth was mistaken in his transcendental intimations, for "Space-time has no beginning and no end," but still there is the "momentary flower," with all that *that* means to man, the "creature to whom meaning matters." We must set about finding the meanings that "Science, that simple saint, cannot be bothered" with.

The ideas and sentiments in MacLeish's recent work are as typical now, as much to be expected, as widely shared in liberal intellectual circles today as the ideas and sentiments in his poems of the 1920's were in their decade, or those of the 1930's were in theirs. An intellectual and poetic history of nearly half a century might be written on the basis of MacLeish's work alone. It would not need to omit any major shift of thought or feeling, any change in the cultural and poetic climate, except neo-orthodoxy.

All such a story would have to omit in addition would be the extreme and unpopular positions of reactionary or radical poets, who have gone it alone. Nothing transcendental and extraordinary, and nothing irresponsible, would be expected in the work of a poet who at every stage of his career has given expression to the historical situation as thoughtful people who were immersed in it saw it.

The Transcendental and Extraordinary

> *I think nothing is of any value in books, excepting the transcendental and extraordinary.*
>
> — Emerson, in "The Poet"

> *Objective evidence and certitude are doubtless very fine ideals to play with, but where on this moonlit and dream-visited planet are they found? . . . . The universe is no longer a mere* It *to us, but a* Thou, *if we are religious. . . .*
>
> — William James, in "The Will to Believe"

WHILE Eliot was picturing the emptiness of life in the wasteland and preparing to think and study his way back to Christian orthodoxy, and Aiken was meditating on the snow falling under the arclight and in his mind, two poets who achieved their poetic maturity in the early 1920's were devoting themselves to saying *No* to the naturalistic temper as loudly as they could. Crane and Cummings were of course "of" their age in all sorts of ways, particularly in shared literary experience and aesthetic assumptions; but their whole effort was to use the new poetic forms of expression as weapons against the philosophic trends of the period.

They hoped to show that there was no need to assume what Aiken called "the emptiness of time"; that, contrary to Stevens, one need *not* have "a mind of winter"; that, despite Eliot, the soul was *not* constituted of a "thousand sordid images," so that poetry need not, in order to be truly contemporary, be composed of "thoughts of a dry brain in a dry season." They would write poetry that would have the effect of denying that "April is the cruellest month." Whatever Aiken and Eliot might think, *they* thought there *was* a "word to say." They would search out the word, and say it.

Crane and Cummings are the first openly, consistently, and self-consciously Transcendental poets after Whitman. Dickinson had been Transcendental in some moods, anti-Transcendental in others. Robinson had been a temperamental Idealist and a sort of secret disciple of Emerson, but he feared that Transcendental philosophy could not be defended in his time. Frost kept what he could of Emerson, but kept it well hidden, not to be thought naive. Williams had not yet written the late poems that would restate many of the Transcendental meanings of Emerson and Whitman despite his "realist" theories. Eliot had not yet gotten over his repugnance for everything Romantic, and *his* way of repudiating scientism and naturalism by becoming an Anglo-Catholic did not seem to either Crane or Cummings to be a "live option." So far as either of them knew, he was completely without contemporary poetic allies.

HART CRANE

Allen Tate's Foreword to Crane's *White Buildings* in 1926, a slender volume that collected all that Crane wanted to save of his work up to that time, is in most respects a triumph of critical acumen. It *places* Crane's early work in a way that needs no substantial alteration forty years later, only an addition; and even that is perhaps implied by Tate:

> The poetry of Hart Crane is ambitious. It is the only poetry I am acquainted with which is at once contemporary and in the grand manner. It is an American poetry. Crane's themes are abstractly, metaphysically conceived, but they are definitely confined to an experience of the American scene. . . . Crane's poems are a fresh vision of the world, so intensely personalized in a new creative language that only the strictest and most unprepossessed effort of attention can take it in. . . . Melville and Whitman are his avowed masters. In his sea poems . . . there is something of Melville's intense, transcendental brooding on the mystery of the "high interiors of the sea." . . . Crane's poetry is a concentration of certain phases of the Whitman substance, the fragments of the myth.

In his conclusion, Tate admits what he considers a fault in the poetry he has defended so vigorously: an obscurity that "is structural and deeper." The reason for it, he believes, lies in "the occasional failure of meeting between vision and subject. The vision often strains and overreaches the theme." He finds the fault common since Baudelaire. "It appears whenever the existing poetic order no longer supports the imagination. It appeared in the eighteenth century with the poetry of William Blake."

I said before that we should have to add something to Tate's placing of Crane's early work, but first there must be a slight subtraction. If we delete "poetic" from the phrase "the existing poetic order," the last two of Tate's sentences quoted just above make considerably better sense. It was not the "poetic" order that failed to give Blake support, but eighteenth-century rationalism and its way of getting at the true and the real. It was not the existing "poetic" order that failed to support Crane's imagination — indeed, on the contrary, he felt very much a part of the *poetic* order, drawing heavily on Eliot, for example, for his style — it was early twentieth-century scientific naturalism that made him try to define and exemplify a "logic" of the imagination that would be independent of the claims of "ordinary" logic and "fact." Tate is prevented here from following up his insights by his devotion to Eliot and the idea of "autotelic" art. If poetry and the other arts are never "about" anything, then we must be careful, as critics, to stay, or to seem to stay, strictly within a "poetic" order. (Williams and the Hartpence story once more.)

What we keep waiting for Tate to say, that never comes, is that Crane belongs in the tradition of nature mysticism defined for modern times by Blake and Wordsworth, Emerson and Whitman, and first studied by Bucke and James. In his best and most lasting work, Crane is a poet of mystic experience. The mystical tradition to which he turned in an attempt to articulate his experience was the typically American, and Romantic, and Transcendental "way up," or what Stace calls "extrovertive" mysticism. This was what was available to him, chiefly through Whitman. If it did not entirely fit the needs of his temperament and the implications of all his experience, particularly in his last years, still it provided a sufficient rationale for the best poems in *White Buildings,* particularly for "Repose of Rivers" and most of the "Voyages," which seem to me the greatest mystical poems in America since early Whitman.

Just how conscious Crane was of the tradition in which he was writing in the best poems in *White Buildings* is hard to determine. Early and late, Crane's explanations of his poetry and statements of intention are very tenuously related to the poetry itself. But his 1926 "General Aims and Theories," though defensive in tone and a little cloudy in its reasoning, shows that he knew, at this time, what was *not* his poetic aim at any rate, even though he might find difficulty in stating what it *was*. The statements in this essay often come closer to seeming to fit the poetry he actually wrote than those in the later and more ambitious "Modern Poetry" do.

Crane comments, for example, on the term "absolutist" that has been, he says, applied to him. He seems uneasy about accepting the description. (What poet would not be? What would it mean, anyway? In the American ethos, "absolutist" is always derogatory, even when not so intended.) But he will accept it, he says in effect, if allowed to define it, first by contrast with what he is *not* trying to do, then by positive statement. He is not, he says, an "impressionist" (Imagist?), for the impressionist is not interested in the metaphysical *causes* of his material. He is not a "realist (of the Zola type)" either, or a "classicist." He cites Blake in an effort to explain himself:

Blake meant these differences when he wrote:

> We are led to believe in a lie
> When we see *with* not *through* the eye.

Impressionists and the others, Crane believes, see only *with* the eye. (We recall Emerson's early definition of himself as a "transparent eyeball.")

Turning from these contrasts to his positive statement, Crane takes off from the quotation from Blake:

> It is my hope to go *through* the combined materials of the poem, using our "real" world somewhat as a spring-board, and to give the poem *as a whole* an orbit or predetermined direction of its own. I would like to establish it as free from my own personality as from any chance evaluation on the reader's part. (This is, of course, an impossibility, but it is a characteristic worth mentioning.) Such a poem is at least a stab at a truth, and to such an extent may be differentiated from other kinds of poetry and called "absolute." Its evocation will not be toward decoration or amusement, but rather toward a state of consciousness, an "innocence" (Blake) or absolute beauty. In this condition there may be discoverable under new forms certain spiritual illumina-

> tions, shining with a morality essentialized from experience directly, and not from previous precepts or preconceptions. It is as though a poem gave the reader as he left it a single, new *word,* never before spoken and impossible to actually enunciate, but self-evident as an active principle in the reader's consciousness henceforward.
>
> [Italics are Crane's.]

To have as one's purpose as a poet the discovery of "spiritual illuminations" is to place oneself within the visionary and mystical tradition in poetry. To trust these illuminations to imply "a morality essentialized from experience directly, and not from previous precepts or preconceptions," is to continue the Emersonian adventure — though Crane was presumably not aware of it. To hope to discover a "new *word,*" unspoken and unspeakable, *in* experience, an immanent *logos,* is to associate oneself with the mystical "way up." If Crane was not wholly clear in his mind about these affinities, he was clear enough for *his* purposes, as, earlier, Stephen Crane had been for his.

A late poem, not in *White Buildings,* makes, paradoxically, a "clearer" statement of Crane's central aim as a poet than anything in his prose. The highly condensed, ambiguous, symbolic language of "The Broken Tower" is more forthright than Crane felt he could afford to be in his prose. (So young, so ignorant, and so vulnerable as he was, it is not surprising that his late prose is usually both apprehensive and cryptically assertive, informed by fear of exposure and desire to please.) The poem opens with a description of the poet's dilemma:

> The bell-rope that gathers God at dawn
> Dispatches me as though I dropped down the knell
> Of a spent day — to wander the cathedral lawn
> From pit to crucifix, feet chill on steps from hell.

But the poet, the "sexton slave" of the bells, is not left simply to wander on the cathedral lawn: "The bells, I say, the bells break down their tower." Their "oval encyclicals" cannot be contained in the structure that held them. Their "reveilles" have outleapt the campaniles and become like "terraced echoes prostrate on the plain," to be sought out and articulated by the poet:

And so it was I entered the broken world
To trace the visionary company of love, its voice
An instant in the wind (I know not whither hurled)
But not for long to hold each desperate choice.

My word I poured. But was it cognate, scored
Of that tribunal monarch of the air
Whose thigh embronzes earth, strikes crystal Word
In wounds pledged once to hope — cleft to despair?

The poet, in short, as mystic or visionary, has tried to formulate a "cognate" vision, to rediscover in his own terms, within his own experience, the essential "illuminations" once conveyed by the bells in the cathedral tower. But *is* his *logos,* the "word" he poured out, really "cognate" with the "crystal Word," the *logos* of John's Gospel?

The steep encroachments of my blood left me
No answer (could blood hold such a lofty tower
As flings the question true?) . . .

The poem ends on a note of certainty as the poet "builds, within, a tower that is not stone/ (Not stone can jacket heaven) . . ." The tower within will be built from the "visible wings of silence sown/ In azure circles, widening as they dip" toward "The matrix of the heart." With the promise of this vision,

The commodious, tall decorum of that sky
Unseals her earth, and lifts love in its shower.

Paraphrase is always difficult with Crane, and any attempt to paraphrase these final lines, with their achieved release and promise of renewal, their new hope found in the midst of despair, would surely result only in a desecration. I shall say only what must be obvious: that this is both a poem "about" mystical experience, and a poem that manages to suggest or "evoke" mystical experience, to *become* a simulacrum of mystical experience for the prepared and sympathetic reader. The fact that its images, particularly the lake and swelling tower of the last stanza, may be seen as phallic symbols in no way invalidates the religious reading of the poem. Erotic experience not only supplies, sometimes, the mystic with a language, with analogies; it may be the avenue leading to mystic vision, as Whitman might remind us. "The Broken Tower" places Crane squarely within the Emerson-Whitman tradition.

To return to the poems in *White Buildings*. Many of them are only experimental, several, like "Chaplinesque," are sentimental, and quite often they make the simple seem mysterious by leaving it obscure. "Legend," the first poem in the book, announces the poet's central preoccupation: in the midst of "this cleaving and this burning," while "Realities plunge in silence by," the poet, "not ready for repentance," resolves to spend himself in a search for "the bright logic" by which "a perfect cry/ Shall string some constant harmony . . ." The poem is at once about poetry and about vision, the two being for Crane almost synonymous, as they were for Emerson, and both connected with love.

The bright logic and the harmony promised by "Legend" are most brilliantly achieved in "Repose of Rivers" and in the last five of the six poems that conclude the volume, the "Voyages." In "Repose of Rivers," images of early experiences of death and evil are transformed as suffering is accepted and the wind, which first was heard seething in willows and cypresses, is heard beyond the "gulf gates," blowing across the sea, which is never directly mentioned in the poem.

> . . . There, beyond the dykes
>
> I heard wind flaking sapphire, like this summer,
> And willows could not hold more steady sound.

The first poem in "Voyages," counseling children not to grow up and take voyages, because "The bottom of the sea is cruel," does not prepare us for what follows in the series. The rest of the poems explore the possibilities of growth in time, by attending to the glimpses of eternity afforded by nature, sexual love, and art. The stanza that concludes the second poem also serves to define the purpose of the quest that will continue through the remaining four poems. The sea gives us epiphanies that rend all pieties but that of lovers, who must "Hasten, while they are true, — sleep, death, desire,/ Close round one instant in one floating flower." The petition in the final stanza then follows naturally:

Bind us in time, O Seasons clear, and awe.
O minstrel galleons of Carib fire,
Bequeath us to no earthly shore until
Is answered in the vortex of our grave
The seal's wide spindrift gaze toward paradise.

In the last poem the poet, the seeker, "derelict" and "blinded," but still the "guest" of the sea, which by this point in the poems carries the fused meanings of love, death, and eternity, continues his voyage. Still seeking, his "eyes pressed black against the prow," "waiting, afire," he cannot claim to "speak" — which for a poet would mean to possess and control — the "Word," he can only point to images that *suggest* it, and speak of his conviction *about* it:

It is the unbetrayable reply
Whose accent no farewell can know.

To speak the "name, unspoke" would be to identify and define, and so to claim some kind of control over, the Absolute. The seeker's scruple springs from religious humility. As Ian Ramsey has said in *Religious Language,* commenting on the significance of "naming" in religious situations as a form of disclosure, *labeling* may be done at any time, without implying any commitment on our part to what is labeled,

> But for us, to name in what we call the "full" sense, would mean that it was in our power to will and create a religious situation, and thus to guarantee God, to compel a religious disclosure, and this the religious man would never allow possible. If *we* name, there is no disclosure.

Thus we may feel all the more, reading the poem, that there has *been* a disclosure, just because the Word is never spoken. We hear of "Creation's blithe and petalled word" (*fiat lux*?) and of the "imaged Word . . . that holds/ Hushed willows anchored in its glow," but the Word is not spoken here as it is in the final lines of *The Bridge,* where the ineffable that has disclosed himself *is* named, by the poet, who tells us its name is "Love." There is good New Testament authority for saying that God is Love, but both poetic and religious considerations unite in suggesting that the poet's explicitness here weakens the affirmation he intends to make. Is he perhaps just "labeling" at this point?

"Voyages VI" is both a triumph of Crane's art and an illustration of what he meant when he said that poetry has a "logic" of its own that could give us, not the merely "fictive" music Stevens expected of it, but "a stab at truth." To be sure, "That 'truth' which science pursues is radically different from the metaphorical, extra-logical 'truth' of the poet," Crane later admitted in "Modern Poetry"; yet the poet who articulates "consciousness *sub specie aeternitatis*" is a true seer and a true visionary for all that. Crane would not admit the perfect disjunction between imagination and reality that Stevens assumed as his starting point. The "extra-logical" truth pursued by the voyager is not "scientific," but neither is it in any sense just "imaginary." It is the truth of mystic vision, which every definition falsifies. Along with "Repose of Rivers," "Voyages II," and the "Proem" to *The Bridge,* "Voyages VI" seems to me to be among the great poems of mystical experience in our literature.

Crane never wrote quite so well again. The "Proem" to *The Bridge* is a magnificent poem, but what it attempts is nowhere near so difficult as the attempt in "Voyages VI." *The Bridge* as a whole, though it is surely one of the several finest long poems in our literature, has been felt by almost all its readers to be uneven in the quality of its parts and to fail, despite its brilliance, to achieve the purposes Crane himself stated, and elaborated, for it.

Insofar as the poem *does* fail to achieve its intention, perhaps it is partly because no poem could be expected to achieve all that Crane said he "intended" in this poem. Crane's life was falling to pieces in the late 1920's. Alcoholism and inversion, increasingly rapid swings from exaltation to despair, a deepening sense of guilt, and a growing distrust of the experiences of illumination that had enabled him to write "Voyages," all put him very much on the defensive as he tried to explain to various friends and benefactors, particularly to Otto Kahn, why the major poem was worth waiting for.

He explained too much, claimed too much. Again and again he drew up outlines, explicating in detail poems not yet written, that sometimes never *did* get written. He was, he said, trying for an "assimilation" of all American experience; he was, he believed, "really handling" nothing less than "the Myth of America." He was writing "an epic of the modern consciousness, and indescribably complicated factors have to be resolved and blended." All this, and much more, from just one of Crane's letters to Kahn. If we begin reading the poem with these and other statements of intention in mind, we are likely to conclude that not all the "complicated factors" the poet said he was dealing with did get "resolved and blended" in the poem.

The real intent of the poem, and of the poet as he was writing it, not writing *about* it, emerges clearly enough from the poem itself to make the grandiose and often contradictory explanations unnecessary — though Crane's letters and book reviews of the years before he started *The Bridge* do help to place the poem in its tradition. *The Bridge* grew out of Crane's personal situation and his devotion to Whitman, particularly to the mystical aspect of Whitman's work; out of his desire to provide an "answer" to Eliot's description of modern life as empty of spiritual meaning ("I feel that Eliot ignores certain spiritual events and possibilities as real and powerful now as, say, in the time of Blake. Certainly the man has dug the ground and buried hope as deep and direfully as it ever can be done."); and out of his belief that P. D. Ouspensky's *Tertium Organum,* describing in twentieth-century language what Bucke had earlier called "cosmic consciousness," had provided him with a way of defending mystical experience in an age of science. Whitman, Eliot, and Ouspensky are thus the formative influences behind the poem; and of the three, Whitman is the real source and fountainhead, the indispensable influence.

Precisely at the center of *The Bridge,* if we count the "Proem" as an introduction and "Atlantis" as a coda, is "Cape Hatteras," which Crane once described in a letter as "a kind of ode to Whitman." This section more than any other is the key to the poem's intent. Crane opens the poem with an epigraph from "Passage to India," section eight, the prayer for a vision of God in Whitman's poem. "Bathe me O God in thee, mounting to thee," Whitman first asks, and then, after some lines that describe (more as remembered and desired than as experienced at present) the mystic's sense of union, ends the section with lines that look ahead to the time when, after death, the union of the soul with God will be complete, "The seas all crossed, weather'd the capes, the voyage done." That Crane should select for his epigraph precisely *these* lines is the first key to his intention in "Cape Hatteras," and ultimately to *The Bridge* as a whole.

He might instead, for instance, have chosen Whitman's opening lines in the poem, "Singing my days . . . Singing the strong light works of engineers." With Brooklyn Bridge as his major symbol, why not? Or he might have chosen a line or two from the second section of the poem, celebrating the "myths and fables of eld," especially those of India. Was he not writing what he would call a "Psalm of Cathay," drawing upon the story of Pocahontas as the source of an American myth? Or he might have chosen the lines that close Whitman's third section,

> (Ah Genoese thy dream! thy dream!
> Centuries after thou art laid in thy grave,
> The shore thou foundest verifies thy dream.)

For he too had celebrated Columbus, in "Ave Maria," his first section, and had said, repeatedly, that the poem would show that America was not a "wasteland" but a land particularly favorable for the realization of the dreams of spiritual voyagers.

Crane's choosing to quote just the lines he did, and not some others that might seem equally appropriate, particularly to certain of his stated intentions, can only be called the key to the intention of a poem that I have asserted is thoroughly Whitmanic in intention if Crane knew how to *read* Whitman; which is to say, if the quoted lines are in fact from the climactic section of Whitman's poem, where the various opposites of that poem are united and transcended, and where we get Whitman's resolution of his tensions between the works of engineers and the meanings of myth. An unprejudiced reading of "Passage to India" will show, I believe, that such is in fact the case. "Passage to India" is no more "about" its Suez Canal, transcontinental railroad, and Atlantic cable, or its "primitive fables," than *The Bridge* is "about" the Brooklyn Bridge or Pocahontas. Both poems are "about" union with God, achieved through sensing the immanence of deity in present experience.

If this is so, it is appropriate that "Cape Hatteras" opens, after the epigraph, with lines that evoke a vision of the land, seen *sub specie aeternitatis,* as Whitman saw it, and closes with quotations from and allusions to "Song of the Open Road." Crane's final lines are

> Yes, Walt,
> Afoot again, and onward without halt, —

Not soon, nor suddenly, — No, never to let go
My hand
in yours,
Walt Whitman —
so —

Whitman's poem begins, "Afoot and light-hearted I take to the open road"; moves through intuitions of what it means to be journeying "Forever alive, forever forward"; and ends with the kind of personal pledge of fidelity that Gabriel Marcel has made a keystone of his philosophy (Whitman first called it "cohesiveness" and finally decided to call it "Personalism"):

Camerado, I give you my hand!
I give you my love more precious than money,
I give you myself before preaching or law;
Will you give me yourself? will you come travel with me?
Shall we stick by each other as long as we live?

Between the beginning and the end of "Cape Hatteras," everything is Whitmanic by intention, though whether the poem actually achieves a re-creation of Whitman's vision or merely urges and asserts it, sometimes frenetically, is likely to remain an open question. In the first place, Crane equates the "cosmic consciousness" of the opening lines, with their perspective gained from geologic time, with the effect of reading "you, Walt." This is Whitman interpreted in Ouspensky's terms. In the remainder of the body of the poem, Crane hears radio static as "the captured fume of space," as Whitman thought of the sounds of the Morse code that came through the Atlantic cable, the technological triumph of *his* day; celebrates the circle, "that star-glistered salver of infinity," in good mystic — and Emersonian-Whitmanic — tradition; invokes the spirit of Whitman walking the beach at Paumanok at night, listening to the song of the bird that sings of love and death ("Out of the Cradle Endlessly Rocking"); specifically equates Whitman with Columbus, the one the physical, the other the spiritual, discoverer of America — "Sea eyes and tidal, undenying, bright with myth!"; looks, with Whitman, for "new verities, new inklings" in the hum of dynamos, which produce the "harnessed jelly of the stars"; celebrates the flight of the Wright brothers at Kitty Hawk, as Frost would later do, and the new dirigibles, as Walt had earlier celebrated the engineering triumphs of *his* day; confesses that the main point of his poem — "To conjugate infinity's dim marge" — has perhaps already been better achieved by Walt — "But who has held the heights more sure than thou,/ O Walt"; states the basic reason for his loyalty to the older poet —

> . . . O, something green,
> Beyond all sesames of science was thy choice
> Wherewith to bind us throbbing with one voice;

dedicates himself to "that span of consciousness thou'st named/ The Open Road"; and, finally, accepts as his own subject the charge Whitman gave to future poets —

> . . . thy vision is reclaimed!
> What heritage thou'st signalled to our hands!

The fact that "Cape Hatteras" does in fact give us the clue to Crane's intention in *The Bridge* could be "proved" — so far as any such critical assertion could ever be "proved" — only by a close reading of the whole poem, section by section, line by line. But such a "reading" of the poem would take a small book. We should have to follow in detail the way in which dream in the poem becomes mere apparition or nightmare, only to turn again to dream, which finally becomes vision. We should have to chart the rhythmic, contrapuntal thematic structure of one of the most dense and complex poems ever written by an American. We should have to say whatever *could* be said about the parts — like "Three Songs" — that seem unrelated to the main theme, or at least not clear in their function within the whole poem.

But after all this, the "reading" would have to conclude with another look at the "Proem" and a final inspection of "Atlantis," the concluding section or coda, and rest its case there. If the beginning, middle, and end do not tell us what a long poem intends to say, it is doubtful that any lesser part will.

The Proem, "To Brooklyn Bridge," is the full repayment of Crane's debt to Whitman. Only a Whitmanic poet, living in the new conditions of the 1920's, could have done it. Moving by affirmation and denial, soaring dream and sinking fact, it captures both Whitman's vision and the ideas of the 1920's which seemed to render that vision invalid. It invokes "harp and altar, of the fury fused," but attends just as carefully to the feeling that comes when "elevators drop us from our day." The parabolic curve of the actual bridge becomes at once the "inviolate curve" that suggests the perfect circle of infinity and the ever-ongoing movement of a spiritual open road; for a parabola never closes in on itself, yet always seems to be moving toward the circle's closure. The poem's final line is the climax of the prayer of invocation: "And of the curveship lend a myth to God."

"Atlantis" begins with an epigraph from Plato: "Music is then the knowledge of that which relates to love in harmony and system." Substitute "poetry" for "music" and we get both Crane's idea of what he hoped he had acomplished and a justification for his naming of the Word which, though it is "unspeakable," he still speaks, as the meaning of his major symbol, and of the poem he has built upon it: "Unspeakable Thou Bridge to Thee, O Love." "God is love," John said in his First Epistle. Crane has not been merely "poetic," indulging in personification, in his capitalization of "Thee": he has been true to the meaning of the Scriptural Revelation, as he had said in "The Broken Tower" he hoped to be; and true also to his mother, who was a Christian Scientist. The final lines of "Atlantis" proclaim the God that Crane's contemplation of the bridge's curve had led him to.

Crane's God is very like that of the Christian Gospel, but he has been arrived at, or met, or discovered, by a different route from that taken by Eliot, who struggled to conform his thoughts to "the faith once delivered to the saints." (Whether God has in fact, in very truth, "disclosed" himself to Crane, in the experiences described in *The Bridge,* is a religious, and not a literary-critical, problem.) Crane has been attentive to what has been called "Continuous creation," considered as revelation. He has listened to the "Swift peal of *secular* light" (my italics), and from the listening created an "intrinsic Myth/ Whose fell unshadow is death's utter wound."

That is to say, the light is "secular" because it has come from "nature," not from "Scripture," the Cathedral being no longer able to hold the bells that peal out the light. And the myth is "intrinsic" both because it is the product of native conditions (Pocahontas, the Indiana mother, the bridge) and also because it has been "essentialized from experience directly, and not from previous precepts or preconceptions." Crane's God has been intuited — perhaps it would be better to say "perceived," since that is what the poem in effect says — in experience by that "steeled Cognizance whose leap commits/ The agile precincts of the lark's return." Like Whitman, who found divinity even in "beetles rolling balls of dung," Crane — though with severer fluctuations of faith — has found the Absolute everywhere, even, as Emerson had said in "Merlin I," in "the din of city arts," which for Crane becomes the "martyr's cave" of the subway, where

> The phonographs of hades in the brain
> Are tunnels that re-wind themselves, and love
> A burnt match skating in a urinal. . . .

"Cape Hatteras," we may conclude, does yield the sufficient clue to the intended meaning of the whole poem. But Eliot and Ouspensky also helped to make the poem possible, and to give it the form it finally assumed. Crane's real literary education had begun with his discovery of Pound, as Brom Weber long ago pointed out, but had later continued under the tutelage of Eliot, while his admiration for Pound gradually waned. Early in 1922, before he had read *The Waste Land,* he wrote his friend Tate, "The poetry of negation is beautiful — alas, too dangerously so for one of my mind. But I am trying to break away from it . . ." When he read Eliot's poem in the fall of that year, he at first found it "dead." His work was cut out for him, he thought. He would devote himself to refuting the poem, to showing that "spiritual illuminations" could come even in the waste land. He would answer Eliot in his own idiom, in the older poet's own symbolic techniques. But *his* myth would be "intrinsic" and "secular."

About the same time, probably in 1922, Crane was profoundly affected by his reading of P. D. Ouspensky's *Tertium Organum.* A Russian mystic with mathematical and scientific training, Ouspensky tried to explain the nature of the "higher consciousness," that Bucke had left unexplained, as a way of "perceiving" that transcended the dimensions of space-time. "That which can be expressed," he argued, "cannot be true," because ordinary logic is founded on space-time categories. Truth is never Aristotelian, but always and only the discovery of "the logic of infinity, the logic of ecstasy," whch is necessarily intuitive. Real knowledge is "direct" knowledge; it comes only by "illumination."

Ouspensky devoted a chapter in his book to Bucke's *Cosmic Consciousness,* which had used Whitman as its chief modern example of a man possessing the mystic awareness. Crane already knew and liked Whitman's work, but now he had another reason to go back to it: Ouspensky had told him why it was that Whitman had been able to articulate, as Crane would later say, a myth "beyond all sesames of science" and thus to become "the most typical and valid expression" of the American psyche, writing visionary poetry that reconciled and fused "those forces in America which seem most intractable." Whitman, Crane learned from Ouspensky, had expressed "human consciousness *sub specie aeternitatis.*" No wonder that when Crane came to write *The Bridge* he showed the influence of Ouspensky's language and concepts and offered his hand to Walt as he attempted to do for his age what he thought Whitman had done for his, that is, to bridge the gap between time and eternity, the one and the many, the wholly transcendent and the inertly factual.

The line between Emerson and Whitman, and Whitman and Bucke, and Bucke and Ouspensky, and Ouspensky and Crane, is unbroken, a kind of Apostolic Succession accomplished by the laying on of hands. Crane was hesitant, and became more so with the years, about claiming to be a "mystic," but all his later work, after the earlier poems in *White Buildings,* shows that that is how he thought of himself — or at least how he thought of the "true poet," which he sometimes despaired of being. He had read in Ouspensky that "the founders of the religions of the world have all been bridgebuilders . . . between the *Finite* and the *Infinite,*" and in Whitman, "I inaugurate a new religion." He felt himself suited for an attempt at Whitman's task by his own experience. He wrote Tate in 1923:

> Frank has the real mystic's vision . . . I have also enjoyed reading Ouspensky's "Tertium Organum" lately. Its corroboration of several experiences in consciousness that I have had gave it particular interest.

His view of poetry, whenever he was not driven to making concessions to the naturalistic conceptions of his friends, was thoroughly Emersonian, though he most often cited Blake when attempting to explain it: "Poetry, in so far as the metaphysics of absolute knowledge extends, is simply the concrete *evidence* of the *experience* of knowledge." It was also Whitmanic as well as Blakean:

> The tragic quandary of the modern world derives from the paradoxes that an inadequate system of rationality forces on the living consciousness. . . . my poetry . . . in so far as it was truly poetic . . . would necessarily express its concepts in the more direct terms of physical experience.

(When Whitman had tired of hearing the learned astronomer, he had gone out and looked up in perfect silence at the stars.) The best part of Crane's work may be understood as the attempt of a poet who interpreted his rare mystical experiences in Ouspenskyan terms, and his proper role and function as a poet in Blakean-Whitmanic terms, to create, in his poetry, an alternative to Modernism's "inadequate system of rationality." This, in effect, is what he meant by such statements in letters to friends as "I find nothing in Blake that seems outdated, and for him the present was always eternity," or "I still stake some claims on the pertinence of the intuitions." [1]

But the 1920's were not a good time for such a poet. Like Robinson earlier, Crane did not feel that he *knew* enough to answer his friends. "If I am metaphysical I'm content to continue so," he wrote, defensively, to Yvor Winters, but he grew more and more uncertain, in his last years, when he was being supported for the specific purpose of creating his bridge between the finite and infinite, that his experiences of harmony and unity in apparent chaos could be trusted.

In one way perhaps Whitman's example, which seemed to offer him validation, did him more harm than good. Temperamentally, perhaps, especially in the final years of his short life, Crane had more in common with St. John of the Cross than with Whitman. If he had lived earlier and elsewhere, he might have trusted his mystic experiences, and interpreted them as "a flight of the alone to the alone." "The way down," into the depths of consciousness, was very possibly the only mystic way Crane had ever personally and strongly experienced. His life was too anguished, his experience too scarifying, to encourage frequent perceptions of "immanent divinity." But Whitman's "way up," his nature mysticism, was the only *example* Crane knew. He was forced to interpret his experiences of illumination in terms fundamentally alien to his temperament.

The failure of *The Bridge,* if it did fail, or to the extent that it fails, may have more to do with Crane's being forced into a mystical tradition alien to him — forced by his lack of knowledge of any other, and by his desire to answer Eliot — than with any of the excesses of his personal life on which it has so often been blamed. The excesses, I suspect, were as much effect as cause. Crane's saving experiences had always come from *outside* his normal daily life, or from *within* his deepest self, which may amount to the same thing. In "Voyages VI," for instance, the "imaged Word" comes in the midst of, and apparently despite, the blackness of despair; it makes an "unbetrayable reply" to experience because it is not dependent upon day-by-day experience, but apart from it. Similarly, in "Repose of Rivers," childhood memories of death and evil are transfigured only by the experience of the sea, a glimpse of the eternal. Neither of these poems would prepare us for Crane's attempt, in *The Bridge,* to create his "intrinsic myth" based on the mystic "way up," the affirmation of images.

Rather, they would lead us to expect him to write something like Roy Campbell's translation of a stanza by St. John of the Cross:

> Deep-cellared is the cavern
> Of my love's heart, I drank of him alive:
> Now, stumbling from the tavern,
> No thoughts of mine survive,
> And I have lost the flock I used to drive.[2]

The experiences of hell in *The Bridge* all seem to come when *other people* are around. "Love" to Crane came to mean being beaten up by sailors, or a burnt match in a urinal. There is the story of the aging Whitman going out to lovers' lanes to watch the lovers, to be sure, but we imagine his returning to his littered room without any sense of guilt. Crane came, in the end, before he committed suicide, to feel much more like St. John than like Whitman. When he jumped from the ship into the moonlit Caribbean, perhaps he was aware that his final symbolic gesture aligned him not with Whitman, but with those whose reliance was *only* on God, conceived as entirely separate from His creation. The opening lines in the saint's "Glosa a lo divino," again in the Campbell translation, seem to fit Crane's sense of himself and his situation better than anything in Whitman's work finally does. To the extent that *The Bridge* is an "imperfect" and uneven poem, perhaps the chief reason is that Crane was trying to re-express Whitman's themes without having Whitman's temperament. Here are Campbell's versions of the lines written by the medieval mystic. They need no comment as they relate to Crane.

> Without support, yet well supported,
> Though in pitch-darkness, with no ray,
> Entirely I am burned away.
>
> My spirit is so freed from every
> Created thing, that through the skies,
> Above herself, she's lifted, flies,
> And as in a most fragrant reverie,
> Only on God her weight applies.[3]

E. E. CUMMINGS

The perfect epitaph for Crane was written by Cummings when he heard of Crane's suicide in 1932. Writing his diary of his Russian trip, *Eimi,* he noted Crane's death this way:

> Drunk and becauseless (talking about a cyclone, telling how at last with the disappearance even of impossibility himself found actually himself and suddenly becoming the cyclone; not perishing and not surviving; Being) the poet Hart Crane was able to invent growth's likeness.

In the private language he used in both prose and verse, Cummings is praising Crane for having accomplished what he, Cummings, was still hoping to accomplish, and what Emerson had recommended but seldom achieved: the creation of poems that would be "growth's likeness." Cummings is praising Crane for being *his* kind of poet — "drunk," in the ecstatic, Dionysian tradition, as Emerson had wanted the poet to be, though Emerson had wanted the drunkenness to be only metaphoric, an airy inebriation; "becauseless," or unconcerned with before and after, cause and effect, or any of the categories of abstract reason; inhabiting "Being," or both sensing, and capturing in his work, the transcendent mysteries of the *nowhere* in the *now-here;* "inventing" poems that would not just be "about" Becoming, as *Four Quartets* are "about" mystical vision, but would themselves, in their own movement, be art's *simulacra* of life's Becoming. Cummings is praising Crane for having written verse that could be defined as he later said he wished his own to be: "carnalized metaphysics"; and saying at the same time that the metaphysics carnalized in Crane's poems is the *same* as his own. No poet could praise another more highly.

The interesting thing about the epitaph is how amazingly just and appropriate it is in the terms of its praise. It would be hard to imagine a more "subjective" statement, yet its very subjectivity is the means by which it gets at the heart of the matter, which is the common tradition and common aim of the two poets. How conscious Cummings was of this bond between them when he wrote the statement, we shall probably never know; but that he later came to see that his praise of Crane illuminated himself as much as it did his subject is apparent in the use he made of the statement in his single effort at formal autobiography, *i: six nonlectures*.

Speaking before a Harvard audience twenty years after Crane's death, during his year as poet in residence at his alma mater, Cummings devoted the first three of his six talks to the "growth" of the poet as a man, the last three to the "growth" of the man as a poet. ("Writing, I feel, is an art; and artists, I feel, are human beings.") The fourth talk he devoted chiefly to quoting brief excerpts from his own earlier works, beginning with his first book, *The Enormous Room,* in 1922, and coming up to just before the time of the talk itself. Comments on the excerpts are minimal when there are any at all; the quotations are meant to be self-explanatory revelations of the "not divisible" man-artist who was attempting, in this way, "an exploration of his stance as a writer." The quotations are arranged chronologically, by the date of the book from which they are taken.

Under the date 1933, Cummings read just two excerpts from *Eimi,* without any comment. The first reveals his distrust of "rationalism" and his preoccupation with "growth": "Not to completely feel is thinking . . . to grow is a fate." The second translates these attitudes into poetic terms and embodies them in an example. This second quotation is the praise of Crane. Those who listened to the talk may have been puzzled by the seeming incoherence of the juxtaposition, but in the total context of the printed talks, the reader can see that there is no incoherence, only an omitted transition.

The talks are so eminently readable and quotable, so authentic and open, so nearly the opposite of what Frost learned to do in *his* public lectures — that is, to "fool" his audience, to seem to reveal without revealing — that there is a temptation to quote at length to establish the context I have said makes the two quotations from *Eimi* plain enough in their revelation of the stance of the writer, and sufficiently coherent in their juxtapositions. But I shall quote only the concluding paragraphs of the last lecture:

> So ends the last lesson of a nondivisible ignoramus: a double lesson — outwardly and inwardly affirming that, whereas a world rises to fall, a spirit descends to ascend. Now our ignoramus faces the nonanswerable question "who, as a writer, am I?" with which his nonlecturing career began; and finds himself deluged by multitudinous answers. What would these multitudinous answers say if they could speak as a single answer? Possibly or impossibly this —
>
> I am someone who proudly and humbly affirms that love is the mystery-of-mysteries, and that nothing measurable matters "a very good God damn": that "an artist, a man, a failure" is no mere whenfully accreting mechanism, but a givingly eternal complexity — neither some soulless and heartless ultrapredatory infra-animal nor any un-understandingly knowing and believing and thinking automaton, but a naturally and miraculously whole human being — a feelingly illimitable individual; whose only happiness is to transcend himself, whose every agony is to grow.
>
> Ecstasy and anguish, being and becoming; the immortality of the creative imagination and the indomitability of the human spirit — these are the subjects of my final poetry reading: which (I devoutly hope) may not wrong a most marvellous ode by Keats, and the magnificent closing stanzas of Shelley's Prometheus Unbound.

These are the views of a poet whose "philosophy of life" his earliest critic has described as "transcendental, romantic, prelapsarian, organicist, and individualistic," [4] a description which is perfectly accurate but needlessly tautological. If we could only change "transcendental" to "Transcendental" (Emerson's sense), there would be no need to continue the adjectives. "Transcendentalism" is the proper word for the context in which the two excerpts from *Eimi* make sense, fit together, and reveal both man as writer and writer as man. "Transcendentalism" is the link between Cummings and Crane, the link that permitted Cummings to see Crane's work in terms of the ideal he held for his own, without distorting Crane's.

But Transcendentalism seemed remote, obscure; an "impossible" view for a poet to hold, all during Cummings' lifetime. When, some twenty years after he began to write, critics discovered that Cummings was "Romantic," they used their discovery as a way of dismissing him as irrelevant, if they happened not to like his work; or else apologized for him, defending his right to be "irresponsible" if he wished, if they happened to like it. Even Norman Friedman, whose pioneering critical study of Cummings is sympathetic and helpful, felt it necessary, as we have seen, to keep on adding other adjectives after starting with "transcendental," as though "prelapsarian," "organic," and so on were not all implied by "Transcendentalism" itself.

What Cummings thought he was up to had been made clear first of all in *The Enormous Room,* in 1922, and then in five volumes of poetry between that time and the date of *Eimi,* and then once again more explicitly in that book, from which I shall continue to quote. In the passage that follows, a conversation is recorded between Henry Wadsworth Longfellow Dana (unnamed in the book, for obvious reasons), Boston Brahmin turned Marxist, and Cummings, Boston Unitarian speaking as a Boston Unitarian. "Q" in what follows stands for Dana, "A" for Cummings:

> Q: The whole trouble with you is that, like so many people who were brought up on religion, you can't bear the idea of anything doing away with it.
>
> A: Can't bear the idea of any what doing away with which?
>
> Q: Of science doing away with religion.
>
> A: I see: we're supposed to suppose that the new religion, science, does away with religion, the old religion — tahk.
>
> Q: (snorts): How can you be so perverse!
>
> A: I?

Q: As if religion and science weren't direct opposites!
A: Right you are, colonel: every coin has two sides.
Q: Odear. There you go, utterly confusing the issue —
A: Issue? We've all tried paying with one side and keeping the other side for ourselves, haven't we?
Q: But, my dear chap — can't you possibly be serious?
A: I'm afraid I'm being much too serious, comrade.
Q: No you're not — you're being extremely trivial and very childish and rather cheaply amusing.
A: And I'm quoting Emerson.
Q: Emerson?
A: "When me you fly, I am the wings."
Q: Who said that?
A: Brahma, the sage of Concord, who (inconsiderately) went to Rome and found —
Q: O, of course . . . but to return to our muttons. What you can't seem to realise is this: religion imprisons the human mind, whereas science makes people free.
A: What I can seem to realise is that I'd just as soon be imprisoned in freedom as free in a jail — if that's any help.
Q: You simply won't be serious, will you.

This was in 1933. When, years later, Cummings first went to Brown University to lecture, at the behest of his classmate S. Foster Damon,[5] and was introduced by Winfield Townley Scott as a New England poet in the unbroken line extending from Emerson and Thoreau through Dickinson and Robinson, he was particularly pleased to be called "a direct heir and descendant of the great New Englanders." No wonder, for to be so described was equivalent to being called a true son of his parents, and fidelity to *them* is the burden of the first three of the six Harvard lectures. Cummings inherited his tradition from his home and made a lifelong career out of the juggling feat of keeping intact what he had been given, while still movng on. The feat was rendered less difficult for him than it might have been by the fact that the Emersonian doctrines of self-reliance and self-transcendence were major tenets in the teaching of his father, the Reverend Edward Cummings, a highly successful, respected, and nationally known liberal minister.

For Cummings, being faithful to his personal past, and particularly to the much-loved father, meant continuing to believe in the future. There was no need for him to rebel against a father who taught as articles of faith the independence, freedom, and growth of the self. John Dos Passos, recalling his visits to the Cummings home on Irving Street in Cambridge in his Harvard student days, has stressed the way "the oldfashioned Cambridge household" seemed to provide a link with the past: "I've cherished my recollection of it as a link with the Jameses and all the generations of old New England back to Emerson and Thoreau . . . Cummings improvising on the piano for the edification of his admiring family. Dr. Cummings booming from the pulpit . . ." William James, Cummings tells us in the Harvard lectures, was his father's favorite neighbor — "so true a friend and so great a human being" — and the one to whom Cummings said he might be said to owe his "existence," since it was James who introduced his father to his mother.

Cummings did not say, but might have, that culturally also he owed much to James, and to the atmosphere James both symbolized and embodied. For it was William James more than anyone else in that time and that place who kept alive Emerson's chief meanings and motives, even while he subtly modified some of them as his openness to the evidence seemed to require. Cummings preferred the unmodified to the modified meanings. His poetry and prose give us the purest example of undiluted Emersonianism our century has yet provided. In his Introduction to the new poems included in *Collected Poems* (1938) Cummings had placed himself unequivocally in the Emersonian tradition, but there has been a subsequent failure of even his most sympathetic interpreters to understand this. The paradox must be explained by the fact that in the recent past critics young enough and "modern" enough to be interested in Cummings have had no real firsthand and extensive knowledge of Emerson. "We can never be born enough," Cummings had said. "We are human beings; for whom birth is a supremely welcome mystery, the mystery of growing: the mystery which happens only and whenever we are faithful to ourselves." He had turned, then, to the negations of scientific philosophy and its "parlourgame of real unreality," to the "neutralization of nature" (he did not use the phrase) which I have been tracing through the works of so many of his contemporaries as the "given" from which their work took its departure. Dismissing "the modern temper" sarcastically, as accepted by "mostpeople" but not worthy of consideration by those who, like himself, refused to be defined as anything less than a transcendent person, an illimitable self, sensuous, sensual, healthily *alive,* but no mere "lookiesoundiefeelietastiesmellie," or behaviorist automaton, Cummings had affirmed (whatever "science" may say) that the "self" is a "citizen of immortality." I have partially "normalized" the pointing of Cummings' words.

> Miracles are to come. With you I leave a remembrance of miracles: they are by somebody who can love and who shall be continually reborn, a human being; . . . Nothing believed or doubted; brain over heart, surface: nowhere hating or to fear; shadow, mind without soul. Only how measureless cool flames of making; only each other building always distinct selves of mutual entirely opening; only alive. Never the murdered finalities of wherewhen and yesno, impotent nongames of wrongright and rightwrong; never to gain or pause, never the soft adventure of undoom, greedy anguishes and cringing ecstasies of inexistence; never to rest and never to have: only to grow.
>
> Always the beautiful answer who asks a more beautiful question

To anyone familiar with Emerson's "Circles," it should have been clear many years ago that there was no emphasis or attitude here, not even the refusal to put a period at the end, that had not been foreshadowed in the essay — by which I do not mean to suggest that Cummings necessarily *knew* the essay.[6] The only reference to Emerson in Cummings that I know of is the one already quoted from *Eimi,* where he is referring to the poetry, to "Brahma" in particular. When a biographer finally tells us what Cummings read, it may turn out that he absorbed much of his Emersonianism — the part he did not get from his father — through Whitman. If so, that fact would add another link to the many that connect him with his friend and fellow-rebel Hart Crane.

What is true of Cummings' "metaphysic" is equally true of other aspects of his stance as man and writer. His epistemology is "intuitive" precisely in the Emersonian sense, with the same suspicion of abstraction, the same unconcern for consistency and "mere logic" and "mere fact," the same hope of seeing as with a "transparent eyeball," the same method of preparing oneself to receive nature's epiphanies by relaxed "aesthetic" attention. His aesthetic is exactly as Platonic, and just as organic, as Emerson's, with the same conception of poetry as a means of suggesting what must otherwise remain incommunicable, the same belief that the "argument" (as Emerson called it) must shape the poem, and the same search for a language "of sufficient energy" (as Emerson had put it) to convey the vision.

Cummings' mystical antinomianism is a part of the same inheritance, resting on the same Protestant religious base and issuing in the same suspicion of all moral rules, especially the *don'ts,* of society's "conspiracy" against the individual; in the same belief in the betrayal of spirit involved in the *letter* of every doctrine, every dogma, every conventional ritual; in the same hostility toward business, politics, and organized reform — toward the whole "practical," work-a-day world in short; in the same preference for the innocence and instinctive wisdom of children and animals, the product of an undivided self in which body, mind, and spirit function together; in the same insistence on an unmediated relation between the Self and the Absolute. Emerson's "What I must do is all that concerns me, not what the people think," lies behind Cummings' scorn for "mostpeople." Emerson's "I would write on the lintels of the doorpost, *Whim.* I hope it is somewhat better than whim at last, but we cannot spend the day in explanation," if taken quite literally and combined with Cummings' sense of his isolation from the intellectuals of his time, would sufficiently account for the frequent belligerency of his refusal to explain himself in "mostpeople's" terms. Antinomians do not talk the same language as either "religious" or "secular" rationalists.

Apart from his poetry and prose, and the poetry of the great poets of the past whose work he said he loved, Cummings in his Harvard lectures cited only one book. Not surprisingly, that book was the Bible. He read to his audience the whole story of the woman taken in adultery, as told in the Gospel of John, 8, 1–11. He introduced the passage by calling it "this masterpoem of human perception, whose seventh verse alone exterminates all conventional morality." The key words here are "perception," implicitly defined earlier in the sentence as "feeling," as opposed to "knowing and believing and thinking"; and "conventional" before "morality," which assumes the antinomian's equation of "morality" with "moralism." Truth, he implies, is related always to the concrete, the individual, the empiric; it must be "perceived" (Cummings usually said "felt") in the response of the total self to an always-novel experience. To follow "feeling" is thus to run the risk of coming into conflict with the "rules" of "conventional" (read "unperceptive," "unfeeling," "closed" and "rationalistic") morality.

"He who would gather immortal palms must not be hindered by the name of goodness [that is, what *society* calls or names "goodness," the "goodness" of conventional morality], but must explore if it be goodness," Emerson had written in "Self-Reliance" in the middle of a discussion of how far it might be necessary to go to preserve the integrity of the self. When a friend, years before this, had objected that "these impulses may be from below, not from above," Emerson reports himself as having replied, " 'They do not seem to me to be such; but if I am the Devil's child, I will then live from the Devil.' No law can be sacred to me but that of my nature." The *thrust* of this is against late Calvinism and its theology of the Fall, against conventional morality, against all who valued security above growth. But the *basis* of it is a positive faith, not a suspicion or hostility, a positive faith in the "Trustee" of all self-trust: "We lie in the lap of immense intelligence, which makes us receivers of its truth and organs of its activity."

I have let Emerson explain the assumptions that undergird the Transcendental faith in self-reliance because he does it more briefly and coherently than Cummings, partly perhaps because he had a better mind, partly because his stance was not, did not need to be, so defensive, and so he could speak more directly. But the religious faith that supports the self-trust is the same for both poets. Failure to recognize this has thrown more than one critic of Cummings off the track of his meaning. Several decades of having to pay for the publication of his own books and getting reviews that revealed very little comprehension of what he meant were the price Cummings had to pay for his Transcendentalism. Very probably, during the years when he could not get published, Cummings thought of Emerson's idea that, "Society is everywhere in conspiracy against the manhood of every one of its members . . . For non-conformity the world whips you with its displeasure."

If all this seems to imply that Cummings ought to be thought of as the complete and perfect exemplification of Emerson's idea of the "true poet" in the twentieth century, the implication must be denied. All that has been said so far has concerned only the *what* of the poems, not the *how;* and even the *what* has been isolated only in its larger outlines. What, in general, Cummings was saying in his poems, what the tradition of this very traditional "experimental poet" is, what kind of clarity lay behind his so often remarked obscurity — all these *whats* are a necessary preliminary to an intelligent reading of the poems, but preliminary only. They are ways of getting at his "metre-making argument."

Cummings said in the Harvard lectures that "perhaps fifteen" poems really were adequate expressions of his stance as artist and man. Surely the number is much larger than that — I should say he wrote at least twice that many highly successful and uniquely memorable short poems — but the most generous guess would put the number at a small fraction of the total number of poems he committed to print. His *Poems, 1923–1954* contains some six hundred poems and was followed by *95 Poems* and the posthumous *73 Poems.* If a tenth of all these should be thought worth reading by the end of the century, this self-described "failure" will have made it into the ranks of lasting poets, without ever having made any concessions to greater popularity.

Despite his dedication to growth, movement, and inventiveness, despite too his reputation as a daring experimenter in verse forms, Cummings tended to lack inventiveness. He repeated himself, writing hundreds of versions of essentially the same poem, especially in the 1930's, when he felt most deeply alienated from his culture and from most of his colleagues. He relied too much and too often on a few simple tricks to jog the imagination, to wake the reader up and make him participate in the poem. His private typography, for instance, amusing and sometimes expressive at first, became tiresome in the end, like Ezra Pound's reliance on misspelling to create the tone of his letters. His use of low dialect to create satirical effects was too easy and limited a device. His "shaped" poems only now and then benefit very much from being shaped as they are. These and other idiosyncratic stylistic tricks too often seem merely self-indulgent or worse — substitutes for fresh insight.

The chief device was more than a device, and often worked for him very well — his dislocation of syntax and breaking up and reconstituting of words — but even this, though perhaps helpful to other poets in encouraging other kinds of freedom, has not proved, in itself, an experiment from which any other poet has felt he could directly learn anything. It was "more than a device" for Cummings because, for one thing, it was expressive of his feeling that ordinary statement, subject as it is to the conventions of logic and logical syntax, could not contain the feeling-tone of even "ordinary" experience, and could not begin to suggest the sense of the miraculous that he so often wanted to convey. It was functional, for him, for another reason, too; by outraging linguistic convention, it might force that freshness of *perception* he thought was the means to illumination. When he opened a poem with the line "i thank You God for most this amazing," in which "most" modifies both what precedes and what follows — very unsatisfactorily from the point of view of logical clarity of predication — he was emphasizing the nonlogical quality of the statement by the ambiguities of the syntax. "Most" actually intensifies the whole line and also suggests the chief reason why he thanks God: It hovers over "this amazing" to make it move toward being *most* amazing. In this poem, one of his own favorites, the device works, but all too often it seems a rather easy trick.

Cummings' best poems are usually his love poems and his religious poems, both more often than not written as disguised and more or less disarranged sonnets. (Once again, to make minor personal adaptations in an old and rigid form was hardly to be a "daring" experimenter. His friend Williams could not approve.) The love poems are generally, after the 1920's, religious in tone and implication, and the religious poems very often take off from the clue provided by a pair of lovers, so that often the two subjects are hardly, if at all, separable. What makes them memorable at their best is the peculiarly Cummingsesque combination of sensuality and feeling for transcendence. Cummings had no less contempt for a "Platonism" that was not "of this earth" than he had for a "realism" that denied wish-dream. Like Emerson before him, he thought he knew that "God IS" because He could be found — sensed, *felt* — in experience. Cummings wrote some of the finest celebrations of sexual love and of the religious experience of awe and natural piety produced in our century, precisely at a time when it was most unfashionable to write such poems.

By contrast, his poems of social criticism often sound thin and petulant. They are seldom more than amusing, and often not even that. For the most part, they depend upon the stock response and elicit a stock response — not that of Philistia, of course, but that of Bohemia. "A salesman is an it that stinks, excuse" is likely to provide "food for thought" only to salesmen who do not read Cummings and have never reflected on the fact that to pretend heartiness and personal warmth for the sake of manipulating the potential customer and thus making a sale is to cease to function as a person and to become an embodiment of economic forces. So with most of Cummings' other satiric poems. They are likely to continue to impress only the very young and the partially read. A poet cannot afford simply to "feel" when writing satiric poems.

It is common today to deny that Cummings developed as a poet, but the denial will hold only if we accept a rigidly intellectualistic or a rigidly formalistic idea of what a poet's "development" must be. It is true that neither in ideas, nor in characteristic style, is there any *great* difference between *Tulips and Chimneys* in 1923 and *73 Poems* in 1963. There is no sudden reversal of belief such as may be seen in Eliot, no gradual shift from a dazzling impressionism to argument and abstraction, as in Stevens, no turning to another type of poem, as in Robinson. But there is "development," of just the type we ought to hope for from a poet of Cummings' type.

The development is in changing attitudes and deepening awareness, a deepened sense of what it meant to be a Transcendental poet, with a corresponding dropping away of defensive-offensive sallies into ideas and criticism. In the last poems, the old devices are used less wastefully, and the old sense of mystery finds more concrete embodiment. Cummings was always at his best when he was "rendering death and forever with each breathing," but in the end he less often depended on pure rhetoric to give content to his abstractions, his "death," "forever," "breathing." *95 Poems* (1958), his finest single volume, will illustrate.

The poems in the book form a loose sequence, something Cummings had often experimented with before, never so successfully, with a metaphoric use of the seasons, reversed from the order in which the "mind of winter" had conceived them, as the basic ordering principle. That is to say, they begin with Fall, go into Winter, and end with Spring. As in Thoreau's organization of *Walden,* Cummings' seasons are "seasons of the soul" — of man's life; so that the Fall poems are poems of old age and approaching death, the Winter poems the poems of death, and the Spring poems the poems of rebirth. At the same time, another organizing principle is being observed. The Fall poems are those of loneliness, of solitude, and of the separated self; the Winter poems are concerned with loss of self; and the Spring poems are concerned with a new "self" which is a "we." In this book, for the first time, Cummings really moves beyond Emerson; for Emerson was apparently never really able to re-learn what "we" means, after the shock and deprivation of the death of Waldo.

The first poem in *95 Poems* is "1 (a," in which, within the parenthesis, a leaf falls; and, outside it, everything is unitary and singular, "loneliness," as it might be typed to suggest (the letter l and the figure 1 being the same on the typewriter) the death of the separated self, contained in the image of the leaf loosened from the tree, fluttering down to earth alone. Whether or not Cummings was inspired to write "1" of *95 Poems* by the anonymous "Death-Song" on page sixty-one of Peter Beilenson's *Japanese Haiku,* I do not know. But the relationship is very close, and significant enough to make a point of, whether there was any influence from Haiku to Cummings or not. The Haiku poem goes like this:

Leaf alone, fluttering
  Alas, leaf alone,
  fluttering . . .
Floating down the wind.

Cummings' poem follows:

1(a

le
af
fa

ll

s)
one
1

iness

The Haiku poem is imagistic (in a completely non-Poundian, nonhistoric "Imagistic," sense), Cummings' poem an incomplete *statement:* [This is] Loneliness (with an illustration included within the statement): (a leaf falls). What is implied in the Japanese poem — the loneliness — is *stated* by Cummings; what is stated in the Haiku — the fluttering of the leaf — is implied by Cummings by the irregular flutter of the right-hand margin of the poem that is shaped to look like what it says.

Later poems in the volume move through "THANKSGIVING (1956)" (with the old brashness and anger dominant once again, as "democracy" refuses help to Hungary), through the beautiful Christmas poem, "from spiralling ecstatically this," through poems of early Spring like the magnificent "stand with your lover on the ending earth," to the last poem in the book, appropriately written in rhythms imitative of swinging in an old-fashioned rope swing in a tree, and in the language of a child — "if up's the word; and a world grows greener." The ideas in this last poem are the ones we have become familiar with, as we are with the poet's adoption of the attitude of the innocent child. But the development of the poet is apparent too — in the increased sense of structure which led him to arrange his book, which he expected to be his last, with this poem at the end; in the controlling metaphor of the swing, which not only orders the language and rhythms of this poem but implies that the book which has thus ended is *about* something which has not ended and will not end; and in the broadening of the appeal at the end from "just the two of us" (the lovers of the early poems) to the "we" which is the last word of the poem, and of the book, and which includes anyone who wants to be included.

Cummings' poetry is romantic, intuitive in precept and in method, and rhetorical as opposed to Imagist-Modernist. It is essentially a "poetry of statement," as Wordsworth's was and as Emerson's was — but very complex, personal, ambiguous, and dense statement, at its best, statement which challenges the reader to complete it by first participating in the making of it and then carrying it on in himself, as his own, the gift to his self of another self. New Critical techniques of analysis do not work with such verse. There is nothing that literary positivism can get hold of — just Emersonian "Primary intuitions" and despised rhetoric to help their transfer. No wonder all the New Critics ignored Cummings for thirty years, except Blackmur, who damned him for not writing the way Ransom and Eliot had taught poets to write, for using general instead of specific words, for being, in short, a "Romantic" poet instead of a Modernist.

Whether Cummings is a "major poet" or not, I should not like to venture even a guess. But that he is a poet to cherish and reread, I should like to assert as strongly as I can. He and Hart Crane were the only important poets in the 1920's and 1930's who clearly and openly continued our major poetic tradition. That Crane's life was deeply troubled and ended in suicide, and that Cummings was perhaps more nostalgic for his childhood than was good for his personal growth, and for his poetry, has nothing to do with the kind of evaluation I am trying to make. When Crane wrote "My hand/ in yours,/ Walt Whitman,/ so — " and Cummings, in his last, posthumous, volume, wrote,

> seeker of truth
>
> follow no path
> all paths lead where
>
> truth is here

both were returning to the fountain.

CHAPTER XX

Irony and Orthodoxy

The development of American democracy toward a welfare state has proceeded so rapidly partly because the ideological struggle was not unnecessarily sharpened.

— Reinhold Niebuhr, in *The Irony of American History*

My life is determined not only by the love for living beings but also by the love for values — truth, beauty, righteousness — and these two kinds of love may come into conflict.

— Nicolas Berdyaev, in *The Destiny of Man*

. . . A purely naturalistic and anti-religious view of the world does not logically follow from science. But from this nothing follows as to the truth or falsity of naturalism. For we have to remember the old principle that a true conclusion is often supported by illogical arguments. The naturalistic view of the world may be true although the modern mind has reached it by a series of thought transitions in which the logic has been faulty.

— W. T. Stace, in *Religion and the Modern Mind*

Agrarian Protest

In the introductory "Statement of Principles" which he wrote for *I'll Take My Stand: The South and the Agrarian Tradition: By Twelve Southerners,* John Crowe Ransom touched on what would ultimately be revealed as the central objection of the Agrarians to technology when he remarked, without special emphasis, "Religion can hardly expect to flourish in an industrial society. Religion is our submission to the general intention of a nature that is fairly inscrutable; it is the sense of our rôle as creatures within it." Technology, he felt, gave us "the illusion of having power over nature" and made us "lose the sense of nature as something mysterious and contingent."

It is not hard to imagine how Emerson, who had a very strong sense of nature as mysterious and contingent, might have replied to this. To suppose that man's "power over" nature is an illusion, he might have said, is itself an illusion. Man has had the power since he learned how to wield a club. When he discovered fire, and again when he invented the wheel, he increased that power enormously. But power "over" nature is the wrong way to put it. Nature itself supplies the power by which spirit uses matter for its own ends. Thus Emerson, speaking out of his Transcendental assumptions, might have commented. Wallace Stevens, not happy with the Transcendental aspects of Emerson's terminology, would still, I think, have given qualified approval to the sage's critique and gone on to add some remarks of his own. Power to order and control nature, he might have wanted to add, is not simply a product of technology. Man alters, and to the extent that he does so, "controls," nature, the sum of things, when he writes a poem or sings a song, or when he acts freely to create anything that did not exist before he created it. Others today might want to agree with Stevens but add a further comment, drawn from the Existentialists, or simply from the mood of the 1960's. To the extent that it increases man's power, they might say, technology increases the burden of his responsibility. Man makes decisions. Once made, the decisions become a part of his fate. To suppose that "man creates himself" is no doubt to exaggerate, but to see the thrust of the idea as directed just as much against the deterministic naturalism of the late nineteenth and early twentieth centuries as it is against religious submissiveness is surely no error.

The point of these imaginary criticisms of Ransom's statements in *I'll Take My Stand* is not to try to show that the Agrarians were wrong in defending their "old-fashioned" and "undeveloped" region against the encroachment of what they correctly understood to be the dominant urban and technological trends of our society, but simply to put their thought in a larger perspective than that afforded by the events of 1930, when their book came out. There is nothing peculiarly Southern about being fearful of "the machine in the garden." Thoreau had had his doubts about the factory system and the railroad, and, with some stylistic changes, we could imagine Hawthorne writing large sections of Ransom's "Statement of Principles." Jefferson was certainly no typical conservative, religious or otherwise, but he too had thought, with Ransom, that "the culture of the soil is the best and most sensitive of vocations, and that therefore it should have the economic preference and enlist the maximum number of workers."

All this ought to remind us that very few American artists of stature in any period have strongly approved of the social reality in which they have found themselves. When they have not simply ignored it, or fled it as expatriates, they have generally denounced or ridiculed it. From the standpoint of the majority of the people at any time, the "radicalism" of the artist, whether he is of the "party of memory" or of the "party of hope," has seemed dangerously impractical when not actually subversive of accepted values. "Liberal" or "conservative," looking to the accomplishment of an ideal not yet achieved or longing for a better state in process of being lost, our writers have usually looked to Scripture or to nature, or to both at once, for the terms by which to measure society's failures. From Emerson's complaint that "things are in the saddle and ride mankind" to Robinson's caustic comments on a shopkeepers' culture and Frost's conservative distrust of everything popularly called "Progress," the line is almost unbroken. The reaction of the "twelve Southerners"—and of others not in the book who would later come to take essentially the same position, Tate and Brooks, for example—was no more extreme than that of Eliot or Cummings or the Marxist poets of the 1930's. One wonders whether any actual society has ever been good enough for the artist, the saint, or the philosopher to *want* to save it?

Curiously, it may seem, Ransom gave industrialization's threat to the arts less space than he gave its threat to religion. "The general decay of sensibility" and the decline in "the amenities of life" get only three sentences apiece of about the same length; together, the two are overshadowed by Ransom's comments on the economic and social factors pushing our society in a direction that could only lead us, he believed, "to expect in America at last much the same economics as that imposed by violence upon Russia in 1917." "Creeping socialism," with its dehumanizing effects, and the "Cult of Science," with its unrealism about man and nature, ought equally to be resisted, he thought, by those concerned for the preservation of "genuine humanism," which was not an "Abstract system" but a way of life possible only in a traditional society.

These are the ideas in *I'll Take My Stand* that are immediately important for the poetry of Ransom and Tate, and the early poetry of Warren. Other aspects of the book would no doubt seem more important to the historian or to the sociologist — the argument for a static-hierarchical social structure, for example, which Ransom — not in his Introduction but in the first essay of the twelve — refers to as an "establishment," in which everyone knows and is content with his place; or the defense of humane segregation by Warren in his contribution; or the curious assumption of all the writers that the way of life they were defending would be favorable to the writer — curious in view of the fact that before their own work, the South had produced very little literature worth more than passing mention.

But all these and other aspects of the book, except the religious and philosophic ones, have slight relevance to the poetry of the three Southerners of this chapter. The *manner* of Ransom's poetry is aristocratic, "chivalric," to be sure; as Hart Crane once remarked, perceptively, in a letter to Tate, Ransom's work mediates between that of Hardy and that of Wallace Stevens, the mannerist of our poetry. But the poems mock their own manner. Tate's poetry is always in effect simply elegiac, with no more connection with "reactionary" politics than would be implied in any poet's nostalgia for the ways of his youth and his people. Warren's poetry at first is "about" Original Sin, and the consequences of ignoring it, as "Idealists" do; later, it is about the search for identity or "definition"; later still, about life's "promises." At no time is it of such a nature that it would not be a critical irrelevance to bring into a discussion of it talk of the Southern "caste system," White Citizens' Councils, or the Negro Revolution. The writings of Niebuhr and Jung are more useful in a discussion of Warren's poetry than anything in *I'll Take My Stand,* including his own contribution, which, as he has recently confessed, now embarrasses him.

The chief reason for paying attention to *I'll Take My Stand* as a preliminary to describing and assessing the poetry of Ransom, Tate, and Warren is that it is a convenient means of placing them in their tradition — or, in the case of Warren, of seeing what tradition he started in, and a convenient way also of relating that tradition to its counterpart, the "Adamic" tradition, as it has been called. Emerson, despite his contempt for materialism, either as a way of life or as a metaphysic, had spoken of the technological advances of his day as "miracles." Whitman, though to be sure not when he was writing in his best vein, had "accepted" science and sung the praises of "the strong light works of engineers." Following suit, Hart Crane had written a hymn to Brooklyn Bridge, asserted that traffic lights condensed the light of the stars, and thought of aviation as a metaphor for spiritual exploration. From the standpoint of the Southerners, all this was very naive.

They were not alone in the stand they took. Yvor Winters would soon blame Hart Crane's suicide on the influence of Emerson's ideas on the vulnerable poet. The Fugitive gesture was a Southern version of Eliot's declaration of several years before that he was Anglo-Catholic, Classicist, and Royalist: in short, not at home in *this* social world.

JOHN CROWE RANSOM

Ransom's first book of verse, *Poems About God,* appeared in 1919, with an apologetic Introduction explaining its theme and title:

> The first three or four poems that I ever wrote (that was two years ago) were done in three or four different moods and with no systematic design. I was therefore duly surprised to notice that each of them made considerable use of the word God. I studied the matter a little, and came to the conclusion that this was the most poetic of all terms possible; was a term always being called into requisition during the great moments of the soul, now in tones of love, and now indignantly; and was the very last word that a man might say when standing in the presence of that ultimate mystery to which all our great experiences reduce.
>
> Wishing to make my poems as poetic as possible, I simply likened myself to a diligent apprentice and went to work to treat rather systematically a number of the occasions on which this term was in use with common American men.

Ransom has never chosen to reprint any of the poems in this first volume, for reasons that are not difficult to imagine in view of his later manner. The early poems are straightforward and open, vulnerable poems, poems irony could easily destroy. Though they are mostly dramatic in intent, the voice of the poet himself may be heard in them even when the words are those of characters allowed, supposedly, to speak for themselves. Thus the farmer in "One Who Rejected Christ" is made to say,

I'm not like other farmers,
I make my farming pay;
I never go in for sentiment,
And seeing that roses yield no rent
I cut the stuff away.

In view of what Ransom has said in his Introduction about "God" as "the most poetic of all terms," it is clear that he lets the farmer speak only that he may reveal and condemn himself; the authorial voice sounds so loud in the background we can hardly attend to the farmer's own words. *He* says nothing about rejecting Christ, but the title tells us that rejecting "sentiment" and "roses" is equivalent to rejecting the Lord, or perhaps only that one who would reject them would reject Him also. The only thing that is *not* clear about the poem is whether the reason why the farmer must be condemned is poetic or religious. Or is there no difference?

Several years later, in the *Fugitive* period (the magazine lasted from 1922 through the end of 1925), Ransom found out how to keep the reader from asking such questions. Technically, stylistically, the poems in *Chills and Fever* in 1924 strike one as having hardly anything in common with the poems of the first volume. The manner is no longer direct and serious, but elegant, witty, evasive, noncommittal. Irony has become the single mood, producing a tone at once wry and wistful, nostalgic and skeptical, mannered and amused at its own artificiality. Everything fights with everything else: the deliberately archaic diction (*bruited, leman, twirleth, halidom, thole,* to be *worsted*) with the colloquial and factual (*ten frozen parsnips, deep in the belly, bandy-legged, rotten teeth*); the formal, traditional meters (heard in the background, occasionally observed) with the actual cadences; the mincing manner with the intruded violence. The ideal is not believed in, and the fact is emotionally rejected, in this verse. An equilibrium, a precarious balance, is achieved by the narrowest of margins. All this was potential in *Poems About God,* in the attitudes *behind* the poems. Now the attitudes need not be searched out; the poet has found a style in which to express them without becoming vulnerable. The style has become both sword and armor.

Most of Ransom's best poems are in this slender volume. (Since the 1920's, he has written only an occasional poem, some half-dozen in all during forty years.) "Bells for John Whiteside's Daughter," "Winter Remembered," "Miriam Tazewell," "Here Lies a Lady," "Necrological," "Blackberry Winter," "Spiel of the Three Mountebanks," and "Captain Carpenter" are all masterpieces, triumphs of stylistic control of emotions so strong that loss of control seems always imminent.

Ransom's last collection of wholly new poems came out in 1927. *Two Gentlemen in Bonds* contained "Persistent Explorer," "Dead Boy," and "Antique Harvesters," the last two being among his best, each of the three developing an aspect of the religion-and-culture theme soon to be expatiated on in *I'll Take My Stand.* The persistent explorer, for instance, who is also a "pilgrim" with a "rueful grin/ Spread over his lips," is searching for meaning in nature:

> The noise of water teased his literal ears
> Which heard the distant drumming and thus scored:
> Water is falling — it fell — therefore it roared.
> However: That is more than water I hear!

When the explorer comes to the waterfall, sight and insight, seeing with and through the eye, are neatly balanced:

> He went still higher, and on the dizzy brink
> His eyes confirmed with vision what he had heard:
> This is but tumbling water. Again he demurred:
> That was not only water flashing, I think.

In the next stanza further thought tells him that "It was water, only water . . . the insipid chemical H_2O"; but this conclusion too seems dubious, and the next stanza turns back again to the possibility that nature may *mean* something: "Its thunder smote him somewhat as the loud/ Words of the god" and "Its cloud of froth was whiter than the cloud/ That clothed the goddess . . ."; yet, though "The cloud was, but the goddess was not there."

This is the end of the fifth stanza and of the first half of the poem. The sixth ends this part of the exploration negatively:

> Tremendous the sound was but there was no voice
> That spoke to him. Furious the spectacle

But it spelled nothing, there was not any spell
Bidding him whether cower or rejoice.

The remaining five stanzas comment on the failure of the search ("What would he have it spell? He scarcely knew"), conclude that the mythic tenants of the mind must be beaten down; and resolve, since "There were many ways of dying" and "many ways of living too," to continue the search for meaning elsewhere. In these stanzas the explorer is called a "pilgrim," but a realistic and stoical one, neither naive nor ironic: "He did not sit upon a rock and die," and "no unreasonable outcry" came from lips that had started to shape a "rueful grin" before "he drew them in."

"So be it." Nature has been "neutralized." There is no point in continuing to question it. The alternative to despair is to "seek another country, — as he would do." The geographic metaphor here foreshadows the praise of the South for continuing European patterns of culture, in contrast to what is called simply the "American" way, in Ransom's essay in *I'll Take My Stand* several years later. Not expressed in the poem, but implied by it when we put the poem in the context of the other poems and the prose, there is the judgment that the dominant Adamic tradition of trust in self and nature, and in the unfallen self's ability to find revelation in nature, has been mistaken from the beginning. But if this exploration must be given up, exploration of another kind must continue. Naturalism, the poem implies, is not enough. "Persistent Explorer" foreshadows the careers of Tate and Warren and the whole later religious movement of neo-orthodoxy.

"Dead Boy" is a more perfect poem from the point of view of Ransom's own critical standards. It is less "philosophic," less open, less paraphrasable. The tension between its "structure" and its "texture" — between the simple story it tells and the seemingly irrelevant details of the telling — is stronger. The speaker here never resolves anything or explicitly reveals his own attitude. Its irony is not, as it was in the first part of "Persistent Explorer," achieved by balancing separately stated attitudes. Now it is implicit in every line, almost in every word. And the implicit subject is smaller—the way of life that supports the meanings not found in nature by the explorer.

There are two ways of looking at and feeling about life, the poem says in effect, the way of "kin" and all that that somewhat archaic word implies, and the way of "transaction." The speaker in the poem exists in "the world of outer dark" where transactions govern, so that his view of the "antique lineaments" of the dead boy's forebears is a distant one, and he knows more than the boy's "foolish neighbors." But he is close enough to the world of kin to feel with the mother that a son, even a son with a "pasty face," need not be "beautiful, nor good, nor clever" for his death to pierce a mother's heart — an insight the abstract intelligence of his adopted country affords him no means of arriving at.

The whole thematic point of the poem — the contrast between two views of life, reflecting two ways of life — is revealed in the diction of the opening line, though we are only fully aware of it after we have read the whole poem: "The little cousin is dead, by foul subtraction." The world of human ties and human meanings — Ransom's "genuine humanism" — is suggested by "cousin," a word smacking of hearth and altar. "Subtraction" gives us the world of "objective" reason, utilitarian calculation: the world without absolutes, which has so far seduced the speaker that at first he joins in the "objective" estimate of the boy, rather than in the mother's grief: "A pig with a pasty face, so I had said." But when the "little man" is "quite dead," the speaker joins, in spirit, in the ritual of mourning, sharing the grief of "the sapless limbs, the shorn and shaken." One of the reasons, it seems to me, why "Dead Boy" is one of Ransom's half a dozen finest poems is that the emotion in it is controlled but *not* disavowed. The language of the funeral ritual ("the Lord hath taken") is not quite the speaker's own, but the feeling which prompts it seems to be accepted without any irony: "shorn and shaken" maintain the speaker's distance from his subject, but do not ridicule the emotion already expressed by the speaker's "O friendly waste of breath!"

"Antique Harvesters" presents the case for traditional Southern culture more effectively than anything Ransom said in his contributions to *I'll Take My Stand.* The title is followed by "*(Scene: Of the Mississippi the bank sinister, and of the Ohio the bank sinister.)*," as though the poem that is to follow were a play to be acted out. Several things are accomplished by this. First, by using "sinister," a word which once meant simply "left" but now means "evil," Ransom places the action geographically — the left banks of the two rivers, seen from a vantage point north and east; in short, the scene of the action is the Old South. At the same time, the archaism permits Ransom to address his readers directly, saying in effect, if you are thoroughly modern, what is about to be described will look "sinister" to you. The device is reminiscent of Eliot's "You, hypocrite lecteur," and also of his use of "antique," shifting from positive to negative connotations of the word, in "A Game of Chess" in *The Waste Land*. Finally, "sinister" also establishes the speaker's *own* vantage point, which is *within* the modernism that condemns the culture of the South as "sinister": unless he were looking down from the north, he could not describe both banks as "left." The tension of conflicting emotions within him that *this* suggests is never relaxed.

The poem opens with a wry question and closes with what is technically an affirmation, but one in which the tone denies the sense of what is being affirmed. The opening lines seem quite straightforward:

> Tawny are the leaves turned but they still hold,
> And it is harvest; what shall this land produce?

Here only the inverted word order of the first clause suggests the language of ceremony, with the inevitable attendant question: Is the ceremony an empty one? Is this language "ceremonious" rather than "ceremonial"? But these questions, which will become the crucial ones later in the poem, are only lightly suggested at this point, so that one is inclined to take the speaker's question as a real one and to answer it — that is, to move outside the poem, something that Ransom's poems constantly try to forbid us to do. The answer here would be, of course, a part of the intention behind rather than within the poem; this land has produced, or will produce, Ransom, Tate, Warren, Brooks, Faulkner, Eudora Welty, Carson McCullers, Flannery O'Connor, and others.

Nothing, we find out as we read further — if we had not guessed it from knowing Ransom's other work, after *Poems About God* — nothing could be more irrelevant to the limits of meaning established by the poem itself than any such roll-call of Southern writers. I have said that the poem makes Ransom's "case" for the values of Southern culture, but only when we stand very far back from the poem can we see that it is true. The poem celebrates values which may conflict with our "belief," or arouse the reaction of "disbelief"; but it moves so completely by indirection, it so carefully refrains from really affirming anything, its irony is so pervasive, that it makes us feel that to move outside it even for a moment, even finally, would be crass in the extreme. As I have said, even what appears to be an affirmation at the end really affirms nothing, so that "belief" continues to be irrelevant:

> True, it is said of our Lady, she ageth.
> . . . .
>   and if one talk of death —
> Why, the ribs of the earth subsist
>   frail as a breath
> If but God wearieth.

The archaic language here ("ageth," "wearieth"); the cultural archaism of "our Lady," suggesting the knight's devotion to his lady, the "religion" of courtly love, and perhaps also, though less immediately, another "our Lady," "Mary, Mother of God"; the quaint conceit of the earth as having "ribs" like the harvesters, and like them being sustained by God — all this has the effect of retracting the "plain prose" sense of the statement. The statement is a "pseudo-statement" after all. The poem is a closed system. Art is autotelic. One must not ask what it "means," or look for "sincerity." Williams and the Hartpence story again: "That, madam, is paint." It is not surprising that Hart Crane wrote Tate that the volume containing "Antique Harvesters" did not impress him very much. Ransom, he felt, "exploits his 'manners' a great deal."

The poem is perfect according to the standards of the time. It might have been used to illustrate how a poem should be written according to New Critical method as expounded by Brooks and Warren in the original edition of *Understanding Poetry.* (Later editions have hedged more and more on the principles which gained the book its fame and made it so influential.) The poem also discourages every critical fallacy condemned by the authors of the graduate student's bible, *Theory of Literature,* which in 1948 summed up the implications of the practices of poets who were *avant-garde* in the early 1940's. It is at once a perfect period piece and a perfect poem of its kind regardless of period.

But if its final effect is to celebrate rite and ritual, is it irrelevant to ask what the ritual is meant to symbolize? Ritual is shared symbolic action. As mutual action, it binds together; as symbolic, it expresses and points. Fox hunting is a ritual, and the fox in the poem is called a "lovely ritualist," but presumably the fox wouldn't see it quite this way. Is racial injustice a part of the ritual, or merely the price that must be paid for it? Is racial strife a necessary or an accidental part of the harvest?

The critic who would ask such questions as these could point to some of Ransom's own critical terms as his justification. Ransom's call for an "ontological critic," for example, rests upon his assumption that poetry offers a kind of knowledge, as presumably it does, though what kind cannot be established by the merely negative statement, "Not the kind that science offers." If poetry's truth is "of the heart," as Hawthorne had said earlier and Faulkner would later say, then what makes it improper to inquire the heart's reasons? Ransom's own criticism offers no answer to such questions, and it would be unprofitable to pursue them further, but they will have served their purpose if they have suggested both the very close relationship between his poetry and New Critical theory, and some of the unresolved contradictions within a theory that insists that poetry is "knowledge" but forbids us to ask, "knowledge of what?"

Ransom's poetry will outlast his critical theory. His influence has been enormous, particularly during his many years of teaching at Kenyon and editing *The Kenyon Review* — all out of proportion, really, to his actual accomplishments as a critic. He taught a generation how to write poems and how to criticize them: Do both, he said in effect, in such a way that the Positivists can never find you out and pin you down. In an age unfriendly to myth and rite as well as to poetry, defend all three, he said, protecting yourself as you do so by irony. You will thus be helping to maintain that "genuine humanism" that is not so much a philosophy as a "way of life" resting ultimately on the mythic God who thunders, the God of "orthodoxy."

The strategy aimed at invulnerability is itself vulnerable. The irony that protects one from attack also prevents one from attacking. Irony is not a mood that encourages exploration. Ransom himself has not proved to be a persistent explorer — though of course, he never said he *was*; his poem has a *persona*, another device useful for protection in an unfriendly place. He will be remembered as a distinguished minor poet who, chiefly in his early youth, wrote a small number of perfectly wrought, finely textured poems that are likely to be remembered a long time.

An important element in Ransom's thinking about literature was his equation of "romantic" not only with "idealistic" and "Platonic," but also with "wishful." Pound and Eliot had first taught Modernists to despise the nineteenth century, for reasons more or less similar to Ransom's, but it remained for Ransom to attempt to express the rejection more philosophically than they generally had. In *God Without Thunder,* he argued that orthodox Christian doctrine gave us a truer myth than the "god without thunder" of secular progressivism and technology. His argument, pretty clearly, was inspired by his desire to defend the South's position of conservatism in religious matters, after the Scopes Trial had exposed the region to the ridicule of Northern writers. The Tennessee law forbidding the teaching of evolutionary theory in the public schools, tested in the Scopes case, was no doubt in itself a mistake, he admitted; but the *spirit* that prompted the law, the South's preference for orthodoxy, was preferable to the spirit that prompted the North to worship Progress and Science.

It was preferable, he argued, just because it fitted experience better. Platonists, Puritans, and Transcendental Idealists all look right through the world to the Ideal, thus conforming it to the patterns of their own thought and wish. But the world's body is thick, not thin; opaque, not transparent; full of mystery and contingency, and evil and suffering that cannot be explained away. Original Sin and the Fall make better sense of history than the myth of an unfallen Adam in the unspoiled garden of the New World. Barlow was simply wrong in his expectation of unending progress now that we were free at last of kings and priests. Twentieth-century history was a sufficient refutation of any such idealism that ignored the reality of evil in man and contingency in nature. "Orthodoxy" was to be preferred not as "revealed" but as simply saner and truer. The metaphysical pluralism it led to was both humbler and finally more realistic in its assessment of the power of reason than any form of philosophic monism.

Such a line of thought, which parallels Eliot's at so many points, would certainly have implications for a theory of literature, but Ransom never systematically worked them out. In book reviews and occasional addresses written during the 1930's he often appeared to be referring to a system that did not yet exist — and in fact never would. But when he collected his occasional pieces in *The World's Body* in 1938, he wrote a Preface that made explicit many of the assumptions governing the pieces that follow in the book but that had been written over a number of years.

There are, he explained in the Preface, two kinds of poetry, a kind that does what poetry properly can do and a kind that aspires to be "what poetry properly is not." Only the first kind, he thought, ought to interest us. It is always "the act of an adult mind; and I will add, the act of a fallen mind, since ours too are fallen." The other, or inferior and improper kind of poetry, which cannot interest us because it is not the act of an adult and fallen mind, ought really to be called

> heart's-desire poetry. If another identification is needed, it is the poetry written by romantics, in a common sense of that term. It denies the real world by idealizing it: the act of a sick mind. A modern psychologist puts a blunt finger in a rather nasty manner upon this sort of behavior. It indicates in the subject a poor adaptation to reality; a sub-normal equipment in animal courage; flight and escapism; furtive libido.

If this is what "romantic" meant at the time, we can understand why Williams had been so deeply offended four years earlier when Stevens had called *him* a romantic. A "realist" could hardly be expected to like having it implied that he was poorly adapted to reality. The kind of poetry Williams wanted to write was centered on the "things" that are the substance of "the world's body." For him as for Ransom, the world was thick, not thin, and to idealize the world in poetry was to play both the world and poetry false. But he would have agreed only in part with the way Ransom went on to describe "true" or antiromantic poetry:

> The true poetry has no great interest in improving or idealizing the world, which does well enough. It only wants to realize the world, to see it better. Poetry is the kind of knowledge by which we must know what we have arranged that we shall not know otherwise [as Stevens was saying at the same time]. We have elected to know the world through our science, and we know a great deal, but science is only the cognitive department of our animal life, and by it we know the world only as a scheme of abstract conveniences. What we cannot know constitutionally as scientists is the world which is made of whole and

> indefeasible objects, and this is the world which poetry recovers for us. . . .
>
> For such moderns as we are the poetry must be modern. . . . [It is] by its thickness, stubbornness, and power [that the world must impress itself on modern poetry].

When the merely persuasive elements have been identified in this statement, we discover that a cognitive function is claimed for poetry, but that the only positive identifying mark of peculiarly poetic knowledge is that it concerns itself with "whole and indefeasible," and thick, stubborn, and powerful, "objects"; that is, not with the reasons for them (their "causes") or the purposes they may serve, or their relations, or their meanings, just with the *objects,* left whole, not analyzed; and "indefeasible," which is to say, not to be seen through, experienced as transparent, "idealized." Everything else this passage — so much like the scientism of Pound — says about poetic knowledge is negative, a series of exclusions: The knowledge given by true poetry is *not* abstract, it does *not* improve or idealize, it is *not* "cognitive" (even though it somehow "knows"), it is *not* schematic, it is *not* convenient.

Though this is a description of poetry conceived, as Ransom says elsewhere, as giving "ontological" knowledge, the one thing it tells us nothing intelligible about is ontology, the branch of metaphysics that studies the nature of Being. What the passage *does* tell us about is the kind of poetry Ransom liked and wanted more of: a poetry fact-centered, realistic (in the modern sense; nominalistic in the medieval), visual but not visionary; a poetry in which nature is conceived as *out there,* unordered, opaque, making no particular sense; with the poet related to this world as an "I" to an "It." This is the kind of poetry the passage calls for. It is also, in effect, a description of Tate's most famous poem, "Ode to the Confederate Dead," which Tate had worked on for a decade or so and completed several years before Ransom wrote his Preface to *The World's Body.*

ALLEN TATE

In the 1925 poem Allen Tate inscribed to Robert Penn Warren and titled "To a Romantic," Tate had characterized the essential element in romantic naivety as the ignoring of death: "You think the dead arise/ Westward and fabulous." Determined not to be romantic himself, Tate built his famous elegy around the conflict between antiromantic knowledge, identified with "indefeasible" objects, and "romantic" feelings. "What shall we say who have knowledge/ Carried to the heart?" the speaker asks toward the end of the poem, when the feelings have finally been subdued by the knowledge. The speaker says nothing after this, except to wonder whether he should set up the grave in the house — which would seem to imply the idea that the romantics were unacquainted with death, in the same way that the shorter poem had.

Ransom described the poet as wanting to "see" the world better — more sharply, precisely, realistically, he implied. Tate's "Ode to the Confederate Dead" is characterized by the density of its visual and auditory imagery. Ransom thought the world the poet would "see" would be "thick" and "stubborn." Tate's "Ode" presents a world which the speaker in the poem can make nothing meaningful out of at all, or in which he can discover no meaning acceptable to his feelings. Ransom warned against "heart's-desire" poetry and described "true poetry" as "the act of an adult mind . . . and . . . a fallen mind." What this last qualification was intended to mean is not clear to me, but Tate does end his poem with a reminder of the Fall, alluding to the serpent and the Tree of Knowledge, which has diminished to a mulberry bush; and the "adult mind" and the "heart's desire" fight it out all the way through the poem.

In the passage from *The World's Body* quoted above, Ransom did not specify that "true poetry" must be characterized by "paradox" and "irony," though an ironic attitude is implicit in what he says about the poet and the world he gives us knowledge of. In Tate's "Ode," *everything* is ironic and paradoxical — "bones" are "verdurous," "felicity" is "grim," "sacrament" is "casual," "chivalry" is "furious," "speculation" is "mute," "eternity" is, after all, only "seasonal." It is irony that dictates the choice of "rumor" to describe the all-too-clear message of the falling leaves, "immoderate" to describe the heroic past and its vision, and "gentle" to describe the green serpent. Every flight is followed immediately by a descent; everything suggests its opposite. We are likely to feel, before the end, that such an inveterate clash of opposites justifies H. D.'s harsh condemnation of this mode in *The Walls Do Not Fall*.

The reader whose feelings have not been totally benumbed by

the violence of the wrenching they have been subjected to will find, I think, that the ending lifts the poem above simple irony, though the largest ambiguities remain unresolved. *Is* speculation a curse that "stones the eyes," destroying "vision" and leaving only the indefeasible objects, all of them spelling death and only death? If we *were* to "set up the grave/ In the house" and live with the knowledge of death, *would* "vision" be recovered? What do the wind-driven leaves of autumn's desolation say to us, and what shall we say of them? The poem does not end with

> We shall say only the leaves
> Flying, plunge and expire

but goes on to suggest that we are our own victims, much as Eliot's Prufrock, who knew too much, had been. The poem protects itself against the doctrinaire reader who would want to dissolve its ambiguities.

The "Ode" is Tate's single masterpiece, but the rest of the poems in the slender volume that collects most of his work, *Poems, 1922–1947,* are nearly all what we may call "accomplished" poetry. The range of feeling is narrow, whatever the subject, and "romantic irony" is never absent for long. As a result, the poems tend to run together in the mind to make one continuous poem in which one listens for the Word no longer heard and tries to look but cannot for the darkness, knowing the feeling of being

> subterranean
> As a black river full of eyeless fish
> Heavy with spawn; with a passion for time
> Longer than the arteries of a cave.

Nearly all of the poems could end as "The Meaning of Death: An After-Dinner Speech" ends, "We are the eyelids of defeated caves."

We are then — so far as we are the caves as well as the lids — in total darkness, presumably. But if the lid should open to admit the light? The possibility had always hovered in the background of Tate's dark early poetry, and in 1953 it seemed to have been realized. In that year the *Sewanee Review* published what it described as "Part VI of a poem of some length, now in progress." "The Buried Lake" is a dream allegory, in a form used by Chaucer and Dante, celebrating "light Lucy, light of heart," the poet's "Lady of Light." Written in Dante's *terza rima,* it is sometimes obscure, chiefly in the privateness of its personal references, but never obscure in the way of paradox and irony.

The poem was written after the poet had remarried and been converted to Roman Catholicism, after years of half-hearted Anglicanism. It marks the end of a style based on exploiting the conflicts between feeling and thought produced by "the modern temper." Eliot had renounced the style thirteen years earlier and H. D. had denounced it in 1944. No outstanding poet under sixty has found the style useful for what he had to say since Tate turned away from it in "The Buried Lake." No further parts of Tate's poem have yet appeared.

ROBERT PENN WARREN

Even Robert Penn Warren's early poetry is much less well described by Ransom's theories than Tate's "Ode" is. It is often ironic, but not constantly so. It is full of paradoxes, indeed paradox is at the center of it, but it moves generally toward the resolution of paradox. It is dense with specific images of "the world's body," but it wants always to do more than "see" the world more sharply, it wants to understand it. It is never patrician in tone or manner, as Ransom's is. It is regional only in the sense that Warren, born in Kentucky, returns again and again to personal memories of childhood, as he does in the series of poems called "Kentucky Mountain Farm." It makes no defense of the culture of the South as against that of some other region. It is not bookish, or learned, or primarily "mythic." So far as it is "orthodox," its orthodoxy appears to be a way of feeling and remembering, not a theoretical position adopted for prudential reasons. Ransom's justification of orthodoxy, by contrast, seems wholly prudential.

"Love's Parable" offers a way into the early poems that removes a good deal of their often-remarked obscurity. As Howard Nemerov has pointed out, the lovers in the poem are man and God. It is Warren's "Fortunate Fall" poem; the "prince whose tongue, not understood,/ Yet frames a new felicity" is Christ, come to cure our alienation from ourselves and each other. The Fall occurs over and over, in each life and each period, but though a dreamed-of original innocence can never be restored, "weakness has become our strength" and hope arises from the "sullen elements" of "self that cankers at the bone," "for there are testaments/ That men, by prayer, have mastered grace."

There is nothing ironical about this poem, not even about these concluding lines, which it would be impossible to imagine either Ransom or Tate writing. The poem is open to the point of being defenseless. Its metaphysical quality is not merely a literary manner but an expression of a way of thinking. Such images as "the fungus eyes/ Of misery" that "spore in the night" are interpreted in generalized statements: "ripe injustice," exploitation of nature, and "hatred of the good once known" are more abstract ways of pointing to the outward evidences of the Fall. The "inward sore/ Of self" produces evil and allows us to see only evil, in ourselves and in nature. Here, as so often later in his career, Warren is in effect rewriting Hawthorne for our time. The closest literary parallel, thematically, to "Love's Parable," is "Young Goodman Brown."

Like Hawthorne, Warren translates the received Faith into psychological terms. C. G. Jung and Reinhold Niebuhr supply all the theoretical framework necessary for drawing out the largest meanings of many of the novels and most of the poems through *Brother to Dragons* in 1953. Over and over, Warren re-tells the archetypal story of "My Kinsman, Major Molineux," in which Hawthorne has his young man confront the ambiguities of sin and sorrow, protest his innocence, discover his complicity, and finally, Hawthorne at least permits us to believe, find a more mature basis for hope than could be found in the Adamic illusion of innocence. Warren's people, like Hawthorne's, break out of the prison of self only when they discover what Hawthorne called "the brotherhood of guilt." As Warren puts it, when man sees himself as a "brother to dragons," he is ready to start moving toward the "glory" it is his destiny to seek.

"Original Sin: A Short Story," a later poem than "Love's Parable," is both less interesting for what it reveals of Warren's chief continuing preoccupations and attitudes, and more typical of the voice we expect to hear in Warren's mature work. A realistic allegory enriched by personal comment and observation, it personifies Original Sin as a repeated nightmare that "takes no part in your classic prudence or fondled axiom" but poisons them nevertheless. Original Sin is a nightmare connected in memory with the wen grandfather used to finger on his forehead as though he treasured the deformity, a nightmare that has grown so familiar it is no longer really frightening:

It tries the lock; you hear, but simply drowse:
There is nothing remarkable in that sound at the door.

There is irony in this poem, but, as so often in Eliot, it is directed by the speaker at himself. He is grateful that the nightmare figure never comes in the daylight to shame him before his friends. He thinks it has nothing to do with "public experience or private reformation." Though he would like to be rid of it, his attempts to escape it by moving and leaving no address have been ineffectual. Hoping to escape the past, in which the nightmare figure mysteriously originated, he finds himself taking "a sly pleasure" in hearing of "the deaths of friends," but the pleasure does not last, and the "sense of cleansing and hope" it brings is delusory. By the end of the poem the speaker has become Everyman, seeking to maintain his innocence by projecting his guilt, denying it as a part of his own identity.

The new voice we hear in this poem is colloquial, easy, assured, humorous and serious in rapid shifts, moving between the folksy and the metaphysical. It takes its cadences from the rhythms of folk poetry while it gets its themes from philosophers and theologians. It moves constantly away from the poetic and the literary, returning only to make a fresh start away. The opening line of each stanza sets the pattern to be departed from.

Nodding, its great head rattling like a gourd . . .

Except for the initial trochee, this is a regular iambic line with five feet; but the final line of the stanza has moved, as though forced by the urgency of the need to speak, much closer to prose rhythms —

It acts like the old hound that used to snuffle
your door and moan.

This is a long way from the voice we heard in "Love's Parable":

Then miracle was corner-cheap;
And we, like ignorant quarriers,
Ransacked the careless earth to heap
For highways our most precious ores;
Or like the blockhead masons who

Burnt Rome's best grandeur for its lime,
And for their slattern hovels threw
Down monuments of nobler time.

Between the two poems, Warren has found his own voice. But the change is nothing like the radical reversal we note between Tate's earlier work and "The Buried Lake." It is a matter, rather, of gradual self-discovery, gradual definition of the self-image.

"The Ballad of Billie Potts" is the triumph of Warren's new voice and manner, and, as it seems to me, one of the finest long poems in our literature. The mythic overtones in its tale of another Fall enacted in another "land between the rivers" are only lightly suggested in the background, played down by the poet's introductory note ("When I was a child I heard this story from an old lady. . . ."), and countered by the tone both of the narrative itself and of the inserted authorial meditations on the action. Since *The Waste Land* we have tended to think of mythic poetry as "bookish," but the very last thing "Billie Potts" suggests is the library.

Vachel Lindsay in his "Simon Legree," the first poem in his Booker T. Washington Trilogy, had used the folk rhythm Warren adopted for the narrative sections of "Billie Potts." As Lindsay handles the form, it sounds like this:

Legree he sported a brass-buttoned coat,
A snake-skin necktie, a blood-red shirt.
Legree he had a beard like a goat,
And a thick hairy neck, and eyes like dirt.
His puffed-out cheeks were fish-belly white,
He had great long teeth, and an appetite.
He ate raw meat most every meal,
And rolled his eyes till the cat would squeal.
. . . .

But he went down to the Devil.

Unfortunately, with a lapse of taste and feeling not untypical of him, Lindsay directs that this be read "in your own variety of negro dialect." That the language is Southern dialect, having nothing to do with race or color, Warren knew when he described Big Billie in the same folk language and the same folk rhythms:

Big Billie Potts was big and stout
In the land between the rivers.
His shoulders were wide and his gut stuck out
Like a croker of nubbins and his holler and shout
Made the bob-cat shiver and the black-jack leaves shake
In the section between the rivers.
He would slap you on your back and laugh.
. . . .

They had a big boy with fuzz on his chin
So tall he ducked the door when he came in,
A clabber-headed bastard with snot in his nose
And big red wrists hanging out of his clothes. . . .

Warren's handling of the form is a little freer than Lindsay's, a little less "literary." He is closer to his subject, writing without any suggestion of the condescending attitude that comes out in Lindsay's unfortunate note on the dialect in his poem. (But Lindsay's condescension appears only in the note, not in the poem itself.) If one had never read any of Warren's verse and knew of him only as the third member of the Ransom-Tate-Warren trio, a Vanderbilt man, contributor to *I'll Take My Stand* and co-author of the most influential New Critical textbook, *Understanding Poetry,* he might be surprised by "Billie Potts," which has behind it the work of Lindsay, Mark Twain, and J. R. Lowell. Of the poets with whom he is most commonly linked, Warren is at once, and paradoxically, the most "liberal" and pragmatic, in ideas and attitudes, and the most "traditional" in a literary sense, after his earliest volume, in choosing to work within traditions developed by earlier American writers, rather than, for instance, those of the French Symbolists or the English metaphysicals.

Traditionalism in this sense is as true of Warren's prose fiction as it is of his verse. His historical romances and allegories have their closest counterpart in the work of Hawthorne, as "Billie Potts" continues the work of Lindsay. Tate's early description of his friend as a "romantic" was prophetic. Despite Warren's continued suspicion of idealists who try to make the world fit a pattern in their mind, despite his affinity with the ironic vision of neo-orthodox theologians, for whom man is "fallen," there has always been a part of his sensibility that drew him toward our own nineteenth-century writers and away from Ransom and Modernist practice.

"The Ballad of Billie Potts" consists of two distinct parts, the folk legend itself and an enclosed, separate commentary, by the "I," set off by parentheses. The speaker is not in any significant sense a *persona* but the poet himself, who interrupts his narration to speculate on its meaning. The narrative tells of the murder of Little Billie by his parents, who didn't know who it was they were killing. The past is vividly present in the narrative sections, as little distant from us as the poet's art can make it. In the parenthetical commentaries the past recedes into the background while the present takes its place in the foreground. Imaginative identification is broken as the tale is acknowledged as remote, legendary, literally an old woman's tale, containing motives and meanings we can only partially understand and partially imagine:

> (Leaning and slow, you see them move
> In massive passion colder than any love:
> Their lips move but you do not hear the words. . . .)

Ransom and other New Critics have thought that the formal unity of the poem is damaged by these breaks in the narrative in which the poet enters his own poem to address the reader directly, but it seems to me that to wish the author's comments away is to wish for a completely different kind of poem. Though the poem is called a "ballad," only the narrative parts could really be so described. Warren's assumption in the poem is the opposite of Pound's in the *Cantos:* the "facts," he knows and says, do *not* speak clearly, univocally, "for themselves." His method acknowledges his assumption. The manner of the poem is closer to Whittier's in "Snowbound" or Emerson's in "The Titmouse" than it is to Pound's.

The poem's subject is man (Billie Potts, Warren, the reader) trying to discover his identity, and so to understand his destiny, by defining the nature of his guilt and his innocence. "Billie Potts" is an exercise in moral philosophy executed in a form alternately narrative and meditative or discursive. No literary model for such a form existed, so that a judgment that it lacks formal "unity" cannot be drawn from an idea of the "requirements of the form," as several critics dissatisfied with the poem have tried to do. Traditional literary *genres* begin to be meaningless with the English Romantic movement and have been increasingly inapplicable ever since, even in British literature. In American literature, they have been almost totally irrelevant since Emerson. In "Billie Potts," Warren created a new form involving a double focus, alternately bringing history close by imaginative identification, in the narrative parts, and holding it at a distance so that it may be understood by the mind, in the discursive parts. Put yourself in Billie's place, the form says ("Think of yourself riding away from the dawn"); but also, don't forget that the limits of the poem are the limits of the imagination ("There was a beginning but you cannot see it").

Between the narrative parts, which involve the reader directly, with an immediate and unselfconscious identification, and the discursive parts, which turn the reader back upon himself, asking him to ponder what he is reading, asking him *why* he has been identifying himself with the characters in the poem, and what *that* means — between the verses in parentheses and those outside, there are, nevertheless, all kinds of linkages. A single example will have to do. In the following passage, we begin with the "I" of the poem commenting on the remoteness in time and cultural conditions of his own characters, and end with his return to his narrative. The contrast in diction, style, and formal *genre* between the part before the parenthesis and the lines that follow is striking, but at the same time an identity is suggested:

> Beyond your call or question now, they move
> . . . .
>
> And breathe the immaculate climate where
> The lucent leaf is lifted, lank beard fingered, by no
> breeze,
> Rapt in the fabulous complacency of fresco, vase, or
> frieze:
>
> And the testicles of the fathers hang down like old lace.)
>
> Little Billie was full of piss and vinegar
> And full of sap as a maple tree . . .

In general, the discursive parts utilize all the resources of poetry to create the *stasis* of art, the stasis of a frieze or fresco in which whatever seems to move, moves only in the imagination. The characters, we feel in the discursive sections, are at once dead and immortal, living on only in the "immaculate climate" of art. One thinks of Faulkner's use of this theme — art as achieving its formal clarity only by "lying" — in the opening story of *The Unvanquished,* and of Aiken's repeated speculations on the theme in his early verse. The shock of the lines about Little Billie that immediately follow the parenthesis in the passage quoted above is functional. In the parenthetical lines omitted from the quotation, the subject is defined as the relations of the generations, and particularly of fathers and sons, each "betraying" the other. The line about the testicles of the fathers gives us the quintessence of the conflict in a single image. Now, after the parenthetical meditation, we return to the story that has motivated the meditation, with the observation that lusty young Billie, about to come into conflict with his father, is "full of piss and vinegar" and "full of sap," folk ways of suggesting the connection of exuberant self-confidence and vitality with genital vigor. The folk expressions are at once less vivid and, in context, more expressive than the last line within the parenthesis. Now that we have been prepared, we realize the poetry implicit in folk speech.

"The Ballad of Billie Potts" makes really clear for the first time Warren's role as a bridging figure between the Fugitives and the more persistent and rooted romantic and transcendental tradition of Emerson, Whitman, Lindsay, Hart Crane, and Cummings. Though the story he tells in the poem reminds us of the archetype of the Fall, the "Original Sin" constantly reenacted by the generations, and so of the "orthodoxy" of Ransom and Tate, and before that of Eliot, the poem ends in hope, not in resignation. It is not our guilt that needs definition. For Warren, as for Hawthorne before him, *that* is obvious enough, needing only to be admitted, not defined, not necessarily even "understood." It is our "innocence" that needs — in this century at least, Warren thinks — "new definition":

> For the beginning is death and the end may be life,
> For the beginning was definition and the end may be
> definition,
> And our innocence needs, perhaps, new definition,
> And the wick needs the flame
> But the flame needs the wick,
> And the father waits for the son.

Brother to Dragons is a reworking and expansion of "Billie Potts" in both theme and form. Formally, the chief difference is that Warren's comments no longer make up a separate poem within the poem. Instead, he himself, in his own person as "R.P.W.," has now become one of the characters in his own tale. His commitment to his characters and to his art are now not two things but one. In effect, the form of the poem says, art is a process of self-discovery and self-realization, in which man and artist cannot ultimately be separated. (As Cummings said, "An artist I feel is a man." As Berryman said, referring to Eliot and others, poetry aims "at the reformation of the poet." As Emerson said, poetry affords the poet, and his readers, a "purchase" by which we may move life into a larger circle.) The form of *Brother to Dragons* implies the artist's double responsibility, to his art, and to himself as a person. Insofar as it points toward the art as something "made" (the tale is taken from history, but it can come alive for us only through the poet's art), the form acknowledges the partial truth of Modernist theory and practice. But insofar as "R.P.W." takes personal responsibility as a man for what he has made, and what he has "discovered," or "seen," in the course of, and through, the making, the form of the poem rediscovers our great tradition by going back to Emerson's idea of the poet as *man naming,* just as the scholar is "man thinking."

Once again, as in "Billie Potts" and in most of the novels, the central action of the poem is violent and terrible. Warren retells the story, which actually occurred, of how Jefferson's nephew, living in the "unspoiled" West among what ought to have been, from the Adamic point of view, the purifying and spiritually exalting influences of Nature, brutally murdered a slave for a trivial offense. Warren departs from history only to imagine motives, and to imagine the effect this event must have had on Jefferson's thinking. (Actually, there is no mention of the event in Jefferson's papers, though he could not have failed to be aware of the widely publicized infamy of his sister's son. Could he not bring himself to face it?)

Again, as in "Billie Potts," the real concern, despite the horror of the event itself, is not with "illustrating" man's "guilt." Warren simply takes it for granted that we are all guilty, and involved in each other's guilt, whether we choose to think about it in psychological or in theological terms. What the poem tries to discover, as "R.P.W." tells us toward the end of his effort, is "an adequate definition" of the "glory" involved in "the human effort." How can we recover a sense of the self as transcendent? Is man, really and finally, only a "brother to dragons," a physicochemical machine plagued by a curiously unnecessary "inner monologue," or is he, potentially at least, "made in the image of God," and a son of God? After Dickinson's doubts, Frost's diminutions, and Stevens' denials, must we, if we are to be honest, admit that the idea of "the transcendent self" has been lost forever?

The title of the poem acknowledges the assumptions from which such thinking as this starts and points in the direction it will take. In the Book of Job, 30:29, Job says, "I am a brother to dragons, and a companion to owls." The context shows that this is not a humble admission but a bitter complaint: I am being *treated*, by God, as though I were such as these, whereas in fact I am a just man deserving a better fate, deserving particularly an answer to my questions. Everyone, Job has said earlier in the chapter, holds me in derision, and the Lord himself seems to be treating me as though I were nothing but dust and ashes. Who is guilty in my case, Job in effect is asking as he passionately asserts his innocence, who but God himself?

Warren's poem starts by assuming that there is a real, and not just apparent "problem of evil," as well as a "problem of guilt." The "problem of evil" is the philosophers' and the theologians' term for what is also called "the problem of pain," which means the problem of unmerited suffering. Suffering that seems to be built into the nature of things becomes a "problem" when we think of nature as teleological. Melville had concentrated, at least insofar as he took Ahab's side, on the "problem of evil" in *Moby-Dick*. Hawthorne normally preferred simply to leave this problem a mystery and concentrate on the "problem of guilt," which is a metaphysical problem in the same sense that the problem of evil is *only* if we assume that man is "naturally good," or "unfallen."

As to the problem of guilt, the poem answers with Warren's idea of "complicity." We have all wished more evil than we have been able to do, as Hawthorne said long ago in "Fancy's Show-Box." Lilburne, the murderer, was peculiarly unfortunate chiefly in having the power and the opportunity to act out his wish. Still, it is also true that we have wished more good than we could accomplish, as well as more evil. We must believe in our responsibility, despite the cogency by which deterministic lines of thought may explain away Lilburne's guilt and our own.

As to the "problem of evil," again Warren bridges the gap between Emerson and Melville, or Cummings and Eliot. God never explained to Job. He merely overwhelmed him with his power and glory. Reason provides no clear or certain answer to this problem, which, as Gabriel Marcel has insisted, is not properly called a "problem" at all but a "mystery." Nevertheless, to say that the question of why there is unmerited suffering is "meaningless," as Sidney Hook has recently said it is to ask "What is the meaning of life?" is to stultify the human effort before it begins.

The "moral order" and the "natural order" are not the same order, Warren's poem says:

> No, what great moral order we may posit
> For old Kentucky, or the world at large,
> Will scarcely account for geodetic shifts.
> There was an earthquake, sure. But it just came.

In the moral order, self-transcendence depends first upon the recognition and acceptance of personal guilt, and then on moving toward the ideal. As Jefferson says, after he has first been forced by the crime to lose his faith in natural goodness and fall into despair, and then to think and feel his way back toward hope:

> To find? Oh, no!
> To think to find it as a given condition of man
> Would be but to repeat, I now see,
> My old error. I have suffered enough for that.
> Oh, no, if there is to be reason, we must
> Create the possibility
> Of reason, and we can create it only
> From the circumstances of our most evil despair.
> We must strike the steel of wrath on the stone of guilt,
> And hope to provoke, thus, in the midst of our coiling
> darkness
> The incandescence of the heart's great flare.
> And in that illumination I should hope to see
> How all creation validates itself,
> For whatever you create, you create yourself by it,
> And in creating yourself you will create
> The whole wide world and gleaming West anew.

Or as "R.P.W." puts essentially the same conclusion in more general and inclusive terms,

> We have yearned in the heart for some identification
> With the glory of the human effort, and have yearned
> For an adequate definition of that glory.
> To make that definition would be, in itself,
> Of the nature of glory. This is not paradox.
> It is not paradox, but the best hope.
>
> It is the best hope, because we have,
> Each, experienced what it is to be men.
> We have lain on the bed and devised evil in the heart.
> . . . .
> But we must argue the necessity of virtue:
>
> In so far as man has the simplest vanity of self,
> There is no escape from the movement toward fulfillment.
> And since all kind but fulfills its own kind,
> Fulfillment is only in the degree of recognition
> Of the common lot of our kind. And that is the death of
> vanity,
> And that is the beginning of virtue.
>
> The recognition of complicity is the beginning of
> innocence.
> The recognition of necessity is the beginning of freedom.
> The recognition of direction of fulfillment is the death
> of the self,
>
> And the death of the self is the beginning of selfhood.
> All else is surrogate of hope and destitution of spirit.

Brother to Dragons is a philosophic poem cast in the form of dramatic narrative. The first question to ask about a philosophic poem is, what does it mean? This is the enabling question. The poem seems not to have been widely understood, judging from most of the comment it has elicited. But whatever its success as a poem may ultimately seem to be, it is certainly a central *document* in American poetry. It represents, I strongly suspect, a conscious effort at accommodation and synthesis of the several strands of American literary tradition.

At any rate, whether Warren consciously aimed at such an effect or not, his poem achieves it. Whether we use the historian's labels, the "Jeffersonian" and the "Hamiltonian," or the philosopher's "idealist" and "realist," or such reminders of a divided past as the "light" and the "dark" traditions, or "the party of hope" and "the party of memory," or the "liberal" and the "conservative" — however we name the chief traditions in our culture, they all are remembered and reconsidered, and drawn upon for whatever insight they embodied that still seems valid, in this poem. The only "tradition" positively dismissed as without value is the recent one of deterministic naturalism.

Brother to Dragons aspires to greatness and almost reaches it. It seems to me that its only significant flaw lies in its partial failure to take us fully enough, and sympathetically enough, into the mind of Lilburne. We are asked to recognize our complicity with him by virtue of a shared nature; but our temptation, recognized in the poem and philosophically, but not, with complete success, I think, *aesthetically* countered, is to dismiss Lilburne as mad, or a mere victim, or else a fiend. Insofar as we either deny him any responsibility, or think of him as pure satanic intention, we are denying him his humanity, denying that he is "like us." Warren says we must not do this, and we feel the wisdom of his advice, but we may still guard our secret reservation: but *I* wouldn't have done *that,* we say. Perhaps Warren would have done better to have followed Coleridge's example in "Rime of the Ancient Mariner" and invented a less terrible crime, instead of using the historical one that seems to cast its perpetrator in the role of maniac. History is often hard to imagine and even harder to believe.

The three volumes Warren has so far published since *Brother to Dragons* continue his steady progress toward the romantic, the direct, the personal, and the visionary in poetry. They have been widely condemned by reviewers for carelessness in technique, for addressing the reader directly with an appeal for intuitive understanding, and for implying that their author believes a poem is something *said* rather than something *made*—for their "romanticism," in short.

That some real tendency in Warren's poetry is being pointed to in all these complaints is clear, whether the tendency should be cause for complaint or not. The first poem in *You, Emperors, and Others,* for instance, is titled "Clearly About You," and begins this way,

> Whoever you are, this poem is clearly about you,
> For there's nothing else in the world it could be about.
> Whatever it says, this poem is clearly true,
> For truth is all we are born to, and the truth's out.

If this, the first of a series of eight poems under the general heading of "A Garland for You" — that is, for every reader — seems to violate the proprieties of "Impersonal" poetry as we have been taught them, the last poem of a later series called "Some Quiet, Plain Poems" does so even more violently in its undisguised offering of the *personal. What,* no *persona?* the critic asks, when he reads,

> Long since that time I have walked night streets, heel-
> iron
> Clicking the stone, and in dark in windows have stared.
> Question, quarry, dream — I have vented my ire on
> My own heart that, ignorant and untoward,
> Yearns for an absolute that Time would, I thought, have
> prepared,
>
> But has not yet. Well, let us debate
> The issue. But under a tight roof, clutching a toy,
> My son now sleeps, and when the hour grows late,
> I shall go forth where the cold constellations deploy
> And lift up my eyes to consider more strictly the
> appalling logic of joy.

Or looking for the "wit," "irony," and "paradox," and finding none in the poems gathered as "Short Thoughts on Long Nights," the reviewer whose only criteria are Modernist and New Critical wonders what to say about "Nightmare of Mouse":

It was there, but I said it couldn't be true in daylight.
It was there, but I said it was only a trick of starlight.
It was there, but I said to believe it would take a fool,
And I wasn't, so didn't — till teeth crunched on my skull.

Or about the poem that follows, "Nightmare of Man":

I assembled, marshaled, my data, deployed them expertly.
My induction was perfect, as far as induction may be.
But the formula failed in the test tube, despite all my skill,
For I'd thought of the death of my mother, and wept; and weep still.

The reviewer might of course say that they "move" him, but that would be "impressionistic." What would *Understanding Poetry,* in the stern purity of its first edition, have said about these poems? It would be an amusing and profitable exercise to write out a destructive analysis of "Nightmare of Mouse" and "Nightmare of Man," complete with unexplained references to the damaging effect on the poems of their lack of irony and to the embarrassing directness of their statements, in the manner of the Brooks and Warren textbook that pioneered in bringing New Critical doctrine to the teachers of literature.

When Warren's later poems *are* ironic or ambiguous, the irony or the ambiguity seems not to be a matter of style, a device invented in the making of the poem, to make it "work" better, but a concession style makes to the nature of nature. Thus the negative statements in "The Necessity for Belief," the last poem in *Promises,* suggest their opposites, as though they were merely "willed"; and the third and last lines are so nicely balanced on the razor edge of ambiguity that we hardly know whether to read "scarcely" as "just barely" or as "not quite." But these ambiguities have been thoroughly prepared for in the earlier poems in the book, and now they seem not so much a manner of style as a recognition of fact. "Belief" is unquestionably necessary, the poem says, and yet, in our time, hardly possible, or, perhaps, not quite impossible:

The sun is red, and the sky does not scream.
The sun is red, and the sky does not scream.

There is much that is scarcely to be believed.

The moon is in the sky, and there is no weeping.
The moon is in the sky, and there is no weeping.

Much is told that is scarcely to be believed.

However we take this, the poems in Warren's recent volumes are the work of a man on the move, a seeker, of a seeker in personal memory, in personal experience, in the sight of his children sleeping, or in the images of nature, for clues to an adequate definition of the glory that potentially is man's. At times his search seems to be taking him, despite his respect for pragmatic ways of thinking, back to something like the conviction of Edward Taylor, who might have written one of the lines in "Go It, Granny — Go It, Hog!" — which is part of one of Warren's finest late poems, "Ballad of a Sweet Dream of Peace." The hogs, the devourers, *time* made incarnate in *flesh,* are eating Granny, or the ghost of Granny, again, or still, or always, in the middle of Central Park. The realistic or skeptical mind rejects the possibility:

Any hogs that I slopped are long years dead,
And eaten by somebody and evacuated,
So it's simply absurd, what you said.

But the believing mind, which is also the imaginative and dreaming mind, replies, and this is the line that Taylor might almost, with some stylistic and some theological changes, have written:

You fool, poor fool, all Time is a dream, and we're
all one Flesh, at last. . . .

Of course Taylor would have wanted to exclude Unbelievers from the "we," and he would have used "one Flesh" as a conceit for the Body of Christ in Heaven, or the Church Triumphant. But he and Warren would understand each other if they stood in colloquy.

The new poems in Warren's 1966 volume, *New and Selected Poems,* provide the most striking evidence that this poet ought to be thought of in terms of the metaphor for the poet favored by Emerson, Whitman, and Gabriel Marcel, man on the road, *Homo Viator*. "Homage to Emerson: On Night Flight to New York," in this volume, shows us a poet who has long understood Taylor now seeking to understand Emerson also. Emerson's essays lie open on the lap of the speaker in the poems as he flies eastward in the pressurized cabin at 38,000 feet. How can he square the hope they speak of with his present experience?

Warren's most recent poems ask us whether it is possible, honestly, for us to reverse the trend toward rationalistic alienation that has been dominant for the past century among our poets, who are, for Warren, as for Emerson, our *seers,* our *diviners*. In "Emerson's Smile," and in the Emerson series as a whole, the poet asks whether there is any real *reason* to smile. If there is, can *we* find Emerson's secret?

Of R. P. Warren it ought to be said, as Robert Frost once said of himself, that the career of this one-time "Fugitive" suggests "not a flight but a seeking."

PART SEVEN

After Modernism

CHAPTER XXI

Transition

The collected editions are now settled comfortably on the shelves, some, even, gathering a little dust. The authors of some of those books are dead. We are witnessing, in other words, the end of a poetic era, the end of "modernism," that school of which the Founding Fathers were Eliot, Pound, and Yeats.

—R. P. Warren, in *A Plea in Mitigation: Modern Poetry and the End of an Era,* 1966

Signs of the End of Modernism

BY the middle of the 1950's there were many signs that Modernism in poetry had run its course, and in the Sixties the revolt was full-fledged. True, Eliot himself had turned away from it as early as 1943 in *The Four Quartets*, but Eliot, likened to the pope by rebellious John Ciardi, was beginning to be so much out of favor with most younger poets that they missed the significance of his renunciation. Not until Lowell's *Life Studies* in 1959 did it seem to many observers of the poetic scene that a definitive death sentence had been pronounced on what had so recently been avant-garde.

By the 1960's so many voices had joined in protest against Modernism, particularly in its Eliotic aspects, that we seemed to be hearing a chorus. With Eliot out of favor and Williams in as models, the Sixties press dedicated itself to spreading the news of the revolt. More and more young poets of distinction or promise of it raised their voices to tell us that there could be no more "poetry of the library," dependent on obscure mythic allusions and the voice of a persona for its effect, and no more "impersonal" or "autotelic" poetry.

James Dickey found that what was "suspect" in such poetry was its artificiality, its lack of direct expression of passion and commitment on the part of the poet, and the absence in it of any suggestion of personal "communion" between poet and reader. Howard Nemerov advised the poet to cultivate "attentiveness and obedience" as he listened to "nature" and learned to see and say "certain simplicities." Denise Levertov joined in calling for "attentive listening" and remembered that it was Emerson who had first advised "asking the fact for the form." Karl Shapiro exalted Whitman and engaged in angry polemics against Eliot, his work, and his influence. Critics, unable to ignore such voices as these—as they had the voices of protest raised in the Fifties—began to speak of "the new romanticism" and soon even of "naked poetry." It seemed very evident that the best young poets had no intention of letting their "individual talent" be shaped and dominated by awareness of the whole Western Christian cultural and poetic "tradition." Our long tradition seemed to the poets making the news to falsify their own experience, as it had earlier seemed to do to the private experience of Emerson and Whitman.

The self, nature, and current social problems became typical subjects of the new poetry. If the poet was religious, he would be more likely to turn to the Old Testament, or to India or China, than to Western Christendom with its amalgam of Greek rationalism and Hebrew piety. Allen Ginsberg's *Howl*, appearing contemporaneously with Lowell's *Life Studies*, added the prophetic note to Lowell's apparent endorsement of autobiography as a subject proper to poetry. Theodore Roethke, approaching the height of his powers in the Fifties, had already made private experience and the personal response to nature his subjects in the late 1940's, with *The Lost Son and Other Poems*, which seemed at the time to be merely eccentric, and now he continued the private note in his celebrations of childhood, love, and personal religious experience in *Words for the Wind* (1958). "Autotelic" poetry had seemed possible so long as theology held firm—as it had seemed to during the Neo-Orthodox decades, as it had for Eliot, Auden, and the early Lowell—but when religious belief was shaken, a new, untraditional search for meaning came to seem necessary, and along with it, necessarily, a new kind of poetry.

New "Schools" of the Sixties and Seventies

AND so we have had the "Beats" (Ginsberg, Ferlinghetti, and others) in the 1950's; the "Confessional" poets, with Plath and Sexton in the lead in the 1960's and 1970's; the "Black Mountain" school, led by Charles Olson, in the 1960's; and the "Deep Image" (Robert

Bly and others) and "New York" (John Ashbery and others) schools dominant in the Seventies. These "schools" seemed sharply distinct at the time and kept fashionable critics busy for years explaining and justifying them, but as we look back over the poetic history of the past third of a century, what the "schools," particularly of the Fifties and Sixties, had in common comes to seem more important than what they quarreled about. They shared both a repudiation of our cultural past and a distaste for present society, each school in its own way doing what Olson called "clearing away the junk of history."

Searching for values that could be lived by, for truths that could be believed in, the Beats went "on the road"—a road that only superficially resembled Walt's open road—or took to drugs and meditation. They turned Eastward to escape the Judeo-Christian tradition (Ginsberg, Snyder), while the Confessional poets turned inward, to the depths of their psychic torture. The Black Mountain poets exalted the primitive and mythic, renouncing civilization and culture as we have known it (Olson, Duncan, Creeley). Bly and others explored the Surrealist "deep images" that C. G. Jung had studied and seemed for a while to find there the meanings that could no longer be found in the world of outward experience.

Or, with a deeper skepticism about the power of the mind to know, or language to express, any objective meaning, Ashbery and others, in what is sometimes called, with questionable justice, the New York school, in effect rediscovered something like Eliot's idea of "autotelic" poetry, stripped of Eliot's religious and cultural assumptions, and wrote "self-referential" poems that seemed designed, like so much avant-garde contemporary fiction, as language games only, poems in which words had ceased to have referential value, poems of the mind alone with itself. When MacLeish had written long before that a poem "should not mean but be," he had meant to rule out only overt didacticism: a poem should "mean" by what it *was*. When the possibility of discovering any kind of reliable meaning or value in our lives is systematically denied by poems, poetry becomes only a pastime, preferable perhaps to solitaire for some.

Repudiation, fresh search, and finally a giving-up of the search: this would seem very nearly to sum up our poetic history in the years since the Second World War, so far as that history found expression in the poetic schools or movements that have made the news. But with every year that passes the schools seem less important and the work of certain poets who transcended the aims and limitations of any school more important. The period after the death of the great Modernists would seem hardly worth recalling if it were not for the work of a few poets who cannot be summed up by any of the preceding tags.

Four Transitional Poets

THE early post-Modernist poets I have chosen to treat at some length, partly because their poetry seems to me most likely to continue to be read and valued by future generations, partly because they seem the best spokesmen for the still-significant aspects of the experience of the recent past, are Theodore Roethke, John Berryman, Robert Lowell, and Richard Wilbur. They are likely to strike us as having little in common, but such an impression would be misleading. All of them are deeply aware of, and find things to value in, the past, even while being acutely aware that the past is past, though to be sure this sense of living in a radically new and different age is least apparent in the work of Wilbur. None of them makes, or wishes to make, that total break with the past, with the "junk" of history, called for by Olson, or repudiates culture with the Beats, or gives up the attempt to transcend the self by responding to value and meaning in the world outside the self, as so many later poets seem to have done.

Of the four, Lowell, with his sharp break from Modernism after his brilliant early Modernist and Catholic period, was the most influential; Roethke, who found his own way slowly outside the main currents of poetic fashion and was slow to be recognized for the great poet he was, the least. Berryman, perhaps the most complex and tortured of the four and the least sure of his own voice when he finally found it, tried to return in the end, before his suicide, to the faith that Lowell had begun with and renounced publicly in *Life Studies*. (The stresses that Berryman endured may help to explain why so many modern poets have ended in suicide—Jarrell, Plath, Sexton, Berryman.) None of them issued manifestoes or attracted overt disciples, though Lowell's *Life Studies* seemed to lend support to the later Confessional poets. Wilbur remains the most conservative and traditional of the four, so much so indeed that he may seem misplaced here. Unlike most of our later poets, all four at some time in their careers wrote from within the Judeo-Christian framework of religious faith, Lowell at the beginning, Roethke and Berryman at the end, and Wilbur all the way through so far.

THEODORE ROETHKE

Though Roethke's major debt in his first volume, *Open House* (1941), would seem to be to the great Modernist Yeats, in the end he probably came the closest of any of the chief post-Modernist poets to repossessing the essential ways of knowing and feeling of our major poetic tradition, the tradition defined by Emerson, Whitman, and Dickinson. Emerson would probably have felt that Roethke came closest among his contemporaries to being the "true" poet he had described. Roethke was a Transcendental poet, a nature poet, and a poet of the transcendent self conceived both as representative and as defined by its capacity for growth. He was a poet dedicated to a new or "high" kind of "seeing," ultimately to illumination or mystic vision, a realization in experience, not in theory, of what Emerson referred to as the seer "becoming" what he sees. He was a poet who hoped to speak both for and to his time by discovering his own identity—and then creating a new identity capable of moving in a larger circumference by recognizing, accepting, and including within the self more "things," more of "fate," more of the tough resilience of the "not-me."

An explanation by one of Roethke's most sympathetic and penetrating critics of a key term that Roethke shared with Emerson will perhaps offer the quickest way into the subject. "The spirit," Ralph J. Mills, Jr., writes, as Roethke means it,

> is perhaps the bloom, the last and highest glory of the self and so becomes the guiding and motivating principle in its experience, its ascent on the scale of being. . . . The spirit as essence of the organic self seeks finally to go beyond that self's circumference. . . . The spirit retains its central position and yet seems to step outside itself, to merge with things other than itself. Thus the spirit is fluid, can expand indefinitely, a potentiality that is fundamental to mystical experience.

Mr. Mills does not say so—perhaps only because it is not relevant to his point at the moment—but his explanation of what Roethke means by "spirit" reads like a summary of Emerson's views of the same subject as they are expressed in "Circles." The same sort of relationship would appear if one were to attempt to explain what Roethke means by "nature," though to be sure in this case Roethke, like Whitman before him, was always concrete in his approach to nature, while Emerson much of the time seems only to be recommending concreteness.

But I shall let Roethke himself say some of these things that link him so closely with Emerson. I shall draw upon his prose explanations of himself and his work, so that there may be no suspicion that a poem is being misinterpreted or that the speaker is not Roethke but a persona like the old woman in "Meditations of an Old Woman" who is at once the poet's mother and, by identification, a projected part of the poet himself.

From Roethke's college sophomore essay, "Some Self-Analysis":

> I have a genuine love of nature. . . . I know that Muir and Thoreau and Burroughs speak the truth. . . . I am influenced too much, perhaps, by natural objects. I seem bound by the very room I'm in. . . . [But] when I get alone under an open sky where man isn't too evident,—then I'm tremendously exalted and a thousand vivid ideas and sweet visions flood my consciousness.

Writing years later about his early childhood in his statement in *Twentieth Century Authors*, Roethke had this to say, which helps to explain the sentiments in the college essay:

> There were books at home and I went to the local libraries . . . ; read Stevenson, Pater, Newman, Tomlinson, and those maundering English charm boys known as familiar essayists. I bought on my own editions of Emerson and Thoreau.

Again, speaking later still to students at a college symposium on "Identity," the poet quotes a part of his poem "Dolor," then comments, in words that might have come from "Self-Reliance":

> This poem is an exposition of one of the modern hells:

> the institution that overwhelms the individual man. The "order," the trivia of the institution, is, in human terms, a disorder, and as such, must be resisted.

At the same symposium, he sometimes seemed to be remembering both Emerson and Thoreau at once, as when he said,

> The human problem is to find out what one really *is*: whether one exists, whether existence is possible.

And once at least he *was* remembering Thoreau. Quoting a part of an early rejected poem that included the lines "I keep the spirit spare" and "The deed will speak the truth / In language strict and pure," he commented, "All this has been said before, in Thoreau, in Rilke." Roethke had, it would appear, no admiration for the poetry of either Emerson or Thoreau, but he must have remembered and respected Emerson from his early exposure to him, and he certainly knew and respected Thoreau.

He differed with both of them too, of course, as any modern must. Something of his criticism of Thoreau is revealed in his comment that the spirit need not be "spare"—need not save itself for only the highest moments of illumination: "it can grow gracefully and beautifully like a tendril, like a flower. I did not know this at the time." But his differences from Emerson and Thoreau are more strikingly apparent when we compare his view of friendship and love with that of the two older poets, and when we contrast his awareness of both moral and natural evil with their typical denial of the ultimate reality of either. Guilt and darkness are admitted and explored in Roethke's work; they are usually denied, repressed, explained, or pushed into the background in the public work (as contrasted with the private statements in journals) of Emerson and Thoreau.

One of the most striking differences between Roethke and Emerson may be discussed in theological terms. Remembering how Emerson had described in *Nature* his unexpected sense of unity with the scene while crossing the bare, muddy common in late winter, a passage that suggests many Emersonian lines in Roethke's poetry, we find the distinction that must be made between the two when we read on a few sentences further in Emerson:

> There . . . [in the woods] I become a transparent eye-

> ball; I am nothing; I see all; the currents of the Universal Being circulate through me; I am part or parcel of God.

With this we may compare Roethke's statement in his essay "On Identity":

> The second part of this feeling, the "oneness," is, of course, the first stage in mystical illumination, an experience many men have had, and still have: the sense that all is one and one is all. This is inevitably accompanied by a loss of the "I," the purely human ego, to another center, a sense of the absurdity of death, a return to a state of innocency.
>
> This experience has come to me so many times, in so many varying circumstances, that I cannot suspect its validity: it is *not* one of the devil's traps, an hallucination, a voice, a snare. I can't claim that the soul, my soul, was absorbed in God. No, God for me still remains someone to be confronted, to be dueled with: that is perhaps my error, my sin of pride. But the oneness, Yes!

Though Emerson was not, ultimately, in his most typical stances, a pantheist, he felt impelled, both by personal necessity and by his sense of the requirements of thought in his time, to obscure the differences between theism and pantheism. Roethke, by contrast, like Hawthorne when he wrote "Night Sketches" and Melville when he created and sympathized with Ahab, preferred to risk enduring the "dark times" that come when one does not blur such distinctions. When he added his own comment on his poem "In a Dark Time" to those made by Ransom, Babette Deutsch, and Stanley Kunitz in Ostroff's symposium, *The Contemporary Poet as Artist and Critic*, Roethke remarked:

> Another reason makes any comment of mine unseemly: the nature of the poem itself. It is the first of a sequence, part of a hunt, a drive toward God: an effort to break through the barrier of rational experience; an intention not unmixed with pride, as Mr. Kunitz has pointed out, accompanied by a sense of exhilaration, and only occasional seizures of humility (in the usual sense of the word). This was a dictated poem, something given, scarcely mine at all. For about three days before

> its writing I felt disembodied, out of time; then the poem virtually wrote itself, on a day in summer, 1958.
>
> Presumably, in the poem, the self dies, for a time at least. I was granted an insight beyond the usual, let us say. To speak of it further is a betrayal of the experience. One forces the self, with all its trappings of vanity and guilt, its "taste," as Mr. Kunitz would have it, upon what seems to me the essential otherworldliness of the poem: one defiles whatever purity has been achieved.
>
> I take the central experience to be fairly common: to break from the bondage of the self, from the barriers of the "real" world, to come as close to God as possible. If the clumsy paraphrase or running comment which follows reveals even one incidental insight about spiritual experience, it will have served its purpose. I write, then, not to enhance the poem, or to quarrel with other interpretations, but to find out further what really happens when one attempts to go beyond "reality."

It is not possible, of course, to "go beyond 'reality' " if "reality" means "all that is." But "reality" for a poet and a person, if not for technical philosophy, means "what I believe to be, or experience as, 'real,' that is, not imagined or wished by me." One's sense of what *is*, of what exists, is a conditioned sense. Roethke's quotation marks around "reality" in the statement just quoted are his concession to more naturalistic views than his; they make the word mean, in his sentence, "so-called reality," or "that limited sense of reality given us by ordinary experience, a sense that is transformed or expanded by mystical experience."

Beginning with *The Lost Son and Other Poems* in 1948, Roethke sought to achieve a fuller apprehension of reality by bringing childhood memories into full consciousness and reliving them. Returning to the completely personal might provide a way of enlarging the person to include the impersonal. Remembering both the anxieties and the exhilaration of the child on top of a greenhouse might provide a way of moving beyond the anxieties of the adult world, and so a way to a more complete recognition of the dimensions of reality. "To love objects"—which as often threaten us as nourish us—"is to love life," Roethke once jotted in his notebook. The end result of loving objects, he said in a late poem, in Whitmanic imagery and diction, is an unexpected joy:

I lose and find myself in the long water;
I am gathered together once more;
I embrace the world.

Roethke's explanation of the action in "The Lost Son," the title poem of his 1948 volume, makes clear the ultimate purpose of the movements downward, backward, and inward that comprise the poem. After describing all his poems included in John Ciardi's *Mid-Century American Poets* as complete in themselves, "yet each in a sense . . . a stage in a kind of struggle out of the slime; part of a slow spiritual progress; an effort to be born, and later, to become something more," Roethke went on to say of "The Lost Son" that in it the protagonist is "hunting, like a primitive, for some animistic suggestion, some clue to existence from the subhuman." Then, like Emerson before him, he used the metaphor of *seeing* to convey his sense of how the suggestions, the clues, might come:

> These he sees and yet does not see: they are almost tail-flicks, from another world, seen out of the corner of the eye. In a sense he goes in and out of rationality; he hangs in the balance between the human and the animal.

Or as he said later in the same statement, "I believe that to go forward as a spiritual man it is necessary first to go back"—back into earliest childhood memories, into the subliminal or barely conscious, back into the child in nature and the child as nature.

This was Roethke's way of searching for the "real." "Reality," Stevens once jotted in his Notebook, "is the spirit's true center." Roethke of course agreed. Who would disagree? But Stevens at first meant by "reality" something abstractly philosophic or rationally cognitive, something that could be "known" by an act of mind alone; and then, because what was "known" this way was intolerable, he meant by "reality" the ultimate nothingness that could not really be "known" at all. (Could it even be imagined?) Roethke made "reality" his "spirit's true center" as much as Stevens tried to do, and was as much aware of the darkness and terror of the personal depths he explored as Stevens was of the darkness of the "real" as he conceived it. But Roethke sought for a new understanding of reality by the methods of embracing, incorporating, and, finally, achieving a new way of "seeing." Periods of terrible darkness as he embraced the otherness and darkness of "things" were the price he had to pay for his progress.

In the poems in *The Lost Son*, Roethke's version of Transcendentalism is mostly implicit, but by the time of *The Far Field* he was ready to state it openly. "All finite things reveal infinitude," we read in the last section of the title poem of the volume. The hope that this might be found to be so had motivated the lost son's immersion in "the muck and welter, the dark, the *dreck*" of memory. *The Far Field* records the successful conclusion of a quest for ultimate meaning found not by "knowing" in the way we associate with Stevens, or by "believing" in the way we associate with Eliot and the early work of Robert Lowell, but by self-transcendence: by spiritual growth of the self to the point where it can "see" Being shining through Becoming. "So to be is to know," Emerson had said. Roethke's poetic career illuminates what Emerson meant.

It should not be necessary at this point to quote once more from Emerson, Thoreau, and Whitman in order to show that by the end of his career Roethke had recovered and made fully his own the Transcendental faith in God's immanence that began to be lost with Dickinson and that could be kept, in part, by Frost, only by being disguised or hidden. Nor would there be any point in quoting at length from Roethke's last poems, as could so easily be done, to show how often Emerson or Thoreau or Whitman might almost, granting the differences of idiom and cadence between their work and his, have written the lines. I shall give just two examples then of Roethke's closeness in theme and image in his last work to each of the three earlier poets.

To Whitman, especially in "Out of the Cradle Endlessly Rocking," we may compare this from Roethke's "Meditation at Oyster River":

> Now, in this waning of light,
> I rock with the motion of morning;
> In the cradle of all that is,
> I'm lulled into half-sleep
> By the lapping of water,
> Cries of the sandpiper.

(In a later poem in the volume, "The Abyss," Roethke invokes Whitman's presence much as Hart Crane had in "The Bridge," echoing, as he does so, several parts of "Song of Myself": "Be with me, Whitman, maker of catalogues: / For the world invades me again, / And once more the tongues begin babbling. / And still the terrible hunger for objects quails me.")

To Whitman again, this time from Roethke's "The Meadow Mouse":

> I think of the nestling fallen into the deep grass,
> The turtle gasping in the dusty rubble of the highway,
> The paralytic stunned in the tub, and the water rising,—
> All things innocent, hapless, forsaken.

To Thoreau this time, his poetry, but even more his prose, *Cape Cod* for example, from Roethke's "On the Quay":

> What they say on the quay is,
> "There's no shelter
> From the blow of the wind,
> Or the sea's banter,—
> There's two more to drown
> The week after."

Or this, from "In Evening Air":

> A dark theme keeps me here,
> Though summer blazes in the vireo's eye.
> Who would be half possessed
> By his own nakedness?
> Waking's my care—
> I'll make a broken music,
> or I'll die.

Finally, to Emerson. Here the verbal parallels are rarer, and probably unconscious for the most part. But not always, it would seem: "Whether the bees have thoughts, we cannot say, / But the hind part of the worm wiggles the most." This in effect, whether Roethke thought about it or not, amounts to a comment, partly critical, on Emerson's "Humble Bee" and a reaffirmation of the idea in his lines on the worm that strives upward through the spires of form.

More commonly, Emerson's meanings are reaffirmed by Roethke without any suggestion of direct indebtedness, as in the line that echoes a line in Whitman's "There Was a Child Went Forth" but at the same time illustrates what Emerson meant by the imagination's being a kind of seeing that becomes what it sees. The line is from "I Waited": "And I became all that I looked upon." Whitman's line goes, "And the first object he look'd upon, that object he became." Or again, the ending of "Journey to the Interior," to cite a final example, expresses the same general meaning and uses some of the same key images as Emerson's poem about the titmouse that survived and sang in the winter storm, with the darkness coming, because his bones were made light by the "Arctic air" that filled them. Earlier, the speaker in Roethke's poem has immersed himself in desiccating memories of a journey in which things moved past the threatened and helpless self and the dust lay thick on his eyelids, but now, having heard "A slight song, / After the midnight cries," he concludes, less confidently than Emerson had concluded "The Titmouse," to be sure, but with at least the beginnings of a new knowledge:

> As a blind man, lifting a curtain, knows it is morning,
> I know this change:
> On one side of silence there is no smile;
> But when I breathe with the birds,
> The spirit of wrath becomes the spirit of blessing,
> And the dead begin from their dark to sing in my sleep.

To suppose that once we have located Roethke in the mystical or visionary tradition that begins with Vaughan, Traherne, and Blake and includes Emerson and Whitman, we have sufficiently accounted for his work, would be as serious a mistake as not recognizing that he belongs in that tradition. Roethke also criticized, modified, enriched, and extended the tradition, in part by drawing upon resources outside it, or even hostile to it, in part by proceeding on the inward journey initiated by the earlier poets farther than they had, or deeper into what had been repressed. To try to avoid suggesting the sort of diminution of Roethke's superbly original achievement that would be implied by pigeonholing him as just another Transcendentalist, I shall list some of the most important ways in which he differs from earlier poets in the tradition. To simplify, I shall let Emerson stand for the tradition and draw some contrasts between Emerson and Roethke.

First, Roethke's situation as a man of the middle of the twentieth century was obviously different from Emerson's. Freud had intervened, and neo-orthodoxy, and Eliot and Yeats. Sometimes Roethke sounds more like Hawthorne, fascinated by the darkness, than like Emerson. (His "Dreams drain the spirit if we dream too long" makes the point Hawthorne made in "Night Sketches.") Roethke's "correspondences" storm too steadily to yield easily or quickly to interpretation. Like Robinson, Roethke praises the darkness for enabling him better to see the light: "In a dark time, the eye begins to see."

Second, quite apart from his seemingly greater awareness of the duality of nature as both threat and revelation (how unaware of this was even the early Emerson, really?), Roethke was finally, as I have already suggested, more traditional or "orthodox" than Emerson in his religious ideas. He never writes as though God were *only* immanent, or only the creation of the mind or imagination, as Emerson occasionally does. In Roethke, the eye sees what it does not in any ontological sense create. He could write "God's in that stone" without confusing the stone and God, or supposing that the laws that governed the stone were the same as those governing the spirit.

"The eternal seeks, and finds, the temporal," he could write at last, even though the whole body of his work is the evidence of his own seeking. Emerson, again, cannot be imagined writing Roethke's line in "The Marrow," "Brooding on God, I may become a man." Still less can we imagine Emerson's praying the prayer in the final lines of the third stanza:

> Lord, hear me out, and hear me out this day:
> From me to Thee's a long and terrible way.

A good deal of the time Roethke is closer to Traherne in his religious feeling and thought than he is to Emerson or Whitman. In some degree, and in his own way, Roethke recovered certain aspects of the traditional faith that had been lost in Emerson.

Closely related to this affinity of Roethke's with the seventeenth century and also working against his absorption in American Transcendentalism is the impact Yeats and Eliot made on him, particularly the latter. His fondness for Yeats could be reconciled without too much difficulty with the Emersonianism already implicit in *The Lost Son* and often explicit in *The Far Field*, but his absorption of Eliot's *Four Quartets* had a quite different effect on his work. Yeats, visionary and metaphysical, prompted loving tributes and conscious imitation. For a while in the early 1950's his influence interrupted the natural development of Roethke's style toward free and organic forms, forcing a return to the formal practices of *Open House*, his first volume. Eliot, by contrast, seems to have modified somewhat Roethke's thinking and feeling about religious matters.

Most of Roethke's critics have noted and several have commented on the echoes of *Four Quartets* in the first poem in *North American Sequence*, "The Longing." But the relationship between Roethke's poem and Eliot's is more than a matter of Roethke's including a few conscious echoes of Eliot. "The Longing" depends upon *Four Quartets* just as clearly as *The Bridge* rests upon "Passage to India." It is a comment on, and partial criticism of, the earlier poem. It agrees in part, as in

> Lust fatigues the soul.
> How to transcend this sensual emptiness?

Especially it agrees about the nature of man's longing: "I long for the imperishable quiet at the heart of form"—Eliot's "still point" at the center of the dance. But it disagrees with what it takes to be the older poet's excessive emphasis on man's guilt, and on the "paleface"—the institutional and authoritarian—

> Old men should be explorers?
> I'll be an Indian.
> Ogalala?
> Iroquois.

Nevertheless, Roethke's "redskin" version of the faith Eliot had meditated on and presented in *Four Quartets* does not amount to anything like a rejection of that faith. The increasing emphasis on God's transcendence—without any diminution of the emphasis on his immanence—in Roethke's last poems surely reflects in part at least the influence of Eliot. In Roethke's last half-dozen years,

Yeats's influence, both on Roethke's style and on his feeling and thinking, was in process of being replaced by two new ones and an older one, by Eliot, Whitman, and Blake. Of the three, Eliot's influence must be taken as qualifying Roethke's Emersonianism and his debt to Whitman and Blake.

A final distinction between Roethke and his earliest American poetic ancestors whose vision he modifies and corrects while keeping it alive: Roethke's work, especially if approached developmentally, could be studied very rewardingly in Buberian terms of the search for reality in relationships. Roethke's preoccupation with the self is more like Whitman's than Emerson's or Thoreau's in two respects: The self takes itself as representative, and the self finds itself, discovers its deeper identity, in love, which requires a full acceptance of the reality of other selves, and not just human ones. The necessity of "dying to the self" continually, if psychic, moral, and spiritual growth is to go on, was "discovered" by both Whitman and Roethke, though more consciously, with the benefit of modern psychiatry, by Roethke, to be sure. The point is that either a Buberian or a more orthodox psychological approach to Roethke's career would uncover an element largely absent in Emerson. Emerson could relate to the cosmos, and to the natural scene as he encountered it in woods and sky; but, as he often admitted, he generally found himself uneasy, forced back into himself, in the presence of people.

But enough, and I should hope more than enough, of such cautionary contrasts between Roethke and Emerson. In his own way, his own terms, in the way possible in our time, after all that has happened since Emerson, Roethke re-expressed many of Emerson's fundamental beliefs and insights. "The Small" and "A Walk in Late Summer" are not distorted by being called great Transcendental poems. "Root Cellar," in *The Lost Son and Other Poems,* concludes, "Even the dirt kept breathing a small breath." "Moss Gathering" concludes with the gatherer's sense of guilt for "pulling off flesh from the living planet," a feeling based on a sentiment that may be found everywhere in Whitman and is often implied, though not developed, in Emerson.

What troubled Roethke most in his "drive toward God" was what had troubled Emerson and Whitman, the "stupor of knowledge lacking inwardness." The same impulse lies behind his backward and downward explorations that prompted Emerson's command to the scholar,

Thou shalt not try
To plant thy shrivelled pedantry
On the shoulders of the sky.

Again and again, in poems and in prose, Roethke stated his agreement with the sentiment in the closing lines of Emerson's "April":

The south-winds are quick-witted,
The schools are sad and slow,
The masters quite omitted
The lore we care to know.

Even when Roethke seems farthest from Emerson, it is often the case that he is far not from the Emerson who wrote a great deal of poetry that has not been read in recent years but from the diminished and caricatured Emerson of modern scholarship and criticism. A line like "By dying daily, I have come to be" immediately suggests Whitman's "O Always Living, Always Dying" to be sure, rather than Emerson; but that is partly because we are not likely to remember Emerson's "The Titmouse," which embodies a part of Roethke's meaning in its images.

In his series of poems on the presence of Yeats, Roethke wrote lines that draw together the several strands of his heritage and would probably have pleased not only Emerson and Whitman but Eliot and Yeats as well:

I've the lark's word for it, who sings alone:
What's seen recedes; Forever's what we know!—
Eternity defined, and strewn with straw,
The fury of the slug beneath the stone.

The final stanza of this poem, "They Sing, They Sing," suggests at once his closeness to and distance from Emerson, his affinity with Whitman and Dickinson, and his disagreement with Stevens, at least before Stevens' very last years:

The edges of the summit still appall
When we brood on the dead or the beloved;

Nor can imagination do it all
In this last place of light: he dares to live
Who stops being a bird, yet beats his wings
Against the immense immeasurable emptiness of things.

ROBERT LOWELL

When Elizabeth Bishop reviewed Robert Lowell's *Life Studies* in 1959 she expressed her admiration in a comment that can take us a good way toward identifying the sensibility that characterizes all of Lowell's work, early and late. "Somehow or other," Miss Bishop wrote, "in the middle of our worst century so far, we have produced a magnificent poet." The sense that this is the "worst century" lies behind the tense and savage verse of the volumes before *Life Studies* and is often openly expressed in Lowell's later poems. In Lowell's work, consciousness and conscience come together and produce a tension very nearly unbearable.

As Roethke renewed for our time much of what was central in Emerson and Thoreau and Whitman, so Robert Lowell has continued his famous ancestor's social and historical awareness and moral earnestness. Though his poems are often as frankly personal as Roethke's, their probings inward and backward into memory are always set in a context of moral judgment operating in terms of social and historical fact. Perhaps no major poet writing today is further from the spirit of Emerson and Whitman, or more continuously aware of the evil that becomes apparent when we survey the "thoughtless drift of the deciduous years" that is history, as his ancestor put it, than is Robert Lowell.

Two poems written almost exactly a century apart on the same subject will serve to illustrate both Robert Lowell's distance from Emerson, Whitman, and Roethke and his closeness in certain essential respects to his poetic ancestor. Between J. R. Lowell's poem of 1865 on those who lost their lives fighting in the Union Army, "Ode Recited at the Harvard Commemoration," and Robert Lowell's "For the Union Dead," there are of course all sorts of differences of length, scope, intention, and, naturally, style; but the two are united by a striking family likeness, for all that. Both are marked by what the older poem calls "the passion of an angry grief"; both find small comfort or none in the spectacle that individual life presents when seen in historical perspective; both admire "the stalwart man" who exercises "man's lovely, / peculiar power to choose life and die," as the later poem puts it; both, finally, are very dark poems.

To be sure, the elder Lowell felt required by the occasion to affirm at last that Harvard's dead had not died uselessly, but the bulk of his poem is about the difficulty of achieving even the limited affirmation it does express. "Our slender life runs rippling by, and glides / Into the silent hollow of the past," expresses in idea and image the dominant feeling in the poem, "Is earth too poor to give us / Something to live for here that shall outlive us?" the older poet asks. And again,

> Was dying all they had the skill to do?
> That were not fruitless: but the Soul resents
> Such short-lived service, as if blind events
> Ruled without her, or earth could so endure.

The earlier poet bases his attempted affirmation that the deaths were not "fruitless" on his faith in the destiny of the "Nation / Drawing force from all her men. . . . She that lifts up the manhood of the poor, / She of the open soul and open door, / With room about her hearth for all mankind!" Finding the spirit of the nation exemplified in Lincoln, "the first American," he cannot find it in him to call deaths for such an ideal "fruitless." But even this (one might think inadequate) ground for hope has been lost to the younger poet. "For the Union Dead" opens with the lines,

> The old South Boston Aquarium stands
> in a Sahara of snow now. Its broken windows are boarded.
> The bronze weathervane cod has lost half its scales.
> The airy tanks are dry,

and closes with these—

> The Aquarium is gone. Everywhere,
> giant finned cars nose forward like fish;
> a savage servility
> slides by on grease.

The sense of loss and decline expressed in the contemporary poem is at once personal ("I often sigh still / for the dark downward and vegetating kingdom / of the fish and reptile"), and social ("The ditch is nearer" now that received the hero's body). "Space is nearer," too:

> When I crouch to my television set,
> the drained faces of Negro school-children rise like
> balloons.

Everything conspires in the later poem to make the figures of the Union dead seem, year by year, increasingly remote from us. The statues "of the abstract Union Soldier / grow slimmer and younger each year," while "on Boyleston Street, a commercial photograph / shows Hiroshima boiling / over a Mosler safe, the 'Rock of Ages' / that survived the blast."

The older poet expressed, in very different style, a very similar sense of time's destructiveness:

> The mighty ones of old sweep by,
> Disvoicëd now and insubstantial things,
> . . . .
> To darkness driven by that imperious gust
> Of ever-rushing Time that here doth blow.

And he found it very difficult to resist the conclusion that "The cunning years steal all from us but woe." The younger poet, tougher perhaps, or at any rate less hopeful, does not try to resist it.

The dominant historical awareness that so often forms the explicit subject of Robert Lowell's later poems was equally present in the earlier ones, though sometimes less openly. When Lowell was converted to Roman Catholicism in 1940, the year of his graduation from Kenyon College, where he had been taught by Ransom, he was reversing family and New England history in a most dramatic way. It need imply no questioning of the genuineness of the poet's religious feelings to say that the conversion was perhaps as much a gesture of rejection and disavowal as it was an acceptance. In effect, it said that the poet refused to accept the role thrust on him, refused to be a passive victim of what seemed to him the decline of Puritanism into Unitarianism and of Unitarianism into moralism and of moralism into secularistic accommodation. Like Eliot's earlier conversion, Lowell's was a dramatic acting out of a judgment at once personal, social, and historical.

The Roman Catholic point of view and modes of feeling that inform *Land of Unlikeness*, *Lord Weary's Castle*, and *The Mills of the Kavanaughs*, the three volumes Lowell published between 1944 and 1951, and that often supply the imagery and allusions in these works, are complemented by a metaphysical style of such taut and packed brilliance that Lowell was quickly recognized as outstanding among the younger poets who were continuing the tradition of Eliot, Ransom, and Tate. His returning to strict syllabic prosody at a time when Williams was insisting that "syllable-counting" implied naivety in poet or critic was the formal counterpart of his turning to the clear and authoritative dogmas of a church that his ancestors had left before they ever came to this country. Both the style and the faith, as we find them in the early poems, are modes of external order; and both imply the judgment that New England's Protestant and organic-Transcendental traditions were by 1940 bankrupt. There were for Lowell, as Stevens would say, no Transcendentalists at *this* end of the road.

Many of the poems in the early volumes make such judgments as these explicit. Salem harbor, once famed for its far-sailing ships, is now the place where "sewage sickens the rebellious seas." Concord is where "Ten thousand Fords are idle . . . in search / Of a tradition." "Mr. Edwards and the Spider" and "After the Surprising Conversions" take off from passages in Jonathan Edwards and go on to imply a negative judgment of Puritanism. The Puritans, it seems, were capitalists and individualists.

Lowell's Catholic period ended in the late 1940's with several years of mental illness. The doctrines that had ordered experience for the man and given the poet a point of view from which to criticize both new and old New England had apparently not brought the man lasting relief from the agony of conscientious consciousness. When *Life Studies* appeared in 1959, eight years after *The Mills of the Kavanaughs*, it opened with "Beyond the Alps," to which was attached an explanatory note: "On the train from Rome to Paris. 1950, the year Pius XII defined the dogma of Mary's bodily assumption." Commenting in the poem on the papal ruling, Lowell, speaking now in his own voice rather than in one of the many voices heard in the earlier volumes, writes,

> The lights of science couldn't hold a candle to Mary
> risen—at one miraculous stroke,
> . . . .
> But who believed this? Who could understand?

"Much against my will," Lowell confesses in this poem, "I left the City of God where it belongs." In a poem included later in *For the Union Dead* in which he returns to a favorite earlier subject, Lowell first writes, in "Jonathan Edwards in Western Massachusetts," that "Edwards' great millstone and rock / of hope has crumbled," and then he goes on to define hope and faith in his own new terms:

> Hope lives in doubt.
> Faith is trying to do without
> faith.

Life Studies is in effect an examination of the resources available to the poet in his effort to "do without faith" and still avoid "despondency and madness," to use the phrase that Lowell assigns to Delmore Schwartz in one of the poems, and that John Berryman chose for the title of his discussion of Lowell's "Skunk Hour." Between "Beyond the Alps" and "Skunk Hour," which concludes the volume, are many "subtle, strong, terrible poems," to quote Berryman again, and an autobiographical prose fragment, "91 Revere Street," relating the poet's memories of his childhood with his parents and relatives and their friends. Such memories as these, it would seem, could provide no resources at all for avoiding despondency and madness. The despised ineffectual father, the hated domineering mother, the family quarrels, the loved dying grandfather—everything is told, and everything is bitter in the mouth and terrible. ("I used to sit through the Sunday dinners absorbing cold and anxiety from the table.")

Much that the poet has confessed so openly the critic who respects him would find it embarrassing to repeat and analyze. These memories, like many of the later poems, are too personal and too terrible to be discussed impersonally: They evoke either silence or confession. They make us wonder, in our depressed moods, whether psychic conditioning may not be a sufficient explanation of our destinies. Roethke's poems honoring his mother and father, and celebrating his childhood life in northern Michigan, stand in sharpest contrast to Lowell's bitter and guilty memories.

Life Studies is carefully arranged to announce and justify Lowell's great decision to leave "the City of God where it belongs." The three poems that follow the announcement in the first poem comment on private and public madness, as seen in Marie de' Medici, the election to the presidency of Dwight D. Eisenhower, and the thoughts of a mad Negro in confinement. After this come the memories, in the prose fragment, of life as it seemed to the only child of the unhappy couple on Beacon Hill. This is the "reality," it is implied, out of which both the personal destiny and the poems have grown.

"Part Three" of the volume consists of poems offering tribute to four writers Lowell admires, with the proper qualifications, who got along without faith: Ford Madox Ford; George Santayana, who is said to have "found the church too good to be believed"; Delmore Schwartz, who is quoted as the first to say, "We poets in our youth begin in sadness; / thereof in the end come despondency and madness"; and Hart Crane.

After this we come to "Life Studies" proper, fifteen poems divided into two groups, the first group treating childhood memories, the second, experiences in the present:

> These are the tranquillized *Fifties*,
> and I am forty. Ought I to regret my seedtime?
> I was a fire-breathing Catholic C.O.,
> and made my manic statement,
> telling off the state and president, and then
> sat waiting sentence in the bull pen
> beside a Negro boy with curlicues
> of marijuana in his hair.

Lowell's later volumes seem to me to show a falling-off of power. More and more he turned to translations, imitations, adaptations—for instance to dramatizing versions of stories by Hawthorne and Melville in *The Old Glory* (1965), in which the verbal brilliance he had long before demonstrated could not compensate for the impoverishment of meaning as "Endecott and the Red Cross," "My Kinsman, Major Molineux," and "Benito Cereno" were adapted for the stage, in the process being reduced to political tracts on such conscientious issues of the decade as racism. Reading them today, we can approve the ethical messages they carry even as we miss the subtleties of Hawthorne's and Melville's classics.

In much of his late work, Lowell's conscience seems to make full consciousness almost unbearable. As he wrote in the first published version of a poem which marks a recent tendency to return to stricter forms than those of *Life Studies*, "Waking Early Sunday Morning," he felt wholly cut off from the kinds of discoveries Roethke was making in his final decade:

Empty, irresolute, ashamed,
when the sacred texts are named,
I lie here on my bed apart,
and when I look into my heart,
I discover none of the great
subjects: death, friendship, love and hate—
only old china doorknobs, sad,
slight, useless things to calm the mad.

In the same version of this poem, Lowell characterized his family's Protestant faith, which he no longer felt obliged by Max Weber's description of the development of "the Protestant ethic" to hate, as impossible but much to be desired. Writing of the early hymns in which the Bible was "chopped and crucified," and in which there were none of "the milder subtleties / of grace or art," he concludes,

Yet they gave darkness their control,
And left a loophole for the soul.

The combination of nostalgia and despair in parts of this poem is too noticeable not to be remarked on. "Hope lives in doubt," he had written earlier, but what if social conditions give no ground for hope?

Pity the planet, all joy gone
from this sweet volcanic cone;
peace to our children when they fall
in small war on the heels of small

war—until the end of time
to police the earth, a ghost
orbiting forever lost
in our monotonous sublime.

When Lowell revised "Waking Early Sunday Morning" for inclusion in *Near the Ocean* (1967), he omitted the stanza beginning "Empty, irresolute, ashamed," quoted previously, and heavily revised many others, with the general effect of making the poem seem a little less dark, or at least less despondent. In the new stanza the idea is the same but the references are less personal and the tone is different:

When will we see Him face to face?
Each day, He shines through darker glass.
In this small town where everything
is known, I see His vanishing
emblems, His white spire and flag-
pole sticking out above the fog,
like old white china doorknobs, sad,
slight, useless things to calm the mad.

The last half of the new volume consists of translations, held together, the poet tells us in a note, by the theme of the "greatness and horror" of the Roman Empire. Here Lowell's historical sense and his conscience find expression in an often macabre way. But "For Theodore Roethke," a strong tribute to one who is called "the ocean's anchor, our high tide" and who is said to have "touched the waters under the earth, and left them quickened with . . . [his] name," suggests the continued aptness of a hopeful reply the poet made several years ago to another poet's comment on "Skunk Hour": "With Berryman too, I go on a strange journey! Thank God, we both come out clinging to spars, enough floating matter to save us, though faithless."

JOHN BERRYMAN

Like his contemporaries Robert Lowell and Theodore Roethke, John Berryman began his career as a late Modernist, but unlike

Roethke he was unable to find universal meaning in his private experience, and unlike Lowell he lacked the confidence in himself that a clean break with the past would have required.

So, after winning fame with *Homage to Mistress Bradstreet* after a long and undistinguished apprenticeship, he went on until almost the end of his life writing what was intended as "impersonal poetry," *The Dream Songs*, insisting as strongly as he could that "Henry," the persona of the "Songs," was "an imaginary character (not the poet, not me)," though the mask was ill-fitting, more and more transparent, and even toward the end apparently forgotten. Not until almost the end of his life could he bring himself to admit that in *Love and Fame* his subject was "solely and simply myself. Nothing else. A subject on which I am expert. . . . so I wiped out all the disguises and went to work." But as John Heffenden has correctly said, "the poet is everywhere at the centre of his work." Perhaps the reason why after *Homage* he could never create a convincing persona is that he could seldom respond fully or for long to the value and meaning of others, or the other, as Roethke could to nature and to transcendent values and Lowell could to history, past and present, and to others besides himself.

Berryman succeeded best in making his "private experience" seem "universal" (Eliot's formula for the aim of poetry) through the creation of a convincing persona in *Homage to Mistress Bradstreet*. We hear two voices in *Homage*, Anne Bradstreet's and the poet's, with hers dominant always, even in the poet's comments. As Berryman imagines his subject thinking of her childbirth pains, her sicknesses, her fatigue, her desire and her guilt about it, with time and death never far from the forefront of her consciousness, we can recognize the preoccupations that will dominate Berryman's later poetry, but without any such loss of belief in the ostensible subject, Anne Bradstreet, as we feel in the later *Dream Songs* about "Henry." The Puritan poet and Berryman seem to have merged into a single consciousness, with the modern poet's reminders that he cannot, for instance, share the comfort of her religious beliefs further strengthening the reader's sense that her words bring us the way Anne Bradstreet herself must have thought and felt. We are likely to finish the poem feeling that human experience in any age is very much the same, despite differing belief systems.

Berryman's learning, which sometimes later seems to be paraded to impress, is never obtrusive in this poem, though the attached "Notes," reminiscent of Eliot's Notes to *The Waste Land*, would convince us that the poet has read everything pertinent to his subject if we needed convincing. I suspect that Berryman was helped by the fact that Bradstreet was an historical figure about whom many outward facts are known, so that he could freely imagine, and identify himself with, only the hidden inner life. The result is a brilliant tour de force in stanzas that remind us of Bradstreet's own in "Contemplations," in diction that seems just right always, whether she is lamenting her failure to *feel* what she believed or Berryman seems to be interpreting her experience for her, as we may suspect is happening when we read that "pioneering is not feeling well." *Homage to Mistress Bradstreet* does not suffer by comparison with Lowell's achievement in such earlier poems as "Mr. Edwards and the Spider" and "After the Surprising Conversions," which probably helped Berryman to find his subject here.

In the interminable *Dream Songs*, which Berryman thought of as his major work and referred to as an "epic," there were no facts of history to discipline his imagination, no other real self to try to empathize with. "Henry" is a vaudeville stereotype of a white comedian "in blackface," a persona in whom Berryman's interest is sporadic at best and who is more and more forgotten as the poems continue, not real enough to engage either Berryman's imagination or ours. Even the dialect he sometimes speaks in seems contrived and unbelievable—

> Henry sats in de bar & was odd,
> off in the glass from the glass,
> at odds wif de world & its god,
> his wife is a complete nothing,
> St Stephen
> getting even.
>
> Henry sats in de plane & was gay.
> Careful Henry nothing said aloud
> but where a Virgin out of cloud
> to her Mountain dropt in light,
> his thought made pockets & the plane buckt.
> 'Parm me, lady.' 'Orright.'
>
> Henry lay in de netting, wild,
> while the brainfever bird did scales;

Mr Heartbreak, the New Man,
come to farm a crazy land;
an image of the dead on the fingernail
of a newborn child.

The Dream Songs can be thought of as an "epic," as Berryman himself referred to the series, only if the epic hero is taken to be Berryman himself. Still, though it is not really a poem but a series of loosely related poems with neither unity nor development, and though it is only in the most superficial sense an example of the "impersonal poetry" that Berryman still apparently thought the modern poet ought to produce, it not only brought the poet many of the most distinguished awards but is still, in some parts, rewarding to read—when Berryman looks and listens and thinks, forgetting his alcoholism, his alternate self-pity and self-deprecation, his doubts and fears, his poses and pretenses. The three poems on Frost, for example, are worth anthologizing, and many others worth rereading. For Berryman really was not only "sick" (like both Roethke and Lowell) but both truly brilliant and very learned. Many of the later songs, when the poet seems to have forgotten about "Henry," may be read as moving specimens of "confessional poetry" by a poet who was not taken in even by any of his several selves. As he would write in the "Afterword" to *Love and Fame*, in which he dropped the elusive "Henry" persona and wrote frankly about himself ("Reflexions on suicide, & on my father, possess me. / I drink too much."), "This guy is unreal" (to himself?), though "more convincing than he knows: His insecurity about his fame (over-brandishing) matches his insecurity over his 'true' (exposed as false by his repeated infidelity to it) love he is so proud of, and we have before us an existential man." This is Berryman the excellent reader and perceptive critic viewing from a distance the persona/self he has both created and exposed, or created by exposing, giving us a "reading" of his own work, a reading notable for both its intelligence and its honesty. "Our affect" as readers, he tells us, correctly, is likely to be "recognition and pity for his unhappiness."

Love and Fame did not please the critics and inspired no academic explications of buried learning, as *The Dream Songs* have. Its plain style seemed both uncharacteristic of Berryman and "unpoetic," and the frankness of its self-revelations suggested to several critics the "psychoanalyst's couch" more than the poet's study. But it was Berryman in his critical "Afterword," and not his disappointed critics, who was right about this volume which, after exposing the emptiness of the "love and fame" he had tasted, ends with "Eleven Addresses to the Lord," poetic prayers which acknowledge all the difficulties of prayer for modern man. Written in the plainest of styles, these prayers are likely to move all but dogmatic secularists. In them, stylistic flourishes would be a false note and learning a vanity.

A very sick man by the time he wrote them, Berryman had given up at last any attempt to be "the invisible poet" that his temperament had never for long allowed him to be, certainly not in *The Dream Songs*. The result, for unprejudiced readers, was just what he said it could be: "recognition and pity," pity not just for Berryman but for all of us, and not just pity but also respect, as these prayers recall the impressive achievements that are not emptied of significance for us, his readers, as they were for Berryman as he faced a no-longer-pseudocomic "Mr. Bones."

RICHARD WILBUR

A poet more unlike Roethke, Lowell, or Berryman than Wilbur would be hard to imagine. Ignoring dates and poetic generations, we would surely want to place him in other company. The youngest of the four, he is yet the most conservative, so much so indeed that it is impossible to see him as representative of mid-century poetry, as, each in his own way, the others are. Wilbur never writes poetic autobiography, straight or slightly disguised, with Roethke or Berryman, or makes a sharp break with his own or the poetic past, with Lowell. Toward Modernism as Eliot had embodied it he continues to maintain the attitude of the "grateful inheritor," discriminatingly appreciative, like Roethke, of the achievements of the great Modernist poets, critical only of those Modernist theories and practices that seem to him "reductive" in limiting the resources of the poet. He insists on playing "the whole instrument"; otherwise, he tells us, he has no "program."

Wilbur is also the most vocal antiromantic among established younger mid-century poets. Almost alone among poets of his generation, he continues to think of himself as writing "Impersonal" poetry in which not the poet but a *persona* speaks, or attitudes are set up and played off against each other. It is difficult to think of another major poet today who would say, as Wilbur did in 1964,

> I've always agreed with Eliot's assertion that poetry "is not the expression of personality but an escape from personality" . . . I've thought of the poem . . . as "a box to be opened," a created object, an altar-cloth, a Japanese garden or ship of death. Not a message or confession.

But such professions of Wilbur's loyalty to Modernist theory as this come to seem somewhat misleading when we have read all the poetry. True, Wilbur writes in traditional forms and places a high valuation on "classic"—a favorite word of his—wit and balance, and he never writes confessionally, but though he rejects romantic *ideas* about poetry, his own poems have very little in common with those of early Eliot or Pound. His Eliotic conception of the poet's role does not prevent his work from often being closer in theme, and occasionally even in style, to that of romantic and visionary poets of the past than is true of any of the others we have been considering except Roethke. The affinities between Wilbur's poetry and that of Dickinson and Frost are often striking, but not, perhaps, altogether surprising. What we would not be prepared for if we had read only Wilbur's prose is his frequent affinity, *thematically*, with Hart Crane, with Cummings, and even, oddly enough, it may seem, with Emerson. This, I should suppose, *is* surprising in a poet more devoted to the antiromantic stance than any poet who has emerged since Auden achieved his fame in the 1930's.

Despite all the Stevensian wit, elegance, and learning, the verbal and other devices that distance the poems from poet and reader alike in Wilbur's controlled, highly conscious poems, our impression when we have read through all the volumes of original verse Wilbur has so far published is that Wilbur's basic assumptions and attitudes and his recurrent preoccupations have much more in common with those of both the American Transcendental and the English Metaphysical poets than they have with the dominant patterns of assumption and attitude in Modernist poetry. When Wilbur sounds most like Stevens, he is likely to be saying something that either Emerson, or George Herbert, or both, might have said, and that Stevens cannot be imagined as saying.

It is not Wilbur's way to give the appearance of being wholly open and unguarded in his infrequent prose statements of intention, but in a statement he contributed to Howard Nemerov's *Poets on Poetry* in 1966, Wilbur had this to say about the poems he had chosen to include and comment on in his self-analysis—a statement which tells us a good deal about why his work, despite its different manner and different style, so often reminds us of poems by Emerson, Dickinson, or Frost, or by George Herbert, Vaughan, or Traherne, and almost never reminds us, except most superficially, of any poem by Pound or Stevens:

> The three poems I have included here ["A Baroque Wall-Fountain in the Villa Schiarra," "Two Voices in a Meadow," and "Love Calls Us to the Things of This World"] all have to do (a critic might say) with the proper relation between the tangible world and the intuitions of the spirit. The poems assume that such intuitions are, or may be, true: they incline, however, to favor a spirituality which is not abstracted, not dissociated and world-renouncing. A good part of my work could, I suppose, be understood as a public quarrel with the aesthetics of Edgar Allan Poe.

With none of Roethke's passionate obsessiveness but with the same conscious acceptance and utilization of past poetic achievements, Wilbur, like Roethke, bridges the gap between Eliot and Crane, Edward Taylor and Emerson. Wilbur's poetry is catholic in several senses of the word, though he would be justified in protesting at this point, that he has not made a "program" even of so inclusive a position as catholicity.

Many of Wilbur's most memorable poems begin by acknowledging what he has called the "discordancy of modern life and consciousness" and move toward a resolution that implies an unstated resource of faith, somewhat in the Frostian manner. Thus "A World Without Objects Is a Sensible Emptiness" opens with a description of "the tall camels of the spirit" heading away from the oases toward the unbroken emptiness of the desert, seeking "the whole honey of the arid / Sun." Like those who look straight out to sea in Frost's "Neither Out Far Nor in Deep," the camels of the spirit turn toward "the land of sheer horizon, hunting Traherne's / *Sensible emptiness*, there where the brain's lantern-slide / Revels in vast returns."

In the middle stanzas of the poem the "connoisseurs of thirst" are addressed as "beasts of my soul" and warned against the dangerous pleasures of mirage, of visions "that shimmer on the brink / Of absence." Finally, they are adjured to turn:

> Back to the trees arrayed
> In bursts of glare, to the halo-dialing run
> Of the country creeks, and the hills' bracken tiaras made
> Gold in the sunken sun,
>
> Wisely watch for the sight
> Of the supernova burgeoning over the barn,
> Lampshine blurred in the steam of beasts, the spirit's
> right,
> Oasis, light incarnate.

"A World Without Objects Is a Sensible Emptiness" reveals Wilbur's characteristic stance and the loyalties that are always behind, and sometimes expressed within, his poetry. Rejecting the mystic "way down," the "flight of the alone to the alone," in favor of the way of incarnation, the poem could also be described as rejecting Poe's "destructive transcendence" in favor of Emerson's vision of immanent spirit. Paralleling thematically not only Frost's "Neither Out Far Nor in Deep" but "Kitty Hawk," it yet is closer not only in its Metaphysical style but in its theme to a number of poems by George Herbert. Wilbur has frequently been rebuked for lack of open commitment, but there is surely commitment enough in this poem.

The Emersonian aspect of Wilbur's thought, evident in a muted way as a minor strain in "A World Without Objects," is clearer in "Attention Makes Infinity" and "The Beautiful Changes." In the first of these, the poet begins by acknowledging the distinction between the transcendental and the actual, dream and fact, the "lightly looming air" and "the forest's manifold snare." In our ordinary moments, when we perceive with no more than the usual attention, it seems that

> Air is refreshment's treasury; earth seems
> Our history's faulted sink, and spring of love;
> And we between these dreamt-of empires move
> To coop infinity away from dreams.

This ordinary reality, with its dichotomy between earth and air, is not good enough. If we will pay full "attention" in moments when sight and insight combine, the poem goes on to say, we may prevent the "foundering" of "the kingdom of air" in the unillumined actual. When the wind of the spirit blows, we are to be wholly attentive. We must learn to *see* how "Earth's adamant variety is remade" and "every yard, alive with laundry white, / Billowing wives and leaves, gives way to air" in moments when airy spirit transforms and remakes solid earth. At such moments,

> The hanging dust above the streets is staid
> And solid as the walls of Central High.

The poem ends with a stanza that would seem quite opaque unless it were read as affirming both the transcendence and the immanence of spirit, as though the poet were remembering both George Herbert and Emerson, and perhaps Hart Crane too in the final lines:

> Contagions of the solid make this day
> An infiniteness any eye may prove.
> Let asphalt bear us up to walk in love,
> Electric towers shore the clouds away.

"The Beautiful Changes" is even more clearly Emersonian in what it has to say to us. Its subject is the relation of beauty to the perception of beauty, a subject Emerson had treated in "Each and All" with a different point in mind. Since its emphasis is epistemological, it does not have to stress the importance, as "Attention Makes Infinity" does, of remembering the "otherness" of Ultimate Being, or God, or the Over-Soul. *That* idea is built into the poem from the beginning.

"Beauty" was one of Emerson's terms for the Over-Soul, or God, the "eternal generator of circles." Reality, he thought, when apprehended without illusion, was both Good and Beautiful. Wilbur's poem starts with this assumption, notes in passing that the experience of beauty is dependent upon the exercise of imagination, and then proceeds to develop the theme that beauty is *there*, whether we see it or not.

Emerson of course had wavered, and sometimes appeared to

contradict himself, on this point. "The eye is the first circle; the horizon which *it forms* [my italics] is the second" is the unpromising way he begins his magnificent essay "Circles," though it is not long before we find him contradicting himself by speaking of "the eternal generator" of circles who "abides," whether we see the circles and grow into them or not.

"The beautiful changes," Wilbur's poem says,

> . . . as a forest is changed
> By a chameleon's tuning his skin to it;
> As a mantis, arranged
> On a green leaf, grows
> Into it, makes the leaf leafier, and proves
> Any greenness is deeper than anyone knows.

Emerson's point in "The Titmouse," exactly. Admitting the overwhelming reality of the "not-me" provides the only way of being able to continue to sing in the wintry blast.

The new note of the poem's last stanza, in which the lover addressed in the whole poem is described as

> Wishing ever to sunder
> Things and things' selves for a second finding, to lose
> For a moment all that it touches back to wonder

is no less Emersonian in its basic inspiration, though Emerson would no doubt have made the same point by talking about Love in the abstract, without addressing a lover. That one must approach nature in terms of love and wonder was, of course, one of his most insisted-upon themes in prose and verse.

The fact that some of the images of the poem also may remind us of Cummings only reinforces the points I have been trying to suggest, that the poem is basically Emersonian in its point of view and is thus within the chief tradition in our poetry. Cummings might have written—many times did almost write—"Your hands hold roses," or that fully submissive attentiveness to nature "makes the leaf leafier" and the "greenness . . . deeper." And Williams might have thought of the image of the chameleon to express his idea that we must not impose our ideas on things but find our ideas in things.

The well-known "Love Calls Us to the Things of This World" is perhaps Wilbur's finest effort to bridge the gap between Edward Taylor and Emerson. "For there is no might in the universe / That can contend with love," Emerson wrote in some lines "Written at Rome, 1833," but in "Days" and elsewhere he had also written of his failure to live up to what he knew in his moments of insight. Emerson knew a good deal about what Wilbur calls in the poem "false dawn" and "the punctual rape of every blessed day." He had been, perhaps, less ready than George Herbert, Edward Taylor's favorite poet, to think of his frustrations in the image of a "pulley" by means of which God makes us desire Heaven. Wilbur, like Dickinson in "There's a Certain Slant of Light," is apparently remembering Herbert in this poem ("The eyes open to a cry of pulleys"), but he also seems to be remembering Poe and Emerson, and choosing between them:

> Let there be clean linen for the backs of thieves;
> Let lovers go fresh and sweet to be undone,
> And the heaviest nuns walk in a pure floating
> Of dark habits,
> keeping their difficult balance.

If in its final effect "Love Calls Us" seems a more "orthodox" and "Catholic" poem than an Emersonian one—though, as I interpret Emerson, it *is*, ultimately, Emersonian as well as "orthodox"—a still uncollected poem, "The Proof," will illustrate Wilbur's increasing tendency to write openly about his basic commitments. "Proof," as Robert Lowell wrote of the poem when he first read it, might have been written by George Herbert—or, if Taylor's metrics had been a little more regular, by Edward Taylor:

> Shall I love God for causing me to be?
> I was mere utterance; shall these words love me?
>
> Yet when I caused his work to jar and stammer,
> And one free subject loosened all his grammar,
>
> I love him that he did not in a rage
> Once and forever rule me off the page,

But, thinking I might come to please him yet,
Crossed out *delete* and wrote his patient *stet.*

The formal contrast between "Proof" and Wilbur's earlier poem "Junk," which appeared in the 1961 volume *Advice to a Prophet*, is enormous, but no more than we should expect perhaps of a poet of Wilbur's intelligence, traditionalism, and conscious ecumenicity. Written in an adaptation of Old English alliterating verse, "Junk" opens with lines that seem a conscious echo of Frost's "The Axe Helve":

An axe angles
from my neighbor's ashcan;
It is hell's handiwork,
the wood not hickory,
The flow of the grain
not faithfully followed.

In the end, the poem has moved from Frost back to Emerson, though now there is no suggestion that the poet is consciously echoing. The "Junk and gimcrack," the "jerrybuilt things"—"And the men who make them / for a little money"—will all "waste in the weather / toward what they were." Time will dispose of them, but destruction is only one side of the process:

The sun shall glory
in the glitter of glass-chips,
Foreseeing the salvage
of the prisoned sand,
And the blistering paint
peel off in patches,
That the good grain
be discovered again.
Then burnt, bulldozed,
they shall all be buried
To the depths of diamonds,
in the making dark

Where halt Hephaestus
keeps his hammer
And Wayland's work
is worn away.

Wilbur's "reconciling" position is the central fact about his work, not his Impersonal, autotelic theory or his other antiromantic ideas, which often seem defensive in origin. His fondness for Emily Dickinson, his extremely perceptive and sympathetic interpretation of her work in his essay "Sumptuous Destitution," and his frequent closeness to her in sensibility in his poems, as well as his public praise of Whitman as a religious poet, are all further bits of evidence, if any more were needed, of his reconciling role.

"October Maples, Portland," will serve as a final example. The poem expresses Emerson's typical stress on God's immanence in language more traditional and "churchly" than Emerson generally cared to use. A light "we thought forever lost," reflected from the autumnal leaves, "redeems the air," we read, and "Where friends in passing meet, / They parley in the tongues of Pentecost." The Holy Spirit, in short, which to Emerson seemed sufficient, without Scripture, speaks now as always through man and nature—the "General Revelation," as the eighteenth-century theologians liked to call it.

But in the poem the Spirit alone is not sufficient. "It is a light of maples, and will go," though not before it leaves "a lasting stain." "So Mary's laundered mantle," the last stanza begins, gave its color to the rosemary bush on which it was spread, so that its blossoms "could not choose but to return in blue." That "blue is Mary's color" most modern poets had to learn from Eliot. The General Revelation needs the Special Revelation of the Bible to complete it, the poem says openly enough. As for the "pretty tale" of Mary's mantle and the rosemary bush, it may still, "like all pretty tales . . . be true." The irony of "pretty" before "tales" is the only defensive guard the poet throws up against the hostile reader's finding him out.

It is not surprising, since he conceives of his role as that of "poet-citizen," that Wilbur thinks of his poems both as artifacts, things he has made, and as "tests" of the limits of the communicability in our time of a vision many of his readers consider to be "outmoded":

> Is it possible, for example, to speak intelligibly of angels in the modern world? Will the psyche of the modern reader consent to be called a soul? The poem which I have just presented ["Love Calls Us"] was a test of those questions.

Four Post-Modernists

DUNCAN, NEMEROV, DICKEY, LEVERTOV

OF the four post-Modernist poets whom I shall treat more briefly, only Robert Duncan's work seems to be saying "yes" to Wilbur's question. Only in Duncan do we find God-language used seriously, with even a reference to the way the doctrine of the Trinity can be found meaningful by being translated. But a significant qualification is attached to the way this historic Christian doctrine can be used: doctrine arises from myth, and though myth, all myths, convey Truth about the Real, it is a Truth we can "apprehend" but not know. Translated, propositionally stated doctrines are not to be believed but treasured as clues to the unseen world of post-Einsteinian physics and Whitehead's "occasions." Duncan's work anticipates *The Tao of Physics.*

Reading Duncan's hermetic poems, we are reminded everywhere of his association with Olson and "projective verse," of his deep respect for Pound, of his part in the "San Francisco renaissance," yet also of Whitman's desire to write a "new Bible" that would help us to move "Towards an Open Universe," with stress on the "open," and of Whitman's "personalism" too. (Unlike Whitman, of course, is Duncan's heavy reliance on the occult and his normal failure to look long and carefully at the actual. His is a difficult poetry.) Like Whitman again, he seems to spend much of his time listening for the "God-step at the margins of thought," wondering, as Whitman had before him, "Who is it goes there?" "Apprehensions" are his goal, not ideas. Perhaps with the aid of Greek myth he will be able to find the words to enable us, his readers, to apprehend the answer. Words are the ultimate manifestation of Duncan's "Emergent Deity," so that only in poetry can religion live, for the imagination and dreams are noetic and poetry their means of expression. Though Duncan's poetry seemed radically new at first, it may curiously strike us now as the product of a bizarre blend of Poe and Whitman.

I would suppose it might be impossible to find two poets more completely unlike in temperament, tone, and subject matter than Robert Duncan and Howard Nemerov, but if they shared no more than their common rejection of the notion that poetry is "autotelic" they would earn the label "post-Modernist." Speaking of a change that came about in his own mature poetry, Nemerov puts the matter this way, in typically modest and tentative fashion:

> The second change is harder to speak of; it involves a growing consciousness of nature as responsive to language, or to put it the other way, of imagination as the agent of reality. This is a magical idea and not very much heard of these days even among poets—practically never among critics—but I am stuck with it. . . . I not so much look at nature as I listen to what it says.

His early verse, before this change came about, he confesses, had shown "more than traces of admired modern masters—Eliot, Auden, Stevens, Cummings, Yeats," in a style governed by "notions drawn . . . chiefly from T. S. Eliot." He did not, he says, strive to achieve an original poetic voice, but by 1962, in *The Next Room of the Dream*, he was participating in the spirit of the times by declaring, tongue in cheek, that poetry did not need to be learned or difficult, written to be studied rather than read, in his good-humored take-off of *The Waste Land*, "On the Threshold of His Greatness, the Poet Comes Down with a Sore Throat," complete with elaborate Notes and even a further "Note on the Notes."

Still, though he might be amused by the notion that poetry must be difficult and though the natural world entered more and more frequently into his poetry, he was suspicious of the too-easy revelations achieved by the new nature-romanticism. "Elegy for a Nature Poet" gently ridicules poets who find sermons in every stone and "just another allegory" in "any old bird." "The Human Condition" as he sees it is more complex, as a number of the poems in *The Blue Swallows* (1967) say in different ways. He does not, as Stevens seems to have thought, "know" that the world is "alien," so that we can only "imagine" meaning, but neither are we given any unambiguous revelation but are left anxiously waiting. Writing in traditional forms, with rhyme and meter, he could respond to the certainty of others that "God is dead" with an uncommitted but amused wit in "Sunday":

The odds are six to one He's gone away;
It's why there's so much praying on this day.

Nostalgia for a time when religious faith was firm enough to be lived by is frequent in these poems:

Our fathers lived on these
Desperate certainties;
Ate manna in the desert, it is said,
And are dead.

"Grace to Be Said at the Supermarket" includes the mock-serious petition

That we may look unflinchingly on death
As the greatest good, like a philosopher should.

But the nostalgia is saved from any touch of sentimentality by humor at once skeptical and gentle. As skeptical of "scientific fact" as he is of religious dogma, Nemerov in his latest volume (*Sentences*, 1980) continues his graceful, thoughtful, often ironic comments on the fashions and follies of the times, as in his playful comment "On the Soul," "A kid can get a hard on from pure thought," or, in "The Ark," his conclusion that it's

As though to say that grace may simply come,
While works, to work at all, have to be tried.

Nemerov's feeling for the wisdom and achievements of the past and his sense of the similarity of the human condition in all times presumably is sufficient to account for his preference for evolution over revolution. It is not surprising that he appears to have attracted no followers. So quiet, civilized, self-mocking, and well-educated a voice urging moderation, good sense, and making do with what we have is never likely to start a cult. But some of the poems in *The Blue Swallows*, I suspect, will still be read and enjoyed when the work of the more radical post-Modernists has been forgotten.

The poet we may well be reminded of as we read the work of

James Dickey is certainly not Duncan or Nemerov but Roethke, whom Dickey has called "the greatest poet this country has produced." Personal memories, especially those of childhood, have always been his best subject, so it was not surprising when he chose to entitle his contribution to the Nemerov volume *Poets on Poetry* "The Poet Turns on Himself." But the self we find in Dickey's poems is not an encapsulated self writing "Confessional" poetry but a self who often speaks to us most strongly out of a self-transcending awareness of all those others with whom he finds himself drowning. An attempt to reach them, to speak to them words from the common speech which they will find true to *their* experience, is the key to his style.

Reminding us often of Emerson in "The Poet" in his ideas about poetry (the true poet will dare "to write his autobiography in colossal cipher, or into universality. . . . The expression is organic, or, the new type which things themselves take when liberated"), Dickey also reminds us of Whitman in his identification with those who presumably do not read poetry, all the "thieves, nightwalkers, truckers, and drunkards" whose cries reach only "Those few who transcend themselves, / The superhuman tenderness of strangers" ("Them, Crying," in *Buckdancer's Choice*). Though he has said that what he is trying to do in his poems is to tell his own story, if it is to be told truly that story must include the experience of all those suffering from "Angina," "Diabetes," "The Cancer Match," and "Madness." The most pervasive feeling to emerge from Dickey's poems is that of one conscious of living on the edge himself, and so able to identify with the sick, suffering, and dying. As he has said of the poet of our time,

> Beneath his words is this sense of battling against universal dissolution, of the loss of all he and other men have been given as human beings, of all they have loved and been moved by.

With the poet writing from this sense of things, it is not surprising to read lines like these in "The Cancer Match," in *The Eye-Beaters, Blood, Victory, Madness, Buckhead and Mercy* (1970):

> Night!
>   I don't have all the time
> In the world, but I have all night.

I have space for me and my house,
  And I have cancer and whiskey
    In a lovely relation.

Or these, from the title poem of his earlier *Helmets* (1964), in which drinking from the helmet of the dead prompts a foxhole prayer, awakening "My nearly dead power to pray," so that

Some words directed to Heaven
Went through all the strings of the graveyard
Like a message that someone sneaked in,
Tapping a telegraph key
At dead of night, then running
For his life.

In his two most recent volumes of verse both sides of Dickey's temperament, his preoccupation with self and his ability and desire to imagine the experience of others, find strong expression. In *The Zodiac* (1976) he adapted and made his own a long poem by a Dutch alcoholic amateur astronomer who was killed at sea in the Second World War. He finds it easy to identify with his alter ego, for his first really distinguished volume had been *Drowning with Others*, he had been a flyer in two wars, and had been called, he tells us, a "mystic" because, like his Dutch counterpart, he had thought and written often of

    Religion . . . death, and the stars:
I'm holding them all in my balls, right now.
And the old *aquavit* is mixing them up . . .

In the same poem he tells us of his intention to keep on with the search:

So long as the hand can hold its island
    Of blazing paper, and bleed for its images:
    Make what it can of what is:

    So long as the spirit hurls on space
The star-beasts of intellect and madness.

His most recent volume, *Puella* (1982), must have come as something of a surprise to many of his readers, for in it the poet whose poems had so often reminded us of condensed versions of his prose volume *Self-Interviews* and who had seemed at times to take excessive pride in his tough masculinity now showed himself able to imagine the experience of another very unlike himself, in this case the consciousness of the growing girl to whom the book is dedicated. But in a curious way *Puella* may remind us that it is by the poet who wrote *Drowning with Others* many years before, for like that earlier volume we find it dealing, once again, with what the poet has described as the frequent subjects of that work, "dream, hallucination, fantasy, the interaction of illusion and reality," and find it also exemplifying the poet's ideal of "the 'open' poem," free from all artifice and aimed at "presentational immediacy."

In Denise Levertov's long, distinguished, and prolific career we find two strains at work fighting it out for dominance, that of the musing dreamer nostalgic for her Judeo-Christian heritage as the daughter of a Jewish convert who became an Anglican priest, and that of the intensely committed political activist who would make of her poems instruments for public good. The first strain is suggested by the titles of several of her volumes—*With Eyes at the Back of Our Heads*, *The Jacob's Ladder*, *O Taste and See* ("that the Lord is good," Psalm 34), *Candles in Babylon*—and is expressed in the title poem of *Relearning the Alphabet* in the poet's description of herself as "stumbling / (head turned) / back to my origins / . . . . Jerusalem." The title poem of *The Jacob's Ladder* contrasts the ladder climbed by Jacob with the one that must be climbed today, no mere "radiant evanescence" but built of stone, "solidly built," with sharp angles against which a man trying to climb "must scrape his knees, and bring / the grip of his hands into play." The result of a successful climb will be that "the poem ascends." The most recent expression of this strain in "Mass for the Day of St. Thomas Didymus" ("Doubting Thomas," the disciple who wanted hard evidence of Christ's Resurrection) appears to strike once again the more personal note found in "Relearning the Alphabet." It is perhaps significant that this long poem was both separately published and included in *Candles for Babylon* (1982), where it is paired with "Many Mansions."

Beginning with the Vietnam war the poet's effort "to make / of my song a chalice / of Time, / a Communion Wine" is interrupted by the poems of social protest. Righteous anger often seems the dominant emotion in these poems, as it does especially in "A Poem at Christmas, 1972, during the Terror-Bombing of North Vietnam," which begins "Now I have lain awake imagining murder," goes on to recount a dream of the poet's throwing napalm into President Nixon's face, and concludes with the wish "O, to kill / the killers!" But with Vietnam over at last the occasional poems tend to give way to poems like "Human Being," which opens *Life in the Forest* (1978):

> Human being—walking
>   in doubt from childhood on: walking
>
> a ledge of slippery stone in the world's woods
> deep layered with wet leaves—rich or sad: on one
> side of the path, ecstasy, on the other
> dull grief.

Still, even the most recent volumes contain many "political" poems, with the nuclear "Age of Terror" replacing Vietnam as focus. *Candles in Babylon* begins with the poet

>   hoping
> the rhyme's promise was true,
> that we may return
> from this place of terror
> home to a calm dawn and
> the work we had just begun

and closes with "The Many Mansions," which expresses the poet's resolve not to forget, in her preoccupation with terror, suffering, and grief, that the world contains beauty and mysteries too, the stuff of vision:

> What I must not forget
> is the knowledge that vision gave me.

Though many of Levertov's most perfectly realized and moving poems are expressive of the grief that dominates *The Sorrow*

Dance and finds frequent expression elsewhere, the shape of the career as a whole so far seems to emerge from the conflict between conscientious protest and a never wholly forgotten effort to climb Jacob's ladder toward religious vision. The poems of political protest will date, and those devoted to the tasted and seen only rarely substantiate the "vision" that must not be forgotten, but still the body of work as a whole remains an impressive expression of the plight of the morally and politically committed poet-citizen in our time, or perhaps any time, as MacLeish's had been for an earlier time. Torn between her desire to make her poems what she has called "messages," poems that are sometimes entitled "speeches" for specific occasions, and the never wholly forgotten desire to recover as much as possible some part of her religious heritage, Levertov has charted the private and public experience, and the aspirations, of a great many readers in our time.

CHAPTER XXII

"For the Time Being"

> *Veracity therefore is that which we require in poets,—that they shall say how it was with them, and not what might be said.*
>
> —Emerson, in "Poetry and Imagination"

It was Emerson again who found the right words for the obvious truth that the inner life of an age is revealed in the poetry it produces, when he said that "the experience of each new age requires a new confession," and the poet is the age's spokesman, its "Sayer" who finds the words to express the dimly felt, the half-recognized feelings and thoughts of his time. The anxieties and dark preoccupations of this fearful age of ours that finds hope for the future so hard to maintain, when, as Hayden Carruth has put it, "Fear and Anger in the Mindless Universe" (*From Snow and Rock, from Chaos*) may seem the only authentic emotions—these feelings have found direct or indirect expression in the work of the majority of our most widely recognized and honored poets, six of whom I shall treat as representative; while at the same time the curious fact that life, and even the possibility of hope, persist despite time and entropy finds its expression too, most notably, I think, in the work of the two "visionary" poets I shall treat.

"Mortal Acts, Mortal Words"

KINNELL, MERRILL, WRIGHT, MERWIN

THAT people are mortal is hardly a discovery, but when the anticipation of death is constant and dominant and belief offers no defenses against fear, we get a new kind of poetry, the poetry of the end, when, as Galway Kinnell has written, everything we value seems to be going "into time and ruin." What is known to be coming can be accepted in various ways, one of which is expressed in Kinnell's early "Hunger Unto Death," a very dark poem it seems to me. (Why has suicide been the way out for so many poets of the recent past?) Kinnell's poetry is an open, relatively defenseless, expression of the feeling of so many today that death is the only true reality, more "real" than love, which doesn't last because we don't last. All concrete perceptions move always "towards the emptiness" ("Poems of Night") that is all that can be seen under "The old, shimmering nothingness, the sky."

Turning from looking to listening as we prepare to spend "Another Night in the Ruins" with Kinnell, we hear only the unacceptable, or nothing at all: "I listen. / I hear nothing." Our dreams become nightmares, endurable because they can be shaped into poems and we can come to realize, as we move toward "home ground," that "love is very much like courage, / perhaps it *is* courage, and even / perhaps / *only* courage." Kinnell seems to me to be writing moving and memorable poetry of courageous despair.

James Merrill would never write a line like Kinnell's about "the space / where tears stream down across the stars," preferring to take his despair with elegance and wit, urbanely, but he too, like his distinguished contemporary W. S. Merwin, has devoted himself to watching the movement of "Dear light along the way to nothingness." Like Berryman before him, he finds the making of poems helpful in "braving the elements," and his own feelings both enhanced and debased by "the sickness of our time." Now that we can no longer pretend to *discover* "form" or meaning, we can at least create it, and "Form's what affirms." As we find ourselves "Flying from Byzantium" instead of sailing to it, we can take some comfort in the realization that there are still poets writing: "Far off a young scribe turned a fresh / Page, hesitated, dipped his pen." With Merrill as his chronicler, the young scribe is in distinguished company.

James Wright's poems record the same losses and fears, but unlike Merrill, Wright is not content with meaning that can only be created, not found, and created only in art, not in our lives. His way of handling his grief is less brittle than Merrill's, his defenses less apparently contrived. Memories of childhood ("Beautiful Ohio") and of earlier poets who somehow managed to keep faith and hope alive nourish him in poems like "Lighting a Candle for W. H. Auden" and "The Morality of Poetry," which begins with a line from Whitman, whose spirit he admires and tries to recall as he stands "waiting for the dark," and "Trying to Pray," which begins with the lines

> This time, I have left my body behind me, crying
> In its dark thorns.
> Still,
> There are good things in this world.
> It is dusk,

and ends with the world and the mind no longer completely at odds:

> I touch leaves.
> I close my eyes, and think of water.

Not content with the darkness he finds himself in so much of the time and seems able to accept, he hears a call "For light, for light! and evening falls." As wheat "leans back toward its own darkness," he leans back toward his own dark "Beginning." Without the help of the beliefs that supported Whitman and other earlier poets, self-described once as an "infidel"—a word that has lost meaning for most younger poets—Wright managed to discover enough light and beauty in his own life in the world to produce lovely poems that, unlike those of Kinnell and Merrill, do not break decisively with our major poetic tradition.

Though the voice we hear in W. S. Merwin's poetry never seems to be that of the poet himself, as it does in Kinnell's and Wright's, still the speaker seems chiefly preoccupied with similar subjects and feelings, particularly the loss of belief in the great myths and the feeling of emptiness that comes with that loss. After his first volume, *A Mask for Janus* (1952), with its explicit allusions to "Easter" and "many mansions," Merwin becomes much more guarded in his allusions to what has been lost as he achieves a style that might be described as that of *The New Yorker*, where so many of his poems have first appeared—tight-lipped, understated, indirect. But his real subject, though not, usually, the ostensible one, continues to be what happens in the heart when, with religious belief impossible, we find ourselves "Walking at night between the two deserts / Singing."

We are singing, presumably, just "for the hell of it," though it sometimes seems "only yesterday" that we thought we saw "The saints marching in." "The Present" is a time when "Naturally it is night" and only "the light worships its blind god." The abyss yawns beneath us, "a gulf / Beyond reckoning. It begins where we are." (But Merwin does not tell us, as Kinnell might and Plath did, that the experience of "the / Abyss over which we float" is the only valid one.) Still, those "peaks on the horizon" are not the promised land but only the tip of an iceberg. "Caught in the magnetism / Of great silence, thinking: this is the terror / That cannot be charted," we continue to stare at them. At least they shine in light, "Offering snow to the darkness" like the speaker in "Whenever I Go There" in *The Lice.* Though we try to avoid asking the great questions, even those we dare to ask get riddling answers or none at all, as in "Some Last Questions" (*The Lice*): "What is the silence / A. As though it had a right to more."

Still, whether we have "a right to more" or not, the title of Merwin's next volume, *A Carrier of Ladders*, suggests his continuing preoccupation with what happens when "the deities go," as do also many poems in *The Compass Flower*, despite their complete avoidance now of what could still be mentioned a quarter of a century before in *A Mask for Janus*. The prayers can be heard now at night in "the sound / of blood rushing in an ear" in "Migration," and worlds are created only to be destroyed in "Robin." Still, "we survived / we survivors / without knowing why." "Vision" is short enough to be quoted entire, and distinguished enough as an example of Merwin's style and preoccupation to deserve it, though it is more direct in its treatment of its subject than is usual in his work:

> What is unseen
> flows to what is unseen
> passing in part
> through what we partly see

we stood up from all fours
far back in the light
to look
as long as there is day
and part of the night

The Two Worlds

ROBERT BLY

THOUGH the imagery of a good many of the most highly praised and successful poets of the past decade or so often depends on a vocabulary drawn from Jung's Analytical Psychology, it is Robert Bly who seems to have read Jung most seriously and thoughtfully. But only in such early poems as "A Man Writes to a Part of Himself" in *Silence in the Snowy Fields* (1962) does he appear to be simply translating Jung's concepts into poetic terms. The part of himself being addressed in that poem is Jung's "anima image," the archetypal female "other" within us males hidden in the "cave" of the unconscious "like a wife" uncared for and "starving." The final line of the poem, "How did this separation come about?" asks the question pondered by Jung in many works, which provide the clues we need to understand the poem's images of *wife*, *water*, *cave*. The poem seems to draw uncreatively on Jung's doctrine of the "Collective Unconscious" and its "archetypes."

Later poems show Bly still drawing heavily on Jung's theory and vocabulary but concerned to bring the two worlds, conscious and unconscious and inner and outer, together somehow in a way that can be personally experienced, not just known about. Bly's next volume, *The Light Around the Body* (1967), broadens and personalizes the theoretic background, especially by drawing on the mystical writings of Boehme, supplemented by sentences from Freud and church liturgy in the epigraphs that open each of the volume's five sections except the one devoted to poems on the Vietnam war.

Now and then in this volume Bly ceases to depend on Jung and speaks to us in a language made familiar by earlier poets: "I am drawn / To the desert . . . to the landscape of zeroes." Still, though,

Jung's explorations of the occult and Gnostic doctrines seem to offer the only hope of meaning to Bly, as they have in the recent past to so many of the religiously minded. The two worlds must somehow be brought together, as they are not by a culture in which "The ministers lie, the professors lie, the television lies, the priests lie. . . . / These lies mean that the country wants to die" (*The Teeth Mother Naked at Last*, 1970).

Beginning with *Old Man Rubbing His Eyes* in 1975, psychological concepts and mystical speculations recede into the background of poems that are openly personal and imagistic in a way that seldom needs translating into theory. "Well that is how I have spent this day. / And what good will it do me in the grave?" The theoretic "death wish" of earlier poems becomes the fear of the farmer who begins each day with "the / knowledge that he is not strong enough to die," and of the poet, who knows that "To live is to rush ahead, eating up your own death, / like an endgate, open, hurrying into night." In an age of total unbelief, when only the cows seem to believe the promises of "*their* savior," consciousness has become an almost unbearable burden. Meanwhile, as "Dreams press us on all sides," even insect heads may seem to "hold sand paintings of the next life."

The seasons of Bly's later poems tend to be fall and winter and the landscape snowy, but there seems to be some comfort to be found in nature, if not in culture, in those moments when the poet can sense "the consciousness *out there* among plants and animals," as he explains in the preface called "The Two Presences" which opens his recent *This Tree Will Be Here for a Thousand Years*, in which he returns to his early subject matter, nature. When this "second consciousness," as he calls it, can be truly felt and adequately expressed, if only in a few poems, the two worlds seem to come together, so that "what is inside and what is outside merge," resulting in the poems that Bly himself prizes.

Ideas like those in this preface, following as they do the religious implications of the Jungian archetypes in the earlier poetry, have prompted some critics to call Bly a "mystic," but though such a label seems not wholly misleading, Emerson's definition of the poet in visionary terms seems more apt. The poet's insight, Emerson wrote, could come only "by the intellect"—Bly's "consciousnesss" —"being where and what it sees." Or as Bly puts it more tentatively and literally in this preface, "It's helpful if you're writing about a pine to go to the pine, or about a tunnel to go to the tunnel, and I've noticed how difficult it is to write poems in this genre at a desk."

The reason why it is helpful, Bly implies in the same preface, is that whereas the accepted assumption today is that "human intelligence stands alone facing a world that appears sometimes hostile, sometimes inviting, but that actually possesses neither intelligence nor consciousness," Bly himself sometimes feels the presence of that "second consciousness" outside himself.

But the "melancholy tone" Bly senses in the "second consciousness" of nature, reminding him of Lucretius' "the tears of things" as they circle downward like the falling leaves, differentiates this experience of "union" sharply from the experience of "union" of mystics in the past, in all cultures, which has always been described as joyful. Death dominates both consciousnesses for Bly, even in his new, somewhat mystical, stance.

"As We Know"

JOHN ASHBERY

WHILE Bly in Minnesota invites experiences of melancholy union, John Ashbery, the chief of the so-called "New York School," accepts the long-dominant concept of an "alien universe" and writes from within it. Nature has no meanings, or none at least that we can possibly know, and there is no "second consciousness" responsive in any way to the questions that man's mind asks. The Descartean dualism of the lonely mind looking out at something wholly other remains not only unchallenged in his poetry, it informs and dominates his every poetic gesture. Ashbery is the poet of the self-enclosed, self-referential poem.

In the early volume *Some Trees* in 1956 we find the position stated that *As We Know* restates, less directly, in 1979. Some trees seem to mean something, but the poet cannot say what they mean. Sometimes the earth itself, our planet, has seemed to be gliding through bright leaves, but we know, "of course," that "she . . . was only an effigy / of indifference," or if a miracle, then "a miracle / Not meant for us." Mind cannot know, or words say, what meaning there is, if any. The poet registers impressions, not truths, and poems are not "about" anything but the play of the mind. Of all contemporary poets, Ashbery is probably the closest to Stevens in his major phase, before his late poems.

The difficulties many readers have found in Ashbery's poems are reduced greatly when we understand that the words in them that seem to refer to the world outside the mind are not being used referentially. The "rivers and mountains" that supply the title of another early volume are not the real rivers and mountains we have experienced but *ideas* of rivers and mountains existing in the poem only. Poetry as it must be written now, Ashbery has long seemed to feel, should be no more "representational" than the abstract visual arts. It is probably not accidental that Ashbery writes as an art critic. The rivers and mountains, even the cities and the land we have looked for and thought we found, exist only on paper, complete with other man-made objects "processed / To look like ferns." The apparently most solid and real things poets once seemed to be talking to us about in their poems are only chimeras, mental projections, words carefully arranged and printed on paper, as paintings are painted on canvas.

Ashbery's is the new "autotelic" poetry with an added disclaimer: not only is the poet no prophet but there *are* no prophets. No one can say what anything means. The mind is shut inside itself, impervious, sealed off from reality. So far as we know, the sun is as likely to blacken a landscape as to light it. Poetry then has no more noetic value than philosophy or theology; it is a form of enjoyable play, like the other arts, and must not be asked to do what it cannot do. A successful poem will not *say* that we cannot know, it will demonstrate it by its shape and movement.

We should not be surprised then when we come upon Ashbery poems like "It Was Raining in the Capital," in *The Double Dream of Spring*, in which we not only cannot find out which capital it is raining in but are given no clue to the identity of the "it," "she," and "other" that form the subjects of a whole stanza. The reason why we cannot find out what the poem is about is of course that it is not "about" anything outside the poem, unless it should be the mood suggested by the final stanza:

> The sun came out in the capital
> Just before it set.
> The lovely death's head shone in the sky
> As though these two had never met.

Sometimes the assumptions behind this style, in which words have only the slipperiest referential value or none at all, are hinted at, as they seem to be in "Rural Objects" in the same volume. Rural objects once seemed to have value and even meaning when belief posited a future which allowed us time to enjoy the passing moment. But with that belief—the belief that kept Frost looking for "epiphanies," for instance—now lost, we can see that it was "just a cheap way / Of letting you off." Knowing this, we can understand better the answer to the question the poem opens with, "Why can't this moment be enough for us as we have become?"

Ashbery is presumably writing about himself in "A Man of Words" in *Self-Portrait in a Convex Mirror*—words, not meanings, for the meanings seemingly found by older poets form a "story worn out from telling." All the verbal gestures are theatrical in this poetry, the product of conscious art, not to be taken as revelation of anything except that the garden will soon fill up with snow. Convex mirror or not, these poems are no "diary," with its references to external events:

> All diaries are alike, clear and cold, with
> The outlook for continued cold. They are placed
> Horizontal, parallel to the earth,
> Like the unencumbering dead. Just time to reread this
> And the past slips through your fingers, wishing you were
> there.

But it is not only poets we cannot trust: "knowledge" itself assails us with its "stench," and the senses provide only apparent revelations. We have not known before "how little there was to learn" ("Houseboat Days"). What is poetry today therefore if not "Trying to avoid / Ideas, as in this poem?" The "linear style" has been given up because there is really no story worth the telling: poetry is a form of play, which at least in some sense takes us outside our otherwise sealed-in selves. If it is a sort of "Ivory Tower," it is at least all we have, now that all the legends we once believed have been recognized as only "legendary" ("The Vegetarians").

All this is summed up in the title poem of *As We Know*. Our awareness that we don't "know" anything at all about what most matters to us is presumably the unstated antecedent of the "it" in the first line and of the "it" that later is said to have "crept up on us" and stolen the evil out of evil, the mystery out of romance, the life out of life. Such reductionism is the price of epistemological sophistication. If John Ashbery's poems typically seem opaque, it is because, as he sees it, life itself is opaque and the poet must write out of that slender knowledge.

Starting from a total distrust of the power of mind and language to discover or convey objective meaning, and too sophisticated to indulge in the nostalgia of a Bly, Ashbery has written a large body of impressive poetry that, while it seems a rejection of most of what Emerson and Whitman believed about poetry, has, presumably without the poet's intending it to, exemplified Emerson's idea of the poet as spokesman: Ashbery's poems give masterly expression to the deep skepticism of many of the most thoughtful in our time.

"The Condition of True Naming": The Poet As Visionary

MEANWHILE, several less fashionable poets, only recently or even just now being "discovered," have continued to express Emerson's sense of life's possibilities, despite the ambiguities that render certainty impossible. Assuming cautiously, with all the necessary qualifications, the ability of the senses and the mind to know, with logic aided by intuition and imagination, and of the proper words to express, what is at once real and meaningful to us, they choose characteristically to explore the becoming of beings immersed in time. Distrustful both of comforting past beliefs ("wishful thinking"?) and of the power of unaided intellect, the "mere understanding," to fashion reasonable new ones, they still seem to find that private experience can be, *may* be, both rewarding and revealing, even if we don't have any certain answers and find ourselves living in a dark and threatening time.

It should go without saying that they can make no such extravagant claims about the poet's ability to "save" us as their poetic ancestors, Emerson and others, made. Yet they still manage to write as though they shared Emerson's belief that the poet's words can "enhance the great and constant fact of Life," as he put it, and so be helpful to those who often find themselves "blinded and lost." But even the guarded and qualified affirmations that emerge from their work require that they turn their attention away from current events and the man-made world to "nature," as revealed either by science or in experience. Emerson of course had faced the same necessity as he struggled with loss of belief much earlier, in an age that now seems to us less dark than ours. As another visionary poet, Roethke, wrote, "In a dark time, the eye begins to see."

"Persistences"

A. R. AMMONS

For Ammons, Roethke's late turn toward the language and thought of Christian tradition has apparently always seemed impossible, however often he may find himself "perishing for deity." Religious beliefs of whatever sort, Eastern or Western, anthropomorphic or Transcendental, are like mirages, existing somewhere between fact and delusion. Mirages, as he knows, must be counted among natural phenomena to be found and reckoned with throughout human history, not fully understood to be sure but too well documented to be dismissed merely because what they seem to reveal is not literally "there." Certain natural conditions seem to favor their occurrence—in the Arctic, in the desert—but since they can be experienced by whole groups of people at once, the crew of a ship in the Arctic, for example, it is not easy to dismiss them as totally groundless, wholly subjective, delusions.

The snow-covered mountains seen in the distance that are not where they seem to be are no doubt somewhere, relocated presumably by some trick of the refraction of light, so that though the *apparent* mountains are "insubstantial," without substance or mass, they are still "real," not a figment of disordered senses, even if always receding when approached. They share something of the quality of the visionary religious faiths that built temples in the desert, where the wind wears them away, turning them to ruins, "our own ruins," making constant rebuilding necessary. Unable either to prevent the constant eroding or to disprove "the theorem of the wind," we rebuild in the ruins, "in debris we make a holding as / insubstantial and permanent as mirage."

So ends "Persistences," the last poem in *A Coast of Trees*, on a note that should remind us of the way Ammons had announced his poetic intentions some thirty years earlier in "So I Said I Am Ezra," in his first volume, the poem later chosen to open both the *Selected*

Poems and the *Collected Poems*. The Old Testament Ezra was a minor prophet remembered chiefly for his connection with the rebuilding of the Temple after the Babylonian Exile, a learned scribe who devoted himself to study of the laws of Yahweh, laws revealed to his modern successor not on any mountain but chiefly by the sciences, with the help of Eastern religion, but not, as he says and implies throughout the whole body of his work, with any "finality of vision." (That he could have been thinking of a more recent Ezra is of course possible, for Pound too thought of himself as a kind of prophet, but Ammons' heavy concentration in his later work on religious and metaphysical themes makes this seem to me the less likely guess. See especially the poem entitled simply "For Harold Bloom" with which he opens *Sphere*.)

Ammons may be described as a religious visionary poet, late twentieth-century style. ("Religious" here points to temperament, sensibility, preoccupations, without describing precise theological beliefs.) He belongs in the company of Blake, Wordsworth, Whitman, Yeats, visionaries all despite their many differences. Like them, he has sought for order and meaning where there is apparently only disorder and no meaning, for the lasting in the universal decay, for the sacred in the secular; sought knowing that "reality" is more than meets the eye—if the eye is conceived as the lens of a camera capable of simply reproducing the visible aspects of what is "out there" —knowing that both belief and constructive imagination are at work even in the most literal visual perception, allowing us to see this and not that and helping to shape what we do see.

"Visionary" has always been and remains an inherently ambiguous word, either a word of dismissal or a word of praise. Through the centuries of its use it has mirrored the ambiguities of our situation, the cruel uncertainties about what we can really know or be sure of. A vision may be a revelation or a delusion. A "visionary" either sees more, better, or deeper than we generally do, or he thinks he sees what is not really there at all but merely wished for and so "projected." If he thus confuses wish with reality, he is the opposite of a "realist," who keeps his feet on the ground of fact and indulges in no wishful thinking. But realists have a tendency to equate reality with the status quo and with existing knowledge, while the visionary, for example one with a vision of a better world, may help it to come into being, or he may glimpse implicit patterns of meaning where the explicit seems to reveal to the "realist" only disorder and no meaning.

Epiphany or delusion? Insight or fantasy? "Time will tell," we say, but we cannot wait around long enough for the decision to come in. Even if it later proves to be revelation, the revelation will remain, in our time, teetering on the brink of delusion. There is no way for the visionary to play it safe: he may always turn out to have been not a seer or prophet but a fool. Ammons knows this well and never lets us forget it: he is a realist, he insists, determined to face facts—whatever "facts" are, and whatever they may mean. Our not knowing what they are, or mean, permits him to play the fool and tell himself, half seriously, that he is Ezra, but there is no magic in the words as a formula. They will not prevent either the poet or the meanings he tries to discover from falling "out of being . . . into the night."

As another early poem, "Turning a Moment to Say So Long," tells us, the visionary search for light involves more than running the risk of being a fool; it requires a deliberate plunge into the dark water. The poem begins this way:

> Turning a moment to say so long
>   to the spoken
>   and seen
>   I stepped into
> the implicit pausing sometimes
> on the way to listen to unsaid things
> At a boundary of mind
>   Oh I said brushing up
>   against the unseen
>   and whirling on my heel
>   said
>   I have overheard too much
> Peeling off my being I plunged into
> the well. . . .

In the poem's last lines the speaker finds "night kissing / the last bubbles" from his lips. Not content, with the Frost of "For Once, Then, Something," to look into the well and remain in doubt about whether the gleam he seemed to see there was truth or a pebble of quartz, Ammons in this poem faces the fearsome cost of any "finality of vision." In this he shows himself in the true line of visionary poets, as Frost was not.

But he is not always in the mood for such imaginative explorations of the darkness. Most of the time, except in the late *Snow Poems*, he is content to savor what the day or the hour offers and explore the implicit possibilities of further meaning. "Corsons Inlet," one of his finest poems, is more typical of his early poetry than "Turning a Moment." It tells us what he saw on a morning's walk along the shore, where sea and land, the One and the many, merged and possibilities of seeing a wider order teased him. He began the walk already knowing what he had written in an earlier poem, "Hymn," that achieving a vision of the One would require a twofold movement in opposite directions, both out and up "farther than the loss of sight / into the unseasonal undifferentiated empty stark," and also staying "with the earth / inspecting" its minutest forms, "down where the eye sees only traces." For he knows, speaking of the One, that "You are everywhere partial and entire / You are on the inside of everything and on the outside." In traditional religious terms, which he normally avoids, these lines would imply the simultaneous Immanence and Transcendence of deity.

The walk, he tells us, both liberated him from the "binds of thought" and confirmed his belief that the "Overall is beyond me," so that though he "reached no conclusions" about it, he ended "willing to go along, to accept / the becoming," confident that though everything we experience is "a congregation / rich with entropy: nevertheless, separable, noticeable as one event, / not chaos." The poem ends with none of the possibilities closed off and the visionary quest to be continued:

I see narrow orders, limited tightness, but will
not run to that easy victory:
still around the looser, wider forces work:
I will try
to fasten into order enlarging grasps of disorder, widening
scope, but enjoying the freedom that
Scope eludes my grasp, that there is no finality of vision,
that I have perceived nothing completely,
that tomorrow a new walk is a new walk.

The search for a more inclusive vision that emerges as the dominant theme of "Corsons Inlet," implicit throughout Ammons' work, becomes explicit in *Tape for the Turn of the Year*, his diarylike record of how his days went for a little over a month one Christmas season. In both form and substance the poem shows Ammons determined to continue his role as one of the "poets of reality," even though fully aware of how feeble is our grasp of Reality—to what extent the very concept of it is necessarily a construct for which we must assume the responsibility. If our concept shuts out mystery or the possibility of experiencing the sacred, it is clearly false, one of those "binds of thought" the poet had found himself liberated from during his walk around Corsons Inlet. We must keep our minds and eyes open, for

> if we looked only by
> what we know,
>   we couldn't turn our
>   heads:
>   if we were at the
>   mercy of what
> we understand,
> our eyes couldn't see:
>
>   discovery is
>   praise &
> understanding is
> celebration:

In *Sphere*, another book-length attempt to create a poetic form ("poetry is art & is / artificial") that would realize "reality's / potentials," Ammons begins his poem with scientific language describing the sex act that reductively shuts out "praise" and "celebration" but ends it with language drawn from our explorations of space that has the opposite effect: "we're gliding," or being glided. Praise and celebration are possible again as we realize that "we're clear: we're ourselves: we're sailing." Religious awe is implied in these final lines, so that it is not surprising to find the poet who has described himself as a poet of "lean belief" writing, in the later long poem "Hibernaculum," lines that both mean something very like what

Emerson had meant in his "Bohemian Hymn" and anticipate the philosopher Robert Nozick in his recent *Philosophical Explanations*:

I address the empty place where the god
that has been deposed lived: it is the godhead: the
yearnings that have been addressed to it bear antiquity's

18

sanction: for the god is ever re-created as
emptiness, till force and ritual fill up and strangle
his life, and then he must be born empty again:

accost the emptiness saying let all men turn their
eyes to the emptiness that allows adoration's life:
that is my whole saying, though I have no intention to

stop talking: . . .

"Hibernaculum": a protective coating or cover which enables an organism to hibernate and thus survive the cold of winter. But if the winter should last too long or the cold be too severe, the organism may not survive, or, surviving, be unable to "praise" or "celebrate." The impulse to adore may die before the physical organism. If the organism should be A. R. Ammons, talking to us in verse, we might then expect *Snow Poems*, in which we find the poet taking no more walks, keeping his distance from the sea, and limiting his close inspection of nature to glancing out his study window and listening to weather reports on the radio. Now the tension between the poet's catching glimpses of "the windy rivers of the Lord" and his determination to remain a "realist"—a tension that made "Corsons Inlet," *Tape*, *Sphere*, and other earlier poems exciting reading—is gone, along with the precarious balance he had earlier maintained between fact and possibility. It is prudent not to look too closely in the direction of the light and settle for a more limited vision, for the poet knows now that "sight / feeds on a / medium / whose / source blinds." With his protective coating thick enough in this volume to keep out not only the cold but the light too, the result is a thick book of dull, tired poems that prompt us to wonder, does Ammons write too much?

Fortunately, that question receives a negative answer in *A Coast of Trees,* in which we are likely to feel that Ammons has never written better. Once again the poet, outside his hibernaculum now, is able to explore the nature of that "reality" that "is, though susceptible / to versions, without denomination"—in the several senses of the word—and to wonder "how are we to find holiness" with only "helplessness our first offer and sacrifice," as we seek "a composure past / sight." The tension between the visual and the visionary that was characteristic of the best earlier poems has returned in these opening lines of the title poem with which the volume opens and is maintained throughout until the book closes with "Persistences." The result is a number of the finest poems Ammons, or anyone else, has written in our cold time, with "Easter Morning" the finest of all. Now we find the poet taking another walk, meticulously noting what there is to see, and letting his imagination play with the implications of the seen.

The characteristic implications of Ammons' work as a whole so far are recognizably Emersonian-Whitmanic, so far as that is possible in the late twentieth century. Nature, of which we are a part, is what we must try to see as truly as possible, and understand, without supposing we have banished mystery. The sciences can help us greatly in this effort, without answering all the questions we find ourselves asking. Nature, from what we can see on a walk to what we can know of the physical cosmos, exhibits both order and disorder, purpose and entropy, but Ammons says he chooses to keep open the "possibility" of meaning. Keeping possibility open means avoiding dogmas, which are as likely to originate in science in our time as they were likely to originate in church history in Emerson's: we must not forget that we don't "understand" the "forces" to which we are subject. Remembering this, we may keep the life of "adoration" going while still avoiding wishful thinking, a difficult balancing act at best and impossible at times, as it was for the poet in *The Snow Poems.*

Crude as such a summary of his characteristic themes and attitudes must be, it may serve the purpose of reminding us that Ammons is engaged in reworking, and thus keeping alive, a long tradition in our poetry, a tradition that is alive not only in what he has to say to us but in how he says it, in the expressive forms he has invented for his verse, reminding us of Emerson's advice to the poet that he look to the fact, or the meaning, for his form. A single example of this from Ammons' verse: his justification of his frequent use of the very short line is that the requirements of the traditional long line, especially when rhymed and arranged in stanzas, may compromise the poet's specific perceptions of specific objects, thus preventing him from looking to the fact for the shape and quality of the image or its meaning. In this, as in so many other ways, Ammons is trying to do for our time what Emerson and Whitman did for theirs.

"Staying Alive in a Clear-cut Forest"

DAVID WAGONER

I shall end this very selective and deliberately, though reluctantly, incomplete survey of notable and, as it seems to me, representative poets of the present with a poet never praised or recognized as Ammons has been or so explicitly responsive to the intellectual, especially the scientific, climate of our time, a formalist poet furthermore outside the Emerson-Whitman-Williams free-form tradition that has been dominant in the recent past and is continued by Ammons and others—yet in his own way an authentic follower of Emerson's plea that we turn to Nature for our Scripture and learn to read its meanings, recognizing that "Natural facts are symbols of spiritual facts." David Wagoner's best poems of experience in the wilderness are neo-Transcendentalist visionary poems that do not suffer by comparison with Ammons' "Easter Morning," "A Coast of Trees," or "Persistences."

Wagoner's starting point, like that of Ammons and so many other poets today, is apparently his assumption that contemporary culture is bankrupt, and traditional monotheistic religious beliefs impossible, so that our problem is how to stay alive in a clear-cut forest. (Might one be an "animist"?) Clear-cutting forests is no doubt profitable in the short run for the companies that do it and perhaps for the society that permits it, but, like strip-mining, it renders the earth less habitable and in the long run amounts to a kind of suicide. Yet even in our man-made wastelands, in which not only forests but meanings and values have suffered clear-cutting, some forms of life survive if they are tough enough and don't need too much nourishment or security.

We might guess then that Wagoner would reject "visionary" as descriptive of his work, saying that unlike visionaries he keeps his feet on the ground. He is a poet, he might say, not a Prophet or a Seer. At any rate, like Ammons, and Williams earlier, he never tires of reminding us that he is a "realist." Like Ammons too he feels he has to reject his boyhood religious upbringing. But also like Ammons, he is as skeptical of the power of the mind to banish mystery by creating new and better, because more "scientific," dogmas than the discarded ones as he is of the truth of historic orthodoxy. His stance is consistently pragmatic and empirical: taking nothing for granted except the fact that we are somehow still alive in the ruins, what may we learn, or relearn, from personal experience, not from past belief or current theory, that may be helpful to us as we try to avoid finding ourselves totally lost? For Wagoner, the best place to explore this question seems to be outside contemporary urban culture.

It is not surprising then that Wagoner's most distinguished poems are his "nature" poems. But the label "nature poet" is likely to be belittling in our time, and Wagoner writes as if he were well aware of that, guarding himself in many ways against such a label, which could be taken to mean "romantic escapist." Most effective as protections against such dismissal are the stance and tone of the speaker in his nature poems. We may expect a visionary poet to soar quickly into the transcendental and a "nature poet" to ignore the dangers, threats, and disorder in nature, but the speaker in these poems habitually looks down before he looks up, giving the facts, not always reassuring, of here and now, the close at hand, his fullest attention before he looks up or off into the distance, keeping his footing carefully on firm ground as he speaks to us in the tone one would use in writing a practical guidebook giving directions and instructions about how to get where we want to go, from here to there. Though I have suggested Wagoner's relation to Transcendentalism, "transparency" may be a better word to suggest what seems to be happening in his best poems than "transcendence": meaning seems not to rise above but to shine through natural things and situations. But no doubt this is only a contemporary way of saying what Emerson meant but did not often achieve in his own poems.

Many of Wagoner's nature poems explicitly warn us against making the error Emerson can be accused of, seeing in nature only what it suits us to see, in effect remaking reality in our own image. Wishful thinking is a constant temptation, and we must guard against when the Black Death, the Hundred Years' War, the breakup of feudalism, and the declining authority of the Church with its two rival popes made it difficult or impossible for many to keep alive hope for the future of "this life." In England, this was the century when anchorites, hermits, and reclusive contemplatives and mystics thrived and *The Cloud of Unknowing* was studied as a source of hope for "the life to come." Which was "the worst century?" Ms. Tuchman seemed to be asking.

Now that "God is dead" for most of our poets and they can find no refuge in contemplation of the life to come elsewhere, they must live and write here and now, in the time of our century's great and small wars, the memory of the Holocaust and the threat of nuclear, environmental, or population-explosion disaster, and the specter of a planet sometime perhaps as dead as the moon. As Hayden Carruth has written, "Everyone is scared to death, everyone is seeking evasions; poets the same." Poets who might find Carruth's words an overstatement would be likely to agree with Howard Moss's description of the poetic situation in the title of one of his volumes, *Writing Against Time*. Solipsism, "surrealism," and a new regionalism flourish as poets seek either to avoid their dread or to find values to live by in the mind alone or in private experience of nature, the home, memories of their ancestors, the small town or region—anywhere but in public life or the future. The Vietnam war was the last national experience to call forth a considerable body of poetry, and it was poetry of protest. Whitman's celebrations of national beliefs and hopes seem simply irrelevant to most poets of the present, though Douglas Crase in an impressive first volume, *The Revisionist* (1982), seems to be saying that with suitable revision, Whitman's love of and hope for the land and its people may still be experienced.

Poets today often wonder what they can write about that will not seem evasive or escapist. Philip Levine speaks for many of them in "Words" (*7 Years from Somewhere*) when he finds himself "searching / again for words / that will make / some difference," and, "finding none," concludes that "Nothing needs to be said," with the word "nothing" now ambiguously suggesting both the words themselves and the memories and meanings they seek to convey.

Still, much fine poetry continues to be written and Emerson's idea of the poet as the "Sayer" for his age seems as true as ever. If poetry is no longer a cohesive cultural force as it was in Longfellow's and Whittier's time, the number of poets, of small presses, and of volumes published seems to increase every year as the hope that science, or technology, or our culture will somehow save us declines. As the poets tell us how it has been, and is, with them, we can find our own experience raised to consciousness and clarified. Though distrust of the power of language to convey real meaning that can be shared and alienation from our culture both seem to be increasing, there are still distinguished poets like Maxine Kumin, Mary Oliver, and Denise Levertov who might be described as Seekers, searching memory and present experience for meaning, and a number of younger ones like Dave Smith, Robert Pinsky, Lawrence Lieberman, and Peter Balakian who manage to make strong verse expressive of a kind of muted celebration of values that may still be retrieved or found afresh—to name only some of the best poets not as old or as famous as R. P. Warren, who in his old age continues to celebrate the experience of *becoming*.

The questions these and many other poets are asking as they seek the meaning of their experience are not wholly different from the questions Edward Taylor and Emerson both asked in their different ways, though the questions are asked in different terms and today's poets cannot share either Taylor's or Emerson's confidence that he knew the answers. But what Philip Levine has called the "questions / without answers" go on being asked, and asked best by our poets.

Postscript

THE "Present" of American poetry that this volume's subtitle promises it will treat refuses to stand still long enough for its outlines to be drawn clearly. In its state of becoming, it offers constant surprises. Poets one had written off as finished delight us with fresh bursts of poetic energy while unknown poets bring out first volumes of great promise. Except that it is very much alive and offers great variety, there are no really safe generalizations about the poetry of the always-changing present. Any attempt to treat it must be wholly open-ended. This volume should end with some blank pages, to be filled by each reader when the present has become safely past.

But I'd like to venture a prophetic note in this inconclusive ending. It seems to me very possible, even likely, that in the blank pages yet to be written the names of Denise Levertov and James Dickey will figure more prominently than they have in this or the preceding chapters, for both have recently brought out impressive new volumes. Both reached the height of their fame in the Sixties when they were in their forties, and both have now demonstrated their staying power, Levertov in *Candles in Babylon* and Dickey in *Puella*. And another name likely to figure in those blank pages: Stanley Kunitz, who has given us pleasure for so long and received so little attention in this and other stories of our poetry.

But enough of prophecy. How the poetic present will look from the backward glance is now anybody's guess.

Appendix

Appendix

A Note on Whitman's Mysticism

THE trouble with the "mystic," Emerson wrote in "The Poet," comparing him unfavorably with the "true poet" he envisaged, is that he "nails a symbol to one sense, which was a true sense for a moment, but soon becomes old and false." The true poet is a better mystic than those commonly recognized as mystics, for he does not make this mistake. He knows that

> all symbols are fluxional; all language is vehicular and transitive, and is good, as ferries and horses are, for conveyance, not as farms and houses are, for homestead. Mysticism consists in the mistake of an accidental and individual symbol for an universal one. . . . And the mystic must be steadily told, All that you say is just as true without the tedious use of that symbol as with it. . . . The history of hierarchies seems to show, that all religious error consisted in making the symbol too stark and solid, and at last nothing but an excess of the organ of language.

The chief example Emerson gives of a "tedious" use of symbols he takes from Jacob Boehme, whose system of theosophy leans heavily on alchemy for its terms and concepts. Boehme's "system" is likely to strike most modern readers as it did Emerson, as indeed tedious and unnecessary. Still, it is typical of the confusions to be found in almost all the discussions of mysticism I am acquainted with that Emerson should at one and the same time demand that the "true" poet *be* a mystic (that is, have all the characteristics of insight, transport, experience of union, etc., that are associated with mysticism); sometimes, in other essays, refer to the poet as a "mystic"; and yet, in "The Poet," condemn the "mystic" for being an inferior poet.

Like many other writers on the subject since, Emerson in "The Poet" is identifying "mystic" with a certain type of mystic, particularly with the medieval Western variety. The crux of the matter would seem to be that though Emerson liked, and recommended, mysticism, he did not want to seem to be recommending mysticism which in any degree fitted itself into a traditional Christian frame of reference or that seemed in any sense, however heretical, to support that world view. More so than Whitman, Emerson thought it *essential* that the creeds of orthodox Christianity be recognized as false.

The kind of mysticism he wanted, and for which he sometimes felt he could not use the term that seemed to him to have become too thoroughly attached to medieval Christianity to be usable any more, was what I have called "the way up," the *via affirmativa.* This is implied in his description of what he says is the chief use to us of the true poet: "For as it is dislocation and detachment from the life of God that makes things ugly, the poet, who re-attaches things to nature and the Whole, — re-attaching even artificial things and violation of nature, to nature, by a deeper insight, — disposes very easily of the most disagreeable facts."

We may be thrown off the track of his meaning here by the unfortunate — for us — way he ends his sentence, but if we can put to one side for a moment our suspicion of any "easy" way of disposing of "disagreeable facts," we shall see that, *in context,* the meaning is that the poet as mystic "sees through" the ugliness to the beauty that remains hidden from ordinary sight. Beauty, for Emerson, *includes* truth and goodness, and *is* ultimate Reality, unconditioned Being — that is, God, or "divine spirit."

So the poet, by re-attaching things to the whole — which means seeing the divine in everything, even in apparently ugly or evil things — redeems the world from meaninglessness, which Emerson took to be the same as ugliness. The poet does this by means of what Emerson calls here merely "a deeper insight"; but elsewhere in the same essay, and generally throughout the early writings, this "insight" turns out to be a kind of "illumination," granted, not willed, essentially, in short, a mystic vision.

Two differences are apparent between Emerson's idea of poetic vision and the illumination granted traditional Western mystics, neither of them crucial except to one who is committed in advance to a belief that determines how the "true" mystic must proceed and what he must discover. First, for Emerson, the "deeper insight" is granted, not in any sense, even a preliminary one, achieved; so that it cannot be "practiced," and there are no steps or stages, no "mystic way" that can be recommended to novices.

It just "happens" to those who have opened their human doors. And second, it does not involve the essential, even if only preliminary, negation of self and world that is typically associated with Western mysticism. What Emerson would have the poet negate is only the *superficial* self and the *apparent* world.

This last difference is, to be sure, not wholly clear-cut, for some form of negation is involved, it would seem, in all varieties of mystic experience. But the difference is real, even if not absolute, as a comparison of Emerson with St. John of the Cross will make clear. The metaphors of the saint's first poem, "Canciones del alma . . . ," suggest first a movement into darkness, then an ascent into light. The total movement might fairly be called "the flight of the solitary soul to God." St. John's full title, as translated by Roy Campbell, reveals enough about this mystic way to make the contrast with Emerson's way clear: "Songs of the soul in rapture at having arrived at the height of perfection, which is union with God, by the road of spiritual negation."

For Emerson in his early period — the period that produced "The Poet" — the world is not dark but only seems to be when we do not perceive the light shining within it. The poet does not so much "ascend" as "penetrate" by the power of his vision — penetrate to the values inherent in experience. But insofar as he may be said to "ascend" — and Emerson's frequent use of "higher" and "lower" metaphors to describe poetic vision makes us see that some kind of ascent *is* involved — when he ascends he takes the whole world with him. This is not what St. John meant by the road of spiritual negation, if we take the metaphors of his poem seriously.

The metaphors are sexual: the saint lies finally in the arms of Christ his lover. Now Emerson theoretically sanctioned, and Whitman practiced, the poet's use of sexual images. But the difference between this mystic way and the way that is implicit in Emerson and explicit in Whitman is clear: St. John uses the images of "secular" love as a way of expressing what would otherwise be inexpressible about "divine" love. There is no implication that secular love may lead to or reveal divine love. In contrast, for Whitman (and for Emerson too, theoretically, in the center of his thought) love as experienced in the world is not to be taken by the poet as valuable only insofar as it supplies him a language in which to talk about something else. If it is, as symbol, a vehicle, to use Emerson's word in his criticism of traditional mystics, it is a vehicle of revelation, the meanings of which are intrinsic.

Or to say it another way, language is "vehicular and transitive" for Emerson — and Whitman — not only when it attempts to convey mystic experience of the "divine," which is beyond time and place, but when it applies to "secular" experience. "Secular" experience itself has ceased to be secular for Emerson and become ineffable. Thus when Whitman writes about sexual experience, two things ought to be perfectly clear: On the one hand, he is not writing about love in a way which a behavioristic reductionist could approve, but on the other hand, he is not using the images of love merely as tropes.

This difference between Whitman and St. John of the Cross in the way each uses sexual images takes us to the heart of the distinction between the *via affirmativa* and the *via negativa.* Emerson's "nature mysticism" and Whitman's "erotic mysticism" are both versions of the affirmative way. Whether mysticism itself offers a valid kind of knowledge or only evidence of psychological aberration; and whether, supposing it to be accepted as offering valid knowledge, "nature mysticism" and "erotic mysticism" are valid forms of "true" mysticism, are, fortunately, questions that do not need to be answered, so far as the purposes of a critical history of American poetry are concerned. I should suppose that from a purely rational — a "publicly demonstrable" — point of view, we could say, "Nobody knows."

Nevertheless, I might as well say explicitly what has presumably been sufficiently obvious from the terms of my discussion of the poems, that personally I am not disposed to question the genuineness of Whitman's mystical visions. This is one of the reasons why I find most of the books on mysticism I have read unsatisfactory in various degrees and various ways. Mystics, I find, generally make much better sense to me than theoreticians of mysticism.

Rudolph Otto's *Mysticism East and West,* for example, devotes considerable space to trying to show that mysticism of Whitman's type (Emerson is Otto's example; he does not mention Whitman by name) is not "true" mysticism but a sham, which is really only "seeking and striving after 'sensations' and 'experiences.' " Calling it "voluntaristic mysticism," he says it boils down to "excited emotionalism" and "intoxicated eroticism." How does he know this? He says the reason is that such mysticism as this claims to experience an *immanent* God, while "true" Western mystics have experienced a *transcendent* (wholly other) God; and the two concepts of God he believes to be completely different in content. The two "mysticisms" therefore cannot both be called "mysticism." One of them must be true, one false.

Whitman could have told him what was wrong with this, if only Otto had read him. If the mystic's experience contains any truth at all, the method of logic-chopping dichotomous definitions will never reveal or identify that truth, especially if, as in Otto's case, the key definition reflects a hidden value judgment. I might add that Otto seems to be conveniently forgetting that Christian thought from the earliest days has insisted on the paradox, or mystery if you will, that God is *both* transcendent, the Creator, not to be identified with his creation as pantheism would have it, *and* immanent, within the world, informing it at every point. As St. Paul puts it in "Ephesians," "One God and Father of all, who is above all, and through all, and in you all." One of the chief functions of the doctrine of the trinity is to protect this mystery of a God who is both transcendent and immanent from those who would settle for an either-or solution. (Incidentally, the Old Testament contains hints of the same paradox or mystery, so that Otto is wrong about Judaism as well as about Christianity.)

The trouble with Evelyn Underhill's better and more useful *Mysticism,* so far as there is any trouble, is that though the book is subtitled "A Study in the Nature and Development of Man's Spiritual Consciousness," it is really not man's spiritual consciousness that interests the author but the Christian's, and the orthodox Christian's at that. She tries hard not to be dogmatic or exclusive, but her unconscious model is the Medieval Christian mystic.

As soon as she moves beyond the circle of allowable deviations from orthodoxy, she begins to write absurdities. "Such a perception of the Divine in Nature [as Blake's], of the true and holy meaning of that rich, unresting life in which we are immersed, is really a more usual feature of Illumination than of Conversion." So? What this seems to mean, translated, is that only Christians — the already converted — have a right to experience Nature as the garment of God.

Naturally, with such a model in mind, she finds Whitman not a true mystic. Trying to give him his due nonetheless, she writes: "Amongst modern men [Why "modern"? Because *real* mysticism ended with the end of the Middle Ages? She seems not to realize what this, if so, does for her argument for mystic experience as a valid way of knowing.] . . . Amongst modern men, Walt Whitman possessed in a supreme degree the permanent sense of this glory ['the glory of God . . . in all His visible creation']. . . . But evidences of its existence and the sporadic power of apprehending it are scattered up and down the literature of the world." In other words, this sort of perception is so common that even if experienced "in a supreme degree," it can't be "real mysticism."

This seems a strange sort of argument, that what seems like mystic perception can't be real because it is so common. Strange, that is, unless there is a hidden premise involved, and of course there is: Once again, only trinitarian orthodoxy can produce the real thing. Thus Blake is out, Wordsworth is out, Whitman is out. Thus what I have taken to be a difficult problem is, according to Miss Underhill, no problem at all.

She might have had a greater awareness of the problematical if she had read Whitman more, or read him with as much understanding as she demonstrates when treating more orthodox mystics. To say for instance that Whitman had a "sense" of the Divine in Nature is inadequate even as description — or perhaps we ought to say that it disguises evaluation *as* description. For it might mean only that he "believed" in it, or was "appreciative" of it. But he claimed to have *experienced* the Divine in Nature, and his poetry makes good his claim, as far as literature can ever make good such a claim. The description would more nearly approach being adequate if Whitman had written only "Passage to India," for there we get the impression of him as a religious poet who *hopes* some day to pass on to "more than India."

Mysticism, in short, though very fine on the mystics Miss Underhill's faith leads her to approve of, is hardly of any use at all on anyone else. A student of mysticism who would put Whitman and Tennyson into the same sentence as "amongst those who cannot justly be reckoned as pure mystics," thus betraying at once a blindness to the special qualities of two very different poets and an excessively narrow idea of what "pure" mysticism is, hardly inspires trust as a guide to the mystical aspect of Whitman.

James Miller, whose interpretation of "Song of Myself" as "inverted mysticism" is explicitly based on Miss Underhill's book, *has* read Whitman, and read him with deep understanding. But though his interpretation has great value in relating Whitman to an earlier tradition, and in doing so highlighting aspects of the poem's meaning and structure too little or not at all noticed before Miller did his work, yet there is a certain inappropriateness in forcing the parallel between the poem's stages and the stages of the mystic way so far as Miller must for the sake of his thesis. An "inverted" mystic ought to be standing on his head, but Whitman stood on feet mortised and tenoned in the granite of his own experience as illumined by Transcendental doctrine.

If Miller's analogy with the traditional Western mystic way seems to me a little forced, Malcolm Cowley's analogy with Indian religion is interesting and suggestive, but partially misleading. Admitting that Whitman knew very little of Indian doctrines at the time when he wrote "Song of Myself," Cowley takes the poem to be an "inspired prophecy" of knowledge that only became known in this country much later.

But why multiply mysteries? All of Whitman's chief doctrines may be found in Emerson. He did not need to be "inspired" in Cowley's sense: He knew perfectly well what Emerson's doctrines were, and he agreed with them. As for Emerson himself, his relation to the Orient has long been studied and known. He knew less about Eastern religions than any reputable Orientalist today, but enough to believe that they confirmed thoughts and attitudes he had developed out of Western resources, including Quakerism.

Nevertheless, it should not surprise us to find many parallels between the thought of both Emerson and Whitman and that of the Eastern mystics. Both William James and his most eminent American successor as a student of religious experience, W. T. Stace, have argued convincingly, against Otto and Underhill, that at a certain (still meaningful) level of generality, the reports of all mystics, East and West, finally agree. Stace makes this point briefly in *Religion and the Modern Mind* and more fully, and in more technical terms, in *Mysticism and Philosophy*. I find it interesting that T. S. Eliot's religious orthodoxy did not prevent him from arriving at the same conclusion.

Since Cowley's essay was published, a whole book has appeared devoted to developing Cowley's argument. V. K. Chari's *Whitman in the Light of Vedantic Mysticism* (Lincoln: University of Nebraska Press, 1964) seems to me helpful insofar as it supplies further reasons for believing that "to get at Whitman's meanings we must read his verse as mystical verse," but unhelpful insofar as it emphasizes his closeness to Vedanta exclusively, ignoring aspects of his work which are more Western than Eastern.

Of the two poets, Emerson and Whitman, Emerson seems to me closer, doctrinally, to the East — though to be sure this strain in his thought emerges only sporadically in his poetry. His tendency at times to view Nature as *maya* and his frequent near-approaches to pantheism take him closer to Buddhist and Hindu religious thought than, as I read him, Whitman ever came. I cannot imagine Whitman's having written "Hamatreya," for instance. His feeling for the individual, and his stubborn, unrationalized sense that the "appearances" of experience *must* contain some kind of "reality," both of these subphilosophic attitudes of his separate him from Buddhism and Vedanta and unite him with his Quaker background. Whitman believed in personal immortality, not in the disappearance of the enlightened individual in the All.

Start with the Sun by Miller, Slote, and Shapiro is a pioneering work that promises more than it delivers in its effort to get Whitman's erotic mysticism understood in its own terms and not as an "inversion" or corruption of something else. The book finds too many enemies to fight and seeks out allies too incautiously. It is not really necessary, in order to understand and appreciate Whitman, to condemn wholesale "Modernism" in literature, even if "Modernism," or the " new Puritanism" as Miss Slote prefers to call it, turns out to be chiefly comprised of Pound, Eliot, and Stevens.

Like a blast from a sawed-off shotgun, the book's negations turn out to be effective only at very short range. Or to change the figure — and a book of this sort can only be briefly described in metaphors — the authors have too many axes to grind, and try to grind them all at once, with the result that none of them gets very well sharpened. Though the book makes a contribution by suggesting some of the affinities between Whitman and Oriental mysticism, on the one hand, and between Whitman and some modern writers like D. H. Lawrence and Hart Crane on the other, yet it is chiefly as a tract calling for a new romanticism that the book will be remembered.

Still, one essay in it, Karl Shapiro's "Cosmic Consciousness," seems to me to cut the preliminary blazes on a trail that, though still ill-defined, is surely pointed toward better understanding. Writing more as a poet responding to another poet than as a critic, writing not at all as a scholar, Shapiro gives us a record of a personal voyage of discovery that contains much that may be shared by those with other interests and other biases. Starting from R. M.

Bucke's *Cosmic Consciousness,* from whom he takes not only his title but his central thesis, Shapiro moves on to Buddhism, then to what he calls a "science mystic," P. D. Ouspensky — who is one of the direct links between Whitman and Crane, for Ouspensky devoted a chapter of *Tertium Organum* to Bucke's book, and Crane read Ouspensky — to end finally with Wilhelm Reich and Robert Graves.

This admittedly subjective journey through one poet's notebook leads to conclusions far closer to what Whitman himself would have recognized as like his own than any that might be derived from Otto or Underhill — or from the article on mysticism in the latest *Encyclopedia Britannica,* which is sheer gibberish. Shapiro writes:

> We must admit at once that we cannot know Whitman through modern criticism. . . . [We must see Whitman as the] chief modern exponent of cosmic consciousness, as Blake was a half-century before him. . . . Nature Consciousness or cosmic consciousness is being forced upon the attention of the world from every side; the deep vein of mysticism has been opened again and the age of pure rationalism seems to be on the wane. . . . A tremendous synthesis is in the making between modern science, the ancient psychologies [*sic*] of the past, and what we call poetry or art. . . . The artist seems to be the nexus between the scientist and the mystic. . . . [There is] a certain unity of aim between poetry, mysticism, and science. . . . [At the center of the literature of cosmic consciousness are those works] usually classed as mystical writings.

Though this starts too many hares to be tracked down, though it indulges in philosophic generalizations that seem not absolutely required for an understanding of Whitman's mysticism, though it all seems even more relevant to Hart Crane than to Whitman, still, with these and whatever other reservations, it is clear that Shapiro has left us in a situation in which it is possible to begin to understand the subject.

The best aids to an initial movement beyond this point of readiness are Bucke's *Cosmic Consciousness,* first published in 1901, and William James's chapter on mysticism in his *Varieties of Religious Experience,* first published in 1902. The two books by W. T.

Stace mentioned earlier in connection with Cowley's oriental interpretation of Whitman should be noted again at this point, for in effect Stace restates James in contemporary philosophical language. For readers who find the nineteenth-century aspects of the thought and style of Bucke and James a barrier to sympathetic understanding, Stace may offer the best starting point for further study. But since there is not much in Stace that was not stated somewhere in James, I shall comment only on Whitman's two nineteenth-century interpreters.

James thought so well of Bucke's book that he wrote the author a long letter, now quoted on the jacket of the ninth edition but missing from James's son's edition of the letters, to say that he thought the book did "a very high service indeed" to both psychology and religion and to beg leave to cite the book in his forthcoming lectures on mysticism. Friend and former biographer of Whitman, Dr. Bucke writes as an advocate of the man he considers the world's chief example of cosmic consciousness. More or less equating Whitman and Jesus as supreme examples of the higher awareness, he gives Whitman the edge in the comparison because he was determined not to be "mastered by it."

But the book survives all its silliness, all the unexamined nineteenth-century stereotypes of ideas, all the unbounded optimism. (In 1900 it seemed to Dr. Bucke that "The immediate future of our race . . . is indescribably hopeful," just because the faculty he was writing about seemed to be becoming more and more common). Its fundamental qualities are its blend of objectivity and sympathy, of passionate identification and fairness, in the treatment of a vast range of material. Its discussion of the distinguishing marks of cosmic consciousness reads at one and the same time like a simplified and generalized version of the mystic way described by Underhill and a sensitive description of the mystical core of "Song of Myself." The following is an example of the depth of Bucke's understanding of Whitman:

> . . . The simple and commonplace with him included the ideal and the spiritual. So it may be said that neither he nor his writings are growths of the ideal from the real, but are the actual real lifted up into the ideal.

James's *Varieties of Religious Experience* is still so far as I know the best book on its subject. On Whitman, if we compare it with Bucke's treatment, we find it at once more distanced from its subject, less "dated" in some of its ruling assumptions, but also less penetrating in some ways. Whitman for James is an example of the religion of "healthy-mindedness," of the "primacy . . . of vague expansive impulse over direction" in what he calls the "faith-state," and of one who had "sporadic" mystical experience. But though James finds no reason to question the "genuineness" of Whitman's mystical experience, he does not find himself wholly in sympathy with the conclusions Whitman seems to him to draw from the experience: "His optimism is too voluntary and defiant; his gospel has a touch of bravado . . ."

Beyond Bucke and James there is only one work that, in my own efforts to understand the subject, has proved to be essential to a grasp of both the historical dimension and the inner meaning of Whitman's mysticism. I say *beyond* Bucke and James, not *better than,* because it is not to be compared with them since it is utterly different; it is *beyond* Bucke and James in the sense that it is *later than* and *less obvious than* they are. I refer to Eliot's *Four Quartets.* (By accident I discovered Stace's work late and found in it confirmation of the already seen but no wholly new insights.) Karl Shapiro noticed, angrily, several years ago that *Four Quartets* is not a mystical poem, only a *religious* one — and, he might have added, a philosophic and theological one of great learning and great subtlety. That is precisely *why* it is so helpful. If it were a mystical poem, it would be only another *example* of a class of which we have examples aplenty. Rather, it is — and, I should suppose, was intended to be — a meditative poem, a series of meditations on the nature of time and eternity, experience and reality, the many and the all, the dance and the still point — in short, on the subjects of mystic experience.

One of its two epigraphs, quoted from Heraclitus, "The way up and the way down are one and the same," was the clue that first started me to thinking about the relation of Whitman's form of mysticism to that of the older mystical tradition. What I take to be the poem's final intent — that the epiphany that was missed in the rose garden *can* be recovered, that revelation is constantly renewed for those prepared in awareness — seems to me now, a number of years later, not so very different from the final meaning of Whitman's whole body of work. I would go further and say that despite the enormous — and from some points of view crucial — differences between the two poems, "Song of Myself" and *Four Quar-*

tets are far more similar poems than we have realized, in more ways than I shall take time to detail here. But only this: Each seeks in personal history for clues to the meaning of life and death; each finds that clue in mystical experience, Whitman apparently reporting an actual experience of his own, Eliot speculating on, and imaginatively recreating, the experiences of others; and each comes to the conclusion that whatever appearances may indicate, come what may the fire and the rose, suffering and love, are one.

To begin with Karl Shapiro and then work through Bucke, James, and Stace to Eliot, as I have in this Note, seems to me as good an order as any, but it is the reverse of the order of my own reading. My understanding of Whitman, such as it is, took its start, years ago, from Eliot's poem; then, long after I thought it was "complete" (had become stabilized), was stimulated by James Miller's "inverted mysticism" interpretation in his *Guide,* partly to agree and partly to try to decide why I disagreed; Miller's essay sent me looking for a better jumping-off place than Underhill's *Mysticism,* and I read Martin Buber and reread Bucke and James with profit, though without feeling that I had yet penetrated the depths; some time after this, my understanding was drastically reorganized and clarified by Patrick White's novel *Riders in the Chariot,* which showed me, artistically, how "the way up" and "the way down" could be thought of concretely as "the same," not just because they arrive by different routes at the same "end" but because the routes themselves so often run parallel; and which also led me to think further about the connection between Blake and Whitman. My understanding finally reached its present, no doubt temporary, resting place out of the experience of rereading Emerson and Whitman simultaneously.

I hope it is not necessary to say that I do not mean to suggest that an understanding of Whitman's mysticism can be reached *only* in this way. Though I have argued that the interpretation Whitman put upon his mystical experience came to him primarily from Emerson and Emersonianism, as understood by a man brought up in the tradition of Quaker Christianity, our way into an understanding of his mystical ideas need not follow the road of his growth. In particular, Miller's insight into the parallels between "Song of Myself" and the accounts by earlier mystics of their experiences may be useful for another purpose than that to which Miller puts it. Instead of limiting its application to an attempt to explain the *structure* of "Song of Myself," we might use it as a starting point for an investigation of *thematic* parallels between the writings of earlier mystics and *Leaves of Grass* as a whole.

For if we assume, with Bucke and others, that Whitman's decisive (and perhaps only) mystical experience occurred in June ("Song of Myself," section five, "I mind how we lay in June," as the first edition has it), possibly in 1853, as Bucke surmises, then we must not only read "Song of Myself" as an imaginative recreation and interpretation of his experience, but most of the rest of *Leaves of Grass* as the product of the illumination achieved in the experience. When we think of the work this way, the bravado James complained of in the "optimism" no longer seems a vice, or a special quality which separates Whitman from other mystics. Eckhart, for one, often makes statements similar to Whitman's about how things appear to the illuminated mind. After the experience of illumination, he finds great joy in the world, which he now sees as completely radiant with the divine light; indeed, God seems to him so brightly to shine through all his creatures that there is a sense in which he can say flatly that all has "become" God.

Or Jacob Boehme: "For those who . . . are in process of birth, have we written this book. . . . We see . . . that every life is essential. . . . Fierce wrathful death is thus a root of life . . . for out of death is the free life born. . . . But the will to anguish, which gives birth to the anguishful nature, and which is called Father, *that* it is impossible to search out" (Whitman: "I understand God not in the least") . . . "For the angelic light-world, and also this our visible world, must have the essence of dark death for their life and source; there is a continual hunger after it" (Whitman: "Come, lovely and soothing death").

Still, though such parallels as these might be indefinitely multiplied, there seems to me always to remain in such comparisons our sense of a decisive difference between Whitman and the Medieval mystics, a difference that remains unaccounted for by the parallels. The decisive break between Medieval and later mystics came, I suppose, with the discovery of the *self* that found expression in the Renaissance and Reformation. At any rate, the later mystics always seem to me much closer to Whitman than the earlier. Closest of all perhaps are Blake and Vaughan.

Blake's insistence on the "divinity" of man, his rejection of Lockean rationalism, his ideas about children and the body, his concept of the imagination as constitutive of reality, and his emphasis on the centrality of direct or intuitive ("aesthetic") apprehension as the way to a realization of transcendence — all these aspects of his thought bring him close to Whitman. But whether these parallels are relevant to a discussion of "mysticism" or not is a question not so easily decided.

One of Blake's most recent interpreters, Northrop Frye, shies away from the word. I shall let him explain why:

> The usual label attached to Blake's poetry is "mystical," which is a word he never uses. Yet "mysticism," when the word is not simply an elegant variant of "misty" or "mysterious," means a certain kind of religious technique difficult to reconcile with anyone's poetry. . . . If mysticism means primarily a contemplative quietism, mysticism is something abhorrent to Blake . . . ; if it means primarily a spiritual illumination expressing itself in a practical and (in spite of its psychological subtlety) unspeculative piety, such as we find in the militant monasticism of the Counter-Reformation, the word still does not fit him. But if mysticism means primarily the vision of the prodigious and unthinkable metamorphosis of the human mind just described [i.e., "the realization in total experience of the identity of God and Man in which both the human creature and the superhuman Creator disappear"], then Blake is one of the mystics. (*Fearful Symmetry,* [Princeton: Princeton University Press, 1947], pp. 7, 431, 432.)

Though Frye is making it as difficult as possible in these remarks to relate Blake and Whitman as mystics, the relationship is apparent even so. If Blake never used the word "mystical," Emerson, we may recall, listed his objections to it forcibly. Calling mysticism a "technique," precisely in the manner of Otto and Underhill (except of course that a positivist does not believe in the *validity* of any such technique), closes a question which James's "experience" leaves open. Note, in this connection, that Frye's only examples of "real" mysticism other than Blake's kind are Oriental ("contemplative quietism") and late Medieval ("militant monasticism," "Counter-Reformation"). Clearly, his gambit here (he himself calls his way of handling Blake's mysticism a "gambit") is to adopt the position of the enemy for strategic purposes. Finally, note "vision": If Whitman's failure to develop a "technique" separates him from Medieval and Oriental mystics, so his failure to elaborate a private myth, a "vision" such as we find in Blake's prophetic books, his relying instead, in "Song of Myself" for instance, on the Biblical Crucifixion and Resurrection, presumably separates him from Blake.

Nevertheless, though Frye's words are all heavily loaded with naturalistic assumptions that make it seem best to him not to discuss mysticism in the body of his work but to relegate it to an appendix, in which he defines the term in such a way as to make it seem to apply validly only to Blake, the parallel between Blake and Whitman *as mystics,* even if we accept Frye's too narrow third definition, is still apparent. Both deserve to be called Transcendental mystics.

The parallel between Vaughan and Whitman as mystics is finally, I think, closer than that between Blake and Whitman, despite the humanistic emphasis that the latter two share. I shall let the author of the only book on the mystical aspects of Vaughan's poetry — and a very good book it seems to me — prepare the way for a comment of my own. I quote from R. A. Durr's Appendix on "Poetry and Mysticism," in his *On the Mystical Poetry of Henry Vaughan* (Cambridge: Harvard University Press, 1962):

> When it happens that a man breaks through — is brought through — the narrow confines of his conventional nature, his ego, or "outer man," when perhaps suddenly, in the twinkling of an eye, the gates of his perception hitherto set to admit only such data as wear the badge of "a priori" definition open toward their full dimension, "then comes the light!" Then he enters the land of the living, Reality flows in, and he sees that "things," *Natura naturata,* are the products of man's abstracting intellect, and that Nature, the manifold universe, is the single and glorious signature of the Divine Life that informs it. Thereafter his life is in the country of the Real, and what he seeks to depict through his use of the language of symbolism is always that numinous region, Reality unnamed and unnameable. To be sure, he looks at the same tree we do, but for him it is realized, and so transfigured, for he sees the light of eternity shining through

and composing its very life. Our tree is unreal only insofar as it is a delimitation and frustration of "tree's" real being and glory, "sicuti est." But for the seer, as for Whitman, "a leaf of grass is no less than the journeywork of the stars." Things become, in their *Istigheit*, as Eckhart would say, surcharged with "meanings" not other than, but transcendent of, their materiality, or, more exactly, their finitude. For him, as for Thomas Traherne, "Eternity was manifest in the Light of Day, and something infinite behind everything appeared . . ." (*Centuries of Meditations,* III, 3).

Others have entered that land of morning and light Vaughan knew, and they have tried to describe it, often with precision and eloquence but rarely with the effect of poetry. The Pseudo-Areopagite has left us a mystical theology, and the records of Plotinus, Bernard, Hilton, St. Teresa, Boehme, and others are available, and all are full of symbols. But they are descriptions and analyses of the *via mystica, containing* its symbols; they are not themselves symbolical formulations; they do not commonly partake of the reality they represent. The verses of St. Teresa are fervent and sincere statements about God and the way of her knowing Him; but they are not poetry. Their interest derives mainly from experiences she has more adequately related in her prose works. The verses are not imitations, re-enactments, of that experience; they have no power of their own. Not, of course, that reading Vaughan gives us title to the name of mystic. No art can reproduce the experience of life itself; it is never in that sense real. But Vaughan's poetry *is* able to give us an experience, of the kind we call esthetic, correspondent to what he underwent: it has a power, a life of its own, born of those illimitable and nearly intangible interrelationships of image, diction, tone, rhythm, and so forth, to the effect of which we assign the name of poetry.

Both St. Teresa in her prose and verse and Vaughan in his poetry are concerned with a unique and profound human event, but while the saint has drawn us a helpful map, often lovely in line and color, of the place she had been, the poet has shown us, even though in a glass darkly, something *of,* as well as something *like,* that region itself. St. Teresa's prose refers always to the event outside itself; Vaughan's poetry, though it, too, has reference to that event in life, is in itself an event, not identical with, but symbolical of, the actual experience, partaking "of the reality which it renders intelligible." We must settle for something like Susanne Langer's "symbolic transformation of experience," for while a clear perception of the nature of the transformation — how the effect of poetry is different from the experience it is about — may not readily be had, still we now understand that a symbol is more than a sign, its relation to the experience it represents more than analogous (insofar as "analogy" denotes only a set of resemblances between the attributes of things fundamentally disparate). By choosing that term we acknowledge that Vaughan's poetry is itself an experience, an act, and not merely a system of counters for an experience. We assert that our interest is in Vaughan's mystical poetry — not simply in his mysticism nor yet again only in his artistry. We cannot know the dancer from the dance.

But the poet and the mystic do have something in common that is of the essence. It is not — as with Vaughan, for example — that the poet necessarily writes out of a transcendent experience, though much great poetry does so emanate. It is rather that the poet (taking the term in its broader application to all creative artists) and the mystic are they who break through, or are brought through, the crusts of convention, the veils of maya — all that vast configuration of assumptions, artifacts, and categories, that we mean by culture; break through and by the excellence they own face existence with an open mind. They are the ones who know the thing itself; they build, sometimes by first destroying, our human world and find our meaning in the *prima materia* of experienced Reality. They are turned to immediate Reality; we are turned to them. That is why the true poet and the genuine mystic speak with authority, and not as the scribes. They do not need to concern themselves with what this or that important person has affirmed; they turn themselves to what they have known and speak

> from that. We depend on them not as we have come to depend upon the technician, for our ease and convenience, but for the life that is not fed by bread alone.
>
> What I have said above sounds hyperbolic, but I am not attempting a thorough analysis of the relation between poetry and mysticism, an analysis that would call for many qualifications, explanations, and developments — and at great length. I want only to intimate more fully what would otherwise have existed in this essay as assumption. Yet it is necessary to enter into at least one qualification here, for what I have said so far pertains more nearly and fully to the great geniuses of the religious life than to the poets, though in its broadest sense it does pertain to them. The mystic's vision is ultimate; he has known Reality; the poet's may be ultimate, and then the lines of demarcation between them are more difficult to draw (though obviously one has to do with the poet's superior powers of communication). But more often the poet has not penetrated to the very essence of being and knowing. His vision is normally tangential and fugitive in comparison, but it is a genuine vision: he has the strength and genius to see with his own eyes and proclaim the truth of what he sees. But — as is implicit in what I have written — most fundamentally important and valuable, as I see it, is the truth the religious genius whom we call a mystic has discovered; for what he knows is not partial and peripheral and subject to change; it is not one man's opinion or "view of life"; it is all there is to know, and all we need to know. When a vision of this kind combines with large powers of expression the highest poetry results.
>
> To me, Henry Vaughan was one of the very rare men in human history who, having been graced with intuitions of Reality, possessed both the genius and the training that enabled him to formulate his vision in words of poetic effect.

I have quoted Durr's Appendix in full this way for several reasons. First, he has provided what I take to be a sufficient answer to Frye's objection that mysticism is "difficult to reconcile with anyone's poetry." It may be that Frye's positivism is the chief source of his difficulty. Second, Durr's discussion is suggestive of the approach to Whitman that may be found in both Bucke and James, yet, in the third paragraph, in the discussion of the event, the artistry, and the poetry, moves a step beyond both. Durr's trope, "We cannot know the dancer from the dance," is implied in the approach I have made to Whitman. This problem, which is simply not discussed by Bucke or James, is crucial if we are to move beyond them toward a fuller understanding of what Whitman's poetry is all about. Third, Durr's discussion, particularly in the first paragraph, closely parallels Emerson's ideas, as they may be found in "The Over-Soul," "Spiritual Laws," "The Poet," and elsewhere.

Durr's Appendix is a general discussion of poetry and mysticism, only incidentally related to Vaughan before the final paragraph. But earlier in the book, in his discussion of the themes of childhood and nature in Vaughan's work, and in his relation of that work to Biblical tradition, and to immanent and transcendent ideas of God, he says much about his poet that would apply, with only a moderate amount of translation of terms, to Whitman.

What this suggests to me is that there really *is* a tradition — which has been inadequately recognized and described — a tradition of Western, and mostly but not exclusively modern, mysticism that because of its emphasis on the immanence of God deserves to be called the *via affirmativa.* It may or may not deny His transcendence: Blake did, ultimately, as Frye understands him; Vaughan and Whitman did not. This mystic way reached its greatest flowering in the Romantic Movement; but I do not take Romanticism to be a dead fact belonging to literary historians. When this mystic way was *most* romantic, and most divorced from, or unaware of, its sources, I have called it Transcendental mysticism. But a comparison of Emerson's religious thought with that of Paul Tillich suggests that the end result of his Romantic revolt was less "unorthodox" than he thought it, or wished it, to be.

The source, from which Emerson felt completely estranged, is Biblical. Not solely Christian; *Biblical.* Jewish Hasidism as interpreted by Buber is a form of the *via affirmativa.* Buber's own thought, so deeply influenced by Hasidism, seems to me, theoretically at least — though Buber, like Emerson before him, prefers not to be called a mystic — a version of the affirmative way.

Notes

Notes

Chapter I

1. "New England was founded at a period when almost everyone who could read at all, read poetry, and many attempted to write it . . ." S. E. Morison, *The Intellectual Life of Colonial New England* (New York: New York University Press, 1956), p. 210.

2. I have taken my examples of anagrammatic elegies from H. S. Jantz, *The First Century of New England Verse* (Worcester: American Antiquarian Society, 1944), and Kenneth B. Murdock, *Handkerchiefs from Paul,* Cambridge, Mass.: Harvard University Press, 1927).

   But even a cursory examination of the holdings of the Harris Collection and the John Carter Brown Library of the Brown University Libraries, the American Antiquarian Society, the Harvard libraries, and the Boston Public Library will suggest that there are discoveries remaining to be made in Puritan verse despite the pioneering work of Murdock and Jantz. The work of John Danforth seems especially worthy of reprinting and study.

3. Since Taylor normally wrote his "Preparatory Meditations" before he presided at the service of Holy Communion, or The Lord's Supper, in his church, and since this service was normally held in the morning, while his wife died in the evening of the day given by Taylor as that on which the Meditation was composed, it would appear that the poem does not mourn his wife's recent death but anticipate her coming death.

   Internal evidence in the poem seems to me to suggest that the common assumption that the poem *refers* to her death is not rendered unacceptable by the discovery that she died in the evening while Taylor composed the poem in the morning of the same day. See Donald E. Stanford, "An Edition of the Complete Poetical Works of Edward Taylor" (Ph.D. dissertation, Stanford University, 1953).

4. Though Barlow's verse is imitative, at least the form he chiefly used, the Popean heroic couplet, is not inappropriate either to his subjects or to his talents. The other "Connecticut Wits" — or "Hartford Wits," or "Yale Poets," for they were all Yale graduates — were either less fortunate, or less talented, or both. Trumbull, Dwight, Humphreys, and Hopkins wrote most of their many works in the form perfected by the age of neoclassicism and reason, the couplet, either pentameter ("heroic") or tetrameter ("Hudibrastic"); but what they had to say often seems to demand a form less brittle and rationalistic. Federalists and Calvinists, they wrote Biblical paraphrases, historical allegories, satires, long descriptive poems, and would-be epics, all in the same verse patterns, which come to seem extremely mechanical, and often unfitted to accomplish their intentions, before they are through with them.

   Inspired by their desire to defend religious and political conservatism and by patriotism (a newly independent country should have its own literature and be celebrated in epic verse), the others in the group generally lacked both Barlow's wit and his occasional felicitous use of the developing American idiom. John Trumbull, a lawyer after a brief period of teaching at Yale, was famous in his time for *The Progress of Dulness* and *M'Fingal;* Timothy Dwight, grandson of Jonathan Edwards and distinguished president of Yale, wrote *The Conquest of Canaan, The Triumph of Infidelity,* and *Greenfield Hill.* Several of the Wits collaborated on *The Anarchiad,* a satirical attack on the liberal thought of the time.

   While Edward Taylor's poetry foreshadows Emerson's, both thematically and in its impatience with the demands of form, and sometimes suggests the earlier work of Robert Lowell, the verse of the Connecticut Wits is, except in subject matter, quite outside the main stream of American poetry. In effect, it is minor British neoclassic poetry written by American nationals. Imitativeness extends to every aspect of the verse, even to the use of pronunciations of rhyming words impossible in American English but carried over uncritically from the practice of English poets like Pope and Charles Churchill, who could claim the justification of spoken usage. Thus Dwight in *Greenfield Hill* rhymed "smile" and "toil," not intending a consonantal rhyme but simply following uncritically the usage of poets who no doubt had *heard* pronunciations that licensed the usage.

The contemporary fame of these poets is adequately suggested by their prominence in *American Poems* (1791), one of our earliest anthologies, but their work is "American" only in intention and subject. Perhaps the time was not right, or perhaps they had not the imagination to assimilate the American experience deeply enough to have it affect the formal qualities of their verse. They speak, at any rate, with an affected British accent while writing about American, or Biblical, subjects. Awkward and sometimes crude as he is, Edward Taylor is a finer poet than any of the Wits.

Chapter II

1. William Dean Howells, many of whose critical judgments still seem so sound that we ought to feel uneasy about dismissing any of them lightly as totally mistaken, once wrote to Whitelaw Reid that he considered Lowell's "The Cathedral" "by far the greatest poem yet written in America, and of its kind there have been none to surpass it anywhere" (Whitelaw Reid Papers, Library of Congress). When he reviewed the poem, Howells was somewhat more cautious. He called it "the noblest poem which Mr. Lowell has yet written," which might have seemed rather meaningless as praise if he had not gone on to add that in his opinion Lowell was "not less than the greatest of living poets in his mental reach." See George Monteiro, "Howells on Lowell: An Unascribed Review," *New England Quarterly,* XXXVIII:508–509 (Dec. 1965).

2. That Whittier himself was at least partially conscious of the sharp divergence in outlook between his own poem and Emerson's "The Snowstorm" is suggested by his selecting for his first epigraph for the poem when it was first printed (1866) and later in his collected poems a passage he identifies as from "Cor. Agrippa, *Occult Philosophy,* Book I, chap. V." The passage follows:

    > As the Spirits of Darkness be stronger in the dark, so Good Spirits which be Angels of Light are augmented not only by the Divine light of the Sun,

> but also by our common Wood Fire: and as the Celestial Fire drives away dark Spirits, so also this our Fire of Wood doth the same.

Then follows, as second epigraph, the first verse-paragraph of Emerson's poem — nine lines, ending with "enclosed/ In a tumultuous privacy of Storm." It is only after this point in Emerson's poem that the speaker invites those seated around "the radiant fireplace" to leave their places around the fire and look out the window at the work of the storm. "Come see the north wind's masonry," the opening line of the second verse-paragraph, opens the important part of the poem for Emerson but not, clearly, for Whittier.

Chapter III

1. In "Emerson" in his *Discourses in America* Arnold writes:

> And, in truth, one of the legitimate poets, Emerson, in my opinion, is not. His poetry is interesting, it makes one think; but it is not the poetry of one of the born poets. I say it of him with reluctance, although I am sure that he would have said it of himself; but I say it with reluctance, because I dislike giving pain to his admirers, and because all my own wish, too, is to say of him what is favourable. But I regard myself, not as speaking to please Emerson's admirers, not as speaking to please myself; but rather, I repeat, as communing with Time and Nature concerning the productions of this beautiful and rare spirit, and as resigning what of him is by their unalterable decree touched with caducity, in order the better to mark and secure that in him which is immortal.
>
> Milton says that poetry ought to be simple, sensuous, impassioned. Well, Emerson's poetry is seldom either simple, or sensuous, or impassioned. In general it lacks directness; it lacks concreteness; it lacks energy. His grammar is often embarrassed; in particular, the want of clearly-marked distinction

between the subject and the object of his sentence is a frequent cause of obscurity in him. A poem which shall be a plain, forcible, inevitable whole he hardly ever produces. Such good work as the noble lines graven on the Concord Monument is the exception with him; such ineffective work as the "Fourth of July Ode" or the "Boston Hymn" is the rule. Even passages and single lines of thorough plainness and commanding force are rare in his poetry.

2. Alvin Rosenfeld's doctoral dissertation, "Emerson and Whitman," Brown University, 1967, recounts, for the first time fully, the story of the relationship of the two men, a relationship that lasted over many years and meant much to both of them, but especially of course to Whitman. The literary impact of Emerson on the 1860 edition of *Leaves of Grass* is the subject of the second half of the dissertation. Evidence for the generalizations I make but do not support in this chapter may be found in Rosenfeld's work.

3. The sense in which Transcendentalism in its early phases really *was* a "Saturnalia of Faith" is illuminated by Mircea Eliade, *The Sacred and the Profane: The Nature of Religion* (New York: Harper and Row, 1959), especially chapter four. The author does not discuss Transcendentalism as such, but what he has to say about "Human Existence and Sanctified Life" throws light on aspects of Concord Transcendentalism that have too often been overlooked.

4. Though Emerson liked to express his rebellion against his religious inheritance in the strongest possible terms, his sense of his continuity with the religious tradition behind him, existing in tension with his need to rebel, often comes out in his letters and journals — not nearly so often in his public writings — in curious ways. In his letter accepting the invitation to address the graduating class of the Harvard Divinity School in 1838, six years after he had resigned his pastorate, for instance, he still speaks of the "Christian ministry" as "our calling." For the complete letter, see the *Emerson Society Quarterly,* no. 28, III Quarter, 1962, part 2.

5. I am not blind to the objections that may be raised to Emerson's view that by opening our human doors, we may prepare ourselves to see God. We may instead be preparing ourselves to be annihilated. A friend who read the manuscript of this chapter objected at this point.

> The question I must ask as a Jew living after Auschwitz is: What about the experience of extreme suffering, extreme cruelty, extreme dehumanization? Is God present also then and there? What would RWE say? Or why did he not say anything at all? Why did he choose essentially to ignore the theological implications inherent in the depths of awful experience, terrible and terrifying experience? After reading Elie Wiesel's *Night,* for instance, I find Emerson almost totally unsatisfactory in this regard — to the point where he has almost nothing to say to me whatsoever in precisely that area where he wants so much to be heard, and where you personally seem to find him at his greatest. Nothing in Emerson's poetry or prose reconciles me to this aspect of Emersonianism.

I can think of no answer I would like to make to this objection. I can only say that I believe we have not yet, under proper conditions, tried Emerson's way. Translated into more traditional religious terms, that way means in effect that the most important thing for us to do is to listen for the voice of the Holy Spirit, as it speaks to us in history, in our personal history.

It is perhaps not irrelevant to note that the objection to Emerson, that "opening" may destroy us, is equally telling against Martin Buber and many of the religious Existentialists.

6. Emerson's "Orientalism" had long roots in his own and his family's past, but it still seems true to say that the chief ingredients in the formation of his original Transcendental views were his personal experience, his Puritan inheritance, and his reading in seventeenth-century literature, especially in the writings of the Quaker mystic George Fox.

In "A Dissertation on Emerson's Orientalism at Harvard" by K. W. Cameron (Friends of the Dartmouth Library, Hanover, N. H., 1954; reprinted in *Emerson Society Quarterly,* no. 32, III Quarter, 1963), we are told that Emerson's grandfather, the Rev. William Emerson, joined the Asiatic Society of Bengal in 1799, with the hope, apparently, that Asian literature might throw light on the question of whether the Old Testament could be trusted as literal history. While Emerson himself was a student at Harvard, some twenty articles on Eastern lore appeared in *The Edinburgh Review* and *The Quarterly Review.* Emerson probably read them. In his senior year at Harvard Emerson would have been introduced to the parallels and contrasts between Berkelian and Hindu versions of Idealism by Stewart's *Elements of the Philosophy of the Human Mind,* which he was required to study.

Nevertheless, the closest parallels between Emerson's thought and Eastern mysticism are not with Hindu religion but with Zen Buddhism, which remained unknown in this country until the present century. A sound discussion of the relationship between Emerson's thought and Zen may be found in Robert Detweiler, "Emerson and Zen," *American Quarterly,* XIV:422–438 (Fall, 1962).

As for Emerson's relation to German romantic philosophers, often cited as the other "source" of his Transcendentalism, recent Emerson scholarship, for instance the Stephen E. Whicher and Robert E. Spiller edition of *The Early Lectures of Ralph Waldo Emerson* (Cambridge: Harvard University Press, 1961), makes no longer tenable the notion that Emerson imported to this country a European philosophic movement. See, for example, the lecture on George Fox in *Early Lectures.* Emerson found support for his ideas, *after* he had developed them, in both European and Oriental thought.

Writing not simply of Emerson but of the other American Transcendentalists too, René Wellek recently had this to say:

> Essentially, in a history of ideas, American Transcendentalism, it seems to me, should not be coupled with German philosophy; nor, of course, should it be described as a result of German idealism. This does not mean a summary dismissal of

> the existing contacts and sympathies; it is rather a conclusion based on the simple fact that none of the Transcendentalists ever adopted the specific tenets of German idealism as, for example, they were adopted and elaborated later in England by thinkers such as Edward Caird or in America by Josiah Royce. The Transcendentalists were merely looking for corroboration of their faith. They found it in Germany, but ultimately they did not need this confirmation. Their faith was deeply rooted in their minds and in their own spiritual ancestry.
>
> "Emerson and German Philosophy," in *Confrontations: Studies in the Intellectual and Literary Relations Between Germany, England, and the United States During the Nineteenth Century* (Princeton: Princeton University Press, 1965), p. 212.

7. Students of Augustine have told me they cannot find in his works the description of the nature of God as a circle whose center is everywhere and circumference nowhere. It may well be that Emerson's source of this mystical commonplace was the Cambridge Platonist Henry Moore, in Book One, Chapter IV of his *An Antidote Against Atheism* (London, 1662). Moore entitles the chapter in which the definition appears, "The Immortality of the Soul," a subject much on Emerson's mind in the years when "Circles," in which he uses the definition in a key position, was gestating. Emerson chose as his first epigraph for "The Over-Soul" a poem by Moore.

   See *Philosophical Writings of Henry Moore* ed. F. I. Mackinnon (New York: Oxford University Press, 1925), p. 69: ". . . the *Idea of absolute Perfection.* The latter whereof some ancient Philosophers endeavoring to set out, have defined God to be *a Circle whose Center is every where.* . . . Which *Ubiquity* or *Omnipresence* of God is every whit as intelligible as the overspreading of *Matter* into all places."

   I am indebted to Professor David H. Hirsch for calling this passage to my attention.

8. Emerson seems here to be using the archaic form of "always" to express *both* his meanings at once: "in all ways" and "at

all times." Though the received opinion that he is not to be valued as a conscious craftsman is not wholly mistaken, this is one of many examples of his care for the right word.

9. Arnold's obtuseness about "The Titmouse" is a little hard to understand, in view of the explicitness — a damaging explicitness, I should suppose, in the opinion of most modern readers — the complete explicitness of Emerson's conclusion, with its *sursum corda* message of trust. Discussion of this poem will be found in chapter X, Frost, for the sake of making a comparison between it and Frost's "The Oven Bird."

   In his lecture on "Emerson" in *Discourses in America* Arnold had this to say about "The Titmouse":

> Emerson's "Mayday," from which I just now quoted, has no real evolution at all; it is a series of observations. And, in general, his poems have no evolution. Take, for example, his "Titmouse." Here he has an excellent subject; and his observation of Nature, moreover, is always marvellously close and fine. But compare what he makes of his meeting with his titmouse with what Cowper or Burns makes of the like kind of incident! One never quite arrives at learning what the titmouse actually did for him at all, though one feels a strong interest and desire to learn it; but one is reduced to guessing and cannot be quite sure that after all one has guessed right. He is not plain and concrete enough, — in other words, not poet enough — to be able to tell us. And a failure of this kind goes through almost all his verse, keeps him amid symbolism and allusion and the fringes of things, and, in spite of his spiritual power, deeply impairs his poetic value. Through the inestimable virtue of concreteness, a simple poem like "The Bridge" of Longfellow, or the "School Days" of Mr. Whittier, is of more poetic worth, perhaps, than all the verse of Emerson.

10. Milton's *Paradise Lost,* Book II, is often cited as the source of the name and character of the "truth-speaking" young

angel Uriel in Emerson's poem. Though Emerson was no doubt familiar with Milton's treatment of Uriel, it seems to me likely that Milton's source was also Emerson's. See the Apocryphal II Esdras, IV, which begins, "And the angel that was sent unto me, whose name was Uriel, gave me an answer, and said, Thy heart hath gone too far in this world, and thinkest thou to comprehend the way of the most High?"

The speaker in the chapter asks for clear answers on the origin and meaning of evil and the destiny of man, whose life is filled with "astonishment and fear." Uriel's answers constitute reminders that man cannot understand the ways of the Lord — not, at least, until he goes "down into the deep" of the sea, and "into hell" and "up into heaven"; the ways of the Lord are not our ways.

Chapter IV

1. "The Method of Nature," delivered as a lecture in 1841, published in *Nature; Addresses and Lectures* in 1849. Emerson prepares his reader for the metaphor of being spoken to from behind by such abstract considerations as the following:

> Not thanks, not prayer, seem quite the highest or truest name for our communication with the infinite, — but glad and conspiring reception, — reception that becomes giving in its turn, as the receiver is only the All-Giver in part and in infancy; I cannot, — nor can any man, — speak precisely of things so sublime, but it seems to me, the wit of man, his strength, his grace, his art, is the grace and the presence of God. It is beyond explanation. When all is said and done, the rapt saint is found the only logician.

Chapter VI

1. The fullest discussion of Whitman's debt to Emerson is Alvin Rosenfeld's in the doctoral dissertation referred to in the notes to Chapter III, above. My treatment of Whitman has been influenced by Rosenfeld's discoveries.

2. In a long talk with Whitman in 1856, while the two walked on the Boston Common, Emerson urged Whitman to remove the "Calamus" and "Children of Adam" poems from his forthcoming second edition, not because they were "shocking" or "immoral," but because, as he said, in Whitman's account of the meeting, they would certainly interfere with the reception of the work, and he wanted the book to be *read* as widely as possible. He also felt that these poems were not *essential* to what Whitman had to say.

   He was, as so often, right, it seems to me. Most readers since then seem to have found these poems simply boring — with one or two exceptions, such as "The Terrible Doubt of Appearances" and "There Was in Louisiana . . ."

   Nevertheless we should, I think, admire Whitman for refusing to accede to Emerson's prudential argument for excluding them.

3. I have used the expression "the transcendent self" as the title of Part Three, Whitman and Dickinson, rather than the "Transcendental" self, partly in an effort to suggest the connection of the two with Emerson without insisting on it too much — that is, without seeming to say that Emerson's Transcendentalism accounts for *all* the meanings and values of the two later poets. Transcendentalism is the point from which both of them start, but neither of them can be subsumed under the term as Emerson defined it, especially, of course, not Dickinson. The development of Whitman's religious attitudes ran parallel with the increasingly formal shapes his verse took after the Civil War. A sign of the direction in which his thought was moving is his increased use of the word *God* in the late poems. Though there was no sharp break in his development, there is a considerable difference in tone and attitude between the poems in the 1855 edition of *Leaves of Grass* and, say, "Passage to India," his last major poem. By contrast, Dickinson's development is neither so clear nor so consistent, as we shall see. She seemed for a long time to be moving away from Emerson and his view of the self as containing and contained in the divine, but in the end she reaffirmed at least a part of what he had believed about the self and its destiny.

   For both of these poets the self is central in their thought and their work, and the self is conceived as transcending time and place, transcending all the "facts" that could be used to describe it. Yet it would be an oversimplification to ascribe to either of them, without several kinds of qualifications, an exclusively and wholly Emersonian view of the self. Dickinson in particular sometimes denied the basic assumption on which Emerson had rested his view of the self, the assumption that "God IS." In some of her work at least the self we find implied might better be called "transcendent" — that is, more than its behavior, not exhausted by "scientific" description — but not "transcendental" — that is, not in touch with, or a part of, Absolute Reality or the Divine.

"Transcendent," then, as a description of the self, any self, as it is found in the work of these two poets, seemed to be specific enough to point toward attitudes they shared — and shared with Emerson — but vague enough, or ambiguous enough, to include them both, while at the same time distinguishing them both from later, more naturalistic, poets like Frost, in his earlier work, and Williams. "The transcendent self" therefore seemed a happy invention, preserving an intentional ambiguity, until I ran across it, some months after first writing it, in James's 1898 Ingersoll lecture, *Human Immortality*. There I found it used as a short-hand expression for the belief that personal identity continues after death, a meaning that would be appropriate enough in talking about Whitman, especially in his later work, but less so in talking about Dickinson. Thus James's use of the phrase, in this book, if taken as normative, destroyed the ambiguity I had been at such pains to guard.

I have since been unable to think of any better phrase to say what I want the title of Part Three to say, and so have decided to keep this one, hoping that not too many readers are familiar enough with James's little book to remember the meaning *he* gave the words. Anyway, I would argue, if confronted with the charge that I have debased a phrase which James used properly, that James's meaning is too narrowly conceived, too much conditioned by the terms of the Ingersoll lectures, which had as their purpose providing support for the belief in "the Immortality of Man." I would suggest that even this phrase itself is ambiguous enough to be interpreted in a variety of ways, only one of which would involve belief in the endless continuation of personal identity after death.

Paul Tillich's comment on what he calls the "popular" belief in personal immortality conceived as endless survival after death seems to me relevant at this point, as a way of suggesting that James's use of "transcendent" need not be considered authoritative. Tillich seems to me the subtlest modern apologist for "orthodox" Christian doctrine, and he intends to speak from within the faith when he writes:

> It is our destiny and the destiny of everything in our world that we must come to an end . . . Repressing the consciousness of our end expresses itself in several ways . . . Many people . . . hope for a continuation of this life after death . . . [This belief] replaces eternity by endless future.
>
> But endless future is without a final aim; it repeats itself and could well be described as an image of hell. . . .
>
> The Christian message acknowledges that time runs toward an end, and that we move toward the end of that time which is our time . . . There is no time *after* time, but there is eternity *above* time.
>
> — "The Eternal Now," in the book of the same title.

Tillich's "above time" is the same expression Emerson used in the key passage in "Self-Reliance" extensively quoted in the opening part of this chapter. Paul Lauter has pointed out how often Emerson anticipated Tillich in his theological emphases.

4. I am indebted to Professor Barry Marks for parts of my interpretation of this poem.

Chapter VII

1. At least three of the poems assigned by Johnson to 1860 and 1862 seem to reflect Dickinson's reading in Emerson's last book of essays. *The Conduct of Life,* published in 1860,

marked the end of Emerson's creative life. In it he shows a much stronger concern with limitation, with fate, than he had earlier. ("Once we thought, positive power was all. Now we learn that negative power, or circumstance, is half. . . . The book of Nature is the book of Fate.")

"Fate," if we may judge from the fact that it figures in all three of the poems that appear to reflect Dickinson's reading of *The Conduct of Life,* must have been her favorite essay in the book. In addition to "Faith is a fine invention" (1860) and "I had not minded — Walls" (1862), "The Brain — is wider than the Sky — " (1862) also seems to echo "Fate."

2. The way an artist may draw upon, and fuse, disparate "sources" to make something new is well illustrated by "A Route of Evanescence." In addition to the Bible, Shakespeare, and Emerson, Higginson should probably also be listed as a "source" for this poem. A key parallel in imagery between the poem and Higginson's Nature essay, "The Life of Birds," which appeared in *The Atlantic Monthly* in September 1862, makes it seem likely that the essay was an even more direct "source" than the others.

   In his article Higginson finds the beauty and meaning of nature particularly apparent in the hummingbird, and he speaks of the whirring song made by its wings, which beat too fast to be distinctly seen except as a round blur. (X, 368) It may be that this detail was not in the first instance observed by Emily Dickinson but read about in Higginson's essay.

   This possibility is strengthened by the fact that Johnson assigns to "about 1862" another poem in which the poet writes of a hummingbird and images it as a "wheel," this time picturing it as *riding* upon the "wheel" of its wings. We know that beginning in 1862, Dickinson made a point of reading all of Higginson's writings as they appeared. That she read "The Life of Birds" and drew from it the image that is crucial in both poems, and then, in the later and much greater poem, managed to freight the image with the meanings it carries in Emerson and the Bible, seems to me very likely.

3. That "The Road was lit with Moon and star — " (Johnson

1450, assigned to "about 1878") should be interpreted as a tribute to Jesus is, of course, not undeniably apparent within the poem itself. Only a complete reading, in chronological order, of all of Dickinson's later poems and letters would disclose all the reasons for reading the poem this way.

The many poems in which the poet puns on "sun-son," for instance — a pun common in earlier poetry and available to her also in Isaac Watts's hymn books — are relevant to the interpretation. Again, in "The Poet" Emerson had pictured the poet, the representative man, as *on the road, "homo viator,"* as Gabriel Marcel would have it; and in a number of late poems Dickinson interprets Jesus as "representative man" traveling through time to eternity. Traditionally, "tree" may be used for "cross"; the "Hill," capitalized, may be Calvary, the hill of the Crucifixion; Jesus, the poem implies, "endorsed the sheen" of life even though his "shimmering" (not clearly defined) "ultimate" nature is "unknown" — that is, theologically, is he "God" or "man"?

But if his "ultimate" is "unknown" in some sense, the poet is still certain of his *humanity:* He is, without doubt, the poem says, "Terrene," that is, human like us. The Theology implied in the poem might be called Unitarian, if we used that term in the sense in which it would apply to Theodore Parker, the Christian Transcendentalist, whose work had so much impressed the poet years before.

4. Both imagistic and verbal echoes, and particularly the *order* of them in the poem, make it clear that the "Governor Pyncheon" chapter in Hawthorne's *The House of the Seven Gables* is behind Dickinson's "I heard a Fly buzz — when I died — ." In the chapter, the Judge sits dead in the ancestral chair while light fades until only the window's faint shape may be seen in the darkness. Then even that light is gone. The Judge's eyes are open, but he too, like the speaker in the poem, "could not see to see." Meanwhile, the storm outside continually shakes the old house "like a wrestler" (in the poem this becomes "the heaves of storm"), though between blasts, there is often an unearthly stillness (in the poem, "the Stillness in the Air/ Between the Heaves of Storm — "). The chapter ends with "one of your common house-flies, such as are always buzzing on the window-pane"

crawling up the Judge's nose toward his wide-open sightless eyes, while the light of morning comes in through the window. (In the poem, "and then it was/ There interposed a Fly — / With Blue — uncertain stumbling Buzz — / Between the light — and me — / And then the Windows failed — and then/ I could not see to see — .") Like the dead Judge, the speaker in the poem is unable to see the light.

That Hawthorne's chapter is more hopeful in tone than the poem is suggested by the way the poem ends in final darkness, while the chapter ends in light, though not for the worldly Judge. In effect, the poem ends at the darkest midpoint of the chapter, where the narrator exclaims, "There is no window! There is no face! An infinite, inscrutable blackness has annihilated sight! Where is our universe? All crumbled away from us; and we, adrift in chaos, may hearken to the gusts of the homeless wind, that go sighing and murmuring about, in quest of what was once a world!"

The poem is about the experience of death, which the poet, or speaker, imagines herself undergoing. The chapter in the novel is about the death of the "unrighteous" Judge; the "righteous" *will* — and do — "see light." Psalm 49, which pictures the unrighteous as going into eternal darkness while the righteous awake to "see the light" (King James translation) was almost certainly in Hawthorne's mind when he wrote his novel. A reading of it would help one distinguish the intended meaning of Hawthorne's chapter from that of the poem which draws upon it.

I think we may anticipate that future students of Dickinson's work will discover other poems in which Hawthorne's influence is discernible.

5. Two of Dickinson's poems, 1669 and 1733, undated by Johnson, seem to me possibly to concern a religious experience unlike any of the experiences noted in her other poems on religious subjects. These two *may* at least, though I should not say they *must,* be read as about "experience" rather than about "belief." The first of them is brief enough to quote entire:

> In snow thou comest —
> Thou shalt go with the resuming ground,

The sweet derision of the crow,
And Glee's advancing sound.

In fear thou comest —
Thou shalt go at such a gait of joy
That man anew embark to live
Upon the depth of thee.

Number 1733, beginning "No man saw awe, nor to his house," appears to draw a parallel between Moses' confrontation with God in the burning bush and an experience which has happened to the speaker recently, an experience so overwhelming that "breathing is the only work/ To be enacted now." That the "awe" of the first line refers to God is clear not only from the development of the poem as a whole, with its culmination in the story of Moses, but in the fact that "awe" is referred to in the second line as "he" —

No man saw awe, nor to his house
Admitted he a man
Though by his awful residence
Has human nature been.

The last stanza, with its explicit statement that what Moses saw, the speaker has seen ("this"), seems difficult to interpret unless it refers to a personal religious experience —

"Am not consumed," old Moses wrote,
"Yet saw him face to face" —
That very physiognomy
I am convinced was this.

Reading the two poems this way raises, to be sure, a number of problems. They are, for one thing, when read this way, untypical of her. For another, if they refer to a major religious experience, why are there not others, a whole cluster, referring to it also? Why do not letters refer to the experience, if there was one?

The difficulty I find in reading the poems in any other way than as referring to a personal religious experience, and yet the difficulties that arise when they *are* so read, suggests to me that Dickinson's late religious development needs further study and clarification. I am indebted to Mrs. Sally Pierce for the suggestion that these poems may refer to a late religious experience, which E. D. was too uncertain about, and too humble, to refer to except in her "private diary"—that is, her poems.

Chapter VIII

1. For a revelation of the sort of man who would write this sentence about the relation of his Aeolian harp and his poetry, see "Herman Melville through a Child's Eyes," by Mrs. Frances Thomas Osborne, his granddaughter, in the *Bulletin* of the New York Public Library, 69:655–660 (Dec. 1965). Mrs. Osborne writes of the Aeolian harp that fascinated her as a small child visiting her grandfather's home, "The other intriguing thing was the music of the Aeolian harp on the windowsill. The wind blowing through it must have reminded grandpa of the wind in the rigging at sea. In *White-Jacket* he mentions an Aeolian harp as a cure for the blues."

Whatever his Aeolian harp may have meant to him in his last years, it certainly did not cure the blues. When he had written *White-Jacket* he had been very much closer to Emerson in thought than he was when he wrote *Battle-Pieces.* Even when he wrote *Moby-Dick* Emerson still seemed worth combating. By the time of *Battle-Pieces,* nature's vagrant "music," made audible by the Aeolian harp, seemed to him still worth listening to, though he now connected nature's airs with what was to him the pure tragedy of the Civil War. By the time recorded by his granddaughter, the wind-harp was a relic of the past, a keepsake from a time when nature, and life, had seemed to have meaning.

Though Mrs. Osborne does not intend to suggest it, her account of the ways of her grandfather suggests to me that by the end of his life Melville was quite "sick," as we should say, emotionally. The withdrawal, the "distancing," apparent in *Battle-Pieces,* is also apparent in Mrs. Osborne's anecdotes about the strength of his inner revery, which made him once forget her presence so completely that he forgot that he had taken her to the park, as a little child, and permitted him to walk home alone without her. Mrs. Osborne comments on the incident, "It must have been wonderful to have had an imagination strong enough to carry him away so far that he could lose a [favorite] grandchild in the big city and never know it." By this time, of course, Melville was completely uninvolved, not only with the people he had written about in *Battle-Pieces,* but even with those he was thought to love.

2. Ian Ramsey, in *Religious Language: An Empirical Placing of Theological Terms,* has, in effect, rehabilitated the fundamental assumptions of Paley's thought for our time. But he has done it from the point of view of, and working with the methods of, the philosophical analysts of the present day, who are generally as rationalistic in assumptions and procedures as were the Latitudinarian theologians of the eighteenth century. In Lanier's time and place, the "argument from design" had come to seem untenable to most thinking people. Lanier was attempting to bulwark his Christian faith with an "outmoded" argument.

   Curiously enough, Lanier was very much aware of, and very fond of, Emerson. He went out of his way to praise "Each and All" in his lectures on the novel. On March 29, 1880, he wrote to his publisher, Scribner's, to thank them for the picture of Emerson he had received: "I wish to acknowledge a special obligation for the portraits in this volume. That of Emerson, over which I have lingered most, glorifies the book, and carried it at once among my treasures." (Manuscript in the Alderman Library at the University of Virginia.)

3. In my discussion of Crane I am indebted, as I hope I have already made clear, to Daniel G. Hoffman's *The Poetry of Stephen Crane* (New York: Columbia University Press, 1957), as, I think, all future critics of Crane's poetry must be. Crane has been fortunate in his recent critics. Robert W. Stallman's monumental labors and John Berryman's critical biography also put all of us in their debt.

   I would take issue with only one idea in Hoffman's book, an idea quite unessential from the point of view of the purposes and achievement of his book — though essential from the point of view of *this* book. In his introduction to the subject of Crane's poetry, Hoffman stresses, properly I think, Crane's alienation and its contribution to his originality. Crane may be described, Hoffman argues, by listing his "repudiations." So far so good. But Hoffman describes Crane's first and most important "repudiation" in this way:

> First, Crane repudiates most of the involvements of the will with society. If, as Lionel Trilling suggests, the work of the novel is to deal "with reality and illusion in relation to questions of social class," even in his prose Crane would seem to be outside the tradition in which the preponderant authority of fiction as an art resides. The social order, as his contemporaries Henry James and William Dean Howells conceived of it, is almost wholly absent from Crane's work.

Hoffman goes on to say that this "repudiation" which is true of his fiction is even *more* true of his poetry. But what about the assumption, taken from Trilling, on which the argument for Crane's very special quality is said to rest? "*If* . . . the work of the novel" — What novel? Certainly not the American long fictions. Jane Austen, surely. Most English novels, perhaps. But if most of the great American novelists have shown themselves very little concerned with "questions of social class," where does that leave this argument for the *originality* of Crane's work?

Supposing it should be discovered that none of the major American poets up to Crane's time, and very few since, have paid much attention to "society" as Lionel Trilling defined it. What tradition would Crane *then* be outside of? But enough of rhetorical questions. Anyone who has a first-hand knowledge, not simply of the poems most commonly anthologized but of the collected poems, of the chief American poets through the end of the nineteenth century must find it perfectly clear that even if Trilling's description of the work of "the" novel were thought to fit the *American* "novel," or whatever one chooses to call it — and it does *not* fit — it certainly bears no relationship at all to American *poetry.*

Only the weakest American poets — weakest in terms of the quality of their poetry as art — have ever shown much concern for "society," and even *they* have never been concerned, except satirically or ironically, with the kind of society implicitly defined by Trilling's remark; that is, with a static, hierarchical, caste society conceived as an absolute and unchanging reality.

Exceptions? They are few and insignificant from an aesthetic point of view. Among the Puritans, none, of course. In the eighteenth century, the Federalist "Hartford Wits" or "Connecticut Wits" sometimes wrote on social themes, but even they, satirizing dullness, or religious infidelity, or political radicalism, showed little concern with social classes as such; they were interested in intellectual or political or religious differences, and they treated these from a conservative position, but their test of "reality and illusion" was supramundane when it was not explicitly Biblical. Anyway, they were not very good poets, for the most part, nor very typical of the main stream of American poetry. Barlow, in the *Columbiad,* to be sure, concerned himself with the future of his country, but always in the abstract, and always in terms of the promise it held that "society" in Trilling's sense would soon be done away with.

There are, I believe, *no* nineteenth-century exceptions worth mentioning. Lowell wrote on political and moral issues in *The Biglow Papers,* but the Mexican and Civil Wars treated in the first and second series of poems, with their related questions of freedom and slavery and the rights of the individual conscience in an evil time, have nothing to do with what Trilling calls "reality and illusion in relation to questions of social class." Whitman's feeling for others, when it is not merely theoretic — "en masse" — is completely individual and Transcendental. Man tramping the open road is not *concerned* with "social classes," except insofar as, if he were to meet any evidence of their existence, he would reject and spurn them. Emily Dickinson, though born to a patrician heritage, as Amherst counted such things, could not possibly have been less concerned with what Trilling says must be the literary artist's main concern. Trilling's statement, then, I conclude, bears no conceivable relation to important American poetry before the twentieth century, not even to the work of those who have been thought to represent the "conservative" or anti-Adamic tradition of Hawthorne, Melville, and Faulkner.

It does not even apply, in our century, to Eliot, who for a while toyed with the idea of a neo-Christian society with fixed orders; for the distinctions in Eliot's ideal social order are religious, not secular. They have, as he tries very hard to make clear, nothing to do with the social classes found in a capitalist society. They add up, finally, to a sort of revived Puritan ideal of a theocracy, or government of God, or by those close to God. Nothing could be further from Trilling's idea. Trilling's idea is purely secular, and American poetry has *not* been secular, whatever the faith it turned to, implicitly or explicitly, in its appeal over the head of society. It has always been, as we might say, "supramundane," if we let Trilling's idea stand for the "mundane." All of our best writers, without exception, have been concerned to discover an authority more ultimate than that of "social classes."

Emerson, Whitman, and Dickinson are the American poets whose work must determine our definition of "the tradition." Stephen Crane by no means repudiates that tradition. Indeed, he renders it down to purity and simplicity. Narrowing it as much as he does, he perhaps impoverishes the tradition; but he is still within it, not outside it.

Chapter IX

1. In *Pragmatism: A New Name for Some Old Ways of Thinking* (1907), James expressed a view of and an attitude toward Spencer probably very like the one that Robinson had heard him express in class in the early 1890's. That James's evaluation of the popularizer of Darwinian notions has proved acceptable to later philosophers does not make it any more surprising that Robinson, given the kind of student of philosophy he was in the early 1890's, should have been angered and alienated. James wrote of Spencer in "The Present Dilemma of Philosophy," the opening "lecture" of *Pragmatism,*

> It is the essential meagreness of *what is suggested* by the usual rationalistic philosophies that moves

> empiricists to their gesture of rejection. The case of Herbert Spencer's system is much to the point here. Rationalists feel his fearful array of insufficiencies. His dry schoolmaster temperament, the hurdy-gurdy monotony of him, his preference for cheap makeshifts in argument, his lack of education even in mechanical principles, and in general the vagueness of all his fundamental ideas, his whole system wooden, as if knocked together out of cracked hemlock boards — and yet the half of England wants to bury him in Westminster Abbey.

2. I suspect that Robinson's poem may owe something to Emerson's second poem on Monadnock, the shorter "Monadnoc from Afar." If so, both the convergence of the imagery in the opening lines of the two poems, and the divergence of the attitudes expressed from that point on would be typical of Robinson's relationship with Emerson. Emerson's poem:

> Dark flower of Cheshire garden,
> Red evening duly dyes
> Thy sombre head with rosy hues
> To fix far-gazing eyes.
> Well the Planter knew how strongly
> Works thy form on human thought;
> I muse what secret purpose had he
> To draw all fancies to this spot.

Robinson wrote his poem (quoted on p. 280) while at the MacDowell Colony at Peterborough, New Hampshire. The mountain directly to the west of Robinson's cottage in the Colony is Monadnock. The trees west of Robinson's cottage had been cut down to permit an unobstructed view of the mountain, which thus formed the background of Robinson's favorite view. Monadnock is also no doubt the "hill" over which the man against the sky climbs in the poem of that name. A slender anthology of New England poems which name, celebrate, or use this not very high, but still impressive, mountain could be made.

3. The experiences of Robinson's childhood and young man-

hood were even more traumatic and terrible than we had known before the appearance of the reminiscence by Chard Powers Smith, *Where the Light Falls: A Portrait of Edwin Arlington Robinson* (New York: Macmillan, 1965). Though the author's style and manner often throw one off, and though he tends to make his whole case suspect by interpreting too many of Robinson's poems as reflecting too literally and directly Robinson's personal experiences, still there can be, as I see it, no doubt that the reminiscences themselves contained in parts one and four of the book may be trusted.

Insofar as the thesis of the book, as developed in parts two and three, depends upon Smith's frequent statement that "Legend has it . . . ," it is of course open to question. But I think we ought to realize that while those who played a part in the tragedy of the Robinson family are still alive, we cannot expect them to permit the use of their names when they talk freely about a family history more tragic and terrible perhaps than that of any other major American poet.

Chapter X

1. Emerson is confusing the common black-capped chickadee with the tufted titmouse, as the spring and winter songs of the bird, quoted toward the end of the poem, make clear. The "nature note" thus is not only "rare" but mistaken. Still, the lesson he learns is not invalidated by the mistake, for both birds are noted for their curiosity and friendliness, their lack of fear of people, and their presence in the winter in southern New England.

2. In Emerson's "Fate" we find not only the general theme of "Sand Dunes"—that "thought" counters "fate," that "mind" makes for freedom despite nature's "ferocities" (Emerson's word) — but the very images and some of the words in which the ideas in the poem are expressed.

3. The Middlebury anecdote was reported to me by Mrs. Grace S. Davis, Curator of the Abernethy Collection of American Literature. For the Dartmouth talk, see "Robert Frost on 'Extravagance'" in the March 1963 number of the *Dartmouth Alumni Magazine*. The talk was delivered on the evening of November 27th, 1962. Frost died on January 29, 1963.

   The subject of Frost's specific debts to Emerson and Thoreau in specific poems remains to be explored. Since we know that Frost continued to read both writers all his life, it would be surprising if a large number of his poems did not reflect his reading. For example, I suspect that "After Apple Picking" owes a good deal to Emerson's essays "Intellect" ("If you gather apples . . . you shall still see apples . . .") and "Experience" ("Sleep lingers all our lifetime about our eyes. . . . All things swim and glitter").

Chapter XI

1. These three "rules" were also mentioned by F. S. Flint in his "Imagisme" note in the March 1913 issue of *Poetry* magazine. Flint does not claim credit for them; he simply reports them as common property of the Imagists. Pound for once, I think, did not claim too much for himself when he attributed them to a mutual agreement arrived at by himself, H.D., and Richard Aldington, who would later become, briefly, H.D.'s husband.

2. Emerson's affinity with one of the chief characteristics of *haiku* — the wiping out of the distinction between the "self" and the "thing" observed by the self, is implied everywhere in his early work. Consider the implication of the italicized clause in the following passage from "The Method of Nature," delivered as a lecture in 1841. The italics are mine.

> Therefore man must be on his guard against this cup of enchantments, and must look at nature with a supernatural eye. By piety alone, by conversing with the cause of nature, is he safe and commands it. And because *all knowledge is assimilation to the object of knowledge, as the power or genius is ecstatic, so must its science or the description of it be.*

Haiku poems, which Emerson had no opportunity to know about, imply an "ecstatic" relation between "knower" and "known" in the sense in which Emerson means "ecstatic" here.

Chapter XII

1. Neither of the two existing books on Imagism treats H.D. as other than, or more than, an Imagist. In 1931, when H.D.

published her *Red Roses for Bronze,* she was embalmed by Glenn Hughes (*Imagism and the Imagists*) as "The Perfect Imagist," despite the fact *Red Roses for Bronze* contains no Imagist poems. Twenty years later, more than a half-dozen years after she had bade farewell to both Modernism and Imagism in *The Walls Do Not Fall,* Stanley K. Coffman, Jr., in *Imagism,* continued to treat her as "the perfect Imagist," though he acknowledged, without specifying, that she escaped the label: "Only H.D. wrote consistently the kind of verse that Pound at first demanded of the Imagists, and neither she nor Pound confined themselves to this early idea." True. But some years before, H.D. had denounced and caricatured the idea. One may conclude that H.D. has not been *read,* even perhaps by those who have written about her.

Chapter XIV

1. I take the term "creative translation" from J. P. Sullivan, *Ezra Pound and Sextus Propertius: A Study in Creative Translation* (Austin: The University of Texas Press, 1964). Chapter I surveys scholarly opinion on the question of whether Pound ought to be thought of as translating or as adapting.

2. In the last twenty years or so, a great deal of scholarship has been devoted to the *haiku* and to the meanings they express. R. H. Blyth has devoted four volumes to the subject (*Eastern Culture,* Tokyo: Hokuseido Press, 1949), and many others have written extensively on the subject. The only conclusion to be drawn from all this scholarship is that Pound had only the faintest inkling of what *haiku* are all about.

   Blyth lists thirteen characteristics of *haiku,* of which the first, and most important, is selflessness, or "interpenetration with all things." This "loss of self," as we in the West might call it, is of course precisely what does *not* happen in "In a Station of the Metro," in which the speaker sees people as *things* and compares them with other *things,* both types of things beautiful, but wholly outside him, an object of his experience. Here, and everywhere else in his poetry, Pound expresses Western rationalistic and dualistic categories.

Support for this statement may be found wherever one turns in modern scholarship on Zen and its various expressions in art, of which the *haiku* form was only one. See, for example, Kenneth Yasuda, *The Japanese Haiku* (Tokyo: Charles E. Tuttle Company, 1957); and Nancy Wilson Ross, *The World of Zen: An East-West Anthology* (New York: Random House, 1960), especially the section called "Zen and the Arts," in which the subsection on *haiku* poetry is written by Alan Watts. Paul Reps, perhaps the best contemporary Western expositor of Zen, has asked, in introducing his fine compilation of Zen and pre-Zen writings, "Dare we open our doors to the source of our being? What are flesh and bones for?" Later he translates what is often rendered as "nothingness" as "No-thingness, spirit." (Paul Reps, *Zen Flesh, Zen Bones: A Collection of Zen and Pre-Zen Writings* (Garden City: Doubleday Anchor Books, 1961), pp. xv, 160. Pound would presumably have thought such a question meaningless, and such a translation mistaken.

In Ross's anthology, which devotes a whole section to the "universality" of Zen, citing quotations from Western writers who shared the Zen spirit, neither Fenollosa nor Pound is mentioned. Nor is either of them mentioned in F. S. C. Northrop's encyclopedic *The Meeting of East and West: An Inquiry Concerning World Understanding* (New York: Macmillan, 1946). If this seems to us surprising, in view of the length (531 pages) of Northrop's book and his purpose, which is to survey the entire subject, we have a greater surprise in store for us: Van Meter Ames, who saw aspects or reflections of Zen almost *everywhere* in American literature, even in rationalists like Paine and Jefferson, did *not* see it in Pound. *Zen and American Thought* (Honolulu: University of Hawaii Press, 1962.) Ames's very broad conception of Zen, which *permits* him to see it in writers like Paine, has been questioned by D. T. Suzuki, the chief Japanese scholarly authority on the subject; see William Barrett, ed., *Zen Buddhism: Selected Writings of D. T. Suzuki* (Garden City: Doubleday Anchor Books, 1956), pp. 259–260.

The reasons why neither Pound nor Fenollosa appears in any modern discussion of Zen and its art forms are not hard to discover. As D. T. Suzuki says (Barrett, *Zen Buddhism,* p. 105), one of the marks of "Satori, or Enlightenment" —

or mystical awakening — is a "Sense of the Beyond. Terminology may differ in different religions, but in satori there is always what we may call a sense of the Beyond; the experience indeed is my own but I feel it to be rooted elsewhere." In his *Mysticism: Christian and Buddhist* (New York: Harper, 1957), p. xix, Suzuki also says that he finds the thoughts of "Meister Eckhart as representative of Christian mysticism" coming closest to the central meaning of Zen and Shin. "Eckhart, Zen, and Shin thus can be grouped together as belonging to the great school of mysticism." But Pound built a career on his rejection of any sort of mysticism, however loosely defined. It ought not to be necessary to say that what he rejected he did not understand.

If Pound's "scientific positivism" makes him seem, to those who understand Zen as mystical, not to have penetrated the meaning of what he wrote so much about, his alienation from Nature — the "not-me" — makes him seem equally irrelevant as an interpreter of the Zen art forms to those who interpret Zen more "naturalistically," or "pantheistically." For those who reject the "mystical" analogy between Zen and Western religion, there remains what has been called "interpenetration," the empathic identification of subject and object, seer and seen, knower and known.

Once again, it should not be necessary at this point to stress Pound's vehement insistence on exactly the opposite of what the "naturalistic" interpreters of Zen see as its chief meaning: the achievement of a way of seeing that might be called "the way of the innocent eye" — Emerson's way, in short. For a contemporary view of "the innocent eye" approach to a sense of relatedness, see, in addition to the last chapter of this book, *The Education of Vision* in the "Vision and Value Series," edited by Gyorgy Kepes (New York: Braziller, 1966–). For a contemporary account of the nature and meaning of mystical experience, see W. T. Stace, *Religion and the Modern Mind* (Philadelphia: Lippincott Keystone Book, 1960; originally published 1952), pp. 275–276; and his *Mysticism and Philosophy* (Philadelphia: Lippincott, 1960), *passim.* But James's *Varieties* is still the unsurpassed classic in the field.

In view of Karl Shapiro's attraction to Zen-like mysticism in Whitman, Bucke, and Henry Miller, and his unqualified condemnation of Eliot for praising and promoting Pound, I find it interesting that Eliot himself recognized that Pound's response to foreign literatures — to literature generally, he *ought* to have said — was purely *technical,* which is to say, superficial. Writing in his Introduction to *The Literary Essays of Ezra Pound,* Eliot, after praising Pound's criticism as indispensable, added, seemingly as an afterthought, "The limitation of Pound's kind [of criticism] is in its concentration on the craft of letters. . . . When we want to try to *understand* [italics mine] what a foreign literature means, or meant, to the people to whom it belongs . . . we must go elsewhere."

I am aware of the fact that Earl Miner, in "Pound, Haiku, and the Image" (reprinted in Walter Sutton, ed., *Ezra Pound: A Collection of Critical Essays* ["Twentieth Century Views"], [Englewood Cliffs, N. J.: Prentice-Hall, 1963]), has presented an argument contrary to the one above. Miner believes that Pound's knowledge of *haiku* was deep and penetrating, and that it did significantly influence his idea of the image: "I hope to show how this one form of Japanese poetry has influenced Pound's theories of poetic imagery, and has offered him techniques which have exfoliated into all his writing."

I remain unconvinced. In the first place, Mr. Miner accepts Pound's ideas as though their truth were self-evident. ("We have Pound's own words to attest to his absorption in *haiku* about 1912.") Citing Pound's explanation of how he wrote "In a Station of the Metro," in which Pound referred to the example of Japanese "hokku," Mr. Miner concludes that "Pound's indebtedness to *haiku* is as definite as it is profound," since from the *haiku* form Pound got the idea for what he called "superposition" — juxtaposing two images without comment. The remainder of the essay is concerned with technicalities of form.

It is theoretically possible, of course, to begin with the *form* of an art and move to an understanding of its *meaning.* But Mr. Miner gives no evidence of being interested in form as expressive. (Pound *was,* in his limited and rigid way; he thought of the imagistic way of writing as expressive of "scientific realism," which of course has nothing whatever to do with intuitive and mystical Zen poetry.)

I surmise that there are two reasons why Mr. Miner did not reach a correct conclusion. First, he gives no evidence in the article of having thought about the significance of the fact that *haiku* are one of the Zen art forms. Second, he writes as though he were under the spell of the Modernist defensive rationalization that "form," or "style," or "craft," or "technique" is ALL there is to say about literature. (Eliot kept saying this; Pound kept saying this; Williams kept saying this — why shouldn't it be true?)

Of course, Pound's own language in the Vorticism essay makes clear the limits of his understanding. He speaks of "hokku" poems as "imagistic," without indicating that their "imagism" is in any way different in its implications from the way *he* had defined Imagism several years before. He speaks of the way they place "one idea on top of another," thus revealing at once two odd notions: that poetry, like sculpture, is an essentially *spatial* form; and that *haiku* poems deal with "ideas," which are precisely what they try to avoid as they concentrate on apprehending the "thinginess of the thing," as Williams might have said. Pound's own words make it perfectly clear that he could not have been more mistaken about what it was he was citing as authority for his own practice.

That it was not necessary, merely because of lack of detailed knowledge, to miss the meaning of oriental literature, even if one had far less "knowledge" of it than Pound, is shown by the examples of Emerson and Whitman. For a "case" much closer in time to Pound, consider Lafcadio Hearn. (See Beongcheon Yu, *An Ape of Gods: The Art and Thought of Lafcadio Hearn* [Detroit: Wayne, 1964].)

The reason why Pound missed the meaning of *haiku* and *Noh* plays can only be guessed at, of course, but I would suggest that, apart from the rigidity of his personality, he believed in a crude scientific positivism, in what I have called "scientism." A poet is not required to be a philosopher, but if he makes philosophic claims for his poetry, and particularly if he insists that there is a "method" behind and within his poems, he has made it obligatory upon us to judge him as a "philosopher" — that is, to judge the rightness or wrongness, the logic or illogic, of his *ideas.* If, after he has made the "scholarly" claim, scholars find him ignorant, and not only ignorant but in temperament, tone, and method a bad scholar, he can hardly claim exemption from "scholarly" judgment — that is, from those who know more than he did of his cherished "facts."

3. The literary editor of *The Boston Evening Transcript* during these years was William Stanley Braithwaite, a quadroon, as Pound no doubt knew. Pound's racism was not, as some of his friends argued in his defense at the time of the Bollingen Award affair, a late development.

Chapter XV

1. Modernism might be said to have begun with the assumption that science had proved false the idea of the self as transcendent. If the soul could not be found in the laboratory, one would have to look *beyond* the individual self to find real values — to the impersonal "Cause," the redeeming Institution, or the super-personal Way. Eliot and Pound, along with many in their generation, sought for something to fill the gap left by the evaporation of the idea of "the transcendent self."

Chapter XVI

1. Emerson and Stevens often approach each other so closely in their views of poetry and imagination, and sometimes of other subjects too, that it is tempting to push the parallels in their thinking to the point of seeing Stevens as the modern Emerson. But it seems to me that we ought to proceed in this direction with considerable caution, even though there is room for much more exploration of the relationship of the two than has yet been undertaken. When they sound most alike, they may at times really mean crucially different things, even by the same words.

   S. F. Morse, in *The Southern Review* (1965), has discussed some of the Emerson-Stevens parallels, including the similarities between the former's *Nature* and the latter's "Academic Discourse in Havana." Mr. Morse points out, in a cautionary note, that "Stevens never acknowledged any debt to Emerson, nor did he regard the poet as a prophet. . . . One cannot make Stevens an heir of Emerson. . . ."

One might go further than this, to say, first, that Stevens was conscious of the real contrast between his own "realism" and Transcendental Idealism; and, second, that in his thinking about the contrast, he showed a partial misunderstanding of Transcendentalism and the kind of writing it produced, so that he ended by making the contrast more complete than it actually was. The following passage from Stevens' Introduction to a volume of poems by S. F. Morse reveals a conception of Transcendental writing that approaches caricature. Praising Morse for being a truly New England poet, Stevens mentions Thoreau, whom Morse has quoted, and then goes on:

> One of his poems, "The Track into the Swamp," relates to one of the abandoned roads, the lost roads, of which New England is so full. We have been accustomed to think that at the far end of such roads the ghosts of the Transcendentalists still live. Obviously they do not live at this end. Mr. Morse is not the ghost of a Transcendentalist. If he has any use at all for Kant, it is to keep up the window in which the cord is broken. He is anti-transcendental. His subject is the particulars of experience. He is a realist; he tries to get at New England experience, at New England past and present, at New England foxes and snow and thunderheads.

To praise a poet for being "anti-transcendental" because he is interested in "the particulars of experience" — especially to do so when Thoreau is the Transcendentalist in mind! — is to reveal oneself as very remote from the books that might have corrected the notion that Transcendentalists were not interested in "particulars." If Stevens read Emerson and Thoreau in his youth, in college for example, as presumably he would have, there is no evidence that I know of in his prose or verse that he retained any real knowledge of them. I suspect that he was unaware of the often close parallels between his own thought and that of Emerson.

It is of course possible to hold that Stevens ought to be

thought of as Emerson's "heir" even though Stevens himself would not have thought so. In "The Central Man: Emerson, Whitman, Wallace Stevens" (*The Massachusetts Review,* Winter, 1966), Harold Bloom argues persuasively precisely to this effect. Having asserted that "Emerson evaded and Whitman abandoned their mutual sense of centrality" (the "central man" has been defined as "most authentic when he ebbs, and merges himself, wrecked, as part of the sands and drift, man absolute, but man on the dump, a savior who could not save himself"), Mr. Bloom writes, "The heir of both these bards . . . is Wallace Stevens, whom it is no longer eccentric to regard as the ironically balanced fulfillment of the American Romantic tradition in poetry."

There are many insights in Mr. Bloom's very personal and committed article, but it seems to me that the plausibility of his claim that Stevens is Emerson's true "heir" and "fulfillment" rests in part upon his isolating a strain in Emerson's thought, the pure "humanist" strain, which is not only more prominent in Emerson's later work, when he was taking in sail, as it were, after Waldo's death, than it is of his early, more creative period, but exists even in the late work in a theistic context that qualifies its meaning.

It is significant that the passage from Emerson that Mr. Bloom quotes is from a *Journal* entry written in 1846, in which Emerson is remembering the faces that have "stamped themselves in fire" on his heart — Waldo's, no doubt, and his first wife's, and perhaps his brother's. The thrust of the passage (which begins, "We shall one day talk with the central man" and ends, "I dreamed and did not know my dreams.") is toward a vision of the unity and timelessness of man, toward what R. P. Warren suggests in *Promises* when the dreaming or visionary voice in "Ballad of a Sweet Dream of Peace" says in reply to the literalist voice, "You fool, poor fool, all Time is a dream, and we're all one Flesh, at last."

Though Emerson speaks in the entry of "these great secular personalities" — Socrates, Dante, and "the Saint Jesus" are among those mentioned — the force of the word "secular" as he uses it here is philosophically neutral, meaning merely "existing in time." All those mentioned in the passage are dead, no longer existing in time. The passage as a whole may be interpreted as closer to the endings of "Monadnoc" and "Threnody" than to Stevens' "Asides on the Oboe," to which Mr. Bloom compares it, even though Stevens uses the phrase Emerson had used, "the central man." The Emersonian passage is visionary in a religious sense. Its central metaphor is a dream.

By contrast, when Stevens uses the words "the central man," he does so to suggest an ideal realizable in *time,* the ideal of "The impossible possible philosopher's man,/ The man who has had the time to think enough . . ." The lines immediately preceding this definition of the "central man" of the future suggest that the passage as a whole ought to be read as indicating Stevens' awareness of, and reply to, the neo-orthodox religious trend of the time — 1940. A year before Stevens composed the poem, Reinhold Niebuhr had published his two-volume work *The Nature and Destiny of Man,* which immediately began to have a very large influence. If Stevens is replying to neo-orthodoxy, then Niebuhr may be thought of as the "you" addressed in lines that summarize the convictions behind his restatement of Pauline theology:

> If you say on the hautboy man is not enough,
> Can never stand as god, is ever wrong
> In the end, however naked, tall, there is still
> The impossible possible philosopher's man. . . .

It seems clear to me that the thrust of Emerson's passage is toward a vision of timelessness, while that of Stevens is toward the ideal of a more perfectly rational secular man. If this is so, the differences between the two are at least as important as the fact that both make use of the same words to describe the man they envision. On the other hand, it is also true that the Emerson of *Conduct of Life* is closer to Stevens than the Emerson of the early works is; and that the Stevens of the last years moved, in some respects, back toward Emerson; so that an argument for their agreement on philosophical matters would find its best evidence in very late Emerson and very late Stevens.

Chapter XVII

1. In the course of a speech he gave in 1958, when he was eighty, Sandburg illustrated a point by quoting Emerson at length, from memory. An early favorite, Emerson was apparently coming back into the foreground of his attention in these years when he was writing the poems in *Honey and Salt.* It was the vision shared by Emerson and Whitman that he had come back to. See Harry Golden, *Carl Sandburg* (New York: World Publishing Company, 1961), p. 39.

Chapter XIX

1. Crane's letters, from which I have been quoting, are now, fortunately, readily available in a paperback edition: Brom Weber, ed., *The Letters of Hart Crane, 1916–1932* (Berkeley: University of California Press, 1965). I have quoted from pp. 322 and 324 of this edition.

2. The lines being translated here are the following:

   En la interior bodega
   De mi amado bebị y cuando salía
   Por toda aquesta vega,
   Ya cosa no sabía,
   Y el ganado perdị, que antes seguía.

3. St. John's second line, rendered by Campbell as "Though in pitch-darkness, with no ray," seems to me more powerful in the original. "Sin luz y a oscuras viviendo" may be translated as "without light, living in and toward darkness."
   The lines being translated by Campbell are the following:

   Sin arrimo y con arrimo,
   Sin luz y a oscuras viviendo,
   Todo me voy consumiendo.

   Mi alma está desasida
   De toda cosa criada,

Y sabre si levantada,
Y en un sabrosa vida,
Sólo en su Dios arrimada.

4. Norman Friedman, *E. E. Cummings: The Art of His Poetry* (Baltimore: Johns Hopkins Press, 1960), p. 66.

5. In *i: six nonlectures* Cummings writes of S. Foster Damon, under the rubric "Let us now consider friendship": "who opened my eyes and ears not merely to Domenico Theotocopuli and William Blake, but to all ultra (at the moment) modern music and poetry and painting." (P. 50.)

6. After reading these cautious sentences, Mrs. Cummings wrote me that Cummings had read and reread his favorite Emerson essays over and over all his life, marking his copies so freely that he finally bought fresh copies and gave his original ones to the Harvard Library, where they may now be studied.

Bibliography

Bibliography

I. *The Poets Treated*

A list of their works
in verse and prose referred to, quoted from, or drawn upon

The following list of works is not intended as a complete, or even as a "selected," bibliography of American poetry. A number of excellent bibliographies of the subject are easily available, the most recent and one of the most useful being that included in Allen, Rideout, and Robinson, eds., *American Poetry* (New York, 1965) [an anthology].

The following list includes only those titles alluded to, referred to by name, quoted from, or consciously drawn upon without being named or alluded to in this book.

ANNE BRADSTREET, 1612–1672.

The Tenth Muse Lately Sprung up in America. Or Severall Poems, Compiled with Great Variety of Wit and Learning, Full of Delight. London, 1650.

(The first volume of original verse by an American poet.)

Several Poems Compiled with Great Variety of Wit and Learning, Full of Delight. Cambridge, 1678.

(A revised edition of *The Tenth Muse,* with new poems added.)

The Works of Anne Bradstreet, Jeannine Hensley, ed. Cambridge, 1967.

PHILIP PAIN, dates unknown.

Daily Meditations: or, Quotidian Preparations for and Considerations of Death and Eternity. Cambridge, 1668. (The first volume of original verse by an American poet printed in America.)

MICHAEL WIGGLESWORTH, 1631–1705.

The Day of Doom. London, 1662.

EDWARD TAYLOR, c. 1642–1729.

The Poems of Edward Taylor, D. E. Stanford, ed. New Haven, 1960.

LEMUEL HOPKINS, 1750–1801.
The Democratiad. Philadelphia, 1795.

JOHN TRUMBULL, 1750–1831.
The Progress of Dulness. New Haven, 1772–1773.
M'Fingle. Hartford, 1782.

PHILIP FRENEAU, 1752–1832.
The Poems of Philip Freneau, F. L. Pattee, ed. Princeton, 1902–1907, 3 vols.
Poems of Freneau, H. H. Clark, ed. New York, 1929.

TIMOTHY DWIGHT, 1752–1817.
The Conquest of Canaan. Hartford, 1785.
The Triumph of Infidelity. "Printed in the World," 1788.
Greenfield Hill. New York, 1794.

JOEL BARLOW, 1754–1812.
The Vision of Columbus. Hartford, 1787.
Hasty Pudding. Hartford, 1796.
The Columbiad. Baltimore, 1807.

WILLIAM CULLEN BRYANT, 1794–1878.
The Poetical Works of William Cullen Bryant, H. C. Sturges, ed. New York, 1903.

RALPH WALDO EMERSON, 1803–1882.
Poems. Boston, 1847.
May-Day and Other Pieces. Boston, 1867.
Parnassus (edited by Emerson). Boston, 1874.
The Complete Works of Ralph Waldo Emerson, Edward Waldo Emerson, ed., 12 vols. Boston, 1903–1904.
The Journals of Ralph Waldo Emerson, Edward Waldo Emerson and Waldo Emerson Forbes, eds., 10 vols. Boston, 1909–1914.
The Early Lectures of Ralph Waldo Emerson, Whicher, Spiller, and Williams, eds., 2 vols. Cambridge, 1961–1964.
The Journals and Miscellaneous Notebooks of Ralph Waldo Emerson, Gilman, Ferguson, *et al.,* eds., 6 vols. to date. Cambridge, 1960–1966.

HENRY WADSWORTH LONGFELLOW, 1807–1882.

Voices of the Night. Cambridge, 1839.

Christus. Boston, 1872.

The Complete Poetical Works of Henry Wadsworth Longfellow, Cambridge edition, Horace E. Scudder, ed. Boston, 1893.

JOHN GREENLEAF WHITTIER, 1807–1892.

The Complete Poetical Works of John Greenleaf Whittier, Cambridge edition, Horace E. Scudder, ed. Boston, 1894.

OLIVER WENDELL HOLMES, 1809–1894.

Poems. Boston, 1836.

Poems. Boston, 1849.

The Complete Poetical Works of Oliver Wendell Holmes, Horace E. Scudder, ed. Boston, 1895.

The Writings of Oliver Wendell Holmes, Riverside edition, 13 vols. Boston, 1891.

EDGAR ALLAN POE, 1809–1849.

Tamerlane and Other Poems. Boston, 1827.

Al Araaf, Tamerlane, and Minor Poems. Baltimore, 1829.

The Poems of Edgar Allan Poe, Killis Campbell, ed. Boston, 1917.

JONES VERY, 1813–1880.

Essays and Poems, Ralph Waldo Emerson, ed. Boston, 1839.

Poems and Essays, Clarke and Bartol, eds. Boston, 1886.

Bartlett, William I., *Jones Very: Emerson's "Brave Saint."* Durham, 1942. (For further poems, not in Clarke and Bartol.)

HENRY DAVID THOREAU, 1817–1862.

The Collected Poems of Henry Thoreau, Carl Bode, ed. Baltimore, 1964.

Walden. Boston, 1854.

Cape Cod, S. E. Thoreau and W. E. Channing, eds. Boston, 1865.

The Writings of Henry David Thoreau, Walden edition, Horace E. Scudder *et al.,* eds. Boston, 1906.

J. G. HOLLAND, 1819–1881.

The Marble Prophecy, and Other Poems. New York, 1782.

JAMES RUSSELL LOWELL, 1819–1891.

A Fable for Critics. Boston, 1848.

The Biglow Papers: First Series. Boston, 1848.

The Biglow Papers: Second Series. Boston, 1867.

The Complete Poetical Works of James Russell Lowell, Horace E. Scudder, ed. Boston, 1897.

HERMAN MELVILLE, 1819–1891.

Typee. New York, 1846.

White-Jacket. New York, 1850.

Moby-Dick. New York, 1851.

Battle-Pieces. New York, 1866.

Clarel. New York, 1876.

John Marr and Other Sailors. New York, 1888.

Timoleon. New York, 1891.

Collected Poems, H. P. Vincent, ed. Chicago, 1947.

WALT WHITMAN, 1819–1892.

Leaves of Grass. New York, 1855. (Revised and enlarged editions: 1856, 1860, 1867, 1871, 1876, 1881, 1888, 1889, 1891–1892.)

Leaves of Grass: Readers' Edition, Blodgett and Bradley, eds. New York, 1964.

The Collected Writings of Walt Whitman, Allen, Bradley, *et al.,* eds. New York, 1961–? (The definitive edition, in progress.)

FREDERICK GODDARD TUCKERMAN, 1821–1873.

Poems. Boston, 1860.

Poems. Boston, 1864.

Poems. Boston, 1867.

The Sonnets of Frederick Goddard Tuckerman, Witter Bynner, ed. New York, 1931.

The Complete Poems of Frederick Goddard Tuckerman, N. Scott Nomaday, ed. New York, 1965.

HENRY TIMROD, 1828–1867.

The Poems of Henry Timrod. New York, 1873.

EMILY DICKINSON, 1830–1886.

Poems by Emily Dickinson, Mabel Loomis Todd and T. W. Higginson, eds. Boston, 1890.

Poems by Emily Dickinson, Mabel Loomis Todd and T. W. Higginson, eds. Boston, 1891.

Poems by Emily Dickinson, Mabel Loomis Todd, ed. Boston, 1896.

The Poems of Emily Dickinson, 3 vols., variorum edition, Thomas H. Johnson, ed. Cambridge, 1955.

The Letters of Emily Dickinson, 3 vols., Thomas H. Johnson, and Theodora Ward, eds. Cambridge, 1958.

The Complete Poems of Emily Dickinson, Thomas H. Johnson, ed. Boston, 1960. (Johnson's one-volume edition, the one normally quoted in this book.)

SIDNEY LANIER, 1842–1881.

The Science of English Verse. New York, 1880.

The Centennial Edition of Sidney Lanier, 10 vols., C. R. Anderson, ed. Baltimore, 1945.

HARRIET MONROE, 1860–1936.

The Difference, and Other Poems. Chicago, 1924.

EDGAR LEE MASTERS, 1869–1950.

Spoon River Anthology. New York, 1915.

The Great Valley. New York, 1916.

Songs and Satires. New York, 1916.

Toward the Gulf. New York, 1918.

Starved Rock. New York, 1919.

Doomsday Book. New York, 1920.

WILLIAM VAUGHN MOODY, 1869–1910.

Poems. Boston, 1901.

Gloucester Moors and Other Poems. Boston, 1910.

The Poems and Plays of William Vaughn Moody, 2 vols., J. M. Manly, ed. Boston, 1912.

(With Robert Morse Lovett), *A History of English Literature.* New York, 1902.

EDWIN ARLINGTON ROBINSON, 1869–1935.
The Torrent and the Night Before. Boston, 1896.
The Children of the Night. Boston, 1897.
Captain Craig and Other Poems. Boston, 1902.
The Town Down River. New York, 1910.
Van Zorn. New York, 1914.
The Porcupine. New York, 1915.
Collected Poems of Edwin Arlington Robinson. New York, 1937.
Thoreau's Last Letter, With a Note by Edwin Arlington Robinson. Amenia, New York, 1925.
Selected Letters of Edwin Arlington Robinson. New York, 1940.
The Letters of Edwin Arlington Robinson to Howard George Schmitt, Carl J. Weber, ed. Waterville, Maine, 1943.
Untriangulated Stars: Letters of Edwin Arlington Robinson to Harry de Forest Smith, 1890–1905, Denham Sutcliffe, ed. Cambridge, 1947.

STEPHEN CRANE, 1871–1900.
Maggie, A Girl of the Streets. New York, 1893.
Black Riders. Boston, 1895.
The Red Badge of Courage. New York, 1895.
War Is Kind. New York, 1899.
The Collected Poems of Stephen Crane, Wilson Follett, ed. New York, 1930.

AMY LOWELL, 1874–1925.
A Dome of Many-Colored Glass. Boston, 1912.
Some Imagist Poets: An Annual Anthology. Boston, 1915–1917.
Pictures of the Floating World. Boston, 1919.
A Critical Fable. Boston, 1922.
Complete Poetical Works. Boston, 1955.

TRUMBULL STICKNEY, 1874–1904.
The Poems of Trumbull Stickney. Boston, 1905.

ROBERT FROST, 1874–1963.
A Boy's Will. London, 1913.
North of Boston. London, 1914.

ROBERT FROST, *continued*

Mountain Interval. New York, 1916.

New Hampshire: A Poem with Notes and Grace Notes. New York, 1923.

West-Running Brook. New York, 1928.

The Complete Poems of Robert Frost. New York, 1949.

In the Clearing. New York, 1962.

"Robert Frost on 'Extravagance,'" *Dartmouth Alumni Magazine.* March 1963.

Selected Letters of Robert Frost, Lawrance Thompson, ed. New York, 1964.

Selected Prose of Robert Frost, Hyde Cox and E. C. Lathem, eds. New York, 1966.

CARL SANDBURG, 1878–1967.

Chicago Poems. New York, 1916.

Cornhuskers. New York, 1918.

The Family of Man, with Edward Steichen. New York, 1955.

Honey and Salt. New York, 1963.

VACHEL LINDSAY, 1879–1931.

Collected Poems. New York, 1925.

WALLACE STEVENS, 1879–1955.

Harmonium. New York, 1923.

Ideas of Order. New York, 1935.

Parts of a World. New York, 1942.

Three Academic Pieces. Cummington, Mass., 1947.

The Necessary Angel: Essays on Reality and Imagination. New York, 1951.

The Collected Poems of Wallace Stevens. New York, 1954.

Opus Posthumous, S. F. Morse, ed. New York, 1957.

WILLIAM CARLOS WILLIAMS, 1883–1963.

Poems. Rutherford, N.J., 1909.

The Tempers. London, 1913.

Al Que Quiere! A Book of Poems. Boston, 1917.

Kora in Hell. Boston, 1920.

Collected Poems, 1921–1931. New York, 1934.

An Early Martyr and Other Poems. New York, 1935.

The Complete Collected Poems of William Carlos Williams. 1906–1938.

WILLIAM CARLOS WILLIAMS, *continued*

Selected Poems, Randall Jarrell, ed. New York, 1949.

Collected Later Poems. New York, 1950.

Collected Earlier Poems. New York, 1951.

The Autobiography of William Carlos Williams. New York, 1951.

The Dog and the Fever: Translated by William Carlos Williams and Raquel Helene Williams. Hamden, 1954.

Desert Music. New York, 1954.

Journey to Love. New York, 1955.

The Selected Letters of William Carlos Williams, J. C. Thirlwall, ed. New York, 1957.

I Wanted to Write a Poem, Edith Heal, ed. Boston, 1958.

Paterson. New York, 1963.

SARA TEASDALE, 1884–1933.

Strange Victory. New York, 1933.

The Collected Poems of Sara Teasdale. New York, 1937.

ELINOR WYLIE, 1885–1928.

The Collected Poems of Elinor Wylie. New York, 1932.

EZRA POUND, 1885–

A Lume Spento. Milano, Italy, 1908.

Personae of Ezra Pound. London, 1909.

Exultations of Ezra Pound. London, 1909.

Des Imagistes. New York, 1914.

Cathay: Translations by Ezra Pound. London, 1915.

Lustra of Ezra Pound. London, 1916.

Hugh Selwyn Mauberley. London, 1920.

ABC of Reading. London, 1934.

The Cantos of Ezra Pound. New York, 1948.

The Pisan Cantos. New York, 1948.

The Letters of Ezra Pound, D. D. Paige, ed. New York, 1950.

The Literary Essays of Ezra Pound, T. S. Eliot, ed. New York, 1954.

Section: Rock-Drill: 85–95 de los Cantares. New York, 1955.

Thrones: 96–109 de los Cantares. New York, 1959.

H. D. (HILDA DOOLITTLE), 1886–1961.
Collected Poems. New York, 1925.
Red Roses for Bronze. Boston, 1931.
The Walls Do Not Fall. London, 1944.
Tribute to the Angels. London, 1945.
The Flowering of the Rod. London, 1946.
By Avon River. New York, 1949.
Tribute to Freud. New York, 1956.
Selected Poems. New York, 1957.
Bid Me to Live. New York, 1960.
Helen in Egypt. New York, 1961.

JOHN GOULD FLETCHER, 1886–1950.
Irradiations: Sand and Spray. Boston, 1915.
Goblins and Pagodas. Boston, 1916.
"The Orient and Contemporary Poetry," in Arthur E. Christy, ed., *The Asian Legacy and American Life.* New York, 1945.
The Burning Mountain. New York, 1946.

ROBINSON JEFFERS, 1887–1963.
Flagons and Apples. Los Angeles, 1912.
Californians. New York, 1916.
The Selected Poetry of Robinson Jeffers. New York, 1938.

MARIANNE MOORE, 1887–
Poems. New York, 1921.
Selected Poems, with an Introduction by T. S. Eliot. New York, 1935.
What Are Years? New York, 1941.
Nevertheless. New York, 1944.
Collected Poems. New York, 1951.
Like a Bulwark. New York, 1957.
O To Be a Dragon. New York, 1959.

T. S. ELIOT, 1888–1965.
Prufrock and Other Observations. London, 1917.
Poems. London, 1919.
The Sacred Wood. London, 1920.
The Waste Land. New York, 1922.
Poems, 1909–1925.

T. S. ELIOT, *continued*

Thoughts After Lambeth. London, 1931.
Murder in the Cathedral. London and New York, 1935.
The Idea of a Christian Society. New York, 1940.
Four Quartets. New York, 1943.
Notes Towards the Definition of a Culture. New York, 1949.
The Cocktail Party. New York and London, 1950.
The Confidential Clerk. New York, 1920.
The Elder Statesman. New York, 1959.
Collected Poems, 1909–1962. New York, 1963.

JOHN CROWE RANSOM, 1888–

Poems About God. New York, 1919.
Chills and Fever. New York, 1924.
Two Gentlemen in Bonds. New York, 1927.
(Contributor to) *I'll Take My Stand.* New York, 1930.
God Without Thunder. New York, 1930.
The World's Body. New York, 1938.
The New Criticism. New York, 1941.
Selected Poems. New York, 1945.
Poems and Essays. New York, 1955.
Selected Poems. New York, 1963.

CONRAD AIKEN, 1889–

Turns and Movies. Boston, 1916.
The Jig of Forslin. Boston, 1916.
The Charnel Rose. Boston, 1918.
Senlin. London, 1925.
Preludes for Memnon. New York, 1931.
Time in the Rock. New York, 1936.
And in the Human Heart. New York, 1940.
Brownstone Eclogues and Other Poems. New York, 1942.
Divine Pilgrim. New York, 1949.
Sheepfold Hill. New York, 1953.
Collected Poems. New York, 1953.
Statement in *Poets on Poetry,* Howard Nemerov, ed. New York, 1966.

ARCHIBALD MACLEISH, 1892–

Pot of Earth. Boston, 1925.
New Found Land. Boston, 1930.

ARCHIBALD MACLEISH, *continued*

Conquistador. Boston, 1932.
Frescoes for Mr. Rockefeller's City. New York, 1933.
Poems, 1924–1933. Boston, 1933.
Public Speech. London, 1936.
The American Story. New York, 1944.
Songs for Eve. Boston, 1954.
J. B.: A play in verse. Boston, 1958.

EDNA ST. VINCENT MILLAY, 1892–1950.

Renascence. New York, 1917.
Collected Poems. New York, 1956.

E. E. CUMMINGS, 1894–1963.

The Enormous Room. New York, 1922.
Eimi. New York, 1933.
i: six nonlectures. Cambridge, 1953.
Poems, 1923–1954. New York, 1954.
95 Poems. New York, 1958.
73 Poems. New York, 1962.

HART CRANE, 1899–1932.

White Buildings. New York, 1926.
The Bridge. New York, 1930.
Collected Poems of Hart Crane, Waldo Frank, ed. New York, 1933.
The Letters of Hart Crane, Brown Weber, ed. New York, 1952.

ALLEN TATE, 1899–

Stonewall Jackson. New York, 1928.
Poems, 1928–1931. New York, 1932.
Reactionary Essays on Poetry and Ideas. New York, 1936.
Reason in Madness. New York, 1941.
Poems, 1922–1947. New York, 1948.
On the Limits of Poetry. New York, 1948.
Poems. Denver, 1961.

ROBERT PENN WARREN, 1905–

John Brown. New York, 1929.
Pondy Woods and Other Poems. New York, 1930.
Statement in *I'll Take My Stand*. New York, 1930.

ROBERT PENN WARREN, *continued*

Thirty-six Poems. New York, 1935.

(With Cleanth Brooks) *Understanding Poetry*. New York, 1938.

Eleven Poems on the Same Theme. Norfolk, Conn., 1942.

Selected Poems, 1923–1943. New York, 1944.

Brother to Dragons. New York, 1953.

Segregation: The Inner Conflict in the South. New York, 1956.

Promises. New York, 1957.

You, Emperors, and Others. New York, 1960.

The Legacy of the Civil War: Meditations on the Centennial. New York, 1961.

Selected Poems: New and Old: 1923–1966. New York, 1966.

THEODORE ROETHKE, 1908–1963.

Open House. New York, 1941.

The Lost Son and Other Poems. New York, 1948.

Statement in *Mid-Century American Poets*, J. Ciardi, ed. New York, 1950.

Praise to the End. New York, 1951.

Words for the Wind: The Collected Verse of Theodore Roethke. New York, 1958.

I Am! Says the Lamb. New York, 1961.

Statement in *The Contemporary Poet as Artist and Critic*, Anthony Ostroff, ed. Boston, 1964.

The Far Field. New York, 1964.

On the Poet and His Craft: Selected Prose of Theodore Roethke, Ralph J. Mills, Jr., ed. Seattle, 1965.

The Collected Poems of Theodore Roethke. New York, 1966.

JOHN BERRYMAN, 1914–1972.

Homage to Mistress Bradstreet. New York, 1956.

Berryman's Sonnets. New York, 1967.

His Toy, His Dream, His Rest: 308 Dream Songs. New York, 1968.

Love and Fame. New York, 1970.

Henry's Fate. New York, 1977.

ROBERT LOWELL, 1917–1977.

Land of Unlikeliness. Cummington, 1944.

Lord Weary's Castle. New York, 1946.
Poems: 1938–1949. London, 1950.
The Mills of the Kavanaughs. New York, 1951.
Life Studies. New York, 1959.
Imitations. New York, 1961.
Statement in *The Contemporary Poet as Artist and Critic*, Anthony Ostroff, ed. Boston, 1964.
For the Union Dead. New York, 1967.
Near the Ocean. New York, 1967.

ROBERT DUNCAN, 1919–
The Opening of the Field. New York, 1960.
Roots and Branches. New York, 1964.
"Towards an Open Universe," contribution to *Poets on Poetry*, Howard Nemerov, ed. New York, 1966.
Bending of the Bow. New York, 1968.

HOWARD NEMEROV, 1920–
The Next Room of the Dream. Chicago, 1962.
The Blue Swallows. Chicago, 1967.
Sentences. New Brunswick, N.J., 1972.
Collected Poems. Chicago, 1977.
"Attentiveness and Obedience," contribution to *Poets on Poetry*, edited by himself. New York, 1966.
Reflexions on Poetry and Poetics. New Brunswick, N.J., 1972.
Figures of Thought. Boston, 1978.

RICHARD WILBUR, 1921–
The Beautiful Changes and Other Poems. New York, 1947.
Ceremony and Other Poems. New York, 1950.
Statement in *Mid-Century American Poets*, J. Ciardi, ed. New York, 1950.
Things of This World. New York, 1956.
Advice to a Prophet and Other Poems. New York, 1961.
The Poems of Richard Wilbur. New York, 1963.
"Proof," *Atlantic Monthly*, 213:62 (March, 1964).
Statement in *Poets on Poetry*, Howard Nemerov, ed. New York, 1966.
Walking to Sleep. New York, 1969.

JAMES DICKEY, 1923–
Drowning with Others. Middletown, Conn., 1962.
The Suspect in Poetry. Madison, 1964.

Helmets. Middletown, Conn., 1964.
Buckdancer's Choice. Middletown, Conn., 1965.
Poems, 1957–1967. Middletown, Conn., 1967.
The Eye-Beaters, Blood Victory, Madness, Buckhead and Mercy. New York, 1970.
The Zodiac. New York, 1976.
Puella. New York, 1982.

DENISE LEVERTOV, 1923–
The Double Image. London, 1946.
Here and Now. San Francisco, 1957.
With Eyes at the Back of Our Heads. New York, 1959.
The Jacob's Ladder. New York, 1962.
O Taste and See. New York, 1964.
The Sorrow Dance. New York, 1966.
Relearning the Alphabet. New York, 1970.
To Stay Alive. New York, 1971.
The Freeing of the Dust. New York, 1975.
Life in the Forest. New York, 1978.
Light Up the Cave. New York, 1981.
Candles in Babylon. New York, 1982.

A. R. AMMONS, 1926–
Expressions of Sea Level. Columbus, Ohio, 1963.
Corsons Inlet. Ithaca, N.Y., 1965.
Tape for the Turn of the Year. Ithaca, N.Y., 1965.
Northfield Poems. Ithaca, N.Y., 1966.
Selected Poems. Ithaca, N.Y., 1968.
Uplands. New York, 1970.
Briefings. New York, 1971.
Collected Poems. New York, 1972.
Sphere. New York, 1974.
Diversifications. New York, 1975.
The Snow Poems. New York, 1977.
A Coast of Trees. New York, 1981.

ROBERT BLY, 1926–
Silence in the Snowy Fields. Middletown, Conn., 1962.
The Light Around the Body. New York, 1967.
Teeth-Mother Naked at Last. San Francisco, 1970.
Old Man Rubbing His Eyes. Greensboro, N.C., 1975.
This Tree Will Be Here for a Thousand Years. New York, 1979.

JAMES MERRILL, 1926–

The Country of a Thousand Years of Peace. New York, 1959.
Water Street. New York, 1962.
The Fire Screen. New York, 1969.
Braving the Elements. New York, 1972.
Nights and Days. New York, 1973.

DAVID WAGONER, 1926–

Straw for the Fire. New York, 1974. (Selections from Roethke's Notebooks.)
Collected Poems. Bloomington, Indiana, 1976.
Who Shall Be the Sun? Bloomington, Indiana, 1978. (Poems based on American Indian myths.)
In Broken Country. Boston, 1979.
Landfall. Boston, 1981.

JOHN ASHBERY, 1927–

Some Trees. New York, 1956.
Rivers and Mountains. New York, 1966.
Self-Portrait in a Convex Mirror. New York, 1975.
The Double Image of Spring. New York, 1976.
Houseboat Days. New York, 1977.
As We Know. New York, 1979.
Shadow Train. New York, 1981.

GALWAY KINNELL, 1927–

What a Kingdom It Was. Boston, 1960.
Poems of Night. London, 1968.
Body Rags. Boston, 1968.
The Book of Nightmares. Boston, 1971.
The Avenue Bearing the Initial of Christ into the New World: Poems, 1946–1964. Boston, 1974.
Mortal Acts, Mortal Words. Boston, 1980.

W. S. MERWIN, 1927–

A Mask for Janus. New Haven, 1952.
The Drunk in the Furnace. New York, 1960.
The Lice. New York, 1967.
The Carrier of Ladders. New York, 1970.
The Compass Flower. New York, 1977.

JAMES WRIGHT, 1927–1980.
The Green Wall. New Haven, 1957.
The Branch Will Not Break. Middletown, Conn., 1963.
Shall We Gather at the River. Middletown, Conn., 1968.
Collected Poems. Middletown, Conn., 1971.
The Blossoming Pear Tree. New York, 1977.
This Journey. New York, 1982.

II. *The Secondary Works*

A list of anthologies, books, and articles, that are mentioned by name, alluded to, or consciously drawn upon in this book

ANTHOLOGIES.

Allen, Donald M. *The New American Poetry, 1945–1960.* New York, 1960.

Allen, Rideout, and Robinson, eds. *American Poetry.* New York, 1965.

Anon. *Five Young American Poets.* Norfolk, 1941.

Beilenson, Peter. *Japanese Haiku.* Mount Vernon, 1956.

Benet, William Rose, and Norman Holmes Pearson, eds. *The Oxford Anthology of American Literature.* New York, 1938.

Braithwaite, William Stanley Beaumont, ed. *An Anthology of Magazine Verse and Year Book of American Poetry.* Boston, 1913–1929.

Burnett, Whit, ed. *This is My Best.* New York, 1942.

Ciardi, John. *Mid-Century American Poets.* New York, 1950, 1952.

Clark, Harry Hayden. *Major American Poets.* New York, 1936.

Haraszti, Zoltan, ed. *The Bay Psalm Book,* facsimile edition. Chicago, 1956.

Holland, Dr. J. G. *Illustrated Library of Favorite Song.* New York, 1873.

Leary, Paris, and Robert Kelly, eds. *A Controversy of Poets.* New York, 1965.

Matthiessen, F. O., ed. *The Oxford Book of American Verse.* New York, 1950.

Murdock, Kenneth B. *Handkerchiefs from Paul.* Cambridge, 1927.

Smith, Elihu, compiler. *American Poems Selected and Original.* Litchfield, 1793.

Stedman, E. C. *An American Anthology, 1787–1900: Selections Illustrating the Editor's Critical Review of American Poetry in the Nineteenth Century.* Boston, 1900.

Warner, Charles Dudley, ed. *Library of the World's Best Literature,* Vol. 13. New York, 1897.

BOOKS AND ARTICLES.

Adams, R. P. "The Failure of Edwin Arlington Robinson," *Tulane Studies in English,* XI (1961), 97–151.

Anderson, Charles R. *Emily Dickinson's Poetry: Stairway of Surprise.* New York, 1960.

Anon. "Eastern Personal Time," *London Times Literary Supplement,* July 1, 1965, p. 558 (Robert Lowell).

Anon. *I'll Take My Stand: The South and the Agrarian Tradition: by Twelve Southerners.* New York, 1930.

Arnold, Matthew. *Discourses in America.* London, 1889.

Asselineau, Roger. *The Evolution of Walt Whitman.* Vol. I: *The Creation of a Personality;* vol. II: *The Creation of a Book.* Cambridge, 1960–1962.

Atkins, Elizabeth. *Edna St. Vincent Millay and Her Times.* Chicago, 1936.

Barnett, Lincoln Kinnear. *The Universe and Dr. Einstein.* New York, 1948.

Bartlett, William J., *Jones Very: Emerson's "Brave Saint."* Durham, 1942.

Benton, Joel. *Emerson as a Poet.* New York, 1883.

Bewley, Marius. "Death and the James Family." *The New York Review of Books,* Nov. 5, 1964 (the likeness of *The Diary of Alice James* to the poems of Emily Dickinson).

Bingham, Millicent Todd. *Ancestors' Brocades: The Literary Debut of Emily Dickinson.* New York, 1945.

Bishop, Jonathan. *Emerson on the Soul.* Cambridge, 1964.

Blackham, H. J. *Six Existentialist Thinkers.* New York, 1952.
Bloom, Harold. "The Central Man: Emerson, Whitman, Wallace Stevens." *The Massachusetts Review,* 7:23–42 (Winter, 1966).
Blyth, R. H. *Zen in English Literature and Oriental Classics.* Tokyo, 1942.
———. *Eastern Culture.* Tokyo, 1949.
Boehme, Jacob. *Six Theosophic Points, and Other Writings, with an Introductory Essay . . . by Nicolas Berdyaev.* Ann Arbor, 1958.
Bogan, Louise. *Achievement in American Poetry.* Chicago, 1951.
Breit, Harvey. *The Writer Observed.* Cleveland, 1956.
Brooks, Cleanth, Jr., and R. P. Warren. *Understanding Poetry.* New York, 1940.
Brown, Rollo Walter. *Next Door to a Poet.* New York, 1937.
Buber, Martin. *I and Thou.* New York, 1937.
———. *Between Man and Man.* London, 1947.
———. *Tales of the Hasidim.* New York, 1947–1948.
Bucke, Dr. Richard Martin. *Cosmic Consciousness: A Study in the Evolution of the Human Mind.* Philadelphia, 1901.
Butterfield, Herbert. *Christianity and History.* London, 1950.
———. *History and Human Relations.* London, 1951.
Cary, Elisabeth L. *Emerson, Poet and Thinker.* New York, 1904.
Caton, Charles E., ed. *Philosophy and Ordinary Language.* Urbana, 1963.
Chari, V. K. *Whitman in the Light of Vedantic Mysticism.* Lincoln, 1964.
Coffman, Stanley K., Jr. *Imagism, a Chapter for the History of Modern Poetry.* Norman, 1951.
Cook, R. L. *The Dimensions of Robert Frost.* New York, 1958.
Cooke, G. W. *A Bibliography of James Russell Lowell.* Boston, 1906.
Culler, Jonathan D., ed. *Harvard Advocate Centennial Anthology.* Cambridge, 1966.
Davidson, Edward H. *Jonathan Edwards: The Narrative of a Puritan Mind.* Boston, 1966.
Davie, Donald. *Ezra Pound: Poet as Sculptor.* New York, 1964.
Detweiler, Robert. "Emerson and Zen," *American Quarterly,* XIV (Fall, 1962), 422–438.
Dickey, James. "Introduction" to *Selected Poems of E. A. Robinson.* New York, 1965. "Theodore Roethke." *Poetry Magazine,* CV (Nov., 1964), 119–122.

Donoghue, Denis. *Connoisseurs of Chaos.* New York, 1965.
Durr, R. A. *On the Mystical Poetry of Henry Vaughan.* Cambridge, 1962.
Eastman, Max. *The Literary Mind.* London, 1931.
Eaton, Walter Prichard. "Forgotten American Poet," [Tuckerman] *Forum* 41:62–70, January 1909.
Eddington, Sir Arthur Stanley. *The Nature of the Physical World.* New York, 1928.
Edwards, Jonathan. *Freedom of the Will.* Boston, 1754.
Eliade, Mircea. *The Sacred and the Profane: The Nature of Religion.* New York, 1959.
Eliot, T. S. "From Poe to Valery," in *On Poetry and Poets.* London, 1957.
Erikson, Erik H. *Childhood and Society,* 2nd edition. New York, 1963.
———. *Insight and Responsibility.* New York, 1964.
Fenollosa, Ernest. *Epochs of Chinese and Japanese Art.* London, 1912.
Fiedler, Leslie A. *Waiting for the End.* New York, 1964.
Fiske, John. *Through Nature to God.* Boston, 1899.
Frazer, Sir James George. *The Golden Bough.* London, 1911.
Fromm, Erich. *Psychoanalysis and Religion.* New Haven, 1959.
Frye, Northrop. *Fearful Symmetry.* Princeton, 1947.
Fussell, Edwin S. *Edwin Arlington Robinson: The Literary Background of a Traditional Poet.* Berkeley, 1954.
Gelpi, Albert J. *Emily Dickinson: The Mind of the Poet.* Cambridge, 1965.
Godwin, Parke. *The Life and Works of William Cullen Bryant.* New York, 1883.
Gregory, Horace and Marya Zaturenska. *A History of American Poetry, 1900–1940.* New York, 1946.
Griffith, Clark. *The Long Shadow: Emily Dickinson's Tragic Poetry.* Princeton, 1964.
Harding, Walter. *Thoreau: A Century of Criticism.* Dallas, 1954.
Hart, Bernard. *The Psychology of Insanity.* Cambridge and New York, 1912.
Hart, James D. *Oxford Companion to American Literature.* New York, 1965.
Hayakawa, S. I. *Language in Action.* Madison, 1939.
Herbert, George. *The Works of George Herbert.* Oxford, 1941.

Hick, John, ed. *Faith and the Philosophers.* New York, 1964.
Higginson, T. W. "The Life of the Birds," *The Atlantic Monthly,* X (September 1862), 368–378.
———. *Short Studies of American Authors.* Boston, 1880.
———. *Contemporaries.* Boston, 1899.
———. *John Greenleaf Whittier.* New York, 1902.
Hoffman, Daniel G. *The Poetry of Stephen Crane.* New York, 1957.
Holmes, Oliver Wendell. *Ralph Waldo Emerson,* American Men of Letters Series. Boston, 1885.
Hook, Sidney, ed. *Religious Experience and Truth.* New York, 1961.
Howells, William Dean. *Literary Friends and Acquaintance.* New York, 1900.
Hughes, Glenn. *Imagism and the Imagists.* Stanford, 1931.
Hyman, Stanley Edgar. *Poetry and Criticism: Four Revolutions in Literary Taste.* New York, 1961.
Ives, Charles. *Essays Before a Sonata.* New York, 1920.
James, Alice. *The Diary of Alice James,* Leon Edel, ed. New York, 1964.
James, Henry, *et al. In After Days: Thoughts on the Future Life.* New York, 1910.
James, Henry. *Notes of a Son and Brother.* New York, 1914.
James, William. *The Principles of Psychology.* New York, 1890.
———. *The Will to Believe, and Other Essays in Popular Philosophy.* New York, 1897.
———. *Human Immortality* (Ingersoll lecture of 1898). Boston, 1898.
———. *The Varieties of Religious Experience.* New York, 1902.
———. *Pragmatism: A New Name for Some Old Ways of Thinking.* New York, 1907.
———. *The Meaning of Truth.* New York, 1909.
———. *Essays in Radical Empiricism.* New York, 1912.
Jantz, H. S. *The First Century of New England Verse.* Worcester, 1944.
Jarrell, Randall. *Poetry and the Age.* New York, 1953.
Jenkins, MacGregor. *Emily Dickinson, Friend and Neighbor.* Boston, 1930.
Johnson, Thomas H. *Emily Dickinson: An Interpretive Biography.* Cambridge, 1955.
Jung, C. G. *Psychology and Religion.* New Haven, 1938.

———. *The Undiscovered Self.* New York, 1957.

Kenner, Hugh. *The Poetry of Ezra Pound.* Norfolk, Conn., 1951.

Knowles, David. *The English Mystical Tradition.* London, 1961.

Kreymborg, Alfred. *A History of American Poetry: Our Singing Strength.* New York, 1929.

Kunitz, Stanley J., and Howard Haycraft, ed. *Twentieth Century Authors.* New York, 1955.

Leyda, Jay. *The Years and Hours of Emily Dickinson.* New Haven, 1960.

Longfellow, Samuel. *Life of Henry Wadsworth Longfellow, With Extracts from His Journals and Correspondence,* 2 vols. Boston, 1886.

Lowell, Amy. *Tendencies in Modern American Poetry.* Boston, 1917.

Mackinnon, F. I., ed. *Philosophical Writings of Henry Moore.* New York, 1925.

MacLeish, Archibald. *Poetry and Experience.* Boston, 1961.

MacLeish, Bogan, and Wilbur. *Emily Dickinson: Three Views.* Amherst, 1960.

Marcel, Gabriel. *Homo Viator.* Paris, 1944.

———. *The Mystery of Being.* London, 1950.

———. *Being and Having: An Existentialist Diary.* New York, 1965.

Martz, Louis. *The Poetry of Meditation.* New Haven, 1954.

Mason, Lowell, ed. *Christian Psalmody.* Boston, 1843.

Matthiessen, F. O. *American Renaissance.* New York, 1941.

Miller, James E. *A Critical Guide to Leaves of Grass.* Chicago, 1957.

Miller, James, Bernice Slote, and Karl Shapiro. *Start With the Sun.* Lincoln, 1960.

Miller, J. Hillis. *Poets of Reality.* Cambridge, 1965.

Miller, Perry. *The New England Mind.* Cambridge, 1953.

———, ed. *Consciousness in Concord.* Boston, 1958.

Mills, Ralph J. *Theodore Roethke.* Minneapolis, 1963.

Monroe, Harriet. *A Poet's Life.* New York, 1938.

Monteiro, George. "Howells on Lowell: An Unascribed Review," *New England Quarterly,* XXXVIII, no. 4, December 1965, 508–509.

Morison, S. E. *The Intellectual Life of Colonial New England.* New York, 1956.

Morse, S. F. "Wallace Stevens: The Poet and the Critics," *The Southern Review,* Vol. I, no. 2, April 1965, 430–446.

Murdock, Kenneth. *Literature and Theology in Colonial New England.* Cambridge, 1949.

Nemerov, Howard. *Poets on Poetry.* New York, 1965.

Niebuhr, Reinhold. *The Nature and Destiny of Man.* New York, 1941.

Northrop, F. S. C. *The Meeting of East and West: An Inquiry Concerning World Understanding.* New York, 1946.

Ogden, C. K., and I. A. Richards. *The Meaning of Meaning.* New York, 1923.

Osborne, Frances Thomas. "Herman Melville Through a Child's Eyes," *Bulletin of New York Public Library,* 69:10 (December 1965), 655–660.

Ostroff, Anthony. *The Contemporary Poet as Artist and Critic.* Boston, 1964.

Otto, Rudolph. *Mysticism East and West.* New York, 1932.

Ouspensky, P. D. *Tertium Organum.* New York, 1922.

Paul, Sherman. *Emerson's Angle of Vision.* Cambridge, 1952.

———. *The Shores of America: Thoreau's Inward Exploration.* Urbana, 1958.

Pearce, Jane, and Saul Newton. *The Conditions of Human Growth.* New York, 1963.

Pearce, Roy Harvey. *The Continuity of American Poetry.* Princeton, 1961.

Pearson, Karl. *The Grammar of Science.* London, 1895.

Pickard, Samuel T. *The Life and Letters of John Greenleaf Whittier.* Boston, 1894.

Ramsey, Ian T. *Religious Language: An Empirical Placing of Theological Phrases.* London, 1957.

Reps, Paul. *Zen Flesh, Zen Bones: A Collection of Zen and Pre-Zen Writings.* New York, 1966.

Richards, I. A. *Science and Poetry.* London, 1925.

Richards, Laura E. *E.A.R.* Cambridge, 1936.

Rieff, Philip. *The Triumph of the Therapeutic; Uses of Faith After Freud.* New York, 1966.

Rosenfeld, Alvin. "Emerson and Whitman: Their Personal and Literary Relationships." Doctoral Thesis, Brown University Library, 1967.

Rosenthal, M. L. *A Primer of Ezra Pound.* New York, 1960.

Ross, Nancy Wilson. *The World of Zen: An East-West Anthology.* New York, 1960.

Rusk, Ralph L. *The Life of Ralph Waldo Emerson.* New York, 1949.

Shephard, Esther. *Walt Whitman's Pose.* New York, 1938.

Smith, Chard Powers. *Where the Light Falls: A Portrait of Edwin Arlington Robinson.* New York, 1965.

Stace, Walter Terrence. *Religion and the Modern Mind.* Philadelphia, 1952.

———. *Mysticism and Philosophy.* Philadelphia, 1960.

Stallman, R. W., and Lillian Gilkes. *Stephen Crane: Letters.* New York, 1960.

Stanford, Donald E. "An Edition of the Complete Poetical Works of Edward Taylor," Doctoral Thesis, Ann Arbor, University Microfilms, 1954.

Stein, Arnold. *Theodore Roethke: Essays on the Poetry.* Seattle, 1965.

Stepanchev, Stephen. *American Poetry Since 1945.* New York, 1965.

Stewart, Dugald. *Elements of the Philosophy of the Human Mind.* Philadelphia, 1793.

Sturges, Henry C. *Chronologies of the Life and Writings of William Cullen Bryant, with a Bibliography of His Works in Prose and Verse.* New York, 1903.

Sullivan, J. P. *Ezra Pound and Sextus Propertius: A Study in Creative Translation.* Austin, Texas, 1964.

Sutton, Walter. "A Conversation with Denise Levertov," *Minnesota Review,* Vol. 5, nos. 3, 4 (October and December 1965), 322–338.

Sutton, Walter, ed. *Ezra Pound: A Collection of Critical Essays.* Englewood Cliffs, 1963.

Suzuki, D. T. *Studies in Zen.* New York, 1955.

———. *Zen Buddhism: Selected Writings of D. T. Suzuki,* William Barrett, ed. Garden City, 1956.

———. *Essays in Zen Buddhism.* London, 1958.

Thompson, Lawrance, ed. *Selected Letters of Robert Frost.* New York, 1964.

Tillich, Paul. *The Eternal Now.* New York, 1963.

Traubel, Horace. *With Walt Whitman in Camden.* Boston, 1906.

Trent, W. P. "Verse Writers of the Seventeenth Century," in *A Brief History of American Literature.* New York, 1905.

Tyler, Moses Coit. *A History of American Literature, 1607–1765.* New York, 1878.

Underhill, Evelyn. *Mysticism.* New York, 1911.

Wagner, Linda. *The Poems of William Carlos Williams.* Middletown, 1964.

Ward, Theodora. *The Capsule of the Mind* (Emily Dickinson). Cambridge, 1961.

Watts, Isaac. *Psalms, Hymns, and Spiritual Songs.* Boston, 1804.

Wegelin, Oscar. *Early American Poetry.* New York, 1930.

Wellek, Rene. *Confrontations: Studies in the Intellectual and Literary Relations Between Germany, England, and the United States During the Nineteenth Century.* Princeton, 1965.

Wellek, Rene, and Austin Warren. *Theory of Literature.* New York, 1949.

Wentz, Walter Yeeling Evans. *The Tibetan Book of the Dead.* New York, 1957.

Whicher, George Frisbie. *This Was a Poet.* New York, 1938.

Whicher, Stephen E. *Freedom and Fate: An Inner Life of Ralph Waldo Emerson.* Philadelphia, 1953.

Whitehead, Alfred North. *Science and the Modern World.* New York, 1925.

Wilkinson, Marguerite. *The Way of the Makers.* New York, 1925.

———. *New Voices: An Introduction to Contemporary Poetry,* revised edition. New York, 1928.

Wilson, Edmund. *Patriotic Gore.* New York, 1962.

Winters, Yvor. "Jones Very and R. W. Emerson: Aspects of New England Mysticism," in *In Defense of Reason.* New York, 1947.

———. "A Discovery" ["The Cricket" by Tuckerman] *Hudson Review,* III (Autumn, 1950), 453–58.

Yasuda, Kenneth. *The Japanese Haiku.* Tokyo, and Rutland, Vermont, 1957.

Yu, Beongcheon. *An Ape of Gods: The Art and Thought of Lafcadio Hearn.* Detroit, 1964.

Zola, Emile. *The Experimental Novel and Other Essays.* Trans. from French by Belle M. Sherman. New York, 1893.

Index

Index